Life Assurance & Pensions Handbook

Life Assurance & Pensions Handbook

Twenty-second edition

2006/07

Chris Marshall
LLB(Hons), FCII

taxbriefs
financial publishing

Taxbriefs Limited
2-5 Benjamin Street
London EC1M 5QL

Tel: 020 7250 0967
Fax: 020 7251 8867
e-mail: info@taxbriefs.co.uk
http://www.taxbriefs.co.uk

ISBN 1-905482-05-1

Printed and bound in Great Britain by Biddles Ltd, King's Lynn, Norfolk

ABOUT THE AUTHOR

Chris Marshall is the Legal and Technical Services Manager for the Life Assurance Division of the Legal & General Group. He joined Legal & General in 1969 after obtaining an Honours Degree in Law at Liverpool University; he worked in various departments of the Legal & General's Life Group including claims, marketing and a number of years as Compliance Officer. He deals with new product development, policy drafting, trusts, taxation and other legal matters. He has been a tutor of the Chartered Insurance Institute and is also the author of a number of their text books. He frequently lectures on insurance and tax planning. He is a member of the ABI Taxation (Life Policies) Panel.

Contents

A An Introduction to Life Assurance

It is not for nothing that life assurance companies have, from time to time, been given awards for gobbledegook. Over the several hundreds of years of the industry's existence, many obscure terms for different types of policy have evolved. Most of these are still in common use today. Therefore, it is not surprising that the subject of life assurance often seems puzzling to the general public. Although the formal definition of a life policy given below implies that life assurance contracts are wholly concerned with the longevity of individuals, in fact life assurance has evolved into a complex but efficient vehicle for investment and tax planning. It can cover such diverse topics as the repayment of house purchase loans, planning for school fees and the provision of lump sums for retirement or income throughout a desired period. In addition, life offices also offer a range of contracts which, strictly speaking, are not life assurance but which also depend, in some way, on an individual's life or health. These contracts include income protection (also known as permanent health insurance) and annuities and will be dealt with later in this book. This chapter explains the basic principles underlying life assurance and runs through the main types of policy available; all offices' policies differ in detail, but are based on these main types.

The last two sections deal with annuities which, while not being life assurance, do depend on the duration of human life and are offered by most life offices.

1 Basic Principles

1.1 Definition of a life policy

The formal definition of a life policy is that it is a contract between an insurance company (the 'life office') and an individual or individuals, where payment by the life office in return for premiums paid depends in some way on the duration of a human life or lives. The sum payable under a life policy is called the 'sum assured', and this will become payable either upon the death of the 'life assured' (see below) or his survival to the end of an agreed period.

The premium paid will depend on the type of cover required and the age and sex of the life assured, together with state of health, occupation and any other factors which may affect the underwriting of the policy (underwriting being the process whereby the life office assesses proposals, decides whether to accept the risks and, if so, at what rate of premium). All these aspects will be explained in greater detail in later chapters.

1.2 The writing of policies

There are certain technical ways in which a policy can be drawn up (ie 'written') and these need to be explained.

1.2.1 The life assured

The person on whose life the contract depends is called the 'life assured'. However, although the assured, who owns the policy, and the life assured are frequently the same person, this is certainly not necessarily the case.

A policy on the life of one person but effected and owned by someone else is called a 'life of another policy'.

1.2.2 Joint life policies

Policies can be effected jointly by two assureds – eg husband and wife – on their joint lives. Furthermore, although the vast majority of joint life policies have two lives assured, it is theoretically possible to have more if insurable interest (see Chapter B) exists. Practically any type of life policy can be effected on a joint life basis.

There are two fundamental kinds of joint life policy – first death and second death contracts. A joint life first death policy pays out on the death of the first life assured to die. First death term assurance and family income policies are used for family protection purposes. First death endowments are commonly used in connection with house purchase arrangements.

A joint life second death policy pays out on the death of the second life assured to die. These are sometimes called joint life last survivor contracts. They are frequently used in inheritance tax planning (see Chapter L) and also sometimes for investment purposes.

A joint life first death policy will always be more expensive than a joint life second death policy because the death claim is payable at an earlier time and therefore the element of premium which pays for the death risk is higher.

There is no limit to the number of lives assured it is possible to have. A number of offices have group life policies (often arranged by an employer) where payment is made on the death of any of the lives assured. Many offices offer investment bonds on multiple lives, payable on the death of the last to die.

1.2.3 Contingent policies

A contingent life assurance is a type of assurance where payment is only made on the death of the life assured if a certain other condition (the contingency) is also fulfilled. The usual condition is that the life assured must die during the lifetime of another person (the counter-life). The policy would thus pay out on the death of A (the life assured) only if it occurs during the lifetime of B (the counter-life). Premiums will depend on the age, sex and health of the life assured and the counter-life.

Policies can be issued to cover other contingencies when the premiums will depend on the contingency involved.

1.3 Types of policy

This chapter briefly describes the various types of life policies which exist. Later chapters deal with their role in tax planning and, where relevant, more detailed descriptions will then be given.

Strictly speaking, there are three different classifications of life assurance policy: term assurance, whole life and endowment. The first, term assurance, consists of policies which are taken out as a means of insuring against the possibility of death within a specific period. The premiums payable are solely for the purpose of providing life cover as a form of protection.

Both whole life and endowment are effectively making an investment that becomes payable at a future date, either on death or earlier. The premiums payable are for the purpose of providing a mix of life cover and investment and, as such, have cash-in, or 'surrender', values; it is because of this surrender value that these policies are known as 'substantive'. In the case of whole life policies, a payout will occur on the death of the life assured, whenever this takes place. On the other hand, an endowment policy will mature, and pay out a sum of money, after a fixed period, or on earlier death.

In addition to these plans, life offices also offer annuities and health insurance cover. These are dealt with in depth in sections 6 and 7 and Chapter E.

1.4 Premium rates

As a general rule premium rates increase with age. Life assurance premium rates for females are cheaper than those for males because their life expectancy is greater, and therefore their chances of dying at any given age are less than those of a male of the same age. As a general proposition, rates for females are equivalent to those for males some three or four years younger. Correspondingly, annuity payments for females are less than for males, because the life office will, on average, be paying out for a longer period.

Under the Gender Recognition Act 2004, anyone who has legally changed their gender by obtaining a gender recognition certificate is treated as being of the new gender. This does not mean that an insurer has to insure them at ordinary rates (or at all). Any change of gender has no effect on any existing policy, as the Act provides that the change does not affect anything done before that, eg the terms of a pre-existing contract.

Premiums can be single or regular. Regular premiums can usually be paid monthly or annually.

2 Term Assurance

Term assurance is the most basic type of life assurance. As explained earlier, it consists of policies which are taken out as a means of insuring only against death within a specified period. The premiums provide life cover only. Many term assurances include critical illness cover and terminal illness cover (see Chapter E).

2.1 Level term assurance

The simplest form of term assurance is level term assurance. This provides that the life office will only pay out the sum assured if the life assured dies during the term of the policy, ie before the expiry date. The sum assured does not vary during the term of the policy and once it has expired the policy has no value.

This is the cheapest form of life assurance, since the cover is only temporary and there is normally no surrender or cash-in value available on early termination. If a premium is unpaid, the policy will lapse at the expiry of the days of grace.

2.2 Renewable term assurance

Some term assurances are 'renewable' in that, on the expiry date, there is an option to take out a further term assurance at ordinary rates without evidence of health, as long as the expiry date is not beyond, say, age 65. Each subsequent policy will have the same option. Thus, instead of purchasing a 20-year term assurance, a 45-year-old man might effect a five-year renewable term assurance which gives him the option of renewing every five years. Whenever the policy comes up for renewal the premium will increase, since it is based on the then age of the life assured. If the insured takes up this option, whatever the state of the life assured's health and life expectancy, the life office cannot decline it.

2.3 Convertible term assurance

This is a level term assurance with an option which enables the assured to convert it, at any time during its existence, to a whole life or endowment assurance without further evidence of health. The premium for the new policy will be that normally applicable to a whole life or endowment assurance policy for a person of the life assured's age, at the time of conversion.

If the original policy was issued with some form of extra premium, then the premium for the new policy will be similarly treated. Often, part-conversion is allowed as well as total conversion. If only part of the policy is converted, the sum assured on the first policy will be reduced by the amount of the sum assured on the new policy.

The premiums charged for convertible term assurance will be slightly higher than for ordinary level term assurance, to allow for the cost of the conversion option.

2.4 Decreasing term assurance

Decreasing term assurance has a sum assured which reduces each year (or possibly each month) by a stated amount, decreasing to nil at the end of the term. Although cover decreases each year, the premium remains constant. Premiums are sometimes payable for a shorter period than the policy term itself, because otherwise there would be a temptation for the assured to lapse the policy in the last year or two, when the sum assured has reduced to a comparatively low level. For a 25-year policy, some life offices would impose a premium paying period of 20 years.

Premiums for decreasing term assurance are either slightly cheaper than for a level term assurance for the same initial sum assured and term, or the same, but payable for a shorter period. Some decreasing term policies also have a conversion option, although this is limited to the sum assured remaining at the time of conversion. These policies can be used to cover the IHT liability on a potentially exempt transfer – see Chapter L.

2.4.1 Mortgage protection policies

These are a type of decreasing term assurance used specifically for mortgage protection. The sum assured reduces at the same rate as the capital outstanding under a house purchase mortgage on a repayment basis. Most offices design their policies so that the sum assured will repay the loan in full provided interest rates do not exceed 10% during the life of the mortgage. It is normally the cheapest way of covering such a loan.

2.5 Expanding term assurance

Because of inflation, a term assurance with a level sum assured gives a reducing amount of real cover as the value of money declines year by year and, consequently, attempts have been made to combat this by introducing term assurance policies with some form of escalating sum assured.

Some offices offer policies where the sum assured can be increased each year by a set percentage (often 10%) of the original sum assured. Other offices have short-term policies which can be renewed at the end of the term, for a higher amount; for example, the holder of a five-year level term assurance may have the right at the end of the five years to effect a new policy for a sum assured of up to 50% more than the original.

Whenever the sum assured is increased, the premium is correspondingly raised. In addition, because the life office is giving the right to increase the cover substantially without any medical evidence, the initial premiums for these increasable contracts are higher than those for ordinary level term assurances for comparable sums assured. Furthermore, short-term policies with renewal options usually provide for the premium to be based on the life assured's age at renewal.

Some offices have guaranteed insurability options enabling the sum assured to be increased on events such as marriage, birth of a child or increase to a mortgage.

Many of these policies incorporate conversion options. Cover can usually continue up to age 60 or 65.

2.6 Index-linked term assurance

The problem with the expanding policies described above is that the real value of the cover is only maintained if the actual rate of inflation is at least matched by the rate of escalation. In addition, because inflation is continuous, any policy which has increases only every three or five years can become seriously out of date towards the end of that period, if inflation is high. The only real way to solve this problem is to link the cover to the rate of inflation. This has been done in recent years, through index-linked term assurances.

Some offices provide the option for the sum assured and premium to be increased each year by the increase in the Retail Prices Index (RPI), possibly up to a maximum increase of 10% in any year. Other policies provide cover that is level for, say, five years with a right on expiry to effect a new policy without evidence of health, for a sum assured increased to match the rate of inflation over the previous five years.

A common feature of this type of policy is that if a policyholder does not exercise the right to increase the cover, the sum assured is frozen at that level and future index-linking is not allowed. However, at least one company has a contract whereby the sum assured and premiums are index-linked automatically, although the company can review premiums upwards over the rate of inflation if it wishes.

2.7 Unit-linked term assurances

Some offices issue unit-linked term assurances. These are term assurances in the sense that the sum assured is only payable on death during the term of the policy. However, they work very much like the regular premium unit-linked whole life policies explained in section 4.

Each month's premium will buy units and each month enough units are cancelled to pay for that month's life risk – ie the difference between the death sum assured and the value of units. There are two types of contract: guaranteed and reviewable.

2.7.1 Guaranteed policies

On a guaranteed policy the premium was fixed at outset and bought a fixed sum assured payable on death during the term. If the units did not perform well enough to maintain the life cover, it continued anyway and the life office effectively stood the loss. If units over-performed the assumptions made in the policy costings, then the value of the units left in the policy at the expiry date was payable in cash to the policyholder. A decrease in mortality costs could also produce a cash sum at expiry. Guaranteed policies are now not readily available.

2.7.2 Reviewable policies

On a reviewable policy there will be regular reviews to see how unit performance is going. If the units perform exactly as per the growth rates assumed in the policy costings, the sum assured can be maintained for the term of the policy. If the units over-perform there will be a cash value in the policy which the policyholder can take at the expiry of the term. If the units under-perform, then the premiums would be increased or the sum assured reduced. Premiums are based on current assessments of future mortality and if these prove inadequate, the life office can increase the rates at each review date.

Premiums on the reviewable contract are therefore cheaper than on the guaranteed contract but could rise in the future if mortality costs increase. On the other hand, the premiums on the guaranteed contract are fixed no matter what happens to mortality rates.

Some of these policies have options to index-link the cover periodically without medical evidence. This is valuable as it enables the client to maintain the real value of the cover.

However, it is usual for the option to be cancelled if it is not elected when it becomes available. Many policies also have an increasing cover option enabling the policyholder to increase cover on events such as marriage or the birth or adoption of a child. A number of offices offer an option to convert to whole life or endowment.

2.7.3 Moneyback policies

Some unit-linked protection policies are sold as moneyback protection policies or 'no claims bonus' policies. They are actually endowments with a very high death sum assured and a maturity value which should equal the total premiums paid at the end of the term, if the units perform as assumed. They are often sold in the direct market on the basis that if you die, your family get paid, and if you don't, you get your money back. They are aimed at relatively unsophisticated clients who perceive term assurance as a waste of money because there might not be a claim. The maturity value is not guaranteed and the value of units attaching at any time would be available as a surrender value.

2.7.4 Term 100 plans

Sometimes term assurances to age 100 are used as a cheap alternative to whole life assurance, although there is always the danger that the life assured will survive beyond that age.

2.8 Family income policies

Instead of having a term assurance paying out a lump sum on death, it is possible to have a policy which pays out an income instead. This type of contract is known as a family income policy, because it is intended to replace the income which the life assured would produce for his family if he was still alive.

The term 'family income' is, in a way, a misnomer since the policy is really written to provide a capital sum by instalments for a selected period, to avoid liability for income tax on each regular payment. The policy pays the selected level of 'income' each year from the death of the life assured until the expiry date of the policy. Instalments can usually be paid monthly, quarterly or yearly – and often a commuted value or lump sum will be available at death in lieu of the instalments. This lump sum is often not guaranteed in advance, and will depend on interest rates prevalent at the time. These policies are relatively cheap because the cover, in effect, decreases over the term of the policy – the nearer the life assured gets to the expiry date, the less will be the total of instalments payable. As a consequence the premium paying term may be shorter than the policy term.

2.8.1 Escalating family income policies

As has already been explained, a term assurance with a level sum assured provides a decreasing level of cover in real terms and, of course, this is equally true of family income policies. Thus, a number of offices market family income policies where the income benefit increases automatically, at a prearranged rate, during the term of the policy.

The income benefit might increase each year by 3%, 5% or 10%, simple or compound. In some cases the increases will stop if a claim arises and in some cases they may continue throughout the claim-paying period. The latter type will be more expensive, but will be a better foil for inflation. Either type will be more expensive than a level family income policy. Premiums will be level, even though the cover increases.

Some family income policies can be index-linked in a similar way to term assurances (see section 2.6).

3 Investment-Linked Policies – the Basics

With all the policies described so far, there is no investment element in the premiums, from the point of view of the policyholder. The policies are for the purpose of protection only, and, because this protection is for a limited period, a payout by the life office is not inevitable. However, as has already been stated, life assurance can be used as an effective investment medium. In the case of whole life policies, as has been explained, a payout will occur on the death of the life assured – whenever this takes place. On the other hand, an endowment policy will mature and pay out a sum of money after a fixed period – usually ten years or more.

Both whole life and endowment policies can be for a guaranteed return only, in which case they are known as non-profit. Alternatively, the return can be linked to the office's investment performance – and there are two ways in which this can be done.

The first is by having a 'unit-linked' policy, where benefits are directly affected by investment performance. The second is by having a 'with-profits' policy, where the link with investment performance is indirect. Both whole life assurance and endowment assurance can be either unit-linked or with-profits.

3.1 Unit-linked policies

Unit-linked policies were introduced as a way of offering investors policies where values are directly linked to investment performance. The way this is done is by formally linking the value of the policy to units in a unitised fund run by the life office. Alternatively, the link can be to the units of a unit trust. The values of the units directly reflect the values of the underlying assets of the fund, and fluctuate daily (or perhaps monthly) according to the performance of those investments. Unit-linked policies vary enormously, but all operate on the same principle, ie all or part of the premiums will be applied to purchase units in the fund at the price ruling at the time of payment. The future value of the policy will then fluctuate according to the value of the units allocated to it.

3.1.1 Pricing structure

Many funds operate on a dual-price structure – ie each unit has two prices, the offer price and the bid price.

- **The offer price** – this is the price which the office uses to allocate units to a policy when premiums are paid – ie if the offer price is £1 and the whole of a £100 premium is to be applied to buy units, it will buy 100 units.

- **The bid price** – this is the price the office will give for the units if the policyholder wishes to cash in or claim under the policy. This is lower than the offer price, ie 100 units can be cashed in for £95 if the bid price is £0.95.

There is commonly a 5% difference between the offer and bid prices. This is known as the 'bid–offer spread' and is, in effect, a charge made by the life office to cover its expenses in setting up the policy. There is also usually a monthly management charge, typically one-twelfth of 1%, which is deducted from the fund before the prices of the units are calculated.

Some offices now offer products (particularly single premium ones) with no bid–offer spread, but with penalties for early surrender to recoup the additional expenses incurred in the early years of the contract. These products may prove more beneficial to clients who continue their policies to the expected maturity or expiry date.

There may be two types of units in any given fund, initial (or capital) units and accumulation units. Initial units have a higher monthly management charge (say, one-third of 1%) than accumulation units (say, one-twelfth of 1%). Initial unit prices are thus lower than accumulation unit prices. Initial units are used for the early years of regular premium unit-linked policies, where additional initial expenses need to be recouped. As with the bid–offer spread, the initial/accumulation unit structure is, in reality, a form of charge imposed by the office. Initial units have become much less common over the last few years for new policies, but are still seen on older policies.

Another form of charge is the non-allocation period. This is a period during which premiums do not purchase units – eg during the first year of a whole life policy.

3.1.2 Funds

Most offices offer a variety of funds to which a policy can be linked. The most usual funds are as follows:

- **Equity (or Ordinary Share) Fund** – invested in ordinary shares quoted on the London Stock Exchange.
- **Fixed Interest (or Gilt) Fund** – invested in securities which carry a fixed rate of interest, normally UK government securities and local authority issues.
- **Property Fund** – invested in real property, usually commercial and industrial premises. However, because of the high capital cost of a single building, a small fund may invest in other media, such as ordinary shares in property investment or development companies, while it builds up enough capital to purchase a further building.
- **International Fund** – invested in assets abroad, usually shares on foreign stock markets.
- **Cash Fund** – invested in the short-term money markets such as bank deposits and Treasury Bills, usually to provide a temporary refuge for the investor who requires a high degree of security.
- **Index-linked Gilt Fund** – invested in UK government index-linked securities.
- **Building Society Fund** – invested in building society deposits.

Many offices have introduced more specialised funds such as a Far Eastern Fund or a European Fund.

The fund with the best performance will vary from time to time. This has led to the concept of the Managed Fund where the office's managers invest in whichever of their funds they feel is best at any particular time.

An extension of this idea is the 'switching facility' offered by many offices. This facility gives the policyholder the option to switch the investment from one fund to another. For example, a policyholder with a policy linked to the equity fund could, if he wished, switch into another fund where he considers prospects to be better. A small charge may be levied for this service, but it does allow the investor to, as it were, back his own judgment. The switch could be of existing units, or for future premiums only.

Obviously, the value of units can fall as well as rise and therefore it is possible for the policy to fall in value, unlike a conventional policy. Thus, while the potential yield of a unit-linked policy may be higher than that of a non-linked contract, the risks are greater.

Most funds are valued daily, weekly or monthly and the policyholder can regularly follow the progress of the investment, because unit prices are published in the *Financial Times* and other leading national daily newspapers. In any event, the life office generally issues periodic statements to its unit-linked policyholders showing the number and value of units allocated. Some life offices even have links to funds run by other product providers.

3.1.3 Unitised with-profits funds

Most offices have unitised with-profits funds. These are really with-profits investments (see later) expressed as a unit-linked policy. The main difference from the other unit-linked funds is that the unit price is guaranteed not to fall. There are two types of with-profits fund, fixed-price and variable-price. Under the fixed-price system the unit price does not vary. When the annual bonus is declared an appropriate number of extra units, with the same price, are allocated to the policy. These extra units cannot then be taken away. Under the variable-price system the unit price remains static throughout the year, until the annual bonus is declared, when it will rise accordingly and is guaranteed not to fall.

An element of the annual bonus may be guaranteed and there may also be a terminal bonus on a claim by maturity or death. There is a wide variety of unitised with-profits funds from the different life offices, but the aim is to express the traditional with-profits investment as a unit-linked policy, so as to give the policyholder the chance to switch between with-profits and true unit-linked funds. However, most life offices reserve the right to apply a market value reduction factor (MVR) to surrenders and switches out of the with-profits fund. The MVR enables the life office to reduce the surrender or switch value if it would otherwise be in excess of the value of the underlying assets – eg in times of stock market crashes. The object is to protect the interests of those staying in the funds and maintain fairness between those who cash in early and those who stay the full term. For this reason, MVRs are not applied to claims on death or maturity.

The amount of unitised with-profits business being written has increased rapidly as offices have moved away from conventional with-profits business. However, it is usual for offices not to maintain a separate unit-linked with-profits fund but to continue to use the main with-profits fund. With-profits funds will thus contain increasing proportions of unitised business in the future.

3.2 Conventional with-profits policies

The way these policies work is that every year (or, with a few offices, every third year) the life office carries out a valuation of the assets and liabilities of its life fund. This will normally reveal a surplus, part of which can be allocated to the with-profits policyholders, in the form of an addition to the sum assured. This addition, called a bonus or a profit, is usually 'reversionary' which means that it is only payable at the same time as the sum assured, ie on death or maturity. It will, however, increase the surrender value, and most companies will allow bonuses to be surrendered for a cash value which will be substantially lower than the declared reversionary value. The cash value will vary with the age of the life assured, being higher at older ages. Any unallocated surplus can be ploughed into the reserves or paid out to the office's shareholders as a dividend.

The bonus systems of the various life offices vary considerably, and it is not possible to describe all the methods within the confines of this book. However, one fundamental distinction is that between 'normal bonus' and 'terminal bonus'. A normal bonus is declared annually (or possibly triennially) and increases the value of the policy year by year, as it gets older. The bonus is usually expressed as a percentage of the sum assured, and thus the higher the sum assured, the greater the bonus. It can be either simple, based purely on the original sum assured, or compound, based on the sum assured plus previous bonuses. Once allocated, normal bonuses cannot be removed or reduced.

A terminal bonus is different in concept. This is normally only added when a policy becomes a claim, and is not payable on surrender. It is usually expressed as a percentage of the total normal bonuses and will vary in accordance with market conditions.

Most offices operate a system using both normal and terminal bonuses, and the eventual amount payable will thus comprise three elements – sum assured, normal bonus and terminal bonus. Only the sum assured is guaranteed at outset.

When comparing premium rates for with-profits contracts, the bonus rates on offer from the offices and the likely prospects for future bonus rates must also be considered. Obviously, this is very difficult and probably the best that can be done is to look at the past bonus records of the offices concerned, although as events have shown this is not necessarily a reliable guide either. The Principles and Practices of Financial Management (PPFM) document required by the FSA rules gives investors and intermediaries the information required to assess the bonus record and philosophy of each life office.

Premiums for with-profits contracts are always higher than those for the corresponding non-profit contracts for the same sum assured, since they reflect the higher benefits which will be paid out.

Under a with-profits policy, the policyholder does benefit in some measure from the investment performance of the life fund, but the link is not direct and depends on annual valuations of the fund's assets and liabilities, where a multitude of factors are taken into consideration, and the decision of the directors as to how to allocate any surplus. Because of this, the bonuses added to policies only follow investment performance in a very cushioned and distant fashion. Allowance must be made for the guarantees underlying the basic sum assured and previously declared bonuses, and so the bonus structure cannot directly reflect the value of the underlying assets of the life funds. In addition, bonuses are only declared yearly and thus cannot possibly match the daily fluctuations in the values of the assets.

There has been a strong trend for offices to pull out of writing conventional with-profits business, as described above, in favour of unitised with-profits business – covered on page 11. Most with-profits policies currently being sold are unitised with-profits and conventional with-profits policies will become rarer in the future.

3.2.1 With-profits investment

Premiums for with-profit contracts have to be invested with the objective of maximising profits but also bearing in mind security and any underlying guarantees, eg guaranteed death sums assured. Thus the with-profit fund will have an appreciable proportion in gilts for security, plus equities for growth, property for both security and growth and cash for liquidity. The exact mix will vary from time to time according to market conditions and the mix of business.

A major consideration in the declaration of bonuses is the smoothing effect. This is to avoid wild fluctuations in values (which are sometimes seen on unit-linked policies). Thus in good years not all current investment profits are allocated as bonuses, to keep some in reserve for bad years. Conversely in bad years (eg when the stock market has dropped sharply) it may still be possible to declare some bonus out of reserves accumulated in good years. It is this smoothing effect that differentiates with-profits from unit-linking.

The stronger a life office is, the higher the equity content in its with-profit fund is likely to be, and the better it will respond to market upturns. A life office will have to bear in mind when deciding the level of bonus in any year that this may affect the level of new business they will generate. Thus where an office is keen to attract new with-profit business it will want to declare good bonus rates if possible. However, this does not apply to funds which are closed to new business, particularly if the life office as a whole no longer offers new business. Here there is no such incentive and it may be that the investment managers are not so keen, or well paid. Therefore there are concerns about the levels of bonuses that the increasing number of closed funds might pay in the future.

4 Whole Life Policies

A whole life policy is a very simple policy which pays out a sum assured whenever the life assured dies. It is a permanent policy, not limited to an expiry date as is a term assurance. Because a claim will be certain, premiums will be more expensive than a term assurance where a claim is merely possible – or at best probable. Whole life policies are substantive policies, and can often be used as security for a loan, either from the life office or another lender. Many whole life policies now include critical illness cover and terminal illness cover (see Chapter E).

4.1 Regular premium unit-linked whole life policies

These plans have been very popular. Their main advantage is their flexibility, since they offer a variable mix between investment content and life cover. The policies are regular premium contracts, where the initial level of life cover is set, often for the first ten years, on the basis of an assumed unit price growth rate in the fund to which the contract is linked. At the end of this ten years, the policy is reviewed to see how the actual growth rate compares with the assumed growth rate. This determines whether the value of the units allocated at that time will be enough to maintain the sum assured.

Currently 6% is commonly used as the assumed unit price growth rate.

The action taken as a result of this review varies from office to office but usually, if the actual growth rate is higher than that assumed, the sum assured can be increased, and if it is lower either the sum assured is reduced or the premium correspondingly increased. Further regular reviews are made, usually every five years – but possibly more frequently once the life assured reaches age 70 or 75. The level of life cover under these plans is higher than on conventional whole life or endowment policies and, to help pay for this, unit allocation percentages in the early years are very low – sometimes nil for the first two years. Thus, the investment element of the policy takes some time to build up. If the policy is cashed in, the surrender value will be the bid value of the units allocated. If the total unit value overtakes the sum assured, then the higher amount will be payable on a death claim.

The earliest of these policies had a fixed relationship between the premium and the sum assured. However, most versions now allow the policyholder to choose his own sum assured within certain limits, for any given premium. The policyholder may then have the right to adjust his sum assured up or down (again within certain limits) according to his circumstances. Obviously, the more premium that goes into life cover, the less is invested into units. The attraction of this type of plan is that the level of life cover is extremely flexible – enabling a high degree of protection to be given in the early years and then reducing it to give higher levels of investment later in life, when protection for the family may no longer be the main aim.

In order to maintain the qualifying status of the policy (see Chapter D), the minimum sum assured is set no lower than Her Majesty's Revenue and Customs (HMRC) minimum – 75% of premiums payable to age 75. Some offices have higher limits. The maximum sum assured also varies from office to office, but is typically that which can be sustained throughout life based on the assumed unit price growth rate. Other offices allow a maximum of such an amount as can be guaranteed for ten years, based on a relatively low unit price growth rate, eg 3%. A 'maximum cover' whole life policy provides a high level of life cover and, because it is virtually all risk premium, is akin to a term assurance, albeit without an expiry date and with a substantial chance of an increase in premium after the first review date.

If an increase in sum assured is requested, this will be subject to fresh medical evidence – unless the policy has a guaranteed insurability provision.

The cost of the life cover is met by monthly cancellation of units. The amount cancelled is based on the difference between the sum assured and the value of the units, and is usually calculated with reference to the latest mortality tables. Enough units are cancelled each month to pay for that month's life cover. The policyholder can thus benefit from any future improvements in mortality statistics. A further advantage is that, as the value of the units builds up, the cost of the life cover can reduce rather than increase – as it would on a conventional policy. Once the value of the units overtakes the sum assured, deductions for life cover will cease.

Some offices allow policyholders to increase the sum assured regularly, in line with inflation, without medical evidence. This guaranteed insurability provision is valuable, because it enables the policyholder to maintain the real value of the cover. However, some offices cancel this option if it is not used every time it is available. The option may be available every year, every three years or every five years, depending on the office. Usually this option will cease at, say, age 65. Many offices offer additional options such as critical illness cover, permanent total disability cover or even income protection. In these cases the cost of the cover will be deducted monthly from the units allocated to the policy at that time.

Because of their flexibility, these policies have been very popular, and they currently outsell all other types of regular premium whole life policy.

4.2 Single premium unit-linked whole life policies

These contracts (often called bonds) are the simplest form of unit-linked policy. They are normally written as whole life contracts, so that the investor can continue the contract as long as it is required. When the policy is effected, the whole of the single premium is applied to purchase units in the selected fund at the offer price ruling on the day of payment. The policy can then be cashed in at any time – the surrender value being the total value of the units at the bid prices on the day of surrender.

If the life assured dies, the death claim value will be paid out. This is usually 101% of the value of the units, so as to reduce costs and make it easier for older lives to invest by avoiding underwriting, though this varies between offices. Some offices offer more substantial levels of life cover, eg 120% at age 50 or 200% at age 30.

Many contracts allow the investor to pay in further single premiums at any time. This 'topping-up' facility is useful, since it eliminates the necessity of taking out a completely new policy. Most offices offer both single life and joint life second death versions of this contract.

Almost all these policies allow the investor to take an 'income' by taking partial withdrawals each year. These withdrawals are achieved by cashing in however many units are needed to give the withdrawal amount. If the annual amount withdrawn does not exceed 5% of the original investment, the policyholder will pay no tax at that time. There may be some liability to tax if the withdrawal rate exceeds 5% or its duration exceeds 20 years. Although the withdrawals may be treated as income by the policyholder, and be subject to income tax if they exceed the 5% limit, they are in fact capital payments as a matter of general law. Further details are given in Chapter D.

Some offices now offer increased allocations for larger investments – eg 101% for investments over £30,000. There is also a trend towards imposing surrender penalties for early encashment – eg a 5% penalty for first-year surrenders down to 1% for fifth-year surrenders. Bonds are more fully dealt with in Chapter M.

4.3 Non-profit whole life policies

A non-profit whole life policy has a level premium, payable throughout life. It pays only a fixed sum assured, whenever death occurs. There are also policies which offer a cessation of premiums on attainment of a certain age – often 80 or 85. These contracts are slightly more expensive, because premiums will be payable on average for a shorter period. These contracts were very rarely sold over the last few decades, but have recently become more popular in the inheritance tax (IHT) market.

Some life offices now market a simple whole life policy by direct mail offers, typically to the over 50s. The proposal forms tend to be very simple with few medical questions. The sum assured is a fixed sum with no bonus or unit-linking. However, it is common for the sum assured only to be payable if death occurs more than two years after the start of the policy, with only a refund of premiums payable on death within that period. There will usually be no surrender value.

4.4 With-profits whole life policies

These policies are almost the same as non-profit whole life assurances, the only difference being that the amount payable on death is the sum assured, plus whatever profits have been allocated up to the date of death. A terminal bonus is also payable by most offices. Again, premiums can be payable throughout life – or can cease at age 80–85. These policies have largely been superseded by unit-linked whole life contracts, but many are still in force.

4.5 Low-cost whole life policies

These policies are with-profits whole life contracts with a guaranteed level of cover. They are actually written with two sums assured. The amount payable on death is the greater of (a) the basic sum assured plus bonuses, or (b) the guaranteed death sum assured. Bonuses are calculated on the basic sum assured and thus amount (a) increases year by year with the declaration of bonuses until it overtakes amount (b). Consequently, the contract is, in effect, a with-profits whole life policy incorporating a decreasing term assurance element which decreases as the bonuses increase.

Premiums for this type of contract are lower than for ordinary non-profit whole life contracts although the benefits will not be as high as a full with-profits policy.

Some offices allow the difference between the basic and guaranteed death sums assured to be converted into basic sum assured, subject to the appropriate increase in premium.

These policies have also largely been replaced by unit-linked whole life contracts.

5 Endowment Policies

The third basic type of policy is the endowment assurance. Here the sum assured is payable on a fixed date (the maturity date) or on the life assured's earlier death. The standard non-profit endowment assurance provides a level guaranteed sum assured on death or maturity. Because there is certain to be a payout at some stage, endowment assurances are substantive contracts and have cash-in (surrender) values and can be used as security for loans, either from the life office itself or from other lenders.

Level premiums are payable for the duration of the contract. Premiums for endowments are generally more expensive than for whole life assurances, because claim payments are generally made earlier. The shorter the term of the endowment, the higher will be the premium for a given sum assured, because it will be payable for a shorter period. Terms of less than ten years were rare, because of the qualifying rules (see Chapter D), although following the abolition of life assurance premium relief they did become more common for a while.

With the exception of flexidowment policies, the endowment policies described below are only really suitable investments if the investor does not want the money before the maturity date, and will not need to cash in the policy earlier. The best yield on an endowment policy is almost always obtained by waiting until the maturity date. The reasons for this are really twofold. First, cash-in (or surrender) values on life policies are generally on the low side – in many cases the surrender value in the early years of a contract can be less than the premiums paid in. Even in later years, the surrender value is often substantially less than the maturity value. Second, under many offices' bonus structures, a terminal bonus is payable on death and maturity claims – but not on surrenders. Terminal bonuses can form a large proportion of the total claim value.

Endowments can include critical illness cover and terminal illness cover (see Chapter E).

5.1 Unit-linked endowments

A unit-linked endowment policy has a maturity sum assured of the bid value of units payable on the maturity date, plus a guaranteed minimum sum assured payable on prior death. If the value of units is higher than the minimum sum assured at the date of death, the greater amount will be paid.

A specified percentage of each premium is applied to buy units at the offer price ruling on the day of payment. In the first year, either initial units, with their higher management charge, will be allocated, or a relatively low percentage (the allocation percentage) of the premiums paid will be applied to buy accumulation units. Subsequent premiums will buy units at an allocation percentage, which will vary from office to office – but the basis will be that older lives assured receive a lower allocation percentage. As the policy progresses, more and more units will be bought and so its value should continue to rise.

The contract will have at least enough life cover to ensure that it is a qualifying policy. This normally means that the sum assured will be at least 75% of the total premiums payable over the full term of the contract. Thus, on death, the amount payable will be the guaranteed death sum assured mentioned above or the bid value of the units – whichever is the higher.

The maturity value will be the bid value of the units. If the investor wishes to cash in his policy before maturity, the surrender value will also be the bid value of the units. However, if surrender occurs in the early years there may be a discontinuance charge or 'surrender penalty' which has to be deducted from the value of the units before arriving at the final figure. Most surrender penalty charges will only apply during the first ten years.

Policies can be single life or joint life. Savings plans are often written as long-term unit-linked endowments, or ten year endowments with an option to extend for further ten year periods. These plans are frequently issued as a cluster of small individual policies which can be dealt with separately, eg a £50 per month plan might be issued as a cluster of ten £5 per month policies. This increases the flexibility of the arrangement and also has taxation advantages (see Chapter M).

Unit-linked endowments are often used in endowment house purchase arrangements. The guaranteed death sum assured will be the amount of the loan and that will also be the target maturity value, although there is no guarantee that this will be achieved. These contracts often use the unitised with-profits fund. For full details see Chapter F.

5.2 Low start policies

Many offices offer low start unit-linked endowments where premiums start at a low level, rising gradually over a number of years to the full premium. This is aimed at the home buyer who is working on a very tight budget, but who has expectations of salary rises in future years. The premium might increase by 20% pa for five years, or 10% pa for ten years.

5.3 Non-profit endowment policies

These are the most basic form of endowment contract, with level premiums and the payout of only a fixed, guaranteed sum assured on maturity, or earlier death. They are now very rare indeed and will probably not be met in practice.

5.4 With-profits endowment policies

The principles that govern with-profits contracts have already been described in section 3. These also apply to with-profits endowment assurances, where the amount payable on maturity or earlier death would be the guaranteed sum assured, plus the bonuses. If the policy runs to maturity, bonuses will be higher than if it becomes a death claim – because they will have been added for a longer period.

As with whole life assurances, it is not possible to guarantee what the eventual payout will be, because of the variable nature of future bonuses. Estimates can, however, be made using the FSA prescribed rates and the office's own charging structure.

Premiums are higher than for non-profit endowments, to reflect the greater benefits that are payable. With-profits endowment contracts used to be the basic element in many savings schemes and house purchase arrangements.

5.5 Low-cost endowment policies

The low-cost endowment contract is, as its name suggests, a low-cost version of the with-profits endowment. This uses a combination of with-profits endowment and decreasing term assurance. As in the low-cost whole life policy, there are two sums assured. The amount payable on death is the greater of (a) the basic sum assured plus bonuses; or (b) the guaranteed death sum assured.

Bonuses are calculated on the basic sum assured, and so amount (a) increases year by year with the declaration of bonuses, and will hopefully overtake amount (b). The term assurance element (which is the difference between the basic and guaranteed death sum assured) will thus decrease as bonuses increase, and will be eliminated once sum (a) is greater than sum assured (b).

The basic sum assured is pitched at such a level that, with the addition of bonuses based on, say, 80% of the office's current normal rates, it will equal the guaranteed death sum assured on the maturity date. The amount payable on maturity is the basic sum assured plus bonuses – and is thus not fully guaranteed.

These policies were introduced as a cheaper way of covering house purchase loans, with the guaranteed death sum assured being equal to the loan. Because the basic sum assured was less than it would be under a full with-profits endowment, the premiums were cheaper – but, owing to the term assurance element, there was a guarantee that the loan would be repaid on death. There was no such guarantee on maturity, but, because of the conservative bonus assumptions used in fixing the basic sum assured, it was expected that the maturity value would exceed the amount of the loan.

Many contracts of this type carried the option for the policyholder to convert the difference between the two sums assured (ie the term element) into basic sum assured. (For a full discussion of the various methods of house purchase, see Chapter F.)

Most offices had low start versions of this contract as well as level premium ones. The low initial premiums did not affect the sum assured or the bonuses, which continued throughout the term of the policy on the normal low cost basis.

This type of contract has now been replaced by the unitised with-profits endowment.

5.6 Flexidowments

Flexidowments are open-ended endowments with profits which can be cashed in without the conventional surrender penalty at any time after ten years.

The surrender value is usually guaranteed, or part-guaranteed, and is more akin to an early maturity value than to the traditional endowment surrender value. For convenience, the policies are usually written as long-term with-profits endowments – say, for 25 years, or to age 65. Some policies of this type have even been written as whole life policies. In whatever way the policy is written, however, its real purpose will be to provide a maturity value at any time after ten years.

Often the flexidowment is issued as a number of small identical policies with a standard premium of, say £1 to £10 per month per policy. This allows just one or two policies to be cashed in whenever required, giving greater flexibility. There are also taxation advantages in this approach, which are explained in Chapter M.

Flexidowments have effectively been superseded by unit-linked endowments.

5.7 Pure endowments

A pure endowment is not truly a life policy, since it provides no life cover. The standard pure endowment is simply a contract which pays out the maturity value if the life assured lives to the maturity date, but pays out nothing if the life assured dies before that date. Some pure endowments may have a surrender value, but many do not. Some pure endowments may offer a return of premiums on death before maturity.

These are very specialised contracts and are used in combination with other policies in capital transfer tax (CTT) and IHT mitigation plans (see Chapter L).

6 Annuities

An annuity is not strictly a life assurance policy as it does not pay out on death; in fact it usually ceases on death. However, annuities do depend on human life and are offered by most life offices. An annuity is simply a contract to pay a given amount (the annuity) every year while the annuitant (the person on whose life the contract depends) is still alive. Annuities are usually expressed in terms of the annual amount payable, although in practice they can be payable monthly, quarterly, half-yearly or yearly. An annuity can be payable in advance or in arrears; eg where an annuity is effected on 1 January 2006 the first annual payment is due on 1 January 2006 if it is in advance, or on 1 January 2007 if it is in arrears.

Where an annuity is payable in arrears, it can either be with proportion or without proportion. This is because each payment is made at the end of the period to which it relates. Thus, when the annuitant dies there will be a period since the last instalment date for which no payment has been made. Under a with-proportion annuity a proportionate payment will be made to cover this period. This is not the case for a without-proportion annuity, where no payment is made.

For any given annuity, an annuity in advance will cost more than one in arrears and one with proportion will cost more than one without proportion. Annuity rates tend to fluctuate much more frequently than life assurance premium rates, as they are much more sensitive to interest rate movements.

Most annuities are paid for by a single premium which is often called the consideration for the annuity. However, deferred annuities are often purchased by regular premiums.

An increasing number of life offices offer increased annuity rates for unhealthy lives. Those who are able to prove that they have a substantially below-average expectation of life can get higher annuities than average lives. At least one office offers higher annuity rates for smokers.

The various types of annuity are described in section 7. Subsequent sections will examine the use, and taxation of, annuities. However, annuities are often used in personal pensions and employee pension schemes. These are dealt with in Chapter P.

7 Types of Annuity

An immediate annuity contract provides, in return for a single premium, an annual payment starting immediately and continuing for the rest of the annuitant's life. Annuity rates have reduced substantially over the last ten years due to declining gilt yields and improving life expectancy.

7.1 Immediate annuities

These contracts are often purchased by retired people who want an income that is guaranteed to last for the rest of their life, no matter how long (or short) that might be.

7.2 Deferred annuities

A deferred annuity is a contract which provides for an annuity to be payable commencing at some future date. The period between the date of the contract and the date the annuity is to commence (often called the 'vesting date' or the 'maturity date') is the deferred period. Often, regular premiums are payable throughout the deferred period. If the annuitant dies during the deferred period the office will usually return the premiums paid, with or without interest. Once the vesting date is reached the annuity becomes payable and will continue for the rest of the annuitant's life.

Often a cash option is available on the vesting date in lieu of the annuity.

Many deferred annuities are effected in connection with pension schemes or personal pension contracts. Full cash options will not be available in those cases. These subjects are fully covered in Chapter P.

7.3 Temporary annuities

A temporary annuity is an annuity which is payable for a fixed period or for the annuitant's lifetime, whichever is the shorter. It thus differs from an immediate annuity which is guaranteed to continue throughout life, hence the term 'temporary annuity'. If the annuitant survives the fixed period, the annuity ceases, as it does if he dies during that period. Rates for temporary annuities are higher than immediate annuities as the average period of payment will be shorter.

7.4 Annuities certain

An annuity certain is simply a contract to pay an annuity for a specified period regardless of whether the annuitant survives. It does not depend on the age of the annuitant as payment is guaranteed for the set period.

7.5 Guaranteed annuities

A guaranteed annuity is an immediate annuity which is guaranteed to be payable for a minimum period, regardless of when the annuitant dies. Thus, an annuity guaranteed for ten years will be payable for life or ten years, whichever is the longer. If the annuitant dies during the guaranteed period the balance of the guaranteed instalments will be payable to the estate, although they may be able to take a commuted cash sum instead. A guaranteed annuity will cost more than the equivalent non-guaranteed annuity as the life office will on average be paying out for longer. The cash value of the balance of a guaranteed annuity on death may be subject to IHT as an asset of the estate.

7.6 Joint life and last survivor annuities

Where an annuity is being used to provide retirement income for a married couple, it would not be advisable to have a single life annuity because, if the annuitant died first, payments would cease and the surviving spouse would be left with nothing. Hence, the existence of joint life and last survivor annuities: these contracts pay an annuity for the joint lifetimes of the two annuitants. Payments usually continue in full after the first death but sometimes reduce by, say, one-third.

These annuities can be in advance or arrears, with or without proportion to the date of the second death, and with or without guarantee – just like single life annuities.

An alternative to a joint life and last survivor annuity is to have two separate annuities. The first would be an immediate annuity on one life and, the second, a reversionary annuity on the other life. The reversionary annuity would provide an annuity for life but commencing only on the death of the annuitant under the immediate annuity.

7.7 Escalating annuities

All the annuities discussed so far are level annuities. However, some offices offer increasing annuities where the instalments increase by a fixed percentage each year. This can help to offset the effects of inflation, although the rate of inflation might well be higher than the fixed rate of increase. It must also be remembered that a level annuity will be much higher for the same premium than the initial level of an increasing annuity.

A number of offices have annuities linked to the RPI where the income will increase (or decrease) each year by the same percentage as the RPI. The initial annuity amount is substantially lower than for a level annuity but there is total protection against inflation.

7.8 Unit-linked annuities

A small number of companies offer unit-linked annuities where the annual income level is linked to the value of units in the selected fund. Initial annuity amounts depend on the investment return assumption used. The lower the assumption, the smaller the initial income compared with ordinary guaranteed annuities, but the greater is the potential for growth. The purchase price is applied to buy a number of units in the fund according to the offer price at the time. The appropriate number of units are cancelled on each payment and so the level of income can vary (up or down) according to the value of units. The annuity will be reviewed periodically and the income varied in the light of the unit performance. Unit-linked annuities are inherently more risky than guaranteed annuities and the client needs to understand that the annuity could fall sharply if there is a market crash. Over the long term, the hope is that the eventual level of annuity will be higher than that provided by a guaranteed level annuity. Some unit-linked annuities have an option to switch to a standard level annuity.

7.9 With-profits annuities

A growing number of offices have with-profits annuities where the lump sum is invested into the with-profit fund. The annuity then depends on the performance of the with-profit fund. The way that most of these annuities work is that an assumed bonus rate is selected at outset which then sets the level of the initial annuity. Thereafter every year the actual return (the declared bonus) is compared with the assumed return. If the returns match, the annuity continues at the original rate. If the actual returns are better than the assumed return the annuity increases, and if the actual return is worse the annuity reduces. If a conservative rate of bonus is assumed the annuity would probably increase each year, although the initial annuity will usually be lower than on a conventional annuity. Most with-profit annuities have some guarantee of minimum annuity and the eventual annuity is likely to be more stable than a unit-linked annuity. In particular, there would be less chance of a dramatic reduction. The higher the selected rate of growth at the outset the greater the risk that the income will fall in later years if the assumed bonus rate is not achieved.

7.10 Capital protected annuities

These are annuities where the total payment is guaranteed to be at least as much as the premium. The effect is that when the annuitant dies, the office adds up all the gross annuity payments made and compares this with the premium. If total payments are less than the premium, the office will pay the balance as a capital sum to the deceased annuitant's estate. This is not subject to income tax, but as part of the estate it might be liable to IHT.

These annuities are more expensive than ordinary immediate annuities but do guarantee that the annuitant will never receive back less than the premium.

7.11 Impaired life annuities

A number of offices offer impaired life annuities. These provide higher than normal annuities for clients with a life expectancy which is below average. The client has to give full details of their health and the proposal will be underwritten. As a result of the underwriting, the office may offer an increased annuity. The increase will depend on the degree of impairment and will be individually calculated.

7.12 Enhanced annuities

Several offices in the impaired annuity market also offer enhanced annuities. These generally do not require the extensive underwriting of impaired life annuities and give higher rates for certain medical conditions (eg anyone who has had cancer) or unhealthy lifestyles (eg smokers). It is estimated that 40% of the population could be eligible for enhanced annuities.

7.13 Uses of annuities

It must be borne in mind that the main disadvantage of most annuities is that the regular income payment is fixed at outset and, because of inflation, can become inadequate after a number of years. This might not matter if the annuity is intended to meet a fixed liability, eg a funding scheme. However, if an annuity is going to be one of the main sources of future income, its declining real value could be a problem. One way of coping with this is to use an escalating annuity, although as seen previously the initial income will be less than that from a level annuity.

7.13.1 Anuities for income

Possibly the most common purpose of an annuity is to provide an income for life, usually after the annuitant's working life has ceased. It is often used to supplement some form of pension. The advantage of a life annuity is that the income is guaranteed for life, so that no matter how long the annuitant lives he will still receive that income. A possible disadvantage is that if the annuitant dies soon after taking out his annuity, he might not have received back anywhere near the purchase price in total annuity payments. Thus some of the purchase price would seem to have been 'wasted'. This possibility can be catered for by effecting a guaranteed annuity (say, for five or ten years) or a capital protected annuity.

The main disadvantage of the level annuity, as already explained, is its declining real value in inflationary periods. This may not be too serious if the annuity is only one element in the person's retirement income but could be serious if it were the sole source of income. If this were the case, an escalating annuity might be more appropriate than a level one.

If the person thinking about an annuity for income is married, then a joint life and last survivor annuity ought to be considered rather than a single life one. A single life annuity might be adequate if the policyholder outlives his or her partner and, in this context, it should be remembered that the statistical evidence is that wives tend to outlive their husbands. If a joint life and last survivor annuity is used, then the income will continue after the first death and will be payable until the death of the survivor.

7.13.2 Annuities for beneficiaries under trusts or wills

Sometimes the terms of a will or trust state that a particular beneficiary shall receive a specified income for life. The executors or trustees could pay this out of the income of the fund as it arose each year but this would involve continued administration and it is often more convenient to purchase an annuity from a life office for the beneficiary. The taxation considerations of such an approach are dealt with in Chapter D section 8.

B Life Assurance Policy Procedures

This chapter traces the life story of a typical ordinary life assurance policy. It does this by dealing first with the procedures for taking out a policy, together with the relevant principles surrounding this. It then goes on to explain the various events that can occur during the life of a policy. Section 7 then deals with the way a policy can be terminated and the relevant legalities.

It must be stressed that the practices of life offices vary in detail and that different types of policy may be dealt with in different ways. However, the procedures described in this chapter are typical of those adopted by the majority of life offices for an ordinary life policy.

Items specifically required by the FSA rules (eg cancellation notices) are dealt with in Chapter Q.

1 The Proposal Form

The basic form used to initiate and then process an application for life assurance is the proposal form. This is a document signed by the proposer which requests the life office to issue a policy and gives the relevant information to enable the office to consider the application and prepare the policy.

The form identifies the life to be assured, gives details of the policy required and gives personal and medical details of the life-to-be-assured. The declaration must be signed to declare the answers to be true and also to give the insurer permission to approach the life-to-be-assured's doctor if any further information is required. The Association of British Insurers' (ABI) Statement of Long Term Insurance Practice requires a warning on the consequences of failure to disclose all material facts and that if there is doubt the facts should be disclosed. The form must also say that a copy of the policy conditions and the completed proposal form are available on request.

An Ownership of Benefits section must be completed if the contract is to be on a life of another basis. The life office will have to be satisfied regarding the insurable interest position and this is the reason for the question on the relationship to the life-to-be-assured. The countersignature of the life-to-be-assured is required to make sure that he or she realises that the policy will be owned by the other, to whom all benefits will be paid. Insurable interest is dealt with later in section 3.

1.1 Access to medical reports

The Access to Medical Reports Act 1988 gives the proposer certain rights and there will be a statement of these rights on the proposal form. The main right is to see the report and request a correction before the doctor sends it to the life office.

2 Underwriting

2.1 The underwriting process

When the proposal form is received by the life office it must go through the underwriting process. Underwriting is the name given to the procedure of assessing proposals and deciding whether to accept the risks, and, if so, at what rate of premium. Each office has its own table of rates for the policies it offers. The rate will vary with age and the policy term. These 'ordinary rates' are based on average mortality experience. If a life proposed reveals features which suggest that there is a significantly above-average risk of death, then the office must investigate further to decide whether the risk can be accepted at ordinary rates, or whether some special terms might be required. The various special terms are explained later in this section (see section 2.2 Under-average lives).

Each life office has its own approach to underwriting and some companies have their own specialities and are known for offering competitive terms for certain impairments. Some offices specialise in term assurances, whereas others are better at other types of risk. Each office will have a maximum sum assured – called a retention – beyond which it will not go without re-assuring some of the risk with another office (by and large, retentions tend to be higher for the larger and older-established offices). Thus, very large sums assured may take time to underwrite because the office will have to arrange the appropriate re-assurance. The need to re-assure will affect the underwriting because the underwriter will have to agree terms with the re-assuring office's underwriter. The value of re-assurance is that it spreads a very large risk among a number of offices.

An underwriter must remember that life assurance contracts are based on utmost good faith. The life-to-be-assured is in possession of all material facts relating to the risk and has a duty to disclose them. However, it is not unknown for material facts to be omitted or only partially disclosed. The subject of utmost good faith and the duty of disclosure is covered in section 3. The job of the underwriter is to recognise defects even if they are not specifically disclosed. Vague answers on a proposal such as 'headache' or 'stomach-bug' may describe some trivial condition. On the other hand, they may reveal something much more serious which may require special underwriting treatment. The underwriter must use his skill to assess whether the proposal can be accepted at ordinary rates, or, if not, at what special terms.

Underwriting is more important for some policies than others. The risk of death is more material for term assurances than for substantive policies. The risk of death increases with age and is thus greater for older lives and longer terms. On substantive policies the cost of the death risk is reduced by the investment reserve building up and therefore underwriting is often more lenient on substantive policies than it is for term assurances.

The first task of the underwriter is to search the office's alphabetical index of proposers to see if any earlier proposals have been received. If so, those papers are obtained.

The proposal form will then be checked to make sure that all questions have been answered and the declarations signed.

The underwriter can now consider the information on the form and decide whether the proposal can be accepted at ordinary rates without further investigation. If this is the case, then it can be passed to the policy issuing department. If the underwriter feels that the proposal cannot be accepted immediately, he can take one of the following courses:

- Obtain further information on which to make a decision.
- Impose some form of special terms.
- Decline the proposal.

Most offices have what are described as non-medical limits under which proposals will be considered without a general practitioner's report or a medical examination being necessary. The office will, however, reserve the right to call for these should the answers on the proposal form warrant this. Limits vary from office to office but a typical age limit would be 'under 40', and for a sum assured 'under £300,000'. These limits will of course relate to the total sum assured for that life, and not just the current proposal. So in the above example, if the proposer already had a £20,000 policy, the limit would be £280,000 for a new proposal. This saves the life office from the expense of automatic medical evidence for all proposals. Long experience has shown that comparatively few cases reveal significant medical defects. However, lives over an office's age limits or sums assured over the limits will automatically require further medical evidence.

If the proposal form reveals any medical factor about which the underwriter wants further information, there are two main ways of obtaining it. The first is the General Practitioner's Report which is a report sent to the proposer's doctor for completion from his records. There is an industry standard General Practitioner's Report developed by the ABI. The second is a medical examination of the life-to-be-assured by a doctor appointed by the office. Most offices have lists of doctors willing to do examinations and they will thus ask one of the doctors in the proposer's area to carry out the examination and send in a report. If the underwriter wants to see copies of the proposer's medical records, this is permitted by the Access to Health Records Act 1990, as long as the life office has the life-to-be-assured's written authority.

With the information from these reports the underwriter should be able to come to a decision. If a further opinion is required, especially where the sum assured is very high, the underwriter can discuss the case with the office's Chief Medical Officer. The Chief Medical Officer will usually be a consultant physician of high professional standing, who can give expert medical advice to the underwriter and may even conduct medical examinations personally in very important cases.

Some offices now use telemedical interviewing. This is an underwriting technique using insurance trained nurses to obtain medical information via the telephone direct from the client. This can speed up the underwriting and reduce its costs.

The underwriter will be on the look-out for any factor which could affect the proposer's longevity. This would include medical factors (eg heart disease), occupation (eg bomb disposal workers) and hazardous pastimes (eg motor cycle racing). It is beyond the scope of this book to go into the details of everything which the underwriter will investigate but basically they will be interested in anything which could reduce the expectation of life to below average.

Those proposers accepted at ordinary rates are termed 'average lives'. However, those assessed by the underwriter as having a materially greater risk of death than average are called 'under-average lives'. Under-average lives should pay a higher than normal premium, otherwise the office's costing assumptions, which are based on average mortality, will be upset. Each proposer should pay a premium appropriate to their own risk.

About 95% of proposers are accepted at ordinary rates. About 4% will have to pay some form of extra premium, or equivalent, and around 1% are declined.

Some offices have introduced 'preferred rates' for proposers who are substantially healthier than average and thus bring a lower risk to the life fund. This is effectively a system of discounted premiums for healthy lives that can score over a certain level in 'healthy lifestyle' tests.

There are a number of different ways of dealing with under-average lives and these are dealt with in the next section.

There is an ABI Statement of Best Practice on HIV and insurance. Underwriters have to take decisions on a case by case basis and assess premiums fairly. They should not ask for excessive, speculative or irrelevant information and must take account of all relevant factors. Underwriters must also stay up to date with developments and statistics and the company must have an agreed policy on dealing with HIV, updated at least every three years.

2.2 Under-average lives

The special terms used by an underwriter to deal with under-average lives are set out below:

2.2.1 Offer ordinary rates for a limited type of policy

If the extra risk is an increasing one becoming more serious in later life, then a proposal might be accepted but only for a policy expiring or maturing not later than, say, age 65. A whole life proposal might be declined, but instead a term assurance expiring at 65 could be offered. A number of health defects are acceptable at ordinary rates if the policy expires before a certain age.

2.2.2 Charge a monetary extra

The monetary extra is an extra premium expressed in terms of a specific amount per £1,000 sum assured. An example would be a motor racing extra of £2.00 per mille. The extra premium may be payable throughout the term of the policy, or only for a limited period, such as a seven-year service flying extra of £2.00 per mille. The limited term extra is used where the extra risk is heavy and immediate, as with aviation (where the bulk of flying is done in early years), or where the risk will decrease with time.

2.2.3 Impose a rating

A rating is another type of extra premium, but is calculated differently from the monetary extra. It is assumed that the life is *x* years older than the real age, and the premium for the rated-up age is charged. Thus a 50-year-old man with moderate asthma might be rated 'plus 4' and be charged the normal premium for a 54-year-old man.

2.2.4 Impose a debt

As an alternative to increasing the premium, a debt can be imposed on the sum assured. This is sometimes offered if the proposer disagrees with an extra premium quoted by the underwriter and wishes to proceed with the ordinary premium. A debt is a deduction from the sum assured. A debt will normally decrease annually. A typical decreasing debt might provide that if death occurs in the first year the sum assured is reduced by a debt of 80%, and that the debt shall decrease by 8% pa for ten years. After the ten years the sum assured will be payable in full. Debts might be suitable for contracts intended for investment where the life cover element might not be too important to the proposer. They can also be used for risks which decrease as time goes on – eg successfully treated tuberculosis.

2.2.5 Exclude the extra risk

Under this method the proposal is accepted at ordinary rates, but death from the extra risk is excluded. For example, a proposal from an otherwise average life who took part in hang-gliding might be accepted at ordinary rates subject to an exclusion for death caused by hang-gliding. The drawback of this method is that cover is not complete, and is in fact not there when it might be needed most. It will usually be used for an occupational or sporting extra risk rather than a medical one.

2.2.6 Postpone the risk

Postponement can be used where the initial risk is such as to render the life virtually uninsurable, but where once the danger period is survived prospects will improve substantially so that acceptance at ordinary rates might then be possible. A postponement may thus be in the best interests of both parties. This method is used, for example, if the proposer is having an operation in the near future. The proposal could be postponed for a while to allow the proposer to recover and to be reassessed at ordinary rates.

2.2.7 Decline the risk

If the extra risk is extremely heavy and there is little prospect of any subsequent improvement, the proposal may be declined (or refused) completely. Most offices do not like to decline proposers and try to offer some special terms if they can, although this is not always possible.

As a result of an agreement made between the ABI and the British Medical Association (BMA), when an insurance applicant is declined or postponed as a result of a medical disclosure they have made on the application form, the life office will give the reason for this to the applicant. If a new, or poorly controlled, medical condition is revealed on the General Practitioner's Report or following a medical examination which was not disclosed on the application, the life office will inform the GP.

2.3 Disability Discrimination Act 1995

Under s19 of this Act, it is unlawful for a provider of services to discriminate against a disabled person by refusing to provide any of its services that are available to the general public or by providing such services on different terms. Insurance is mentioned as one of the services to which the section applies.

This would mean that declining or rating up a disabled person for life assurance would be unlawful. However, under s20, such treatment is lawful if it reflects the greater cost to the insurer in providing insurance to the disabled person and the treatment is reasonable in that light. Thus, any form of special terms (eg an extra premium) is allowable provided it can be justified by actuarial or other statistical or medical evidence. It is not necessary for the terms to be the same as those offered by other insurers, provided the treatment is reasonable.

2.4 Genetic testing

The ABI has published a mandatory code of practice on the use and handling of genetic test information by insurance companies. Important features of this code include:

- Insurance companies will not insist on genetic tests.
- Genetic test results will only affect insurance if they show a clearly increased risk of illness or death. A low increase in risk will not necessarily affect the premium.
- Insurance companies will always seek expert medical advice when assessing the impact of genetic test results on insurance.
- Insurers may take account of a test result only when reliability and relevance have been established by the government's Genetics and Insurance Committee.
- Applicants for insurance will not be asked to take a genetic test, but existing test results should be given to the insurance company when it asks a relevant question, unless it has said this information is not required.
- Existing genetic test results need not be disclosed in applications for life assurance up to £500,000 (including existing cover with that insurer), for life assurance and £300,000 for critical illness, income protection and long-term care cover.
- An applicant will not be required to disclose the result of a genetic test undertaken by another person (such as a blood relative), and one person's test information will not affect another person's application.
- The reason for an increased premium or rejection of an insurance application will be provided to the applicant's doctor on request.
- Insurers will not 'cherry pick' by offering a 'preferred life' lower than normal premiums on the basis of their genetic test results.
- Complaints about a breach of the Code can be made to an independent Adjudication Tribunal.

3 Legal Requirements

In order for a life assurance contract to be legally valid, five requirements have to be complied with. They are:

- Offer and acceptance.
- Premium payment.
- Contractual capacity.
- Insurable interest.
- Duty of disclosure.

These will now be considered in detail.

3.1 Offer, acceptance and premium payment

In order for any contract to be valid, there has to be a definite offer by one party and a definite acceptance by the other party. This applies to life policies as well. An advertisement or prospectus issued by an insurer is not legally an offer; it is an invitation to make offers. When the proposer completes and signs the proposal form, this is the offer. When the life office has underwritten the risk it sometimes issues a 'letter of acceptance' stating that it will issue the policy required at a stated premium provided the first premium is paid by a certain date on the understanding that the state of health of the proposer remains unchanged.

At law the letter of acceptance is not an acceptance at all but a counter-offer (*Canning v Farquhar* [1886] 16 Q.B. 727). This the proposer can accept by paying the first premium within the specified time.

If an under-average life is being offered special terms, these will be specified in the letter. The letter makes it clear that the office is not on risk until it has accepted the first premium. The offer period is usually 14 days, though some offices allow up to 30 days. When the proposer pays the first premium the contract begins and the office is on risk.

If the time limit is exceeded, the offer is withdrawn. Most offices would still accept the first premium within, say, three to four months, provided a satisfactory up-to-date Declaration of Health is supplied by the life (or lives) assured. If there has been any deterioration in health, this should be disclosed to the life office. The office will then obtain full details of the condition and can amend or withdraw its offer.

The first premium will sometimes be paid by cheque, but it is more common for offices to accept a signed direct debit mandate for the first (and subsequent) premiums. It is considered that this is equivalent to a cheque as far as offer and acceptance are concerned.

If it transpires that the cheque bounces or the direct debit is refused by the bank, then the office is not on risk as the first premium has not truly been paid.

3.2 Contractual capacity

Both parties to a life policy must have the legal power to contract. The life office must meet all the requirements of the FSA Prudential Rulebook which sets out the rules for many aspects of the running of life assurance business – particularly authorisation, accounts, valuations and solvency. Foreign life offices may not be authorised to transact business in the UK and therefore do not have to meet the requirements. However, UK policyholders of these offices are not covered by the Financial Services Compensation Scheme which applies only to companies authorised under the Financial Services and Markets Act 2000.

With regard to potential policyholders, there are legal restrictions on the contractual powers of certain classes of person and these are dealt with below.

3.2.1 Minors

A minor in English law is a person under 18[1]. Subject to certain exceptions, contracts made by a minor are not enforceable against him, although he may be able to enforce them; contracts for necessaries and certain contracts of employment beneficial to the minor are enforceable. Other types of contract are valid unless the minor repudiates them either before attaining 18 or within a reasonable time thereafter. Life policies are in this category.

A minor can therefore propose for a life policy if he is old enough to know what he is doing. He could then repudiate it within a reasonable time of attaining 18. Any office granting a policy to a minor is thus taking a commercial risk that the minor will repudiate the policy at age 18 and demand a refund of premiums plus interest. Some offices therefore will not issue policies to minors. Others will but only with the countersignature of a parent or guardian – however, this is not legally watertight and the minor would still be able to repudiate the contract at age 18. Some offices have specific statutory authority to issue policies to minors and these will not be subject to the general law as stated above. Another problem is that a life office cannot safely accept a discharge for surrender from a minor, or make him a loan.

Scottish law is different. Under the Age of Legal Capacity (Scotland) Act 1991, a person under 16 only has legal capacity to enter into a transaction of a kind commonly entered into by persons of his age and circumstances and on terms which are not unreasonable. It would probably be held that a life assurance contract would not be a contract of a kind commonly entered into by someone under 16. Such a contract would therefore be void and a life office would thus take a great risk if it contracted with someone under 16.

In addition, under Scottish law anyone under 21 can apply to the Court to set aside a transaction entered into at age 16 or 17 which is prejudicial. A transaction is deemed

[1] Family Law Reform Act 1969

prejudicial where an adult exercising reasonable prudence would not have done it. Thus, even contracting with 16 and 17-year-olds is not free from problems.

3.2.2 Mentally disordered persons

In general, a contract with a person of unsound mind is binding on him if his disability was not known by the other contracting party. He can however repudiate the contract if the disability was known to the other party. Thus, an office should not grant a life policy to a proposer whom it knows is of unsound mind.

Under the Mental Health Act 1983 the affairs and property of a mental patient can be put in the hands of the Court of Protection and if this is done the patient has no power to contract. The Court of Protection will normally appoint a Receiver who only has the powers specifically given by the court order. The order does not transfer ownership of the patient's assets and is not the equivalent of a power of attorney. It might (or might not) give the power to make investments on behalf of the patient or deal with the patient's existing contracts.

3.2.3 Corporations

A company has a legal identity separate from that of its members. The contractual powers of a company can be found in its Memorandum of Association. Power is implied to do anything incidental to these powers.

Under s108 of the Companies Act 1989 it is provided that the validity of an act done by a company shall not be called into question on the ground of lack of capacity by reason of anything in the company's memorandum. The section also states that in favour of a person dealing with a company in good faith the power of the board of directors to bind the company or authorise others to do so shall be deemed to be free of any limitation under the company's constitution. The effect of this is that companies will be bound by their contracts notwithstanding the fact that technically they may not have power to enter into them. However, it has been considered for some time that a trading company does have the power to effect a policy on the life of a director or employee, subject to insurable interest.

Under s130 of the Companies Act 1989 a proposal form can be executed by a company with its common seal or by the signatures of two directors or a director and the secretary. In practice, most proposals will be signed by an officer or employee of the company preferably with its stamp or seal.

3.3 Insurable interest

A further requirement for a contract of insurance to be valid is insurable interest. For life assurance this means that the assured must have an insurable interest in the life of the life assured.

This requirement was introduced by the Life Assurance Act 1774. This stated that no insurance could be made if the assured did not have insurable interest in the life assured and that no greater sum than that interest could be insured. It also said that the assured must be named in the policy.

The Act did not define insurable interest but case law over the years has established that the assured must stand to be financially worse off if the life assured dies, to a degree capable of valuation and as a result of a legally recognised relationship. A moral duty or an expectation is not legally sufficient.

A life office will usually ask for the relationship between the proposer and the life proposed so that it can be sure that the interest is present on all 'life of another' proposals. Some offices are prepared to issue policies without insurable interest if no life cover is involved – eg single premium unit-linked bonds.

3.3.1 Examples of insurable interest

- A person has an unlimited insurable interest in his own life. Most offices will however refuse a policy which is so large that the proposer could not possibly afford the premium. This would be questionable on best advice grounds anyway.

- A husband has an unlimited interest in his wife (*Griffiths v Fleming* [1909] 1 K.B. 805).

- A wife has an unlimited interest in her husband (*Reed v Royal Exchange Assurance Corporation* [1795] Peake Add. Cas. 70).

- A creditor has an insurable interest in the debtor for the amount of the loan plus accrued interest (*Anderson v Edie* [1875] 29 Digest 346).

- An employer has an insurable interest in the life of an employee but only for the value of services agreed to be given. If the employee is a 'key person' whose special services the company could not easily replace if he died, then the company may have an insurable interest for the loss of profit caused by the key person's death. For more details on key person insurance see Chapter K. Also, if the employer provides a pension scheme which includes death benefits, this in itself will create an insurable interest to enable the employer to insure that liability.

- A partner in business has an insurable interest in the lives of his other partners if the partnership agreement provides that when one partner dies the survivors can buy his share of the business from his estate. Partnership assurance is covered in more detail in Chapter I. Similar principles apply to directors of small companies with similar 'buy-out' provisions – see Chapter J.

- Civil partners (see Chapter H section 8) have had unlimited insurable interest in each other, like spouses, from 5 December 2005.

3.3.2 Examples of situations where no insurable interest exists

- In strict law fiancés and fiancées do not have an insurable interest in each other as this is not a legally binding relationship. However, almost all life offices will agree that insurable interest exists in practice, especially if they are joint borrowers on a mortgage. Also, the Insurance Ombudsman stated he would normally accept that there is insurable interest between fiancés, and no doubt the Financial Ombudsman takes the same view.

- A beneficiary of a will does not have an insurable interest in the life of the testator. He only has a hope of receiving something as he might predecease the testator or the will could be changed so as to exclude him. Even if the will is not changed the beneficiary stands to gain, not lose, by the death.

- A parent has no insurable interest in his child merely because of that relationship (*Halford v Kymer* [1830] 10 B + C 724). Equally a child has no interest on the life of its parent (*Howard v Refuge Friendly Society* [1886] 54 L.T. 644). However, some other factor may provide insurable interest in either case. The situation in Scotland is different in that a child has a right to be supported by its parent and vice versa. Thus, there a child would have an insurable interest in its parent and vice versa, at least for a reasonable amount.

3.3.3 General legal considerations

The case of *Dalby v India and London Life Assurance Co* [1854] 15 C.B. 365 held that a life assurance contract is not a contract of indemnity and that the amount and existence of the interest need only be decided at the commencement of a policy. Therefore, insurable interest need only exist at the date the policy starts and the situation at the claim stage is not relevant. So, if the situation giving the interest ceases to exist at some time during the life of the policy, the assured can still make a valid claim despite the lack of insurable interest at that time.

The Life Assurance Act states that a policy effected without insurable interest is null and void. However, it does not impose any punishment and the effecting of such a policy is not specified to be a criminal act.

It is probable that an insurer can waive the right to void a policy for lack of insurable interest. In the case of *Worthington v Curtis* [1875] 1 Ch.D. 419, the judge said: 'the Statute is a defence to the insurance company only if they choose to avail themselves of it. If they do not, the question of who is entitled to the money must be determined as if the Statute did not exist.'

Unfortunately the situation is not free from doubt, for in *Gedge v Royal Exchange Insurance Corporation* (1900) 2 Q.B. 214, lack of insurable interest was not pleaded, but the Court refused to enforce the contract when it was revealed that there was no insurable interest.

If a policy is issued with no insurable interest, ignorance of the law by both parties is not a ground on which premiums can be recovered by the policyholder (*Harse v Pearl Life Assurance Co* (1904) 1 K.B. 588).

However, premiums can be reclaimed where the parties are not equally at fault. For example, if a representative of the insurer induces the assured to take out the policy by fraudulently representing it as valid, despite lack of insurable interest, the assured can recover premiums paid (*Hughes v Liverpool Victoria Legal Friendly Society* [1916] 2 K.B. 482).

In the case of *Fuji Finance Inc. v Aetna Life Insurance Ltd* (1996), the court decided that a unit-linked bond where the death claim value was the same as the surrender value (ie the total value of units) was still a contract of insurance and thus required insurable interest. The case, although it had some unusual features, probably re-established that an insured cannot recover more than the value of the insurable interest.

3.4 The duty of disclosure

Insurance contracts are contracts of utmost good faith or *uberrimae fidei*. Both parties to a contract have to be of the same mind (*ad idem*) as to the subject matter of a contract. However, in life assurance only the life assured knows all the relevant facts concerning health, occupation and life risks. The life office cannot possibly be expected to know these.

So the law imposes on the proposer the duty of utmost good faith. The proposer must disclose all material facts known by him to the life office and this is commonly known as the duty of disclosure.

3.4.1 Material facts

What is a material fact? The Marine Insurance Act 1906 states that 'Every circumstance is material which would influence the judgment of a prudent insurer in fixing the premium or determining whether he will take the risk'. This principle also applies in life assurance. The duty is voluntarily to disclose, and the proposer cannot withhold a material fact because no specific question was asked on that subject in the proposal form or medical examination. A proposer might, however, be justified in inferring from the fact that the question was not asked that the information is not regarded as material.

For this reason many offices frame their questions fairly widely and may even have a question such as 'Is there any other factor which may affect the risk on your life?' In addition, the Statement of Long Term Insurance Practice – agreed in 1977 with the Department of Trade and Industry – contains the following provisions:

(a) Proposal forms should contain a statement drawing attention to the consequences of failure to disclose all material facts, and pointing out that these are facts that an insurer would regard as likely to influence the assessment and acceptance of a proposal.

(b) Proposal forms should warn that if there is doubt about whether certain facts are material, these facts should be disclosed.

(c) Those matters which insurers have commonly found to be material should be the subject of clear questions in proposal forms.

(d) Insurers should avoid asking questions which would require knowledge beyond that which the signatory could reasonably be expected to possess.

Regarding point (d), it is impossible to disclose what one does not know and a proposer cannot be expected to disclose matters, immaterial in themselves which, if expertly examined further, might lead to information which is material (*Joel v Law Union and Crown Insurance* Co [1908] 2 K.B. 863). The example given by the judge in this case was that one could not expect the ordinary man to disclose an occasional headache, even if it might be regarded by an experienced doctor as a possible symptom of something more serious.

It does not matter that the proposer himself does not consider a particular fact to be material. This point arose in *Godfrey v Britannic Assurance Co Ltd* [1963] 2 Lloyd's Rep 515, where the proposer did not disclose that his doctor had sent him to a hospital for a check-up for a suspected kidney problem. He died of nephritis (a kidney disease). It was held that he knew he had been to hospital for a kidney check-up and it was agreed that he had honestly believed this not to be material. However, the Court said that his belief was irrelevant and that materiality must be judged by what a reasonable man would consider to be of importance. The company was therefore entitled to repudiate the policy.

The case of *Simmer v New India Assurance Co* made it clear that the duty of disclosure is confined to matters within the proposer's actual or presumed knowledge and does not require the proposer to make enquiries as to matters outside this knowledge.

Under s20 of the Marine Insurance Act 1906, a representation as to a matter of fact is true if it is substantially correct, ie the difference between the representation and the actual fact would not be considered material by a prudent underwriter. A representation as to a matter of expectation or belief is true if made in good faith. The belief only has to be honest, not reasonable, although the proposer cannot wilfully shut his eyes to the truth (*Economides v Commercial Union Assurance Company plc*).

The case of *Kelsall v Allstate Insurance Co Ltd* [1986] confirmed that the test of materiality was whether a fact would have been treated as material by a reasonable and prudent insurer, not necessarily the individual insurer in the particular contract.

The House of Lords stated in the case of *Pan Atlantic Insurance Co Ltd v Pine Top Insurance Co Ltd* [1994] S.J.L.B.182 it was not necessary for an underwriter to prove that the non-disclosure had a decisive effect on the prudent underwriter's decision on whether to accept the risk and if so at what premium. But the underwriter did have to show that the misrepresentation induced him into making the contract on those terms. However, where there was misrepresentation there is a presumption of inducement owing to the doctrine of utmost good faith. Thus a proposer would need to prove that the misrepresentation was not an inducement in order to succeed in showing that an undisclosed fact was not material and thus that the contract was valid.

There is no duty to disclose:

- Facts which the office already knows, possibly from a previous proposal.

- Facts which the office ought to know.
- Facts about which the office waives information.
- Facts possible of discovery where enough information has been given to provoke enquiry.
- Facts which lessen the risk.

The duty of disclosure also applies the other way round, in that insurers must disclose all material facts about the insurance to the proposer. For life policies, this will be achieved by the FSA's product disclosure rules – see Chapter Q.

3.4.2 General legal considerations

The duty of disclosure lasts until the contract is completed when the first premium is paid. This was decided in the case of *Looker v Law Union and Rock Insurance Co* [1928] 1 K.B. 554. Looker proposed for a life policy and received an acceptance letter stating the policy would be issued on payment of the first premium, on condition that his health remained unaltered. Before the premium was paid he fell ill. A friend then paid the premium, but Looker subsequently died from his illness. It was held that his estate could not claim as there was a continuing duty to inform the insurers of any material change in the risk. This was not done and so the contract was void.

This case is supported by *Marshall v Scottish Employers' Liability & General Insurance Co* [1901] 85 L.T. 257. Here it was said that it is not sufficient that statements made in the proposal are true on the date when they are made; if any material fact becomes known to the proposer before completion of the contract it must be disclosed.

If a proposer fails to disclose a material fact, the contract is voidable. This means that the office can make the policy void if it wants to or it can continue it (possibly at a higher premium) if the office prefers. However, if an office discovers an undisclosed material fact (maybe on a subsequent proposal) and then continues to accept further premiums it cannot later repudiate liability on those grounds, as it will be held to have ratified the non-disclosure – *Hemmings v Sceptre Life Association Ltd* [1905] 1 Ch. 365.

The case of *Malhi v Abbey Life Assurance Co Ltd* [1994] T.L.R. 2 June 1994 showed that, unless the undisclosed fact was later disclosed to a person authorised and able to appreciate its significance, the insurer did not lose its right to avoid the contract. In this case the proposer did not disclose alcoholism on his first proposal which resulted in a policy. The alcoholism was discovered by the life office following a medical report requested after a second proposal which was then declined. The life office did not check back to the first proposal and did not raise the matter until a death claim was made on that policy. It was held that the life office was still able to repudiate the claim on the first policy due to the non-disclosure.

Often a non-disclosure will only come to light when a claim arises. At law an office can repudiate liability whatever the circumstances but in practice most offices will only refuse the claim if the undisclosed fact is related to the cause of death.

An insurer has no right to damages for a breach of utmost good faith – the only remedy is to avoid the contract. In theory an insurer could have a claim for damages for a fraudulent misstatement under the tort of deceit or under the Misrepresentation Act 1967.

4 The Policy Document

Once the life has been underwritten, the first premium paid and the various legalities complied with, the office can prepare and issue the policy document. Methods of policy production vary but all offices will produce a policy and, possibly, a copy policy if the original is to be held by a lender in connection with house purchase. The policy will be sent to the policyholder, possibly via an intermediary who arranged it.
The policy records all the details of that individual contract, ie:

- Life assured.
- Assured.
- Policy number.
- Policy date.
- Expiry or maturity date.
- Type of policy.
- Premium.
- Sum assured.
- Any special conditions.

It will also contain all that office's standard conditions for that type of policy.

5 Renewals

5.1 Renewal systems

Once a policy has been issued, unless it is a single premium contract, a system will have to be set up to collect future premiums. Premiums can be paid yearly, half-yearly, quarterly or monthly. Under industrial policies premiums can also be paid weekly.

There are a number of ways in which premiums can be collected. The most important are renewal notices, standing orders/direct debits, account collections and physical collection by an agent (industrial assurance).

5.1.1 Renewal notices

This is the simplest method. A renewal notice is sent to the policyholder some two to three weeks before the due date showing the premium due (net of tax relief, if applicable). The policyholder then returns part of the renewal notice with his remittance for the premium. Most offices use computerised systems to prepare and despatch renewal notices. Monthly premiums cannot normally be paid this way.

5.1.2 Direct debits

The most common method of paying premiums is by direct debit.

The direct debit system is a variety of standing order whereby the premium payer authorises the life office to debit premiums directly from the bank account. All premiums are then debited automatically by regular exchange of tapes between the life office's computer system and the bank's computer system. The vast majority of monthly premiums are now paid by this method. Its advantage is its low cost and flexibility which makes it ideal for variable premium contracts such as index-linked ones where the amounts of future premiums are not known at outset.

A few offices still offer non direct debit standing orders, but their use is rare nowadays.

5.1.3 Account collection

Many offices have schemes whereby premiums are collected by a third party, often an employer, on an account basis. A typical instance would be where an employer arranges a life assurance scheme for its employees. Individual policies are issued by the life office to the employees, and the premiums are deducted each month by the employer from the employee's salary. The employer then makes a payment to the life office consisting of the total premiums for all members of the scheme for that month.

5.1.4 Industrial policies

Under industrial policies, premiums are usually collected in cash by an employee, or agent, of the life office who has to complete the policyholder's premium receipt book to show the premium as paid, and pay the premium on to the life office. Industrial premiums can be suspended in some cases without affecting qualification (see Chapter D section 1.1.19 – last paragraph).

5.2 Arrears of premium

All offices have procedures for policies which fall into arrears. When this happens the office will write to the policyholder stating the amount of the arrears and pointing out the consequences of non-payment. If the policyholder pays the arrears within a certain time, the days of grace, the policy will continue although most offices will impose a late payment charge if the amount or the duration of the arrears warrants it. This compensates the office for the interest lost by not having the premium to invest on the due date.

If the arrears are not paid, and the policy has no surrender value, it will lapse at the expiry of the days of grace and the office will cease to be on risk. The days of grace are usually 30, or perhaps 14 for monthly premiums.

If the policy has a surrender value, then the policy's non-forfeiture provisions will come into effect. These vary from office to office, but the following are typical conditions:

- The policy remains in force for as long as the surrender value exceeds the total of outstanding premiums and late payment charges.
- The policy remains in force for one year and then the surrender value becomes payable and death cover ceases.
- The policy is converted on the expiry of the days of grace (or after one year) to a paid-up policy for the appropriate reduced sum assured.
- A unit-linked policy may continue to have units cancelled to pay for the cover and charges until units are exhausted. The policy will then lapse.

Many offices have computerised their arrears procedures so that the computer sends out a reminder automatically once the policy is in arrears for a certain time. If a policy is mortgaged, the office will usually inform the mortgagee if premiums fall into arrears, so as to enable it to protect its interest.

5.3 Reinstatement

Once a policy has lapsed due to non-payment of premiums the office is off risk. The office may later receive a request from the policyholder to reinstate or revive the policy. This may be possible but is entirely at the discretion of the office involved. The office may agree to reinstate the policy subject to payment of all the arrears, a late payment charge and a satisfactory declaration of health. The life assured will have to declare that he is in good health and, as the duty of disclosure is also revived, give details of any deterioration in the risk since the date of the proposal.

If a long period has elapsed since the policy expired, the office may not be willing to reinstate the old policy at the old premium. It may only be willing to consider a new proposal based on the premium rate for the life assured's current age, which may well be higher than the old premium. Reinstatement may have some effect on the qualification status of the policy; this is dealt with in Chapter D.

6 Assignments

An assignment is a transfer of ownership from one person to another. This often happens with life policies and offices have to have methods of dealing with assignments to make sure they can pay the right person and to comply with the law.

There are a number of different types of assignments as follows:

- An assignment by way of sale – A sells a policy to B.
- An assignment by way of gift – A gives a policy to B.

- An assignment into trust – A assigns a policy to trustees B, C and D for the benefit of his children X, Y and Z. Trusts are dealt with in more detail in Chapter G.
- An assignment by way of mortgage – A mortgages his policy to B as security for a loan given to him by B. When A repays B in full, B reassigns the policy to A. Mortgages are dealt with more fully in Chapter F.

The law on assignments of life policies is contained in the Policies of Assurance Act 1867. Assignments may involve taxation consequences and these are dealt with in Chapters C and D.

6.1 The Policies of Assurance Act 1867

This act sets out the law on assignments of life policies and imposes a number of obligations on life offices. It specifies that everyone to whom a policy is assigned must serve a notice of assignment on the life office giving details of the assignment.

The assignee cannot claim from the office until notice has been served. The Act provides that every life policy must show the office's principal place of business where notices can be served.

When served with a notice the office must on request, and for a fee not exceeding 25p, supply a written acknowledgement of receipt of the notice. Most offices do not charge the fee. This acknowledgement is then conclusive evidence of receipt of the notice. The office must have a system for recording notices of assignment. This will enable it to comply with the Act and also pay the right person when a claim arises. It must be stressed, however, that a notice of assignment does not prove the assignee's ownership and the relevant deed of assignment will have to be produced when a policy payment is required. For this reason many offices include a statement to this effect on their acknowledgements.

6.2 Deeds

Under the Law of Property (Miscellaneous Provisions) Act 1989 a deed must be signed by the assignor in the presence of a witness who attests the signature. However, a deed could also be signed at the assignor's direction and in his or her presence by someone else, provided this is attested by two witnesses. Signing can include making one's mark on the deed.

7 Payments

There are a number of ways in which payment can be made under a life policy and different procedures apply to each. These are now dealt with in turn.

7.1 Death claims

A death claim is normally started by the claimant or solicitors to the estate informing the office of the death of the life assured and asking for confirmation of the amount

payable. The office will first check its index of lives assured to discover all the policies on that life. Then the amount payable will be calculated. This may depend on the exact date of death – eg the profits on a with-profits policy or the sum assured under a decreasing term policy will vary with the precise date of death. Unit value on a unit-linked policy will usually depend on the date the office is told of the death, or when proof is received by the office. The office will then reply quoting the amounts payable and stating its requirements for payment.
The main requirements will be:

- Proof of death.
- Proof of age.
- Proof of title.
- Completion of a claim form.

7.1.1 Proof of death

Proof of death in the UK is by an official death certificate. This is a copy, made by the Registrar, of an entry in the Register of Deaths maintained pursuant to the Births and Deaths Registration Act 1953. Only original death certificates should be accepted as proof of death. Photocopy certificates are often submitted but are not often accepted as there is a danger of forgery. There have been cases of life offices being defrauded by paying death claims based on forged 'photocopy' death certificates. A Government minister has stated that while there is no objection to any organisation copying a death certificate for their own records, as a general rule solicitors are not allowed to photocopy death certificates for endorsement and use as evidence of death. It is possible to get as many original death certificates as desired from the Registrar on payment of the appropriate fee.

It is infinitely more difficult to forge original certificates and therefore the Association of British Insurers has recommended offices not to accept photocopy death certificates. Other documents will not normally be allowed as proof of death.

There has been an attempt by the Association of Independent Financial Advisers to introduce a verification form for IFAs to confirm that they have seen an original death certificate, but it is up to individual life offices to decide whether to accept this in lieu of a death certificate.

A UK death certificate contains the following information:

- Date and place of death.
- Full name.
- Sex.
- Date and place of birth.

- Occupation and usual address.
- Name and address of informant.
- Cause of death.

The full name of the deceased together with the date and place of birth, occupation, and address will be checked against the details on the office's files to make sure that it is the life assured who has died.

The office will look at the cause of death shown on the death certificate. There is a possibility that the life assured died as a result of some activity that was excluded from the cover provided by the policy – eg private flying or motor racing.

Also, if death has occurred within a comparatively short period after the issue of the policy, the office should consider the possibility of non-disclosure. If the office suspects that there may have been non-disclosure of a material fact, it will have to make further enquiries. An example of this would be if the life assured died of cancer a few months after effecting the policy. In this case the office would investigate the medical history of the deceased. If the office needs to see the deceased's medical records, this is permitted under the Access to Health Records Act 1990, as long as the office has the written authority of the deceased's personal representatives. If it was discovered that he had been suffering from cancer for the last five years and had been receiving regular treatment for it, but had not disclosed this on the proposal form, this would be a clear case of non-disclosure. The office would therefore have the right to repudiate the claim. If the non-disclosure was fraudulent, the claimants have no legal right to recover premiums. If the non-disclosure was not fraudulent, then premiums can be recovered, but interest on them would not be due. Suicide can often have a bearing on the validity of claims and this is dealt with later.

7.1.2 The Financial Ombudsman Service (FOS) View

While the law provides that any non-disclosure of a material fact renders the contract void and thus entitles the insurer to repudiate the claim, as mentioned in 3.4.2, most offices will only repudiate a claim if the non-disclosure was related to the cause of death. However, life offices also have to bear in mind the views of the FOS to which a complaint may be referred if a claim is refused.

The FOS view is that where non-disclosure of a material fact is fraudulent or deliberate the office can decline the claim, void the policy from outset and refuse to return the premiums. It should also be mentioned that fraudulent non-disclosure is a criminal offence, although the perpetrator may well be dead by the time the life office finds out about this.

If the non-disclosure is innocent, the FOS view is that the life office should meet the claim in full even if, had it known of the non-disclosure, it would have increased the premium or refused to offer cover. FOS says it is likely to conclude that non-disclosure was innocent if the questions on the proposal were not clear or it is reasonable for the

proposer to have overlooked the non-disclosed facts, eg minor childhood illnesses. In any event proposers have no duty to disclose facts of which they are not aware.
The FOS further distinguishes between inadvertent non-disclosure and clearly reckless non-disclosure. The FOS is likely to conclude that non-disclosure was inadvertent if it seems to have resulted from an understandable oversight or moment of carelessness rather than any deliberate act. In such cases FOS may adopt a proportionate approach and work out the premium that would have been paid if the fact had been disclosed. It would then calculate what proportion of the recalculated premium the actual premium was and base its settlement on that proportion. It is difficult to reconcile this approach with the FSA's duty to treat customers fairly (ie those that did tell the truth on the proposal).

The FOS is likely to conclude that non-disclosure is clearly reckless if a proposer appears not to have any regard for accuracy when completing the proposal. Typically the non-disclosed facts will be of significance and were well known by the proposer, but the FOS is unable to conclude that the non-disclosure was deliberate. In these cases the FOS says the office can decline the claim and cancel the policy, but should normally refund premiums.

However, the FOS would clearly look at each case on an individual basis.

7.1.3 Proof of age

Proof of age will be required on a death claim if this was not given when the policy was effected. Proof of age is necessary because premiums vary with the age of the life assured (as described in Chapter A) and if the age differs from that stated on the proposal form then the wrong premium has been charged for the risk.

Age is normally proven by production of an official birth certificate. Some offices may accept photocopies but many insist on originals. If the life assured was born in the UK, a birth certificate can be easily obtained from the Registrar of Births, Deaths and Marriages as long as the approximate date and place of birth are known.
However, for a person born outside the UK proof of age can be more difficult, in that a birth certificate cannot be obtained or may not even exist. This is particularly true of those born in countries where registration of birth was not customary – eg many Asian countries. In such instances an office will require the best possible evidence of age available in the individual circumstances of the case – such as a baptismal, adoption or naturalisation certificate, or a passport.

For a married woman, the marriage certificate will also be required to link the name on the birth certificate with the present name of the life assured.

If it is found that the life assured was older than stated, although practice may vary between offices, then the most usual course of action is to reduce the sum assured payable to that which would have been purchased by the premium actually paid, using the rate for the true age. This may also necessitate recalculating any profits on a with-profits policy, or mortality deductions on a unit-linked policy.

If the age was younger than that stated, again practice will vary. The most usual course is to work out the premium which should have been paid and refund the excess over the premium actually paid for each payment.

7.1.4 Proof of title

Proof of title is the name given to the procedure of the claimant proving his ownership of the policy. If the policy is a life of another contract, the assured will just need to produce the policy document. If it is a trust policy, the trustees will need to produce the policy and the deed(s) appointing them as trustees. Full details of trusts and trusteeship can be found in Chapter G. If an assignee is claiming, he will have to produce the policy and the deed of assignment.

If the policy is an own life policy that has not been assigned, then payment will be made to the deceased's estate. The estate is represented by legal personal representatives who prove their title by means of a document known as a grant of representation, obtained from the Probate Registry. There are two types of legal personal representative and thus two types of grant. If the deceased left a will, then it names persons (executors) whose job it is to administer the estate – collecting all monies owed, such as life policy claims – and distribute the assets as directed in the will. Their grant is called a grant of probate.

If the deceased did not leave a will, the Registry will normally appoint the closest family member willing and able to act as the administrator of the estate. The administrator does a similar job to the executor except that he distributes the assets according to the laws of intestacy[2]. The administrator's grant is called a grant of letters of administration.

The Scottish equivalent of a grant of probate is a grant of confirmation nominate. The equivalent of letters of administration is a grant of confirmation dative, although the representative is called an executor dative, not an administrator. A Scottish grant itemises the property of the estate in an inventory and gives power to collect only the assets specified therein. If an asset is missed out, then the executors have to obtain a further grant, called an eik, in respect of this item.

A legal personal representative must produce the grant of representation to prove title before the office will pay the claim. Sometimes an office is asked to pay a claim before the grant is obtained but this is usually refused as it is not until a grant is obtained that the office can be sure who the legal personal representatives are. If payment was made before the grant was produced, the office could not be sure it was paying the right person, and might face another claim from the real legal personal representatives.

It often takes the legal personal representatives some time to obtain the grant and therefore payment of the claim may be unavoidably delayed. It is fairly common practice, however, for offices to pay interest on death claims from the date of death to the date of payment, although this is not usual for unit-linked policies. The Statement of Long-Term Insurance Practice (see Chapter R) contains provisions for paying interest on claims. An original grant or a court sealed 'office copy' will be required and ordinary photocopies are not usually accepted. A legal personal representative can

[2] *Intestates Act 1952*

obtain as many office copies as desired from the Registry on payment of the appropriate fee.

Sometimes a claimant may say that as the value of the estate is small, no grant will be applied for, and request the office to pay without it. Any such request will involve the office in some risk, however small, of paying the wrong person. The practice of offices varies, but most will pay claims under a certain limit (say, sum assured up to £5,000 or where the value of the estate is less than £20,000) without a grant. Often this will only be done provided payment is made to a surviving spouse. The office would require an indemnity from the claimant to recompense them if they have to make payment again to a subsequent claimant who produces a grant.

Under a joint life first death policy with joint assureds the payment would be made to the surviving assured as the surviving joint tenant. If a claim is made under an own life joint life second death policy, payment would be made to the estate of the second of the assureds to die.

If both lives assured under a joint life policy are killed in the same incident it will be necessary to know for title purposes which of the two died first. This may be clear from the evidence available but if not, s184 of the Law of Property Act 1925 provides that:

In all cases where, after the commencement of this Act, two or more persons have died in circumstances rendering it uncertain which of them survived the other or others, such deaths shall (subject to any order of the court), for all purposes affecting the title to property, be presumed to have occurred in order of seniority, and accordingly the younger shall be deemed to have survived the elder.

Thus if the two lives assured died in the same disaster and there is no evidence to show who died first, s184 would apply and the younger would be deemed to have survived the elder. This view has been confirmed by the House of Lords in the case of *Hickman v Peacey* [1945] A.C. 304 where two brothers were killed in a basement when a bomb struck the house. Payment would thus be made to the estate of the younger life assured.

This rule's application to the distribution of property on intestacy is modified by s1(4) of the Intestates Estates Act 1952. This provides that where an intestate and the intestate's spouse or civil partner have died in circumstances rendering it uncertain which of them survived the other, and the intestate's spouse or civil partner is deemed by s184 of the Law of Property Act 1925 to have survived the intestate, the distribution of the intestate's estate shall take effect as if the spouse or civil partner had not survived the intestate.

The position is different in Scotland where the Succession (Scotland) Act 1964 s31 applies. This states that where two persons have died in circumstances indicating that they died simultaneously, or rendering it uncertain which survived the other, then for all purposes affecting title to property: (a) where the persons were spouses or civil partners, it shall be presumed that neither survived the other; and (b) in any other case it shall be presumed that the younger survived the elder, unless the elder has left a will containing a provision in favour of the younger if he survives the elder and, failing the younger, in favour of a third person, and the younger person has died intestate; in this case it shall be presumed for the purposes of that provision that the elder survived the younger.

Generally speaking, a UK grant must be produced to collect the monies under a UK policy. However, there is an exception provided for in s19 of the Revenue Act 1889. This states that:

Where a policy of life assurance has been effected with any insurance company by a person who shall die domiciled elsewhere than in the United Kingdom, the production of a grant of representation from a court in the United Kingdom shall not be necessary to receive the money payable in respect of such policy.

If a claimant wants to use this section, it will have to be proved that the assured was domiciled outside the UK and that any inheritance tax liability due on the policy monies will be, or has been, met. If the section does apply, then the claim can be paid on production of a foreign grant, or its equivalent, which proves the title of the claimant.

Domicile is not the same as nationality or residence. Domicile is a legal status, although it is treated as a matter of fact by the courts. A person's domicile is the country where he has (or is deemed by law to have) his permanent home. He may be resident in some other country for business purposes and may not have visited his country of domicile for many years.

7.1.5 Procedure

Most claims are initiated by the claimant or his solicitors writing to the office. As explained earlier in this section the office will calculate the claim values on all its policies on that life and reply quoting the values and stating its requirements for payment. Most offices will also send out their claim form for signature by the claimant and return with the documents of proof discussed earlier. When all the requirements have been received, the office will make out its cheque as directed on the claim form and send it to the address specified.

7.1.6 Suicide

The Suicide Act 1961 abolished the rule that suicide was a crime, but did not mention life assurance. The position of a claim where death is by suicide whilst of sound mind is not entirely free from doubt if there is no suicide clause in the policy. One view is that as suicide is no longer a crime, payment should be made. However, it is widely held that it is a fundamental principle of insurance law that an insured cannot recover if, by his own deliberate act, he causes the event insured against. This is supported by the case of *Beresford v Royal Insurance Co Ltd* [1938] A.C. 586. Although this was decided before 1961, the court considered that the rule preventing payment was not that of public policy, but a fundamental implied term of the contract that a person cannot by his own deliberate act cause the event on which the insurance money is payable. It is submitted that this is the correct statement of the law.

This principle cannot apply if the life assured commits suicide whilst insane, as it can be said that he does not have the mental capacity to understand what he is doing. The estate would be able to claim the policy monies in such a case.

If the policy has a suicide clause, then the position depends on its exact wording. Many offices include a clause such as: 'If the Life Assured shall commit suicide within one year from the date of the policy all benefits which would otherwise have become payable shall be forfeited and belong to the insurer'.

Suicide would therefore not be covered if it occurred during the specified period. If it occurred after that period then the office would be liable even if the life assured was of sound mind at that time. This is because by having a suicide clause expressly excluding cover for a limited period, the office is impliedly insuring the risk after that time.

Most suicide clauses protect the interests of assignees so as to render the policy acceptable as security for a loan. A typical proviso would be: 'This suicide condition shall not prejudice the interest in the policy of any third party who shall have bona fide acquired that interest for valuable consideration'.

The general rule of public policy which does not allow a person to benefit from his own criminal act operates to prevent a claim from someone who has murdered another person on whose life he holds a policy (*Prince of Wales Assurance Co. v Palmer* (1858) 25 Beav. 605). This rule, however, does not apply where the murderer was insane (*Re Batten's Will Trusts* (1961) 105 S.J. 529). The rule can also be set aside by the court in appropriate cases under the Forfeiture Act 1982. In one case, the court did this to enable the survivor of a suicide pact to claim under a policy on the life of her partner, whom she had assisted to commit suicide.

7.2 Maturity claims

All offices have procedures for paying claims on maturity of their endowment policies. Most offices have programmed their computers to list every week the policies maturing in, say, eight weeks' time. These lists are then used as a basis for the maturity procedure. For each maturing policy, the office will write to the policyholder, say, a month or six weeks before the maturity date, reminding him of the maturity, quoting the amount payable, listing the requirements for payment and enclosing the claim form. The aim is to receive all requirements before the maturity date so as to enable the office to be able to release its cheque in settlement to reach the policyholder by the maturity date. If the policy has never been assigned, the sole requirement will be production of the policy document. If it has been assigned the relevant deeds of assignment will have to be produced. The office should already be aware of these due to the notice of assignment procedure discussed in section 6. For a trust policy, any deeds of appointment or retirement of trustees will have to be produced.

In most cases, all documents of title and the claim form will be received before the maturity date so that the office will be able to send out its cheque on time, as directed on the claim form. Sometimes a claim will be delayed past the maturity date due, eg to problems in contacting a 'lost policyholder'. Offices are loath to have unpaid claims on the books and make every reasonable effort to contact policyholders, although this is not always easy if the policyholder has forgotten to tell the office of a change of address.

7.3 Surrenders

A surrender occurs when a policy is cashed in before it becomes a claim. When a policyholder asks to surrender his policy, the office will calculate the surrender value and send out its surrender form for signature and return with whatever documents of title are needed. The title requirements will be the same as those for maturities.

When the surrender form is returned with the documents of title, the office will send out its surrender cheque as directed on the form and will cease to be on risk.

A surrender may involve a chargeable gain for income tax. If so, the office may warn the policyholder of this and will have to issue a certificate to the policyholder and possibly a copy to Her Majesty's Revenue and Customs (HMRC). This is explained in Chapter D.

The FSA requires life offices to make sure that endowment policyholders who seek information on surrender values are made aware of the other options available, including the fact that they may be able to sell the policy on the traded market as an alternative to surrendering.

7.3.1 Bonus surrenders

Sometimes a policyholder may wish to surrender just the bonus (or profits) attaching to his policy rather than the whole policy. Most offices will allow this and will pay the cash value of the bonus subject to proof of title and completion of the appropriate form. Normally, the policy will be endorsed to record this transaction.

Bonus surrenders are part surrenders and so may involve chargeable gains under the 5% rules – see Chapter D section 2.4.

7.4 Paid-up policies

If a policyholder can no longer afford to pay premiums, under some policies he may request that the contract be made 'paid up'. This means that no further premiums are payable and cover continues at an appropriately reduced level. Only substantive policies (endowments and whole life assurances) can be made paid up – a term assurance will just lapse if premiums cease. The reduced paid-up sum assured on a non unit-linked policy will normally bear some relation to the number of premiums actually paid as opposed to the total originally payable. Thus if a 20-year endowment was made paid up after premiums had been paid for ten years, the reduced paid-up sum assured would probably be half the original sum assured. Any future bonus would be based on the reduced sum assured.

The office will require the normal proof of title and completion of the appropriate letter of authority to make this alteration. The policy will be endorsed to show the reduced sum assured. Conversion to paid up may increase the likelihood of a subsequent chargeable event. For qualifying policies certified since February 1988, HMRC has refused to allow the policy to give the policyholder the right to make the policy paid up, although policy provisions may allow this to happen automatically if premiums cease.

On unit-linked policies the normal procedure is for the sum assured to be maintained for as long as the value of units in the policy is enough to pay for the mortality cost of the life cover and charges. Thus more and more units will be cancelled to pay for this and the policy may eventually lapse if the units run out before surrender, maturity or claim.

7.5 Loans

It is common for life offices to give loans on the security of their policies. This does not apply to all policies. Loans will not generally be offered on term assurances or unit-linked policies. Offices will often only lend on non-linked policies up to, say, 90% of the surrender value, because it is the surrender value that is the security. Rates of interest charged will vary according to market conditions but are currently between 5% and 12%.

If a policyholder wants a loan, he has to prove his title in the normal way and sign a mortgage deed assigning his policy to the office for the duration of the loan. Under this deed he will promise to repay the loan, to pay interest while it is outstanding and to maintain premium payments. The office will hold the policy for the currency of the loan together with any other documents of title. When the loan is repaid, the office will return the policy and any deeds to the borrower and also formally re-assign the policy to him.

Although a loan may be theoretically repayable on a fixed date, most offices will allow it to remain outstanding, as long as premiums and interest are paid, until the policy becomes a claim or is surrendered. If this happens, the loan, plus any accrued interest, will be deducted from the payment.

Again, chargeable gains can be involved – under the part surrender rules – see Chapter D section 2.4.

Some life offices provide policy loans via an associated bank, rather than directly.

7.6 Lost policies

It often happens on a claim or surrender that the claimant says the policy is lost. The loss of the policy is not crucial as the policy is not the contract itself, merely evidence of it. However, non-production of a policy may indicate that a third party has an interest in it.

For this reason the company will require a proper search to be made, and enquiries undertaken of those who might hold the policy or know of its whereabouts – eg the assured's bank, solicitors or accountants. The office will check its files for any clues as to the policy's whereabouts. Often the policy will be found by this process.

If the policy cannot be found, and the office is satisfied that it is genuinely lost, it may ask the claimant to execute a Statutory Declaration, setting out the circumstances of the loss and stating that the policy has not been assigned. Not all offices will insist on a Statutory Declaration. Payment can then be made on completion of an indemnity from the claimant against any losses to the life office as a result of paying without production of the policy. If the claim is very large, an indemnity policy from another insurance company might be required. Statutory Declarations are made in front of a magistrate or solicitor under the Statutory Declarations Act 1835. There are penalties if the declaration is made knowing it to be false. It should be appreciated that a form of indemnity cannot prevent a subsequent claim from someone else, although it can help the life office recover the payment to the first payee.

7.7 Bankruptcy

Bankruptcy is the name given to the situation where a person cannot (or in some cases will not) pay his debts. The law of bankruptcy[3] provides for a trustee-in-bankruptcy to be appointed to take the bankrupt's property, sell it all and distribute the proceeds to the creditors. Then the bankrupt can be discharged and start life afresh, freed from previous debts. Sometimes the Official Receiver acts as trustee-in-bankruptcy.

When a policyholder becomes bankrupt, he can no longer deal with his life policy and no payments should be made by the office without the permission of the trustee-in-bankruptcy. The trustee will usually notify the office of his interest in the policy and the office will note this in its records.

The trustee can surrender the policy to provide cash for the creditors. If so, he will have to produce the policy, the Bankruptcy Order and either the Order for Summary Administration or the Certificate of Appointment as Trustee as proof of his title. Alternatively, the trustee can keep the policy in force for the benefit of the creditors in case the bankrupt dies. When the policyholder receives his discharge from bankruptcy, ownership of any life policies does not revert automatically to the policyholder, unless and until the trustee-in-bankruptcy assigns them back to him. If one of the owners of a jointly owned policy becomes bankrupt, the trustee will need the consent of the other joint owner(s) to surrender the policy.

The effect of bankruptcy on pensions is dealt with more specifically in Chapter P.

Under the Enterprise Act 2002 for bankruptcies on or after 1 April 2004, there is normally an automatic discharge after one year. Previously the period was three years. For bankruptcies before 1 April 2004 discharge is automatic on 1 April 2005, unless already given. There are provisions to extend the bankruptcy period for serial bankrupts and those who act irresponsibly or recklessly up to 15 years.

[3] Insolvency Act 1986

7.8 Powers of attorney

A power of attorney is a deed executed by one person (the donor) giving another person (the donee or attorney) authority to act for him. This power can be either general or for a specific matter only. Perhaps the most common instance where a power of attorney is given is where the donor is going abroad for some time and wants to give some other person power to handle his affairs in the UK for the period of absence.

The power of attorney must be given in a deed, which must be witnessed by at least one person if signed by the donor. A donor who is unable to sign the deed because of some physical disability can direct another person to sign it on his behalf, and in this case two witnesses are necessary to attest the signature. A person of unsound mind cannot execute a power of attorney.

The law on powers of attorney is contained in the Powers of Attorney Act 1971. The attorney proves his authority by producing the original power of attorney. By virtue of s3 of the Act, a photocopy power of attorney is acceptable providing it is certified as a true and complete copy by the donor, a solicitor or a stockbroker.

An attorney may execute documents with his own signature or by the signature of the donor; eg 'A B by his attorney C D'. The execution clause should include a reference to the power of attorney.

If a power of attorney is given for valuable consideration, or as security for some obligation, it can be expressed to be irrevocable. In this case it cannot be revoked except with the donee's consent, and is unaffected by the donor's death, incapacity or bankruptcy.

A power not given for valuable consideration or as security can be revoked at any time by the donor. It is also revoked automatically if the donor dies, becomes of unsound mind or is adjudged bankrupt.

Section 5 of the Act gives protection to attorneys and purchasers from attorneys who have no notice of revocation. The protection is as follows:

- An attorney who continues to act on a power without knowledge of its revocation incurs no liability to the donor or to any other person.

- Where a power has been revoked and a person without knowledge of the revocation deals with the donee, the transaction between them shall, in favour of that person, be as valid as if the power had then been in existence.

If a person has knowledge of any event, such as death, that would have the effect of revoking the power he is deemed to have notice of the revocation.

When a life office is dealing with an attorney, it will have to satisfy itself: (a) that the power was duly executed; (b) that it is still valid; and (c) that it gives authority for the intended transaction. These facts can be ascertained by production of the power of attorney itself. The office will also have to check that it has had no notice of revocation or of anything that has that effect, such as the death of the donor. If all is in order then the attorney will be able to claim, surrender or borrow under the policy on his signature alone. Section 10 of the Act provides a simple general power of attorney to do anything the donor could lawfully do (except exercising trustee functions).

A power of attorney is normally revoked automatically if the donor becomes mentally incapable. However, the Enduring Powers of Attorney Act 1985 created a special type of power, called an enduring power, which does continue when the donor becomes mentally incapable. The attorney must be over 18 and not bankrupt. An enduring power must be registered with the Public Guardianship Office (PGO) if the attorney believes that the donor is becoming mentally incapable. The PGO will allow registration only if the power meets the conditions of the Act. Once the enduring power has been registered, the attorney can continue to act despite the donor's mental incapacity. The PGO may refuse registration if a receiver has been appointed under the Mental Health Act 1983. The PGO is effectively part of the Court of Protection.

The donor cannot revoke a registered power without the PGO's permission, although it will be automatically revoked by the attorney's bankruptcy.

Sometimes a life office is asked to accept a proposal form signed by an attorney rather than the proposer. Most offices will decline to accept this for any policy involving any life risk because the attorney will not be able to answer the health questions properly as he will probably not have an adequate knowledge of the proposer's medical history. In addition, if the policy is to be under trust, the office should exercise great caution because the effect may be that the attorney is giving away the donor's money and his powers to do so, particularly under the Enduring Powers of Attorney Act 1985, are limited to providing for the needs of those the donor might be expected to provide for. A transaction could be especially dubious if it was to the benefit of the attorney or persons connected with him. An enduring power of attorney is not normally suitable for trustee functions. Under the Trustee Delegation Act 1999 a trustee can delegate his powers to an attorney for only one year. There are provisions in the Mental Capacity Act 2005 to change the law on enduring powers of attorney, but it appears that they will not be implemented until April 2007.

The law in Scotland is different as the Enduring Powers of Attorney Act does not apply in Scotland. Under the Law Reform (Miscellaneous Provisions) (Scotland) Act 1990 every power of attorney given after 1 January 1991 continues in force after the donor's incapacity, unless a contrary intention is expressed in the deed. This is termed a continuing power of attorney. However under the Adults with Incapacity (Scotland) Act 2000 no power of attorney made after 2 April 2001 is a continuing power of attorney unless the deed expressly provides that the attorney's powers should continue beyond the donor's incapacity. Continuing powers have to be registered with the Public Guardian once the donor has lost capacity.

There has been a case *(McDowell v IRC Sp.C.382)* where an IHT plan was declared invalid because gifts were made by an attorney who had no legal power to make them.

It is important to understand that just because a policyholder has appointed an attorney, it does not mean that the policyholder can no longer act on his own behalf (unless he becomes mentally incapable). It also does not change ownership of any policies and the proceeds must be used for the benefit of the donor, not the attorney.

C Taxation

1 **Income Tax**

2 **Capital Gains Tax**

3 **Inheritance Tax**

4 **Corporation Tax**

5 **Value Added Tax**

6 **National Insurance Contributions**

7 **Insurance Premium Tax**

8 **Disclosure of Tax Avoidance Schemes**

This part deals with the main personal taxes – income tax, capital gains tax (CGT) and inheritance tax (IHT). It also covers corporation tax which is the tax payable by companies on their profits together with value added tax (VAT), National Insurance Contributions (NICs) and insurance premium tax (IPT).

It explains the general principles of these taxes but is not meant to provide a comprehensive coverage of all aspects of them. The aim is to give the reader a general understanding of how the taxes work so that the subsequent parts can be more easily understood. The taxation of life and pension policies in particular is covered in detail in the relevant parts – eg Chapters D, O and P.

Tax is administered by Her Majesty's Revenue and Customs (HMRC) which is the new name for the merged Inland Revenue and Customs and Excise.

1 Income Tax

Income tax is an annual tax on income which has to be renewed each year by Parliament. The main Acts containing the principles of the tax are the Income and Corporation Taxes Act 1988 (ICTA), the Income Tax (Earnings and Pensions) Act 2003, the Income Tax (Trading and Other Income) Act 2005 and the Taxes Management Act 1970. However, rates and reliefs will normally be adjusted each year by proposals in the Chancellor's Budget, which are later embodied in the Finance Act for that year. The income tax year, on which taxation is based, runs from 6 April in one year to 5 April of the next. The aim is to charge tax at the rate or rates applicable for that year on the individual's taxable income for that year. A married person's income tax generally does not depend on the spouse's income. The same now applies to civil partners. Each individual is taxed independently on his or her own income, although Child Tax Credit has clouded this principle (as has Her Majesty's Revenue and Customs' (HMRC's) recent successful attack on husband and wife companies). As a broad principle, any person resident in the UK is liable to income tax on world-wide income. Anyone not resident in the UK is subject to income tax on income arising in the UK.

If a person is taxable on the same income in the UK and in another country, then any element of double taxation may be avoided if the UK has a double taxation agreement with the country concerned or, in the absence of a treaty, either the UK or the other country may give unilateral relief.

1.1 Computation of taxable income

The first step in assessing an individual's taxable income is to determine total income for the year. This is the total income from all sources. Items to be taken into account would include any of the following:

(a) Salaries, wages, bonuses, commissions and other remuneration from employment.

(b) Certain fringe benefits received from employment, such as cheap loans and company cars (often called benefits in kind).

(c) Directors' fees.

(d) Professional fees and business profits.

(e) Pensions and annuities.

(f) Some social security benefits.

(g) Share dividends, interest and other forms of investment income.

(h) Rent from land or property.

(i) Profits from any trade.

In respect of (d) and (i) the profits may need to be adjusted to take out certain types of expenditure, eg depreciation, which are not allowable expenses for tax purposes.

1.2 Deductions from income

Once a person's income for the tax year has been calculated, certain allowances can be deducted in order to arrive at the taxable income. The main deductions are as follows:

(a) Payments under a deed of covenant or gift aid to a charity.

(b) Business losses and capital allowances. (Capital allowances are given for certain assets purchased for business purposes, such as plant, machinery, factories and mines.)

(c) Payments into retirement annuity policies up to limits. Personal pension contributions are no longer deductions against income. (For full details see Chapter O.)

(d) Contributions to an approved occupational pension scheme. (For full details see Chapter O.)

In certain cases relief is given for loan interest. These include the following loans:

(a) To buy plant and machinery for use in a business.

(b) To buy a share of a close company or partnership.

(c) To lend on to a close company or partnership for use in the business.

(d) To pay inheritance tax on death.

In these cases relief is allowed at the starting, basic and higher rates, but (a) is available for three years only, and (d) for one year only. A partnership for these purposes includes a limited liability partnership (LLP) – see Chapter I.

1.3 Personal reliefs

Once the individual's taxable income has been arrived at, the taxpayer is then allowed to deduct any applicable personal reliefs before the tax rates are applied. They can be claimed only by UK residents, and citizens of states within the EU, although certain non-residents can claim a proportion of the personal reliefs on their UK income under s278 of ICTA.

The main personal reliefs are as follows (2006/07):

- **Personal allowance** of £5,035 given to all individuals. It is not transferable to a spouse.

- **Age allowances.** These are a series of increased personal and married couple's allowances for taxpayers who are 65 or over. They are as follows:

Age 65 to 74	Personal allowance	£7,280
	Married couple's allowance	£6,065
Age 75 and over	Personal allowance	£7,420
	Married couple's allowance	£6,135

  Relief is given in full for the personal allowance but restricted to 10% for the married couple's allowance, which also applies to civil partners.

  The age allowance is received in full only by those whose total income does not exceed £20,100. Personal pension contributions are deductible from total income for this purpose. If income does exceed this limit, the age allowance is reduced by £1 for every £2 of excess income, although it will not be reduced below the standard personal allowance, or £2,350 for the married couple's allowance. The personal age allowance is reduced before the married couple's age allowance, so that effectively the married couple's allowance will only be reduced if the personal allowance has already been reduced to the standard level.

  The increased personal allowance is available if the individual attains the relevant age during the tax year. The married couple's age allowance is normally given to the spouse/partner with the higher income but the basic allowance (ie £2,350) can be transferred to the other spouse or partner. The reduction in personal age allowance depends solely on the individual's income. The reduction in the married couple's age allowances is determined by the income of the claimant only.

  The married couple's allowance only applies to couples where one of the spouses or civil partners was born before 6 April 1935.

- **Blind person's relief** of £1,660. Available to registered blind people only.

- **Rent-a-room relief.** This gives exemption from tax to gross annual rents of up to £4,250 payable to owner occupiers and tenants who let furnished accommodation in their only or main home. Those who receive gross annual rents over £4,250 can either (a) pay tax on the excess over £4,250 with no relief for allowable expenses, or (b) calculate their profit from letting (gross rents less actual expenses) and pay tax on that profit in the normal way.

1.4 Rates of tax

When an individual has deducted all available personal reliefs from taxable income, the tax rates are applied to the resulting figure to calculate the tax payable. For this purpose the income is divided into three 'bands', and the rate applicable to each band is applied to produce the tax on that band. The final tax is the total of the amounts of tax for each band. The rates and bands are determined annually by Parliament and are usually changed each tax year.

The most important rate is called the basic rate. The basic rate band covers the average earnings of most individuals. All income over the upper limit of the basic rate band is in the higher rate band and is subject to higher rate tax. The current bands are as follows (2006/07):

Taxable income	Rate
£0–£2,150	10%: starting
£2,151–£33,300	22%: basic
Over £33,300	40%: higher

The basic rate on savings interest is 20%. For UK dividends the basic and starting rates are 10%, and the higher rate is 32.5%. For a full explanation of the taxation of dividends see Chapter C section 4.4.

1.5 Tax credits

Two new tax credits were introduced on 6 April 2003 to replace Children's Tax Credit, Working Families Tax Credit and Disabled Persons Tax Credit. These are the Child Tax Credit and Working Tax Credit. They are a bit like social security benefits, but are actually credits payable by HMRC.

1.5.1 Child Tax Credit

This can be claimed by a person or couple who are responsible for a child under 16, or under 19, if in full time education or unemployed. It is paid in addition to Child Benefit and any Working Tax Credit. There is a family element of £545 and a child element of £1,765 per child. There is also an extra £545 for the first year following the birth of a child.

The total is then reduced progressively once total income (joint for a couple) exceeds £14,155 for those entitled to Child Tax Credit only or £5,220 for those entitled to Working Tax Credit as well. The family element of Child Tax Credit is reduced by 6.67% of total income over £50,000 or, if higher, the level of income at which all other entitlements to tax credits are extinguished. For this purpose a couple includes a civil partnership.

The credit is paid directly to the person who is mainly responsible for caring for the children in the family. Payment can be made weekly or every four weeks.

1.5.2 Working Tax Credit

Working Tax Credit is a payment to top up the earnings of working people on low incomes, including those who do not have children. It is payable to those responsible for a child who are over 16 and work at least 16 hours per week and those without children who are over 25 and work at least 30 hours per week. It can also be paid to those without children who are over 16 and work at least 16 hours per week who have a disability, and some over 50s who work at least 16 hours per week.

The amount varies according to the number of hours worked, whether there is a child, whether single or a couple, and total income (joint for couples). There are extra amounts for those with a disability and there is also a child care element for those paying for registered or approved child care. It is reduced progressively for those with incomes over £5,220 per annum. For this purpose a couple includes a civil partnership.

The credit is paid directly by HMRC for employees and the self-employed. Couples can decide which one will get the credit.

1.6 Collection of tax

There are two methods used by HMRC to collect income tax. The first is by direct assessment and the second is by deduction at source.

Direct assessment is used, eg in the case of taxpayers who are self-employed or partners in a business. HMRC will send the taxpayer a tax return in April. The taxpayer must then fill in the details of income and claim any relevant allowances, and return the form to HMRC. For full details of how this system works see the following section 1.7.

1.6.1 Self-employed people

The tax position is as follows:

- The tax for the first tax year of business is based on the profits for that tax year.
- The tax for the second tax year of business is based on the profits for the accounting period ending in that tax year, but if that is not a full year then it is based on the first actual year's profits.
- The tax for the third and subsequent years is based on the profits for the accounting period ending in that tax year.

Relief will be given for any periods of overlap when the accounting period changes or the business ceases. The aim is that the total profits taxed will equal the total profits made. Anyone starting up as self-employed must register with HMRC within three months of the last day of the month in which self-employment began.

1.6.2 Pay as You Earn

The most common example of tax deducted at source is the Pay as You Earn scheme (PAYE). Under this system, an employer deducts the employee's income tax directly from the employee's remuneration and pays it over to HMRC. A system of code numbers, incorporating the allowances for each taxpayer, is used to enable the employer to deduct the correct amount of tax. This system places the burden of collection onto the employer and there are penalties for not complying with the PAYE rules.

1.6.3 Deduction at source – Investment income

Another example of tax deduction at source arises with bank interest where the payer deducts tax at 20% from the income, pays the net income to the investor, and pays over the tax deducted to HMRC. This process is also applied by life offices to the interest content of a purchased life annuity. The investor receives a certificate showing the tax deducted, so that he can reclaim tax from HMRC if income is low enough for some of that investment income not to be taxable or taxable at only 10%. Likewise, if the investor is in the higher rate bracket, HMRC will collect the balance of the tax liability (that is higher rate minus 20%) by direct assessment on the investor. Basic rate taxpayers have no further liability.

1.7 Self-assessment

There is a single tax return to cover all sources of income and capital gains and taxpayers can choose whether to calculate the tax themselves or leave this to HMRC. If no tax return is filed, HMRC can decide the tax due to the best of their information and serve an assessment on this basis. The tax return must be filed by 31 January following the end of the tax year to which it relates, or three months after issue if later. All tax returns include a tax calculation section which must be completed by the taxpayer unless he wants HMRC to calculate the tax, in which case the return must be submitted by 30 September following the end of the tax year.

The payment dates for tax are the same for all classes of income. The first payment on account is due on 31 January of the tax year concerned, with the second payment on account due on the following 31 July, and any balancing payment due on the next 31 January. The first payment on account is one-half of the previous year's tax. The second payment on account is a further half of the previous year's tax. The balance payment will consist of an adjustment calculated by comparing the actual tax liability with the total tax paid in the first two payments. This payment could be to or from HMRC. The balance payment will also include the full amount of any CGT payable. The two payments on account will take into account any tax deducted at source and will not be required if the tax is below certain limits. This is designed to ensure that those people whose tax is almost entirely taken care of under PAYE do not have to make any payments on account. The two payments on account will also have to include any Class 4 National Insurance contributions (NICs).

Payments on account are not required for taxpayers if their income tax liability for the preceding year (net of tax deducted at source or tax credits on dividends) is less than £500 in total, or if more than 80% of their income tax liability for the preceding year was met by deduction of tax at source (eg PAYE) or from tax credits on dividends.

A taxpayer can claim a reduction of the two payments on account if they would lead to an overpayment, although there are penalties for such claims which are fraudulent or negligent. Interest is payable by the taxpayer on late payments and underpayments and by HMRC on overpayments. In addition, there is a fixed penalty for late payments and late filing of returns.

During routine processing, HMRC only checks returns for obvious errors. So, for most taxpayers, their self-assessment will be processed as submitted. However, HMRC has a right to enquire into the accuracy of any return. This could be by random audit or targeted by suspicion. The result of an enquiry may be an amendment to the assessment if HMRC believe that the assessment was incorrect. A HMRC enquiry must normally begin within 12 months of the date of submission of the tax return and therefore a taxpayer who has made full disclosure in the return will know one year after sending in the return that the assessment is final unless there has been fraud or negligence.

A partnership must submit a partnership return showing all the information needed to calculate the profits of the partnership on the normal basis. The return must also show the profit allocation between the partners. The partners must then include their share of the profit on their individual tax returns and include that in their self-assessment calculations. Each partner is solely responsible for the tax due on their share and there is no liability for any other partner's tax. These rules apply to LLPs as well as ordinary partnerships.

The tax due dates for 2006/07 are:

31 January 2007	First payment on account.
31 July 2007	Second payment on account.
31 January 2008	Balancing payment.

In addition, the first payment on account for 2007/08 will be due on 31 January 2008.

Example A

This shows some of the principles involved, and uses 2006/07 rates.

Mr X is married and has an income from his business of £50,000. He has savings income of £2,000. He pays interest of £3,500 on a £50,000 house purchase loan and interest of £1,000 on a loan to buy machinery for his business. He pays £5,000 gross into his personal pension (£3,900 net of basic rate tax deducted at source).

	£	£
Earned income	50,000	
Savings income	2,000	
Total income	52,000	52,000
Less deductions:		
Business loan interest	1,000	
Total deductions		1,000
Taxable income		51,000
Less personal allowance:		5,035
Amount to be taxed		45,965
Tax payable		
First £2,150 @ 10% +	215.00	
Next £36,150 @ 22% +	7,953.00	
Next £7,665 @ 40%	3,066.00	
Total		11,234.00
Less tax already deducted on savings income £2,000 @ 20%		400
Tax due		10,834.00

£1,100 basic rate relief for the personal pension contribution is given at source. Higher rate relief is given by extending the basic rate band by the amount of the gross contribution, ie £33,300 + £5,000 – £2,150 = £36,150.

1.8 A tax trap

The introduction of the 20% rate of tax on interest opened up a tax trap in which many ordinary investors could find themselves paying tax at a top effective rate of 42% on some of their income. It is like the so-called age allowance trap, which is much better known, but it is more serious. Fortunately, there are several ways to escape this high tax charge, including making a pension contribution.

The situation arises because basic rate taxpayers will pay tax on bank and building society interest at 20%. If there is a mix of income, the interest is always treated as if it comes on top of the rest, along with dividends from shares. The 42% tax charge can best be shown by an example.

Example B

Gemma has an income of £38,335 in the tax year starting 6 April 2006, ie £33,300 after her personal tax allowance of £5,035. Of this, £3,000 is interest from the building society account and the rest is her salary. During the year, she is offered a bonus of £1,000 by her employer.

Her tax position is as follows:

Before the bonus	**£**	**£**
Earnings		35,335
Interest		3,000
Total income		38,335
Personal allowance (set against earnings)		5,035
Taxable		33,300
£2,150 earnings taxed @ 10%	215.00	
£28,150 earnings taxed @ 22%	6,193.00	
£3,000 interest taxed @ 20%	600	
Total income tax	7,008.00	
After the bonus		
Earnings including bonus		36,335
Interest		3,000
Total income		39,335
Personal allowance (set against earnings)		5,035
Taxable		34,300
£2,150 earnings taxed @ 10%	215.00	
£29,150 earnings taxed @ 22%	6,413.00	
£2,000 interest taxed @ 20%	400	
£1,000 interest taxed @ 40%	400	
Total income tax	7,428.00	

Extra income tax on £1,000 bonus 420 (42%)

In this example, it is only after Gemma's earnings have been taxed that the taxman turns his attention to her interest. This does not matter when her taxable income is below £33,300, the 40% threshold. But it is crucial when her income is increased by enough to bring her interest to the 40% bracket. The extra £1,000 bonus is taxed at just 22% but £1,000 of interest has been displaced from the 20% band into the 40% band. So, not only is she paying 40% tax on the top £1,000 of her interest, she also has some income under £33,000 on which she is paying 22% tax instead of 20% tax. And that is where the extra 2% comes from. Paying Gemma an extra £1,000 has increased her tax bill by £420 or 42% of the increase. What can she do about it?

The answer is to cut back her taxable income, maybe by making a pension contribution, if she qualifies. For example, if she invested the whole of the £1,000 bonus into a pension plan, she would qualify for effective tax relief of 42%, because the basic rate band is extended by the amount of the gross pension contribution.

Alternatively, she could perhaps switch some of the building society money into a more tax-efficient investment. National Savings certificates (NSCs), Individual Savings Accounts (ISAs) cash element and possibly even investment bonds would all have the desired effect.

1.9 Pre-owned assets tax (POAT)

HMRC acted against certain IHT avoidance schemes by imposing a stand-alone income tax charge from 6 April 2005. This has become known as Pre-Owned Asset Tax or POAT. POAT applies where an individual disposes of an asset but somehow retains the ability to use or enjoy it.

POAT does not apply to the extent that:

- The asset in question ceased to be owned before 18 March 1986.
- The asset formerly owned by a taxpayer is currently owned by their spouse or civil partner.
- The asset still counts as part of the taxpayer's estate for IHT purposes under the pre-existing gift with reservation rules.
- The asset was sold by the taxpayer at arm's length for cash.
- The taxpayer was formerly the owner of the asset only by virtue of a will or intestacy, which has subsequently been varied by agreement between the beneficiaries.
- Any enjoyment of the asset is no more than incidental, including cases where an out and out gift to a family member comes to benefit the donor following a change in their circumstances.

Where POAT does apply there is an income tax charge at the taxpayer's marginal rate on the annual cash value of the benefit – much like a benefit in kind charge for an employee. However, there is a *de minimis* threshold of £5,000 so that if the total annual cash value of all the taxpayer's assets subject to POAT does not exceed £5,000 there is no charge. However, if the annual cash value exceeds £5,000, the charge applies to the total value.

The exact way in which the annual cash value is calculated varies according to the type of asset, as explained below.

It should be noted that this tax is effectively retrospective by 19 years in that something done in March 1986 (which was perfectly legal, sensible and tax effective at the time) could produce a tax charge for 2005/06 and subsequent years.

For land (including the buildings thereon) the charge is on the rental value of the land if it was let commercially, less any payment made by the taxpayer as a result of a legal obligation. Thus the land had to be valued as at 6 April 2005 to establish the rental value and this value will apply for the next five years. After that the land will have to be revalued every five years, and the new value will apply for each subsequent period of five years.

For chattels and intangibles the charge is at the official interest rate, which is aligned with the official interest rate for cheap loans to employees under the benefit in kind rules – currently 5%. Thus chattels had to be valued on 5 April 2005 and every fifth year thereafter (as with land) to establish their open market value. Tax is then charged on 5% of that value.

For intangibles, such as life policies, POAT works in a somewhat different way. Firstly there is a potential POAT charge in respect of any trust where the settlor is a beneficiary in any shape or form, even if he is only a potential beneficiary and never actually receives any benefit. HMRC say that their intention is to tax (in their own words) the 'psychic income' or the nice warm feeling you get from being able to have access to the asset if necessary. Secondly, the asset has to be valued on 6 April in each tax year and then tax is charged on 5% of that open market value. This will often produce no actual tax payable due to the £5,000 threshold, particularly where a life policy has no surrender value.

It appears that the HMRC's main target was firstly 'double trust' house schemes and secondly, defeasible life interest trusts (otherwise known as Eversden Schemes). HMRC has confirmed that the following are not caught by the POAT rules:

- Discounted gift schemes where the settlor retains an absolute right to a defined sum or sums.
- Carve out schemes where an asset is divided in two, one part kept and another gifted, eg critical illness cover (CIC) split trusts where the right to a CIC benefit is kept and the right to the death benefit gifted entirely.
- Gift and loan trusts.
- Will trusts, either as far as the deceased was concerned or created within two years of the death by a deed of variation.

- Equity release schemes done on an arm's length basis.

The charge applies to residents of the UK. For taxpayers who are domiciled in the UK (or deemed to be) the charge will apply to their assets anywhere in the world. For taxpayers who are not domiciled in the UK (or not deemed to be) the charge will apply only to their UK assets. For taxpayers who have become domiciled in the UK (or deemed to be) the charge will not apply to any non-UK assets which they ceased to own before they acquired UK domicile.

Any taxpayer affected by the POAT rules can elect on or before 31 January 2007 to effectively substitute the pre-existing gift with reservation rules for the new income tax charge. The income tax saving would have to be balanced against the IHT disadvantage of the asset being deemed to be in the taxpayer's estate for IHT purposes on death. There are rules to prevent a double IHT charge on the settlor in these circumstances. In practical terms the age and state of health of the settlor will probably be the major factors in the decision as to whether to elect back into IHT to avoid POAT.

2 Capital Gains Tax

Capital gains tax (CGT) is a tax on gains arising from the disposal of capital assets. The charging legislation is in the Taxation of Chargeable Gains Act 1992. The tax is levied on the total of all chargeable gains accruing to a person on the disposal of assets in that tax year, after deduction of allowable losses. Only that proportion of the gain relating to the period after 31 March 1982 is chargeable. Tax is charged on the person making the disposal, not on the person receiving the asset. Spouses and civil partners are taxed separately on their own gains.

2.1 Exemptions

There are many exemptions from the tax. The most important exempt assets, on which no chargeable gain or allowable loss can be made, are as follows:

- An individual's principal private residence.

- Private motor vehicles.

- National Savings certificates and premium bonds.

- Government and most corporate bonds or government-guaranteed securities, held by individuals.

- Most life policies (see Chapter D).

- Capital redemption policies.

- Non-deferred annuities.

- Tangible movable property if the value at disposal does not exceed £6,000.
- Cashbacks given by providers of goods or services as an inducement to purchase those goods or services, eg by mortgage lenders.

In addition, disposals to a charity or to certain national institutions (eg museums) are exempt. Claims can be made for exemptions on disposals of works of art, historic houses and other assets of national interest if certain conditions are satisfied. Disposals by charities, registered pension funds and registered retirement annuity funds are also exempt.

2.2 Disposals

The term 'disposal' has a wide meaning for CGT purposes, and includes any transfer of ownership or the deriving of a capital sum from the asset. It therefore covers sales and gifts, whether absolute or by way of trust or settlement.

Transfers on death and transfers as security for a debt (mortgages) do not rank as disposals. A disposal by one spouse or civil partner to another does not give rise to a chargeable gain, but when the asset is ultimately disposed of the eventual tax liability is calculated by reference to the acquisition cost to the first spouse or civil partner, and holding period of both spouses or civil partners. The spouses or civil partners must be living together.

Disposals also occur in the following circumstances:

(a) The receipt of a capital sum as compensation for damage or injury to assets.

(b) The receipt of a capital sum under an insurance policy for damage, injury or loss of assets.

(c) The receipt of a capital sum for a surrender of rights.

(d) When a beneficiary under a trust becomes absolutely entitled to settled property against the trustees.

(e) The termination of a life interest under a trust by death.

In (d) the trustees would be the persons chargeable, but in (e) no gain arises and the trustees are deemed to reacquire the assets at their market value on the date of death.

On the death of an individual there is generally no tax on the transfer by death, and the beneficiaries of the estate are deemed to acquire the assets at their market value on the date of death.

2.3 Calculation of gain

Tax is only payable if a gain has been made. The first step in working out the gain is to calculate the disposal proceeds. In a sale this is simply the sale price less any incidental costs of disposal such as a stockbroker's commission. If an asset is given away, the disposal proceeds will be the market value of the asset at the time of the gift, again less any incidental costs of disposal. If the disposal is also a transfer of value for inheritance tax purposes, the IHT liability can be deducted in computing the gain on a subsequent disposal.

From the disposal proceeds must be deducted the acquisition cost of the asset. If the asset was bought, then this will be the purchase price plus any incidental costs of purchase; if the asset was acquired as a gift, it will be the market value at the time of acquisition. A further deduction is allowed for any expenditure on the asset for the purpose of enhancing its value, such as the cost of building an extension to a house. The resultant figure is, in crude terms, the 'profit' on the transaction. There is a special indexation allowance that applies to periods of ownership up to April 1998. The base acquisition value or enhancement expenditure is revalued in line with the increase in the retail prices index between the date of acquisition or expenditure and the date of disposal.

The indexation allowance cannot be used to create or increase a loss. It can be used to reduce a gain to zero, but is then effectively lost.

Indexation is only given for periods up to April 1998. For an asset held at 6 April 1998 and disposed of after that date, indexation allowance is given for the period from the date of acquisition to April 1998, but not for the period from April 1998 to the date of disposal. For assets acquired on or after 1 April 1998, no indexation allowance is given at all.

2.3.1 Indexation allowance

Indexation factors to April 1998:

	1982	1983	1984	1985	1986	1987	1988	1989	1990	1991	1992	1993	1994	1995	1996	1997	1998
Jan	-	0.968	0.872	0.783	0.689	0.626	0.574	0.465	0.361	0.249	0.199	0.179	0.151	0.114	0.083	0.053	0.019
Feb	-	0.960	0.865	0.769	0.683	0.620	0.568	0.454	0.353	0.242	0.193	0.171	0.144	0.107	0.078	0.049	0.014
Mar	1.047	0.956	0.859	0.752	0.681	0.616	0.562	0.448	0.339	0.237	0.189	0.167	0.141	0.102	0.073	0.046	0.011
Apr	1.006	0.929	0.834	0.716	0.665	0.597	0.537	0.423	0.300	0.222	0.171	0.156	0.128	0.091	0.066	0.040	
May	0.992	0.921	0.828	0.708	0.662	0.596	0.531	0.414	0.288	0.218	0.167	0.152	0.124	0.087	0.063	0.036	-
Jun	0.987	0.917	0.823	0.704	0.663	0.596	0.525	0.409	0.283	0.213	0.167	0.153	0.124	0.085	0.063	0.032	-
Jul	0.986	0.906	0.825	0.707	0.667	0.597	0.524	0.408	0.282	0.215	0.171	0.156	0.129	0.091	0.067	0.032	-
Aug	0.985	0.898	0.808	0.703	0.662	0.593	0.507	0.404	0.269	0.213	0.171	0.151	0.124	0.085	0.062	0.026	-
Sep	0.987	0.889	0.804	0.704	0.654	0.588	0.500	0.395	0.258	0.208	0.166	0.146	0.121	0.080	0.057	0.021	-
Oct	0.977	0.883	0.793	0.701	0.652	0.580	0.485	0.384	0.248	0.204	0.162	0.147	0.120	0.085	0.057	0.019	-
Nov	0.967	0.876	0.788	0.695	0.638	0.573	0.478	0.372	0.251	0.199	0.164	0.148	0.119	0.085	0.057	0.019	-
Dec	0.971	0.871	0.789	0.693	0.632	0.574	0.474	0.369	0.252	0.198	0.168	0.146	0.114	0.079	0.053	0.016	-

You simply multiply the base acquisition cost of the asset by the indexation factor to calculate the indexation allowance.

For example, Bill bought an asset for £10,000 before March 1982 and held it until after April 1998.

The indexation allowance is £10,000 x 1.047 = £10,470.

2.4 Taper relief

For post-April 1998 periods, indexation has been replaced by a taper relief. The taper relief reduces the amount of the gain according to the length of time the asset has been held since 5 April 1998.

There are two sets of taper relief, one for business assets and one for non-business assets, as follows:

	Gains on business assets			Gains on non-business assets		
No of complete years after 5.4.98 for which asset held	% of gain chargeable	Equivalent tax rates Higher	20%	% of gain chargeable	Equivalent tax rates Higher	20%
0	100	40	20	100	40	20
1	50.0	20	10	100	40	20
2	25.0	10	5	100	40	20
3	25.0	10	5	95	38	19
4	25.0	10	5	90	36	18
5	25.0	10	5	85	34	17
6	25.0	10	5	80	32	16
7	25.0	10	5	75	30	15
8	25.0	10	5	70	28	14
9	25.0	10	5	65	26	13
10 or more	25.0	10	5	60	24	12

A business asset is:

- An asset used for the purposes of a trade carried on by any individual (either alone or in partnership) or by a qualifying company of that individual.
- Assets owned by trustees and used for trade by a partnership of which they or some of them are members.
- An asset held for the purposes of a qualifying office or employment to which that individual was required to devote substantially the whole of his time.
- All shareholdings in unquoted trading companies.
- All shareholdings held by employees in quoted companies (this includes employees of group subsidiaries). If it is a non-trading company, the employee must not hold more than 10%.
- Shareholdings in a quoted trading company where the holder is not an employee but can exercise at least 5% of the voting rights.

Non-business assets acquired before 17 March 1998 qualify for an addition of one year to the period for which they are treated as held after 5 April 1998. So, for example, a non-business asset purchased on 1 January 1998 and disposed of on 1 July 2006 will be treated for taper relief as if it had been held for nine years, ie eight complete years after 5 April 1998 plus one additional year.

2.4.1 Summary

In summary, the gain is:

[Disposal proceeds – (acquisition costs + enhancement expenditure + incidental costs + indexation allowance)] x taper relief percentage.

For assets acquired before 31 March 1982, the acquisition cost is deemed to be the market value on 31 March 1982 and the indexation allowance is for the period from that date to April 1998. In this case no deductions are allowed for incidental costs of acquisition or enhancement expenditure prior to that date. The gain would thus be:

[Disposal proceeds – (1982 value + post-1982 enhancement expenditure + incidental costs of disposal + indexation allowance)] x taper relief percentage.

However, the taxpayer does have the option of using the actual acquisition cost if it is higher than the 1982 value, in which case incidental costs of acquisition and pre-1982 enhancement expenditure are deductible although the indexation allowance is still based on the post-1982 period.

Should a disposal produce a loss, this can be set against any gains in the same tax year. If these gains are insufficient to absorb the loss then the unabsorbed loss can be carried forward to be set against gains in subsequent years until it is fully absorbed. As spouses and civil partners are taxed independently, one's loss cannot be set against the other's gains.

If spouses or civil partners dispose of a jointly-held asset, it will be assumed that each has disposed of half the asset and received half the proceeds.

2.5 Holdover relief

A holdover relief applies to gifts of trading assets (including agricultural property and private company shares) and transfers that attract an immediate charge to IHT (such as gifts into settlements). For the latter, the relief still applies, even if there is no IHT payable because the transfer is within the nil rate band. The holdover relief means that no tax is payable at the time of the gift, but the acquisition cost to the donee is reduced by the amount of the held-over gain. This effectively increases the amount of any gain made by the donee on a subsequent disposal. From 10 December 2003 holdover relief cannot be claimed for disposals to trusts in which the settlor has an interest.

2.6 Reinvestment relief

Reinvestment relief allows people to defer paying tax on any gains if they reinvest those gains in an Enterprise Investment Scheme (EIS) or Venture Capital Trust

(VCT) – see Chapter N. For VCTs, relief only applies for shares issued before 6 April 2004.

2.7 Identification

Special rules apply to assets of the same type and class acquired at different times. These are needed to match acquisitions and disposals to calculate gains.

Disposals of shares, or units in unit trusts, are identified with acquisitions in the following order:

- Acquisitions on the same day.
- Acquisitions within the following 30 days.
- Previous acquisitions after 5 April 1998, identifying the most recent acquisition first. This is called the LIFO basis – last in, first out.
- Any shares held at 5 April 1998 and acquired after 5 April 1982. These are pooled.
- Any shares held at 5 April 1982 and acquired after 5 April 1965. These are pooled separately from later acquisitions.
- Any shares acquired before 6 April 1965.

The effect is that when part of a holding of shares is disposed of, they are deemed to be the most recently acquired ones. This will tend to minimise any taper relief, but as long as share prices increase, it will also minimise chargeable gains.

The identification rules are not relevant to the disposal of an entire shareholding. Nevertheless, there would be different periods for calculating any indexation allowance and taper relief if some of the shares were acquired at different times from the others.

2.8 Calculation of the tax

The tax is based on the net gains arising in the tax year: in other words, gains less allowable losses. The procedure is to add up all the gains made on disposals in the tax year and deduct any losses made in the same year to arrive at a total net gain figure. If net gains do not exceed £8,800 (a maximum of £4,400 for trusts) no tax will be payable. If gains exceed that figure, then the excess is treated as the top slice of income. The part that is in the basic rate band is taxable at 20%, the part that is above is taxable at 40%. Any gain falling within the starting rate band is taxable at 10%.

When working out a taxpayer's income to decide the rate of CGT where there is a chargeable gain on a life policy, it is the top sliced gain that is taken into account – not the whole gain.

Losses are set against gross gains before the application of taper relief. It is therefore best to ensure that losses can be offset against gains that qualify for little or no taper relief.

If an individual's income is so low that it does not exceed their income tax allowances (and thus the income tax rate is effectively 0%), the CGT rate will begin at 10%. Spouses and civil partners each have their own £8,800 exemption, and their tax is calculated separately. The tax is due on the 31 January following the end of the tax year concerned.

Companies are chargeable to corporation tax on capital gains at their corporation tax rate. Authorised unit trusts, open ended investment companies (OEICs) and approved investment trusts are exempt from corporation tax on their chargeable gains. Unitholders or shareholders are, however, liable for CGT when they cash in their holdings. This affects life offices, who may hold units or shares in connection with unit-linked policies. The policyholder's share of gains in a life office's life fund is charged at 20%. Companies and life funds do not get taper relief or any annual exemption, but continue to get indexation allowance.

The following is an example of a CGT calculation to show how the principles work:

Example C

Mr A buys an old picture for £10,000 in January 1988. He has it cleaned and restored in June 2006. This costs £1,000 but reveals that it is much more valuable than originally thought. He immediately has the picture auctioned and it fetches £100,000. The auctioneers' fees are £1,000. Mr A is a higher-rate income taxpayer, but has no other gains that year.

	£	£
Disposal proceeds		100,000
Less acquisition costs	10,000	
Indexation allowance for Jan 1988–April 1998:		
57.4% enhancement	5,740	
Expenditure	1,000	
Disposal costs	1,000	
	17,740	17,740
Gain		82,260
Nine years' taper relief 82,260 x .65		53,469
Less exemption		8,800
Taxable gain		44,669
Tax at 40%		17,867.60

3 Inheritance Tax

The law is primarily contained in the Finance Act 1986 and the Inheritance Tax Act 1984. The 1984 Act is cited throughout this book as the IHTA. Likewise the tax itself is referred to as IHT.

3.1 The cumulation principle

Inheritance tax is a cumulative tax applying to transfers during life and on death. All 'chargeable transfers' (see below for definition) are added up and tax is payable once the threshold of £285,000 is exceeded. However, once a transfer is more than seven years old, it drops out of the cumulation[1]. When a person dies, the value of the estate left is added to the total of chargeable lifetime transfers in the previous seven years, in order to find the tax due. A table of rates is given at the end of this section and an example of a taxpayer's IHT life history is also shown to illustrate the operation of the tax in practice.

3.2 People to whom IHT applies

IHT applies to all the assets of individuals who are domiciled in the UK, whether or not the assets are situated in the UK. For persons domiciled outside the UK, IHT applies only to their assets situated in the UK. However, the domicile rules for general law are extended in two ways for IHT. First, three years' domicile outside the UK are needed to acquire a foreign domicile for IHT. Second, a person is treated as having a UK domicile if he has been resident in the UK in not less than 17 of the previous 20 tax years before the transfer[2].

From 16 October 2002 OEIC and authorised unit trust holdings of non UK domiciled investors have been exempt from IHT.

3.3 Transactions to which IHT applies

Inheritance tax is charged on the value transferred by a chargeable transfer – that is any transfer of value made by an individual which is not exempt (for an explanation of how the value of the transfer is calculated for tax purposes see later). A transfer of value is any disposition made by a transferor by which the value of the estate immediately afterwards is less than it would have been if the disposition had not been made. The tax therefore affects dispositions in the nature of a gift, or part-gift, and does not affect commercial transactions where full consideration is received, as there is then no loss to the estate. There is, in fact, a specific exemption for transactions where there was no intent to confer any gratuitous benefit and the transaction was either 'at arm's length' between unconnected persons or was such as might be expected to be made in those circumstances[3]. Thus, an individual would not pay IHT if he makes a 'bad bargain'.

Where a gift is made by cheque the gift is not complete until the cheque has cleared – *Curnock v IRC* [2003] W.T.L.R.55.

[1] IHTA 1984 s7(1); [2] IHTA 1984 s267; [3] IHTA 1984 s10

Any transfer which is allowable in computing a person's profits for income tax is exempt, and so is a contribution to a registered occupational pension scheme, or personal pension, for an employee.

An interest-free loan is not a transfer of value if it is repayable on demand.

In the recent case of *McDowell vs IRC* (2004 STC (SCD) 22) it was held that gifts purportedly made by the taxpayer's attorney were void as the attorney lacked the formal power to make them, and so were subject to IHT as part of the estate. In this connection it should be noted that the Enduring Powers of Attorney Act 1985 s3 only allows an attorney to make gifts on behalf of the donor if they are to provide for the needs of those the donor might be expected to provide for, or are normal 'birthday and Christmas' gifts. Thus if the taxpayer has lost mental capacity this effectively rules out IHT planning involving gifts or trusts done by the attorney. However, it would be possible for the attorney to apply to the Court of Protection for permission to make such gifts, although this might be time consuming and costly with no guarantee of success.

The tax covers situations where the deliberate omission to exercise a right reduces the value of the estate[4]. This would include the failure to collect a debt. There are a number of provisions in s268 of the IHTA designed to combat avoidance devices using a series of transactions. These 'associated operations' provisions cover transactions whereby a transfer of value is made by two or more operations of any kind affecting the same property. The section attempts to tax the transaction as a whole, disregarding the intermediate steps.

3.3.1 Interaction with capital gains tax

A transaction can, of course, be subject to CGT, as well as IHT, and in this case some double tax relief may be available. In calculating the loss to the estate no account is taken of any CGT (or any stamp duty or additional expenses). Where the CGT (or incidental expenses) is borne by the recipient the value transferred is reduced by that amount.

3.3.2 Lifetime transfers

Once the total of chargeable lifetime transfers in the last seven years has exceeded the IHT threshold of £285,000, tax will become payable at the lifetime rate of 20%.

Tax is primarily charged on the transferor, but can also be paid by the transferee. The amount of tax paid can be affected by who pays the tax (see 'the grossing-up rule', below). Tax is due six months after the end of the month when the transfer is made, or for a transfer made after 5 April and before 1 October in any year, at the end of April in the next year[5].

3.3.3 Potentially exempt transfers

A potentially exempt transfer (PET) is a lifetime transfer made from one individual to another individual, or from one individual into a trust for the disabled[6], or an absolute trust (otherwise called a bare trust).

[4] IHTA 1984 s3(3); [5] IHTA 1984 s226(1); [6] Finance Act 1986 Sch 19-1

If such a gift is not otherwise exempt (see later for the exemptions), it will be potentially exempt and thus no tax will be charged at the date of the gift and it will not count for the donor's cumulation. It does not have to be reported to HMRC. If the donor then survives for seven years, the gift becomes fully exempt and thus escapes tax entirely.

However, if the donor dies within seven years from the date of the PET, it becomes retrospectively chargeable. In this case tax will be chargeable on the value of the PET at the date it was actually made, based on the donor's seven-year cumulation at that date but using the death rates in force at the date of death, subject to a taper relief[7]. The taper relief provides that if the donor survives for at least three years, only a reduced percentage of the full death rates will be used as follows:

Years between gift and death	**Percentage of full charge at death rates**
3–4	80%
4–5	60%
5–6	40%
6–7	20%

Although the taper relief reduces the amount of tax payable, it does not reduce the value of the transfer for the purposes of the donor's cumulation. Thus, the full value of the transfer is included in the donor's cumulation for the purposes of working out the death tax on the estate.

If the value of the PET plus any chargeable transfer in the seven years prior to it does not exceed the IHT threshold, no tax will be payable on the PET itself. However, it will still increase the cumulation for any subsequent chargeable transfer whether during life or on death. Thus the tax on any chargeable lifetime transfer between the PET and death would have to be recalculated using the new cumulation figure.

Because of these provisions most lifetime transfers other than to trusts will be exempt when they are made and will only come into account if the donor dies within seven years. Gifts to trusts other than disabled trusts or absolute trusts cannot be PETs and so are chargeable when made (unless otherwise exempt) at the lifetime rates.

3.3.4 Death within seven years

If a transferor dies within seven years of making a chargeable lifetime transfer, tax at the death rates will apply retrospectively to that transfer. Thus the tax is recalculated using the value of the gift at the actual date of the transfer, the previous seven years' cumulation at the actual date of the transfer but the death rates in force at the date of death.

The position on PETs has been covered above but if the lifetime transfer was not a PET (eg because it was a gift into a trust), some lifetime tax may have been paid at outset. If so, this tax is allowed as a credit against the tax payable at the death rates. The same taper relief applies as for PETs and thus the charge is reduced during the last four years of the seven-year period. It is possible for the lifetime tax already paid to exceed the death tax due to the taper relief – because the life rate is half the death

[7] *Finance Act 1986 Sch 19-2(4)*

rate but the tapered charges are 40% and 20% in the sixth and seventh years respectively. In these cases there will be no extra tax to pay but no refund either[8].

If no lifetime tax was payable because the transfer was wholly in the nil rate band, there will be no extra tax to pay on death as it will still be within the nil rate band – unless a previous PET has retrospectively become chargeable and thereby increased the cumulation to over the IHT threshold.

3.3.5 Relief for drop in value

If tax becomes due on a PET because the donor dies within seven years, there may be relief if the value of the property gifted has dropped since the date of the gift. If the donee still owns the property, the value for the tax calculation will be the market value on the donor's death. If the donee has sold the property to an unconnected person, then the value will be the market value at the date of the sale.

However, this does not apply if the property is tangible moveable property that is a wasting asset (ie having a useful life of 50 years or less).

3.3.6 Transfers on death

Inheritance tax is chargeable on the death of any individual[9]. The tax is chargeable as if, immediately before death, the deceased had made a transfer of value equal to the value of his estate on that date. Changes brought about by death (eg the proceeds payable under a life policy) do, however, have to be taken into account[10].

The estate is the total property to which the deceased was beneficially entitled at death, apart from excluded property. If the deceased has an interest in settled property and on his death the property reverts to the settlor or the settlor's spouse, it is excluded property unless the settlor or the settlor's spouse or civil partner acquired the reversionary interest for money or money's worth. Certain pension scheme benefits are also excluded, as is a reversionary interest in a settlement. A deduction is allowed from the estate for reasonable funeral expenses.

Any property over which the deceased had a general power of appointment is treated as part of the estate, eg a joint bank account where the deceased put in all the money and there were no limits on the amount they could take out. This would also be a gift with reservation (see later).

When two people die in circumstances where it is impossible to say who died first, the general law presumes that the older was the first to die[11]. Thus, if the older person left the property to the younger, two successive tax charges could occur for that property. For IHT purposes, however, it is presumed that they died at the same instant, thus avoiding the double charge[12].

Tax on death is charged at the death scale of rates on the value of the estate sitting on top of the previous seven years' cumulation. The working of this principle can be seen in the example set out at the end of this section. Liability for the tax falls on the personal representatives, who have to pay it before a grant of representation will be issued. Tax is due six months after the end of the month of death, although there are

[8] Finance Act 1986 Sch 19-2(4); [9] IHTA 1984 s4(1); [10] IHTA 1984 s171; [11] Law of Property Act 1925 s184; [12] IHTA 1984 s4(2)

provisions for payment of tax in instalments for certain property such as land[13].

A quick succession relief is available where property in the deceased's estate had passed to him by a chargeable transfer in the five years before his death[14]. The tax charged on death is reduced by a percentage of the IHT paid on the earlier transfer. The percentage varies according to the period between the transfer and death as follows:

Not more than 1 year	100%
1 to 2 years	80%
2 to 3 years	60%
3 to 4 years	40%
4 to 5 years	20%

However, the percentage only relates to the tax on the net increase in the estate of the second to die.

3.3.7 Settlements

The IHTA contains very detailed provisions for the taxation of settled property: the following is a brief outline of the position.

For IHT purposes, settled property includes property held in trust for successive beneficiaries (eg a widow and then child) or for any person subject to a discretion or contingency (eg for a child on reaching age 21). Bare trusts, ie trusts under which the trustees are acting as mere nominees of the beneficiaries, are not regarded as settlements.

As a general rule, gifts into settlements for a disabled person are treated as potentially exempt transfers, whereas gifts into other settlements are chargeable transfers. A beneficiary with a right to income from a settlement was deemed to own the underlying capital for IHT purposes. Thus there can be a tax charge on a change of entitlement to income. For example, when a beneficiary's life interest ends and instead a new beneficiary becomes entitled to income or capital[15]. However this treatment has been changed by the 2006 Budget – see section 3.3.8.

A change in the interest in possession beneficiary under a pre-2006 Budget trust during the outgoing beneficiary's lifetime is deemed to be a PET. Thus an appointment under a flexible power of appointment trust would only be chargeable if the outgoing beneficiary died within seven years of the appointment.

However, there is no charge where property reverts to the settlor or to their spouse or civil partner[16]. Where there is a tax charge on a change of beneficiary, the rate of tax is determined by the old beneficiary's cumulative total at that time. The tax is then payable by the trustees out of the settled property.

Settlements with no interest in possession were treated somewhat differently[17]. An 'interest in possession' is not defined in the Act but is accepted to mean a present right to present enjoyment of the property or the income from it. Thus, in a trust 'for A for life, thereafter to B', A has an interest in possession but B has not. However, in

[13] IHTA 1984 s227-229; [14] IHTA 1984 s141; [15] IHTA 1984 s52(1);
[16] IHTA 1984 s53(3),(4); [17] IHTA 1984 ss58-85

a trust 'for such of X, Y and Z as the trustees may appoint', then no-one has an interest in possession until an appointment is made.

In such discretionary trusts any capital distribution by the trustees is chargeable (the exit charge) and there is also the 'periodic charge'. The periodic charge is a charge falling on every tenth anniversary of the settlement. This subject is covered more fully in Chapter G, section 3.

3.3.8 2006 Budget changes

Before the date of the 2006 Budget – 22 March 2006 – the creation of a trust with an interest in possession, or an accumulation and maintenance trust, was a PET. This was changed by the Budget.

Now the creation during the settlor's lifetime of any trust except an absolute trust or a disabled trust is a chargeable lifetime transfer unless an exemption applies. It could still be exempt under the annual, normal expenditure or spouse exemption. If not, and the transfer is over the nil rate band (taking into account the previous seven years' chargeable lifetime transfers), there is a tax charge at outset of 20% of the excess over the nil rate band. Thus a transfer of £300,000 into a flexible trust where no exemptions were available would generate an immediate tax charge of £3,000 (ie 20% of £15,000) if paid by the trustees. There might be further tax if the settlor died within the next five years (see section 3.3.4). Even if a chargeable lifetime transfer is not over the nil rate band, it still has to be reported to HMRC within a year of outset if it exceeds £10,000, or the donor's cumulation in the previous ten years exceeds £40,000.

In addition, if these trusts are created on or after 22 March 2006, they will be subject to the exit and periodic charges which previously only applied to discretionary trusts, but only if they exceed the nil rate band. The only trusts that will avoid the new rules are those that:

- Are created on death by a parent for a minor child who will be fully entitled at age 18; or
- Are created on death for the benefit of one life tenant in order of time whose interest cannot be replaced; or
- Are created either in the settlor's lifetime or on death for a disabled person.

Accumulation and maintenance (A&M) trusts that existed before 22 March 2006, and where the trust provides that the trust assets will go to a beneficiary absolutely at age 18 (or where the trust terms are modified before 6 April 2008 to provide this), keep the pre-existing PET treatment. Where such A&M trusts do not provide this, they will become subject to the discretionary trust regime from 6 April 2008 for the period between age a18 and 25 and the periodic and exit charges will apply. Ten-yearly anniversaries will depend on the original date of the trust but for the first ten years after 6 April 2008 the charge will reflect the fact that it has not been subject to the new regime for the full ten years. Thus the maximum charge would be 4.2%.

The previous PET rules for interest in possession trusts created before 22 March 2006 will continue until the interest current on that date ends. If someone then takes absolute ownership this will be a transfer by the previous beneficiary as before. If, when that interest comes to an end, the trust continues, this will be treated as a chargeable lifetime transfer by the outgoing beneficiary (if alive) or part of the estate (if on death). Thereafter the trust will be subject to the new regime with the exit and periodic charges. However, any new interest in possession that arises when a pre-22 March 2006 interest in possession ends before 6 April 2008 (whether on death or during life) will be treated as a pre-22 March 2006 interest.

The IHT treatment of trusts is dealt with in more detail in Chapter G, section 3.

3.4 Exemptions and reliefs

The impact of IHT is reduced by a number of exemptions and reliefs and it is important to note the distinction between exemptions and reliefs. An exemption means that the transfer does not count as a chargeable transfer and therefore is neither taxed nor included in the cumulation for the future. A relief is a means by which the value of a chargeable transfer is reduced. It does not remove the transfer from the tax regime but merely reduces or extinguishes its value.

3.4.1 Exemptions

The following is a list of the main exemptions. These exemptions are not mutually exclusive (except (c)) and a transfer may fall under more than one exemption and so be freed from tax partly by one exemption and partly by another. Where an exempt gift is made during life, it does not matter whether the donor survives for seven years or not.

(a) **Transfers between spouses or civil partners.** Transfers between spouses or civil partners, whether during life or on death, are totally exempt. However, if the transferor is domiciled in the UK but the civil partner or spouse is not, the exemption is limited to a total value of £55,000[18]. The spouse must be a legally married spouse, and it should be noted that under English law there is no such thing as a common law spouse. By virtue of s49 of the IHTA, this exemption applies where a spouse or civil partner is given an interest in possession under a trust, eg a life interest under a will trust. A legal case (*Holland v Commissioners of Inland Revenue 2002 sc350*) has decided that the exemption does not apply where the couple were not legally married, even though they had lived together as husband and wife for over 30 years.

(b) **Annual exemption.** A transferor may make transfers of up to a value of £3,000 in any one tax year exempt from IHT. If the whole £3,000 is not used in any year, the balance can be carried forward to the next year. For example if X transfers £1,500 in year 1, he can carry forward £1,500 and have a £4,500 exemption in year 2. However any unused balance is lost if not utilised in the next year – it cannot be carried forward to year 3. This exemption applies only to lifetime gifts[19].

(c) **Small gifts.** Transfers of value made by the transferor, by outright gifts to any person in any one year, are exempt up to a value of £250. This exemption can be used

[18] IHTA 1984 s18; [19] IHTA 1984 s19

any number of times in respect of different donees. The gift has to be outright and this does not include gifts on trust. Again, this exemption is available for lifetime gifts only. It cannot be used as part of a larger gift[20].

(d) **Normal expenditure.** A transfer is exempt if it is shown that:

- It was made as part of the transferor's normal expenditure; and
- It was made out of income; and
- After allowing for all transfers forming part of normal expenditure, the transferor was left with sufficient income to maintain his usual standard of living[21].

Expenditure will have to be habitual or regular to rank as 'normal', and this will obviously only apply during the transferor's lifetime. It will be seen that this exemption could readily be used for payment of premiums into a life policy for the benefit of the intended donee, since the element of regularity is provided by the premium frequency. However, the exemption cannot be used for this purpose if the transferor has also purchased an associated annuity on his life.
The capital content of a purchased life annuity is not treated as part of the transferor's income when applying this exemption to a transfer. If the transferor is taking withdrawals from a single premium bond these payments are not income under the general law, even if the excess over 5% is deemed to be income for income tax purposes.

Following the case of *Bennett v IRC*, payments do not have to be of a fixed amount to qualify as normal expenditure. In this case, a donor instructed her trustees to pay to the donees such of her trust income as was surplus to her financial requirements. This resulted in two annual payments of £9,300 and £60,000. The court held that this was normal expenditure, because the precise instructions given to the trustees established that the very different amounts were part of a pattern of normal expenditure from income, which clearly did not reduce her standard of living.

(e) **Gifts on marriage or civil partnership.** Certain gifts in consideration of marriage or civil partnership are exempt, up to various limits. The limits are as follows:

- £5,000 if the donor is a parent of a party to the marriage or civil partnership.
- £2,500 if the donor is a remoter ancestor of a party to the marriage or civil partnership.
- £2,500 if the donor is the bride or groom, and the gift is made to the other prospective spouse or civil partner.
- £1,000 if the donor is any other person.
This exemption is available only during the donor's lifetime[22].

[20] IHTA 1984 s20; [21] IHTA 1984 s21; [22] IHTA 1984 s22

(f) **Gifts for education and maintenance.** Transfers to a spouse or civil partner or ex-spouse or formal civil partner for his or her maintenance are exempt, as are certain payments for a child's maintenance, education or training. This latter exemption only lasts until the tax year when the child becomes 18, or ends full-time education, whichever is the later. The donee has to be a child (including illegitimate, step and adopted) of the donor. A transfer for a dependent relative of the donor is exempt if it constitutes reasonable provision for the relative's care and maintenance[23].

(g) **Gifts to charities and political parties.** Gifts to charities[24] and political parties[25], whether during life or on death, are totally exempt.

(h) **Gifts for the national benefit.** Certain gifts for the national benefit are exempt. These include gifts to museums, libraries, universities and the National Trust[26].

(i) **Death on active service.** The estate of a member of the armed forces is completely tax-free on death, if death is due to wounds received, or diseases contracted, on active service[27].

(j) **Decorations awarded for valour or gallant conduct that have never been sold.** This covers medals gifted or bequeathed by the original recipient or anyone else, where they have never been sold. If a medal has changed hands for money or money's worth it will be liable to IHT like any other asset.

3.4.2 Reliefs

The following are the main reliefs. Most of these are very complicated and so only a brief outline can be given in this work.

- **Business relief.** This is a relief for transfers of business property[28].

  The relief is 100% for:
  - Interests in unincorporated businesses (including limited liability partnerships).
  - Shareholdings in unlisted companies.
  - Shareholdings in alternative investment market (AIM) companies.

  The relief is 50% for:
  - Controlling shareholdings in fully listed companies.
  - Land, buildings, plant or machinery used wholly or mainly in connection with a company controlled by the transferor, or a partnership of which he was a partner.

  Property has to be owned for two years prior to the transfer to qualify as business property. The relief does not apply if the business consists wholly or mainly of dealing in securities, stocks and shares, land or buildings, or making or holding investments. When valuing business property any asset which has not been used for the business for the last two years or is not required at the time of the transfer for future use for the business must be disregarded. This is to stop business relief being claimed on assets such as large amounts of cash which are not *bona fide* parts of the business. Business property relief is not available if the property is at the time of the transfer subject to a binding contract for sale.

[23] IHTA 1984 s11; [24] IHTA 1984 s23; [25] IHTA 1984 s24; [26] IHTA 1984 s25; [27] IHTA 1984 s154; [28] IHTA 1984 ss103-114

- **Agricultural relief.** This is a relief for agricultural property in the UK, Channel Islands or the Isle of Man[29]. Agricultural property includes agricultural land, growing crops and farm buildings but not the animals or equipment. The relief is 100% for owner-occupied farms and farm tenancies and 50% for interests of landlords in farmland let before 1 September 1995. One hundred percent relief applies to land let on or after 1 September 1995 for transfers made on or after that date. Agricultural relief only applies to the agricultural value of the land, not any development value. The case of *Starke v IRC* held that agricultural property did not include buildings on their own. The property must have been occupied by the transferor for agricultural purposes for the previous two years, or have been owned by the transferor for seven years and been occupied by someone else for agricultural purposes for that time.

  Agricultural relief does not apply if the property is subject to a binding contract for sale.

  If agricultural relief is claimed on property, business property relief cannot also be claimed on the same property.

- **Woodlands relief.** This is a special relief for growing timber in the UK[30]. It applies only to the timber not the land itself, which may in any case qualify for agricultural relief. The relief only applies to transfers on death and works by deferring the tax until the timber is disposed of. However, the occupation of woodlands for commercial purposes would mean that business relief could be claimed at 100%, which is preferable to deferment.

3.5 Gifts with a reservation of benefit

These are gifts made on or after 18 March 1986 where an individual disposes of any property by way of a gift and either possession or enjoyment of the property is not taken by the donee or it is not enjoyed to the exclusion or virtual exclusion of the donor[31]. An example of a gift with a reservation would be where Mr X gives his house to his son but continues to live in it.

If a gift with a reservation is made, then all the normal consequences of a lifetime transfer follow – ie it might be exempt, potentially exempt or chargeable depending on the circumstances. However, when the donor dies the gifted property will be taxed as if it was part of the donor's estate on the basis of its value at the date of death. If any lifetime tax was paid on the original gift, this will be allowed as a credit against the death tax.

For these reasons gifts with a reservation are now generally to be avoided. HMRC has stated that if the donor is a potential beneficiary under a discretionary trust, or even under a power of appointment trust where someone else has an interest in possession, it will regard this as a reservation of benefit. Therefore, the standard advice for clients using these trusts is to make sure that they cannot themselves benefit in any way by excluding them from benefit in the trust deed. The donor can still be a trustee but

[29] IHTA 1984 s115-124; [30] IHTA 1984 ss125-130; [31] Finance Act 1986 s102

should not be able to benefit from any trustee charging clause. The provisions do not apply to gifts which are exempt for the following reasons: transfers between spouses or civil partners, small gifts, gifts in consideration of marriage or civil partnership, gifts to charity, gifts to political parties or gifts for the national benefit. HMRC has also stated that where a gift is made into trust, the retention by the settlor of a reversionary interest under the trust is not a reservation of benefit.

Under section 102B Finance Act 1986 a gift of an undivided share of an interest in land is a gift with reservation unless:

- The donor does not occupy the land; or
- The donor pays the full market rent; or
- The donor and donee share occupation and the donor does not receive any benefit provided by the donee.

To avoid problems if the last exemption is being claimed, the donee should not pay more than their proportionate share of the running costs.

A benefit can be reserved for the spouse or civil partner of the donor but if that spouse or civil partner shares enjoyment of the gift with the donor, HMRC may regard this as a reservation of benefit by the donor.

Prior to the 1986 Budget many regular premium life policies were sold under some form of flexible trust where the donor was a potential beneficiary and thus post-Budget premiums would have been gifts with a reservation. To avoid this an amendment[32] provides that these premiums are not gifts with a reservation, if the policy was effected prior to 18 March 1986 and was not varied after that date so as to increase the benefits or extend the term. An index-linking variation made on or before 1 August 1986 will not count for this purpose. Thus, to avoid IHT problems these policies should not now be varied. Any increase in cover required should be arranged via a new policy under a non-reservation trust rather than by altering the old policy. However, there are POAT problems with these policies – see page 69.

The gift with reservation of benefit provisions could also have caught the placing of the death benefit under a personal or other type of pension policy under trust on the grounds that the pension is reserved for the donor. However, HMRC has stated that it does not regard these arrangements as gifts with a reservation.

It is believed HMRC does not regard an interest-free loan of itself as a gift with reservation. A case (*Sillars v Deeprose* [2004] Spc 401) has held that where an individual transfers a bank account into the joint names of the individual and someone else, and there were no limits on drawing rights, this was a gift with reservation. Thus the whole balance of the account was subject to IHT on death.

[32] Finance Act 1986 s102(6),(7)

3.6 Valuation of the transfer

The value of an asset for IHT purposes is generally taken as the price it might reasonably be expected to fetch if sold on the open market. No reduction of this value is allowable on the ground that the whole property (eg a large shareholding) is theoretically put on the market at one and the same time[33].

Any expenses of the transfer (eg legal costs) are disregarded if they are paid by the transferor, but reduce the value of the transfer if they are paid by the transferee.

Where a chargeable transfer also results in a CGT liability which is paid by the donee, the value for IHT purposes is reduced by the CGT paid.

If a deceased's estate includes listed shares or authorised unit trust holdings which are sold within a year of the death at a lower value than the value at the date of death, then relief is given by recalculating the tax on the basis of the actual sale value.

A similar provision applies to sales of land to unconnected persons within four years of the death, but only if the loss is more than the lower of £1,000 or 5% of the death value.

3.6.1 Related property

Account must also be taken of 'related property'[34]. Related property is property which is either (a) in the estate of the donor's spouse or civil partner, or (b) in a settlement where the donor or spouse or civil partner has an interest in possession. When a donor transfers related property, he is deemed to transfer the value of his proportion of the total value of all the related property. An example of the operation of this is where a husband and wife each own 45% of the shares in a private company. If the husband gave all his shares to his son, he is deemed to have transferred, not the value of a 45% minority shareholding, but half the value of a 90% controlling shareholding. A controlling shareholding is worth more than a minority shareholding and therefore this rule increases the value of the transfer.

3.6.2 The grossing-up rule

One aspect of valuation is the grossing-up rule. This rule applies to transfers where the transferor pays the tax, and stems from the principle that the tax is based on the loss to the transferor's estate. If the transferor pays the tax, his estate is reduced by (a) the value of the asset transferred, and (b) the tax thereon. Tax is therefore calculated on the total of the gift plus the tax. Thus it is necessary to gross-up the net transfer to calculate the tax. This can be made clearer by the following example.

Example D

Mr X decides to make a gross gift of £10,000 and the relevant rate is 20%. The tax is £2,000 and the donee receives £8,000. However, if Mr X wishes the donee to actually receive £10,000 he has to make a larger gift, because the gift is grossed-up for tax purposes. In this case the gross gift would have to be £12,500 with tax of £2,500 (still at a rate of 20%) going to HMRC and the net gift of £10,000 to the donee.

---

[33] IHTA 1984 s160; [34] IHTA 1984 s161

It is important to understand this principle as it is the grossed-up value which is cumulated for future transfers. Grossing-up does not apply if the transferee pays the tax, because the loss to the transferor is merely the value of the asset. It can only apply to lifetime transfers.

The grossing-up formula is that the tax is one-quarter of the excess over £285,000. An example of its use would be if a net gift of £300,000 is to be made the formula would show the tax to be:

$$\frac{1}{4} \text{ x the excess over £285,000} = \frac{1}{4} \text{ x £15,000} = \text{£3,750}$$

The tax is thus £3,750 making the gross transfer £303,750 and this is the figure which will be carried forward for future cumulation. Proof of the calculation is:

$$\text{Tax on £303,750} = 20\% \text{ x (£303,750} - \text{£285,000)}$$
$$= 20\% \text{ x £18,750} = \text{£3,750}$$

Grossing-up is more common than it used to be now that many gifts into trusts are chargeable lifetime transfers rather than PETs.

3.6.3 Valuation of life policies

Under an own life policy, not assigned or under trust, when the life assured dies the proceeds paid on death will be part of the estate.

If a life policy is the subject of a transfer of value during its lifetime, the value based on normal IHT rules would be its market value – usually the surrender value (unless the life assured is known to be in very bad health). However, there is a special valuation rule which applies to life policies[35]. Under this rule the value is not to be less than the total premiums paid under the policy minus any sums previously paid out. The normal market value (surrender value) will be used if it is higher.

This special valuation rule does not apply to term assurances for three years or less, or if the term exceeds three years where:

- Premiums are payable for at least two-thirds of the term; and
- Premiums payable in any one year do not exceed twice those in any other year.

Unit-linked policies are not fully subject to the premiums valuation, in that any drop in the value of units since they were allocated is allowed as a deduction from the total premiums.

If premiums are paid on a life policy for the benefit of someone other than the payer, that is a transfer of value of the amount of the premium. If the premium is paid net of life assurance premium relief, the value is the net premium not the gross, since it is only the net premium that is the loss to the estate.

[35] *IHTA 1984 s167*

If an individual buys a capital protected annuity and puts the return of capital benefit in trust, there has been a transfer of value. The value of this, based on the loss to the estate principle, is the difference between the purchase price of the annuity and the open market value of the right to receive the unprotected annuity payments for the annuitant's lifetime. This open market value is likely to be less than the normal purchase price of such an annuity because a purchaser in the open market would need to buy life cover to protect his investment. Thus, HMRC's view is that the value of the gift for IHT purposes will generally be substantially more than the value of the death benefit which has been gifted.

3.7 Pre-owned assets

The government acted against certain IHT schemes from 6 April 2005 by introducing a stand-alone income tax charge on benefits from pre-owned assets – see section 1.9 of this chapter.

3.8 How IHT works

The following is an example of a person's IHT history, designed to illustrate how the tax works. It uses current rates, thresholds and exemptions throughout, for simplicity.

Example E

		£
Year 1	Gift to son	30,000
	Transfer	30,000
	Annual exemption (year of transfer)	3,000
	Annual exemption (previous year)	3,000
	Non-exempt transfer	24,000
	Not chargeable as a PET	
Year 2	Gift to daughter	30,000
	Transfer	30,000
	Annual exemption	3,000
	Non-exempt transfer	27,000
	Not chargeable as a PET	
Year 3	Outright gift of £10,000 to son on wedding day	
	Transfer	10,000
	Annual exemption	3,000
	Marriage exemption	5,000
	Non-exempt transfer	2,000
	Not chargeable as a PET	
Year 4	Gift of £10,000 to wife. Totally exempt	

Year 5	Outright gift of £18,000 to daughter on wedding day	
	Transfer	18,000
	Annual exemption x 2	6,000
	Marriage exemption	5,000
	Non-exempt transfer	7,000
	Not chargeable as a PET	

Year 6	Discretionary trust set up for grandchildren	400,000
	Transfer	400,000
	Annual exemption	3,000
	Chargeable	397,000
	Over threshold – tax payable – trustees pay	
	Thus grossing-up does not apply	
	Tax is £397,000 – 285,000 x 20% = £22,400	

Year 8 Donor still alive so Year 1 PET becomes fully exempt as donor survived for seven years.

Year 9 Donor still alive so Year 2 PET becomes fully exempt.

Year 10 Donor still alive so Year 3 PET becomes fully exempt.

Year 11 Donor dies, leaving an estate of £200,000. The will leaves £100,000 to his wife, £1,000 to the Royal National Lifeboat Institution and the rest to his children.

(a) Death is within seven years of the Year 5 PET, so that now becomes retrospectively chargeable as a transfer of £7,000. No tax as it is within the nil rate band but it uses up £7,000 of the nil rate band.

(b) Death is within seven years of the Year 6 chargeable transfer. This gift is retrospectively taxable at death rates, based on a transfer of £397,000 with a previous cumulation of £7,000 (ie the Year 5 £7,000 PET).

Thus tax has to be recalculated at the death rates based on the higher cumulation:

	£
	7,000
	397,000
Cumulative total	404,000

Tax at death rates:
£285,000 nil-rated
£119,000 @ 40% = £47,600

But death between four and five years after the gift, so taper relief applies.

Thus the tax is 60% of £47,600 = £28,560. But credit is given for lifetime tax paid. This was £22,400, so the extra tax payable is £6,160.

(c) Death tax is based on the value of the estate at death rates on top of the previous seven years' cumulative total

	£	£
Year 6 trust	397,000	
Year 5 PET	7,000	
	404,000	– over nil rate band
Estate		200,000
Left to wife	100,000	
Left to charity	1,000	
Total exempt		101,000
Chargeable		99,000

The tax is as follows (nil rate band used up):

£99,000 @ 40% = £39,600

3.9 IHT rates 2006/07

Transfers on or within seven years of death

Portion of value	Rate
£0 – £285,000	0%
£285,000+	40%

Other chargeable transfers

Portion of value	Rate
£0 – £285,000	0%
£285,000+	20%

It has been announced that the nil rate band will be £300,000 for 2007/08, £312,000 for 2008/09 and £325,000 for 2009/10.

4 Corporation Tax

Corporation tax is the tax charged on the profits of companies. It also applies to unincorporated bodies, eg clubs and associations, but not to partnerships or LLPs, where the individual partners are subject to income tax. If a company is resident in the UK, the tax is charged on its world-wide profits. If a company is non-resident but carries on a trade in the UK via a branch or agency, the tax applies only to the profits arising in the UK. Corporation tax also applies to the capital gains of companies.

A system of self-assessment, similar to that for income tax, applies to corporation tax. HMRC issues a notice, normally three to seven weeks after the end of the company's accounting period, to file a tax return. The return normally has to be filed within a year of the end of the accounting period. The company's accounts must be sent with the return. Companies must assess their own tax liability, and cannot ask HMRC to do this for them, although HMRC can always disagree with the calculations, and/or make further enquiries. Records must be kept for six years from the end of the accounting period.

4.1 Calculation of profits

Corporation tax is charged in respect of a company's accounting periods on the basis of the profit for each period. It is the profit which is taxed, not the income of the company, and thus most business expenses of a revenue nature are deductible in working out profits. Examples of deductions would be employees' wages, cost of raw materials, office rent, postage and telephone bills and so on. Business entertainment of clients is not deductible, nor is depreciation of fixed assets. However, there is a system of capital allowances for items such as plant, machinery, vehicles, industrial buildings, agricultural buildings, hotel buildings, scientific research expenditure, patents, mines and oil wells. The system is too complex to be explained here but, for example, in the case of vehicles, involves a 25% pa writing-down allowance, on a reducing balance basis with balancing charges possible when items are sold.

Contributions by the company towards a registered occupational pension scheme or personal pension are deductible. Dividends are not allowable deductions. For details of pensions see Chapter O, and for taxation of company-owned life policies see Chapter D, section 2.9 and Chapter K.

4.2 Calculation of tax

When a company's profits have been calculated, the tax rate for the financial year concerned must be applied to find the amount of tax due. The financial year is 1 April to 31 March. The rate of tax for the financial year starting 1 April 2006 is 30%. However, there is a small company's rate of 19% for companies where profits are between £50,000 and £300,000. If profits exceed £300,000 but are less than £1,500,000 then there is a marginal relief, imposing an effective rate of 32.75% on profits between these limits plus 19% on the first £300,000. There used to be a 0% rate but this was abolished with effect from 1 April 2006.

If a company has associated companies, the small companies limits mentioned above are divided by one plus the number of associated companies (companies under common control).

Example F

Examples of tax calculations are as follows:

Company A

	Profits	£100,000		
	Tax	19%	=	£19,000

Company B

Profits	£500,000		
Tax 19% on	£300,000	=	£57,000
+ 32.75% on	£200,000	=	£65,500
Total			£122,500

Company C

Profits	£2,000,000		
Tax	30%	=	£600,000

For companies with profits up to £1,500,000, tax is due nine months after the end of the accounting period, or within 30 days of HMRC issuing the assessment, if later. For companies with profits over £1,500,000, tax is payable in four equal quarterly instalments starting between the sixth and seventh month of the accounting period and based on estimated liabilities.

4.3 Losses

If a company makes a loss in an accounting period, then no tax is payable and a repayment can be claimed for tax paid on an equal amount of profits for the previous year. If this is not possible, the losses can be carried forward to be relieved against future profits.

4.4 Dividends

Companies pay out some of their profit to shareholders in the form of dividends. The dividend comes with a tax credit at 10% of the gross dividend. This is the full liability for starting and basic rate taxpayers. Higher rate taxpayers have a 32.5% liability, resulting in a further 22.5% liability on the grossed-up dividend. Non taxpayers cannot reclaim the tax credit. The gross dividend is the net dividend plus the tax credit. For these purposes, dividends are treated as the top slice of income.

Example G

Company A has two 50% shareholders, X and Z. It makes a net profit of £3,000 and decides to pay £1,500 as dividends and retain the other £1,500 in the company as working capital. The company pays £750 to X and £750 to Z.

X is a basic rate taxpayer and has no further tax liability on the dividend because it is covered by the tax credit. Z is a higher rate taxpayer and is deemed to have received £750 plus a tax credit of 10% of the gross dividend (10/90 of the net dividend), ie £750 + £83.33 = £833.33. His tax liability is £833.33 x 32.5% = £270.83. The tax credit covers the first £83.33, leaving a balance payable of £187.50.

If a dividend is paid to another UK resident company, it does not have to be included in the receiving company's profits, because tax has already been paid. In this case the dividend plus tax credit is known as franked investment income. This can then be passed on as dividends to the receiving company's own shareholders, who receive the benefit of the original tax credit.

4.5 Companies' capital gains

Capital gains made by companies are chargeable to corporation tax. The gain is calculated according to the normal CGT rules (see section 2). The gain is then added to the profits of the company and tax is charged at whatever is the company's corporation tax rate, depending on the level of profits. However, for capital gains within life assurance companies' funds, the policyholders' share of gains is taxed at 20%. Companies, including life assurance companies, do not benefit from taper relief but continue to receive indexation allowance.

Gains can be relieved by losses in the same year, or losses brought forward from previous years. Losses can be carried forward to be set off against future capital gains, but not trading profits.

5 Value Added Tax

Valued added tax (VAT) is charged on the value of supplies of taxable goods and services made in the UK and is also chargeable on the value of imports. VAT is administered by HMRC. From a date to be announced, imports from EU countries will not be subject to VAT, but instead exports to EU countries will be subject to UK VAT.

There are three rates of VAT: zero, 5% and 17.5%. In addition, some supplies are exempt. The standard rate is 17.5% and the 5% rate only applies to a limited range of items, including electricity, gas, coal and oil for domestic use plus energy-saving materials funded by government grants, some residential property conversions, contraceptives and children's car seats.

5.1 Registration

All traders who make taxable supplies of more than the set limits must register for VAT. If the value of taxable supplies in the following 30 days is likely to be at least £61,000, or if the value of taxable supplies in the previous 12 months was more than £61,000, the trader must register. Traders under these limits can register if they wish.

5.2 The VAT system

A registered trader pays input VAT when buying taxable goods or services and must charge customers output VAT on any taxable goods or services sold.

The value of input tax can be offset against output tax and the excess output tax is paid over to HMRC. Where there is an excess of input tax over output tax, VAT may be reclaimed. Some input tax on purchases and expenses cannot be reclaimed:

- Most purchases of motor cars.
- Business entertainment expenses.

Where a business is partially exempt (see below), the amount of input tax that can be recovered is restricted.

A trader may be liable to account for VAT output tax on the value of goods or services supplied to customers even if the trader has failed to add on the extra amount to the price.

The net effect of the VAT system is to pass the charge on to the consumer or to businesses that are not allowed to reclaim the tax.

5.3 Exempt supplies

Certain supplies are exempt from VAT. Output VAT is not charged on such supplies and, in principle, input VAT attributable to such supplies cannot be reclaimed or is restricted.

Exempt supplies include: insurance, finance, education and the provision of burial and cremation services. In general, leases and sales of non-domestic land and buildings are exempt, but with an option to tax, ie make the transaction subject to VAT. A taxable person may choose to charge output tax on supplies of buildings and land which are not used for residential or charitable purposes, but only where the property is used at least 80% for vatable purposes. For VAT treatment of insurance commission see Chapter D section 7.

5.4 Zero-rated supplies

If a business makes zero-rated supplies, it need not charge VAT on supplies but it can reclaim input tax. Many supplies are zero-rated, including:

- Most food or drink – but not catering, restaurant meals or hot take-away food.
- Domestic supplies of water and sewerage.
- Books and most other publications.
- Supplies of services by contractors when constructing new domestic buildings or buildings for charities.
- Alterations to certain buildings where listed building consent is needed.
- Public transport of passengers.
- Drugs, medicines and aids for the disabled.
- Clothing and footwear for children.
- Exports of goods and certain services.

5.5 Collection of VAT

Registered traders normally will have to submit VAT returns, and pay any VAT due, every three months. However, traders who regularly reclaim VAT from HMRC may apply to submit monthly returns.

Tax on imports has to be paid at the time of importation, unless special arrangements are set up.

Traders with turnover of £1,350,000 a year or less can complete annual returns only, making monthly VAT payments on account.

5.6 Bad debts

Most businesses have to account for VAT at the date that the invoice for the supply takes place (known as the tax point). If a person fails to pay, there is normally no immediate relief for the trader, who is still required to pay the VAT due. There are exemptions:

- Many retailers operate a special retail scheme. This is broadly based on the level of turnover in a period; non-payments would therefore not be included.
- Traders with turnovers of not more than £660,000 may opt to account for VAT on a cash basis. Bad debts would not be included.
- Traders can claim bad debt relief for VAT on debts which are more than six months old. The debt must have been written off in the trader's accounts, ie it must have been transferred from the debtor's ledger to a VAT bad debt account.

If the bad debt is paid in full or in part, the trader must account for output tax on the cash which is received.

6 National Insurance Contributions

National insurance contributions (NICs) are compulsory contributions to the state social security system and are effectively a tax. For the self-employed and employees (but not employers), NICs cease at state retirement age even if the individual works beyond that date. There are four classes of NICs.

6.1 Class 1

Class 1 NICs are related to an employee's earnings and are normally paid by both the employee and employer. No contributions are payable if the employee's earnings are less than the contributions threshold. NICs are payable on all gross earnings, including salary, overtime, commissions and bonuses. Employers' Class 1A NICs are payable on all benefits in kind which are subject to income tax.

6.1.1 Earnings and contribution thresholds

- **The Primary Contribution Threshold,** set at £97 per week for 2006/07, is the level of earnings above which employees have to pay Class 1 NICs.

- **The Secondary Contribution Threshold,** set at £97 per week for 2006/07, is the level of earnings above which employers have to pay Class 1 NICs.

- **The Lower Earnings Limit (LEL),** set at £84 per week for 2006/07, establishes the minimum level of earnings needed for an employee to be entitled to contributory social security benefits (eg basic state pension). In NIC calculations the LEL is relevant for calculating contracting out rebates, even though it is below both the primary and secondary contributions thresholds.

- **The Upper Earnings Limit (UEL),** set at £645 per week for 2006/07, establishes the maximum level of earnings on which an employee has to pay full rate NICs and the upper level of earnings for State Second Pension (S2P) calculations and contracting out rebates. Employers' NICs are not subject to the UEL ceiling.

- The weekly, monthly and annual thresholds and limits for 2006/07 are:

	Weekly £	**Monthly** £	**Annual** £
Lower earnings limit	84	364	4,368
Primary contribution threshold (Employee)	97	420	5,044
Secondary contribution threshold (Employer)	97	420	5,044
Upper earnings limit	645	2,795	33,540

6.1.2 Employee contributions

For the first £97 per week, employee contributions are nil.

- For earnings between £97 per week and £645 per week, the employee pays NICs at 11% (contracted in rate) or 9.4% (contracted out rate).

- For earnings in the band between the LEL (£84 per week) and £97 per week, a contracted out employee is entitled to a rebate of 1.6%, ie a maximum rebate of 21p per week. This is firstly used to reduce the employee's NICs, but if the rebate is greater than the employee's NIC liability, the excess is applied to reduce the employer's NIC liability.

- For earnings over £645 per week there is a contribution of 1% with no limit.

6.1.3 Employer contributions – contracted in

- The employer pays no NICs on earnings of up to £97 per week.

- The employer pays 12.8% on earnings over £97 per week.

6.1.4 Employer contributions – contracted out

The rates used differ according to whether contracting out is on a money purchase or final salary basis. In either case the NIC reduction applies to earnings between the LEL and UEL only.

- For all schemes the employer pays no NICs on earnings of up to £97 per week.
- For contracted out money purchase schemes, the employer pays 11.8% on earnings between £97 per week and £645 per week, ie a 1% reduction. In addition the employer is entitled to a rebate of 1% on earnings between £84 per week and £97 per week. This rebate is offset against the employer's total NIC liability.
- For contracted out final salary schemes, the employer pays 9.3% on earnings between £97 per week and £645 per week, ie a 3.5% reduction. In addition the employer is entitled to a rebate of 3.5% on earnings between £84 per week and £97 per week. This rebate is offset against the employer's total NIC liability.
- Above £645 per week, there is no contracting out reduction and the full 12.8% rate applies in all cases.

6.2 Class 2

Class 2 NICs are flat-rate contributions of £2.10 a week (£109.20 a year) for a self-employed person, if their self-employed earnings are £4,465 a year or more.

6.3 Class 3

Class 3 NICs are voluntary flat-rate NICs payable by individuals who would otherwise fail to qualify for full retirement pension and certain other benefits because they have an insufficient Class 1 or Class 2 contribution record. The flat rate is £7.55 a week (£392.60 a year).

6.4 Class 4

Class 4 NICs are payable by the self-employed on their profits for the year. It is chargeable on profits between £5,035 and £33,540 at the rate of 8%. There is also an extra 1% on profits over £33,540 with no limit. Class 4 contributions are not payable by self-employed people over pension age or under 16.

7 Insurance Premium Tax

Insurance premium tax (IPT) applies to most general insurance premiums. The tax is charged at the rate of 5%. The tax is under the control of HMRC but is collected by the insurer along with the premium and then paid over to HMRC regularly in bulk. Insurances which are not taxable are as follows:

- Long-term insurance (ie life, income protection and pensions).

- Reinsurance.
- Motor insurance for vehicles for the disabled.
- Commercial ship and aircraft insurance.
- Lifeboat insurance.
- Foreign or international railway rolling stock insurance.
- Goods in foreign or international transit insurance.
- Insurances of risks outside the UK.

Where a life policy contains an incidental element of general insurance, it is exempt from IPT if the total premium does not exceed £500,000 and no more than 10% of the premium is attributable to the general insurance element.

There is a special rate of IPT of 17.5% for insurances sold by suppliers of specified goods and services (eg mechanical breakdown insurance and insurance sold with TV and car hire). Similar insurance purchased from an insurance broker or agent who is not a supplier of these goods (or direct from an insurer) is still taxed at 5%. All travel insurance is subject to 17.5% IPT.

Insurance premium tax applies to medical insurance written in the long-term fund. This applies to private medical insurance, and does not affect critical illness cover (CIC) or income protection insurance.

8 Disclosure of Tax Avoidance Schemes

The Finance Act 2004 contains provisions requiring disclosure of tax avoidance schemes to HMRC from 1 August 2004. The object is to give HMRC earlier and better intelligence on schemes, enabling the government to make swifter and more targeted responses to certain tax avoidance arrangements if it considers any action is desirable.

The rules currently apply only to income tax, corporation tax and CGT plus stamp duty land tax on commercial property, although there are separate rules for VAT. A tax avoidance scheme is any scheme giving a tax advantage which includes any relief, repayment, avoidance, reduction or deferral of tax.

The promoter of a disclosable tax avoidance scheme must notify the Anti-Avoidance Group (Intelligence) of HMRC within five business days of launching the scheme. Full details must be given including how the scheme works and how the tax advantage is gained. If the promoter is not UK resident or there is no promoter because the taxpayer has thought of the scheme themselves, the taxpayer must make the disclosure.

Where a scheme is disclosed, HMRC may issue a reference number, although this is not a clearance and does not mean that the scheme is effective. The promoter must then give the reference number to the client who must disclose it on the relevant tax return. There is a penalty of £5,000 (plus possibly £600 per day) for failure to comply.

D The Taxation of Life Assurance Policies and Annuities

1 The Qualifying Rules

2 Income Tax on Policy Benefits

3 Life Assurance Premium Relief

4 Clawback

5 Capital Gains Tax

6 Taxation of Life Funds

7 Tax Aspects of Commission and Fees

8 Taxation of Annuities

This chapter deals with the various aspects of the taxation of life assurance policies. It deals first with the qualifying rules and the taxation of policy benefits. Next the rules regarding tax relief on premiums paid in and the situations in which relief can be 'clawed back' are considered. Then, the subjects of capital gains tax, tax on life funds and tax on commissions are discussed.

Finally the chapter deals with taxation of annuities.

1 The Qualifying Rules

The qualifying rules are relevant to the possibility of a tax charge on policy payments (see section on Income Tax on Policy Benefits). The qualifying rules are contained in Schedule 15 of the Taxes Act 1988 and are set out below. The rules are also relevant for life assurance premium relief (see later).

If the policyholder so requests, the life office must issue a Qualifying Life Assurance Policy Certificate (QLAPC) for a qualifying policy[1]. This gives policy details and states that it is a qualifying policy in the opinion of the issuing office. This form may be needed for any claims from Her Majesty's Revenue and Customs (HMRC) in connection with tax relief on premiums or tax on the benefit. The rules are as follows:

1.1 Exempt policies

Two categories of policy are exempt from the qualifying rules.

The first category consists of policies which have as their sole object the provision, on death or disability, of a sum substantially the same as that outstanding under a mortgage of the policyholder's residence or business premises[2].

This would apply only to a decreasing term policy where the sum assured decreases as the mortgage is repaid. It would not apply to an endowment house purchase policy as this aims to repay the loan on maturity as well as death.

The second category consists of policies issued in connection with a sponsored superannuation scheme (where at least one-half of the cost is borne by the employer) or an approved pension scheme. The scheme must have been established before 6 April 1980.

1.1.1 Whole life policies

All the following tests must be met[3]:

- The policy must secure a capital sum on death (or on death or earlier disability) and no other benefits. Participation in profits, surrender values, annuity options, increasability options, waiver of premiums on disability, and disability benefits of a capital nature do not count as other benefits.

- Premiums must be payable at annual, or shorter, intervals for at least ten years, or until earlier death (or disability).

- The total premiums payable in any one year must not exceed twice the total premiums payable in any other year. Total premiums payable in any one year must not exceed one-eighth of the total premiums payable over the whole term (or over the first ten years where premiums are payable throughout life).

- For policies effected on or after 1 April 1976 the capital sum on death must not be less than 75% of the premiums which would be payable if death were to occur on

[1] Taxes Act 1988 Sch 15 para 22; [2] Taxes Act 1988 s266(10)(a); [3] Taxes Act 1988 Sch 15 para 1

the life assured's 75th birthday. Where the sum assured can be paid as a lump sum or as a series of sums, the rule will operate on the smallest total payable.

1.1.2 Endowment policies

All the following tests must be met[4]:

- The policy must secure a capital sum payable on survival to the end of the term, or earlier death (or disability). Other benefits may be included, except those of a capital nature payable before death, disability, or survival. Surrenders and bonus encashments are ignored for this purpose.

- Premiums must be payable at annual, or shorter, intervals for at least ten years, or until earlier death (or disability). The term of the policy must be at least ten years. HMRC has confirmed that where a life office posts a maturity cheque slightly in advance of the maturity date solely to ensure that the policyholder receives the cheque as close as possible to the maturity date, they will not treat this fact alone as breaching the qualifying rules.

- The total premiums payable in any one year must not exceed twice the total premiums payable in any other year.

- The total premiums payable in any year must not exceed one-eighth of the total premiums payable over the whole term.

- The sum assured on death must be at least 75% of the total premiums payable if the policy ran for its full term. Where the sum assured is payable by instalments, the total of the instalments is used for this purpose, rather than any cash alternative which might be offered by the office on maturity. However if a cash option is quoted in the policy then this is taken instead. For policies effected on or after 1 April 1976 the 75% is reduced by 2% for each year by which the age of the life assured at outset exceeds 55.

1.1.3 Term assurance policies – over ten years

All the following tests must be met[5]:

- The policy must secure a capital sum on death (or on death or earlier disability) and no other benefits. Participation in profits, surrender values, annuity options, increasability options, waiver of premiums on disability, and disability benefits of a capital nature do not count as other benefits.

- Premiums must be payable at annual or shorter intervals for at least ten years, or three-quarters of the term, whichever is the shorter.

- The total premiums payable in any one year must not exceed twice the total premiums payable in any other year.

- The total premiums payable in any one year must not exceed one-eighth of the total premiums payable over the whole term.

[4] Taxes Act 1988 Sch 15 para 2; [5] Taxes Act 1988 Sch 15 para 1

- For policies effected on or after 1 April 1976 the capital sum on death must be not less than 75% of the premiums which would be payable if death were to occur on the life assured's 75th birthday. Where the sum assured can be paid as a lump sum or as a series of sums, the rule will operate on the smallest total payable. However, a term assurance which has no surrender value, and which does not run beyond age 75, is exempted from this rule.

1.1.4 Term assurance policies – ten years or less

All the following tests must be met[6]:

- The policy must secure a capital sum on death (or on death or earlier disability) and no other benefits. Participation in profits, surrender values, annuity options, increasability options, waiver of premiums on disability and disability benefits of a capital nature do not count as other benefits.

- The policy must provide that any surrender value must not exceed the premiums paid.

- The term must not be less than one year.

1.1.5 Joint life policies

When applying the 75% rule for whole life and term assurances to joint life policies, the 75th birthday to be used is as follows[7]:

- Joint life first death policy, the older life.

- Joint life second death policy, the younger life.

A joint life second death policy does not qualify if premiums cease on the first death, since they may not then be payable for the minimum period of ten years. The policy will qualify if premiums are expressed to be payable until the first death or the expiry of ten years, whichever is the later.

1.1.6 Family income policies

These policies are term assurances so the qualifying rules relevant to term assurances apply to them. Sometimes whole life and endowment policies may incorporate family income benefits. If they do they will qualify provided that either (a) the basic assurance and income benefit would have qualified separately, or (b) the rules for whole life or endowment policies, as the case may be, are met by the combined policy[8].

1.1.7 Contingent policies

These policies are usually payable on the death of the life assured provided that another person (the counter-life) is still alive. For qualification purposes they are treated in the same way as if payment did not depend on the contingency. Thus, they will normally have to meet the rules for term assurances or whole life policies.

[6] Taxes Act 1988 Sch 15 para 1; [7] Taxes Act 1988 Sch 15 para 1(5); [8] Taxes Act 1988 Sch 15 para 9

1.1.8 Friendly society policies

The qualifying rules are modified for friendly society tax-exempt policies issued (or varied) on or after 19 March 1985. The policy must be for a term of at least ten years and premiums must be level and payable at annual or shorter intervals for at least ten years. However, the term can be reduced to five years for an assured under 18 if premiums do not exceed £13 in any year. Payment can also be made after five years if it is one of a series of payments falling due at intervals of not less than five years, and the amount of any payment, other than the final payment, does not exceed four-fifths of premiums paid in the interval before its payment. Commutation of premiums is allowed after half the term, or ten years if earlier, and also if the policyholder ceases to reside in the UK. Any term or whole life sum assured must be at least 75% of total premiums payable up to age 75. Any endowment sum assured must be at least 75% of total premiums payable, subject to the normal age 55 rule[9].

1.1.9 Industrial assurance policies

There are special rules for industrial assurance policies[10]. An industrial policy that fails the normal rules will still qualify if it complies with the following conditions:

- The total sum assured under the policy, together with all the individual's other non-qualifying industrial policies, does not exceed £1,000.
- Premiums meet the normal ten-year, 'twice times and one-eighth' rules.
- No capital sum, other than on death or surrender or one allowable under the point below, can be payable in the first ten years.
- If the policy provides a series of payments:
    - The first payment must not be due in the first five years and the others must be at intervals of at least five years.
    - The amount of any payment, other than the final payment, must not exceed four-fifths of the premiums paid in the interval before payment. This condition does not apply to policies issued before 6 April 1976 or to policies issued after 6 April 1979 in substantially the same form as policies so issued before 6 April 1976.

The distinction between industrial business and ordinary business was abolished from 1 January 1996. However, policies effected before 1 December 2001 still benefit from these rules. In addition, if premiums on a policy are no longer collected door-to-door, an increase in the benefits to reflect the lower cost of collection to the insurer will not trigger any adverse tax consequences.

1.1.10 Double death benefit policies

HMRC's interpretation of the qualifying rules is that policies which can pay a capital sum on each of two (or more) deaths, or can pay capital sums on both diagnosis of a critical illness and a subsequent death, cannot be qualifying policies.

[9] Taxes Act 1988 Sch 15 para 3; [10] Taxes Act 1988 Sch 15 para 7

1.1.11 Children's policies

Policies on the lives of children frequently have life cover deferred, say, to age 16. However, in order to qualify, the policy must provide that if life cover is deferred to age 16 or some lower age, any payment made on death during the deferred period must not exceed the total premiums paid.

1.1.12 Connected policies

Where the terms of any policy provide that it is to continue in force only so long as another policy does so, neither policy is a qualifying policy unless, if they had constituted together a single policy, that single policy would be a qualifying policy[11].

In addition, a policy is not regarded as a qualifying policy if it was issued on or after 26 March 1980, and is connected with another policy, and the terms of either provide benefits greater than would be reasonably expected if any policy connected with it were disregarded[12]. The rule applies where one of the two policies would, by itself, be uncommercial.

HMRC has stated that the following arrangements are not affected by this rule:

- Where a policy charge is reduced – or higher unit allocation allowed – when the policyholder is taking out more than one policy, provided that this treatment is intended only to reflect a saving in office expenses.

- Where an insurance is split into a number of separate policies, each of which is a qualifying policy providing identical benefits for an identical premium (this practice is known as clustering or segmentation).

- Where, owing to the issue or existence of other policies, a policy is issued on terms which do not take into account an exceptional risk of death, or where less than normal underwriting information is sought.

- Where a policy is issued simultaneously with a temporary purchased life annuity which is intended to fund the premiums (known as a back-to-back arrangement).

- Where a policy is issued in the exercise of an option in a convertible term assurance which will remain wholly or partly in force.

1.1.13 Extra premiums and debts

When applying the qualifying rules, any extra premiums charged for any exceptional risk of death or disability (whether medical or otherwise) can be disregarded[13]. HMRC has confirmed that this applies to the removal as well as the imposition of a loading. The same applies to any debt on the sum assured, imposed for any such exceptional risk. This treatment only applies if there is evidence of an exceptional risk of death or disability. It does not apply merely because the proposer declines to provide medical evidence or the insurer decides not to ask for any. When applying the 75% rule any loading for paying premiums more frequently than annually can also be ignored.

[11] *Taxes Act 1988 Sch 15 para 13;* [12] *Taxes Act 1988 15 para 14;* [13] *Taxes Act 1988 Sch 15 para 12*

From 1 December 2001 if a policy provides for payment other than annually, without providing an annual amount, 10% of those premiums can be disregarded for the 75% test.

1.1.14 Free gifts

HMRC has issued a press release stating that the provision of a free gift by the life office for taking out a policy may in some circumstances infringe the qualifying rules.

However, HMRC also issued an extra-statutory concession stating that so long as the total cost to the insurer of all gifts provided in connection with an insurance (and for this purpose a cluster of policies will be treated as one insurance) does not exceed £30 no account will be taken of gifts in:

- Assessing whether a policy is qualifying; or
- Calculating any chargeable gain.

1.1.15 Premiums paid from maturity proceeds

If the maturity proceeds of an endowment assurance which was (or would have been if effected after 19 March 1968) a qualifying policy are retained by the life office and transferred to pay the single or first premium under a new policy for the same policyholder, then:

- If the new policy is a single premium one it will qualify, unless it is an endowment for less than ten years.
- If the new policy is a regular premium contract, the first premium transferred from the old policy can be ignored when applying the qualification rules.

The same applies to a single or first premium, paid by transferring the surrender value of a previously qualifying policy which has been in force at least ten years[14]. The new policy must be issued by the same office as the maturing one. A wholly-owned subsidiary does not count as the same office for this purpose. However, where two offices have merged, HMRC will consider it the same office. The new policy must be issued to the holder of the maturing policy although it need not necessarily be on the same life.

1.1.16 Backdating

If a policy is backdated by up to three months, it will be regarded as having been made on the date to which it is backdated[15]. This rule applies for qualification, clawback and chargeable gains. However, if the policy is backdated more than three months, it will be regarded as having been made on the date the contract was actually completed. This may result in an otherwise qualifying policy being non-qualifying – often because the 'one-eighth' rule will be broken, due to well over one year's premiums being payable in the first actual year of its existence.

For example, if a 15-year endowment, completed on 1 January 2006 with an annual premium of £100, were backdated four months, the amount due in the first actual year

[14] Taxes Act 1988 Sch 15 para 15; [15] Taxes Act 1988 15 para 1(8), 2(3)

of risk would be £200 (ie £100 due 1 January 2006 plus £100 due 1 September 2006). The policy would thus fail the one-eighth rule as 200/1,500 is greater than one-eighth.

1.1.17 Reinstatement

If a qualifying policy lapses due to non-payment of premiums, this can affect its qualifying status. If it is reinstated within 13 months this is ignored and the policy can continue to qualify but only if the policyholder gets exactly the same policy as he had before. Thus, if the premium is increased because of a health problem revealed on a declaration of health, it is treated as a new policy. If reinstatement occurs after 13 months then it is also treated as a new policy which may prevent it qualifying – eg if there is less than ten years still to run.

1.1.18 Policy options

Before 1 April 1976, if a policy contained contractual options, it was tested for qualification at outset without regard to the options and was retested if and when an option was exercised. This basis continues for policies issued before that date and the qualification status when an option is exercised is tested according to the variation rules explained later in this section.

Policies effected on or after 1 April 1976 are tested at the outset taking the options into account[16]. All the hypothetical policies which could result from the exercise of a contractual option must be looked at to see whether they would qualify. The basic policy only qualifies if all the hypothetical policies arising from its options would also be qualifying.

For this reason, most policies containing options now have a clause to the effect that:

The right to exercise any option given under this policy is limited to making such changes in the terms of this policy and/or substituting a new policy as are compatible with the requirements of paragraph 19(3) Schedule 15 Taxes Act 1988 for a qualifying policy.

1.1.19 Substitutions and variations

A policy effected on or before 19 March 1968 is not subject to the qualifying rules on a variation, except if the variation is to increase the benefits or to extend the term of the policy. Where the term of an endowment is reduced and the premiums consequently increased, this is regarded as an increase in the benefits. The same applies to the addition of profits to a non-profit policy, unless the sum assured is correspondingly reduced.

If a post-19 March 1968 policy (or a pre-1968 policy in the cases mentioned above) is substituted or varied then it has to be re-tested under the rules contained in paragraph 17 of Schedule 15 to the Taxes Act 1988. In these rules 'the old policy' means the policy prior to the substitution or variation and 'the new policy' means the policy after the substitution or variation.

[16] *Taxes Act 1988 Sch 15 para 19*

The rules are as follows:

- If the new policy would, apart from this provision, be a qualifying policy, but the old policy was not, the new policy is not a qualifying policy unless the person making the insurance was an infant when the old policy was issued, and the old policy was one securing a capital sum payable either on a specified date falling not later than one month after attaining 25 or on the anniversary of the policy immediately following attainment of that age.

- If the new policy would, apart from this provision, be a qualifying policy and the old policy was qualifying, the new policy is a qualifying policy unless:

  - It takes effect before the expiry of ten years from the effecting of the old policy; and

  - The highest total of premiums payable for any period of 12 months expiring before that time is less than one-half of the highest total paid for any period of 12 months under the old policy, or under any related policy issued less than ten years before the issue of the new policy ('related policy' meaning any policy in relation to which the old policy was a new policy, any policy in relation to which that policy was such a policy and so on).

- If the new policy would not, apart from this provision, be a qualifying policy, and would fail to be so by reason only of the ten-year premium term, 'one-eighth', or 'twice times' rules, it is nevertheless a qualifying policy if the old policy was a qualifying policy and:

  - The old policy was issued more than ten years before the taking effect of the new policy, and the premiums payable for any period of 12 months under the new policy do not exceed the smallest total paid for any such period under the old policy; or

  - The old policy was issued outside the UK, the circumstances being as follows:

    (a) The person in respect of whom the new insurance is made became resident in the UK during the 12 months ending with the date of its issue.

    (b) The issuing company certify that the new policy is in substitution for the old, and that the old was issued either by a branch or agency of theirs outside the UK or by a company outside the UK with whom they have arrangements for the issue of policies in substitution for those held by persons coming to the UK, and that the new policy confers on the holder benefits which are substantially equivalent to those which he would have enjoyed if the old policy had continued in force.

Where the new policy referred to in the above rules is one issued on or after 1 April 1976, then in determining its qualification that part of the first premium payable which derives from the value of the old policy is left out of account.

These rules apply to both contractual and non-contractual substitutions and variations.

HMRC's view is that if a variation goes to the root of a contract, that makes it a new contract rather than a variation of an existing contract. Examples would be the conversion of a convertible term assurance into an endowment or the addition or removal of a life assured. Adding new conditions to critical illness cover without charge is not a significant variation.

A reduction in premiums in the first year of the policy will not be regarded as a significant variation, provided that the reduction leads to an appropriate reduction in the sum assured and that any excess of premium is used to pay further premiums within the first year of the policy or returned to the policyholder or retained by the insurer with no value being credited to the policyholder – Extra Statutory Concession A41.

If, under a term assurance for ten years or less, the original sum assured is reduced to less than half, or the term is extended to cover an additional period (but the total term is still not more than ten years), any resulting reduction in the rate of premium to less than half is not treated as leading to disqualification under the rules above – Extra Statutory Concession A45.

Switching from one unit-linked fund to another is not a significant variation, nor is switching to or from with-profits.

By a concession in February 1997, HMRC stated that no account would be taken of an alteration to a qualifying policy in certain specific circumstances. This is aimed at cases where insurers have decided that it is uneconomical to collect premiums on old policies because of the small sums involved. This might particularly be the case on industrial policies. In these cases, if the insurer does stop collecting premiums, the alteration will not be regarded as making the policy non-qualifying. This will only be the case if the alteration itself is not a chargeable event and the alteration results from a decision by the insurer that it will not collect further premiums from any of the holders of a number of policies of the same type, provided the policy has been in force for at least 20 years. The benefits provided by the policy after the alteration must be substantially equivalent to those payable before the alteration, and the premiums under the policy must not have been reduced to a nominal amount on the exercise of an option if that reduction is connected with a right to make partial surrenders.

Where policies are transferred to a different insurance company under a court approved business transfer scheme, a variation under the scheme will not affect qualification status if the only change is to the basis on which the economic return to policyholders is calculated, eg from with-profits to unit-linked.

1.2 Certification

No policy effected on or after 1 April 1976 can qualify, even if it meets the rules, unless it is certified as qualifying by HMRC or conforms to a standard form of policy which has already been so certified[17]. Furthermore, no additional policy wordings are allowed unless they have been certified by HMRC as compatible with a qualifying policy.

Thus, all policy forms and wordings for qualifying policies have to be submitted to HMRC for certification. If a life office wishes to introduce a new policy it will have to get it certified before it can claim it qualifies.

Certification is at the discretion of HMRC and is not mandatory, even if the policy meets the qualifying rules. However, the discretion must be exercised reasonably – *Monarch Assurance plc v Inland Revenue Commissioners*.

HMRC uses a system of reference numbers for identification purposes and the relevant reference number must be shown on a QLAPC form.

Policies do not need to be re-certified where there is a change of name of the insurer, or a transfer of business to another insurer and the terms of the policy are unchanged. However, HMRC does need to be informed of the change.

1.3 Offshore policies

From 17 November 1983, a policy issued by a non-UK life office cannot be certified and thus will not qualify until either:

- The life office becomes UK authorised and premiums are payable to a UK branch; or

- The policyholder becomes resident in the UK and the life fund income is chargeable to UK corporation tax.

These policies are known as 'new non-resident policies' and a pre-17 November 1983 policy will become a new non-resident policy if it is varied after that date so as to increase the benefits or extend the term.

1.4 Change of life assured

Where, as a result of a change in the life (or lives) assured, a qualifying policy is replaced by a new qualifying policy, then for the purposes of clawback and income tax on the benefit the policies are treated as a single policy starting at the date of the first one[18]. This reduces the chance of any chargeable gain arising by preventing the ten-year period starting again. However, this only applies if no consideration is received by any person as a result of the replacement policy. HMRC considers that if a salesman gets commission on the new policy, this is consideration so the rule does not apply. A change of life assured sometimes happens on divorce and HMRC considers that a divorce settlement (unless it results from a court order) is also consideration.

If paragraph 20 does not apply, HMRC considers that a change of life assured is so fundamental a change as to make it a new contract commencing on the date of the change. This may result in it being non-qualifying – eg if less than ten years to run.

[17] Taxes Act 1988 Sch 15 para 21; [18] Taxes Act 1988 Sch 15 para 20

2 Income Tax on Policy Benefits

Income tax on policy benefits is popularly known as 'chargeable gains' and because of this is frequently confused with capital gains tax (CGT). What the legislation (Income Tax (Trading and Other Income) Act (ITTOIA) 2005 ss461-546 and what remains of Taxes Act 1988 ss539-552) aims to do is charge to income tax (usually at the higher rate only) gains arising from life policies in certain circumstances. The legislation affects all life policies, capital redemption policies and purchased life annuities effected after 19 March 1968 and also policies effected prior to then, if they are varied after that date so as to increase the benefits or extend the term. The income tax charge effectively takes precedence over any CGT charge by virtue of s37 Taxation of Chargeable Gains Act 1992.

Qualifying policies are treated much more favourably as, broadly, only gains in the first ten years are taxable whereas all gains under non-qualifying policies are taxable. Exempt policies are not taxable. It must be remembered that in this context qualifying means qualifying as per the rules in Schedule 15 of the Taxes Act 1988 and does not mean eligible for tax relief. In other words, eligibility for tax relief has no relevance to chargeable gains. Certain group life policies are also exempt from these rules. These are group term assurances not running beyond age 75, with no surrender value, payable only to an individual or charity (whether direct or via a trust) and where no life assured can benefit. Life policies issued in connection with a registered pension scheme are exempt.

Tax is only payable if:

- A chargeable event occurs; and
- A chargeable gain arises therefrom; and
- When the gain is added to the taxpayer's total income for that year it falls partly or totally within the higher rate tax bracket (subject to exceptions for some life annuities, certain policies owned by Lloyd's members, tax-exempt friendly society policies, and offshore policies).

These factors will now be dealt with in turn.

2.1 Chargeable events – life policies

The chargeable events for a non-qualifying life policy are[19]:

- Death (if it gives rise to a benefit).
- Maturity.
- Surrender.
- Certain part surrenders and part assignments (see below).

[19] *ITTOIA 2005 s484(1)*

- Policy loan if the policy was effected after 26 March 1974.
- Assignment for money or money's worth.

The chargeable events for a qualifying life policy are as follows[20]:

- Death (if it gives rise to a benefit).
- Maturity.

But only if the policy is made paid-up within ten years, or three-quarters of the term if sooner.

- Surrender.
- Certain part surrenders and part assignments (see below)
- Policy loan at non-commercial rate of interest, if policy effected after 26 March 1974.
- Assignment for money or money's worth.

But only if it occurs during the above period or the policy has been made paid-up within that time.

The time limits run from the commencement of the policy, or from any variation by which premiums are increased[21], unless the increase is solely due to a variation in the life or lives assured or the exercise of an option under a policy entered into on or after 1 April 1976[22].

Assignments or reassignments by way of mortgages are ignored, as are assignments between spouses or civil partners living together[23]. The insurer can assume that spouses and civil partners are living together unless it knows otherwise. If a policy issued prior to 26 June 1982 was assigned for money or money's worth before that date, no subsequent event can be a chargeable event. However, this does not apply if – after 23 August 1982 – the policy is reacquired by the original beneficial owner, a further premium is paid, or a policy loan is given[24].

An assignment in connection with a divorce or pre-nuptial settlement is an assignment for money's worth. However, if it is a result of a divorce court order it is not for money's worth, even if the court is only ratifying an agreement reached by the divorcing parties.

[20] ITTOIA 2005 s485; [21] ITTOIA 2005 s485(6); [22] Taxes Act 1988 Sch 15 para 20; [23] ITTOIA 2005 s487; [24] ITTOIA 2005 Sch 2 para 102

HMRC has been told by another government department that there would be a court order for almost every divorce involving property. Thus it has agreed that a life office can assume that an assignment as part of a divorce settlement is under a court order, and thus is not a chargeable event, unless it definitely knows otherwise. The life office does not have to make enquiries into the circumstances of the assignment. An assignment as part of a separation settlement under a court order is similarly not a chargeable event.

A policy loan at a non-commercial rate of interest on a qualifying policy is not a chargeable event if it was made before 6 April 2000 by the issuing office to a full-time employee for house purchase or improvement. A loan to buy a life annuity where the interest is eligible for tax relief is not a chargeable event.

Under s500 of ITTOIA 2005, if a loan is a chargeable event it is treated as a part surrender and the gain is calculated as set out in the rules for part surrenders in section 2.4. If a loan is treated as a part surrender then repayment is treated as an additional premium. Any unpaid interest added to the loan is a further part surrender.

Payment of a critical illness benefit or a terminal illness benefit is not a chargeable event and so cannot give rise to a tax charge.

2.2 Chargeable events – life annuity contracts

The chargeable events for life annuity contracts are as follows[25]:

- Total surrender (or the taking of a cash option in lieu of annuity instalments).
- Payment of a capital sum on death if contract effected on or after 10 December 1974.
- Assignment for money or money's worth.
- Certain part surrenders and part assignments (see below).
- Policy loan, if contract effected after 26 March 1974.

For details of the tax charge on the annuity instalments see section 8.

2.3 Calculation of chargeable gain

When a chargeable event occurs a calculation must be made to see if a gain has arisen. A chargeable gain arises under a life policy in the following cases[26]:

- On maturity or surrender – if the amount paid out, plus any capital payments, exceeds the premiums paid plus the total gains on previous part surrenders or part assignments. Where the sum assured is payable by instalments the amount taken for the calculation is the capital value of the instalments.

[25] ITTOIA 2005 s484(1) and s542 Taxes Act 1988;
[26] ITTOIA 2005 ss491-497

- On death, if the surrender value immediately before death, plus any capital payments, exceeds the premiums paid plus the total gains on previous part surrenders or part assignments.
- On assignment, if the price received, plus any capital payments, exceeds the premiums paid plus the total gains on previous part surrenders or part assignments.

Where the chargeable event is an assignment between persons connected with each other, the gain is based on the market value, not the price received. This would affect assignments to a spouse, civil partner, brother, sister, parent, child or grandchild.

Capital payments are any benefits of a capital nature (other than those attributable to a person's disability) paid under the policy prior to the chargeable event (ITTOIA 2005 s495(3)). Where a policy pays out on each of two (or more) deaths, there will be a chargeable event on the first death because such a policy cannot be qualifying. In practice, no gain is likely to arise because, as explained in (b) above, the gain is calculated by reference to the surrender value immediately prior to death. However, in calculating the gain on the chargeable event caused by the second death, the benefit paid on the first death will be taken into account as a capital payment. This is likely to produce a significant chargeable gain on the second death. In the case of a group life policy, the chargeable gain on successive deaths will continue to increase with each death benefit which is paid – unless the policy is an excepted group policy – see section 2, second paragraph.

Where a chargeable event occurs on a second-hand policy there is no credit given for the purchase price paid by the current owner. The calculation of the gain still depends on the total premiums paid even though some of these would have been paid by the original owner.

Where a critical or terminal illness payment is followed by a payment on death, the illness benefit itself is not a chargeable event and does not have to be taken into account in the calculation of the death gain as a relevant capital payment. This is because s493(3) disregards sums attributable to a person's disability in calculation of chargeable gains.

Gains can also occur on part surrenders and part assignments and the special rules for these are explained in the next section.

Chargeable gains occur on life annuities in the following cases[27]:

- **On surrender** – if the amount paid out, plus any capital payments, exceeds the premiums paid in (reduced by the capital element of any annuity instalments paid out) plus the total gains on previous part surrenders and part assignments.
- **On assignment** – if the consideration received, plus any capital payments, exceeds the premiums paid in (reduced by the capital element of any annuity instalments paid out) plus the total gains on previous part surrenders and part assignments.

[27] *ITTOIA 2005 ss491-497*

The receipt of a cash option instead of the annuity is treated as a surrender. The part surrender and part assignment rules also apply in theory to life annuities, although in practice they are very rarely part surrendered, or part assigned.

2.4 Part surrenders

A part surrender (which would include a bonus encashment or a loan) can be a chargeable event if it exceeds a certain limit[28]. The law looks at the total part surrenders in any policy year and not to individual part surrenders. A chargeable event only occurs if at the end of a policy year the value received exceeds the sum of the 'allowable elements' – the annual 5% allowances, described below.

Each policy year there is an allowance of 5% of any premium paid in that year plus 5% of any premium paid in previous policy years, subject to a maximum allowance of 100% for any premium. However, no allowance is given for any policy year prior to the first policy year falling wholly after 13 March 1975. Any allowance not used can be carried forward to future years. So an investor with a single premium policy can withdraw 5% of the single premium each year for 20 years without a chargeable event occurring.

Under this system, at the end of each policy year the total of part surrenders is compared with the accumulated allowances. If the surrenders exceed the allowances a chargeable event has occurred and the amount of the excess is the chargeable gain. When this happens the allowances which have accumulated so far are deemed to have been used up and the process of cumulative allowances will start again. A gain can thus only occur on the last day of a policy year.

When a policy is terminated by death, maturity or full surrender, then the period from the previous policy anniversary to the termination (which may not always be a full year) is treated as the final year. If that final year begins and ends in the same tax year, then the final year and the year preceding it shall together be treated as one year.

On the final termination of the policy there is a 'sweep-up' calculation to tax the total profit under the policy. If the termination is a chargeable event, a chargeable gain will arise if the total of the final proceeds plus any previous partial surrenders exceeds the total of premiums paid plus any chargeable gains arising on any previous part surrenders. Withdrawals under the 5% limit are thus tax-deferred rather than fully tax-free.

If a policy is owned jointly, the chargeable gain produced by a withdrawal in excess of the 5% limit is shared between the joint owners even if it is actually paid to just one of the owners.

The way the system works will be made clearer by the following example:

[28] ITTOIA 2005 s507

Example A

Calculation involving a five-year single premium policy:

Policy date 1 January 2001 *Single premium £10,000*

1 Part surrender 31 December 2001, £500
No chargeable event because it is not over 5% of single premium
2. Part surrender 31 December 2002, £1,000
Chargeable event because it exceeds 5% of single premium
Chargeable gain is excess over 5% of single premium = £500
3 Maturity of policy 1 January 2006
Maturity value, £14,000

Maturity of non-qualifying policy is chargeable event

		£
Chargeable gain	= maturity value	14,000
	+ part surrender 1	500
	+ part surrender 2	1,000
Total		15,500
Less single premium		10,000
		5,500
Less previous chargeable gain		500
Chargeable gain at maturity		5,000

Chargeable events on part surrenders occur at the end of each policy year, not each time a part surrender is made. Thus, if withdrawals are actually paid monthly on a unit-linked bond, there is one chargeable event on the last day of each policy year, not 12 chargeable events each year. The chargeable gain is deemed to be the income of the individual who owns the policy at the time of the chargeable event, unless the policy is under trust. The policy owner might be different from the person who actually received the withdrawals.

If a policy is assigned during the policy year the calculations are done first with regard to withdrawals made before the assignment (for which the assignor is liable) and then for withdrawals made after the assignment (for which the assignee is liable).

2.5 Part assignments

The part surrender rules also apply to assignments of part of the rights of a policy, but only if it is for money or money's worth. However this does not apply to assignments between spouses or civil partners living together. A part assignment is any assignment where one of the assignors is also one of the assignees – eg A and B to A, or A to A and B. Frequently on a divorce one of the owners of a joint life policy will assign his or her rights to the other ex-spouse, and as this is for money's worth it could create a chargeable gain unless it is as a result of a court order. The value to be used is the surrender value of the rights being assigned – eg half the surrender value in the usual case of one joint owner assigning his half share in the policy to the other. In this case half the surrender value would have to be compared with any available 5% allowances to decide whether a gain had arisen.

If a policy is part assigned for consideration any gain caused by the part assignment is taxable on the part assignor, although the date of the chargeable event for income tax purposes is still the end of the policy year.

2.6 Taxation of gain

Once a chargeable event has occurred and a chargeable gain has arisen, then the tax can be calculated. Normally the gain will only be subject to the higher rate of income tax. The person chargeable to tax is the beneficial owner of the policy[29]. However, if it is mortgaged, the mortgagor is chargeable and if it is under trust, the creator of the trust or the trustees, or in certain circumstances the beneficiaries of the trust, are chargeable as explained below.

For an individual policyholder, the tax is calculated as follows on a life policy[30]:

(a) Top-slice the gain by dividing it by the number of full years between the date the policy was effected and the date of the chargeable event. If the gain is on a part surrender (or part assignment), the period is the number of full years back to the start of the policy from the first part surrender (or part assignment) or back to the previous part surrender (or part assignment) giving rise to a chargeable event for a second or subsequent part surrender (or part assignment).

(b) Add the top-sliced gain to the individual's total income for that tax year.

(c) Calculate the tax liability on the total income including the top-sliced gain remembering that the lower rate of 20% applies to the gain (rather than the basic rate of 22%).

(d) Calculate the tax liability on the income without the top-sliced gain.

(e) Deduct the figure in (d) from the figure in (c) and this difference is the theoretical tax liability on the top-sliced gain.

(f) Deduct tax at the lower rate of 20% on the amount of the top-sliced gain from the figure in (e) so that the balance represents higher rate tax only.

(g) Multiply the figure in (f) by the number of years used in the top-slicing procedure to give the actual tax liability on the whole gain.

Top-slicing is only of any benefit to policyholders who are not already higher rate taxpayers on the basis of other income. Personal pension contributions do not reduce total income for this purpose, but the basic rate band is extended by the gross contribution. Top-slicing applies only to individuals, not trustees or companies.

[29] ITTOIA 2005 ss464-472; [30] ITTOIA 2005 s535

The calculation can be made clearer by the following examples. These use the current tax rates and ignore personal and other allowances and reliefs for the sake of simplicity.

Example B

A five-year endowment policy effected 1 July 2001 with a single premium of £10,000

Policy matures on 1 July 2006
Maturity value £15,000
Maturity of non-qualifying policy is a chargeable event

			£
Chargeable gain = maturity value	=	£15,000	
Less single premium		£10,000	5,000
(a) Top-slicing – number of full years is 5			
Top-sliced gain = $\frac{\pounds 5{,}000}{5}$	=	£1,000	
Individual's other taxable income that tax year	=	£20,000	(all earnings)
(b) Total income			21,000
(c) Income tax with gain £2,150 x 10%	=	£215.00	
+£17,850 earnings x 22%	=	£3,927.00	
£1,000 gain x 20%	=	£200.00	
	=	£4,342.00	
(d) Income tax without gain £2,150 x 10%	=	£215.00	
+£17,850 x 22%	=	£3,927.00	
		£4,142.00	
(e) Difference between (c) and (d)	=	200	
(f) Less 20% tax on top-sliced gain £1,000 x 20%	=	200	
Total	=	0	

There is therefore no tax liability in this case because even with the addition of the top-sliced gain the individual's income for that tax year was below the higher rate tax threshold of £33,300.

Example C

Using the same policy as in Example B **£**

(a) Top-sliced gain is £1,000 as in Example A
Individual B's other taxable income is £40,000 (all earnings)

(b) Thus total income is	£40,000 + £1,000	=	£41,000.00
(c) Income tax with gain	£2,150 x 10%	=	£215.00
	£31,150 earnings x 22%	=	£6,853.00
	£7,700 x 40%	=	£3,080.00
			£10,148.00

(d) Income tax without gain	£2,150 x 10%	=		£215.00
	£31,150 earnings x 22%	=		£6,853.00
	£6,700 x 40%	=		£2,680.00
				£9,748.00
(e) Difference between (c) and (d) =			400	
(f) Less 20% tax on top-sliced gain				
	£1,000 x 20%	=		200
Tax on top-sliced gain		=		200
(g) Therefore tax liability on whole gain				
	£200 x 5	=		£1,000

It will be seen that the effective rate of tax on the gain is thus:

	%
Top rate of tax	40
Less lower rate tax	20
Effective rate on gain	20

ie tax is £1,000 which is 20% of gain of £5,000.

If a gain is made on a tax-exempt friendly society policy or an overseas life assurance businesses policy, there is no lower rate credit and the full rate of tax is payable. For life annuities there is no lower rate credit if made after 26 March 1974 and in an accounting period of the insurer beginning before 1 January 1992.

Where two or more gains are made in the same tax year, the gains are added together and the top-slicing is done by adding up the appropriate fractions of each individual gain – s537 Income Tax (Trading and Other Income) Act 2005.

If a policy is owned jointly, s469-472 ITTOIA 2005 splits the gain in the same proportion as the ownership regardless of the person to whom the money was actually paid. Each owner would thus be taxed (or not) on his or her share of the gain. If the joint owners are married to each other (or civil partners of each other), HMRC consider that s282A Taxes Act 1988 overrides the ITTOIA 2005 provisions so that each would be taxed on half the gain. However, if they hold the policy in unequal shares they can make a declaration under s282B to enable them to be taxed on their actual shares.

It may be advantageous for a higher rate tax-paying spouse to assign a policy before the chargeable event so that the gain forms part of a lower or basic rate tax-paying spouse's income. This would avoid any tax bill even if the higher rate tax-paying spouse has been taking 5% withdrawals for years. The assignment to the other spouse would not itself be a chargeable event or a chargeable transfer for inheritance tax.

Another way of avoiding or reducing tax on a chargeable gain is to make a personal pension contribution which has the effect of increasing the basic band by the amount of the gross pension contribution and thus reducing the chance of the top-sliced chargeable gain putting the total income into the higher rate tax band. In this way tax relief can be obtained on the pension contribution itself, plus the 20% saving in tax on the chargeable gain.

It is possible that part surrenders in excess of the 5% allowances can produce 'artificial' gains. For example, consider a unit-linked bond taken out for £10,000 which grows after one year to £11,000 and where a part surrender of £5,000 is made at the end of the first year. The chargeable gain is £5,000 less 5% of £10,000 – ie £4,500. However, the bond has really only grown by £1,000. Nevertheless, these artificial gains are taxed if the policyholder is a higher-rate tax-payer. Thus, very large partial surrenders should be avoided if possible.

The situation would be even worse if the bond had dropped in value to £9,000 and a part surrender of £5,000 was taken. The chargeable gain would still be £4,500, even though in reality there has been a loss of £1,000. Tax can thus actually be paid on losses, for example, £900 in this case (£4,500 @ 20%).

Some relief is allowed by s539 ITTOIA 2005 for this type of situation. This provides that, if on the eventual final termination a loss arises, then the policyholder is entitled to a corresponding deduction from his other income for that tax year as long as it does not exceed the previous chargeable gains. The deduction operates for higher rate income tax only and would have the effect of reducing the tax otherwise payable on his other income for that year. This is called 'relief for deficiencies', and only applies where individuals (not trustees) are liable. The law in this area was changed with effect from 3 March 2004 so that relief is only given if the previous chargeable gain was the deemed income of the individual claiming the relief. This change applies to policies dated on or after 3 March 2004 and to policies effected before then if, on or after that date, they are varied so as to increase the benefits, or assigned. Insurers are not required to report deficiencies to the policyholder or HMRC.

The chargeable gain is included in a taxpayer's income (without top-slicing) in order to calculate entitlement to age allowance (see page 62), Child Tax Credit (see page 63), and Working Tax Credit (see page 63). It may thus reduce, or even eliminate, a taxpayer's eligibility for these allowances.

Under s465 ITTOIA 2005 any individual who is not resident in the UK in the tax year in which the gain is chargeable will not have to pay tax on it (and the same applies to companies).

For chargeable events on or after 6 April 2004 the basic rate credit reduced to 20% to reflect the lower tax on the life fund. Higher rate taxpayers thus have a 20% liability on the gain, but basic rate taxpayers have no further liability. There is no relief for any losses, and a loss on one policy cannot be set against a gain on another policy.

2.7 Trust policies

Originally the rule was that if a policy was subject to a trust, the person chargeable was the individual who created the trust, although he could recover the tax from the trustees. If the creator of the trust was dead and had died in a tax year prior to the year of the gain, there was no-one on whom HMRC could tax the gain – the so-called 'dead settlor trick'.

This rule was changed in the Finance Act 1998. The situation is now as follows:

- If the individual who created the trust was both alive and UK resident immediately before the chargeable event, the gain is treated as part of that individual's income. He or she can recover any tax paid from the trustees.

- If the individual who created the trust was dead, or resident outside the UK, immediately before the chargeable event and the trustees are resident in the UK, the trustees are chargeable on the gain. The charge is at the rate applicable to trusts, which is 40%, resulting in a 20% liability for a UK policy, after allowing for the lower rate credit. This tax cannot be reclaimed by the trust beneficiaries, even if they would not be liable in their own right because they were well below the higher rate threshold. Where one (or more) of the trustees are not UK resident, they are treated as UK resident if the settlor was UK resident, ordinarily resident or domiciled at the time the trust was created.

- If the trustees are not resident in the UK, any UK beneficiary receiving a benefit under the trust from the gain will be taxable on that amount at his or her tax rates, via s740 Taxes Act 1998, but without top-slicing relief or lower rate credit.

Where there is more than one settlor the gain is chargeable on each settlor in proportion to the amount contributed to the trust.

These rules apply to chargeable events which occur on or after 6 April 1998. They do not apply to policies effected prior to 17 March 1998, where the trust was also created prior to this date and the creator of the trust died before then. For these cases, the dead settlor trick will still apply, as long as the policy was not varied on or after 17 March 1998 so as to increase the benefit or extend the term.

For chargeable events on or after 9 April 2003 where the trust is a charitable trust the charge is on the trust (not the settlor) and at the lower rate, leaving no tax to pay on a UK policy.

2.7.1 Lloyd's members

If a life policy is held by a member of Lloyd's as part of his Lloyd's trust fund, the gain is chargeable as trading income, not under s465. Thus the full gain is chargeable as income, with no top-slicing relief or notional lower rate tax credit.

2.7.2 Offshore policies

When a new non-resident policy (see section 1.3) pays out, there will be a chargeable event for income tax purposes as it is a non-qualifying policy. However, the chargeable gain is reduced by multiplying it by the following fraction:

$$\frac{\text{number of days policyholder was resident in the UK}}{\text{total number of days policy has run}}$$

Thus, the whole gain is chargeable if the policyholder was resident in the UK for the whole term of the policy. However, if he or she was resident for, say, five out of the ten years the policy was held, only half the gain is chargeable. If the policyholder was resident outside the UK the whole time, the chargeable gain is zero. However, there is no time apportionment if the policy has ever been held by a non-resident trustee – in such cases the whole gain is chargeable.

Where a gain arises it is charged to starting and lower as well as higher rate tax. The number of years used for top-slicing is reduced by the number of complete years for which the policyholder was not resident in the UK. The number of years to be counted goes back to the policy date for all chargeable events – including all part surrenders and part assignments (unlike an on-shore policy). Top-slicing only applies to higher rate tax – it cannot be used to reduce the tax from lower to starting or nil rates.

The effect of this is to make UK policyholders with offshore policies liable to income tax at their highest rate(s) on the whole of their gain, with some relief for any periods spent outside the UK during the term of the policy. This reflects the fact that, in principle, no UK tax is paid on the underlying life fund.

However, the charge is reduced to higher rate minus lower rate if:

- The insurer is based in a country which is a member of the EU or the EEA; and
- In its home state the insurer is taxed on the investment income and gains accruing for its UK policyholders at a rate of not less than 20%; and
- The insurer has not reinsured the investment content of the policy.

The remittance basis for non-UK domiciled taxpayers does not apply to such taxable gains. Thus gains made on offshore policies by non-UK domiciled UK residents are taxable, whether or not they are remitted to the UK.

2.8 Administration of the tax

The taxation of chargeable gains is not the responsibility of the life office and all policy payments would be made without deduction of tax. It is the responsibility of the policyholder to declare the gain on the tax return for the tax year in which the chargeable event occurred.

The life office has to issue a chargeable event certificate to the policyholder, unless it is satisfied that no gain has occurred.[31] The certificate has to be issued before the end of three months after the latest of:

- The date of the chargeable event.

[31] *Taxes Act 1988 s552*

- The end of the policy year for a part surrender or part assignment.
- The written notification of a death or assignment.

The certificate must show the following details:

- The policy number.
- The nature and date of the chargeable event.
- The end of the policy year for a part assignment.
- The amount of the chargeable gain.
- The number of years for top-slicing.
- The amount of lower rate tax treated as already paid.
- If the event is a full assignment the amount of any relevant capital payments, the total premiums paid, the value of any previous part assignments and the total previous chargeable gains caused by part surrenders or assignments.

The information on the certificate will enable the policyholder to complete the details on the tax return. A certificate must be sent to each policyholder for a jointly held policy, although only one certificate is required where the policyholders live at the same address, or are trustees. For a death claim on an own life policy, HMRC has agreed that the certificate can be sent to whoever is dealing with the estate, although it should still name the deceased policyholder. The certificate must be sent to the policyholder even if they are not the person chargeable, eg the trustees on a trust policy where the settlor is alive and UK resident.

A certificate must also be sent to HMRC within three months of the end of the tax year in which the event occurred if the chargeable event is a full assignment, or the gain (plus connected gains) exceeds half the basic rate limit for the tax year concerned – ie currently £16,650. HMRC may also request a certificate in any other case. A certificate sent to HMRC must be in the form specified by them. The certificate will enable HMRC to tax a policyholder who omits to declare the chargeable gain on the tax return.

HMRC has the power to audit a life office's system used to produce these certificates, and regulations specify what records a life office must keep for this. Special rules apply to offshore life companies which are required to have a UK tax representative to issue the relevant certificates.

When a life office receives notification of an assignment it is entitled to assume it is not for consideration unless it is told otherwise.

2.9 Policies held by companies

Sometimes, companies effect life policies; indeed, it is quite possible for a company to take out any type of life policy. The taxation provisions also apply to policies held on trusts created by a company, or held as security for a debt owed by a company. The situation is as follows:

- Policies effected before 14 March 1989:
  - If the policy is qualifying and provided the policy matured or was surrendered on or after ten years (or on death) so that no chargeable event occurs, there is no tax liability on the company.
  - If the policy is non-qualifying, or a chargeable event occurs on a qualifying policy, a tax liability will still not arise even if the company is a close investment company.
  - Policies varied on or after 14 March 1989 so as to increase the benefits or extend the term will be treated as policies effected on or after 14 March 1989 and so be subject to the rules applying to such policies.
- Policies effected on or after 14 March 1989:
  - For a qualifying policy the definition of chargeable event is made the same as for a non-qualifying policy. Thus, virtually all payouts will be chargeable events.
  - If the chargeable event results in a chargeable gain it is treated as income of the company and is thus subject to corporation tax. However, unlike individuals, companies get no effective credit for the tax paid on the underlying life fund and no top-slicing. Thus, the whole gain is taxed at the company's corporation tax rate, giving a substantial element of double taxation. Therefore, the effective total rate of tax is up to 35.2% at the small companies' rate (19%) and up to 44% at the full corporation tax rate (30%) for 2006. There will also be no top-slicing to possibly stop the gain pushing the company into a higher rate of corporation tax.
  - These provisions apply only if the gain is not otherwise chargeable. Thus, the rules will not apply to key person term policies, which will still be taxable in full (not just on the gain) because they are 'otherwise chargeable' – see Chapter K.
  - If the company is a close investment company the tax rate will be 30%.
  - If the policy is a qualifying endowment held as security for a debt owed by a company the treatment is slightly modified. In deciding whether a gain has arisen, the amount of the debt can be used instead of the total premiums if it is higher.

    However, this only applies if:

- The policy has been held as security for the debt continually since being effected;
- The sum assured is not less than the original debt;
- The sum payable is used to repay the debt; and
- The loan was to purchase land for the company's trade, or the construction, extension or improvement of buildings for the company's trade.

The effect of this is that there will only be a tax charge if the policy payout exceeds the loan, and the charge will only be on the excess. HMRC has confirmed that 'held as security' covers mortgages by deposit as well as formal assignments.

2.9.1 Capital redemption bonds held by companies

From 10 February 2005 capital redemption bonds held by companies have been taken out of the chargeable gains regime and made subject to corporation tax under the loan relationship rules. Under these rules, tax is payable annually on the year by year profit from the bond as shown in the company's accounts. This applies whether the bond is encashed or not. Bonds held on 9 February 2005 are treated as having been assigned for consideration on that date at their then value, with any chargeable gain that arises on this deemed assignment deferred until subsequent maturity or surrender.

2.10 Second-hand policies

Chargeable gains have to be considered when policies are sold.

2.10.1 Taxation on the seller

If a qualifying policy is sold after at least ten years (or three-quarters of the term, if sooner), the sale is not a chargeable event and there is no income tax liability.

If a qualifying policy is sold within the ten-year period (or three-quarters of the term), the sale will be a chargeable event. If a non-qualifying policy is sold, the sale will always be a chargeable event.

If the sale is a chargeable event, the seller will make a chargeable gain if the sale price exceeds the total premiums paid. The gain will then be subject to higher rate income tax minus lower rate tax resulting in a maximum rate of 20% on current rates (subject to top-slicing relief).

2.10.2 Taxation on the buyer

If the buyer holds a qualifying policy to maturity (or death claim), there is no chargeable event and thus no income tax liability. If the buyer holds a non-qualifying policy to maturity (or death claim), this is a chargeable event. There will be a chargeable gain if the maturity value (or surrender value immediately prior to death on a death claim) exceeds the total premiums paid by the buyer and the seller. The purchase price paid by the buyer does not enter into the calculation and neither does any chargeable gain on the original assignment. If a gain arises the buyer will pay income tax at the higher rate minus the lower rate subject to top-slicing relief.

Whether or not the policy is a qualifying policy, there is also a disposal for capital gains tax purposes. In practice this will normally mean a capital gain arises under a qualifying policy and an allowable capital loss under a non-qualifying contract, although this is restricted to the real economic loss under the policy.

2.11 Personalised bonds

For a description of personalised bonds see Chapter M section 3.8.

HMRC had long disliked personalised bonds and acted against them in the Finance Act 1998 by imposing a penal tax on a deemed gain. The deemed gain is 15% of the total premiums paid at the end of a policy year plus the total deemed gains from previous years less any chargeable withdrawals. The effect of this is to tax the policyholder as if the investment was yielding 15% compound, regardless of any actual growth. However, it is worse than this, as the deemed gain is on top of the normal tax charge which would arise on a part surrender. The deemed gain can be deducted from a final termination gain. For an onshore policy, there is a credit for the lower rate tax paid by the life fund. The normal rules for chargeable gains apply to the deemed gain, except that there is no top-slicing relief.

The intent seems to have been to extinguish these bonds, which is what has happened, at least as far as UK resident investors are concerned.

3 Life Assurance Premium Relief (LAPR)

In certain cases, income tax relief can be obtained on life assurance premiums. This relief is popularly called LAPR and is referred to as such frequently throughout this book. The relief was abolished for all policies effected after 13 March 1984[32]. Furthermore, any policy effected before then will lose relief completely if it is varied after that date so as to enhance the benefit or extend the term.

Full details of eligibility are given in previous editions of this book. However, some aspects need to be considered because relief is still available for premiums paid on policies effected on, or before, 13 March 1984.

3.1 Payer of the premium

The premium must actually be paid by the life assured, spouse or civil partner. For this purpose spouse includes a person who was the spouse at the time the policy was effected, unless the marriage was dissolved before 6 April 1979. Relief cannot be given on a policy, eligible in all other respects, if a third party pays the premiums. If premiums come to the life office via a third party, such as a broker or employer, relief can be given if the office is satisfied they came ultimately from the life assured, spouse or civil partner, eg a deduction from salary scheme for employees.

[32] Taxes Act 1988 s266(3)(c)

3.2 Residence

In order to pay premiums net of tax relief, the payer must be resident in the UK[33]. HMRC has stated that for this purpose residence means actually having one's home in the ordinary sense in the UK and that a person who goes abroad on business or pleasure will be regarded as a UK resident only if the visits abroad are for short periods[34]. Residence for tax relief is thus not necessarily the same as that for other taxation purposes. It should be remembered that the United Kingdom does not include the Channel Islands or the Isle of Man.

Members of the armed forces or their spouses and civil partners are treated as UK residents[35]. Other persons resident abroad, such as diplomatic staff or civilian employees of the armed forces, may be taxed as UK residents but cannot pay premiums net of relief. However these, and some other policyholders resident abroad, may be able to claim relief direct from HMRC under s278 of the Taxes Act 1988. This covers anyone in the following categories:

- Commonwealth citizens, or EEA nationals.
- Persons who are, or have been, employed in the service of the Crown or any missionary society or in the service of any territory under Her Majesty's protection.
- Residents of the Isle of Man or the Channel Islands.
- Previous residents of the UK who are now resident abroad for the sake of their own health or that of a family member.
- Spouses or civil partners of individuals who were in the service of the Crown.

In these cases relief can be claimed direct from HMRC (not the life office) even if the individual has no UK income. The amount of UK income is only relevant for the £1,500 or one-sixth of income test (see next section).

When a policyholder leaves the UK permanently, he will remain eligible to deduct tax relief from his premiums up to the end of the tax year of his departure – that is the next 5 April. Premiums will have to be paid in full from then on. Where a policyholder returns to the UK permanently from a foreign residence, he will be entitled to tax relief by deduction from the date of his return. He may also be able to claim tax relief from HMRC for premiums due and paid in full between the previous 6 April and the date of return.

3.3 Limits of relief

The total amount of premiums on which relief can be obtained in any year is £1,500 (gross) or one-sixth of a person's total income, whichever is the greater[36].

The limits mentioned above do not operate as a limit on the deduction from premiums, as a life office would not know if the one-sixth limit was being exceeded. Tax relief may therefore be deducted regardless of the size of the premium and it is up

[33] Taxes Act 1988 s266(5); [34] Inland Revenue Statement LAPRI; [35] Taxes Act 1988 s266(9) FINS 33-35; [36] Taxes Act 1988 s274(1)

to HMRC to ensure that the limits are not exceeded. If the limits are exceeded, HMRC can recover the excess tax relief from the policyholder, and prevent excess relief in the future by means of a 'paragraph 4 notice'. This is a notice to the policyholder, and the life office, specifying that premiums must henceforth be paid in full with no deduction.

If a life office receives a paragraph 4 notice from HMRC, it must make arrangements to collect premiums without deduction of tax relief, with effect from the date specified in the notice. Any complaint from the policyholder concerning this would have to be referred to HMRC.

Total income for LAPR is the total income from all sources, less all charges and other deductions, but before any personal allowances. The capital element of any purchased life annuity is not income for this purpose.

3.4 Administration of the relief

Relief is given by deduction from the premiums[37]. An eligible policyholder who pays premiums under a pre-14 March 1984 policy which satisfies all the conditions for relief can deduct the relief from the premium and pay the life office the net premium. The current rate of relief is 12.5%. The rate of relief is not linked to any rate of income tax and the rate can be altered in the Budget each year. Illogical though it may seem, a policyholder does not have to be a taxpayer in order to deduct the relief.

Thus, if an eligible policyholder has a qualifying policy with a premium of £100 he can deduct £12.50 and pay the office the net premium of £87.50. The life office is bound to allow the deduction but will be reimbursed by HMRC. Each month the life office submits a block repayment claim to HMRC for the tax relief deducted on that month's premiums.

The operative date for the relief is the due date of the premium and not the date it was actually paid[38]. This rule becomes relevant whenever the rate of relief is changed.

The policy document itself will show only the gross premium since this is the contractual premium between the office and the policyholder. It would not be possible to show the net premium, because the rate of relief might change in the future and the policyholder might become ineligible – for example, by residing abroad. However, renewal notices will show the net premium in appropriate cases and arrangements have been made with the banks for net premiums to be collected at the current rate without getting a new mandate each time the rate changes.

It should be noted that the premium must actually pass from the payer to the life office for relief to be given[39]. A number of consequences stem from this principle. Where premiums are deducted by the life office from a surrender value, maturity value or loan payment, relief is not allowed and premiums must be deducted gross. However, as a concession, HMRC allows premiums to be deducted from a death claim net of

[37] Taxes Act 1988 s266(5) F/N 37; [38] Taxes Act 1988 s266(4); [39] Taxes Act 1988 s266(5); see also Watkins v Hugh Jones [1928] 4TC94 and R v Income Tax Special Commissioners exparte Horner [1932] WN 266

relief. Similarly, relief by deduction is not allowed where a premium is paid by some form of internal transfer in the life office's records – eg an annuity 'feeding' a life policy. In these cases, the annuity will have to be paid into the annuitant's bank account and the premiums paid out again for net premiums to be paid. If a policyholder pays premiums net of commission (ie 'own-agent' cases) the relief is calculated on the net of commission premium, not the gross premium[40].

3.4.1 Adjustments

The system of tax relief by deduction makes it possible for too much or too little relief to be given. As already explained, the limits for relief are not limits on deductions. If HMRC discovers that the limit is exceeded, perhaps through the details of life policies revealed on a taxpayer's annual return, it can use the 'paragraph 4 notice' procedure to prevent over-allowance of relief by requiring premiums on some (or all) of the taxpayer's policies to be paid gross. As an alternative, the relief can be recovered by the self-assessment regime.

It is also possible for a policyholder not to receive all the relief to which he is entitled. This can happen in a number of ways. One example is for joint life policies, many of which are effected by fiancés. These are ineligible for tax relief and so the life office collects the premiums gross; but the lives assured may then marry and forget to tell the life office of this for some time. Once the marriage certificate has been produced, the office can allow net premiums, but some premiums may have been paid gross between the date of the marriage and the notification to the life office. The law provides that any relief allowable but not given in this type of case can be claimed from HMRC special office at Bootle[41].

A certificate from the life office showing the gross premiums paid, plus a QLAPC form, will normally be required by HMRC before payment will be made.

3.4.2 Loss of tax relief on pre-1984 policies

As has already been stated, only policies effected on or before 13 March 1984 are eligible for LAPR. However, even then a policy will lose relief if it is altered after that date so as to increase the benefits or extend the term[42].

Examples of alterations regarded as removing eligibility are as follows:

- Reduction of the term of an endowment accompanied by an increase in premiums.
- Addition of disability or accidental death benefits.
- Addition of any new option.
- Extension of the premium-paying term for a whole life policy whose premiums were payable for a limited period.

Examples of alterations which do not affect eligibility are as follows:

40 Inland Revenue Statement of Practice 4/97 FIN 40;
41 Taxes Act 1988 sch 14 para 6; 42 Taxes Act 1988 sch 14 para 8(4)

- Reduction in the term of an endowment – premiums remaining unchanged and sum assured correspondingly reduced.
- Conversion of a without-profits policy to with-profits or unit-linked – premiums remaining unchanged and sum assured correspondingly reduced.
- Commutation of future premiums – although this is a significant variation for qualifying purposes which may disqualify the policy anyway.
- Switching of funds on a unit-linked policy or conversion to or from with-profits.
- Removal of a debt, premium-loading or exclusion, imposed because of an exceptional risk of death – even if premiums increase as a result.
- Change (up or down) in the death sum assured on a unit-linked policy where the premium does not increase and there is a corresponding increase or decrease in the proportion of premiums going to investment in units.

Where there is a change of life assured on a pre-14 March 1984 policy, LAPR will be preserved (other things being equal) if the revised policy provides benefits substantially equal to the original policy – Taxes Act 1988 Schedule 14 para 8(6).

If an alteration does remove eligibility, it is the whole premium which is disallowed, not just the increase in premium. Policies which provide for automatic increases (eg low start endowments) are not caught by these rules.

However if a pre-14 March 1984 qualifying policy is issued to someone who is ineligible, ie a non-UK resident or unmarried couple, the policyholder can subsequently become eligible for relief if circumstances change, even if this is after 13 March 1984, eg by return to the UK or by marriage.

4 Clawback

The clawback legislation was designed to 'claw back' some or all of the LAPR given in certain cases. It only applies to qualifying life policies effected after 26 March 1974 and before 14 March 1984. It does not apply to industrial policies.

Clawback only applies to surrenders, part surrenders or policy loans at a non commercial interest rate on the second or subsequent time that this happens. It is thus very rare these days so details are no longer given in this book. Full details can be found in previous editions of this book, if they are required.

5 Capital Gains Tax

Capital gains tax aims to tax gains realised on the disposal of capital assets. It is often called CGT for short. However, life policies and annuities are normally exempt from this tax. A disposal is not subject to CGT unless the policy has at any time been acquired by any person for actual consideration. For this purpose premiums do not count as actual consideration, and neither does a post marriage disposal. A post marriage disposal is one made in the course of the dissolution or annulment of a marriage or civil partnership, by one party to the other, made with the approval, agreement or authority of a court.[43]

Thus, where the ownership of a life policy does not change there can be no CGT liability. Tax can only be charged if a policy is sold or otherwise assigned for some consideration, ie not if it is gifted or mortgaged. The tax is not charged on the assignment – although this could be a chargeable event for income tax purposes. Tax is only charged to the assignee on a subsequent disposal. The following rank as disposals for this purpose:

- Payment of sum assured (on death or maturity).
- Payment of surrender value.
- Payment of the first instalment of an annuity.
- A further assignment for value, or as a gift.

Where a policy is subject to the tax the gain is calculated by deducting from the proceeds of disposal the market value on 31 March 1982 if the policy was held on that date, or the acquisition cost if acquired since then. Also allowed as a deduction is an indexation allowance representing the effects of inflation from March 1982 or acquisition whichever is later to April 1998. In addition, any incidental costs of acquisition or disposal (such as legal fees) are allowed, as are premiums paid by the assignee from March 1982 or acquisition whichever is later. All these items (except disposal costs) can benefit from indexation. Taper relief might also apply depending on how long the policy had been held by the disposer. The acquisition cost is the purchase price paid for the policy (with indexation allowance). The disposal proceeds of a life policy would be the sum assured, surrender value or market value as the case may be. The disposal proceeds of a deferred annuity will be the market value of future payments. Immediate annuities and pensions are exempt from the tax.

It would be possible for the same event to be a chargeable event for income tax and a disposal for CGT – eg the surrender of a post-1982 non-qualifying policy by someone who had bought it. However when working out the CGT, any amount charged to income tax on the disposer (ie the chargeable gain) is deducted from the disposal proceeds to avoid double taxation[44].

Stand-alone critical illness policies are not considered life policies by HMRC and would not give rise to any CGT liability[45].

A life office does not have to inform the policyholder or HMRC when a disposal subject to CGT occurs.

[43] Taxation of Chargeable Gains Act 1992 s210 F/N 43; [44] Taxation of Chargeable Gains Act 1992 s37; [45] Taxation of Chargeable Gains Act 1992 s204(1)

5.1 Second-hand policies

Capital gains tax is most commonly paid on life policies in connection with second-hand policies (see Chapter M section 6) when the buyer eventually receives the proceeds of the policy.

There is no CGT on a seller who is the original owner. However, when the buyer makes a claim under the policy, this is a disposal by someone who is not the original owner and who acquired the policy for actual consideration, and so CGT may be payable.

The CGT situation takes no account of whether the policy is qualifying or not, although the taxable capital gain is reduced by any amount which is subject to income tax (ie a chargeable gain). Thus, it is unlikely that the same policy will be subject to income tax and CGT.

For CGT purposes, the disposal proceeds will be the maturity value or death claim value as appropriate. The buyer can then deduct the purchase price and expenses plus all premiums he has paid plus indexation allowance to April 1998 on all these items to work out the gain. Taper relief might also apply. If the gain exceeds the annual CGT allowance of £8,800 (taking into account any other gains that year), the excess will be subject to CGT at 10%, 20% or 40%, depending on which band the gain takes the buyer's income into.

Example D

Graham bought a house in 1986 with the aid of a 20-year endowment mortgage for £25,000 – premium £90 per month. As a result of receiving an unexpected legacy from a long-lost aunt, he repaid his mortgage in 1990. The endowment policy was then surplus to requirements. The life office quoted him a surrender value of £2,500, but Graham managed to sell the policy on the second-hand market for £3,000.

Selling the policy in the first ten years was a chargeable event, but there was no gain, because the sale price was less than the total premiums paid.

The maturity of the policy in 2006 will not be a chargeable event, so the buyer will not be liable for income tax. The buyer will, however, make a CGT disposal by receiving the maturity value. He will have a CGT liability on the gain which will be the maturity value *less* the sale price paid and premiums paid by the buyer from 1990 to 2006. Indexation allowance will also be given on the sale price and these premiums (up to April 1998) and taper relief for the period since then plus the added year because the buyer owned the policy before 17 March 1998.

In the past it has been possible for the CGT charge to be avoided by the buyer gifting the second-hand policy straight away to a trust or a member of his family who would thus have been exempt from the CGT charge as they had not acquired it for money or money's worth. This loop-hole was closed for disposals on or after 9 April 2003 by the Finance Act 2003, and thus the CGT charge will still apply in these circumstances.

6 Taxation of Life Funds

It should not be forgotten that the UK life office's life fund which underlies all its life policies is subject to taxation. The taxation of the life fund is complex, but from the policyholder's point of view the effect is that the fund pays tax on dividend income from overseas at 20%, interest income at 20%, and at 20% on property rental income and offshore income gains. Tax on UK dividends is covered by the 10% tax credit. If the fund sells any assets at a profit (after indexation allowance), it pays tax on any capital gain at the rate of 20%. Thus the funds that underlie investment policies have effectively borne tax at approximately the lower rate.

However the I-E principle applies so that these rates are only charged on the income (I) after deduction of expenditure (E). So the actual effective rates on the fund are somewhat lower than the nominal rates.

The tax on the fund cannot be reclaimed by a policyholder, whatever their personal rate of tax.

6.1 Overseas Life Assurance Business (OLAB)

For overseas assurance business (OLAB) a UK life office is only taxed on the profit it makes from writing the business. It is not taxed on the income and gains from the investments in the OLAB fund. OLAB funds can thus grow faster than ordinary UK funds – called basic life assurance and general annuity business (BLAGAB).

OLAB is business with a policyholder not residing in the UK. However, trust policies cannot be OLAB business unless the settlor and all the beneficiaries are non-residents (or a charity). Group policies can only be OLAB business if they provide benefits for overseas employees or their families.

In this context residing is not the same as resident. It is a more permanent concept (like ordinary residence), where a person's vital interests – economic, domestic and social – are centred. So an individual could be residing in the UK for OLAB, but could be not resident for other tax purposes. If the policyholders are trustees, all the trustees must reside outside the UK. If it is a discretionary trust, all beneficiaries must reside outside the UK or be a charity. If it is not a discretionary trust, at least 65% of the beneficial interest must be for non-UK beneficiaries.

Term assurance business with a non-resident policyholder done in a life office's accounting year starting on or after 1 October 1999 must be done as OLAB and not as BLAGAB. This led some offices who did not wish to run OLAB funds to cease doing term assurance business with non-UK residents. However it can still be done as BLAGAB if the policy is under trust and one or more of the beneficiaries are resident in the UK.

Business other than term assurance (ie whole life and endowment assurance) can only be done in an OLAB fund if the life office obtains the relevant certificate. For a British citizen the certificate must state that the policyholder was not resident in the UK when the contract was made and specify the country of residence. There must also be an undertaking to notify the office if the policyholder begins residing in the UK or the policy becomes subject to a trust. For policyholders who are not British citizens the certificate must state the country of residence and that the life office has no knowledge making it reasonable to assume that the policyholder was residing in the UK. The office must have the information to back up the certificate.

When the life office becomes aware that the identity of the policyholder has changed, a further certificate is required for the new policyholder if it is to continue to be OLAB business. If a life office learns within 18 months of the policy date that the policyholder was resident in the UK within 12 months of the policy date, OLAB status is lost. Otherwise the policy does not lose OLAB status if the policyholder later becomes UK resident. If the life office finds out that the policyholder's original statements about residence were incorrect, the policy has to be recategorised as BLAGAB from the outset.

An OLAB policy is not a qualifying policy, and is treated for tax purposes as a new non-resident policy (see the beginning of section 2 and section 2.7.2) if effected on or after 17 March 1998, or varied on or after that date so as to increase the benefit or extend the term. Thus any chargeable gain will be taxable at starting and lower rates, as well as the higher rate.

The life office must keep records to show that the OLAB rules were satisfied for at least six years after the termination of the policy, and these can be audited by HMRC.

7 Tax Aspects of Commission and Fees

Where an adviser is paid commission by a life office for selling a policy, the commission is a trading receipt subject to income tax (or corporation tax if the adviser is a company). This has no effect on the client although, as commission effectively comes out of the premium if the client is getting tax relief on the premium (eg on a personal pension), it could be argued that the client is in effect getting tax relief on the commission, although less is being invested in the policy because of the commission. However, some advisers do not take commission but instead charge the client a fee and use the commission foregone to improve the policy benefits. For the adviser the fee is a trading receipt for income tax purposes in the same way as commission. The private client will not be able to get tax relief on the fee he pays to the adviser and a business client (such as a sole trader or a partner) will have to persuade HMRC that the fee was an expense incurred wholly and exclusively for the purposes of the business for relief to be given. Most clients are unlikely to be successful in this.

Where commission is paid on indemnity terms, the whole amount advanced is taxable as a receipt in the year of payment, despite the fact that some might have to be repaid if the premiums ceased within the initial commission period (*Robertson v Commissioners of Inland Revenue*). Any unearned indemnity commission later reclaimed by the life office would be deductible as a business expense in the year in which that happened.

An HMRC Statement of Practice (SP4/97), issued on 27 November 1997 stated that if an independent financial adviser (IFA) or a company representative rebated commission to a policyholder, either in the form of cash or as an enhancement of the policy terms, the rebated commission is a taxable receipt of the intermediary. However, this would be tax neutral for the intermediary, as he would be able to claim an equivalent amount as a business expense, because it was passed onto the policyholder as an expense of doing the business. Any rebate passed onto the policyholder is not taxable on the policyholder provided he or she is an ordinary retail customer. Where a discounted premium is paid, the discount is not a taxable receipt of the policyholder or the intermediary. Where a 'menu-style' commission arrangement applies, the fact that an intermediary chooses *x*% as the commission rate, rather than *x*+%, does not make the difference a taxable receipt.

If the policyholder is an IFA or a self-employed company representative, any commission earned on his own or his family's policies is still a taxable business receipt.

When life office employees receive commission arising from their employment (ie because they are employed to sell) on policies including their own, this is subject to PAYE. Where an employee pays a net of commission or discounted premium on his own policy, this is in theory a fringe benefit subject to income tax. However, HMRC accept that where the discount is not greater than the sum of (a) the commission which would otherwise have been paid by the insurer on selling the policy to a third party, and (b) the anticipated profit on the policy, then no taxable benefit arises. This effectively means that there would be no tax liability in the vast majority of cases.

Where a policyholder pays a discounted premium under a qualifying policy, it is the discounted premium which is used in applying the qualifying rules. For chargeable gains, the rules are as follows.

- Where a policyholder pays a gross premium and receives commission, the chargeable event gain is calculated using the gross premium without taking the commission received into account.

- Where commission is reinvested in a policy, the amount reinvested is included as a premium paid when calculating the chargeable gain.

- Where a policyholder nets off commission from the life office in respect of his own policy and the commission is not taxable on him, the chargeable event gain is calculated using the net premium paid to the life office.

- Where a policyholder pays a discounted premium, the chargeable gain is calculated using the discounted amount of premium paid.

- Where extra value is added to the policy by the insurer (eg bonus units), the premium for the purposes of calculating the chargeable gain is the amount paid by the policyholder without taking the extra value into account.

But income tax is not the only tax to be considered as there is also a VAT aspect. Commission paid for arranging insurance is exempt from VAT under VAT Act 1994 Schedule 9 Group 2. The exemption includes most services provided by insurance agents and brokers, such as introductory services and claims handling. Research, design, advertising and similar services are not included in the exemption. Neither is selling a list of names and addresses for a flat fee.

Thus the fees charged by an IFA network to its appointed representatives are not subject to VAT. However, if a network does not provide Financial Services and Markets Act (FSMA) authorisation and only provides marketing or compliance support services to directly authorised IFAs the fees are subject to VAT. The European Court of Justice decision in the Arthur Andersen case ruled that if an insurance company outsources back office functions this service is not exempt from VAT. This will typically affect administration and claims handling services (unless the service provider has also introduced the policyholder to the insurer).

The VAT treatment of fees is similar, although if the fee for advice covers other areas (eg tax planning) it will be liable to VAT.

8 Taxation of Annuities

For taxation purposes, annuities can be broken down as follows:

- **Purchased life annuities** – partly taxed as savings income and partly tax-free.
- **Purchased annuities certain** – partly taxed as investment income and partly tax-free.
- **Pension annuities** – taxed in full as earned income.
- **Deferred annuities** – taxed as a purchased life annuity when annuity taken.
- **Annuities for beneficiaries under trusts or wills** – taxed in full as investment income.
- **Cash sum payable under a guaranteed annuity** – income tax-free.

8.1 Purchased life annuities

8.1.1 Definition

Any annuity dependent upon human life can be a purchased life annuity except those in the following categories (ITTOIA 2005 s718):

- Any annuity already treated as part capital and part interest – ie annuities certain (see next section).

- Any annuity for which the premiums are eligible for life assurance premium relief, or retirement annuity relief.
- Any annuity purchased in pursuance of any direction in a will or by virtue of a will or settlement.
- Any annuity purchased in connection with a sponsored superannuation scheme, or any other annuity purchased by any person in recognition of another's services in any office or employment, sometimes called a Hancock annuity, or a personal or stakeholder pension annuity.
- Any annuity resulting from a pension sharing order.

8.1.2 Capital and interest elements

Purchased life annuities are split into a capital element (the 'capital content') and an interest element. The capital content is deemed to be a part return of the annuitant's original capital and as such not taxable. Only the interest element is taxable. The relevant legislation is contained in s720 ITTOIA 2005.

The capital content of each payment is fixed at outset and remains constant throughout the duration of the annuity. It is based on the purchase price (or consideration) and is calculated by dividing the purchase price by the annuitant's expectation of life for the age at outset. This is derived from mortality tables prescribed by HMRC. Thus, if an annuitant survives for the exact expectation of life, the whole of the purchase price will have been received back – tax-free.

The capital content will vary according to the age and sex of the annuitant and whether the annuity is with or without proportion, with or without guarantee, and in advance or in arrears. Life offices have agreed tables of capital contents with HMRC and are able to quote them on request. The younger the annuitant, the lower will be the capital content because the greater the expectation of life.

Where, on a variable annuity, the capital content exceeds the initial amount of the annuity, then the excess may be carried forward as an addition to the capital element in the following year's payment.

The split does not apply to a trader for whom the annuity is a receipt of the trade.

8.1.3 Procedure

To obtain purchased life annuity treatment (PLA), the life office will supply the annuitant with HMRC form PLA 1. This is filled in by the annuitant and returned to the life office which then completes the declaration that the annuity is a PLA and inserts the capital content. The form is then sent to the life office's Inspector of Taxes who, if satisfied, sends form PLA 3 to the annuitant to confirm this, and form PLA 4 to the life office to authorise them not to deduct tax from the capital content. Thenceforth the office will only deduct 20% tax from the interest content and all the taxation details mentioned in section 8.8 will apply to the interest content only.

8.2 Purchased annuities certain

Purchased life annuity treatment is not available to annuities certain as they do not depend on human life – they are payable for a set term, regardless of the death of the annuitant. However, for many years they have been treated as comprising part capital and part interest, with only the interest content being taxable. As the annuity has a fixed term the total payment is known in advance and the capital content can be easily worked out so that when multiplied by the number of payments it will equal the purchase price. Many offices will quote the capital and interest elements on the policy or show them on a separate schedule. The life office must deduct tax at 22% (not 20% as for purchased life annuities) from the interest content.

However, this procedure does not apply if the annuity is paid to someone other than the person who provided the purchase price. The reasoning is that if the annuitant has not paid for the annuity there can be no return of capital. Such an annuity would thus be wholly taxable.

If a person wanted to buy an annuity certain for another, the best course of action might be to give the purchase price directly to the donee. The donee could then use that money to purchase the annuity and thereby gain the advantage of the capital/interest split.

8.3 Pension annuities

If an annuity is being paid as a result of a pension scheme, personal or stakeholder pension or self-employed retirement annuity contract, then it cannot be accorded PLA treatment and will be taxable in full. For tax purposes a pension annuity is recognised as wholly earned income.

Often, some form of cash commutation may be available on retirement. If required this can be used to buy a purchased life annuity and gain the benefit of the tax-free capital content, and 20% tax deduction.

The PLA can even be bought from the same office as the pension, as long as the policyholder has a legal right to the cash sum. For most pensioners who want to maximise their after-tax income it will be beneficial to commute the maximum amount of the pension (taxable in full) for cash and reinvest it in a PLA where it will be partly tax-free. Further details of this will be found in Chapter P.

8.4 Deferred annuities

Some non-pension deferred annuities provide at maturity for the policyholder to have the choice of a life annuity or a cash sum. If the annuity is chosen then it will be taxable as a purchased life annuity, the capital content being based on the cash option. If the cash option is taken then this is a chargeable event (the deferred annuity being a non-qualifying policy) and there could be a liability to tax.

Where a gain arises on a life annuity effected on or before 26 March 1974 it is subject to higher rate tax as for a life policy (see section 2).

Where a gain arises on a life annuity effected after 26 March 1974 but before the life office's accounting period beginning on or after 1 January 1992, it is subject to basic rate tax as well as higher rate tax.[46]

However, if the annuity is effected in a life office's accounting period beginning on or after 1 January 1992, there is only a higher rate tax charge.[47] This is to recognise the increased tax payable by the life office on the annuity fund from that date.

8.5 Annuities for beneficiaries under trusts or wills

If an annuity is purchased from a life office for the beneficiary of a will or trust, then such an annuity cannot be treated as a purchased life annuity. This is because annuities purchased as a result of a direction in a will or settlement are specifically excluded from PLA treatment by s718 of ITTOIA 2005. The life office will thus deduct basic rate income tax from the whole annuity payment and the beneficiary may also be subject to higher rate tax if applicable.

If an annuity is payable under a direction in a will, the beneficiary can legally demand the capital value of the annuity. If this is paid to him as a cash lump sum he could then buy an annuity on his own behalf and thus gain the benefit of PLA treatment.

8.6 Structured settlements

Sometimes annuities are paid in settlement of a claim for damages in a personal injury action, often called 'structured settlements'. These annuities can be paid without deduction of tax and without becoming taxable in the hands of the recipient – s731 ITTOIA 2005.

This facility is used where someone is awarded damages for personal injury – for example, as a result of a motor accident or medical negligence claim. The damages could be awarded as a lump sum, in which case any income it produced after investment would be taxable in the normal way. Alternatively, instead of a lump sum, the defendant might agree (or be ordered) to pay by way of a structured settlement. Under a structured settlement the defendant buys the successful plaintiff an annuity with some or all of the lump sum. The annuity would be purchased from a life office, but would be wholly non-taxable. Thus the life office would pay instalments in full with no deduction of tax, and the recipient would not be taxed on them, or have to include them in the computation of tax on any other income. Payments can be made to the plaintiff or someone else, eg parent or trustees, on his behalf. The facility also extends to payments made under the Criminal Injuries Compensation Scheme and by the Motor Insurers' Bureau. The exemption does not apply if the defendant is awarded a lump sum and voluntarily decides to buy an annuity with it.

8.7 Immediate care annuity

Where an impaired life annuity is being used for long-term care purposes (often called an immediate care annuity) and payments are made direct to the care provider or local authority in respect of the provision of care, there is no income tax liability on the annuitant – s725 ITTOIA 2005.

[46] ITTOIA 2005 sch 2 para 109; [47] ITTOIA 2005 s530

8.8 Administration of Tax on Annuities

8.8.1 Deduction of tax

As explained above, the taxation treatment of annuities varies but where some portion is taxable the life office must deduct income tax and pay the annuitant the net of tax amount[48]. The office will provide the annuitant with a certificate showing how much tax has been deducted, and then account to HMRC at regular intervals for the tax deducted.

For a PLA, tax is deducted at 20%, which satisfies the full liability for basic rate taxpayers. Starting rate taxpayers can reclaim 10%. Higher rate taxpayers will have a further liability of 20%, ie 40% less the 20% already deducted. For other non-pension annuities (eg annuities certain and annuities for beneficiaries under trusts or wills) tax will be deducted at the basic rate of 22%. Higher rate taxpayers will have a further liability of 18%. If any higher rate tax is payable, the annuitant's Inspector of Taxes will collect this directly from the annuitant following the submission of the tax return after the end of the tax year.

If the annuitant's total income is low enough for the total tax bill for the year to be less than the tax deducted by the life office, he will be entitled to make a repayment claim from his Inspector of Taxes. This he can do at the end of the tax year using the certificate of tax deduction supplied by the life office. Alternatively, it might be possible for the annuity to be paid without deduction of tax and this is explained below.

Under s282A of the Taxes Act 1988, a joint annuity owned by spouses or civil partners is regarded as income to which they are beneficially entitled in equal shares. Thus, under independent taxation, one might pay higher rate tax on their half of the annuity and one might be able to reclaim the tax on their half. If an annuity is actually owned in unequal shares and they make the appropriate declaration under s282B (HMRC Form 17) the tax can be based on the actual beneficial interests.

It might be considered advantageous for one spouse to assign his or her interest in an annuity to a lower taxpaying spouse. However, HMRC consider that an annuity is a right to income; thus, any assignment will be ineffective for tax purposes.

Pension annuities are taxed as earnings with the pension provider operating a PAYE system which effectively deducts income tax at the appropriate rate via a system of code numbers.

8.8.2 Payments of annuities without deduction of tax

In order to avoid large numbers of comparatively small repayment claims, HMRC has made arrangements with the life offices for annuities to be paid without deduction of tax in certain circumstances. This only applies where the annuitant's total income is below certain limits which are revised each year. The limits for the tax year 2006/07 are as follows:

[48] *Taxes Act 1988 s349*

Age of annuitant		If entitled to married couple's allowance
Under 65	£5,035	–
65 to 74	£7,280	£11,210
75 or over	£7,420	£11,381

In order to participate in this arrangement the annuitant has to complete HMRC form R89. The life office will forward the form to HMRC which, if it is satisfied, will authorise the office to pay the annuity without deduction of tax.

This arrangement only applies to annuitants resident in the UK. However, similar arrangements can be made by non-residents with the Chief Inspector of Taxes (Claims) if the annuitant is:

- A Commonwealth citizen.
- A person who is or has been employed in the service of the British Crown.
- A person employed in the service of any missionary society or of any state under the protection of Her Majesty.
- A resident of the Isle of Man or the Channel Islands.
- A person previously resident in the UK but living abroad for reasons of the health of himself or a member of his family resident with him.
- A widow whose husband was in the service of the British Crown.
- A national of a state in the EEA.

HMRC has said it is willing to allow payment without deduction of tax on joint annuities where only one of the annuitants is below the tax threshold. The office would thus deduct tax from half the annuity and pay the other half gross.

8.8.3 Double taxation

An annuity payable to an annuitant resident abroad may be subject to UK tax and also to tax in the country of residence. This double taxation may be mitigated if there is a double taxation treaty between the UK and the other country. Many treaties allow some exemption from UK tax if the annuity will be taxed abroad. Such annuities can be paid without deduction of UK tax under the provisions of the Double Taxation Relief (Taxes on Income) (General) Regulations 1970 (SI No 488).

E Health Insurance

This chapter deals with those types of insurance which cover a person's health rather than their life.

1 Income Protection

Income protection, also sometimes still known as permanent health insurance (PHI), differs from life assurance in that it may have no death sum insured but instead pays out when the insured is unable to work due to illness or accident. It provides a regular income (weekly or monthly) to replace that which the insured may no longer be able to earn for himself. The office is thus insuring a person's health rather than his life.

Some employers may have sick pay schemes for their employees and these schemes may be insured by a group income protection policy with a life office. If a person is not covered by one of these schemes he can take out an individual policy. There are some 20–30 life offices in this market and the policies all vary in detail. This section explains the types of policy available, the usual conditions and restrictions, the proposal and claims procedures and the taxation treatment. This section deals mainly with individual policies, although group schemes are covered in section 2.

Currently, only about 11% of workers in the UK have any income protection cover and the majority of those that do have it arranged for them by their employer under some type of group scheme. This is somewhat surprising because, for every individual of working age who dies, 14 have been off work for more than six months. The risk of being seriously injured or ill is much greater than the risk of dying and the fact that income protection policies are sold much less frequently than life policies indicates that it is a somewhat underdeveloped market.

There is an Association of British Insurers (ABI) Statement of Best Practice for Income Protection Insurance (see Chapter R).

1.1 Incapacity

Income protection policies are written so that the benefit only becomes payable whilst the insured is incapacitated as defined in the policy.

1.1.1 Definition of incapacity

All offices have different definitions of incapacity and some offices use more than one. The following are typical definitions:

- **Own occupation:** The insured will be considered to be incapacitated if in the opinion of XYZ Life he/she is, by reason of illness or accident, totally unable to perform his/her own occupation(s) and is not following any other employment.

- **Suited occupation:** The insured will be considered to be incapacitated if in the opinion of XYZ Life he/she is, by reason of illness or accident, totally unable to perform any occupation(s) to which he/she is suited by education, training or experience.

- **Any occupation:** The insured will be considered to be incapacitated if in the opinion of XYZ Life he/she is, by reason of illness or accident, totally unable to perform any occupation whatsoever.

- **Activities of daily living (ADLs):** The insured will be considered to be incapacitated if in the opinion of XYZ Life he/she is, by reason of illness or accident, unable to perform, without the direct assistance of a third party, four or more of the following functions: dressing or undressing, washing and bathing, eating, climbing stairs, shopping, preparing food. Some insurers now use an 'activities of daily working' or ADW definition instead. This is similar to an ADL definition, but ADW definitions tend to vary more between insurers and there is no ABI standard definition.

- **Key person:** The insured will be considered to be incapacitated if in the opinion of XYZ Life he/she is by reason of illness or accident, totally unable to perform his/her own occupation within the company.

These different definitions give different levels of cover. Of the first three, the 'any occupation' definition is the most restricted and theoretically the cheapest. The first is the widest and theoretically the most expensive. The ADL definition can be used in cases where the insured has no earnings, eg a houseperson.

Some insurance companies now use a two tier approach in which the 'own occupation' definition applies for the first two years of incapacity, but thereafter the 'suited occupation' test applies.

There has been a legal case where the court decided that an insurer's 'any occupation' definition was ambiguous, and so should be interpreted in favour of the policyholder, not the insurer. The Financial Ombudsman Service (FOS) will also take this into account, as well as the reasonableness and clarity of the definition, although each case will be treated on its individual merits, both as regards the policyholder's claim and the exact wording of the clause.

1.2 Deferred periods

Most offices provide that benefit will only be payable once the insured has been incapacitated for a specified period known as the deferred or waiting period. The longer the deferred period, the cheaper will be the premium – since the duration and frequency of claims is thereby reduced. The standard deferred periods are four weeks, eight weeks, 13 weeks, 26 weeks, 52 weeks and 104 weeks or their monthly equivalent. Most offices offer a choice of these periods. Some offices offer a two-year deferment period and two friendly societies offer 'Day One' cover.

Some offices offer stepped deferred periods for employees whose employers give them full pay for say X weeks of incapacity, followed by half pay for a further X weeks. The policy payment thus commences after the first X weeks, and then increases appropriately after the second X weeks.

If an insured becomes incapacitated, receives benefit, recovers and then becomes incapacitated again from the same cause, many offices do not re-apply the deferred period and benefit will recommence immediately.

At least one office has a 'crisis cover' provision on its four-week deferred policies. This allows for the benefit to become payable immediately if the insured is in hospital for more than seven days.

1.3 Proportionate benefit

In most cases benefit will cease once the insured recovers and returns to work. However, it may be that the incapacity is so serious that the insured cannot return to their previous occupation. The definition of incapacity will mean on the face of it that it would probably be financially better for the insured to stay sick rather than seek a less onerous and less well paid job. For example, a manual worker might not be able to continue a job involving heavy physical labour but might be able to do a lower paid job involving lighter or clerical duties.

To encourage claimants to return to work, many offices include a proportionate benefit clause in their policies. This will provide that if, having been incapacitated from the previous occupation, the insured engages in another occupation then benefit will continue proportionate to the reduction in earnings.

A number of offices also have a similar provision where the insured returns part-time to the previous occupation. These provisions in effect make up part of the loss of earnings involved in the rehabilitation of the insured. They define the level of previous earnings for this purpose, usually in terms of the average earnings for the year or six months prior to incapacity.

1.4 Limitation of benefits

To ensure that an insured will not be better off financially by claiming, most offices put a limit on the benefit payable and this will operate regardless of the nominal benefit insured. The usual limitation is that the monthly benefit is limited so that the total of all income benefits (thus including other income protection policies) shall not exceed a specified limit between 50% and 75% of the insured's average monthly earnings in the year before incapacity, often less the Single Person's Long Term State Incapacity Benefit.

For higher levels of cover over, say, £50,000 pa, the limit will probably be reduced even further to between 25% or 35%. There may also be a fixed monetary limit on benefit, eg £120,000 pa and there may also be a relatively low maximum for houseperson's cover, eg £15,000 pa.

This can mean that, although the benefit insured might be, say, £10,000 per month, if this is excessive in relation to the insured's earnings, the limitation clause can operate so as to reduce the claim payments to the specified level. When selecting a policy, therefore, the benefit should be set at the right level to ensure that a claim can be paid in full, unless allowance is being made for future increases in earnings.

Before 1996 when income protection benefits were taxable, the maximum benefit was often linked to 75% of pre-incapacity earnings. Some individuals may now have excessive income protection cover, as that limit will still apply even though new policies have lower limits.

1.5 Exclusions

Most companies have exclusions in their policies, and no benefit will be paid for incapacity arising from an excluded cause. The most common exclusions are:

- War, invasion, act of foreign enemy, riot or military or usurped power.
- Intentional self-inflicted injury.
- Taking alcohol or drugs other than under the direction of a registered medical practitioner.
- Participation in any criminal act.
- Pregnancy, childbirth or any complications arising therefrom.
- Aviation other than as a fare-paying passenger on a normal flight.
- Failure to follow medical advice.

Virtually all companies have some form of AIDS exclusion. Some only exclude claims due to AIDS, AIDS-related diseases or HIV infection, whereas others make the whole policy void if the insured is diagnosed as HIV positive.

1.6 Foreign residence and travel

Benefit will often only be payable whilst the insured is permanently resident within areas known as 'geographic limits'. The geographic limits vary from office to office but will be at least the UK and the Republic of Ireland, and will usually extend to the EU or Western European countries and often to USA, Canada, Australia, New Zealand and other countries where reliable medical reports in English may be obtained. The trend is to widen the limits.

It is common for offices to continue to provide cover if the insured travels or resides temporarily outside the limits but benefit will not then be payable for more than, say, six or three months. It is also fairly usual to provide for cancellation of the policy if the insured resides outside these limits for more than a set period, usually between three months and a year.

1.7 Change of occupation

Many offices require the insured to notify them of any change of occupation. The office can then decide whether to continue the insurance and if so at what premium. If the insured changes to a more risky job, then an increased premium would be likely. Companies without such a policy condition have to underwrite at outset the risk of changing to a more hazardous occupation.

Many offices treat unemployment as a change of occupation and would be very reluctant to continue the policy as there are no longer any earnings to protect. Sometimes the definition of incapacity may change to being based on ADLs.

1.8 Assignment

Many offices provide that the policy is not assignable or that if it is assigned it becomes void.

1.9 Death sum assured and PTD

Some policies pay out a cash lump sum on death or on permanent and total disability (PTD). Such benefits are not taxable.

1.10 Expiry dates

The standard procedure is for the policy to expire at age 60 or 65. Most offices restrict the maximum expiry age to 65, or to 60 for females and 65 for males. Many policies now take the form of a renewable contract which is written for a five-year term, with a right to renew on expiry. This will be cheaper in its earlier years but more expensive later on in comparison with the traditional policy, as after each five years the premium is recalculated on the insured's then age and the insurer's then rates. The right to renew exists, regardless of the policyholder's state of health, up to normal retirement age and the level of cover can be increased every five years by up to 50%.

The minimum term is usually five years. No matter how many claims are paid, the insurer cannot cancel the policy as long as premiums are paid.

1.11 Increasing policies

Any policy effected for a fixed benefit will become less valuable as time goes on due to the effects of inflation. Thus, many offices offer policies with some form of increasability provision.

There are three basic variations on this:

- An option to increase the benefit, without evidence of health, every three or five years by a specified percentage. The maximum benefit levels of these options are normally limited by the insurer and can only be taken if the insured is below a certain age. The increased premiums, of course, depend on the benefit and are based on the insured's age and the office's rates at the time.

- An automatic increase in benefit of a stated percentage, every year (or every three or five years). Premiums will normally increase by the same percentage.

- Index-linking, whereby the benefit is increased each year by the annual increase in the General Index of Retail Prices or the national average earnings index (NAEI), and premiums are correspondingly increased. Often benefits also increase in line with the index during a claim. Sometimes the index is the NAEI before a claim and the RPI during a claim. This method follows inflation much more closely than the other types.

Some offices have a guaranteed insurability option enabling the insured to increase the benefit without medical evidence if he receives a salary rise due to promotion or a job change.

1.12 No claims bonus

Some offices have a no claims bonus payable at expiry, if no claims have been made. Some also provide a payment on death of a sum such as the last year's premiums.

1.13 Unit-linked policies

A number of offices have unit-linked income protection policies available. These are effectively non-qualifying life policies. After an initial, say, two-year non-allocation period premiums buy units in the selected fund. Each month the appropriate number of units are cancelled to pay for that month's cover. Every three or five years the policy is reviewed to see whether the unit growth rate has met that assumed in the initial costing, in much the same way as unit-linked whole life policies. In general terms, if units have under-performed the premiums will have to be increased. If units have over-performed then the policy will build up a cash value which can be surrendered for cash or paid out on final termination. Such payments will incur the normal taxation consequences for non-qualifying life policies, ie chargeable gains are subject to higher rate income tax. Usually, however, there would be no tax to pay as the cash sum would be less than the total premiums paid.

Several offices will allow critical illness cover (see section 7) to be added to unit-linked income protection.

Some offices have automatic index-linking of the benefit with the premiums increasing appropriately on every review date. The review would then incorporate the cost of the extra cover. Some policies pay out the unit value on death before expiry.

1.14 Reviewable premiums

Traditionally income protection premiums were guaranteed at outset for the whole policy term. However, many companies now operate policies giving the insurer the right to review premiums every three, five or more years. This avoids the costs of guaranteeing premium rates for the life of the contract and gives the office the ability to increase premiums if there is a deterioration in claims experience. Reviewable premiums tend to be cheaper than guaranteed premiums. Offices with such policies have stated that premiums will be reviewed on an overall rather than individual basis. The insurer cannot refuse to renew the policy as a result of the policyholder's claims. The disadvantage for the policyholder is that he does not know what he might have to pay for future cover, although he will not have to be re-underwritten as he would on a completely new policy. Some offices allow the policyholder to index-link the cover on a review date.

One office also provides an annual cover review to check that the policyholder is maintaining the correct percentage of income protection in relation to earnings as selected at the outset. If further cover is required, premiums will have to increase, but fresh underwriting is not required.

1.15 Limited payment term or budget income protection

Aimed primarily at 'blue collar' occupations, these policies typically have a simplified structure, lower maximum benefit and claims are paid for a period of two to five years only. Some policies also cover unemployment and there are single premium versions available, although these are usually written as short-term annually renewable general insurance policies. Confusingly, they may also be marketed as 'income protection'.

2 Group Income Protection

As well as the individual policies discussed above, a number of offices offer group income protection policies whereby groups of employees are covered. These are sometimes known as long-term incapacity or disability contracts. Often the employer will pay the premiums and the insurer will pay claims to the employer who will then pay it out to the employee under the terms of their contract of employment rather than as a policy benefit. The terms of these policies roughly follow those of individual policies although benefits are commonly expressed as a set percentage of the member's salary.

Usually premiums are cheaper than for individual policies (as administration costs are lower) and underwriting easier (especially if membership is compulsory) as large numbers will be joining thus reducing the chances of selection against the office. Many group arrangements are set up in conjunction with pension schemes. The premiums are normally costed on a single premium basis so that the employer pays each year a single premium appropriate to the combination of sums insured and the age and sex of all the members.

Some group income protection schemes have a continuation option giving employees who leave the right to effect an individual continuation policy. However, claims experience has been bad on these continuation policies, so the option will therefore increase the cost of the group scheme.

3 Specialised Income Protection Policies

A number of policies are marketed for special situations. Among the most important are the following:

- **Key Person Income Protection** – whereby an employer can insure against loss of profits due to the incapacity of a key person. A variant of this is locum income protection typically allowing a doctor or lawyer to employ a locum to do their work if they become ill or incapacitated.

- **Mortgage health insurance** – a no restrictions, no frills contract to pay a homebuyer's mortgage repayments whilst he is incapacitated. The benefit level may vary with mortgage interest rates. Such policies are often written as annually renewable general insurance, with benefit lasting one to two years only. However, one office does offer cover under which payments could continue throughout the balance of the mortgage term.

- **Incapacity options on life policies** – not true income protection but merely payment of the sum assured on incapacity rather than death – see section 7.

- **Waiver of premium benefit** – not true income protection but an option under a life or pension policy whereby premiums are waived during incapacity, the sum assured or pension being unaffected. It thus protects the insured against inability to pay premiums due to loss of earnings caused by incapacity.

- **Combined health insurance** – a package which combines income protection and critical illness cover, and maybe private medical insurance and long-term care cover. The income protection element of this pays out a percentage of the sum assured each year for five years if the insured is unable to follow any occupation. These are sometimes now known as a menu plan as policyholders choose benefits from a menu of possible options.

3.1 Holloway policies

These are income protection insurance (IPI) policies named after George Holloway, a 19th century MP and social reformer, who founded the Holloway Friendly Society. A number of friendly societies offer these policies and may insure occupations that other insurers would not. Some societies offer an immediate benefit with no deferred period thus making them particularly suitable for the self-employed. Regular bonuses may be added over the term of the contract out of the societies' profits and these would be unaffected by claims. The policies may have a low surrender value and possibly a cash value on expiry at retirement. Many societies have no loading for females and rate all occupations the same and therefore are more competitive for riskier occupations, but not necessarily so for less risky occupations. Maximum benefits are usually between 50% and 75% of pre-disability earnings, but may reduce progressively the longer the claim period lasts. The object of this is to give a growing incentive to return to work.

4 Income Protection Underwriting

4.1 Income protection rates

Income protection rates vary with age, sex, occupation and deferred period. As one gets older, the chances of being incapacitated increase, and so premiums are more expensive. Statistics show that, on average, females suffer more ill-health than males and thus higher premiums are usually charged for them. Most offices add a 50% loading to male rates, but some have separate (higher) rates for females. Many offices also load the rates for smokers.

Occupation is a crucial factor for two reasons. First, some occupations have a higher risk of incapacity from accident or illness than others and, second, it is easier to return to work with some degree of incapacity in some occupations than in others. For example, not only is a manual worker more likely to be incapacitated than an accountant, but it is also easier for an accountant to work with, say, a broken arm than it is for a manual worker. Thus, most offices have a rate structure depending on classes of occupation.

A typical rate structure would be as follows (the higher the class, the higher the premium):

Professional
Some offices have a 'super' rate class for some white collar professions.

Class 1
Managerial, executive, administrative and clerical workers.

Class 2
Shop workers; skilled light manual workers in non-hazardous jobs; garage, hotel and catering workers.

Class 3
Skilled workers in non-hazardous manual jobs, butchers, policemen.

Class 4
Skilled workers in hazardous jobs or heavy manual workers.

Rate tables are usually based on Class 1 with extra premiums for the other classes. Many companies will not grant policies to those in very hazardous jobs – such as miners, explosives workers and members of HM Forces. Housepersons and those between jobs are not always insurable as they have no earnings to protect, although some offices will provide a limited benefit, based on ADL tests.

The longer the period of deferment, the cheaper is the premium because claims will be less frequent and of shorter duration.

4.2 Proposals

The underwriting of an income protection proposal differs from a life proposal in that the underwriter is looking at the risk of the proposer being incapacitated through illness or accident rather than the risk of death. Income protection proposal forms thus differ from life policy proposals. Therefore there will probably be more questions about health and occupation and some offices automatically ask for a general practitioner's report as a minimum.

The underwriter will process the proposal form in the same way as explained in Chapter B, except that he will be looking at the risk of illness or accident rather than the risk of death. The same methods can be used to obtain further information. If the life is under-average, an extra premium could be charged, the life rated up or only longer deferred periods offered. If the life followed some hazardous pursuit this could be the subject of an exclusion, but a debt would not be used.

5 Income Protection Claims

Most policies state that the insured should give written notice of a claim as soon as possible, although some offices specify a time limit. When a claim is made, the office will often not take any action until the deferred period is up. Then a claim form will be sent out for completion by the insured and his doctor. This will give the office the information to decide whether the insured is incapacitated according to the definition in the policy. Most offices reserve the right to have their own doctor examine the insured, which can be done for very large or dubious claims. Premiums are often waived during the claim period.

If the claim is accepted, the office will start to pay the benefit. The claim form will have a question to ascertain the insured's other incapacity benefits and previous earnings so that the limitation of benefits clause can be operated.

Benefit may be payable weekly or monthly. The office will usually require periodic medical certificates for the duration of the claim, to establish that the insured is still incapacitated. Once incapacity ceases the benefit payments will also stop. If an insured becomes permanently incapacitated then the office will continue paying benefit regularly until the expiry date of the policy, probably without any further medical evidence. A few offices have budget plans with a maximum claim period of two, three or five years, but most will pay benefit up to the expiry date if the insured does not recover.

Some offices use incapacity counsellors to visit claimants in order to assist in their rehabilitation and to monitor claims. In some cases, rehabilitation may be started even before the deferred period expires, as experience has shown that it is most effective if set up as soon as possible. Much will depend on the nature of the illness or disability.

There is considerable evidence that claims experience for most offices has worsened in the last few years. The ABI runs a register of IPI claims to reduce the risks of multiple claims by people grossly overinsuring themselves.

6 Income Protection Taxation

This section describes the taxation treatment of the various types of income protection policy, both as regards the premiums paid in and benefits paid out.

6.1 Taxation of individual policies

Income protection benefits are exempt from tax and so benefits are paid gross for all claims.[1] The policy must be a genuine health insurance where there is a risk that the insurer could make a loss if claims exceed premiums, rather than some type of investment in disguise.

[1] ITTOIA s735

Benefits are not tax-free if premiums have qualified for tax relief as a deductible business expense – eg a doctor insuring against the costs of employing a locum to do his work whilst he is ill. In these cases, full income tax relief is due on the premiums as an allowable business expense, and any benefits payable are fully taxable as business receipts. If used to pay for a locum, such sums would themselves be offset against the business's taxable profits, although the locum would pay tax on their income as usual.

6.2 Taxation of group policies

Many group income protection contracts are sold in association with a pension scheme. Premiums paid by the employer will normally be allowable as a business expense for corporation tax, and the premiums will not count as part of the employees' remuneration for income tax purposes, nor will they attract national insurance contributions (NICs). However, if the scheme is contributory, the employee will not be allowed relief on his contributions. If a group policy includes controlling directors, controlling shareholders, or their close relatives, Her Majesty's Revenue and Customs (HMRC) will only allow tax relief provided that they represent only a small proportion of the membership and that their benefits are reasonable in relation to those of senior employees.

Under most schemes, claim payments are paid to the employer without deduction of tax by the life office but are taxable in its hands as income. However, when payment is passed on to the employee it is taxable under PAYE and thus allowable to the employer as a business expense. In this way the employer will not, in effect, pay any tax on the claim. The employee will receive the payment net of tax and NICs under the PAYE system. If the claim payments are paid gross direct to the employee or to the employer on trust for the employee then they are treated as part of the employee's remuneration and so taxed as earned income[2].

If the employee pays part of the premium, then this treatment will only apply to such part of the claim 'as it is just and reasonable to regard as attributable to the employer's contributions'. The balance would be non-taxable as with individual income protection benefits.

7 Critical Illness Cover

Critical illness cover (CIC) pays out a lump sum on the diagnosis of a critical illness. The market for this type of insurance is highlighted by the fact that someone under 65 is five times as likely to suffer a critical illness than to die. CIC now outsells income protection.

Each CIC policy will specify exactly what illnesses are covered. The scope of cover can vary from office to office, but virtually all offices cover the following conditions:

- Life-threatening cancer

[2] ITEPA 2003 s221

- End stage kidney failure
- Heart attacks with evidence of coronary heart disease
- Loss of hearing, speech or sight
- Loss of limbs
- Major organ transplants
- Multiple sclerosis
- Permanent and total disability
- Stroke

Other commonly covered problems are:

- AIDS/HIV
- Alzheimer's disease
- Aorta graft surgery
- Aplastic anaemia
- Bacterial meningitis
- BSE/CJD
- Cardiomyopathy
- Cardiovascular disease
- Coma
- Coronary artery bypass graft (CABG)
- Dementia
- Diabetes mellitus
- Heart valve replacement
- Hodgkin's disease
- Liver failure
- Motor neurone disease
- Paralysis
- Parkinson's disease
- Severe burns
- Terminal illness
- Thrombosis
- Valvuloplasty

Each office will have its own definition of illnesses covered, although the ABI has a set of standard definitions for core illnesses which its members must meet as a minimum standard. These are divided into core conditions and additional benefits, not all of which currently have a model definition. A few offices have a menu-style contract enabling clients to choose from a list of conditions for which they would like cover.

Very few offices cover AIDS or HIV in general terms, although a number will cover these conditions if they are contracted by a medical professional, firefighter or police officer in the course of their duties or as a result of a blood transfusion in a UK hospital.

Where there is no life cover, most offices require the life assured to survive diagnosis by, say, 14, 28 or 30 days before the claim is payable. Single life and joint life cover is available, and some offices also offer to extend the cover to such of the life assured's children as are under 18, but over 30 days old, without any extra underwriting, although a more limited sum assured is payable (typically £10,000–£25,000) and the number of conditions covered may be lower. The onus is on the policyholder to prove that a CIC claim is payable and the appropriate medical evidence will be required, at the policyholder's expense.

CIC is available as a stand-alone contract or as an optional extra on a term assurance, whole life or endowment policy.

The ABI has a Statement of Best Practice for CIC to help insurers provide clearer product information and to enable different types of policies to be compared.

Improvements in medical science and treatments have led to some illnesses becoming much less critical than previously, and so the market periodically reviews what illnesses should be covered and how they should be defined. Insurers thus from time to time revise their policy wordings, although any changes would not affect any policy already issued unless that was allowed for in the policy conditions.

7.1 Stand-alone CIC

Many offices offer stand-alone CIC with no life cover. These policies can be guaranteed or reviewable, often written as a unit-linked plan. A guaranteed policy provides a fixed benefit for a fixed premium. A reviewable policy is like a reviewable term assurance, and therefore premiums could increase in the future because of poor investment performance or bad claims experience.

A few offices have policies which pay regular instalments of capital rather than a lump sum (much like a family income policy). Some offices offer increasibility options, index-linking and waiver of premium benefit on CIC policies.

Because of the much higher risk to the life office, premiums are higher than those for basic life cover. Underwriting may also be tighter.

7.2 Combined life assurance and CIC

If CIC is added to a life policy it is usually effectively an 'accelerated death payment' made during life as an alternative, not an addition to, the death sum assured. The sum assured would thus be payable on death or diagnosis of a critical illness, whichever occurred first. If there were a CIC payout, there would not be a further payment on subsequent death.

Some companies have a facility for the client to buy back lost life cover if he or she survives for, typically, two years from the date of the CIC claim. This is useful on policies where the CIC benefit is an advance payment of the death sum assured. The premium for buying back the cover is based on the ordinary rates for the life assured's age, despite the fact that a CIC claim has been paid which probably means that the life assured's health would make it very difficult to get life assurance in the normal way.

Where CIC is added to a unit-linked policy, the morbidity risk premium is usually paid for by cancellation of units in the same way as the mortality costs. Many advisers recommend that CIC is added to mortgage endowments so that the loan can be repaid on critical illness as well as death. This usually means only a relatively small premium increase.

7.3 Reviewable CIC

There is a trend towards reviewable CIC products as the cost of guaranteed premiums increases, due to possible future medical advances in diagnostic techniques. Reviewable premiums are generally 15 to 55% cheaper than guaranteed ones and the gap is widening. The policies would be reviewed every five or ten years on then current rates, based on general advances in medical science not on individual circumstances or individual lives assureds' health.

7.4 CIC taxation

The tax situation on payment of a critical illness benefit is the same whether the policy is qualifying or not. This is because payment on diagnosis of a critical illness is not one of the chargeable events (see Chapter D section 2) listed in the legislation. There is, therefore, no tax on the payment, even if the policyholder is a higher rate taxpayer. HMRC has agreed that payment of a critical illness benefit is not a relevant capital payment[3]. It has also confirmed that these policies are not subject to CGT.

In addition, the Treasury has ruled that stand-alone critical illness policies should be written as income protection contracts. Thus, as a critical illness payout would be taxed as an income protection benefit, it will be tax-free.

7.5 CIC policies under trust

Care needs to be taken if a life policy with a critical illness benefit is put into trust. If the whole policy is under trust for the client's beneficiaries the life assured himself could not receive any critical illness benefit. However, a trust can split the critical illness benefit rights from the rights to the death benefit. The former can be retained by the life assured and the latter given to the chosen beneficiaries. HMRC have confirmed that the arrangement is not a gift with reservation (see Chapter C). Many offices have these 'split trusts'. CIC split trusts are not subject to the POAT charge, as they are effectively carve outs.

If the donor under a life policy with a critical illness benefit under a split trust did not claim the critical illness benefit on diagnosis of an insured illness, HMRC could claim

[3] ITTOIA 2005 s495(3)

this was transfer of value under the omission to exercise a right provision (s3(3) IHT Act 1984).

7.6 Group CIC

Some offices offer group CIC to employers with a choice of a flat sum assured, or a sum assured that is a multiple of salary. Employees normally have to be aged between 16 and 65 to be eligible. There is usually reduced underwriting, but pre-existing conditions are often excluded. The illnesses covered tend to be the same core conditions as for individual contracts.

If the employer pays the premium it is taxable on the employees as a benefit in kind, but is allowable against corporation tax as a business expense. If the benefit is paid, it is usually paid direct to the employee and is tax-free.

8 Terminal Illness Cover

Terminal illness cover is a rider benefit added to a basic life policy. Some offices offer it free on policies over a certain sum assured. Otherwise it will result in a small additional premium.

It is similar to critical illness cover and provides that the sum assured is payable if the life assured is diagnosed as suffering from an advanced or rapidly progressing incurable disabling terminal illness, where the life expectancy is less than 12 months in the opinion of the life office. However, if the cover is part of an endowment policy and the 12 months would take the policyholder to beyond the maturity date, the advance payment would not usually be paid. The terminal illness payment is, in effect, an accelerated death benefit.

Terminal illness cover can be added to term assurance, but does not normally apply in the last 18 months of the contract. However, if a terminal illness payment is made and the life assured then lives beyond the expiry date, it will not have to be refunded to the life office.

The aim is that if a terminal illness is diagnosed, the life assured will get a lump sum and be able to spend the last few months in relative luxury. However, a counter argument might be that the life assured could be too ill to spend it.

If a policy with terminal illness cover is written under trust, the life assured cannot receive the money because it would belong to the beneficiaries, unless a split trust is used as described in the previous section for CIC.

9 Long-Term Care Insurance

Long-Term Care Insurance (LTCI) aims to provide a planned way to pay for some or all of the cost of long-term care required because of long-term illness or extreme old age requiring medical care. Long-term care costs can include domestic help, physical aids (such as stair lifts), medical services and nursing home care. There are state benefits available, such as Disability Living Allowance and Attendance Allowance, but these rarely cover all the non nursing costs of long-term care. In addition, some benefits are means tested and no help is given if an individual's assets exceed a certain level. There is therefore a need for insurance products to prevent undue reliance on state benefits which might not be available when needed. For further details of state benefits – see Chapter H section 6. The average cost of private nursing care in 2003 was £455 per week.

As with most forms of insurance, the earlier the policy is started the lower will be the cost. A 1999 Royal Commission report indicated that about 20% of men and 33% of women willl require long-term care at some stage. The market for LTCI is potentially very large, although current sales are low.

There are two basic types of LTCI contract – pre-funded insurance and immediate care insurance.

9.1 Pre-funded insurance

Pre-funded contracts provide for a benefit to be payable in the future when care is needed in return for a lump sum or regular premiums. Benefit is triggered when the insured is unable to perform a certain number of ADLs. The ADLs will be defined in the policy, and the ABI has a model set of ADL definitions, but typical ADLs are:

- **Mobility:** – the ability to move from room to room in your home.
- **Washing:** – the ability to keep yourself clean.
- **Dressing:** – putting on and taking off your clothes.
- **Feeding:** – the ability to eat when food has been prepared for you.
- **Toileting:** – the ability to get on and off the toilet or commode yourself.
- **Continence:** – bowel and bladder control to maintain personal hygiene.

Low-cost (or budget) plans tend to pay out if the insured is unable to perform three or more ADLs or is cognitively impaired (eg has Alzheimer's disease) for, say, three months and this situation is likely to be permanent. Top of the range plans with higher premiums tend to pay out when the insured is unable to perform two or more ADLs.

The 'traditional' LTCI plan is a pure insurance contract with underwriting at outset, a premium guaranteed for five or ten years, an unlimited benefit period, but a maximum annual benefit (eg £30,000 pa). Payments are tax-free and can be made to a care provider direct or to a family member. Policies do not have surrender values and premiums could rise on review after any guaranteed period if the claims experience of the insurer is poor. Policies may include escalation options and waiver of premium. Most policies have exclusions such as alcohol and drug abuse, self-inflicted injuries and HIV/AIDS.

Most offices have now withdrawn from the pre-funded sector of the market.

9.2 Investment-linked policies

Pre-funded insurance can also be investment-linked whereby a lump sum is invested into a unit-linked fund from which each month a risk premium is deducted by cancelling units to pay for that month's cover.

If a claim is made, the policy pays out the selected benefit and if the insured dies there is a death benefit based on the value of units remaining. The plan is costed on an assumed growth rate of units with periodic reviews, as a result of which poor investment performance or bad claims experience could necessitate a reduction of cover or an additional premium. Many investment-linked policies are set up through offshore insurers, and can also incorporate additional inheritance tax mitigation. However, even UK based funds, which are technically income protection funds, will pay little or no tax within the funds.

Investment-linked LTC policies have virtually disappeared from the marketplace due to low sales and market falls.

9.3 Immediate care insurance

These policies provide cover for people who already need care by guaranteeing future payments towards the cost of care for as long as necessary in return for a lump sum premium. In effect these plans are impaired life annuities and so the poorer the health of the insured the greater will be the annuity for the same lump sum. The annuity will continue even if the annuitant recovers.

These annuities are currently taxed in the same way as purchased life annuities (see Chapter D section 8) although the interest content is much higher than a normal annuity because of reduced life expectancy. Where an impaired life annuity is being used for long-term care purposes (often called an immediate care annuity) and payments are made direct to the care provider or local authority in respect of the provision of care, there is no income tax liability on the annuitant. This exemption applies only if the annuity meets the condition at outset, and cannot be used for an existing 'ordinary purchased life annuity'. One of the purposes must be the provision of personal and/or nursing care due to mental or physical impairment, injury, sickness or other infirmity expected to be permanent.

Home reversion and home income (lifetime loan) schemes (see Chapter F section 6.1) can also be used to raise funds for long-term care.

There is also an immediate care plan involving the investment of a lump sum in a series of non-qualifying endowments. Each month one policy is encashed to provide a regular income for as long as the insured lives. The plan is taxed under the chargeable events regime for non-qualifying policies – see Chapter D.

One company has an LTCI policy written as a lump sum income protection plan which pays out direct to a care provider as long as the insured is unable to perform two or three ADLs. The benefit is tax-free in the same way as income protection.

9.4 Regulation

Originally only LTCI which had an investment element was fully within the FSA Conduct of Business (COB) rules. However, since 31 October 2004 all LTCI products have been subject to specific FSA regulation – see Chapter Q section 4.7.

10 Personal Accident and Sickness Insurance

Personal accident and sickness policies are in the same general market as income protection, but they are inherently different. They are usually annual contracts rather than permanent ones. Cover lasts for one or two years only and an insurer can decline to renew the policy at the end of the year even if the insured offers a premium. This contrasts with income protection where the insurer must maintain the cover up to the expiry date, as long as the insured continues to pay premiums.

Personal accident and sickness insurance is therefore classified as short-term or general insurance under the FSA Prudential Rulebook. It can be bought as stand-alone cover or as an optional extra on household insurance, motor insurance or holiday insurance. Policies can cover accidents only or accidents and sickness.

At the end of each year's cover, the insurer can decide whether to offer renewal terms or not. A bad claims record could cause an insurer to decline to renew a particular contract. As the insured's duty of disclosure revives at each renewal, the insurer must be told of any new material facts such as a health problem. This could lead an insurer to decline renewal.

In some cases a policy is written on a rolling monthly basis. This means that the insurer can change the terms, increase the cost or refuse renewal at perhaps just one month's notice although, in practice, this will rarely happen.

Most policies have a schedule of benefits with fixed lump sum amounts that are payable for specific injuries and permanent total disablement and a set weekly amount for temporary disablement. Weekly benefits are normally limited to a specified total period, usually from 26 to 104 weeks. This is again different from income protection where benefit may carry on until expiry which could be some 30 years away.

Personal accident and sickness insurance is considerably cheaper than income protection but is in no way a substitute because of its temporary nature. It is much more suited to specific and temporary risks such as holidays and business trips abroad.

10.1 Redundancy cover

Many offices also offer redundancy cover in connection with a mortgage which can be valuable as it protects the client from inability to maintain mortgage payments due to redundancy. Cover is usually limited to say two years' payments and there are often numerous conditions to ensure claims can only be made for genuine involuntary redundancy. Redundancy cover is often combined with accident and sickness cover and marketed under the initials ASU (Accident, Sickness and Unemployment).

11 Payment Protection Insurance

The object of payment protection insurance is to protect a client against inability to keep up payments on some form of credit agreement due to sickness, accident or unemployment. The credit could be a house purchase mortgage, car loan, domestic appliance credit sale, personal loan or any other form of credit agreement.

These contracts are often sold by the lender or dealer as part and parcel of a credit agreement. Common features of these contracts are:

- They are short-term (or general) insurances.
- Benefit may be limited to a relatively short period, eg two years.
- Benefit is usually limited to the loan repayment plus interest.
- Premiums may be monthly or annual, but are sometimes payable as a single premium added to the loan.
- The policy term is the same as the loan term.
- Eligibility is often restricted to UK residents under 65 in paid employment or self-employment.
- Existing conditions at outset are often excluded, whether known about or not.

There has been some criticism that contracts that are sold by the lender or a dealer are poor value for money, especially where the single premium is added to the loan, so that interest is payable on that as well as the original loan. Often much cheaper and better contracts could be obtained on the open market.

12 Private Medical Insurance (PMI)

PMI provides cover against the costs of private medical treatment. This is valuable because in many areas there are NHS waiting lists for operations. Many people prefer to have operations done privately to avoid waiting lists and to get treatment at a time and place to suit them, but are discouraged by the costs involved. PMI can enable them to get private medical care when required, with a consultant and at a hospital of their choice, with the costs being paid for by the insurer.

A PMI policy will pay out when the insured needs private medical treatment. It will fund the costs of accommodation (patients usually, but not always, get their own room), nursing charges, theatre fees, drugs and dressings, doctor's and consultant's fees. Some providers have links with hospitals to provide the treatment.

All providers' contracts vary in detail, but there is a broad division of the market into budget plans, standard plans and comprehensive plans.

12.1 Budget plans

Many insurers offer budget plans with low costs, no extra benefits, and limits on the cover for different types of treatment. Often premiums can be reduced if the insured pays the first part of each claim. Cover is mostly restricted to the costs of accommodation, drugs, dressings and doctors' fees, with outpatient treatments, home nursing and private ambulance services not covered. There may well be limits on the cost of treatment covered in any one year.

12.2 Standard plans

These cost more than budget plans but give wider cover. More items are covered, with longer claim periods and higher limits. There is often a wider choice of hospitals.

12.3 Comprehensive plans

These plans are the most costly, but give the fullest cover; claim periods can be longer, with higher limits and often a wider choice of hospitals. Services such as home nursing and private ambulances are covered. Most plans also cover the costs involved in a parent needing to stay at the hospital with a child who is ill or injured. Other items covered may include alternative medicine, dental treatment, travel abroad and cash payments for nights spent as an NHS patient. Policies may cover a whole family, not just one individual.

12.4 Health cash plans

There are healthcare plans that pay a fixed cash sum for each day spent in hospital, plus fixed cash sums for specified treatments including optical services and dental treatment. There will often be a waiting period of up to six months before claims can be made, and pre-existing conditions are usually excluded. These low-cost plans give the patients money to help pay for medical care, rather than providing a full indemnity against the cost of private medical care, as with proper PMI contracts.

12.5 Administration

Contracts can be arranged individually or by groups. A high proportion of the market is group cover arranged by employers for selected classes of employee, such as senior managers. In this case the scheme will cover all employees above a certain grade, with the employer paying the premiums and providing the scheme as a benefit of employment. Group premiums are lower than individual premiums to reflect the lower costs of group processing and the bargaining power of a large group. There may well be reduced underwriting for groups of more than 20–50, or no underwriting at all if the cover is automatic for all those at work on a given day in a large group.

If the employer pays the premium, this is normally a benefit in kind, and so the employee will have to pay income tax on his share of the overall premium. The premium would be a deductible expense for the employer's corporation tax. However the premium is also subject to employer's national insurance contributions.

Individual contracts can be fully underwritten or accepted without medical information subject to a moratorium. This typically means that medical conditions present in the five years before the start of the policy are excluded from cover for say the first two years of the policy. This reduces the real value of the cover but makes it simpler and cheaper to obtain. However the effect of this should be clearly explained to the client. Premiums have been rising in recent years because of increased claims. Traditionally PMI policies are annually renewable so premiums may increase substantially each year. However some insurers now offer policies where premiums are fixed for say five or ten years, no matter how many claims are made. There is also a lump sum premium option.

When a claim is made the insured will need to provide the appropriate evidence of medical need and costs. Payment will often be made direct to the hospital or doctor. Claim payments are tax-free.

PMI is short-term insurance under the FSA Prudential Rulebook. There is an ABI Statement of Best PMI Practice.

13 Health Insurance Choice

The different types of health insurance each have their advantages and disadvantages, and are not directly comparable. Each has its own objectives and they should be regarded as possible elements of an overall protection plan, rather than alternatives or competitors.

The table overleaf illustrates some of the relevant factors:

	Advantages	Disadvantages
Income protection	• Pays income if unable to work • Income continues until recovery or until retirement age • Income tax-free for individual policies • Cover permanent until expiry	• Cover limited to a percentage of earnings • Cover costly for high risk groups • Full underwriting for individual policies
CIC	• Pays a lump sum to ease problems of serious illness • Pays out regardless of ability to work • Payment tax-free • Useful for mortgage cover	• Illness definitions may vary • Lump sum may not cover loss of earnings for long-term illness • Advance payment of death sum assured, resulting in loss of life cover, if a rider benefit on a life policy
LTCI	• Can enable wider choice of care • Will pay out when care required • Can avoid relying on state and local authority benefits • Payment tax-free	• Cost is high • Protection-only plans usually have no value on death or surrender • May depend on investment growth rate • Benefits may not be guaranteed for life
PA	• Low cost • Payment made on illness or injury, or in some cases unemployment • Payment tax-free	• Cover can be declined at end of year • Low limits on benefit • Income payments limited to maximum of two years
PMI	• Relatively inexpensive for large groups • Pays out when medical treatment needed • Avoids reliance on NHS waiting lists • Freedom of choice of hospital, consultant and date	• Can be expensive for individuals especially at older ages • Pre-existing conditions often not covered • Cover varies making comparisons difficult • Premiums generally increase faster than inflation due to increased claims and medical costs • Cost rises dramatically at older ages

F Mortgages

For many people, the purchase of a house will be the biggest financial transaction of their lives. Not only does the purchase involve a large sum of money but, in the vast majority of cases, the purchaser will also have to borrow some or all of the purchase price. This chapter deals with the sources of that finance, the security required, the different methods of repayment and their taxation consequences.

1 Arranging the Finance

Finance for house purchase is offered by banks, building societies and specialist lenders. Many previous building societies have demutualised and become banks. Some life offices offer home loans through their bank subsidiaries.

1.1 The cost of finance

All lenders charge interest on their loans and this is the major element in the cost of the finance. Most lenders have variable interest rates, and tend to alter their rates around the same time. There is no longer any tax relief on loan interest.

It is not always possible to directly compare interest rates between lenders because of differences in the way the charges are calculated. Some banks and building societies calculate the interest due on the reducing balance on a daily basis, but others charge interest on the outstanding balance at the beginning of each year, despite the fact that, because repayments are made monthly, some capital will be repaid during the year. Thus, the true rate of interest under the 'building society system' is higher than the apparent rate. As an example, an apparent rate of 6.5% on a 25-year mortgage equates to a true rate of 6.90%. Because of these differences, probably the best way to compare rates is to find out the actual amount in cash of each monthly interest payment. Some lenders offering flexible mortgages are making a virtue of charging interest on a daily basis. The government's CAT standard for mortgages requires daily interest calculations.

One factor that must not be forgotten is any possible arrangement or setting-up fee. Many lenders charge an arrangement fee, typically £200–£500. Some will also charge a completion fee.

Mortgages and mortgage advice are now regulated by the FSA – see Chapter Q section 11.

1.2 Security for the loan

All lenders will require the borrower to mortgage the house to them for the duration of the loan. This means that the legal title to the house is assigned to the lender but the borrower retains the right to live there. When the loan has been fully repaid, the lender has to reassign the house to the borrower. This right to reassignment on repayment is known as the borrower's 'equity of redemption'. The word equity is also used to describe the difference between the value of the house and the amount of the loan. For example, if a £100,000 house is bought with a 90% mortgage, the borrower's equity of 10% will be worth £10,000. However, if in five years' time the value of the house rises to £130,000 the borrower is then said to have an equity of £40,000.

If the borrower defaults on his payments, the lender is entitled to apply to the courts for a possession order to sell the house to recover the loan. There may be practical problems in removing the borrower to gain vacant possession and this is usually an option of last resort for a lender. If a lender does sell the house, it is only entitled to keep the amount owed and must pass any balance of the sale price after expenses to the borrower. Thus, in the above example, if the lender sells after five years it can only keep the loan capital of £90,000 together with any outstanding interest and expenses. On the other hand, if the sale price is less than the loan the borrower will still owe the lender the difference. It is not possible to just hand the keys to the lender and be free from any further responsibility.

2 Types of Mortgage

There are basically five methods of paying off a mortgage in common use:

- Repayment mortgages.
- Endowment mortgages.
- Pension mortgages.
- ISA mortgages.
- Interest-only mortgages.

2.1 Repayment mortgages

Under a repayment mortgage the borrower makes level monthly payments to the lender throughout the term of the mortgage. Each payment consists partly of interest and partly of capital. The interest content is at its highest in the first year and gradually, as more and more capital is repaid, the interest content falls and the capital content correspondingly increases. The amount of outstanding capital falls faster and faster as the years pass and by the end of the mortgage term the whole capital has been repaid. Although payments are said to be level, they will vary each time the lender alters the rate of interest.

Life assurance is not always required by the lender for a repayment mortgage, although cover for the contingency of the borrower dying before the loan is repaid is strongly recommended. A widow may be unable to continue the payments to the lender, particularly if she has children to support. In order to avoid the possibility of losing the house, life assurance should be effected when the loan is made.

The cheapest method is a decreasing term policy, where the initial sum assured is the amount of the loan but this decreases each year as the amount of capital outstanding reduces. The policy expires at the end of the term of the mortgage.

An alternative is a level term assurance. This costs only slightly more than a decreasing term assurance but gives better value for money, because the excess over the outstanding loan will provide a handy cash sum for the borrower's family.

An increasing number of mortgages are being paid for by the earnings of both partners. In these cases, a joint life policy ought to be effected. The cost will be little more than a single life policy and the advantage is that the loan will be repaid if either of them dies.

A major advantage of the repayment method is its simplicity. It is also the most widely available and is often the cheapest method. There is no chance of there being any extra lump sum for the borrower at the end, but neither is there any danger of a shortfall. A disadvantage is that if the borrower moves after a few years, this usually means repaying the existing loan and taking out a new one. Most of the payments in the early years are interest and thus not much capital has been repaid.

2.2 Endowment mortgages

With this method, life assurance (and possibly critical illness cover – CIC) is an integral part of the package – not an optional extra. Repayments are made in two parts: interest payments to the lender; and premiums to a life office under an endowment policy. No capital is repaid to the lender during the term of the mortgage; it will be repaid by the maturity value of the endowment policy which may be mortgaged to the lender at outset. Because no capital is repaid during the term of the mortgage, the monthly payment to the lender is wholly dependent on the interest rate charged. As well as paying off the mortgage on maturity (subject to satisfactory investment returns), the endowment will also pay it off on prior death. Again, if both partners are paying for the mortgage, the policy ought to be on their joint lives.

These days few lenders demand a full legal mortgage of the endowment policy. Some lenders just keep possession of the policy document, having effectively an equitable mortgage by deposit. It is backed up with a power of attorney from the borrower in the main mortgage deed of the property to give the lender power to deal with the policy. However, a number of lenders do not hold the policy at all and rely on the borrower repaying the loan himself from the proceeds of the policy on maturity.

There are a number of different types of policy which can be used for an endowment mortgage. The simplest type would be the non-profit full endowment where the sum assured is the amount of the loan, but this is virtually never used. The next simplest policy is the with-profits full endowment. Here, the sum assured is the amount of the loan, but there are also profits payable on death or maturity which form a handy cash sum for the borrower's family. This method is fairly expensive and thus not often used, but it does guarantee to pay off the loan on maturity.

2.2.1 Unitised with-profit endowments

A shrinking number of life offices offer unitised with-profit endowments for mortgage repayment, and many lenders now accept them. The idea is the same as a conventional endowment in that the policy may be mortgaged to the lender for the duration of the loan to provide the funds to pay off the loan on maturity or earlier death.

However, under a unit-linked endowment, premiums are allocated (often after an initial non-allocation period of a year) to purchase units in the with-profit fund. The percentage of premiums applied to buy units varies between offices and is often lower in the early years, to reflect the life office's initial expenses. Every month, as another premium is paid, more units are bought depending on the unit price at the time. Also, each month a number of units are cancelled (again at the current price) to pay for the life cover that month. The life cover for this purpose is the difference between the guaranteed death sum assured and the current bid value of the units so far allocated. Thus, as the total unit value rises, the life cover required reduces, although the cost of each £1,000 of cover will rise each year with increasing age, and so life cover deductions will fluctuate each month. The contract is close in effect to a low-cost conventional with-profits endowment which it has largely replaced.

The policy has a guaranteed death sum assured equal to the amount of the loan, and the maturity value will be the total bid value of the units at the maturity date. The premium for any given loan is calculated so that if the units grow at an assumed growth rate, usually around 5–6% pa (after annual charges), the maturity value will be enough to repay the loan in full.

Thus, if the units grow at a faster rate, there will be a surplus on maturity; and if growth is less than that, there will be a shortfall. For this reason, the life office will review performance at specified intervals, generally after ten years and then at five yearly intervals to compare the actual growth rate with the assumed growth rate. If the actual growth rate is higher then the policy will normally be left as it is. But if it is lower then premiums will have to be increased appropriately or an equivalent top-up policy effected. Some offices guarantee a maturity value equal to the loan if unit growth is at least the assumed rate each year, but as this depends entirely on the investment performance of the funds concerned the guarantee is not worth a great deal. The assumed growth rate need not be a FSA projection rate, but most offices now adopt the FSA central return rate (6% pa) as a basis for their calculation, as recommended by the Association of British Insurers (ABI).

If the policy's surrender value reaches the amount of the loan before maturity, then the policyholder will have the funds to pay off his loan early if he wants to. This is a potentially valuable option not provided by conventional endowments, although the corollary of this is that if unit growth is less than that assumed, the policyholder will have to increase his premium (or possibly extend the term of the loan if the lender agrees) and so faces an uncertain future commitment.

2.2.2 Low start endowments

Some offices offer low start endowments whereby premiums start at a low level and rise to the full premium over a period of years. The object is to reduce the cost in the early years as this is the time the borrower is most likely to be hard up. The eventual full premium is higher than for an ordinary policy, to compensate for the lower premium in the early years.

However, the initial premium cannot be lower than one-half of the full premium for qualification reasons (see Chapter D). In other respects, the policy is a standard endowment. A typical low start endowment would have premiums increasing by 20% pa simple for five years, or 10% pa simple for ten years, the full premium being payable for the balance of the term.

2.2.3 Low-cost endowments

A popular type of endowment for a mortgage has been the low-cost endowment, sometimes called a 'bonus reinforced' or 'build-up' policy. In practice it has largely been replaced by the unitised with-profit policy, although many existing low-cost endowments remain in force. This was a with-profits endowment where the basic sum assured was not the amount of the loan, but that sum assured which, with the addition of profits calculated on what were thought to be conservative assumptions, would produce a maturity value of at least the amount of the loan. This made it much cheaper than a full endowment. If profits exceeded those assumed, the balance at maturity would be paid to the borrower. On its own, this would not necessarily provide sufficient life cover to repay the loan on death before the profits had risen to a high enough amount. Thus, the policy incorporated a decreasing term element which guaranteed a minimum death sum assured of the amount of the loan. This term element reduced as profits increased and fell away once the basic sum assured plus profits exceeded the loan. Thus, full cover was given for a much cheaper premium than a full endowment.

Most offices structured their policies so that the loan would be repaid on maturity if annual bonuses were maintained at, say, 80% of the current level throughout the term of the policy. Terminal bonuses were not normally taken into account as they are more volatile. Thus, there should still have been enough funds to repay the mortgage even if the investment performance was not maintained at then current levels. These policies were accepted by virtually all lenders. The assumption used needed to have no relation to any FSA growth rate used for projection purposes.

The higher the assumption the cheaper the premium, but the greater the risk of not achieving a maturity value sufficient to repay the loan. The maturity value, unlike the death benefit, was not guaranteed.

Illustrations of endowment mortgages involving projections of the ultimate maturity value must now only be done at both the FSA assumed rates of 4% and 8% and, if required, at the rate needed to exactly repay the loan. The appropriate FSA wordings must also be used.

Policies could be effected on a joint life first death basis where there are two joint borrowers, eg a married couple. However, sometimes two single life policies are recommended rather than one joint life policy. Each policy has a death sum assured that is enough to repay the loan, but is targeted for a maturity value of half the loan. The advantage is that if the couple separate or divorce, each party has their own policy which they can take with them when they split up.

2.2.4 Unit-linked endowments

Some offices have mortgage endowments which can be linked to a full range of funds, not just the with-profit fund. These are true unit-linked endowments where the policyholder can choose the fund (or funds) to which the policy is linked, although many life offices suggest the managed fund as the standard link.

Some offices offer both a level premium and a low start unit-linked endowment mortgage plan. The low start version would start low and increase by a stated amount each year (say, 20% for five years), although still using the normal assumed growth rate and unit growth review procedures.

The policy operates like a unitised with-profit endowment, but the review procedure will probably be more crucial, because unit performance is likely to be more volatile than the with-profit fund, with its smoothing effect.

Most offices' policies incorporate a standard unit growth rate assumption fixed at outset but some offices let the policyholder choose the growth rate, within limits. The premium thus depends on the policyholder's own estimate of future investment performance. If the office outperforms the policyholder's estimate, the loan can be repaid early. If the office under-performs, this will be picked up at a policy review and premiums increased as necessary.

A unit-linked endowment mortgage has fewer guarantees than a with-profits endowment mortgage but a correspondingly better prospect of a higher overall return to balance against the increased risk.

Illustrations of unit-linked endowment mortgages involving projections of the ultimate maturity value must only be done at both the FSA assumed rates of 4% and 8% and, if required, at the rate needed to exactly repay the loan. The appropriate FSA wordings must also be used.

2.2.5 Reviews

Reviews are important on all mortgage endowments, particularly unit-linked ones. The purpose of the review is to see whether the policy is on target to repay the loan at maturity, and if not to give the policyholder a chance to do something about it, eg increase premiums or effect a top-up policy. Falling investment returns and bonus rates have led offices to recommend increased payments in some cases. As bonus rates have fallen, so more policies are projected to show a shortfall at maturity. There is an ABI Code of Practice for Mortgage Endowment Reviews.

As a result of potential and actual shortfalls, the endowment mortgage market has declined very significantly in recent years.

2.2.6 Options

Most life offices offer a range of options in their endowment mortgage policies. For old low-cost policies, there is commonly an option to increase the maturity sum assured up to the level of the guaranteed death sum assured on payment of the appropriate increased premium. This effectively converts the policy to a full endowment where all the profits would be available to the borrower on maturity.

2.2.7 Increasability

Almost all offices in the endowment mortgage market offer some form of increasability option on their policies, both with-profits and unit-linked. This option, often called a Further Mortgage Option, enables the policyholder to increase the sum assured, without evidence of health but subject to an appropriately increased premium, if he moves house and obtains a bigger loan from his lender. The increase in sum assured will be limited to the increase in the loan and probably also to an overall monetary limit varying from office to office. This takes into account the fact that the average mortgage only lasts some seven years before the borrower moves to another house and usually increases his loan in doing so. It also helps to reinforce the fact that an endowment policy is not tied to any particular house, or indeed any particular loan. The option is normally included free of charge.

2.2.8 Waiver of premium

Another useful option is the waiver of premium, again available on many with-profits and unit-linked policies. This enables the policyholder to have his premiums paid for him by the life office if he is unable to work due to illness or accident. The option operates in a similar manner to an income protection policy (see Chapter E) in that there will be a deferred period, a definition of disablement, exclusions, and it will only pay out for the duration of the disablement. It is usually only available for lives in certain occupations, below specified ages and will expire at age 60–65 or earlier policy maturity.

If this option is selected, it will mean payment of an appropriate extra premium and, in the case of a unit-linked policy, the monthly deduction from units to pay for the life cover could include an extra to pay for the waiver cover. On joint life policies the waiver option is sometimes available on one life only – usually the main breadwinner.

2.2.9 Critical illness and terminal illness cover

Often diagnosis of a critical illness will substantially impair a borrower's ability to repay the mortgage. Thus, a number of advisers recommend that CIC is incorporated into a mortgage endowment and most offices allow this. Those that do not might offer a stand-alone critical illness policy. This will increase the premium but may well be worthwhile as the chances of suffering from a critical illness are much higher than the chances of death.

Some offices now offer CIC or terminal illness cover as a standard feature of their mortgage endowments. This has the benefit of repaying the mortgage, thus reducing pressure on the life assured's family, at a crucial time. However, under terminal illness cover, if the terminal illness is diagnosed so close to the maturity date that the life assured is expected to survive until that date, the accelerated benefit will not be payable. This is no real disadvantage as the maturity benefit will be paid out soon anyway.

2.2.10 Existing endowment reviews

As a consequence of widespread criticism of endowment mortgages, both by the regulators and the press, at the end of 1999 the ABI announced that during 2000 and 2001 all endowment mortgage holders would be provided with re-projections of their policy benefits based on current FSA investment returns assumptions.

In practice many endowments have been established with premiums based on higher investment return assumptions – in some cases as high as 11%. The result of each policy review depends on the investment assumption used, remaining term to maturity and past performance to the date of the review. Many of the more recently purchased policies are showing a significant shortfall. How this will be addressed will be a matter for the policyholder and the lender to agree. One option is to increase endowment premiums, where policy conditions permit, but policyholders may be unwilling to adopt this course of action.

The fallout from these reviews has seriously depressed the sale of endowment mortgages and encouraged a number of major life offices to end the sale of long-term endowments. Many policyholders have also sought and gained compensation where they were not made aware of the investment risks or where those risks did not match their investment risk profile.

2.3 Pension mortgages

These operate in a similar way to endowment mortgages in that the monthly payment to the lender is interest only and repayment of capital is expected from a life office's policy.

However, the policy in this case is a personal or stakeholder pension contract (explained in Chapter O).

Repayment of the capital will come from the proceeds of the cash commutation available on retirement. The loan term must therefore end between ages 50 and 75. Retirement for this purpose does not have to coincide with actual retirement from work. Because of the statutory prohibition against assignment of the annuity, the pension policy cannot be mortgaged to a lender in the same way as an endowment. If the borrower does not elect to commute for cash and requests full pension, the life office will have to comply. Even if the borrower did take the cash commutation, the life office would have to pay it to him if requested rather than direct to the lender as on a mortgaged endowment. However, the lender will always have the security of the borrower's house to fall back on if repayment is not made as expected.

The premium charged is that premium required to produce a cash sum on the selected retirement date of at least the amount of the loan. This might be based on an assumption of an assumed investment return before charges of around 7% pa. The investment rate assumed need not have any relation to any FSA growth rate used for projection purposes but most offices adopt the FSA central return assumption (7%). It always has to be ensured that the resultant premium is within the statutory limit.

Naturally, these mortgages are only available to those eligible for personal pensions, although that would be most people following A Day.

The advantage of this method is that full tax relief is available on premium payments. Thus, the net cost to a top-rate taxpayer is reduced by 40%. The nil, starting and basic rate taxpayer will all get relief at 22%. When premiums are paid, they go into the office's pension fund, which is free of income tax (although tax credits on UK dividends cannot be reclaimed) and capital gains tax (CGT), and therefore the benefits should grow at a faster rate than on an endowment, which is in the office's ordinary life fund and is taxed. In addition, the cash commutation at retirement is tax-free. The whole arrangement is therefore tax-efficient. Of course, the borrower also receives a pension for life (taxable as earned income), thus increasing the benefits of this method. The borrower must understand that the pension may have to start at the time when the loan is repaid. Waiver of premium insurance is also often included.

One minor drawback to this method is that a personal pension annuity does not provide enough life cover to repay the loan on death before retirement. Most lenders therefore insist on the borrower effecting life cover within the scheme for the duration and amount of the loan. This has the advantage of full tax relief on the premiums but it must be remembered that this counts against the overall maximum for the scheme and therefore may reduce the maximum pension premium. Many offices now provide integral life cover within the personal pension, thereby reducing the cost of cover.

Her Majesty's Revenue and Customs (HMRC) allows personal pension term assurance benefits to be assigned and so a lender can take a full mortgage just as on an endowment policy.

Similar arrangements can be made with individual executive pension policies and smaller group pension schemes. In practice, these cases tend to be small in number, although large in value, being mainly for directors and senior executives.

Some life offices are willing to give loans on the security of their executive and director's pension plans. These loans will be repaid from the cash lump sum on retirement. The life office will require a mortgage of the property and life cover for the amount of the loan.

Illustrations of pension mortgages involving projections of the ultimate cash sum values at retirement must only be done at both the FSA assumed rates of 5% and 9% and if required at that rate, required to exactly repay the loan. The appropriate FSA wordings must also be used.

2.4 ISA mortgages

An ISA mortgage is an interest-only mortgage, where an individual savings account (ISA) is used to provide the capital to repay the loan at the end of the term. However, there is no guarantee that the plan will produce the right amount of money because of the nature of the underlying investments. The advantage is the tax-free growth within the ISA.

ISAs cannot be assigned to lenders. Also an ISA cannot provide life cover and therefore some form of term assurance is usually effected to repay the loan on death. One life office had an ISA mortgage package incorporating a term assurance, which decreased as the value of the ISA increased, so as to repay the loan on death by a combination of the two. This effectively replicated with a tax-free investment fund the benefits provided by a low-cost endowment. Critical illness cover, terminal illness cover, waiver of premium benefit, guaranteed insurability options and payment holidays were also available in the package. The maximum ISA investment is currently £7,000 pa.

Similar plans existed using personal equity plans (PEPs) before 6 April 1999.

Those clients with PEP mortgages had to alter their repayment arrangements on 6 April 1999. In most cases, it was possible to convert straight into an ISA mortgage, leaving the old PEP intact to provide part of the capital at the end of the loan term.

The bad publicity which endowments have received in recent years has given a boost to the ISA mortgage market, although many more mortgages are simply set up as interest only.

2.5 Interest-only mortgages

Some lenders give interest-only mortgages where all they are concerned about is whether interest is paid when due. They are not concerned to see whether the borrower arranges any repayment vehicle for the capital. At the end of the term of the loan the capital must be repaid. If the borrower has not arranged a repayment vehicle he will have to repay it from some other source (eg an inheritance) or arrange another loan or perhaps downsize to a less expensive property. If the capital is not repaid the lender would be able to repossess the house and sell it to recover the capital. Term assurance is recommended for these loans to cover the risk of death during the term of the loan.

2.6 Health and redundancy insurance

As well as providing cover against death during the mortgage term, a borrower should also consider the risk of a serious accident or long-term illness removing his ability to keep up the mortgage payments. For this reason, some offices issue mortgage health insurances where the policy is designed to cover the mortgage payments (including life policy premiums) while the borrower is disabled due to illness or accident. These policies are a type of income protection (see Chapter E) although they usually have few restrictions and simplified conditions.

Many insurers have taken this idea a step further by introducing a policy which also covers redundancy and unemployment. The policy, often described as a mortgage payment protection insurance (MPPI) includes inflation and further mortgage options. Redundancy and unemployment are only covered if they are caused by factors outside the borrower's own control, eg unemployment due to being sacked for incompetence would not be covered. The major disadvantage of these policies is that benefit only continues for a maximum of two years. Thus, permanent disablement and long-term unemployment are not covered. People with continuing income and some self-employed or contract workers may not be able to benefit from MPPI, so care needs to be taken when considering such cover.

The importance of health and redundancy insurance was increased by the 1995 changes to the social security benefit rules. New borrowers after 1 October 1995 do not have their mortgage interest paid for them for the first nine months. Existing borrowers do not have their interest paid for the first two months, and then only half the interest for the next six months. In addition, the maximum loan eligible for benefit payments is £100,000. There is no benefit for anyone with savings of £16,000 or more.

Most MPPI policies are sold by lenders who market branded products underwritten by a general insurer. However, such insurance can also be brought through a broker or direct, when it may often be cheaper.

The ABI and the CML (Council of Mortgage Lenders) have developed a minimum standard of cover for MPPI policies which most insurers (and all ABI members) now adopt.

3 Choosing the Appropriate Method

The question of which method of repayment to choose must rest on the individual circumstances of each case. In some cases, a borrower may not be eligible for a particular method, eg a pension mortgage. In other cases the lender may not be willing to lend on a particular basis, eg a unit-linked policy. Each method has its advantages, ranging from the simplicity of a repayment mortgage to a pension for life on a pension mortgage. Any additional benefits must obviously be taken into account when reaching a decision. Some methods (eg a unit-linked pension mortgage) involve more risks but the chance of a much higher return, and therefore the degree of insecurity the borrower is willing to live with is also a factor to be borne in mind. The issue of risk has come to the fore as a result of the endowment reviews which offices have been undertaking. The realisation that an endowment policy will not always clear a loan has led to a large increase in new mortgages being established on a repayment basis, and a big decline in the endowment market.

Surveys have shown that there is not much difference between the total capital repaid on a repayment mortgage and the average projected surrender value of the endowment in an endowment mortgage. The average borrower in the UK tends to move after seven years, and on a 25-year repayment mortgage around 14% of the capital has been repaid at that point. In practice, the new repayment loan is for a term exceeding the balance on the old one in order to keep monthly payments as low as possible. Thus, it is not uncommon for borrowing, originally planned to be for 25 years, to actually run for 35 or 40 years.

4 Regulatory Requirements

The PIA issued guidance on the use of interest only mortgages with an investment as a repayment vehicle, which is still valid in the FSA era. Advisers must explain clearly to the client the risks involved and must not give the impression that the final value is guaranteed, if it is not. In particular for endowment policies advisers must explain:

- That the projection used to illustrate the capital sum payable on maturity is no more than a projection designed to illustrate the return a customer may receive based on given market assumptions; there is no guarantee that the capital sum illustrated will be achieved.
- That the actual sum payable on maturity will always be dependent on future market performance.
- Associated costs and charges and how they are structured.
- That it may be necessary for the customer to increase the premium payable (on the occasion of a regular premium review or at some other time) to achieve the required capital sum on maturity.
- That if the customer fails to maintain premium payments at the necessary level (or at all) then he or she is responsible for ensuring that an alternative means of repaying the mortgage is in place.
- The consequences of surrendering the policy prior to maturity.

Mortgage advice is now regulated by the FSA – see Chapter Q, section 11.

5 Other Uses

Mortgages are not just used to provide funds for house purchase – they can be used for many other purposes as well. The word mortgage merely means a loan with security. The security might be a house but could be anything. Even where the security is a house the money does not have to be used for house purchase. Many lenders will lend money for other purposes, eg:

- To buy an annuity (see section 6).
- To pay school or university fees.
- To purchase a share in a partnership.
- To purchase shares in a business.
- To pay inheritance tax (IHT).

At present, income tax relief can be obtained on loan interest where the loan is used for the following purposes:

(a) To purchase plant and machinery for use in a partnership where the borrower is a partner, but for three years only.

(b) To purchase plant and machinery used in connection with an office or employment held by the borrower, but for three years only.

(c) To purchase ordinary shares in a close company or to lend it money for use in its business. This only applies if the borrower will have more than 5% of the shares, or any level of shareholding and works for the greater part of his time for the company.

(d) For an employee to purchase shares in his company as part of an employee buy out.

(e) To buy a share in a partnership or lend it money for use in the business if the borrower is or will be a partner.

(f) To pay IHT on death where the borrowers are the legal personal representatives of the deceased, and for the first year of the loan only.

(g) To buy an annuity for a borrower 65 or over where the loan was arranged before 9 March 1999 and is secured on land in the UK or the Republic of Ireland. Up to 10% of the loan can be used for any purpose. See section 6.

For item (g) the loan is limited to £30,000 and the interest can be paid net of 23% tax relief. For the other items there is no limit to the amount of the loan but interest payments have to be paid gross and relief claimed via the annual assessment.

Full tax relief is available for items (a)–(f) so that a higher rate taxpayer can get relief at 40%.

6 Lifetime Loans (Home Income Plans)

Many retired people face the problem of a rising cost of living and a fixed income, usually from a pension. The purchasing power of a fixed pension is swiftly eroded in inflationary periods. Additional capital may thus be needed in order to boost income. For many people, the only significant capital resource they have is the house that they are living in and therefore one option would be to sell up, move to a cheaper house and invest the balance to provide extra income. However, this is a costly and time-consuming exercise, as well as being unacceptable to many people who are happy and settled in a particular house.

The homeowners could just obtain an interest only mortgage to provide a lump sum which could then be invested for income. A number of lenders will offer these loans to elderly people, and some will allow interest to be rolled up until death rather than paid. If interest is rolled up there is a danger that the outstanding capital and interest could overtake the value of the house. However, virtually all lenders now have a 'no negative equity' guarantee which means that the lender will accept the value of the house in full repayment of the loan, ie the loan plus interest on death will never exceed the value of the house. This is a requirement of the trade body SHIP (Safe Home Income Plans). SHIP also insists that the client takes independent legal advice. Inevitably the loan to value ratio on these products is low. The mortgage will have to be repaid at the latest on the death of the homeowner.

Some form of shared appreciation mortgage might also be used under which interest is not charged but the lender shares in the appreciation of the property.

An alternative is the home income plan, which enables elderly people to utilise the capital value of the house to boost income and yet to continue to live there. These plans are only offered direct to the public by a few institutions but can be extremely beneficial for the right type of client.

For this type of plan the lender arranges for a valuation of the house and then, provided it is acceptable as security, lends the homeowner up to, say, 80% of the value of the property. This sum is then used to purchase a life annuity from the office which provides the homeowner with his extra income, usually payable monthly. The annuity will qualify as a purchased life annuity (see Chapter D section 8.1) which means that the homeowner will only be taxed on the interest element. The lender may be prepared to allow up to 10% of the loan to be taken in cash and used for any purpose – possibly buying a further annuity at the best rates available on the market at that time.

The house is mortgaged to the lender as security for the loan, the borrower covenanting to maintain the property in a state of good repair. The borrower has to pay interest on his loan which limits the scope for the arrangement to those in their 80s. Loans arranged before 9 March 1999, qualify for tax relief at 23% on the interest and the borrower has only to pay the office the net figure. Tax relief can be deducted whether the borrower is a taxpayer or not and so the scheme works well for both taxpayers and non-taxpayers. The rate of relief remains at 23% throughout the loan even though the basic rate has been reduced below this level. The interest rate can be fixed or variable and may be different from general market rates. If a life office offered the scheme, the interest rate would generally be different from market rates (8.25% being the usual figure) and was fixed. However the annuity must be bought from the life office. If a bank or building society offered the scheme, the interest rate will usually be the current market rate and variable, but the money can generally be used to buy an annuity from any life office. The maximum loan for tax relief is £30,000.

Fixed rates are preferable because the annuity is also fixed. Variable interest rates could absorb too much of the annuity in times of high interest rates.

The life office will probably deduct the net loan interest from the annuity payment, as well as 20% income tax on the interest content. The balance will be the increase in spendable income. This is illustrated in the following example.

Example A

Male life age 80 attained and female age 75 with a house valued at £100,000 paying tax at the basic rate

	£
Amount of loan	30,000
This buys an annual gross annuity of	3,260
Less tax at 20% on interest element	242
	3,018
Less net annual interest at 8¼% fixed gross	1,906
Total increase in net spendable income	1,112

The capital of the loan will remain outstanding until the death of the borrower, when it can be repaid from the proceeds of the sale of the house, or from the rest of the estate if the heirs wish to retain the house. As the value of the house would normally increase over the years and the loan is limited to, say, 80% of valuation, there should still be a substantial sum passing to the heirs. Some varieties of the plan are protected against early death in that only part of the loan is repayable if death occurs in the first three years. However, this reduces the annuity.

The loan can of course be paid off at any time before death if the borrowers wish to and if they have the resources. In this case the income from the arrangement would increase as loan interest payments would cease. If the house is sold prior to death, the loan would be repaid from the sale price.

Since FSA regulation of mortgages was introduced at the end of October 2004, home income plans are now known as lifetime loans.

6.1 Home reversion plans

The home reversion plan is aimed at the same market as the lifetime loan but works in a different way. There is no loan given; instead the homeowner sells a reversionary interest in the house to the promoter of the scheme. The homeowner retains a legal right to live rent-free in the house for the rest of his life and that of his spouse. Like the home income plan, the homeowner has to covenant to maintain the property in good repair.

The purchaser cannot take possession of the house until the homeowner dies and this is reflected in the price paid for the house which is at a considerable discount to the current market value. The discount depends on the life expectancy of the homeowner(s) – thus the older the client, the shorter the life expectancy and the lower the discount. Discounts for males are lower than females because life expectancy is lower. Discounts for single clients are lower than for couples for the same reason. The client would also have to pay legal fees and a charge.

The homeowner can then use the cash for any purpose he wants. If he wishes to maximise his income, he can buy an annuity from the office offering the best rates at the time. As there is no loan interest to pay, the whole net annuity is spendable income.The following example shows how the plan works.

Example B

Male age 75 attained with a house valued at £150,000 paying tax at the basic rate 22%

	£	£
Sale price (at discount of 47%)	79,500	
Less charge 1.5% of valuation	2,250	
Less legal fees – say	1,000	
	76,250	
This will purchase a gross annuity of		10,292
Less 20% tax on interest content		932
Increase in net spendable income		9,360 pa

A variation on this scheme is where the homeowner gets a slightly lower percentage of the house value at outset but also gets an additional cash sum at a later date to reflect any increase in the property value (this could be, say, 40% of the increase in value at any time after five years).

The advantage of home reversion schemes over home income plans is that the client can do as he wants with the cash realised and, if he chooses the annuity option, can get the best annuity available at the time. There is no fiscally-related maximum limit because it does not depend on loan interest relief which was the limiting factor for pre-9 March 1999 home income plans.

The disadvantage is that the arrangement is final – once the house is sold it cannot be regained and the increase in the value of the house after the sale belongs to the buyer and will not pass to the client's heirs. However this will not be too important if the client has no beneficiaries to leave the house to in his will. Some schemes have an inheritance protection guarantee which provides for a percentage of the property value to be returned to the client's estate if they die in the first four years.

A variant on this plan involves the life office in buying the house for the full market value. The income for the first year depends on the client's age and the value of the house. Thereafter the annuity is linked to the value of the office's 'pool' of houses and is adjusted annually by the movement of that pool, subject to a maximum increase of 12%. The annuity is well below that available on the open market and reflects the fact that the house is being bought for its full value with the client paying only a peppercorn rent for living there. It does, however, enable the client to benefit from any increase in house prices, although it should be remembered that these could fall as well as rise. An additional advantage is that because the capital content agreed with HMRC is higher than the initial annuity, it is tax-free until it overtakes the capital content and will only be taxable on the excess thereafter.

Another scheme involves the selling of the house in tranches. Each tranche buys a five-year temporary annuity at the end of which a new tranche is sold to buy a further five-year annuity, which, if interest rates have not fallen, will be higher as the client is older. At age 85 a lifetime annuity is bought. When the plan is started (which must be at least 65 for a single male) only, say, 25% of the property value would be sold to make sure that the whole property value is not taken up before the client reaches age 85.

Although home reversion schemes are not currently regulated by the FSA, the government has proposed to bring them under FSA jurisdiction and that is expected to happen during the current (2005 onwards) Parliament.

G Trusts

1 How a Trust Works

2 Types of Trust

3 Taxation Considerations

4 Life Policies under Trust

5 Taxation of Life Policies under Trust

A trust is a way of arranging property for the benefit of other people without giving them full control over it. This may be done for reasons of convenience, eg if the beneficiaries are to be minor children who could not appreciate or deal with the property themselves or it can be done for reasons of protection, eg if the beneficiary is to be someone who is mentally incapable. Sometimes a trust is created to preserve flexibility in allocating benefits between a number of people. Often, however, a trust is created to mitigate some form of taxation.

The essence of any trust arrangement is that the trustees have the legal ownership of the trust property, but cannot use it as their own personal property: they have to use it for the benefit of the beneficiaries. In every trust there is therefore this division of ownership. The trustees will be the legal owners and would be entitled to claim against the life office if the trust property included a life policy. The beneficiaries have certain rights which means that although they cannot claim against the life office they can claim against the trustees if the trustees do not act properly and in accordance with the terms of the trust. (For example if the trustees pay sums to people who are not beneficiaries.) It is possible for the same person to be a trustee and a beneficiary.

This chapter looks at how a trust works, the various types of trust which exist and how they are taxed. It then goes on to examine the role of trusts for life assurance purposes and some related taxation considerations.

1 How a Trust Works

Every trust has a settlor, trustees and beneficiaries. These will be dealt with in turn.

1.1 The settlor

The person who puts the property into a trust is called the 'settlor'. The settlor is the original beneficial owner of the property being put into the trust and thus has to transfer legal ownership of it to the trustees. This is usually done by a declaration of trust (sometimes called a 'settlement'). Sometimes additional documentation is needed, particularly in the case of land. Often the settlor will be one of the trustees in order to retain some control over the arrangement.

1.2 The trustees

There can be any number of trustees but, in the case of land held in trust, there must be a minimum of two trustees (unless one trustee is a trust corporation) and a maximum of four[1]; otherwise the number of trustees is usually from two to five.

1.2.1 Duties of trustees

The job of the trustees is to hold the trust property and administer it for the benefit of the beneficiaries, as directed by the trust provisions. They have what are termed fiduciary duties. Trustees should hold the title documents to any trust property (eg share certificates and life policies) and should ensure that they, the trustees, are registered as the legal owners on any relevant registry (eg land registry or register of shareholders of a company). They must make sure that everything they do with the trust property is done for the benefit of the beneficiaries and is authorised by the terms of the trust. The trust deed will usually give the trustees specific powers to deal with the trust property. For example, if a trust fund contains a portfolio of shares, the deed will probably give the trustees power to buy and sell shares as they think fit.

If any cash comes into the trust, the trustees have a duty to invest it, unless it is being paid out to a beneficiary straight away. The Trustee Act 2000 contains a wide general power of investment – see section 1.4.

When a trustee is carrying out his duties, he must use utmost diligence to avoid any loss and he will be liable to the beneficiaries if he acts in breach of this duty. The trustees must keep proper accounts of all trust property. The beneficiaries are entitled to see these on demand and can also require any information about the dealings of the trust that is reasonable. They cannot require to see internal minutes of the trustees. Trustees are liable to the beneficiaries for any loss caused by their default, although in certain circumstances the trustees may be exonerated if they have acted reasonably.

Under the Trustee Delegation Act 1999 a trustee can delegate functions to an attorney by a power of attorney for up to a year. The other trustees must be informed of this.

[1] Trustee Act 1925 s34

1.2.2 Breach of trust

If trustees do something outside their powers or fail to do something the trust requires them to do, this is said to be a breach of trust. The clearest example would be a trustee failing to pay a beneficiary money to which the beneficiary was entitled under the terms of the trust, and using it for personal benefit instead.

If a beneficiary believes that a trustee has committed, or is going to commit, a breach of trust, he or she can take legal action against the trustee. If the court agrees it is a breach of trust it can:

- Grant an injunction preventing the trustee taking that course of action.
- Order the trustee to make restitution by making an appropriate payment to the beneficiary.
- Order the return of any trust property wrongly transferred.

Where a trustee is guilty of a breach of trust, he is liable to compensate the beneficiary for loss caused by that breach but he is not liable for losses which would have been suffered by the beneficiary even if that breach had not been committed (*Target Holdings Limited v Redferns*). Following the case of *Royal Brunei Airlines v Tan*, where a third party assists a trustee to commit a breach of trust or persuades him to do so, that third party is liable to the beneficiaries for any consequent loss. This is only so provided the third party was dishonest and not just negligent. If the third party has been dishonest, he is still liable even if the trustee himself was not acting dishonestly.

1.2.3 Appointment of trustees

Trustees are usually appointed at the outset by the deed setting up the trust. There is no restriction on who may be a trustee, except that they must be 18 or over and sane. Although most trustees are individuals, it is possible to appoint a corporation as a trustee, which can be an advantage in that, unlike an individual, it cannot die. Also, a trust corporation may have within it the professional expertise necessary to run a large or complex trust where investment and taxation advice is required. Banks offer their services as trustees. The disadvantage of a trust corporation is that it will charge for its services and the scale of charges may not make it worthwhile for a smaller simple trust.

If an individual trustee dies, it may be necessary to appoint a replacement. For this reason a trust deed will sometimes name the person (the appointor) entitled to appoint new trustees. This will normally be the settlor. If the deed has no such provision, the power to appoint new trustees is possessed by the surviving trustee(s) or the legal representatives of the last trustee to die[2]. Many trust deeds give the appointor power to appoint new trustees at any time. If not, the Trustee Act 1925 can be used. Section 36 provides that a new trustee can be appointed to replace a trustee who:

- Is dead.
- Remains outside the UK for more than a year.

[2] *Trustee Act 1925 s18*

- Desires to be discharged.
- Refuses to act.
- Is unfit or incapable of acting.
- Is a minor.

If in any trust there are fewer than four trustees, then no new appointment under the statutory power can increase the number of trustees to more than four (s36(6)).

If a trust does not name an appointor, then those beneficiaries of the trust who are of full age and capacity and (taken together) absolutely entitled, can direct a trustee to retire and also direct the trustees to appoint a replacement. If a trustee becomes mentally incapable and there is no-one willing to replace him under s36 of the Trustee Act 1925, then those beneficiaries who are of full age and capacity and absolutely entitled can direct the trustee's receiver or enduring attorney to appoint a specified replacement. These two powers are given under the Trusts of Land and Appointment of Trustees Act 1996. Individual trust wordings can specify that these provisions shall not apply.

1.2.4 Retirement of trustees

If a trustee wishes to retire, he can be replaced under s36 (as above) or, by the use of a Deed of Retirement under s39, he can retire without being replaced. This can only be done if at least two trustees remain, or a trust corporation, and the co-trustees and appointor (if any) must consent in the deed. Some trust wordings give the settlor power to remove trustees.

1.2.5 Death of trustees

As stated above, under s36 a new trustee can be appointed to replace a dead trustee. However, if this is not done, the powers of a deceased trustee can be exercised by the surviving trustee(s) – s18 Trustee Act 1925. If a sole or last surviving trustee dies, then his legal personal representatives can act as trustees. Death of the last trustee does not invalidate the trust.

1.3 The beneficiaries

The beneficiaries under a trust are the equitable owners of the trust property and everything that takes place must be for their benefit. The trustees must balance the interests of different beneficiaries. There are various different types of beneficial interest.

An **absolute interest** means that the beneficiary has a full equitable ownership which cannot be taken away. A **life interest** is where a beneficiary is entitled to the income (or enjoyment) from the trust property for life but is not entitled to the capital. Such a beneficiary is called a life tenant. After a life tenant dies, the property passes to the next beneficiaries who are called the remaindermen. Often, however, the trustees are given power to appoint capital to the life tenant at their discretion. The remaindermen only get a full interest after the death of the life tenant; until then, their interest is known as a reversionary interest.

A **contingent beneficiary** is one whose interest depends on the happening of a particular event (the contingency) which may, in fact, never happen. An example would be A's interest where property is on trust 'for B if he is alive at my death, and if not for A'. A will only benefit if B dies before the settlor.

A beneficiary can be a sole beneficiary or one of several joint beneficiaries. Joint beneficiaries will take in equal shares unless the trust states otherwise.

A beneficiary may be named (eg 'my wife Mrs X' or 'my children X, Y and Z in equal shares') or defined by description or class ('my wife' or 'all my children in equal shares'). Often, beneficiaries are described by class for extra flexibility. Taking the example above, if X, Y and Z were named as beneficiaries, then if a further child, A, was born, he would not be able to benefit from the trust. However, A would be included automatically if the trust was for 'all my children'. The beneficiaries must be described precisely enough, so that at any one time it can be said exactly who is a member of that class.

The beneficiaries cannot control the trustees but they can insist that the trustees act only in accordance with the terms of the trust and the general law. The beneficiaries can insist that the trust accounts be audited by a solicitor or accountant and they have recourse to the courts, if necessary, in the case of a breach of the trust.

It is possible for beneficiaries in some cases to put an end to the trust. Under what is known as the rule in *Saunders v Vautier*[3], if all the beneficiaries are ascertained, if there is no possibility of further beneficiaries, and if they are all of full age and capacity, they can direct the trustees to hand the trust property over to them. This effectively puts an end to the trust, but it does require the unanimous agreement of all the beneficiaries. A settlor cannot generally revoke or dissolve a trust once it has been created.

If a beneficiary is a minor, he cannot demand his share but the trustees have power[4] to apply trust income to any minor beneficiary for maintenance or education. The trustees can also apply capital for the benefit of a beneficiary[5] up to certain statutory limits although these limits can be changed by a particular trust wording.

1.4 Trustee Act 2000

This act came into force on 1 February 2001 and applies to England and Wales only. It sets out some of the duties and powers of trustees, in particular with regard to investment.

It states that trustees have a duty of care to use such care and skill as is reasonable in the circumstances, having regard in particular to:

- Any special knowledge or experience that they have or hold themselves out as having; and

[3] Saunders v Vautier [1841] Beav. 115; [4] Trustee Act 1925 s31;
[5] Trustee Act 1925 s32

- If acting as trustee in the course of a business or profession to any special knowledge or experience that is reasonable to expect of a person acting in the course of that kind of business or profession.

The duty of care applies to matters such as investment, acquiring land, appointing agents, insuring and valuing trust property, subject to anything to the contrary in the trust wording.

The Act gives trustees a specific power to invest anywhere as if they were absolutely entitled to the trust assets. This general power of investment replaced the previous system of approved investments under the Trustee Investments Act 1961 which has been repealed. Trustees must have regard to the standard investment criteria when exercising any power of investment. Trustees must from time to time review investments and consider if, having regard to the standard investment criteria, they should be varied. The standard investment criteria are: (a) suitability to the trust, and (b) diversification as far as is appropriate.

Before exercising any power of investment trustees must obtain and consider proper advice about the way it is exercised. They must do the same on reviews. However this does not apply if the trustees reasonably conclude in all the circumstances that investment advice is unnecessary or inappropriate. Proper investment advice must be given by a person reasonably believed by the trustees to be qualified to give it by ability and practical experience. The general power of investment applies to all existing and new trusts subject to any restriction in a specific trust wording. However no investment restriction in a pre-3 August 1961 trust can restrict this general power.

Trustees may acquire land in the UK for any reason and have the powers of absolute owners over it, subject to any restriction in the specific trust wording.

Trustees can authorise any person to exercise any or all of their delegable functions as an agent. However trustees cannot delegate the functions of distributing trust assets, deciding whether payments come out of income or capital or appointing a trustee. The agent could be a trustee and if two or more people are agents for the same function they must act jointly. However the agent cannot be a beneficiary of the trust. The trustees have specific power to pay an agent for work done for the trust. The trustees will not be liable for the acts or defaults of an agent unless they have failed in their duty of care.

If trustees delegate investment functions they must have a written policy statement for investments and a written agreement with the agent including compliance with the policy statement. Trustees must keep these arrangements under review.

Any trustee who is a trust corporation or a professional (but not a sole trustee) is entitled to reasonable remuneration for services rendered to the trust if each other trustee has agreed in writing, even if those services could be provided by a lay trustee unless the specific trust wording says different. Trustees are also entitled to be reimbursed from trust funds, or may pay out of trust funds, expenses properly incurred by them acting on behalf of the trust.

Trustees may insure any trust property and pay premiums out of the trust and those premiums can come from income or capital.

The Act applies to personal representatives administering a deceased person's estate as well as to trusts created during a settlor's lifetime.

The Act applies to retirement annuity contracts and personal pensions under trust but not to occupational pension schemes. The Trustee Act (Northern Ireland) 2001 introduced similar provisions for Northern Ireland. The Charities and Trustee Investment (Scotland) Act 2005 gives trustees of Scottish trusts a general investment power (subject to suitability and diversification) unless there is something to the contrary in the trust wording. No investment restriction in a pre-3 August 1961 trust can restrict this general power. There is also an advice duty and a delegation power similar to the English Trustee Act 2000, but no review duty.

2 Types of Trust

There are a number of different types of trust and these are dealt with below.

2.1 Absolute or bare trust

This is not really a trust in any true sense. The beneficiary(ies) has an absolute interest and the sole duty of the trustee is to hold the property on behalf of the beneficiary and transfer it to him as required. An example would be a policy on trust 'for X absolutely', where X is an adult. The trustee's duty is merely to claim the proceeds from the life office and pass them on to X. If X was a minor, the trustee would have to invest the money until X reached 18 and then transfer it to him. Absolute trusts are not caught by the 2006 Budget IHT changes.

2.2 Life interest trust

This, as the name suggests, is where the trust involves a life interest. An example would be a trust 'for my wife X for life, and thereafter to my children A, B and C in equal shares absolutely'. In this case, the wife, 'the life tenant', enjoys the income from the trust property for her life, and on her death the trustees can split the property three ways and pay each beneficiary his share. The children, in this case, are 'the remaindermen' and are said to possess 'the reversionary interest', at least until the death of the life tenant.

2.3 Flexible trusts

The trusts discussed previously are all fixed trusts, in that once they are set up the beneficial interests cannot be varied. However, it is possible to have a trust where the beneficial interests can be altered. This is achieved by virtue of a 'power of appointment' whereby the trustees have a power to appoint or vary beneficiaries. A typical wording would be as follows:

On trust for all or such one or more of my wife A B and the children of our marriage in such share or shares as the trustees shall from time to time by deed or deeds revocable or irrevocable appoint and subject to and in default of any such appointment and in so far as any such appointment shall not extend or shall fail for any reason on trust for my wife A B absolutely.

This type of trust is very flexible as it gives the trustees power to vary the beneficiaries within the stated limits. It can thus be adjusted to cater for changing family circumstances. Maximum flexibility can be retained if any appointments are made revocably. The trust wording usually contains a 'gift over' in case an appointment is never made or fails for some reason. The trust also makes provision for what happens to income and capital in the meantime until an appointment is made.

The class of potential beneficiaries can be worded very widely and can thus give the trustees great flexibility in the distribution of the proceeds.

2.4 Revertor to settlor trusts

Many revertor to settlor trusts were created before 1986. These are flexible trusts where the settlor is one of the potential beneficiaries. He can thus recover the trust property himself if required. However, since 1986 this has constituted a gift with reservation for inheritance tax (IHT) purposes, and thus is not now generally recommended.

2.5 Discretionary trusts

A discretionary trust is a flexible trust where beneficiaries are not entitled to either capital or income. Whether or not they receive anything is entirely in the discretion of the trustees. It is thus very flexible, as the trustees can at their discretion appoint a beneficiary to receive capital or income at any time, because the situation makes it appropriate.

2.6 Accumulation and maintenance trusts

An accumulation and maintenance trust is a discretionary trust where one or more beneficiaries will become legally entitled to the capital or the income of the trust property on attaining a specified age of not more than 25. Until then, the income can either be accumulated or it can be used by the trustees for the maintenance, education or benefit of any of the potential beneficiaries. The trust must last in this form no longer than 25 years or be for the benefit of grandchildren of a common grandparent.

2.7 Probate trusts

A probate trust is usually a trust with the settlor having the initial interest in possession plus access to capital as a potential beneficiary. Thus during the settlor's life, he or she effectively has full access to income and capital and thus there is no transfer of value for IHT at outset. When the settlor dies, the trust fund is treated as part of the estate for IHT purposes, but the further provisions of the trust as to who is now the beneficiary come into effect. These trusts are sometimes used for bonds, not for tax planning reasons, but for convenience on death in that the bond is owned by the trustees who can cash it whenever they want without having to produce a grant of representation. This can speed up administration of the estate, but is not as good as funding the IHT liability – see Chapter L.

2.8 Will trusts

A will trust is simply a trust in a will, as opposed to one created during the settlor's lifetime. Like anything else in a will it only becomes effective when the testator dies. Once the testator dies the trust starts and normally the executors of the will are the trustees. While the testator is alive the will can be changed whenever they want and so any asset left in a will trust is still in the testator's ownership, is disposable by them and is subject to IHT as part of the estate. It is common for there to be a nil rate band trust in a will to maximise IHT efficiency.

A straight gift in a will to a minor is effectively a will trust until the child attains age 18.

2.9 Intestacy trusts

If someone dies without a will leaving a spouse/civil partner and children the law imposes a statutory trust. The spouse/civil partner takes personal chattels plus £125,000 absolutely plus a life interest in half the residue. The children take half the residue on reaching age 18 or marrying before that age, plus the other half of the residue on the death of the spouse/civil partner. The administrator(s) will be the trustees of this trust.

3 Taxation Considerations

Taxation considerations are covered in more detail in Chapter C, but the creation of any trust, other than one giving a life interest to the settlor, is a transfer of value for IHT purposes. The amount of the transfer is the loss in value to the settlor's estate and tax may or may not be payable according to whether the settlor's tax threshold has been reached and what type of trust is used.

3.1 Inheritance tax

3.1.1 Interest in possession

If the trust has an interest in possession (see later), then before the 2006 Budget its creation used to be a potentially exempt transfer (see Chapter C) and thus there could only be a tax charge if the settlor died in the next seven years or reserved a benefit.

Once the trust was set up, the trust property was outside the estate of the settlor. If a 'revertor to settlor' trust was used, and the settlor is later appointed as a beneficiary, then a further transfer has been made, although this is exempt from tax[6]. However, the property will then be back in the settlor's estate.

[6] *IHTA 1984 s53(3)*

During the life of a trust, the property for tax purposes is regarded as being owned by the beneficiary with what is called the 'interest in possession'. This phrase means the person who is entitled to the income from the property (if there was any) at the time it arises. If there are two beneficiaries they each have an interest in possession in half the trust fund and so on. Enjoyment of tangible trust property as of right is the equivalent of income.

Where there is a life interest, the life tenant has the interest in possession and, under the flexible trust, the 'gift over' beneficiary has the interest until an appointment is made. Where a beneficiary has an interest in possession and entitlement to income, they are deemed for IHT purposes to own the underlying capital.

When ownership of the interest in possession changes, a transfer of value occurs for IHT purposes. This would happen on the death of a life tenant or an appointment under a flexible trust. The tax charge is worked out using the outgoing beneficiary's rates, but the tax is payable by the trustees out of the trust fund. For example, X is the life tenant of a trust worth £200,000 and also has a personal estate of £200,000. For IHT purposes tax is calculated on the total, ie £400,000. Tax is thus £400,000 – £285,000 x 40% = £46,000. Half is payable by the trustees out of the trust fund and half by the executors out of the estate. This assumes no exemptions or reliefs apply.

If the change in the interest in possession occurs during the lifetime of the outgoing beneficiary (eg by the trustees using their power of appointment) this is deemed to be a potentially exempt transfer and thus will only be chargeable to tax if the outgoing beneficiary dies within seven years.

No IHT is charged when the trustees pay out capital to a beneficiary who has been entitled to an interest in possession (and therefore the income). For IHT purposes, the interest in possession beneficiary is always deemed to own the capital. All the above applies only to pre 2006 Budget trusts.

3.1.2 Inheritance tax on discretionary trusts

If a trust has no interest in possession (ie it is a discretionary trust) the rules are different. The creation of the trust is a chargeable lifetime transfer and thus tax could be payable at 20% if the gift is over the threshold. There may also be further tax to pay if the settlor dies within seven years (see Chapter C). The IHT regime for discretionary trusts during the course of their existence is also different because there is no-one with an interest in possession on whom to base the tax charge.

IHT is consequently chargeable each time a distribution of capital is made to a beneficiary. If this occurs during the first ten years, tax is chargeable at 30% of the lifetime rate that would have been charged on a hypothetical transfer by the settlor using his cumulation just prior to creating the trust. This produces a maximum rate of 6%. However, only X-fortieths of the full rate is charged with X being the number of full three-month periods for which the property has been held on a discretionary trust during the initial ten-year period, before the distribution or appointment.

A similar method is used after the first ten years, except that the rate used is the last periodic charge rate, although the X-fortieths rule still applies, and the maximum rate is still 6%.

As well as a tax charge on distributions, there is also a periodic tax charge on the value of the trust fund whether distributions have been made or not. This will occur on each tenth anniversary of the date of the creation of the trust. The charge is at 30% of the lifetime rates which would have applied to a hypothetical transfer by the settlor using his cumulation just prior to the creation of the trust, plus the value of any appointment or distribution made in the previous ten years.

In many cases, although the maths can be very complicated the tax charge works out at nil. The maximum periodic charge tax rate is 6% (ie 30% of 20%) – and only then of any excess over the nil rate band.

As each trust effectively has its own nil rate band it may be possible to eliminate or reduce the tax by creating a number of almost identical trusts, each on a different day and each with its own nil rate band.

3.1.3 Accumulation and maintenance (A&M) trusts

Before the 2006 Budget, the creation during life of an accumulation and maintenance trust was a potentially exempt transfer. It would only become a chargeable transfer if the settlor died within seven years of setting it up.

This treatment only applied to a trust if it had been in existence for less than 25 years, or one where all the beneficiaries were grandchildren of a common grandparent (or their widow(er)s or children).

3.1.4 2006 Budget changes

Before the date of the 2006 Budget – 22 March 2006 – the creation of a trust with an interest in possession, or an accumulation and maintenance trust, was a PET. This was changed by the Budget.

Now the creation of any trust other than an absolute trust or a disabled trust is a chargeable lifetime transfer unless an exemption applies. It could still be exempt under the annual, normal expenditure or spouse exemption. If not, and the transfer is over the nil rate band (taking into account the previous seven years' chargeable lifetime transfers), there is a tax charge at outset of 20% of the excess over the nil rate band. Thus a transfer of £300,000 into an interest in possession trust where no exemptions were available would generate an immediate tax charge of £3,000 (ie 20% of £15,000) if paid by the trustees. There might be further tax if the settlor died within the next five years. Even if a chargeable lifetime transfer is not over the nil rate band it still has to be reported to Her Majesty's Revenue and Customs (HMRC) within a year of outset if it exceeds £10,000 or the donor's ten-year cumulation exceeds £40,000.

In addition, if these trusts are created on or after 22 March 2006, they will be subject to the exit and periodic charges which previously only applied to discretionary trusts, but only if they exceed the nil rate band. The only trusts that will avoid the new rules are those that:

- Are created on death by a parent for a minor child who will be fully entitled at age 18; or
- Are created on death for the benefit of one life tenant in order of time whose interest cannot be replaced; or
- Are created either in the settlor's lifetime or on death for a disabled person.

Accumulation and maintenance trusts that existed before 22 March 2006, and where the trust provides that the trust assets will go to a beneficiary absolutely at age 18 (or where the trust terms are modified before 6 April 2008 to provide this), keep the pre-existing PET treatment. Where such A&M trusts do not provide this, they will become subject to the discretionary trust regime from 6 April 2008 for the period between age 18 and 25 and the periodic and exit charges will apply. Ten-yearly anniversaries will depend on the original date of the trust but for the first ten years after 6 April 2008 the charge will reflect the fact that it has not been subject to the new regime for the full ten years. Thus the maximum charge is 4.2%.

The previous PET rules for interest in possession trusts created before 22 March 2006 will continue until the interest current on that date ends. If someone then takes absolute ownership this will be a transfer by the previous beneficiary as before. If, when that interest comes to an end, the trust continues, this will be treated as a chargeable lifetime transfer by the outgoing beneficiary (if alive) or part of the estate (if on death). Thereafter the trust will be subject to the new regime with the exit and periodic charges. However, any new interest in possession that arises when a pre-22 March 2006 interest in possession ends before 6 April 2008 (whether on death or during life) will be treated as a pre-22 March 2006 interest.

3.1.5 Summary of 2006 Changes

- The creation of any trust on or after 22 March 2006 is a chargeable lifetime transfer unless it is an absolute trust, or a disabled trust, or otherwise exempt (eg under the annual exemption of £3,000).

- Chargeable lifetime transfers must be reported to HMRC by the settlor if they exceed £10,000 or the settlor's ten (not seven) year cumulation of chargeable lifetime transfers exceeds £40,000.

- When a chargeable lifetime transfer is made there is an entry charge at 20% of the excess over the nil rate band, using the donor's seven year cumulation at outset. Any tax has to be paid within six months after the end of the month in which the chargeable transfer is made, or in the case of a transfer made after 5 April and before 1 October in any year, at the end of April in the next year.

- The entry charge is only at 20% if the trustees pay. If the settlor pays it is effectively at 25% due to grossing-up – see Chapter C section 3.6.2.

- If the settlor dies within five years of the chargeable lifetime transfer. IHT at the death rates is payable (after taper relief) with credit for any lifetime tax paid at outset – see Chapter C section 3.8 year 11 for an example.

- There is a periodic charge on every 10th anniversary of the trust. For a settlor with a nil cumulation at outset, this is simply 6% of the excess over the then nil rate band of the value of the trust at the 10th anniversary. So there is no tax if the trust value is less than the nil rate band. The trustees must do a report to HMRC and pay any tax.

- There is an exit charge every time capital leaves the trust. The trustees must do a report to HMRC and pay any tax.

- The exit charge in the first ten years is based on the entry charge. It is 30% of the effective rate at the outset multiplied by x/40 where x is the number of complete quarter years since the trust was created. So if the entry charge was nil, the exit charge is nil – even if by then the value of the trust has overtaken the nil rate band.

- The exit charge after the first ten years is based on the last periodic charge. It is the effective rate at the last periodic charge point multiplied by x/40 where x is the number of complete quarter years since the last 10th anniversary. So if the last periodic charge was nil, the exit charge is nil – even if by then the value of the trust has overtaken the nil rate band.

- Thus if the value of the trust at all times is less than the nil rate band, there will be no tax payable.

3.1.6 Example of the new rules

Tony Smith sets up a flexible trust with £400,000. Like most clients he has a full nil rate band but has used his annual exemption.

This is a chargeable lifetime transfer which Tony must report to HMRC.

The entry charge if the trustees pay is £400,000 – £285,000 = £115,000 x 20% = £23,000.

If Tony pays the tax, grossing up applies and it will be £115,000 x 25% = £28,750.

Let us assume the trustees pay so the effective rate is $\frac{£23,000}{£400,000}$ = 5.75%

Suppose after six years the trust is worth £450,000 and the trustees decide to distribute it all to the beneficiaries. The exit charge is based on the effective entry charge rate. So it is:

£450,000 x 30% x 5.75% x 24/40 = £4,657.50

However, if instead, the trustees keep the money in the trust until the 10th anniversary when it is worth £500,000 and the nil rate band is £400,000, there will be a periodic charge.

This will be £500,000 – £400,000 x 6% = £6,000

The effective rate is $\frac{6{,}000}{500{,}000}$ =1.2%

Suppose after 11 years the trust is worth £520,000 and the trustees decide to distribute it all to the beneficiaries. The exit charge is based on the last effective periodic charge rate and so is £520,000 x 1.2% x 4/40 = £624

3.2 Trusts and income tax

Trustees are subject to basic rate tax on trust income. If the income is paid over to a beneficiary this is then subject to income tax based on the rates of the recipient beneficiary. Thus, if the beneficiary had unused personal allowances in excess of any income from which tax has already been deducted (eg on bank interest), he could reclaim the tax. This is not possible for the tax credit on UK share and unit trust dividends. Beneficiaries who are higher rate taxpayers have to pay the excess over any tax already deducted or credited.

However, there are some special rules for trust income. If the settlor or the settlor's spouse has retained any interest in the trust, any trust income will be treated as the settlor's for tax purposes unless that income is paid to a charity. If the trust is for the benefit of a settlor's minor, unmarried child then income paid to the child is treated as the income of the settlor, although income of £100 or less is ignored for this purpose. Payments of capital to a child will also be treated as the income of the settlor for tax purposes to the extent that they can be matched against available undistributed income of the settlement. 'Child' includes a stepchild and an illegitimate child. A settlor can claim reimbursement from the trustees of any income tax he has had to pay in respect of a settlement.

Special rules exist for chargeable gains on life policies – see section 5.

3.2.1 Income of accumulation or discretionary trusts

If income of a trust is accumulated, or payable at the discretion of the trustees, a special trust rate of 40% is payable on all income above the first £1,000, which since 6 April 2006 has been only subject to basic rate. The introduction of the £1,000 basic rate band is intended to remove small trusts (one third of all income accumulating trusts according to HMRC) from the burden of accounting for small tax payments. (This tax treatment does not arise if the income is treated as the settlor's or where any beneficiary is entitled to that income.) This could mean that where the total income is less than £1,000 and includes a chargeable gain on a life policy it would eliminate any tax.

Expenses of running the trust are allowed as a deduction for the additional rate, but not the basic rate. Thus, if a trust receives rental income of £2,000 the basic rate tax payable will be £2,000 x 22% = £440. If expenses of £300 have been incurred, the additional rate tax after allowing for the £1,000 basic rate band will be £1,200 x 18% = £216. Any beneficiary receiving this income is deemed to have suffered tax at 40% which may well be reclaimable, depending on their other income. However, this must be covered by tax paid by the trust, which may negate the benefit of the £1,000 basic rate band.

For dividends from shares and unit trusts there is a 10% tax credit which the trustees can use against their trust tax rate, of 32.5% for dividends above the £1,000 basic rate threshold. For dividend income within the threshold, the tax credit would cover the liability. The trustees thus have to pay an extra 22.5% tax if their gross income exceeds £1,000. If the trustees then distribute the dividend to a beneficiary, the beneficiary can only get credit for the 22.5% tax paid by the trustees, and not the 10% tax credit on the original dividend.

3.2.2 Tax returns

If a trust has income or gains one of the trustees must do a tax return in the same way as an individual (see Chapter C). However a new trust with no income or gains does not need to be reported to HMRC, and existing trusts with no income or gains can request HMRC not to issue annual tax returns.

3.2.3 Capital sums out of trusts

If a trust pays capital sums to a settlor, he is chargeable to income tax on any amount up to the undistributed trust income. If the capital sum is in excess of this, the balance is carried forward to match against future undistributed income for the next 11 years. For this purpose a capital sum would include loans and loan repayments.

HMRC has sometimes tried to tax recurrent payments of capital as income in the hands of a trust beneficiary. However, this approach was rejected more recently by the Court of Appeal in *Stevenson v Wishart.*[7] The court held that where payments were made in exercise of a discretionary power over capital, the payments were not turned into income just because they were used for an income purpose. This contrasts with the earlier Brodie decision where capital payments were taxed as income, because the trustees were compelled by the trust wording to advance capital to bring income up to a set level.[8]

3.3 Trusts for the vulnerable

These are trusts for the disabled and trusts for minor children who have suffered the death of a parent (but only where the child has an unconditional entitlement at age 18). Trustees of these trusts can elect to be taxed on the beneficiary's individual circumstances for income tax and capital gains tax. The election must be made jointly with the beneficiary, or their parents/guardian where they are unable to elect on their own behalf. Thus the beneficiary would be able to use their own personal allowances and exemptions. Elections have to be made within one year of the 31 January after the end of the tax year concerned. This provision is in the Finance Act 2005, but back dated to 6 April 2004. This might be able to be used to eliminate or reduce tax on a chargeable gain on a life policy.

[7] *Stevenson v Wishart (1987) STC 226:*

[8] *Brodie's Will Trustees v Inland Revenue Commissioners (1933) 17T.C. 432*

4 Life Policies under Trust

A life policy can be put into trust in three ways:

- By effecting it at outset under one of the statutory trusts.
- By effecting it at outset under a non-statutory trust.
- By assigning an existing policy into a trust.

These will now be dealt with in turn.

4.1 The statutory trusts

The statutory trusts are the Married Women's Property Act 1882 (for England and Wales), the Married Women's Policies of Assurance (Scotland) Act 1880, and the Law Reform (Husband and Wife) Act (Northern Ireland) 1964.

4.1.1 The Married Women's Property Act (MWPA)

The Married Women's Property Act (commonly called MWPA) enables a person to effect a policy on his/her own life under trust from outset merely by expressing it to be for the benefit of his/her spouse and/or children. In other words, the policy itself creates the trust. The Act can only be used where the beneficiaries are restricted to a spouse, civil partner or children, although children includes illegitimate children[9] and adopted children[10], but not stepchildren. The policy has to be a life policy but cannot be a joint life policy as the Act refers to a policy 'on his own life' or 'on her own life'[11]. A joint life policy for the benefit of spouse or children has therefore to be effected under a non-statutory trust.

The procedure required to effect a policy under the Act is to submit a MWPA trust form (or form of request) to the life office at the same time as the proposal form. The form refers to a specific proposal and then names the beneficiaries and appoints the trustees. Normally trustees are given wide powers to deal with the policy and there is a trustee charging clause, in case a professional trustee is appointed.

With regard to trustees, there should always be a trustee additional to the life assured to ensure that there will be a trustee alive to claim the benefits from the life office when the life assured dies. The countersignatures of the trustees are probably not legally necessary, but in practice they are valuable to ensure that the trustees concur with their appointment. Problems could arise on a claim if a trustee was not aware of his appointment. Civil partners could be included as beneficiaries from 5 December 2005 – see Chapter H section 8.

MWPA trust wordings

There can be many variations of beneficiary wordings. Beneficiaries can be named or defined by description. The following are examples of possible wordings to show what can be achieved:

[9] Family Law Reform Act 1969; [10] Adoption Act 1958; [11] MWPA 1882 432

(a) On trust for my wife, Mrs Joanna Jones, absolutely.

(b) On trust for my wife absolutely.

(c) On trust for my wife, Mrs Joanna Jones, for life and thereafter for our children in equal shares absolutely.

(d) On trust for my children in equal shares absolutely.

(e) On trust for my children John Jones, Chris Jones and Fred Jones in equal shares absolutely.

(f) On trust for such of my children as attain age 21 in equal shares absolutely.

(g) On trust for such of my wife and children as the trustees may by deed, revocable or irrevocable, appoint and in default of appointment for the benefit of my wife Joanna absolutely.

If a wife is named – as in (a) – then her interest will continue even if she is later divorced from the life assured. The interest will also pass to her estate if she predeceases her husband[12]. However, if the wife is unnamed – as in (b) – then the beneficiary is the wife of the life assured at the time concerned[13]. This means that, if the life assured divorces his first wife and later remarries, the policy is automatically for the benefit of the second wife. Similarly if children are named, then any future children are excluded, but if they are left unnamed – as in (d) – then future children are automatically included.

The MWPA policy

When the policy is issued it will have a clause on the lines of: 'This policy is effected under the Married Women's Property Act 1882 on the trusts stated in the attached memorandum'. The full trust wording will then be set out on the memorandum attached to the policy.

Once this is done, the trust is fully created and the trustees possess the full legal interest without the need for further documentation.

MWPA trustees

Anyone of full age and capacity can be appointed a trustee. A common arrangement is for a husband to appoint himself and his wife as trustees. He can thereby retain some control over the policy during his lifetime but she, as the surviving trustee, can claim the proceeds on his death by producing the policy and proof of death. If no appointment is made at outset, the assured will be the trustee and on his death this duty passes to his legal personal representatives – although they will need a grant of representation to prove their title. New trustees can be appointed at any time and existing trustees can retire by means of the appropriate deeds as explained below.

[12] *Cousins v Sun Life Assurance Society (1933) 1 Ch.126;*
[13] *Re Collier (1930) 2 Ch.37*

4.1.2 The Scottish Act

The MWPA applies in England and Wales only. The Scottish equivalent is the Married Women's Policies of Assurance (Scotland) Act 1880, as amended by the Married Women's Policies of Assurance (Scotland) (Amendment) Act 1980. There is now no effective difference between the two acts. Civil partners could be included as beneficiaries from 5 December 2005.

4.1.3 The Northern Irish Act

The Northern Irish equivalent of the MWPA is the Law Reform (Husband and Wife) Act (Northern Ireland) 1964. The only real difference is that it is not limited to policies effected by a person on his/her own life – it can be used for a policy effected by a person on the life of his/her spouse or civil partner. In addition, the permitted class of beneficiaries extends to stepchildren and persons of whom the assured is a lawful guardian. Civil partners could be included as beneficiaries from 5 December 2005.

4.2 Non-statutory trusts

If a desired beneficiary is not within the class allowed by the MWPA or if the policy is a joint life one, a non-statutory trust will have to be used. Under the MWPA the policy itself creates the trust, but under a non-statutory trust the documentation must ensure that the trust is completely constituted.

Procedures will vary from office to office, but normally the proposer completes a trust form declaring that the policy is to be under trust and requesting that the office issue it to him as sole trustee.

The life office may incorporate the trust wording into the policy, possibly as an attachment. Once the policy has been issued, the assured can appoint further trustees by means of a Deed of Assignment or Appointment. This will usually be supplied by the life office.

Sometimes there may be a purported appointment of trustees, just by naming them in the trust form or on the policy. Unlike the statutory trusts, this is not fully effective since the additional trustees would not have acquired the legal title and, really, a proper deed of assignment or appointment is required.

Where a joint life, second death policy is being effected under trust it is advisable to appoint a third trustee, who is not a life assured, to make sure there will be a trustee alive when a death claim arises.

4.2.1 Scottish trusts

What has been said so far about trust law is the English law on the subject. Scottish law is somewhat different and, although most of the principles are similar, the Trustee Acts 1925 and 2000 do not apply, the legislation north of the border being the Trusts (Scotland) Acts 1921 and 1961. The Trustee Investments Act 1961 does, however, still apply to Scotland.

Some differences are merely in terminology – for instance, a settlor is called a truster, a life interest is a life rent and a life tenant is a life-renter. There is no maximum number of trustees. The truster has a general implied power to appoint new trustees. If any trustee becomes insane or is incapable of acting due to physical or mental disability or by continuous absence from the UK for six months or more, the remaining trustees can appoint a replacement by a deed of assumption. Scottish trusts can be terminated if all the beneficiaries are of full age and capacity and consent thereto – the authority being *E. Lindsay v Shaw* [1959] SLT (Notes)13.

If a resident of Scotland is effecting a trust policy, then a Scottish Court might say that Scottish law would apply to the trust, even if the life office is in England. For this reason some offices have special trust forms for Scotland.

If a trust is governed by Scottish law, then, in order for it to be valid, delivery – or some other overt act signifying irrevocability – is necessary. Delivery means that the trust property must be physically delivered to the trustees or beneficiaries with the intention of creating a trust. However, instead of delivery, the trust can be registered in the Books of Council and Session. An intimation to the beneficiaries is also deemed to be equivalent to delivery[14].

Thus, one of these acts is required for a non-statutory trust policy in Scotland. It is not required for statutory trust policies, because the Acts specifically enable fully valid trusts to be created.

4.3 Assignment into trust

An existing policy can be put under trust by the policyholder executing a trust deed. In this deed, the policyholder will assign the policy to trustees for the benefit of the intended beneficiaries.

Assignments into trust are not normally supplied by the life office and are usually drafted by a solicitor. Notice of the assignment should be given to the life office and the deed kept with the life policy, since it will be required when a claim is made.

The assignment will be a transfer of value for IHT purposes. This subject is dealt with in more detail in Chapter C.

4.4 Stamp duty

There is no longer any stamp duty on assignments or declarations of trusts of life policies – the stamp duty exemption wording is not therefore required (Finance Act 2003, s125).

4.5 Uses of trust policies

Virtually any type of life policy can be put under trust. Some of the most common reasons are as follows:

[14] *Clark's Trustees v Inland Revenue Commissioners (1972) S.L.T. 190*

- To protect one's family (see Chapter H).
- For school fees provision.
- For partnership protection (see Chapter I).
- For director's share protection (see Chapter J).
- For inheritance tax planning (see Chapter L).

4.6 Trust policies and bankruptcy

As was seen in Chapter B, if a policyholder becomes bankrupt he loses control over his policy, since it passes to the trustee-in-bankruptcy, to use for the benefit of the creditors. However, a policy written in trust is not the property of the bankrupt and so will probably not be affected by the bankruptcy. This fact makes trust policies especially popular for policyholders who are in business, as the protection can usually continue despite the bankruptcy.

A policy under the MWPA (or its Scottish or Northern Irish equivalent) is almost totally protected from a trustee-in-bankruptcy. The trustee cannot claim the policy even if it was effected with intent to defraud the creditors. The only claim a trustee-in-bankruptcy can make is for the premiums paid by the bankrupt, and only then if it can be proven that the policy was taken out with intent to defraud the creditors.

Protection is not so complete for non-statutory trusts or policies assigned into trust. If the settlor becomes bankrupt within five years of the trust the trustee-in-bankruptcy can apply to the court for an order restoring the position to what it would have been had the trust not been created. This in effect would set aside the trust and enable the creditors to receive the benefit of the policy.

However, if the trust was set up more than two years before bankruptcy, it cannot be attacked unless the bankrupt was insolvent at the time of the trust or became so because of it. The bankrupt will be presumed to be insolvent if the trust was for the benefit of a relative or business partner (as it normally will be).

4.7 Claims under trust policies

As the trustees are the legal owners of a trust policy, the life office must deal with them, not the beneficiaries, when any payments are being made. Trustees have an inherent right to claim the policy proceeds on death or maturity. With respect to any other dealing, the trustees should make sure that the trust wording does give them power to do what they are attempting to do.

Most trust wordings give the trustees wide powers, but if the trust wording is silent then trustees probably have power to surrender, convert to paid-up or borrow on the security of the policy under s15 of the Trustee Act 1925. Trustees also have a fundamental duty to protect the trust property and this will probably cover conversion to paid-up or borrowing to pay the premiums.

Any dealings the trustees make must be for the benefit of the beneficiaries. Any moneys claimed from the life office must be passed on to the beneficiaries, or invested for them if they are minors. Any options to convert the policy or effect further policies must be done in such a way that any converted or new policy is subject to the same trust.

When a claim is made by trustees of a life policy, the life office will require proof of their title. The documents of title would be:

- The policy.
- The Deed of Assignment or Appointment of trustees (unless the policy is under the MWPA).
- Any deeds of appointment of new trustees.
- Any deeds of retirement of trustees.
- The death certificates of any trustees who have died.

The signatures of all the trustees will be required on the form of discharge for the claim. Where trustees request payment to themselves or the beneficiaries, the life office can safely do this, but if they request payment to be made to an apparently unconnected third party, the life office should make some investigation before payment, to satisfy itself that no breach of trust is involved.

4.8 Dealings by beneficiaries

A beneficiary cannot claim against the life office because he does not have the legal interest. However, a beneficiary can deal with his beneficial interest under the trust and can assign or mortgage it (at least if he is over 18). Any person acquiring a beneficial interest under a trust policy from a beneficiary should notify the trustees. If all possible beneficiaries under a trust policy are over 18, and of full capacity, they can put an end to the trusts and surrender (or otherwise deal with) the policy under the rule in *Saunders v Vautier*[15].

5 Taxation of Life Policies under Trust

Basically, a trust involving a life policy is subject to the taxation implications explained earlier in Section 3. However, some special rules apply to life policies.

[15] *Saunders v Vautier (1841) 4 Beav. 115*

5.1 Income tax

Life policies do not normally produce income and so the income tax rules explained in Section 3 rarely apply. However, a chargeable event may occur on a life policy under trust and thus a chargeable gain can arise as described in Chapter D.

5.2 Trust policies

The rules for chargeable gains are as follows:

(a) If the individual who created the trust was both alive and UK resident immediately before the chargeable event, the gain is treated as part of that individual's income. He or she can recover any tax paid from the trustees. If a settlor chose not to do this, it would be a transfer of value for IHT as an omission to exercise a right under s3(3) IHTA.

(b) If the individual who created the trust was dead, or resident outside the UK, immediately before the chargeable event and one or more of the trustees are resident in the UK, the trustees are chargeable on the gain. The charge is at the rate applicable to trusts, which is 40%, resulting in a 20% liability for a UK policy, due to the 20% credit.

(c) If the trustees are not resident in the UK, any UK beneficiary receiving a benefit under the trust from the gain will be taxable on that amount at his or her tax rates, but without top-slicing relief.

The 20% tax charge payable under (b) above cannot be reclaimed by the beneficiaries of the trust, even if they are non-taxpayers or basic rate taxpayers in their own right. In these circumstances, it could be advantageous for the UK trustees to retire before a chargeable event, eg a surrender, and be replaced by foreign trustees, eg a Channel Islands or Isle of Man company. The foreign trustees could then cash in the policy, and under (c) above the gain would be taxable on the beneficiaries. This might have the effect of fragmenting the gain if there were multiple beneficiaries, and might well mean that there would be no tax if the beneficiaries were still not higher rate taxpayers. The switch of trustees might thus save 20% tax liability.

Alternatively, the trustees could assign the policy to a beneficiary, free of the trust, before a chargeable event occurred. The policy could then be cashed in by the ex-beneficiary (now assignee and full owner) and tax would be chargeable on him, rather than the settlor or the trustees. If he was well within the higher rate tax threshold this could eliminate any tax liability on a UK policy. He would also benefit from full top-slicing relief which would not be allowed if the policy were in trust and the gain were made by foreign trustees but taxable on the beneficiary under (c) above.
Originally, the rule was that if a policy was subject to a trust, the person chargeable was the individual who created the trust, although he could recover the tax from the trustees. If the creator of the trust had died in a tax year before the year of the gain, there was no-one on whom HMRC could tax the gain – the so-called 'dead settlor trick'. The dead settlor trick still works for policies effected before 17 March 1998, where the trust was also created prior to that date and the creator of the trust died

before then. For these cases, the dead settlor trick will still apply, as long as the policy was not varied on or after 17 March 1998 so as to increase the benefit or extend the term.

For chargeable events on or after 9 April 2003 where the trust is a charitable trust the charge is on the trust (not the settlor) and at the lower rate, leaving no tax to pay on a UK policy.

5.3 Inheritance tax

When a life policy is effected under trust, the settlor makes a transfer of value. The value of the transfer is normally the first premium payable. Thus, if a regular premium policy is effected under trust, the transfer will often be exempt under the £3,000 annual exemption. Further amounts could be claimed as exempt under the 'normal expenditure' exemption, although this will vary from settlor to settlor. HMRC may be reluctant to agree this in the first year of a trust policy since it will not have gained the requisite element of regularity. For details of this exemption, see Chapter C.

When further premiums are paid into the policy by the settlor, these count as further transfers of the amount of the premium on the basis explained above. Thus, policies with annual premiums of up to £3,000 (single) or £6,000 (joint) may involve no chargeable transfers at all. In addition, once a trust policy has been going for a few years it should be easier to claim the normal expenditure out of income exemption since regularity will have been established. You must be able to show that the premium payments are being made out of income, not capital, and do not adversely affect your standard of living.

If a single premium policy is effected under trust, then the single premium is the transfer. This will often be over £3,000 and thus may be chargeable to tax unless otherwise exempt. The normal expenditure exemption will not be available, but it is possible that some other exemption (eg the marriage exemption) could apply. Unless the trust is an absolute or disabled trust, the excess over the exemption(s) will be a chargeable transfer. The lifetime rates (only if over the nil-rate band) will be payable, although if the settlor dies within five years, the death rates will retrospectively apply and any excess will be payable then.

Where premiums are paid net of life assurance premium relief, the transfer of value is the net premium rather than the gross premium because the tax works on the 'loss to the estate' principle. This has been confirmed by an HMRC Statement of Practice. Thus, with life assurance premium relief at 12.5%, a gross annual premium of £3,428 can be exempt because this nets down to under £3,000.

Similarly if a grandparent pays £2,808 into the pension of a grandchild this is the value of the transfer not the grossed up equivalent of £3,600. There is no specific exemption for one person paying a pension contribution on behalf of another, unless it is an employer paying for an employee.

5.3.1 Tax on assignments under trust

If an existing policy is assigned under trust, this is a transfer of value by the settlor. A special valuation rule applies here[16]. The value is deemed to be not less than the total premiums paid (gross of any tax relief), less any sums previously paid out by way of part surrender. The market value, which is normally taken to be the surrender value, will apply if it is higher.

The special premium valuation does not apply to term assurances of three years or less, or where, if the term exceeds three years, premiums are payable for at least two-thirds of the term and the premiums payable in any one year are not more than twice those in any other year. In these cases, the market value applies and this would usually be negligible (unless HMRC knew the life assured was in very bad health).

The special valuation also does not apply fully to unit-linked policies where allowance is made for any drop in the value of units since allocation.

5.3.2 Related policies

In some cases, the transfer of a life policy has to be valued with reference to a related policy. One example is that of 'back-to-back' arrangements (Chapter L section 3.5) where s263 of IHTA 1984 applies.

Back-to-back arrangements are where an individual purchases an annuity on his own life and also a life policy on his own life under trust. Section 263 provides that, if a life policy is effected under trust on or after 27 March 1974 and at that time (or earlier or later) an annuity is purchased on the life of the life assured, then unless it can be shown that the arrangements were not associated a transfer of value occurs. The transfer of value is deemed to be the lesser of:

- The purchase price of the annuity plus the first premium on the life policy.
- The value of the greatest benefit capable of being conferred at any time by the life policy – ie the sum assured.

This section does not prevent back-to-back arrangements, but means that if they are to be successful it must be proved that the life policy and the annuity are not associated. Thus full evidence of health would have to be given for the life policy and each policy issued on normal terms for unrelated policies. This can be more easily proved if the contracts are effected with different life offices.

There is a further provision to the effect that the normal expenditure exemption cannot be used for life policy premiums if the donor has also effected an annuity on his own life, unless it can be shown that the annuity and the life policy were not associated[17].

Also, whenever the normal expenditure exemption is being used, the capital content of a purchased life annuity bought after November 1974 does not count as income[18],

[16] IHTA 1984 s167; [17] IHTA 1984 s21(2); [18] IHTA 1984 s21(3)

and neither do any withdrawals from single premium life policies as although they may be deemed income for income tax purposes they are capital under general law.

5.3.3 Death of life assured

When the life assured dies, and a claim arises under a trust policy, there is no charge to tax because it was not part of the deceased's estate. The beneficiaries will thus receive the money free of tax.

5.3.4 Death or change of beneficiary

If a beneficiary who has an interest in possession under a trust policy dies, the value of that interest is part of his estate for tax purposes. The policy is valued on the market value basis explained earlier, and the tax is based on the deceased beneficiary's rates, but is payable by the trustees out of the trust fund. The premium valuation basis does not apply to transfers on death.

If there is a change in the beneficial interest in possession for some other reason (ie the exercise of a power of appointment), this is deemed to be a chargeable lifetime transfer by the outgoing beneficiary. Tax would be based on the outgoing beneficiary rates, but payable by the trustees out of the trust fund.

For trusts other than absollute or disabled trusts created on or after 22 March these rules no longer apply.

5.3.5 Pension schemes

Any contributions an employer makes to a registered pension scheme for the benefit of employees or their dependants are exempt from IHT[19], as are any other payments that are allowable in calculating profits for income or corporation tax.

Many pension schemes have a death-in-service benefit written under a discretionary trust where the trustees have a discretion as to whom they pay. This discretion is normally exercised in favour of a person nominated by the member. Such death benefits are exempt from tax on the death of the member although the money must be distributed within two years of death[20]. Any other interest the deceased might have had is also exempt[21].

A similar provision applies to widow's or dependant's pensions under personal or stakeholder pensions or section 226 self-employed annuity contracts[22].

Thus, these are not subject to tax when the annuitant dies and the widow's/dependant's pension becomes payable. The placing of personal or stakeholder pension death benefits into trust can sometimes involve a potential tax charge and this is covered in Chapter P section 10.

Payments from registered pension schemes (including pensions term assurances) are not subject to the discretionary trust IHT regime, even for post-2006 Budget cases.

5.3.6 Pre-owned asset tax (POAT)

A life policy could be subject to a POAT charge – see Chapter C section 1.9.

[19] IHTA 1984 s12; [20] IHTA 1984 s86; [21] IHTA 1984 s151; [22] IHTA 1984 s152

5.3.7 The 2006 Budget and existing trust policies

The official HMRC Guidance Note that accompanied the Finance Bill stated the following:

"No-one who wrote a life insurance policy into trust before Budget Day will have to pay an IHT charge. All of these continue to be exempt from IHT as they were before the Budget. The Finance Bill and its Explanatory Note provide complete certainty that the new rules will not apply to life insurances policies entered into before Budget Day, even where the policyholder continues to make payments after the Budget under the original terms of the policy."

Originally there was no such explicit clause in the Bill, but the ABI persuaded the Government to put a clause in the Finance Act 2006. This means that the Budget changes do not apply to a pre-Budget life policy under a pre-Budget trust in respect of a pre-Budget interest in possession or change of beneficiary due to the death of a previous beneficiary. This applies even though premiums continue to be paid post-Budget. This protection even applies if the policy is altered to increase the benefits or extend the term, if it is as a result of rights under the contract that existed before the Budget. Thus if premiums were increased under an indexation option or guaranteed insurability option, the protection would still apply. However if the policy were increased post-Budget as a result of a non-contractual alteration, the protection would be lost.

5.3.8 Protection policies in flexible trusts and the 2006 Budget

The question has arisen as to how protection life policies (term assurance and 'real' whole life) under the standard flexible trust will be affected by the 2006 Budget changes. The answer is probably hardly at all. If such a policy was effected post the 2006 Budget, the situation would be as follows.

The gift is the premium(s) paid by the settlor. These are normally fully exempt under the £3,000 annual and/or normal expenditure from income exemptions. Thus there is no chargeable lifetime transfer at outset, so no report or entry charge. If the life assured dies in the first ten years, and the trustees claim the sum assured and pay it to the beneficiaries, that generates a theoretical exit charge. This is based on the entry charge, so if that was nil, the exit charge is nil even if the sum assured is over the nil rate band.

If on the tenth anniversary the life assured is still alive and in reasonable health, the value of the policy is its surrender value, probably nil or negligible. So the periodic charge is nil. If the life assured dies in the next ten years and the trustees claim the sum assured and pay it to the beneficiaries again, there is a theoretical exit charge. That is based on the last periodic charge, so if that was nil the exit charge is nil, even if the sum assured is over the nil rate band.

The only problem would be if at a tenth anniversary the life assured was dead (or in very bad health) and the trustees had not had time to claim the sum assured or had not yet paid it to the beneficiaries. Then if the sum assured was over the nil rate band the open market value of the trust at the tenth anniversary would be over the nil rate band and thus there would be a charge at 6% of the excess. This would also trigger an exit charge unless the sum assured was paid to the beneficiaries within the next three months.

This problem could occur if the life assured died a day or two before the tenth anniversary or the trustees did not want to pay out the money because of minor or irresponsible beneficiaries. There would be a special problem with family income benefit policies as the sum assured is a stream of monthly payments, rather than a lump sum. This might lead trustees to commute the instalments and pay the beneficiaries out as a lump sum before the next tenth anniversary.

H Family Protection

Probably the most important aspect of financial planning is to protect a person's dependants against the financial consequences of death or disability. This can sometimes be lost sight of in tax-planning operations, but it is of little use devising an extremely good tax mitigation plan if the effects of untimely death on the dependants are ignored.

Protection for a man's family was the original purpose of life assurance. In this area, unlike others such as investment, life assurance has no serious rivals. The object should be to arrange for enough insurance on the life of the breadwinner(s) to enable the dependants to cope financially. The ideal would be to provide an income to replace that provided by the breadwinner, in a manner as tax efficient as possible. This chapter explores ways in which this can be done.

1 State Benefits

The state provides a wide range of social security benefits designed to provide support and care for those in need and especially for those on low incomes. The benefits thus promote the social welfare of the whole country. In general terms, social security benefits are available to all residents of the UK. Advisers should have an awareness of benefits which an individual could obtain free from the state. Anyone who is eligible for a benefit should be encouraged to claim it, as it will probably have been paid for by National Insurance Contributions (NICs) during that person's working life. Advisers should also be aware that some benefits are 'means tested' which means that they are only available to those with incomes or savings below certain levels. This may affect investment advice.

1.1 Main benefits and current rates

This book cannot give all the details of all the benefits available. These can be obtained from any social security office and some Post Offices. However, the main benefits and current rates are as follows.

1.1.1 Basic state pension

See Chapter P section 1.

1.1.2 Income support

This is a weekly payment to anyone aged 16 or over whose income is below a certain level and who is not working 16 hours or more per week and not required to be available for work. The amount depends on age, income, savings and family circumstances. It is taxable for the unemployed.

1.1.3 Jobseekers' allowance

Jobseekers' allowance is available to those claimants who are unemployed and between 18 (16 in some cases) and the state pension age. All claimants must be available for and actively seeking work and sign a jobseeker's agreement setting out the steps being taken to obtain full-time work. Benefit will be stopped if the claimant breaks the terms of the agreement or declines to follow the directions of an employment adviser. The amount depends on age and family circumstances. The payment is taxable and requires either a satisfactory contribution record or a low income means test. There is also a capital means test.

1.1.4 Child benefit

This is a tax-free weekly payment for anyone responsible for a child under 16 (or under 19 if in full-time education). It is currently £17.45 for the eldest child (£17.55 for lone parents with protected rights) plus £11.70 for each other child.

1.1.5 Bereavement payment

This is a tax-free lump sum of £2,000 payable to one spouse or civil partner on the death of the other. It replaced the old Widow's payment from 9 April 2001. It is only payable if the deceased had made sufficient NI contributions or his or her death was caused by their job. It is also a requirement that either the recipient is under state pension age or the deceased was not entitled to a state pension at the date of death.

1.1.6 Widowed Parent's allowance

This is a taxable weekly benefit which replaced the old Widowed Mother's allowance. This is payable to one spouse or civil partner on the death of the other provided the deceased had made enough NI contributions (or his or her death was caused by their job) and the recipient has a child in respect of which child benefit is being paid. The allowance includes a basic payment of £84.25 per week plus an allowance for each dependent child and a possible additional State Second (S2P) pension.

1.1.7 Bereavement allowance

This is a taxable weekly benefit payable for 52 weeks for one spouse or civil partner after the other spouse or civil partner dies. It replaced Widow's pension and can only be claimed by someone aged 45 or over. The full rate is £84.25 per week for someone aged 55 or over but is reduced for those under 55.

1.1.8 Carer's allowance

This is a taxable weekly benefit for people of working age who are caring for a severely disabled person. It is currently £46.95.

1.1.9 Statutory Sick Pay (SSP)

Most people who work for an employer and are sick for at least four days in a row can obtain SSP from their employers for a maximum of 28 weeks in any spell of sickness. The amount is £70.05 per week if gross average earnings are £84 per week or more is taxable and paid by the employer in the same way as wages. Anyone still sick after 28 weeks can receive incapacity benefit.

1.1.10 Incapacity benefit

Where an individual is not entitled to SSP (eg a self-employed person), incapacity benefit is paid for up to 28 weeks at £59.20 per week (if under pension age) or £75.35 per week (if over pension age). After 28 weeks, those receiving SSP transfer to incapacity benefit. For all those still sick after 28 weeks incapacity benefit is payable at £70.05 per week (if under pension age) or £78.50 per week (if over pension age) for a further 24 weeks.

After 52 weeks, the benefit increases to £78.50 per week. The benefit is taxable. There is also a medical assessment carried out between the 28th and 52nd weeks to restrict benefit to those who are genuinely unable to do any reasonable occupation due to a medical reason.

On top of the basic benefit, there are adult dependancy and child dependancy allowances. The benefit is still payable even if an employer keeps on paying the individual's salary in full. The benefit is not paid if state pension is also being paid.

Those claimants receiving the pre-1995 sickness or invalidity benefit payments retain the tax-free status of that benefit.

1.1.11 Minimum income guarantee

This was replaced by the pension credit (see Chapter P section 1.4) in October 2003.

1.1.12 Industrial injuries disablement benefit

This is payable to those who become disabled as a result of an accident at work or an industrial disease. The amount depends on the degree of disability.

1.1.13 Other benefits

The following benefits are also available:

- Housing benefit
- The social fund
  - Maternity payment
  - Funeral payment
  - Cold weather payment
  - Community care grant
  - Budgeting loan
  - Crisis loan
- Free milk (disabled children only)
- Statutory maternity pay
- Maternity allowance
- Guardian's allowance
- Attendance allowance
- Disability living allowance
- Reduced earnings allowance
- Retirement allowance
- Vaccine damage payments
- War Pensions

- Free NHS prescriptions and treatment
- Christmas bonus
- Winter allowance
- Free TV licence (over-75s)

1.1.14 Tax credits

There are also two tax credits, which look like social security benefits but are actually tax credits, from Her Majesty's Revenue and Customs (HMRC) – see Chapter C section 1.5.

1.2 Estimating needs

The amount of life cover needed will vary from person to person. An estimate should be made of how much the family would require to meet the expenses of continuing their present standard of living if the breadwinner were to die. For a spouse, protection might have to last for the rest of his or her life. For children, protection may only be required until they are old enough to be financially independent, say age 18 or 21.

Estimates could be made of what expenses might require lump sum payments (eg paying off debts) and what might require continuing payments (eg general living expenses).

The income needs can be met from either:

- A policy that would provide a lump sum that could be invested to generate an income; or
- A policy where the sum assured is expressed as an 'income' over a fixed number of years (such as family income benefits (FIB) – see below). The FIB approach is particularly suitable where the income is only required on a temporary and foreseeable basis, eg while there are dependent children.

A lump sum may be more appropriate if the cover is required to provide a long-term income for an indefinite period. The capital needs should be provided from lump sum benefit policies.

It is then necessary to calculate the lump sum needed to generate the income required. Annuity rates based on the potential beneficiary's age should provide a good basic indication for long-term income needs. For example, if the annuity rate were £80 per £1,000, the capital needed to generate £10,000 of income over the beneficiary's lifetime would be

$$\frac{£1{,}000}{80} \times 10{,}000 = £125{,}000.$$

When a rough estimate has been made of the amount required, any current entitlements should be ascertained. They could consist of existing life policies, cover under a pension scheme and state benefits. If the current entitlements would not provide the amount required, then more cover should be arranged up to the desired sum.

2 Appropriate Policies

The types of policy most often used for family protection are term assurances, family income benefit policies and whole life assurances. Other aspects to be considered are index-linking, expandability, increasability and pension cover. These will now be dealt with in turn.

2.1 Term assurance

Term assurance is the cheapest form of life cover because the sum assured is only paid out if death occurs before the expiry date. It is 'pure' protection cover with no frills, and as such is suitable for, say, a newly married couple or anyone else where cost is the prime factor.

Quite high levels of cover can be obtained for a comparatively small premium.

The term of the policy should ideally be to the normal retirement date when some form of pension should commence. But if the protection is mainly intended for children, it need only run until the youngest will complete full-time education and gain financial independence.

A number of offices offer a waiver of premium benefit. This is valuable as it protects against the client being unable to pay the premiums due to illness or accident reducing his income.

2.2 Convertible term assurance

Convertible term assurance, as explained in Chapter A, is term assurance with an option to convert to whole life or endowment assurance for up to the same sum assured at any time before the expiry date. This costs more than ordinary term assurance but it does give the right to extend the cover for the duration of one's life, by converting it to a whole life assurance. This can be done at any time prior to the expiry date, but the earlier it is done the lower the revised premiums will be – although of course they will be payable for a longer period. Many convertible term policies are effected to expire at age 60 or 65 and then converted to whole life assurances shortly before the expiry date if protection is still desired.

Alternatively, the policy can be converted to an endowment to use as a savings plan, although this will require a minimum term of ten years from the date of conversion for qualification reasons.

2.3 Family income benefit policies

So far, the policies discussed would pay a lump sum benefit on death. However, often the dependants will require income after the breadwinner's death. This could be provided by investing the lump sum, but then the income would be subject to income tax. There is also the possibility of seeing the capital value of the investment decline as a result of unwise or unfortunate investment, plus the difficulty of the dependent relatives having to actually arrange the investment at a time of bereavement.
A better solution might be a family income policy. On death, this contract pays regular instalments of capital for the balance of the term of the policy. Thus, if the life assured under a 30-year family income policy died after ten years, the instalments would be payable for 20 years. The instalments can be monthly or less frequently. Because they are instalments of capital, no income tax is payable.

Policies are usually written to normal retirement date to protect a spouse, or to the expected completion of full-time education in the case of children.

2.4 Whole life assurances

These policies are more expensive than the three types previously mentioned because cover is permanent – it lasts through life.

Unit-linked whole life policies are very popular for family protection. Because these policies are so flexible, they can be adapted to meet changing family circumstances. At outset the policy could be effected on a 'maximum cover' basis with all the premium going towards the life cover. The policy is at that stage effectively akin to a term assurance. Later on, as finances improve, the mix between cover and investment can be varied as desired. In later life, the policy could be on a 'minimum cover' basis with virtually all the premium going towards the investment into units. For these reasons, unit-linked whole life policies substantially outsell all other varieties of whole life assurance.

2.5 Expandability and index-linking

Any policy with a fixed sum assured will see the real value of the cover it provides decrease as long as inflation continues. The higher the rate of inflation, the greater the drop in the real value of the cover. Thus, family protection cover should be reviewed at least once every three years to see whether it is still adequate. Fresh cover may be required to increase total cover to the same level in real terms, although the premium may have to reflect increased age and/or worsening health.

One way to offset the effects of inflation is to use a policy with an expanding sum assured. As explained in Chapter A, it is possible to purchase term assurance (convertible or level) and family income benefit policies where the sum assured expands at a fixed rate. These cost more than level policies for the same initial amount but maintain their real value better. Nevertheless, it is most unlikely that the fixed rate expansion will exactly match the rate of inflation and thus it is still possible for the real value of the policy to be eroded.

Ideally, term policies should be index-linked to match inflation and a number of offices have an indexation option.

Most offices offering unit-linked whole life assurances have some form of index-linking option for the life cover element.

2.6 Increasability

Many offices offer 'increasability' or 'increasing cover' options. These are options to increase the cover at specified times, up to a specified maximum, without evidence of health. Details vary from office to office but are commonly exercisable on marriage, birth of a child or increase to a mortgage. These can be of assistance in keeping up the real value of the total cover.

2.7 Universal life plans

Universal life plans can be used for family protection. These plans are basically unit-linked whole life policies (described in Chapter A section 4) but with a whole range of bolt-on extras for total flexibility. The idea is that the policyholder pays in what he likes, when he likes and chooses from a whole range of benefits. All premiums paid are applied to purchase units in the selected fund(s) and each month the cost of whatever benefits currently apply is paid by cancelling the relevant number of units.

The range of benefits available usually includes the following:

- Death benefit.
- Annual indexation option to automatically adjust the death benefit (and possibly other benefits) in line with the Retail Price Index (RPI).
- Guaranteed insurability options.
- Waiver of premium benefit during disability.
- Regular 'income' option.
- Facility to suspend premium payments, eg during unemployment.
- Income protection benefits.
- Sum assured payable on disability.
- Hospital income benefits.
- Accidental death benefits.
- Option to add a further life assured, eg on marriage.

- Critical illness cover.
- Terminal illness cover.

Benefits can often be added later as well as chosen at outset.

Because of the range of benefits offered the policies cannot meet the qualifying rules and are thus non-qualifying. However, this does give the policyholder great flexibility with respect to payment of premiums. Most contracts provide for a regular premium, usually monthly, which can be increased or reduced as required, and also allow single premiums to be paid in whenever desired.

Because the policies are non-qualifying, the payments are not tax-free as they would be on a qualifying policy. The income protection, hospital income benefits and critical illness payments are all free of tax. The other benefits are free of basic rate income tax but subject to higher rate tax under the chargeable gains rules – see Chapter D. Thus, for most policyholders there will be no tax to pay as most people will not be in the higher rate tax bracket. Under the 'income' option the normal 5% rules would apply and on the death benefit only the surrender value immediately before death (minus premiums) would be taxable. It is probable, especially in early years or where maximum cover is selected, that the surrender value will be far less than the sum assured and the tax will be zero (because the surrender value is less than total premiums paid) or minimal.

2.8 Pension scheme cover

For anyone who is a member of a pension scheme, the possibility of arranging family protection cover within the scheme should not be ignored. Many schemes provide a death-in-service benefit. This can be arranged on a discretionary trust basis so that it will be free of inheritance tax (IHT) on the member's death. The normal procedure is for the member to complete an 'expression of wish' form telling the trustees who he or she would like them to pay. The trustees would normally comply with these wishes but because of their discretion do not legally have to do so.

Many schemes provide for a widow's pension if death occurs before retirement. This would be payable to her for life and would be taxed as earned income. Protection after retirement can be obtained by arranging for the member's pension to be on a joint life last survivor basis with his wife. Thus, if the husband dies first the pension will continue for the life of the survivor. Again, the pension would be taxed as earned income.

Any amount paid by the member into a registered pension scheme will rank for full tax relief and so can effectively cost less than providing it independently where no tax relief is available. Any contributions by the employer also gain full tax relief as a business expense.

2.9 Personal pension cover

For anyone who is eligible (see Chapter O), the possibility of arranging family protection cover under a personal pension scheme should be investigated. This is because premiums gain full tax relief up to the statutory limits, in contrast to none at all on ordinary life assurance.

Under a personal pension, an eligible person can effect a term assurance or a family income benefit up to age 75. This can be effected under trust just like an ordinary policy. The legislation also allows an individual to effect a spouse's or dependant's pension contract whereby the pension will commence on the death of the life assured and continue for the life of the pensioner. The pension is taxed as earned income. The maximum life cover is governed by the annual and lifetime allowances – see Chapter O. In all cases, the life cover premium counts towards the overall maximum for all pension arrangements.

It is also possible for the death benefit of the individual's own personal pension policy to be put into trust for their family. All modern pension contracts provide a return of fund on death before retirement and this can be a handy lump sum if the policy has been running for some years.

3 Arranging the Policy

When arranging family protection assurance, consideration must be given to the way in which the policies are to be written. If a policy is an 'own-life' contract (where the assured is also the life assured), then it will form part of the estate when the assured dies. This has two disadvantages. First, the sum assured is potentially subject to IHT (see Chapter C). Second, the life office cannot make payment until the legal personal representatives can produce their grant of representation in proof of title. Payment could thus be delayed for some months. There is also the point that unless the life assured has made a will, the proceeds of the policy would be distributed according to the law of intestacy and thus might not pass to the desired dependants.

This is particularly so in the case of a family income benefits policy if it becomes part of a life interest under the law of intestacy. This was illustrated in the case of *Re Fisher, Harris v Fisher*[1], where the deceased had a family income policy on his own life and died intestate. A life interest then arose and it was held that the legal personal representatives had to commute future instalments and invest the cash sum for the beneficiaries. This effectively defeated the whole purpose of the policy.

For these reasons consideration should be given to arranging policies on a 'life of another' basis or under trust.

3.1 Life of another policies

Under a life of another policy, the assured is someone other than the life assured. Because the policy belongs to the assured, it is not part of the life assured's estate on death. The proceeds are thus not subject to IHT and can be claimed simply and

[1] *Re Fisher, Harris v Fisher (1943) 2 A.E.R 615*

swiftly by the assured producing the policy and proof of death. For this reason, many family protection policies are written with the life assured's spouse as the assured – and any premiums paid by the life assured are exempt from IHT.

However, there is a disadvantage in that the life assured has no control over the policy as the other spouse is the full legal owner. Thus, if the marriage were to break down, the assured would keep the policy. The life assured can do nothing about this, except stop paying premiums. If the life assured wishes to maintain a greater degree of control the policy could be effected under trust.

If the policy was designed to protect dependants other than a spouse, then in theory they could be the assureds. This is rarely the case in practice, however, as there are usually a number of dependants, some of whom may well be minors. In these cases a trust policy is the answer.

3.2 Trust policies

Many family protection policies are effected under trust. This has the following advantages:

- The policy is not part of the life assured's estate and thus is not subject to inheritance tax on death. Premiums will be transfers of value for IHT purposes but they will normally be exempt under the annual exemption (see Chapter C).
- The life assured can maintain some degree of control during his lifetime by being a trustee. Further control can be exercised by careful selection of the other trustee(s).
- Payment on death is quick and easy because the life office just pays the surviving trustee(s) on proof of death and production of the policy. There is no need to wait for a grant of representation because the sum assured is not part of the life assured's estate.
- The range of possible trust wordings allows the life assured's exact wishes to be carried out. The proceeds will be paid out exactly in the manner specified in the trust.
- A considerable degree of flexibility can be obtained by using power of appointment or discretionary trusts.
- The policy is in some degree protected against any claims from the life assured's creditors, especially if it is under the Married Woman's Property Act (MWPA) (see Chapter G section 4.1.1).

It is thus common for policies to be effected under trust for the intended beneficiaries, with the life assured and spouse as trustees. The surviving spouse will be able to claim the proceeds very easily on death and pay them out in accordance with the trust wording.

If the intended beneficiaries are all within the permitted class, then the MWPA should be used because of its great simplicity and protection from creditors. However, if greater flexibility of beneficiaries is desired, or it is a joint life policy, a non-statutory trust will have to be used.

Whatever trust wording is used, it should be scrutinised to make sure it does accord with the settlor's wishes as it cannot subsequently be changed. It should also be ensured that the wording includes wide powers of dealing for the trustees, as well as a trustee-charging clause, in case it is desired to appoint a professional or corporate trustee at any time. The effect of the 2006 Budget has been dealt with in Chapter G sections 5.3.7 and 5.3.8.

3.3 Joint life policies

In many families nowadays both spouses contribute to the family budget. Thus, death of either a husband or a wife could bring financial problems. Even if a wife is at home looking after the house and children, her death would bring problems. If she were to die, her husband would have to arrange for the children to be looked after and might even have to move to a part-time or less demanding – and therefore lower-paid – job so that he could do this himself.

Because of this, joint life protection policies have become popular. The policy should be on the joint lives of husband and wife, and would pay out to the survivor on the death of the first to die. As long as the couple are legally married there are no IHT implications.

The cost of a joint life policy may not be much more than the cost of an equivalent single life policy.

Instead of one joint life policy there could be two single life policies, each on the life of one spouse, with the assured as the other spouse. This will cost more than a joint life policy but gives more cover – since after the first death one policy will still remain in the estate of the deceased. The value will usually be negligible for IHT purposes but it can be continued by the surviving spouse who will probably inherit it under the will or the law of intestacy.

Most joint life policies simply have the spouses as the assureds, but it is possible for a joint life policy to be effected under a non-statutory trust if required.

4 Income Protection

So far, we have mostly considered life cover. However, long-term disability due to sickness or accident will also bring financial hardship to a person's family. Thus, income protection should not be ignored. This subject is discussed in detail in section 6 but a few points need to be made here.

The object of the policy is to provide an income while the breadwinner is unable to work due to illness or injury. Thus, the first step is to decide what level of cover the family will need to continue living at the same standard. This may be affected by whatever benefits might be paid by an employer or under a pension scheme, which could possibly provide an acceptable level of income for some while. The benefits provided by the state should also be taken into account. These factors may also limit the payment made by the life office.

Then the deferred period should be selected. This will again depend on the insured's own circumstances. Maybe his employer will continue to provide full pay for the first six months, in which case this should be the deferred period. An insured who was self-employed might need a much shorter deferred period, unless his income was going to continue for some time even if he had to stop work – eg an insurance salesman who has new business commission 'in the pipeline' or large amounts of renewal commission. It should be remembered that the longer the deferred period, the cheaper the cover will be.

The expiry date should be the insured's expected retirement date as the policy is designed to cover his earned income and should thus continue for the whole of his working life.

Selecting the right life office is not as easy as it is with term assurance, because different life offices have varying attitudes to certain types of occupation. For example, many offices are not too enthusiastic to insure salesmen if a very large proportion of their total earnings is made up of commission. Also, exclusions vary from office to office and it is important to check that none of these will adversely affect a particular insured.

5 Divorce

When divorce occurs, this should entail a review of the family protection cover. This is because of the effect it has on existing policies and on the need for cover.

Under the divorce laws, the court can in effect make any order it thinks fit regarding the future ownership of any of the parties' property. An existing life policy can thus be affected by such a court order. If a court orders one party to transfer a policy to the other, or to continue to maintain a policy for the other's benefit, then the policyholder must comply. Notice of any transfer of ownership should be given to the life office. The court can even vary the terms of an existing trust policy[2]. If it does, again this must be complied with and the trustees and the life office notified.

If the court makes no order as to any existing policy, then it will continue as before. Divorce does not of itself destroy the interest of any named person. Thus, if a spouse is an assured, a life assured, a trustee or a beneficiary, this will continue. Practical problems may arise, particularly if ex-spouses lose touch with each other or if there is a degree of ill-will involved. Joint life policies are a particular problem and it will normally be best if some amicable agreement is reached at the time of the divorce. It is often the case that one of the spouses will assign his or her interest in the policy to the other. This might be caught by the part-withdrawal chargeable gains rules – which apply to assignments of part of the policy. Ideally any assignment should be done while

[2] Matrimonial Proceedings and Property Act 1970 s27

the couple are still married and living together. This is because HMRC's view is that an assignment made as part of a divorce settlement (unless it is by virtue of a court order) is for money's worth and thus could be a chargeable event. See Chapter D section 2.1 for further details.

If a spouse is an unnamed beneficiary, then the situation changes. For example, if a policy is on trust for 'my wife absolutely' then divorce will destroy the interest of the original beneficiary as she no longer meets that description[3]. The policy would revert to the estate of the life assured until he remarried, in which case it would be for the benefit of the second wife[4].

When considering joint life or life of another policies it should be noted that if a policy was eligible for life assurance premium relief, this will not be destroyed by a subsequent divorce, if the divorce is after 6 April 1979[5].

The effects of the divorce may mean that some existing policies are no longer required. Thus, unless one party wishes to maintain the cover, the policies can be cancelled and any surrender value claimed.

Alternatively, there may be some need for fresh cover. For example, the court may order the husband to pay a certain amount of alimony to his ex-wife. This will only continue for his lifetime and thus she may wish to protect her interest by insuring his life for an appropriate sum. The court order is legally binding, which gives her an insurable interest she might not otherwise have as she is no longer his wife. The policy should ideally be a whole life assurance, although this may be too costly and a term assurance may be all that can be afforded. This should last at least until the youngest child finishes full-time education. CIC or income protection could be considered to cover the risk of the ex-husband being unable to keep up payments due to disability.

Divorce may well affect rights under a pension scheme, since many provide benefits for 'the spouse' of a member. After a divorce, an ex-wife would lose these potential benefits because she no longer meets that description. For details of pensions and divorce see Chapter P section 13.

6 Long-Term Care

Long-term care products are dealt with specifically in Chapter E, but a few further points need to be made here.

If an individual needs to enter a residential care home, due to illness or old age, nursing care is free as part of the NHS but non nursing costs such as food and accommodation must be paid for.[6] Non nursing costs can in some cases be paid by the local authority, subject to means testing. The costs will not be met if capital or income exceeds certain limits, as individuals will be expected in these cases to use these assets to pay the costs themselves.

[3] Re Collier (1930) A.E.R 447;
[4] Re Browne's Policy, Browne v Browne (1903) 1 Ch. 188;
[5] Taxes Act 1988 Sch 14 para 1; [6] Health and Social Care Act 2001

The current limits mean that those with capital over £21,000 must pay for their own care. Those with capital below £12,750 can have all their costs paid by the local authority up to the standard rate for the area if they have insufficient income. Those with capital between £12,750 and £21,000 or sufficient income have to make some contribution from their own resources. They will be assumed to have income of £1 per week for each £250 in excess of £12,500 and this will be added to the real income to determine the ability to meet the standard rate of homecare fees, with the local authority making up any balance. When assessing this amount the value of a person's house is taken into account but only after the first three months. The local authority can register a charge against the house, but cannot force a sale. The charge would be paid out from the subsequent sale proceeds. The house is disregarded if a spouse, a relative over 60, a child under 16 or a disabled relative is living there. The regime in Scotland is different, providing £145 per week for personal care and £65 per week for nursing care. The £21,000 figure applies only to England and Northern Ireland, it being £19,500 for Scotland and £21,000 for Wales. Similarly the lower figures are £12,000 for Scotland and £14,750 for Wales.

The surrender value of a life policy can be disregarded for the capital test under paragraph 13 of Schedule 4 of the National Assistance (Assessment of Resources) Regulations 1992. A test case (CIS7330/95) has held that a claimant with an investment bond should have that bond disregarded in the capital test because it is technically a life policy. However that would not apply to any proceeds taken from the policy, as they become cash and so lose the protection of the regulations. This treatment has been confirmed in the Charging for Residential Accommodation Guide. This is a guide for local authority assessors when deciding which assets to take account of for the means test. However, if a bond was effected immediately before the claim was made, the deliberate deprivation rule (see below) could be applied.

The question sometimes comes up as to whether an individual can avoid losing this benefit under the means test by assigning, or putting into trust, an investment that might otherwise cause the test to be failed. In principle, the answer is no because local authorities can take account of assets if they believe the person has disposed of them deliberately to avoid them being taken into account. Thus, assigning an investment just before claiming is unlikely to succeed. This is known as the deliberate deprivation rule. However, an investment *bona fide* put into trust years ago would be unlikely to be taken into account. Any asset given away before residential care was even contemplated, or demonstrably for another *bona fide* purpose will almost certainly not be caught. Putting an investment in trust but retaining some benefit in it is also unlikely to succeed, and will be a gift with reservation for IHT purposes anyway.
In practice, the answer may depend on the degree of strictness and determination shown by the local authority. The case of *Yule v South Lanarkshire Council* showed that there is no time limit after which a disposal cannot be taken into account. However the case of *Beeson v Dorset* C.C. held that the local authority must show some subjective evidence of the person's motives to decide there had been deliberate deprivation.

7 Personal Injury Awards

There has been considerable interest lately in personal injury trusts, where a claimant has received compensation for some personal injury but still wishes to receive means tested state benefits. Normally means tested benefits are stopped once a claimant's capital assets exceed £8,000.

However if the compensation is paid into a trust the value of the trust, and the claimant's right under it, are disregarded for the capital means test if the funds of the trust are derived from a payment in consequence of any personal injury to the claimant – Income Support (General) Regulations 1987 46(2). The trust can be created by anyone including the claimant and any type of trust can be used. However if the claimant has a right to income then that income would be taken into account for the income means test. Thus a discretionary trust might be preferable, or the trust could invest in a single premium bond (which is a non-income producing asset) as long as it had power to advance capital. However when payments are received by the claimant from the trust, they become cash and lose the protection of the regulations. However trustees might be able to ensure that only enough income or capital was distributed to take the claimant up to the limit, or used to purchase a possession such as a house or a car.

The trust can be created at any time, even after the compensation has been received as long as the compensation has not been mixed with the client's other assets.

8 The Civil Partnership Act 2004

This came into force on 5 December 2005. A civil partnership is a relationship between two people of the same sex (civil partners) which has been registered under the Act. It is a quasi-marriage relationship and like marriage ends on death, dissolution or annulment. Parental consent is required for any party under 18.

A person is not eligible to be a civil partner if they are:

- Not of the same sex as the other partner.
- Already a civil partner or lawfully married.
- Under 16.
- Within prohibited degrees of relationship, eg close relatives.

The Registrar of Births, Deaths and Marriages issues a civil partnership schedule as evidence of the registration. A court can then dissolve the partnership on the grounds that it has broken down irretrievably (like a divorce). Courts can then make orders regarding property of the civil partners, again like a divorce.

A will is revoked by a subsequent civil partnership, unless done in anticipation of it or if the contrary is expressed in it. A gift in a will to a civil partner is revoked by the partnership's dissolution.

The civil partner will be treated as a spouse for:

- Wills and intestacy.
- Parental responsibility.
- Employment discrimination.
- Housing law.
- Insurable interest.
- Most social security benefits.
- Tax credits.
- Pension sharing.

The Act also extended the beneficiaries of the MWPA, and its Scottish and Northern Irish equivalents, to civil partners as well as spouses and children.

The Act made no other taxation provisions, although various sets of regulations made under the Finance Act 2005 have extended virtually all the spouse exemptions and other provisions of the tax regime to civil partners. These are mentioned in the appropriate places in this work.

I Partnership Protection

1 Partnership Protection Plans

2 Personal Pension Policies

3 Retirement

4 Limited Liability Partnerships

5 Pre-Owned Asset Tax (POAT)

6 The 2006 Budget

A partnership is defined as 'the relationship which exists between persons carrying on business in common with a view of profit, other than by way of membership of a body corporate[1]'. It is thus the carrying on of a business by two or more individuals without using a company. It could be a professional partnership (eg solicitors), a trading concern (eg a shop) or a more physical business (eg plumbers). There is no longer any limit on the number of partners a partnership may have.

Each partner owns a share of the capital and goodwill of the partnership and takes a share of the profits. In the absence of any agreement to the contrary, a partnership is automatically dissolved on the death of a partner[2].

When a partner dies, the partnership is dissolved and ownership of the deceased partner's share passes to his estate. The estate will usually be his widow and/or children. They may not understand the business, nor be able to contribute to it. Indeed, they may wish to withdraw their share of the capital. If they do not, part of their financial future will be provided by the profits of a business over which they have no effective control.

As far as the surviving partners are concerned, they may now have to continue the business with a sleeping partner who makes no contribution to the earning capacity of the business, but who will take a share of the profits.

Thus, it is in the interest of all parties for the surviving partners to buy out the estate's share. The deceased's family will receive a cash settlement with

[1] Partnership Act 1870 s1; [2] Partnership Act 1890 s33

which to provide for its financial future, and the surviving partners are able to keep full control and continue the business. This can best be achieved if there is a proper agreement in force with a way of providing the right amount of cash in the right hands at the right time.

Ideally, all partnerships should have a written agreement to provide a framework for the business and to help avoid disputes. A part of the agreement should cover what will happen on the death of a partner and give the surviving partners legal rights to buy his or her share. It should also set out an agreed basis for valuing the share.

However, having the right to buy the share of a deceased partner is of little use if there is no ready cash available to exercise this right; it is often the case that the surviving partners have no capital resources other than those already tied up in the business. Life assurance is thus a necessity to provide cash on the death of a partner for a modest cost to enable the business to continue. This chapter looks at the different types of partnership protection plans available and goes on to examine problems which have to be faced at retirement.

1 Partnership Protection Plans

Because life assurance is a vital part of partnership protection, many life offices offer partnership protection plans for use with their policies. Details vary from office to office, but there are basically three types of plan:

- Cross option.
- Automatic accrual.
- Buy and sell.

These will now be dealt with in turn but the following points should be considered before any plan is taken out:

- Does it give rights for all parties to carry out the scheme?
- Does it put the right amount of money in the right hands at the right time?
- Does it give any tax relief on the premiums?
- Does it ensure there will be no income tax on the proceeds?
- Does it avoid any inheritance tax (IHT) liability?
- Is the cost distributed fairly among the parties?

1.1 The cross-option method

This method, sometimes called the double option method, consists of an option agreement between the partners backed up by policies under trust. The surviving partners have an option to require the deceased partner's estate to sell and the estate has a corresponding option to require the surviving partners to buy, within a specified period from the death. If either party exercises the option, the other party must comply. The period during which the option can be exercised would be, say, three months.

The surviving partners will buy the deceased partner's interest in the proportions to which they are already entitled on the balance of the partnership. Thus, if there are four partners each with a 25% share in the business, then on the first death the survivors would each buy one-third of the deceased's share, so that the same ratio would be maintained between the survivors.

Because the parties only have options to buy and sell, the agreement is not a binding contract for sale and thus the share of a deceased partner will still be able to obtain business property relief for IHT.

The agreement will specify that each partner must effect and maintain a life policy to provide the sum required to purchase his share, and will provide for the valuation of that share on death. The policy will usually be under a special cross-option trust, with other partners also being trustees.

While double options are generally used for life cover, they are less appropriate for critical illness cover (CIC). A partner who is eligible to make a claim under a critical illness policy may not wish to sell his business interest because:

- His health is such that he can expect to continue working, eg after a mild heart attack.

- He does not want to be faced with a large capital gains tax (CGT) bill on selling his interest in the business.

- He does not want to convert a 100% IHT relievable asset into unrelievable cash.

To overcome these problems it is common to use a single option agreement alongside CIC, giving the critically ill partner the option to sell (a put option), but not providing his fellow partners with the option to buy (a call option). The option agreement can therefore become a long document, with different clauses applying on death or a claim under a critical illness policy.

A single option agreement for CIC may not always be advisable, because a partner who thinks he can recover from his illness may not actually be able to do so. If he cannot recover fully, he may not be able to pull his weight in the business, and his partners may wish to be able to force him to go. A double option agreement with different option periods could therefore be the most appropriate approach. The ailing partner could have an option to force a buy-out in the three or six months following diagnosis of the illness. The other partners could have an option to force a buy-out but only exercisable after a suitable period has elapsed since diagnosis (eg one or two years); by that time the final situation should have clarified so as to enable a sensible decision to be made.

When a partner dies or becomes the subject of a critical illness claim, the trustees will claim the money from the life office and pay the proceeds to the surviving partners. They will then use that money to buy out the share of the deceased or ill partner.

Specimen agreements are usually offered by life offices on the basis that they are suggested drafts for use by the partnership's solicitors, because they will have to be consistent with any existing partnership agreements.

The trust used is often a flexible power of appointment trust. It used to be suggested that alongside his fellow partners, the settlor was nominated as a potential beneficiary in case he ever needed to recover the policy. This could happen if for example the partnership broke up or went out of business before policy expiry for any reason. If that happened, then each partner could be appointed the sole beneficiary of the policy on his life. The policies could then be continued and used for any other purpose, with the other partners retiring as trustees.

Normally, putting the settlor in the trust would make the transaction a gift with reservation, but that would not apply in this case as the whole arrangement would be a *bona fide* commercial arrangement. Partner X is only putting his policy in trust for Y and Z because they are putting theirs in trust for him as part of a commercial arrangement. There is no donative intent. Thus, as it is not a gift, it cannot be a gift with reservation. However, the rules for pre-owned assets tax (POAT – see section 5) now mean that to name the settlor as a potential beneficiary could mean a tax liability arises in certain limited circumstances. In any event a partner's spouse and family should not be included as potential beneficiaries, because this would create a gift with reservation by destroying the commerciality of the arrangement.

Any new partners joining the firm are normally automatically included as beneficiaries of the existing policies. Any new partner would, of course, have to sign a supplemental agreement and effect and maintain a policy on his own life under trust for the existing partners. Possible future changes in the name of the business can be coped with by the use of the words 'and their successors in business'.

The sum assured under each policy should be the amount required to meet the value of the life assured's share of the partnership on death.

The life policy used should be a term assurance to the expected retirement date of the partner. When a partner dies, the trustees will claim the money from the life office and pay it out proportionately to each surviving partner to enable him to purchase his part of the deceased's share from the estate, under the option in the agreement.

1.1.1 Illustration of cost

The following is an illustration of the cost of a cross-option plan, showing how the scheme can work.

The Hans Christian Anderson Partnership

Capital	£400,000		
The partners			
Mr Hans	Age 50	Share 50%	
Mr Christian	Age 40	Share 30%	
Mr Anderson	Age 30	Share 20%	
Normal retirement age	Age 65		
The policies			
Level term assurance	Mr Hans	Mr Christian	Mr Anderson
Policy term in years	15	25	35
Sum assured	£200,000	£120,000	£80,000
On trust for	Mr Christian & Mr Anderson	Mr Hans & Mr Anderson	Mr Hans & Mr Christian
Annual premium	£736	£248	£115
Total premiums	£1,099		

1.1.2 The tax situation

Because each policy is qualifying or has no surrender value there will be no income tax liability on the proceeds. Neither will there be CGT, because the proceeds are payable to the original beneficial owners – the other partners.

If all the partners take part in the arrangement, there will be no IHT either at outset or when further premiums are paid. This is because it can be claimed that the arrangement is a *bona fide* business transaction for full consideration with no gratuitous intent[3]: full consideration being the fact that all the partners are participating. There will be no IHT on the policy on death, since no transfer of value has occurred. There will be no IHT on the partnership share on death, because 100% business property relief applies. If the settlor is excluded as a potential beneficiary, there will be no pre-owned assets tax (POAT) liability.

1.1.3 Distribution of cost

In most partnerships, the ages of the partners are not equal. However, life premiums are of course largely based on age and therefore the older partners will be paying higher premiums but will be less likely to benefit, since they are more likely to die. There will thus be some inequality of cost but, because term assurances are being used, the amounts may well be minimal. It should be remembered that in any partnership arrangement there will always be some element of give and take, although it is possible for the differential in cost to be adjusted according to an agreed formula. Any adjustments can then be made by way of cash payments between the partners. These will normally be small enough to be exempt from inheritance tax under the small gifts or annual exemptions. Alternatively, it could be claimed that they were exempt as a *bona fide* commercial arrangement.

Example A

An example of a distribution of cost formula applied to a three-man partnership of A, B and C.

The cost A should pay is the sum of the following:

$$\frac{\text{Sum assured on A x B's premium}}{\text{Total sum assured} - \text{sum assured on B}} + \frac{\text{Sum assured on A x C's premium}}{\text{Total sum assured} - \text{sum assured on C}}$$

The same principle can be applied to B and C.

Having worked out the costs that each partner should bear, it is then a simple matter to ascertain what payments need to be made between the partners to achieve equity. This can be illustrated using the Hans Christian Anderson Partnership referred to earlier.

[3] IHTA 1984 s10

The cost Hans should pay is the sum of:

$$\frac{\text{Hans's sum assured x Christian's premium}}{\text{Total sum assured – Christian's sum assured}} + \frac{\text{Hans's sum assured x Anderson's premium}}{\text{Total sum assured – Anderson's sum assured}}$$

$$= \frac{200{,}000 \times 248}{400{,}000 - 120{,}000} + \frac{200{,}000 \times 115}{400{,}000 - 80{,}000}$$

$$= \frac{49{,}600{,}000}{280{,}000} + \frac{23{,}000{,}000}{320{,}000}$$

$$= 177.14 + 71.87$$

$$= \mathbf{249.01}$$

The cost Christian should pay is the sum of:

$$\frac{\text{Christian's sum assured x Hans's premium}}{\text{Total sum assured – Hans's sum assured}} + \frac{\text{Christian's sum assured x Anderson's premium}}{\text{Total sum assured – Anderson's sum assured}}$$

$$= \frac{120{,}000 \times 736}{400{,}000 - 200{,}000} + \frac{120{,}000 \times 115}{400{,}000 - 80{,}000}$$

$$= \frac{88{,}320{,}000}{200{,}000} + \frac{13{,}800{,}000}{320{,}000}$$

$$= 441.60 + 43.13$$

$$= \mathbf{484.73}$$

The cost Anderson should pay is the sum of:

$$\frac{\text{Anderson's sum assured x Hans's premium}}{\text{Total sum assured – Han's sum assured}} + \frac{\text{Anderson's sum assured x Christian's premium}}{\text{Total sum assured – Christian's sum assured}}$$

$$= \frac{80{,}000 \times 736}{400{,}000 - 200{,}000} + \frac{80{,}000 \times 248}{400{,}000 - 120{,}000}$$

$$= \frac{58{,}880{,}000}{200{,}000} + \frac{19{,}840{,}000}{280{,}000}$$

$$= 294.40 + 70.86$$

$$= \mathbf{365.26}$$

In summary:

	Actual cost	**Equitable cost**	**Difference**
Mr Hans	736	249.01	+486.99
Mr Christian	248	484.73	–236.73
Mr Anderson	115	365.26	–250.26
Total	1,099	1,099.00	

Mr Christian should thus pay Mr Hans £236.73 and Mr Anderson should pay Mr Hans £250.26 to achieve an equitable distribution. Both these amounts are well under the IHT annual exemption, and are *bona fide* commercial transactions anyway.

A more rough and ready method is to add up all the premiums, divide by the number of partners, and then adjust on that basis. If that was done in the above example, the costs would be as follows:

	Actual cost	**Equitable cost**	**Difference**
Mr Hans	736	366.34	+369.66
Mr Christian	248	366.33	–118.33
Mr Anderson	115	366.33	–251.33
Total	1,099	1,099.00	

Mr Christian could thus pay Mr Hans £118.33, and Mr Anderson could pay Mr Hans £251.33.

1.2 The automatic accrual method

This method is different from the previous one in that it does not involve an actual purchase of a deceased partner's share. In this case, the partners complete an automatic accrual agreement which provides that the partnership will continue on the death of a partner and that a deceased partner's share will pass automatically to the surviving partners, but only to the extent of the proceeds arising under a life policy effected by the deceased partner.

Each partner has an obligation to effect and maintain a policy on his own life for the value of his share. This policy would be a term assurance to retirement date, but does not have to be issued under any form of partnership trust. The idea is that a deceased partner is compensated for the automatic passing of his share to the surviving partners by the sum assured payable to him under his own policy. Each partner's policy is entirely at his own disposal and can be used for any other desired purpose. For example, it could be effected under trust for his children as part of an inheritance tax planning exercise. So long as the policy is kept in force, the policyholder's obligation to his fellow partners is fulfilled.

Only if the policy proceeds on death are less than the value of the partnership share will the surviving partners have to make any payments to the deceased's estate. For example, if the share was valued at £100,000 but the deceased's policy only provided £85,000 then the surviving partners would have to pay £15,000 to the deceased's estate.

Again, there may be some inequality of cost but, once more, adjustments can be made to compensate. The cost of the arrangement would be the same as that illustrated on page 243.

1.2.1 The tax situation

Since each partner effects a qualifying policy, there will be no income tax or CGT on the proceeds. There should be no inheritance tax on the arrangement if all partners participate because it will be a *bona fide* commercial arrangement, and business property relief will apply. POAT tax is not an issue because, if a trust is involved, the settlor will not be a beneficiary.

1.3 The buy and sell method

Some arrangements have been made using buy and sell agreements whereby on death of a partner the survivors have to buy his share and his estate has to sell it.

The major disadvantage of the buy and sell method lies in the absence of IHT business relief. When a partner dies, his share in the partnership is a part of his estate and thus subject to inheritance tax. There is, however, a relief for business property which reduces the value of business assets for inheritance tax purposes by 100%[4]. However, the relief is not available where the property is subject to a binding contract for sale[5]. The existence of a buy and sell agreement means that the deceased partner's share is not business property and thus the relief is not available.

This might not matter if the share passes under the will or intestacy to a surviving spouse or civil partner, as it would then be exempt from tax anyway. But where the share passes to someone else, business property relief is important which is why the cross-option method is usually preferable.

[4] IHTA 1984 ss103-114; [5] IHTA 1984 s113

1.4 Choosing a method

There is no one method best for all situations. Each partnership should be looked at individually and what may be the best answer for one partnership may not be for another.

The buy and sell method has the advantage of simplicity and is easy for all partners to understand, which is extremely important in the practical process of selling a scheme. However, it may have IHT disadvantages if some of the partners are not married or in a civil partnership because of the loss of business property relief. In these cases, the cross-option method might be preferable. However, because this only gives options, it is not totally foolproof, although it is probably the best all-round method.

The automatic accrual method has the advantage of flexibility, since each partner's policy is at his own disposal. However, in practice, it has proved more difficult to sell than the other methods as it is more difficult to understand.

If there is a need to keep the arrangement as simple as possible for a two-partner firm, then each partner could effect a policy on the life of the other partner. The fact of the partnership gives an insurable interest, particularly if there is a buy and sell or cross-option agreement. Alternatively, there could be a joint life first death policy on the lives of both partners, so that on one death the other will receive the sum assured. However, these arrangements are only really suitable if the clients are sure that there will never be any more partners, and the shares are equal.

Perhaps the key thing to be remembered for any plan is that the cover must be kept up to date: the cover should always match the value of the partnership shares. If not, any scheme may partially fail by requiring extra payments from the surviving partners. Thus, policies with index-linking or increasability options are to be preferred over level term assurances.

1.5 Critical illness and terminal illness cover

As mentioned, CIC and terminal illness cover can be incorporated into partnership protection arrangements. Although a partnership is not legally dissolved if one partner is diagnosed as suffering from a serious illness, the problems caused are similar to death. The partner who is ill will probably not be able to contribute to the business any more and will no doubt wish to retire early and take his share of the capital as cash. Incorporating this cover into the policies in any of the previously explained methods will give the other partners the money to buy out the ailing partner to the benefit of them all.

Adding CIC and terminal illness cover to partnership protection policies can, however, cause problems. Any agreement between the parties will need to be amended to cover this as well as death. However, if a partner is diagnosed as being terminally ill and the agreement forces him to sell his share to the other partners for cash he will be exchanging an asset which will attract 100% IHT business property relief on subsequent death for fully taxable cash. Therefore, if this type of cover is required it might be better provided on a personal basis outside the partnership protection agreement.

The question of whether to use a single option or double option agreement has been covered on pages 235-36.

2 Personal Pension Policies

So far, we have dealt with ordinary term assurance policies on which no life assurance premium relief is available. However, partners are eligible for personal pensions and so can arrange their term assurances under that legislation. This enables full tax relief to be obtained on the premiums and, therefore, maximum relief is 40% and the minimum is 22%. These policies are thus effectively much cheaper than ordinary term assurances. Full details of these policies are given in Chapter O.

The maximum premium on which relief can be given the post-A day rules is governed by the annual allowance and the maximum sum assured by the lifetime allowance.

Life cover premiums count towards the overall limit for all pension arrangements. Any term assurance premium will correspondingly reduce the partner's maximum contribution to a pension. This would not normally be a problem but would affect someone who wanted to make the highest possible payment into a pension who was a very high earner.

The legislation allows the term assurance to run to a maximum expiry age of 75, so that the normal range of retirement dates can be accommodated. There is no restriction on the payment of these policies and they can be issued under trust.

As an illustration, we can take the example of the Hans Christian Anderson partnership used previously, and compare the ordinary term assurance cost with the personal pension term assurance cost.

Example B

Suppose Mr Hans was a 40% taxpayer, Mr Christian a 40% taxpayer and Mr Anderson a basic rate taxpayer. The relative costs would be as follows:

	Ordinary term assurance with no tax relief	**Personal pension life cover after tax relief**	**Difference**
	£	**£**	**£**
Mr Hans	736	486	250
Mr Christian	248	164	84
Mr Anderson	115	99	16
Total	1099	749	350

3 Retirement

The problem of an outgoing partner also arises on retirement. The problems are not as acute as they are on death, because the date of a partner's retirement will normally be known well in advance which will make the funding of any liabilities easier.

A retiring partner may often want to leave the business entirely and take his share of the capital with him. The other partners will therefore want to be able to buy him out, to continue the business. It is quite possible to leave this question until retirement, but it is more sensible to do some planning in advance and the buy and sell, cross-option or automatic accrual methods, already discussed, can all be used. In each case the agreement would be altered to provide rights or options on retirement as well as death, and the retirement dates would normally have to be specified.

The life policies to fund the liabilities could be endowments, maturing on the respective retirement dates. Future rises in values could be anticipated by effecting the policies on a with-profits or a unit-linked basis. Personal pension contracts cannot be used, because only term assurances are allowed to be placed under trust. No tax relief is allowed on life policies, but an endowment for at least ten years will still be a qualifying policy. If one of the partners will retire in less than ten years' time, then a ten-year endowment could be effected and surrendered on the retirement date. However, there might be some liability for income tax on a chargeable gain if surrender was within seven-and-a-half years.

An alternative answer would be a unit-linked whole life policy which does not have a fixed maturity date. This could be surrendered whenever required, which might also be useful if some flexibility over retirement dates was required. If surrender values are going to be used, it should be remembered that these are not usually guaranteed, and can fluctuate considerably on unit-linked policies.

Because endowment or whole life policies are required when planning for retirement, the cost is much higher than when planning for death alone. The life policy premiums are substantially higher and the inequalities in premiums, which might be insignificant on term assurances, are quite large. Also, the surrender values can cause problems if a partner leaves the partnership other than on death or retirement.

For these reasons, most partnerships do not use these methods to plan for retirement. A more popular arrangement is to split the planning into separate death and retirement aspects. Death can be planned for by using the methods outlined earlier; and retirement taken care of by using a pension-based approach.

3.1 The pensions approach

Many partnerships plan for retirement by using personal pension contracts. The partnership agreement may insist that each partner pays a certain level of contributions into his own pension plan. Thus, on retirement, he will have built up his own pension and so avoid the continuing partners having to provide him with a pension out of future business profits.

Full tax relief can be obtained on the partner's contributions (up to the statutory maxima) and the pension is taxable as earned income. The contributions are invested in a tax-free fund and there will also be a tax-free cash sum on retirement. Retirement can be at any age from 50 (55 from 6 April 2010) to 75 and most offices provide policies with flexible retirement dates which avoid the necessity of fixing a date too far in advance.

Provisions could be made for the partnership share to pass automatically to the other partners with the retiring partner being compensated by the payout from his pension plan. If this might be inequitable because of a wide discrepancy in the ages of the partners, some adjustment could be made in the partnership's profit-sharing ratio, to enable the older partners to make higher contributions. If the whole of the adjustment is used for a pension premium, there will be no income tax disadvantage as full tax relief is obtainable on the premiums. The change in profit-sharing ratios should not be a transfer for IHT purposes as it is a *bona fide* commercial transaction with no gratuitous intent. It should also avoid any pre-owned assets tax liability.

Alternatively, if some payment has to be made by the continuing partners to the retiring partner, this could be funded by means of a loan linked to the remaining partners' pension plans.

Interest will be charged on the loan, but if it is used to buy a retiring partner's share then it will qualify for income tax relief. Tax relief will be at a partner's top rates and there is no limit on the amount of the loan.

The loan capital can then be repaid by the tax-free cash sum on subsequent retirement. Although it is sometimes possible to let the interest roll-up, it is not recommended as no tax relief can be obtained and the debt could increase rapidly because of the compounding effect – so that it overtakes the potential cash sum.

4 Limited Liability Partnerships

A limited liability partnership (LLP) is a halfway house between a partnership and a limited company. It is a body corporate separate from the partners, which has a separate legal personality, and so can own property in its own right. It has to be registered with the Registrar of Companies and must have a registered office like a company. However in most other respects it is like an ordinary partnership. In particular it is taxed as a partnership and the partners are self-employed individuals, not employees of the LLP. The interest of a partner is business property for IHT. However the liability of the partners is limited to the amount subscribed for the LLP. The partners are not liable for the trade debts of the partnership in their own personal capacity.

The methods of partnership protection explained earlier are equally as applicable to LLPs as to ordinary partnerships.

5 Pre-Owned Asset Tax (POAT)

There is a theoretical possibility of POAT applying to existing partnership share protection policies. This is because normally the settlor is a potential beneficiary of the trust. Thus, even though the policies were not taken out for any IHT motive and are indeed exempt from IHT as a *bona fide* commercial transaction, the trust is within the POAT rules – see Chapter C section 1.9. This is so even though the settlor cannot possibly benefit from a term assurance as he will be dead when a claim arises and during the settlor's life there is no surrender value.

In almost all cases there will be no charge as there is no surrender value and even if there was it would be covered by the £5,000 threshold. However, if on 6 April in any tax year the life assured was dying, but was not yet dead, Her Majesty's Revenue and Customs (HMRC) could allege that the policy had a market value, even though there was no surrender value. There will be very few cases where this could produce a tax charge, especially when term assurance policies are used, and the Association of British Insurers (ABI) is lobbying for a specific exemption for these cases.

There is also a good argument that the POAT rules do not apply anyway. This is because the POAT rues for intangibles (such as life policies) operate via s624 of the Income Tax (Trading and Other Income) Act 2005 (ITTOIA) and the court in the *Jones v Garnett* case stated that there had to be an element of bounty for this section to apply. In partnership protection cases there is no element of bounty as it is a *bona fide* commercial arrangement with no donative intent or effect.

6 The 2006 Budget

Partnership protection policies under trusts other than absolute trusts could be affected by the 2006 Budget even though they are not done for IHT reasons. See Chapter G, sections 5.3.7 and 5.3.8.

J Directors' Share Protection

1 Directors' Share Protection Plans

2 Personal Pension Life Cover

3 Pension Scheme Cover

4 Retirement

5 Alternative Approaches

6 Pre-Owned Asset Tax (POAT)

7 The 2006 Budget

Small businesses that are run as companies have similar problems to partnerships. Many small businesses operate as private companies with a comparatively small number of people owning the company as shareholders and running it as directors. This is particularly the case for family companies. Although a company will not be dissolved on the death of a director, the surviving directors run the risk of his shares passing to someone with no interest in the company, or even to another company which might then be in a position to make a takeover bid.

When a director shareholder dies, his shares will pass to his estate – which will often mean to his widow. She may not want to retain them and may have no knowledge of the business. She could well prefer a cash settlement and if the surviving directors will not, or cannot, buy them, she may try to sell them to someone else, although there may be restrictions on the transferability of the shares in the company's Articles of Association.

The surviving directors will want to keep control of the company and probably would not like the deceased's wife to sell the shares to a perhaps unknown third party with whom they might not be able to work amicably. It will thus be far better for all parties if there is a prearranged scheme for the surviving directors to purchase the shares of a deceased director. Like partnership protection, this will require some advance funding as it is most unlikely that the other directors will all have the required cash when needed.

Life policies can meet this need and many life offices have directors' share protection plans available.

1 Directors' Share Protection Plans

As with partnership protection, the following points must be considered when selecting a directors' share protection plan:

- Does it give rights for all parties to carry out the scheme?
- Does it put the right amount of money in the right hands at the right time?
- Does it give any tax relief on life policy premiums?
- Does it ensure that there will be no income tax on the proceeds?
- Does it avoid any capital gains tax (CGT) liability?
- Does it avoid any inheritance tax (IHT) liability?
- Is the cost distributed fairly among the directors?

The various methods of planning will now be dealt with in turn.

1.1 The cross-option method

This method preserves business property relief for the shares by using a cross-option (or double option) agreement. Instead of giving legal rights to buy and sell, the agreement gives options. The surviving directors have an option to require the deceased director's estate to sell and the estate has a corresponding option to require the surviving directors to buy, within a specified period from the death. If either party exercises the option the other party must comply. Under the agreement each director shareholder must effect and maintain a life policy to provide the sum needed to purchase his shareholding and the agreement will provide for the valuation of that holding. The policy is usually under a cross-option trust with other directors as trustees.

While double options are generally used for life cover, they are less appropriate for critical illness cover (CIC). A shareholder who is eligible to make a claim under a critical illness policy may not wish to sell his shares because:

- His health is such that he can expect to continue working, eg after a mild heart attack.
- He does not want to be faced with a large CGT bill on selling his shares.
- He does not want to convert a 100% IHT relievable asset into unrelievable cash.

To overcome these problems it is common to use a single option agreement for the CIC, giving the critically ill shareholder the option to sell (a put option), but not providing his fellow shareholders with the option to buy (a call option). The option agreement can therefore become a long document, with different clauses applying on death or a claim under a critical illness policy.

A single option agreement for CIC may not always be advisable as a director who thinks he can recover from his illness may not actually be able to do so. If he cannot recover fully he may not be able to pull his weight in the business, and the other directors may wish to be able to effectively force him to go. This could be achieved by a double option agreement with different option periods. The ailing director could have an option to force a buy-out in the three or six months following diagnosis of the illness. The other directors could have an option to force a buy-out but only exercisable after a suitable period has elapsed since diagnosis (eg one or two years) by when the final situation should have clarified so as to enable a sensible decision to be made.

Some life offices have draft cross-option agreements and directors' share protection trusts.

The life policies will be term assurances drawn to the directors' retirement dates and so there may be some inequality of cost but, the directors can make cash payments between themselves to compensate for this.

The surviving directors as trust beneficiaries will use the sum assured to buy the deceased directors' shares in the proportions to which they are already entitled to the balance of the shareholding. Thus if there are four directors, each with a 25% shareholding, then when one dies the survivors will each buy one-third of the deceased's shareholding, so that the same ratio is maintained among the survivors.

The trust is often a flexible power of appointment trust. It used to be suggested that, alongside his fellow directors, the settlor was a potential beneficiary in case he ever needed to recover the policy. This could happen if, say, the company went out of business before expiry for any reason. If that happened then each director could be appointed the sole beneficiary of the policy on his life, with the other trustees retiring, leaving the life assured as sole beneficiary and sole trustee. The policies could then be continued, and used for any other purpose.

Normally putting the settlor in the trust would make the transaction a gift with reservation, but that would not apply in this case as the whole arrangement would be a *bona fide* commercial arrangement. Director X is only putting his policy in trust for Y and Z, because they are putting theirs in trust for him as part of a commercial arrangement. There is no donative intent. Thus, as it is not a gift, it cannot be a gift with reservation. However, the rules for pre-owned assets tax (see section 6) now mean that to name the settlor as a potential beneficiary could mean a tax liability arises in certain limited circumstances (see section 6). In any event a director's spouse and family should not be included as potential beneficiaries, because this would create a gift with reservation by destroying the commerciality of the arrangement.

New director shareholders are normally automatically included in the trust, although they would have to sign supplemental agreements and effect policies on their own lives under the same trust.

The sum assured under each policy should be equal to the value of that directors' shareholding. However, the agreement can provide that, if the policy proceeds are less than the value, the balance can be paid in instalments over a period to ease cash flow problems. The life policy used should be a term assurance written to the expected retirement date of the director. As share values would be liable to rise in the future, an index-linked or expanding term assurance would be preferable to a level one. Increasability options could also be used.

1.1.1 Illustration of cost

The following is an illustration of the cost of a cross-option plan, showing how the scheme can work:

Rustbox Motors Ltd

Total shareholding	**£250,000**	**Retirement age 65**	
The directors	John Rust	(age 55)	Shareholding 40%
	Fred Rust	(age 50)	Shareholding 35%
	Peter Box	(age 45)	Shareholding 25%
The policies	**J Rust**	**F Rust**	**P Box**
Level term assurance			
Policy term in years	10	15	20
Sum assured	£100,000	£87,500	£62,500
On trust for	F Rust & P Box	J Rust & P Box	J Rust & F Rust
Annual premium	£425	£322	£160
Total premium	£907		

1.1.2 Distribution of cost

As the directors are likely to be of different ages, there will be some inequality of cost because the older directors will be paying more with less expectation of benefit. This inequality can be evened out by the directors making cash payments between themselves. With term assurances, these adjustments will usually be small enough to be exempt from IHT under the small gifts or annual exemptions. Alternatively, it could be claimed that they were exempt as a *bona fide* commercial arrangement.

The following is an example of a distribution of cost formula as applied to a company with three directors.

Example A

The cost director A should pay is the sum of the following:

$$\frac{\text{Sum assured on A x B's premium}}{\text{Total sum assured} - \text{sum assured on B}} + \frac{\text{Sum assured on A x C's premium}}{\text{Total sum assured} - \text{sum assured on C}}$$

The same principle can be applied to the other two directors.

Having worked out the costs that each director should pay, it is then a simple matter to ascertain what payments need to be made between the directors to achieve equity.

This can be illustrated using Rustbox Motors Ltd referred to above.

The cost John Rust should pay is:

$$\frac{\text{J Rust's sum assured x F Rust's premium}}{\text{Total sum assured – F Rust's sum assured}} + \frac{\text{J Rust's sum assured x P Box's premium}}{\text{Total sum assured – P Box's sum assured}}$$

$$= \frac{100{,}000 \times 322}{250{,}000 - 87{,}500} + \frac{100{,}000 \times 160}{250{,}000 - 62{,}500}$$

$$= \frac{32{,}200{,}000}{162{,}500} + \frac{16{,}000{,}000}{187{,}500}$$

$$= 198.15 + 85.33$$

$$= \mathbf{£283.48}$$

The cost Fred Rust should pay is:

$$\frac{\text{F Rust's sum assured x J Rust's premium}}{\text{Total sum assured – J Rust's sum assured}} + \frac{\text{F Rust's sum assured x P Box's premium}}{\text{Total sum assured – P Box's sum assured}}$$

$$= \frac{87{,}500 \times 425}{250{,}000 - 100{,}000} + \frac{87{,}500 \times 160}{250{,}000 - 62{,}500}$$

$$= \frac{37{,}187{,}500}{150{,}000} + \frac{14{,}000{,}000}{187{,}500}$$

$$= 247.92 + 74.67$$

$$= \mathbf{£322.59}$$

The cost Peter Box should pay is:

$$\frac{\text{P Box's sum assured x J Rust's premium}}{\text{Total sum assured – J Rust's sum assured}} + \frac{\text{P Box's sum assured x F Rust's premium}}{\text{Total sum assured – F Rust's sum assured}}$$

$$= \frac{62{,}500 \times 425}{250{,}000 - 100{,}000} + \frac{62{,}500 \times 322}{250{,}000 - 87{,}500}$$

$$= \frac{26{,}562{,}500}{150{,}000} + \frac{20{,}125{,}000}{162{,}500}$$

$$= 177.08 + 123.85$$

$$= \text{£300.93}$$

In summary:

	Actual cost	Equitable cost	Difference
John Rust	£425	£283.48	+ £141.52
Fred Rust	£322	£322.59	– £0.59
Peter Box	£160	£300.93	– £140.93
	£907	£907.00	

Fred Rust should thus pay John Rust £0.59 and Peter Box should pay John Rust £140.93 to achieve an equitable distribution.

A more rough and ready method is to add up all the premiums, divide by the number of directors, and then adjust on that basis. If that was done in the above example, the costs would be as follows:

	Actual cost	Equitable cost	Difference
John Rust	£425	£302.34	+122.66
Fred Rust	£322	£302.33	+19.67
Peter Box	£160	£302.33	–142.33
	£907	£907.00	

Thus Peter Box could pay John Rust £122.66 and Fred Rust £19.67.

1.1.3 The tax situation

Because each policy is a qualifying own-life contract or has no surrender value, the proceeds are free of income tax. As the proceeds are payable to the original beneficial owners (the other directors), there will be no CGT liability. The arrangement will be exempt from IHT as a *bona fide* commercial transaction, assuming all director shareholders take part[1]. This applies at outset and when future premiums are paid.

[1] *IHTA 1984 s10*

There would be no inheritance tax on payment of the policy proceeds as no transfer of value occurs at this time.

Because the cross-option agreement is not a binding contract for sale, there will be no IHT on the shares on death because 100% business property relief will apply (assuming the conditions specified in Chapter C are met). If the settlor is excluded as a potential beneficiary, there will be no pre-owned assets tax (POAT) liability.

1.2 The buy and sell method

Some arrangements have been made using buy and sell agreements whereby on the death of a director, the survivors have to buy his share and his estate has to sell it. However, as explained in Chapter I section 1.3 the buy and sell agreement is a binding contract for sale and will thus mean the loss of IHT business property relief on a deceased directors' shareholding. If the shares are not to pass on death to a spouse or civil partner, the cross-option method will be preferable.

2 Personal Pension Life Cover

If a director is not a member of an approved pension scheme, he will be eligible for a personal pension. If the director is eligible, the term assurance can be effected under personal pension rules and top-rate tax relief obtained on the premiums, thus making the cover much cheaper. Full details of these policies are given in Chapter O.

The maximum premium on which relief can be given under the post-A Day rules is governed by the annual allowance and the maximum sum assured by the lifetime allowance.

These premiums count towards the overall limit for all pensions. Any term assurance premium will correspondingly reduce that director's maximum contribution to pension. This will not usually be a problem, but it would affect a director who wanted to make the highest possible payment into a pension. This method can be used for any retirement age up to 75 and the policy can be issued under trust.

As an illustration, we can take the example of Rustbox Motors Ltd used earlier, and compare the cost of personal pension term assurance with ordinary term assurance.

Suppose John Rust is a 40% taxpayer, with Fred Rust paying 40% and Peter Box 22%, the relative net costs would be as follows:

Premiums

	Ordinary term assurance with no tax relief	Personal pension term assurance after tax relief	Difference
	£	£	£
John Rust	£425	£281	£144
Fred Rust	£322	£213	£109
Peter Box	£160	£138	£22
Total	£907	£632	£275

3 Pension Scheme Cover

If a company has a registered pension scheme with a death-in-service benefit, this may be able to be used to provide the life cover required. If, like most schemes, the death-in-service benefit is operated under a discretionary trust, then a director could use his expression of wish form to request the trustees to pay the benefit to the surviving directors in whatever proportions are required to enable them to fulfil their obligations or options under whatever agreement is used. A proviso could be added that if a surviving director failed to exercise his option under a cross-option agreement, then that share should be paid to the deceased's spouse or other beneficiary. This method is not legally watertight but as the fellow directors will all be making the same arrangements it will usually work in practice. There could be a snag if the maximum cover allowed by Her Majesty's Revenue and Customs (HMRC) was less than the value of a directors' shareholding and, if this was the case, other arrangements might have to be made. Premiums for the cover could be paid by the company and would qualify for tax relief as a business expense. Any contribution made by a director would also qualify for full tax relief.

4 Retirement

Problems can also occur on the retirement of a director shareholder. These are not as acute as they are on death, since the date of retirement will be known well in advance – making the funding of any liabilities easier. In addition, whilst many directors wish to relinquish some or all of their working responsibilities as they get older, many like to remain on as shareholders.

If a director wanted to leave the business entirely on retirement, then modified forms of either buy and sell or cross-option agreements could be used, backed by an endowment policy maturing on the retirement date under the relevant trust. Future rises in share values could be anticipated by effecting the policy on a with-profits or unit-linked basis. No form of pension contract could be used, but a qualifying policy could be effected if the period to retirement was at least ten years. If it was less than ten years, a ten-year endowment could be effected with the idea of surrendering it on retirement. However, there might be some liability for income tax on a chargeable gain if surrender was within seven-and-a-half years.

If surrender values are going to be used, it should be remembered that these are not normally guaranteed and can fluctuate considerably on unit-linked policies. As an alternative to an endowment, a unit-linked whole life policy could be used and surrendered when required. This could be valuable because it can cope with a variable retirement date.

If a director wishes to retire but keep his shareholding, then no problem arises until death. This can be planned for by using a whole life policy which will pay out whenever death occurs. The best type of whole life policy for this purpose would be unit-linked whole life assurance, as these have options to index-link the life cover and are extremely flexible. The policy would be issued under a buy and sell, or cross-option trust to coincide with whatever agreement is being used.

The cost of planning for retirement is much higher than just planning for earlier death and thus the inequalities in premiums can be substantial. For these reasons, as with partnerships, not much planning is done on this basis. A more popular alternative is to split death and retirement planning into separate aspects.

Death before retirement can be planned for by using the methods explained earlier, and retirement by using a pension-based approach.

4.1 The pensions approach

Many small companies plan for retirement using some form of pension arrangement. Director shareholders may all agree to effect personal pension policies (usually funded by the company), or the company may set up a registered pension scheme for them. Any contributions made by a director will be eligible for full tax relief and any contribution paid by the company will be an allowable business expense. These contributions are invested in a tax-free fund and the pensions are treated as earned income.

As each director retires, the continuing directors can fund any buyout of the retiring director by using a loan linked to the pension scheme.

Interest will be charged on the loan, but if it is used to purchase a retiring directors' shareholding it will normally qualify for full income tax relief[2]. Tax relief will not be available if the company is an investment company. There is no limit on the amount of the loan for this relief.

The loan capital can then be repaid by the tax-free cash sum when that director retires. It is sometimes possible to let the interest roll up but this is not recommended as no tax relief can be obtained and the debt could increase rapidly due to the compounding effect so that it overtakes the potential cash sum.

[2] *Taxes Act 1988 s360*

5 Alternative Approaches

5.1 Company subsidies

So far, the schemes discussed have involved directors paying their own premiums under whatever life policies are used. However, it is possible for the company to pay these premiums on a director's behalf and if this can be arranged, it can result in savings for the directors.

If the company pays the premium on a director's behalf, HMRC treats this as part of his remuneration for income tax and National Insurance contribution (NIC) purposes. The corollary of this is that the company receives corporation tax relief as a business expense. The personal cost to a director is thus confined to the income tax payable by him on the premium (and an additional National Insurance liability).

The following example will make this clearer.

Example B

Mr Steve Fielding is a director of Fielding, Headley & Co Ltd, shoe repairers. His directors' share protection policy has a premium of £400. If the company pays the premium on Mr Fielding's policy, this is treated as an addition to his remuneration. Thus, his personal cost is just the tax and NICs on £400.

The premium is an allowable business expense for the company, so if it is paying corporation tax at the small companies' rate of 19% the net cost to it is £400 x 0.81 = £324. The total cost would thus be £456 if Steve is a basic rate taxpayer and pays NICs at 11%. However, if the company paid tax at 30%, the net cost to the company would reduce to £400 x 0.7 = £280. In addition, there would be an NIC liability.

This principle can be extended still further and can sometimes be used to eliminate all personal cost to the director; basically this involves giving the director a further rise in salary to enable him to meet his income tax liability on the premium. This again gives rise to an extra National Insurance liability.

5.2 Company share purchase

There is another solution to the problem: the company itself buys its own shares from a deceased or retiring director.

If a company buys the shares of an outgoing director, it must cancel those shares. The authorised share capital is unaltered and thus these shares become unissued share capital. This effectively increases the proportionate shareholdings of the continuing directors and enables them to keep control of the business while giving the outgoing director (or his estate) a cash settlement. This can be seen in the following example.

Example C

Rosenfield, Perry & Co Ltd has an issued share capital of 100 shares in the following proportions:

Mr Rosenfield	25
Mr Perry	25
Mr Patterson	25
Mr Bennett	25

Each director has a one-quarter interest.

Mr Bennett dies from cirrhosis of the liver, the company buys his shares from his estate and then, as it must, cancels them.

The revised shareholdings are still the same but, as the issued share capital has been reduced to 75, each of the continuing directors has a 25/75 or one-third interest.

The immediate practical effect is much the same as if the continuing directors had personally purchased those shares by a buy and sell or cross-option scheme, but the 25 cancelled shares remain available to be issued in the future if required, possibly for issue to a new director.

To enable a company to buy the shares of an outgoing director it would be best to have a written agreement between the company and its directors that this will take place on death or retirement. The agreement could be in a buy and sell form or, if it is desired to retain inheritance tax business property relief on the shares, a cross-option agreement could be used. In each case, the company will be buying, and the outgoing director (or his estate) selling, the shares.

5.2.1 Legal requirements of a company buyout

A number of legal requirements are set out in the Companies Act 1981 and these have to be met before a buyout can take place. The main ones are as follows:

(a) The company's Articles of Association must permit the purchase. Thus, many companies (certainly those formed prior to 1981) will have to change their Articles if they wish to use this method.

(b) The shares purchased must be cancelled (unless it is a listed company), thereby becoming unissued share capital.

(c) If the purchase is on a recognised stock exchange, or on the Alternative Investment Market (AIM), it must be approved by an ordinary resolution of shareholders. The resolution must specify the maximum number of shares to be purchased, the maximum and minimum prices to be paid and the period of execution (not more than 18 months).

(d) Most purchases will be off-market and therefore not subject to requirement (c) above, but instead any contract (or option) to purchase shares must be authorised by a 75% majority of shareholders at a General Meeting of the company. This will not normally be a problem, as the arrangement will be for the ultimate benefit of the other major director shareholders.

In the absence of any change in tax law, the excess of the price the company paid for the shares over the capital originally subscribed would be treated as a distribution by the company. Thus the outgoing director (or his representatives) would be liable for income tax. However, the Taxes Act 1988 allows the payment to be treated as capital if the conditions in s219 (set out below) are met. Thus, the only tax payable would be CGT by the outgoing shareholder on the difference between what he paid for the shares and what he got for them. Even then, this would only apply on retirement (since death is not a taxable disposal for CGT purposes) if the gain after indexation and business assets taper relief was over the annual exemption limit, currently £8,500.

The conditions are as follows:

(a) The company must be an unquoted trading company or the holding company of a trading group. Investment companies, or those dealing in shares or land, are excluded.

(b) The purchase must be for the benefit of the company's trade. It appears that HMRC interprets this fairly broadly and Press Release SP2/1982 states that this would normally include the total buy-out of a deceased or retiring shareholder. It does not matter that the outgoing shareholder (or his estate) will also benefit.

(c) The purchase must not be part of an arrangement, the main purpose of which is tax avoidance.

(d) The outgoing shareholder must be resident in the UK and have held the shares for at least five years. This period includes the ownership of a spouse or civil partner and is reduced to three years where the shares were acquired on the death of an earlier shareholder.

(e) If the company only buys part of the outgoing director's holding, and/or his associates (broadly spouse or civil partner and minor children) also hold shares, then the percentage of all shares held after the purchase by the director and his associates must not exceed 75% of what it was before, or 30% of the reduced share capital. This will not usually be a problem on a complete buy-out.

(f) If the purchase is to enable a deceased director's estate to pay IHT which could not otherwise be met without undue hardship, then if substantially all the cash paid out is actually used to pay the tax within two years of the death, conditions (b) to (e) inclusive do not apply.

A procedure exists under the Taxes Act 1988 s225 for advance clearance to be obtained from HMRC that the purchase is one to which s219 applies and HMRC has 30 days to decide. As capital will usually be leaving the company, clearance must also be obtained under s707 of the Taxes Act 1988. In addition, once the shares have been purchased, the company will have to notify the Registrar of Companies.

5.2.2 The role of life insurance

To fund the purchase the company must first use any available distributable profits and the proceeds of any new share issue. Only the balance can come from capital. The company could just hope that it would have (or be able to borrow) the capital necessary to make the purchase at the required time. However, it will not be known when the payment will have to be made – humans have a habit of dying at unpredictable and awkward times. Also the rules on payment out of capital are fairly onerous. The directors have to make a statutory declaration that the company will be able to pay its debts throughout the following year. This will have to be checked by the company's auditors. The proposed purchase must also be advertised in the *London Gazette* and a national newspaper.

Thus, it will be best for the company to adopt some method of advance funding. For retirement, any type of investment might be used but for death some type of life policy is the only answer. If death is the only thing being planned for, the company can effect a term assurance to retirement date on the life of each of the directors involved. The liability to buy the shares under whatever agreement is used will provide the insurable interest.

If, in addition, retirement were being planned for, an endowment maturing on the retirement date could be used. As an alternative, a unit-linked whole life plan could be used and surrendered on the retirement date if the director is still alive at that time. The policy would be owned by the company and would not need to be under trust. Premiums would be paid by the company but corporation tax relief would not be available, because the policy is not to meet loss of profits on death (see Chapter K). Any chargeable gain under the policy would be treated as income of the company, subject to corporation tax under the Finance Act 1989 provisions (see Chapter D).

6 Pre-Owned Asset Tax (POAT)

There is a theoretical possibility of POAT applying to directors' share protection policies. This is because normally the settlor is a potential beneficiary of the trust. Thus, even though the policies were not taken out for any IHT motive and are indeed exempt from IHT as a *bona fide* commercial transaction, the trust is within the POAT rules – see Chapter C section 1.9. This is so even though the settlor cannot possibly benefit from a term assurance as he will be dead when a claim arises and during his life there is no surrender value.

In almost all cases there will be no charge as there is no surrender value and even if there was it would be covered by the £5,000 threshold. However, if on 6 April in any tax year the life assured was dying, but was not yet dead, HMRC could allege that the policy had a market value, even though there was no surrender value. There will be very few cases where this could produce a tax charge, especially when term assurance policies are used, and the Association of British Insurers (ABI) is lobbying for a specific exemption for these cases.

There is also a good argument that the POAT rules do not apply anyway. This is because the POAT rules for intangibles (such as life policies) operate via s624 of Income Tax (Trading and other Income) Act 2005 (ITTOIA) and the court in the *Jones v Garnett* case stated that there had to be an element of bounty for this section to apply. In directors' share protection cases there is no element of bounty as it is a *bona fide* commercial arrangement with no donative intent or effect.

7 The 2006 Budget

Directors share protection policies under trusts other than absolute trusts could be affected by the 2006 Budget, even though they are not done for IHT reasons. See Chapter G sections 5.3.7 and 5.3.8.

K Key Person Insurance

A company in business has two sorts of assets. First, there are its physical assets – a factory, offices, machinery, stock, motor vehicles and so on. These will virtually always be insured by the company. The second type of asset is the people involved in the business. The success or failure of a business is usually more dependent on its human assets than any other factor. Despite this, very few UK companies insure their key employees. A company will happily insure the managing director's desk but not the managing director himself.

If it is thought necessary to insure the physical assets that produce a company's profit, then surely it is reasonable to insure those human assets which make a vital contribution to profitability? Indeed, the necessary insurance is readily available and is known as key person insurance. As might be assumed from the name, it provides cover against the loss of profits a company will suffer on the death of a key employee. Sales of key person insurance are increasing in this country although it is believed that less than 5% of UK companies have any form of this cover, in contrast to the USA, where the figure tops 25%.

1 The Policy

A key person is any person whose death (or disability) would have a serious effect on the company's future profits.

1.1 The life assured

Examples of key persons could include:

- A **sales director** with valuable foreign contacts which, together with the business they provide, could be lost if he died. This may be particularly true if the business involves negotiations with foreign government officials where personal contact can be all important.

- A **controlling director** who has personally guaranteed loans made to the company by a third party, eg a bank. In these cases, a bank will often insist on life cover as a condition of the loan.

- The **founder of a small company** who may have built it up from nothing and who still provides most of its impetus. In this case, the company might not be able to survive at all after his death.

- A **top research scientist** who is vital to the development of a new product because of his personal expertise and knowledge. With the loss of this scientist it might be impossible to launch the product.

- An **engineer** who is vital to a particular project because of his detailed knowledge. The loss of this knowledge might necessitate the cancellation of the project.

- A **top executive** who has been recruited as a result of an expensive 'head hunting' operation. If he was expensive and difficult to recruit, then finding a worthwhile successor will also be expensive and difficult.

This list is not exhaustive but it does give an indication of the type of people who should be insured. Most companies will only have a few key persons, and some may have just one, but it is thought that this is a somewhat underdeveloped market in this country.

1.2 Types of policy

1.2.1 Term assurance

In essence, key person insurance is loss of profits insurance. Thus, for each key person the company should try to estimate the loss of profit it would suffer on his death. This would include the costs of finding, and training a successor, and loss of business and goodwill in the meantime. The loss may only emerge over a period of years. These requirements would indicate the use of a term assurance written to the retirement date of the key person, possibly with the sum assured payable by instalments.

However, a key person may not always remain a key person. He may leave the company, his effectiveness may decline and as he approaches retirement his successor ought to be recruited anyway. The need for cover is more short-term and so a better answer would be a term assurance for five or ten years. The ideal would be to use a five-year renewable term assurance. The initial premium would be less than that charged for a term assurance to age 65 and the policy could be renewed as many times as needed up to age 65. In the USA it is common to use one-year renewable term assurances on the basis that the risk is more akin to general insurance than traditional long-term life assurance. Escalating or index-linked policies would be valuable to combat inflation.

Some companies now offer a terminal illness option on their key person policies. Under a typical option if the life assured is diagnosed by the life office's doctor as probably having less than a year to live the office will pay out the sum assured. If the life assured survives the one-year period or even survives to the end of the policy term the terminal illness payout is not reclaimed.

1.2.2 Whole life policies

Unit-linked whole life policies are sometimes used for key person assurance. They have the disadvantage that they can be more expensive than term assurances and cover is provided for longer than might be strictly needed. However, they can be valuable in the type of situation where a company is insuring its founder who has no intention of retiring, or a director who has personally guaranteed loans which may continue beyond his retirement date. These long-term liabilities would demand whole life assurance, as most offices restrict term assurance cover to age 80 at the maximum.

If the company goes for the highest level of life cover available (the maximum cover basis), then the contract becomes very much like a term assurance and the premiums are little more than those for a ten-year term assurance and possibly less than those for a longer-term policy. Leading offices in this field now offer index-linking options for the life cover and this, together with the flexibility over the sum assured, has attracted a number of companies to use this route.

There can be some disadvantages: if the investment return has been less than that estimated at outset (often 6%), premiums will have to be increased after ten years if the same level of cover is to be maintained. On the other hand, if the investment return is greater than assumed, then premiums can be reduced or a cash sum built up within the policy. The possibility of future investment gains, if the level of life cover is reduced because of a lessening of the potential loss on a key person's death, may also be attractive to the company. When the key man retires the policy can be surrendered by the company, or given to the key man. If it is given to him when he is still an employee, its current value would be income taxable on him as a benefit in kind.

1.2.3 Comparison of policies

Although term assurance is initially the cheaper solution, this is not necessarily true in the long run. The performance of a unit-linked whole life plan ultimately depends on the growth of the units, and so unit-linked whole life policies may give better or worse value for money in the long run.

The difference in the taxation of term assurances and whole life policies is also relevant to the question of which to choose, both as regards the tax deductibility of the premiums and the taxability of any benefit. This is dealt with in section 2.

Whatever type of policy is used, it should normally be written as a life of another contract with the company as the owner of the policy, paying the premiums and receiving any benefits.

1.2.4 Critical illness cover (CIC)

The serious illness of a key person could cause the company similar problems as their death, because the key person could probably no longer contribute to the company's profitability. CIC is often recommended as an addition to a key person life policy. Alternatively a stand-alone CIC could be effected to cover the key person until retirement date. This would increase the premium, but would give the company better all-round cover against loss of profits.

1.3 Amount of cover

The question of how much cover to buy is always difficult to answer. As stated previously, the company should make some estimate of the financial loss it would suffer on the death of a key person. This is not easy as it often involves future business possibilities and other eventualities which are extremely difficult to quantify.

One 'rule of thumb' type method that has been used is to work out the key person's total remuneration (including any fringe benefits) and multiply that by ten. This is a very hit and miss method. If a key employee is not being paid his true worth it may be too little, if he is close to retirement it may be too much. In addition, it is really looking at the problem from the wrong angle. The cover is basically to replace loss of profits and thus it might be better to look at the problem from the starting point of the company's current gross profit level.

A rough estimate of the key person's contribution to a company's profits can be gained by multiplying the company's gross profit level by the fraction obtained by dividing the key person's remuneration by the company's total wage bill.

If the company's total gross profits are £10 million, the key person's remuneration £100,000, and the total wage bill £4 million, the key person's contribution could be estimated as follows:

$$\pounds 10{,}000{,}000 \quad \times \quad \frac{\pounds 100{,}000}{\pounds 4{,}000{,}000} \quad = \quad \pounds 250{,}000$$

It should then be asked how many years it would take for the company to recover from his loss and the previous figure should be multiplied by this number. If it would take the company four years to recover, the level of cover should be:

$$\pounds 250{,}000 \times 4 = \pounds 1{,}000{,}000$$

This method will obviously not work for a new or unprofitable company although if a company is regularly making a loss more drastic action is required than a key person policy.

A final consideration is the fact that the company will obviously hope for an increase in profits in the future. Thus, the sum assured ought to cater for future increases. This would dictate the use of increasing policies if possible.

1.3.1 Underwriting considerations

Key person policies, by their very nature, involve large sums assured and thus underwriting is usually a significant factor. Firstly, from the health angle, a full medical examination will usually be required and there may be problems if a key person is in poor health. A key person may often do a lot of flying and if much of this is in private or company aircraft this may interest the underwriter. The key person may have to travel to remote places (eg oil rigs) or dangerous areas (eg war-torn countries) and this might involve extra risks which the underwriter will also have to take into account.

For these reasons, it is never safe to assume that a life will be accepted at ordinary rates of premium. If the sum assured is over the life office's retention limit then some part of the sum assured will have to be reassured. The reassurer will have to be satisfied as to the risk and thus it can often take some time to underwrite a key person case.

There is also the aspect of financial underwriting. An office may be happy with the medical risk but not the 'moral hazard'. For example, no office will look kindly on a proposal from a small insurance brokerage to insure one of its salesmen for £1 million. Many offices have seen and refused proposals for large sums assured where there is little serious evidence of justification. A few have also had to pay out very early claims in such cases. For this reason the company will have to produce evidence to justify the level of cover proposed. Insurable interest is still a legal necessity[1] and virtually all offices require proof of this for key person business.

For cases below a certain level (say £250,000) the office would want details of the company, its business, its profits and the contribution of the key person to them, together with his salary and shareholding. For cases over this limit, the life office will probably insist on seeing the last three years' audited accounts and a letter of explanation from the company's secretary or its accountants. For very high sums assured, even more evidence may be required.

These details may take some time to sort out but past experience, both in this country and abroad, has shown that they are a necessary precaution.

[1] *Life Assurance Act 1774*

2 The Tax Position

Before effecting a policy a company will want to be sure of the taxation position regarding both tax relief on the premiums and the taxability of any payment of benefit.

2.1 Corporation tax relief

Unfortunately, the corporation tax situation is not so simple, since there is no direct legislation on the subject of key person policies. The principles were set out as long ago as 1944 by the then Chancellor of the Exchequer, Sir John Anderson. In answer to a parliamentary question he made the following statement:

> *Treatment for taxation purposes would depend upon the facts of the particular case and it rests with the assessing authorities and the Commissioners on appeal if necessary to determine the liability by reference to these facts. I am, however, advised that the general practice in dealing with insurances by employers on the lives of employees is to treat the premiums as admissible deductions, and any sums received under a policy as trading receipts, if (i) the sole relationship is that of employer and employee; (ii) the insurance is intended to meet loss of profit resulting from the loss of services of the employee; and (iii) it is an annual or short term insurance. Cases of premiums paid by companies to insure the lives of directors are dealt with on similar lines.*

2.2 Conditions for relief

As shown above, the broad position is that most term assurances gain relief on the premiums but are taxed on the benefit, whereas any other sort of policy is treated as a capital item and thus does not enjoy relief on the premiums. However, as the Chancellor said, the treatment does depend on the facts of a particular case, and the practice of local Inspectors of Taxes can vary. For this reason, it is very strongly recommended that every company proposing to effect a key person policy obtains confirmation of the tax position, from its own inspector, before completing the arrangement.

2.2.1 General considerations

Concerning the Chancellor's statement, a number of points need to be made. First, it is not possible for a company to forego premium relief to which it is entitled in the hope that this will eliminate tax on the proceeds. Relief on the premiums depends on their allowability as a business expense and this is not affected by whether the expense is actually claimed or not. Therefore, the status of the proceeds as a trading receipt is similarly unaffected.

Second, it is always possible for Her Majesty's Revenue and Customs (HMRC) to tax proceeds of a policy which was not allowed relief, if it can show that the proceeds were not treated as a capital item. This is extremely rare but not impossible.

2.2.2 The Chancellor's conditions

- **Sole relationship**: With regard to the first of the conditions, the sole relationship between company and life assured must be that of employer to employee. Working directors are employees for this purpose but if the life assured has a significant shareholding in the company this may prevent relief being given. This is because the premiums must be 'wholly or exclusively laid out or expended for the purposes of the trade' in order to be a business expense[2]. It has been held that if the life assured has a significant proprietorial interest in the company, that test is failed, since it is partly for the life assured's own advantage[3].

  This requirement would also mean no tax relief where a parent company insures a key person in a subsidiary or associated company. There would also probably be insurable interest problems here.

- **Loss of profits**: The second point in the statement was that the insurance must be to meet loss of profits resulting from the loss of the key person. Thus, any policy with a surrender value would not qualify, because some portion of the premium goes towards investment, thus failing the 'wholly or exclusively' test[4]. This would apply to whole life or endowment policies, even unit-linked whole life policies effected on a maximum cover basis because of their inherent flexibility. The sum assured would have to be reasonable in relation to the probable loss of profits. Convertible term policies may also be disallowed relief on the grounds that the existence of the conversion option means that there must be a purpose other than loss of profits on death and that it therefore fails the 'wholly and exclusively' test. If the policy was effected as security for a loan, it would be disallowed as part of the cost of raising capital.

- **Short-term assurance**: To meet condition (III), the policy must be an annual or short-term assurance. Nobody seems to be exactly sure what this means but it would seem that single premium policies (unless for one year only) would not qualify. It is also suggested that a term assurance to age 65 would fail the test and that the maximum term would be, say, five years. This is a specific area where the views of the company's inspector of taxes may be crucial. Short-term renewable term assurance is probably the answer to this problem.

These principles seem to have been endorsed (without being specifically referred to) in the recent case of *Beauty Consultants Ltd v Inspector of Taxes*.

2.3 Taxation of benefit

On a normal key person term assurance, the sum assured paid on a claim is a trading receipt of the company, and is subject to corporation tax at the company's rate for that financial year. This is logical in that the object of the policy was to replace the loss of profits caused by the death, and those profits would have then been taxable. If the sum assured was based on gross profits, then the fact that the benefit will be taxable does not matter.

[2] Taxes Act 1988 s74(1)(a); [3] Samuel Dracup & Sons v Dakin (1937) T.C. 382;
[4] Earl Howe v Commissioners of Inland Revenue (1919) 7 T.C. 300

If a whole life policy has been used, the proceeds would normally be treated as a capital item and thus not taxable – except possibly under the chargeable gains rules (see below). Any policy effected as security for a loan should also be non-taxable if there was a payout because the sum assured would be a capital item. This was recently confirmed in the case of *Greycon Ltd v Klaentschi* where the life assured was the guarantor of a loan made by a bank to the company.

If the proceeds are to be taxable, then it may be worthwhile to arrange for the sum assured to be payable by several yearly instalments. This might coincide with the gradual emergence of the loss of profits and could be valuable if it might prevent the company's profits exceeding the limit for the small companies' rate of tax (£300,000 at present) by virtue of a large lump sum payment.

For employees with a significant shareholding, there is an inheritance tax (IHT) point to be remembered. This is that on death, although the proceeds may not be subject to corporation tax, they do swell the value of the company and this will be reflected in the value of the deceased's shareholding. A large quantity of cash in the company may reduce entitlement to IHT business property relief. If this is likely to be a problem, it might be better to arrange life cover somehow outside the company – possibly by a pension scheme death-in-service benefit or by an own-life policy under trust (with an appropriately increased salary to finance it).

2.4 Critical illness cover

If CIC is added to a key person policy, HMRC practice seems to be to base the tax treatment on the underlying policy: thus tax relief might be available on term assurance plus CIC, but not on whole life assurance plus CIC. Stand-alone CIC is usually treated as term assurance.

2.5 Whole life policies

Key person whole life policies are covered by the Finance Act 1989 provisions on policies held by companies. They are dealt with in detail in Chapter D but effectively mean that the chargeable gain on the policy is treated as the income of the company and subject to corporation tax.

On a death claim, the gain is based on the surrender value immediately before death rather than the sum actually paid out on death. There is no credit for the tax paid by the life fund and so a measure of double taxation could occur. Where a unit-linked whole life policy is used, the surrender value immediately prior to death will usually be less than the total premiums paid. Thus although death is a chargeable event, there is no chargeable gain and no tax.

Whole life policies effected before 14 March 1989 would not be affected by these rules and would be free of tax.

2.6 Key person arrangement

An example of a key person arrangement could be as follows:

Example A

Mr S. Claus is the 50-year-old managing director of the Christmas Novelty Company Ltd. They decide he is a key person and that they would suffer a loss of pre-tax profit of around £250,000 if he died.

The company thus decides to insure his life and effects a five-year term assurance for £250,000. The life office requests a medical examination but, because it is a large office, does not have to reassure the risk. Mr Claus is acceptable at ordinary rates.

The premium is £594 per year but, because the company has got its Inspector of Taxes to agree that it is a business expense for corporation tax purposes, the effective net cost is £416 pa (assuming tax at 30%).

If Mr Claus dies within the term of the policy, the sum assured of £250,000 will be paid to the company. This will be taxed as a trading receipt in the year of payment and thus the net benefit to the company could reduce to £175,000 if its total profits for that year are high enough to keep it in the full corporation tax bracket. If Mr Claus survives the policy term, the company will have to reassess the situation. If they still need the cover they will need to exercise any renewal option in the expiring policy or effect a new policy. In either case the premium rate for age 55 would be used (assuming underwriting at ordinary rates for a new policy). This would be £968 gross, £678 net of 30% corporation tax relief. However, an increase in sum assured might also be necessary, which would further increase the cost. This procedure would continue until Mr Claus retires, leaves the company, or the need for the insurance ceases. If this happens, the company can simply allow the policy to lapse by not paying the next premium.

3 Key Person Income Protection

So far, this chapter has largely looked at the problems caused by the death of a key person. Similar problems may also occur if he becomes unable to work for a prolonged period because of sickness or accident. However, key person income protection business is not straightforward. This is because of the problems of moral hazard. If a key person in charge of a special project fails, the company could put so much pressure on him that he becomes ill so as to enable them to claim. If a top salesman's new business starts to tail off, it would be very tempting for the company to make a claim by trying to prove (possibly with his assistance) that he was ill. This type of temptation could exist with any key person whose performance started to decline.

For these reasons, underwriters are wary of key person income protection and most offices do not write these policies. If cover can be obtained, it may be restricted – eg a maximum policy term of ten years, a deferred period of a year and a maximum benefit period of five years. The maximum entry age is liable to be fairly low and the definition of disablement tight.

If cover can be obtained, it is understood that the taxation principles in Sir John Anderson's statement will apply, although it did not mention income protection. Thus, premiums would probably be allowed as a business expense. With regard to the benefit, if this was paid out as a periodic sum it would be difficult to avoid the conclusion that it was a taxable trading receipt. If key person income protection cannot be obtained, an alternative might be a life policy that pays out on disability as well as death, eg CIC (see above).

4 Key Person Insurance for Partnerships and Sole Traders

Not all small businesses are companies. Many are partnerships and sole traders. These businesses may also have employees who are key people and their lives can be insured for the same reasons as given above for companies.

In England a partnership is not a legal entity unless it is an limited liability partnership (LLP) and thus the partnership may not be able to effect a policy on the life of an employee. However, the key employee or one or two of the partners could effect a policy on the life of a key employee on trust for all the partners for the time being. The policy would thus effectively be an asset of the partnership. A Scottish partnership would be able to effect the policy, as it is a legal entity north of the border. The partnership would probably pay the premiums and tax relief as a business expense might be available, if the partnership could persuade its Inspector of Taxes that the premiums were a genuine business expense on the normal key person basis – ie that an employee was being insured against loss of profits by a short-term assurance. However, it would be most unlikely that HMRC would agree to tax relief if the life assured was one of the partners.

If the premiums were allowed as a business expense it is probable that HMRC would want to tax the sum assured as a trading receipt. If this was not the case, then the normal chargeable gains rules would apply with the partner who effected the policy paying any tax at his rate. If more than one partner effected the policy, any chargeable gain would be apportioned between them. In most cases it is unlikely that there would be any tax liability as a qualifying policy or a policy with no surrender value would be used. But if there was any tax to pay, the partner who was liable could require the other partners to bear their share of the tax.

A sole trader could effect a policy on the life of an employee on a life of another basis. The tax situation would be the same as that set out above for partnerships. Thus, income tax relief might be available as a *bona fide* business expense with the sum assured being taxable as a trading receipt – or alternatively no tax relief on premiums with the proceeds being subject to the normal chargeable gains rules.

L Inheritance Tax Planning

Inheritance tax (IHT) has already been explained in Chapter C. This chapter explains how the tax can be planned for or reduced using life products.

1 Planning for IHT – Joint Life Planning Points

For married couples and civil partnerships, the major tax liability will occur on the death of the second to die. It should never be forgotten that if the first to die leaves everything on death to the survivor, then effectively the nil rate band on first death has been wasted. An example will make this clearer.

Example A

Mr A has an estate of £400,000 and Mrs A £100,000. Mr A dies leaving whole estate to Mrs A. Mrs A then dies leaving:

£100,000		**Tax**
+ £400,000		
£500,000		£86,000
	Total tax	£86,000

Net amount to children £414,000

Instead, if Mr A's will is altered to leave the nil rate band direct to the children and the rest to his wife, the situation is as follows:

Mr A dies leaving

			Tax
£285,000 to children – nil rated			Nil
and £115,000 to Mrs A – exempt			Nil
Mrs A then dies leaving	£100,000		
	+ £115,000		
	£215,000		Nil
		Total tax	Nil

Net amount to children £500,000.

A saving of £86,000 has been made and the children have benefited from some of the estate earlier. It may not always be possible or convenient to leave assets equivalent to the nil rate band direct to the eventual beneficiaries on first death, but this should always be considered. However, this arrangement will only save as much tax if Mr A dies first. If Mrs A died first the position would be as follows:

Mrs A dies leaving £100,000 to children –		**Tax**
below threshold		Nil
Mr A dies leaving £400,000 to children		£46,000
	Total tax	£46,000

Net amount to children £454,000.

In this case the saving is only £40,000. A better plan might therefore be to redistribute the estates during lifetime to ensure that major savings can be made whoever dies first.

The working of this principle is shown by the following example, using the same family.

Example B

Mr A's estate £400,000, Mrs A's estate £100,000.
Mr A gives Mrs A £150,000 during lifetime. Gift to spouse – tax-free.

On death	**Mr A**	**Mrs A**
Estate left to children	£250,000	£250,000
Less tax	£0	£0
Net estate to children	£250,000	£250,000
Total tax	£0	

Total net to children £500,000 whoever dies first.

If it is practicable, it is always advisable to consider redistributing the total estate between husband and wife to ensure that each is able to use the nil rate band on first death by leaving £285,000 direct to the children rather than to the survivor. In this way, savings of £114,000 can be made (ie £285,000 x 40%). However, it is important to ensure that the surviving spouse will have enough to live on before this exercise is attempted. If spouses automatically leave the whole of their estates to the survivor, that is effectively wasting the nil rate band.

One way of using the nil rate band but retaining flexibility to provide for a surviving spouse is by using a single premium bond. The husband could effect a bond for, say, £285,000 on the joint life of himself and his wife. The husband leaves the bond in his will to the children but under a trust which gives the trustees power to lend or advance money to the widow. The rest of the estate can be left to the wife.

When the husband dies, the bond is free of tax as being covered by the nil rate band. The trustees can cash the bond if they wish. Alternatively, the bond can be continued because it is on the joint lives of both spouses. If the widow requires any money over and above what she received from her husband's will, the trustees can make withdrawals from the bond and either lend them to her interest-free or give them to her.

Interest-free loans might be preferable as these would be a debt on the widow's estate which would reduce the IHT when she dies. Any chargeable gain would be taxable under the special rules for trust policies – see Chapter D section 2.7.

The wife could effect a similar policy so that the arrangement would work whoever died first. During the lifetime of each investor, the bond belongs to them and is not under trust and so can be cashed without any problems if an emergency arises.

2 Planning for IHT – Regular Premium Plans

2.1 Funding for the tax

Inheritance tax is primarily a tax payable on death. It is then that the major liability normally arises and there is frequently a physical problem in finding the cash with which to pay it. The deceased's legal personal representatives must deliver an account to Her Majesty's Revenue and Customs (HMRC) of all the deceased's property before a grant of representation can be obtained. They must also pay the tax due before they get the grant, unless any of it can be paid in instalments[1]. Thus, before they can get the grant, they have to pay the tax – which in practical terms can be a problem because the assets of the estate (which could be used to pay the tax) cannot be released because the legal personal representatives cannot prove their title without the grant, which they cannot get until the tax is paid.

However, if there was a ready source of liquid cash outside the estate, this could provide the deceased's heirs with the funds to pay the tax, obtain the grant and release the assets in the estate. A life policy can achieve this very easily as it is tailor-made to provide cash on death whenever it occurs. For this reason many life policies are effected to fund for IHT. The policy should be written under trust (see Chapter G) for the heirs to the estate so that the policy is not itself an asset of the estate. Therefore, there will be no IHT on the policy itself and payment can be made to the trustees (without waiting for the grant) very soon after the death. The trustees (who will often be the same people as the legal personal representatives) then have the liquid cash to pay the tax straight away.

Let us look at an example of someone who is leaving the whole estate to children to see how this could work.

	£
House	400,000
Contents	10,000
Car	10,000
National savings	10,000
Bank account	5,000
Building society deposit	12,000
Shares	83,000
Total estate	530,000
Tax liability	£98,000

The tax could, in theory, be met by selling some of the investments and withdrawing the money from the various savings accounts, but the legal personal representatives cannot do this without the grant.

However, if the deceased had effected a life policy for £98,000 under trust for his children with his legal personal representatives as trustees, they would be able to get their hands on this cash very swiftly and so pay the tax, obtain their grant and release the rest of the estate.

[1] IHTA 1984 s226(2)

Payment of each premium by the deceased is a transfer of value, but is usually within the annual exemption. It could also qualify as normal expenditure.

Term policies to age 100 are sometimes used as a cheap alternative to whole life policies, although there is always a risk that the life assured will survive past the expiry date.

For the effect of the 2006 Budget, see Chapter G sections 5.3.7 and 5.3.8.

2.2 Preserving the estate

A further problem that arises is that of preserving individual assets within the estate. It is obviously possible for the legal personal representatives in the example above to obtain a short-term loan to raise the cash to pay the tax. However, the loan will have to be repaid from the assets in the estate when the grant is obtained. There may be enough liquidity in the estate to do this but there may be a real problem if major assets have to be sold off to pay the tax.

If we look back to the previous example, it could be that the family wish to keep the house – maybe some of them are still living in it.

Again, the answer would be to effect a life policy under trust for £98,000. This would pay the tax and mean that the family house and assets could be preserved intact which would be a very valuable practical benefit.

For this reason, many individuals who wish to preserve individual items for their beneficiaries effect life policies under trust for those beneficiaries to pay the tax on the assets concerned.

2.3 Policies which can be used for funding and preserving

The cheapest cover is obtained by using a term assurance but because this must expire at some stage, it is not the complete answer. Most life offices will not write term assurances beyond age 80 and so more permanent protection should ideally be arranged.

The natural contracts for this are whole life policies – often unit-linked ones. These have the advantage of greater flexibility for the future with the variable mix between premiums applied to investment or life cover; although there is always the possibility of premiums being increased at a future review date, if unit growth has not been high enough to sustain the desired level of life cover.

Cover is relatively cheap, particularly at the younger ages, and very high amounts of life cover can be obtained for premiums within the exemptions.

Some guaranteed premium non-linked whole life policies have been launched lately for IHT purposes. A number of these have no surrender value, thus effectively being term assurance until death.

2.3.1 Joint life policies

Reference has already been made to the problem for married couples and civil partnerships of the major tax liability occurring on the second death (see section 1). This is because frequently one leaves all or most of the estate to the other. This is exempt as a gift to a spouse/civil partner and therefore no tax is payable at the time. However, there will be a tax liability on the death of the survivor based on the value of his or her own estate plus that inherited from the other.

For this reason, many funding or preservation arrangements are written on a joint life second death basis. The life policy will pay out under trust on the death of the second of the couple to die and provide the cash to fund the tax payable at that time.

An added advantage of a joint life second death arrangement is that the premiums are cheaper than on single life policies, because payment is deferred to the second death. Also a female's expectation of life is greater than a male's and most wives are younger than their husbands anyway.

2.3.2 Sum assured

When planning to fund a potential IHT liability, the amount of that liability should obviously be calculated, as far as this is possible. However, it is not known when death will occur or what the asset values or rate bands will be at the time. Thus, the first step is to work out the tax payable on current rates, if death occurred immediately.

At present, the nil rate band should be indexed each year[2], although the Chancellor can decide to ignore this if he wishes. Indeed, he did so in the last Budget, announcing that the nil rate band for 2007/08 will be £300,000 and for 2008/09, £312,000 and for 2009/10 £325,000. If the value of the estate also increases at the same rate as the Retail Price Index (RPI) and the nil rate band is index-linked, the effect is that the potential tax bill is also index-linked. If the estate grows at a rate faster than the rate of inflation, the potential liability will grow even faster.

If level cover is bought, there is thus a risk that the sum assured will become inadequate to cover the desired tax liability once the policy has been in force for a few years. One way to combat this is to effect a with-profits policy, whereby the amount payable will increase each year by the amount of the bonus to cover the increased liability.

Alternatively, if a unit-linked whole life policy is being used, advantage could be taken of the facility which most of these provide to index-link the life cover.

If a term assurance is being used, then an increasing version might be preferred to a level contract.

2.3.3 Pension arrangements

When looking at funding for IHT or for preserving the estate, the possibility of providing life cover under some form of pension arrangement should not be ignored. Life cover of up to the lifetime allowance can be given under a registered pension scheme and this could be used to fund for the tax.

[2] IHTA 1984 s8

The life cover is usually arranged under trust so as not to be an asset of the estate itself and the trustees of the scheme will be able to pay the proceeds direct to the beneficiaries soon after death.

If the cover is expressed as a multiple of salary as is often the case, it will potentially be an increasing sum (since salary will often increase from year to year) and so will in some measure protect against future rises in the value of the estate and thus the tax payable.

Life cover under pension schemes has to expire by age 75 at the latest, but some offices offer a retirement option whereby the individual has the option to effect a whole life policy at retirement without any medical evidence. This is a valuable option and should be taken if the life cover is to be used for IHT funding.

The option usually costs a small extra premium but is well worth having.

The advantage of pension scheme cover is that the employer will often pay the premium and, even if the scheme is contributory, full tax relief can be obtained by the member on his contributions. In this way tax relief can be obtained at a minimum rate of 22%.

For those who are eligible, similar benefits can be obtained from personal pension life cover (see Chapter O for full details). In this case, the premium is limited by the annual allowance and the sum assured by the lifetime allowance. The policy can be effected under trust for the desired beneficiaries just like an ordinary life policy.

The advantage over an ordinary life policy is that there is full tax relief on the premiums. The disadvantage is that cover must cease at age 75 and there can be no continuation option.

If income withdrawal is taken on a personal pension and the policyholder dies before purchasing an annuity, the remaining fund is paid as provided for in the policy, subject to a 35% income tax charge. If the fund is payable to the estate this would be subject to IHT. However, most drawdown policies would be written under some form of trust, with death benefits passing outside the estate.

HMRC has said that on any personal pension there is a possibility of IHT under the omission to exercise a right provision if the policyholder could have taken an annuity, but deliberately did not exercise that option. It has stated that there will only be a claim where there is evidence that the policyholder's intention in failing to take up the annuity was to increase the estate of someone else. It will look closely at arrangements where the policyholder became aware that he or she was in very poor health and so deferred the date for taking the annuity. Even then a claim would not be pursued where the death benefit was paid to the policyholder's spouse and/or dependants. In addition a claim would not normally be pursued where the policyholder survived for two years or more after making these arrangements. As is usual HMRC reserves the right to examine each case individually.

The discretionary trust regime and 2006 Budget changes do not apply to registered pension schemes (including pension term assurance).

2.3.4 Policies under seal

Most life assurance policies are issued under hand which means that they are UK assets for IHT purposes. However, if a policy is issued under seal, for IHT purposes it is deemed to be situated in the country in which it is physically present. Thus, if a policy under seal is physically located outside the UK, it is deemed to be a non-UK asset. For a UK domiciled policyholder, this makes no difference because UK domiciled individuals are subject to IHT on their worldwide assets. But an individual domiciled outside the UK is only taxable on his UK assets. So a UK policy under hand which was part of his estate will be taxable. But if the UK policy is under seal and physically located outside the UK, it would not be a UK asset, and so a non-UK domiciled policyholder would escape IHT on it.

For this reason policies issued to non-UK domiciled policyholders are often written under seal, although if the policy is issued under trust this would not be necessary as it would not be part of the estate anyway. HMRC's view is that if a policy was originally issued under hand, it does not become a policy under seal by the addition to the document of the company's seal.

2.4 Shifting wealth

Regular premium life policies can be used to shift wealth out of the estate and thus actually reduce tax on death as well as merely funding for it. The technique here is to effect a policy under trust (see Chapter G) for the intended beneficiaries, with a premium that will be exempt. Obviously, the most effective plan will be that which uses the various exemptions available to achieve the highest possible exempt premium. By this means, an appreciable amount can be built up outside the estate which will be free of IHT on death.

The types of policy used for this purpose will probably be endowment assurances – either with-profits or unit-linked.

A unit-linked endowment policy can be used in the knowledge that it will pay out the total value of units to the beneficiaries on maturity, or the guaranteed sum assured on earlier death. The extension option incorporated in these policies can also be used to extend the term of the plan and maximise its efficiency. Because these plans involve some life cover, the proposer needs to be in a reasonable state of health for his or her age. Alternatively, a maximum debt might be imposed so that impaired health would not affect the investment return.

The aim is to use the exemptions to the maximum. In many cases this will mean that a premium of £3,000 pa can be paid to be exempt under the annual exemption (assuming it is not being used in any other way). This can enable large sums to be built up outside the estate over the years. It must be remembered, however, that premature death will reduce the number of £3,000 premiums that can come out of the estate, although the life cover provided by the plan may compensate for this.

In addition to the annual exemption, the normal expenditure exemption can also be used in these cases. The amount of premium that can be claimed as 'normal expenditure' will vary from person to person, but can be substantial for a wealthy individual. To claim this exemption, HMRC must be satisfied that the premium comes from income and does not reduce the donor's usual standard of living. The element of 'normality' may also be a problem, in that HMRC may not accept this in the first policy year, when only one premium has been paid and there is no guarantee that future premiums will be paid – although that is part of the contract between insured and insurer. The task will be easier in the second year and by the third year, when three payments have been made, it is anticipated that HMRC will usually accept the 'normality' element both for future premiums and retrospectively for those already paid. Care should be taken over the amount of the premium, as what may qualify at outset as expenditure out of income may not do so in future, especially if the policyholder's income reduces.

This exemption can be used in conjunction with the annual exemption. For example, a £4,000 premium for a moderately wealthy man may be accepted as totally exempt – £3,000 being annual and £1,000 normal expenditure. In comparison, for a millionaire, a premium of £13,000 might be accepted as totally exempt – £3,000 being annual and £10,000 normal expenditure.

The claim values will be payable free of IHT, because they are outside the estate of the deceased. The policy is qualifying and so there is no income tax on death. Premiums were exempt when paid – thus the estate has been reduced by the total premiums and tax has been saved on this amount at 40%.

There is a potential pre-owned assets tax (POAT) problem with pre-18 March 1986 regular premium policies under trust. It is because in those days the settlor was frequently included as a potential beneficiary and there was no gift with reservation rule to discourage this. The gift with reservation rules contain an exemption for these policies, as long as the policy is not varied on or after 18 March 1986 so as to increase the benefit or extend the term. There is no similar exemption in the POAT rules, so they apply to that proportion of the value of such a policy as is attributable to premiums paid on or after 18 March 1986.

The problem should not apply to policies effected on or after 18 March 1986 as the settlor should not be a beneficiary in these cases (other than for co-director and partnership arrangements).

2.4.1 Joint life policies

For married couples and civil partnerships, it should not be forgotten that each partner has his or her own exemptions. Thus, a joint life second death policy can be effected with each partner paying a share of the premiums in order to maximise the use of the exemptions. If the cost is met half each, a premium of £6,000 pa can be paid enabling each partner to claim the annual exemption.

This does mean that each partner has to pay from their own resources, but for this exemption it can come from income or capital. It frequently happens that a wife does not have sufficient resources of her own to enable her to do this. In these cases a redistribution of estates (see section 1) exercise could be done or the husband could give £3,000 to his wife as and when needed. This gift would be exempt as a gift to a spouse but it is important that there should be no conditions attached to this, ie it must be a gift to her to use however she wishes. If there was a condition that it must be used for the premium, then the arrangement would fall foul of the 'associated operations' rule, and be treated as a gift by the husband of £6,000[3]. It must be remembered however that there could be problems after the first death as only one annual exemption will then be available.

The normal expenditure exemption could also be used by both partners but only if they each have enough income for this purpose. In this case, gifts from a husband to give the wife the resources would not count as income. However, investment income from capital assets given to her by her husband would count.

These sort of plans, both single and joint life, can be very useful if a large portion of wealth is held in shares which would incur a large capital gains tax (CGT) bill if they were sold immediately to effect one of the lump sum plans mentioned later. Annual funding can use the annual exemption, currently £8,800, to avoid CGT altogether.

3 Lump Sum Plans

Some plans on the market involve the investment of a lump sum and these are dealt with in this section.

3.1 Gift and loan schemes

A number of offices have gift and loan schemes. This involves the client executing a deed of gift creating a trust. This is either a chargeable lifetime transfer or will probably be fully exempt (eg under the £3,000 a year exemption). The client then lends the trustees, interest-free, a sum of money (generally much larger than the gift) which they then use to effect a bond. The loan can be repaid to the client in 5% instalments each year by partial encashment of the bond until it is fully repaid. The amount of any loan outstanding at any time would remain in the donor's estate but all future growth would be outside his estate.

When the client dies, the bond pays out the value of the units to the trustees. This is free of IHT as it is not part of the client's estate. The trustees pay whatever remains of the loan back to the client's estate (where it is subject to IHT) and pay the balance to the beneficiaries of the trust. Any higher rate income tax liability on a chargeable gain is payable by the estate at the client's rates.

It would seem that HMRC does not find the plans objectionable, a view supported by its favourable comments on this type of scheme in connection with POAT. In any event the plans do not achieve much that could not otherwise be gained by a potentially exempt transfer (PET) in that the unrepaid loan is always in the client's estate (not just for seven years) and on early death very little will have been saved. Once the loan has been repaid no further payments can be made to the client.

[3] IHTA 1984 s268

A couple of offices offer a plan that is all loan with no 'starter' gift. The settlor creates a flexible trust with a loan to trustees which they then invest in a bond. Because there is no initial gift, this increases the risk of the trustees not having enough money to repay the loan if the settlor dies very soon after effecting the plan. Therefore, one plan's trust wording includes a clause removing a trustee's liability to repay the loan if the value of the investment is insufficient, but most advisers consider that this provision increases the risk of an HMRC attack.

These schemes are not subject to the POAT rules as the settlor will not be a beneficiary of the trust.

With respect to the 2006 Budget changes, the loan repayments to the settlor would not generate an exit charge. The value at a tenth anniversary would be the value of the bond less the outstanding loan. Thus, if as is usual, the original gift is well under the nil rate band, it is unlikely that there will be no exit or periodic charge.

3.2 Single premium life policies

Single premium life policies are really an extension of the regular premium funding approach. However, instead of buying life cover with regular premiums, a single premium is paid into a unit-linked whole life policy. The amount of life cover varies with age but the idea is to make an estimate of the current IHT liability and pay whatever single premium is required to produce this amount of life cover. The premium will be applied to buy units in the fund(s) of the policyholder's choice. Every month enough units are cancelled to pay for that month's cover. The sum assured is worked out as the amount that can be sustained if units grow at an assumed rate (often 6% pa). The policy will be reviewed from time to time and if unit growth is below that assumed, the sum assured will be reduced.

The policy is effected under trust so that the proceeds are free of IHT. A gift is thus made, at outset, of the amount of the single premium and this may involve a chargeable transfer, as it may well be over the relevant exemptions. In addition, because of the single premium, it is a non-qualifying policy and there will be an income tax charge on death if the surrender value immediately prior to death is greater than the single premium[4]. This charge would be at the settlor's rates even though the policy is under trust[5].

Example C

An example will show how the plan works:

Mr A is 60, has an estate of £570,000 and is a 40% income taxpayer.

The IHT on £570,000 at death rates is £114,000. Mr A therefore effects a single premium policy for a sum assured of £114,000. The single premium for this is £43,133. Because the policy is under trust, this is a lifetime gift of the amount of the premium. The first £3,000 of this might be exempt under the annual exemption but the rest would be chargeable, unless an interest in possession trust was used. The policy will

[4] ITTOIA s493(7); [5] ITTOIA s465(3)

pay out £114,000 under trust, free of IHT when Mr A dies – thus enabling his beneficiaries to pay the tax and release the estate.

If death occurred after, say, five years and the fund achieved a unit growth of 6% pa, the surrender value immediately prior to death would be say £48,000 giving a chargeable gain of £48,000 – £43,133 = £4,867. Income tax would be payable on this at Mr A's top rate (40%) minus the lower rate (20%). Thus, the income tax liability would be £4,867 x 0.2 = £973.40. This would be payable by the estate. The income tax bill might be lower or even nil if Mr A died early enough in the tax year before his total income reached the 40% band.

This plan is more effective at younger ages and is subject to an upper age limit, typically 75–80. It can be arranged on a single life or joint life second death basis. One office markets a version of this plan combined with an ordinary unit-linked bond. The bond stays in the client's estate and thus can be used to pay regular withdrawals to the client and as emergency capital if required. The single premium unit-linked whole life plan is written with the sum assured being equal to the total investment. This policy is under a flexible trust which will repay the total investment free of IHT on death, although the normal higher rate income tax consequences as described above still apply. The effect of the plan is to free the whole investment from IHT but give a right to withdrawals and access to a substantial portion of the capital.

These policies are not subject to the POAT rules as the settlor will not be a beneficiary of the trust. The plans could be subject to the 2006 Budget changes unless an absolute trust was used.

3.3 Family wealth trust bonds

Some life offices used to offer bonds under a family wealth trust. This was a trust with an initial defeasible life interest for the client's spouse which enabled the client to be a potential beneficiary of the trust without it being a gift with reservation. This was challenged in the courts by HMRC but it lost. Having lost in court it then changed the law to block the loophole.

The Finance Act 2003 thus provides that it is a gift with reservation where:

- A gift to a spouse or civil partner is made on or after 20 June 2003; and
- The property becomes settled property by virtue of a gift; and
- The trust gives an interest in possession to the donor's spouse or civil partner so that the gift is exempt from IHT by reason of exemption for transfers between spouses and civil partners and the rule which treats an interest in possession as equivalent to outright ownership; and
- Between the date of the gift and the donor's death the interest in possession comes to an end; and

- When that interest in possession comes to an end the beneficiary does not become entitled to the settled property or another interest in possession in it.

Family wealth trusts created before 20 June 2003 are not affected by this legislation and still work as intended for IHT purposes. Details can be found in previous editions of this work if required. However, they are potentially affected by the POAT rules. There is no charge to POAT whilst the spouse of the settlor is still the beneficiary with the interest in possession. However, if the spouse's interest has been removed by the trustees exercising their power of appointment and, say, the children are now the beneficiaries, then the POAT rules apply.

3.4 Split trust bonds

Another way of using a single premium bond is to effect a standard bond under a split trust often called a retained interest trust. The trust splits the beneficial ownership into a gifted portion and a retained portion. The retained portion is held on trust for the settlor absolutely and the gifted portion is held on trust for the intended beneficiaries, usually by a flexible trust. The settlor is not a beneficiary of the gifted portion in any way and thus it is not a gift with reservation.

The IHT situation is that there is a transfer of value at outset. One office offering the scheme states that the transfer of value is that proportion of the total premium represented by the proportion of the gifted portion to the total – ie if £200,000 is invested and 50% gifted and 50% retained, it is stated that the transfer is £100,000. However, HMRC's view is that the value of the transfer must include the bid–offer gap on the retained portion on the loss to the estate principle. Thus, the transfer in the previous example would be £200,000 – £95,000 (the immediate post-transfer value if there was a bid–offer gap of 5% of the retained portion) = £105,000. The transfer might be partly exempt but mostly chargeable.

The settlor can take withdrawals from the bond as income, subject to the normal chargeable gains rules. However, the 5% is related to the total investment not just the retained portion. Thus, in the example above the settlor could withdraw £10,000 pa without incurring an immediate income tax charge.

However, all withdrawals must be deducted from the settlor's portion and thus if that grows at a rate less than the total withdrawal it will erode. Each time a withdrawal is taken, the proportions gifted and retained are re-calculated to reflect the withdrawal and advised to the trustees. In this way, the retained portion can be progressively reduced or even eventually extinguished, leaving an increasing proportion of the bond in the gifted portion. However, no transfer occurs at the time of the withdrawal as this comes entirely from the retained portion.

When death occurs the trustees pay the value of the gifted portion, free of IHT if the donor lived seven years, to the beneficiaries. The balance is paid to the settlor's estate and is subject to IHT therein. Any higher rate income tax charge on the total profit (including all 5% withdrawals taken) is based on the settlor's rate and is a liability of the estate, further reducing it for IHT purposes.

Split trust bonds are not subject to the POAT rules as they are a species of carve-out scheme where the settlor's benefits are held on a bare trust for them.

These plans could be subject to the 2006 Budget changes, as regards the gifted portion, unless an absolute trust was used.

3.5 Back-to-back plans

These plans are a combination of a whole life policy and a life annuity running 'back-to-back'. A lump sum is paid at outset, most of which buys an annuity for the life of the individual. The balance is used to pay the first premium under a whole life policy, effected under trust for the individual's beneficiaries. This is a gift for IHT purposes, but will normally be exempt under the annual exemption. The annuity is paid out, say, yearly, part funding the whole life premium and the rest being available for the individual to spend as income. The annuity is a purchased life annuity and so only the interest content is taxable, the rest being the tax-free capital content.

On death, the annuity ceases and is thus worth nothing for IHT purposes. The life policy pays out free of IHT to the beneficiaries. There is no income tax charge because the whole life assurance is a qualifying policy. These plans are very effective for getting large amounts of capital out of the estate, whilst still giving the individual an income. They are available on a single or joint life second death basis for married couples and civil partnerships.

The individuals have to be in reasonable health because they have to be underwritten for the whole life policy. If both contracts are written by the same life office, it will not be concerned when death occurs because the 'loss' on an early death under the whole life policy is matched by the 'gain' on the annuity contract. However, s263 of the Inheritance Tax Act 1984 (IHTA) applies to back-to-back policies, unless it can be shown that the contracts were not associated operations. If the section applies, the transfer of value is the lesser of the total initial lump sum and the whole life sum assured – which would render the plan totally ineffective. Thus, in order to show that the contracts are not associated, the whole life policy must be underwritten without reference to the annuity. The best way to establish that the two contracts are not associated is to use different life offices, which will also be beneficial in that the best rates for each type of contract can be obtained; it would be unlikely that one office would offer both the best whole life rates and the best annuity rates on the market. If the same office is used for both parts of the plan it is essential that full medical evidence is obtained to underwrite the life policy. The working of the plan can be seen from the following example.

Example D

Mr X is 65 and Mrs X is 60. They are both in good health and have an estate of £400,000. They are basic rate taxpayers with shares currently yielding 2.3%.

Mr and Mrs X take out a back-to-back plan for £40,000. The whole life policy is effected under trust for their children for a premium of £1,400 pa. This is well within their annual exemptions and provides a sum assured of £79,480.

The balance of £38,600 purchases an annuity for their joint lives of £2,550 of which the tax-free capital content is £1,400. The effect on their income is as follows:

Before	**£**
£40,000 shares yielding 2.3%	920
No further income tax as covered by the 10% tax credit	–
Net income	920

After	**£**
Gross annuity	2,550
Less income tax at 20% on (£2,550 – £1,400) = £1,150	230
Net annuity	2,320
Less whole life premium	1,400
Net income	920
Previous net income	920

Thus income has been preserved.
The effect on the IHT position, however, is much more impressive.

Before	£
Estate	400,000
Less IHT	46,000
Net estate to children	354,000

After	£
Estate	360,000
Less IHT	30,000
Net estate to children	330,000
Plus whole life sum assured	79,480
Total to children	409,480
Previous total	354,000
Net gain to children	55,480

A variant on this back-to-back theme is the combination of a purchased life annuity, and a term assurance paying out on death before age 110 (or 50 years if earlier). The effect is very similar to a whole life back-to-back plan, although the term assurance rates and sums assured are guaranteed, so it does not rely on any with-profits return or unit-linked growth rate.

These plans are not subject to the POAT rules as the settlor will not be a beneficiary of the trust of the life policy. The life policy trust could be subject to the 2006 Budget changes unless an absolute trust was used.

3.6 Conversion plans

These are a combination of a single premium unit-linked bond and an annual premium unit-linked policy. The way the plan works is that the major portion of the lump sum pays the single premium for the bond and the balance provides the first premium under the life policy which will probably be a flexible whole life plan under trust for the client's desired beneficiaries. Each year, 5%, say, will be withdrawn from the bond and used to pay all subsequent premiums with any balance being spendable as income. There will be no tax to pay on these withdrawals, at least for 20 years. If the client does not want income, only that amount needed to pay premiums is withdrawn, leaving the balance of the 5% allowances to be accumulated for use when required.

The premiums will be transfers of value but will normally be exempt under the annual exemption. The idea is that money is built up in the life policy which will be free of income tax and IHT. If the units grow by more than the amount withdrawn, then the bond will also grow in value.

On death, the sum assured under the life policy is paid out free of all taxes to the beneficiaries of the trust. The bond also pays out its residual value, although this would be subject to IHT as part of the estate and to higher rate income tax on any chargeable gain as well.

The overall effect is to substantially increase the amount received by the beneficiaries as shown in the following example.

Example E	£
Male aged 50 with an estate of	400,000
On which inheritance tax would be	46,000
Thus net amount passing to beneficiaries	354,000
Invests £50,000 – split two ways	
Single premium bond	48,500
First premium on life policy	1,500
Sum assured on life policy	87,793
Each year 5% of bond withdrawn	2,425
Annual premium on life policy	1,500
Balance spendable as income	£925
Position on death immediately	
Rest of estate	350,000
Plus value of bond (after 5% bid–offer spread)	46.075
Total	396,075
Inheritance tax	44,430
Net estate	351,645
Plus life policy sum assured	87,793
Net amount to beneficiaries	439,438
An increase of	85,438

It will be seen that the effect is that the life policy enables all the tax to be funded and thus substantially increases the net amount received by the beneficiaries. As time goes on, the situation could improve, especially if the unit growth rate exceeds that assumed in the life policy, because that might enable the sum assured to be increased and of course the bond would be growing in value as well – although there would be some higher rate income tax to pay on that.

These plans are not subject to the POAT rules as the settlor will not be a beneficiary of the trust of the life policy.

These plans could be subject to the 2006 Budget changes unless an absolute trust was used.

3.7 Series of endowments

One office has a lump sum plan involving a series of single premium unit-linked endowments maturing at selected yearly intervals to age 100. The policies do not have a surrender value. Each endowment is under trust for the selected beneficiaries of a power of appointment trust on death, but for the investor on maturity. If the investor wants income from the arrangement he can take the proceeds of each policy at maturity. The payment back to the settlor would be exempt from IHT under the revertor to settlor rule.

The arrangement is thus a chargeable lifetime transfer at outset of the total premiums less the value of bond maturities which the client could expect to receive during his lifetime, based on age and state of health at outset. The office can give its opinion of this discounted value, although HMRC may not necessarily agree with the figure. Any chargeable gain on maturity is the liability of the investor, but as there is no surrender value there can be no chargeable gain on death.

The arrangement is not a gift with reservation as HMRC has confirmed that where there is a gift to a trust, the retention by the settlor of a reversionary interest is not a gift with reservation. The retention of the right to the maturity value is effectively a reversionary interest.

One version of this scheme gives the trustees the option to extend the maturity date and incorporates a surrender value. Because of the surrender value, this is a chargeable lifetime transfer at outset of the full premium, not a discounted value. If the trustees do extend the maturity date, the client does not get the maturity value, and the extension is a further gift which would be a chargeable lifetime transfer.

One office has a variation of this scheme involving whole life policies with encashment dates, instead of endowments, to the same effect.

The POAT rules do not apply as the settlor's reversionary interest is held on a bare trust for him.

3.8 PETA plans

A few offices have PETA plans which are a combination of a pure endowment (PE) and a term assurance (TA), and are available on a single or joint life second death basis to investors under 85.

A lump sum is invested into the pure endowment and invested in units in the underlying account which cannot be surrendered. If the unit price has increased at the end of a policy year, the growth is transferred from the underlying account to a separate bonus account. Whatever is in the bonus account can then be taken as withdrawals or left in the account. If withdrawn, it is subject to the normal 5% part surrender rules. The policy is retained by the investor as it is his source of 'income'. If it matures at age 105, the total value of units will be paid out to the investor and this would be subject to the normal chargeable gains rules for income tax and be in the estate for IHT purposes. If the investor dies before age 105, the death sum assured of 0.1% of the premium plus any remaining bonus units is paid to the estate. This amount would be subject to IHT, and possibly higher rate income tax in the unlikely event of it (plus previous 5% withdrawals) exceeding the premium.

The term assurance has a premium of 0.1% of the pure endowment premium and is written to age 110 under trust for the investor's chosen beneficiaries. On death prior to age 110 it will pay out the amount of pure endowment premium to the trust free of IHT (as not in the estate) and income tax (as there is no surrender value prior to death).

The putting of the term assurance into trust is a chargeable lifetime transfer for IHT but at a discounted value to reflect the value of the bonus rights retained. The life office provides its opinion of the discounted value but while HMRC may accept the general basis of the calculation, each case would be considered individually and the exact value might be a matter for negotiation. The discounted value must be reported to HMRC at outset. The standard discounted values are based on normal health for age and sex, and underwriting would be necessary to establish this in individual cases.

The arrangement is not caught by the gift with reservation anti-avoidance provisions in paragraph 7(1)(b) of Schedule 20 of the Finance Act 1986 as the benefit to the beneficiaries does not vary by reference to the benefits accruing to the investor.

Example F

A 69-year-old widow, in normal health has an estate of £500,000. She invests £100,100 into a PETA plan – £100,000 into the pure endowment and £100 into the term assurance and the discounted value is £45,000. The IHT liability is reduced as follows on the basis that all bonus units are withdrawn each year and spent as income:

		Position on death	
	Before the PETA plan	**During years 1–7 of the PETA plan**	**After year 7 of the PETA plan**
	£	**£**	**£**
The PE proceeds	0	100	100
Other assets	500,000	399,900	399,900
Discounted value	0	45,000	0
Total for IHT	500,000	445,000	400,000
IHT	86,000	64,000	46,000
For the beneficiaries			
The PE proceeds	0	100	100

The TA proceeds	0	100,000	100,000
Other assets	500,000	399,900	399,900
Total	500,000	500,000	500,000
Less IHT	– 86,000	– 64,000	– 46,000
Net benefit	414,000	436,000	454,000
Saving		22,000	40,000

One office has a version of this plan using one single premium bond rather than a pure endowment plus a term policy. The bond contains two separate benefits – a death benefit of 101% of the premium and a right to surrender units in a deposit fund, which is fed by investment growth from the main bond fund. Again, the transfer at outset is a discounted value to reflect the value of the growth rights retained. The tax consequences are the same as the PETA plan. Another office has a pure endowment/whole life plan which works in the same way as the PETA plan.

These plans are not affected by the POAT rules as they are carve-out schemes whereby the settlor's interest is in the pure endowment and he is not a beneficiary of the term policy. The term policy could be subject to the 2006 Budget changes unless an absolute trust was used.

3.9 Discounted gift schemes

A number of life offices offer discounted gift schemes which are based on a trust being established with a sum of money before any bond is purchased. The way these work is that the settlor puts a sum of money into trust mainly for, say, his children but specifically instructs the trustees to pay the settlor a fixed sum each year for the rest of his life. The trustees subsequently purchase a single premium bond as an investment of the trust and use the withdrawal facility (often at 5% for income tax reasons) to pay the settlor the specified sum each year.

This is a chargeable lifetime trasnfer at outset of a discounted value being the total amount being put into the trust less the present value of the settlor's right to £x per annum for the rest of his life. This is an actuarial calculation depending on the settlor's age, sex and state of health at the time. Underwriting may be necessary to back up the discounted value, although as with PETA plans HMRC may, or may not, agree with the life office's valuation, which has to be reported to them at outset as a chargeable lifetime transfer.

These plans are not affected by POAT rules as they are carve-out schemes, whereby the settlor's interest is held on a bare trust for him.

These plans could be subject to the 2006 Budget changes as regards the gifted portion unless an absolute trust was used. Payments to the settler do not generate an exit charge. The periodic charge would be based on the value of the bond less the value of the settlor's interest based on the age, sex and state of health at that time.

3.10 Offshore bond

One office has an IHT plan based on an offshore unit-linked capital redemption bond which matures after 99 years. The bond provides a fixed annual withdrawal which cannot be altered and will continue for the life of the investor as long as there are sufficient units in the bond. The bond cannot be surrendered. The bond is written in trust so that the investor retains the right to the withdrawals but all other benefits are held for the beneficiaries of a flexible power of appointment trust which excludes the investor but could include his spouse. The trust beneficiaries will thus be paid the value of units on death or maturity.

The withdrawals are subject to the normal 5% rules. For IHT purposes, the plan involves a gift at outset which will be a chargeable lifetime transfer. The office claims that the value of the gift is a discounted value being the total investment less the value of the rights retained by the investor. The discounted value will vary according to age, sex, state of health and the level of withdrawals. The office will issue its estimate of the value although HMRC would not necessarily agree this.

This is not a gift with reservation as, although the benefits which accrue to the donees vary by reference to the benefits accruing to the donor, this provision (Finance Act 1986 Sch 20 para 7) does not apply because it is a capital redemption policy not a life policy.

These plans are not subject to the POAT rules as they are carve-out schemes whereby the settlor's interest is held on a bare trust for him. The comments in section 3.9 regarding the 2006 Budget changes also apply here.

3.11 Will trusts

Some offices recommend combining single premium bonds with will trusts for a married couple or civil partnership. This is effectively the same idea as making sure the nil rate band is used on first death (explained in section 1 example B). Each individual buys a joint life bond for the nil rate band with the bond being owned solely by the investor. A trust is written into the will so that the bond becomes subject to the trust on death. During the investor's lifetime the bond is the investor's sole property and can be used to provide withdrawals if required.

The will trust only comes into operation on death and is a power of appointment trust giving the heirs (eg children) an interest in possession but with the surviving spouse or civil partner as a potential beneficiary. It also gives the trustees power to make loans to any beneficiary, including the spouse or civil partner. This ensures that the nil rate band is used on the first death, gives the investor access to the investment during life and gives the spouse or civil partner an emergency source of capital if required. The bond will finally pay out to the heirs on the death of the survivor.

Before using this plan it must be ensured that the will trust does not conflict with any other provision of the will.

Because the bond is on joint lives, it continues for the lifetime of the survivor. If the survivor needs access to any of the money the trustees can make an interest-free loan to him or her, getting the cash by making a withdrawal from the bond. This loan would have to be repaid on the survivor's death by the estate to the trust but would be a debt on the estate, thus saving IHT at 40% on that amount. If the loan was interest-bearing and the interest was not paid but rolled up, this would increase the debt and further reduce the IHT on the second death, but this is not always recommended because of the possible income tax implications.

On the second death, the bond would pay out to the trustees who would also collect in any debts owed by the survivor and pay out the total to the will trust beneficiaries (usually the children). Any chargeable gain would be taxable under the special rules for trusts – see Chapter D section 2.7.

These plans are extremely flexible and tax-efficient, and are not affected by the POAT rules as the trust only comes into force on the death of the settlor.

3.12 Equity release schemes

Home income plans (see Chapter F) can be used as a form of IHT planning. A home-owner could borrow money on the security of the house and then gift that amount as a PET to, say, his children. If he survived seven years, that gift would escape IHT and the value of his estate is reduced by the debt secured against the house.

The home reversion plans described in Chapter F can also have IHT advantages, especially where the homeowner does not have enough income and is not worried about not being able to leave the house in their will. What is effectively being done under these schemes is to exchange a capital asset (the house) which might well be a major, and thus highly taxed, part of the estate for an annuity for life, plus the right to live in this house for life. The purchase of the plan is a commercial transaction and so does not attract IHT. On death the annuity ceases and is worth nothing, and the house is not in the estate and thus not subject to IHT.

Equity release schemes with commercial providers are not subject to the POAT rules.

4 IHT Trusts

The IHT plans explained above, both regular and single premium varieties, all depend on some form of life policy under trust. The type of trust used will depend on the exact requirements of each individual client (see Chapter G).

Where the client is certain who the beneficiaries will be, and does not want to be able to change his mind or recover the policy himself, an absolute trust could be used. If a single life policy was being put in trust for spouse or children, the Married Women's Property Act (MWPA) (see Chapter G section 4.1.1) could be used, otherwise a non-statutory absolute trust must be created (see Chapter G section 4.2). The policy would be considered a part of the beneficiary's(ies') estate(s) for IHT purposes.

An absolute trust would also avoid any problems with the 2006 Budget changes.

4.1 Power of appointment trusts

In many cases, however, particularly where large sums are involved, a client will require greater flexibility. For this reason, power of appointment trusts are commonly used with IHT plans. (See Appendix)

There will be a class of potential beneficiaries, from whom the trustees can appoint an actual beneficiary at any time. In the meantime, and until any appointment is made, the beneficiaries will be as specified in the class of actual beneficiaries. If the client wishes to change a beneficiary for any reason, this can be done by the trustees executing a Deed of Appointment naming the new beneficiary. The new beneficiary must come from the class of potential beneficiaries and so it is wise to word this as widely as possible at outset for maximum flexibility. A typical wording of this class might be *'my wife, my children and remoter issue'*. It would even be possible to obtain further flexibility by adding *'and anybody except myself whose name I supply in writing to the trustees at any time'*. The power of appointment commonly lasts for up to two years after the client's death. It will be normal for the client himself to be a trustee and he may have the power to remove existing trustees and appoint new ones in order to maintain full control.

The actual beneficiaries have the interest in possession and are classed as the owners of the policy for IHT purposes. Thus, if such a beneficiary dies, or is replaced under the power of appointment, this is treated as a transfer of value for IHT purposes. Any tax is calculated at the outgoing beneficiary's rates, but is payable by the trustees.

To avoid any problems with the reservation of benefit provisions and the POAT rules, the settlor must keep himself out of both beneficiary classes, although the settlor's spouse or civil partner can be (and frequently is) named as a potential beneficiary.

Power of appointment trusts created on or after 22 March 2006 are subject to the 2006 Budget changes. As a consequence the holder of the interest in possession is not classed as the owner for IHT purposes. There is thus no tax charge when he/she dies or is replaced.

4.2 Revertor to settlor

Since the 1986 Budget it has become unusual for the settlor to include himself as a beneficiary because of the reservation of benefit provisions. The settlor's spouse or civil partner can be included so that the policy could be appointed to him or her, in which case the reservation of benefit provisions would not apply and the revertor to settlor's spouse or civil partner exemption could still be claimed. However, there should be no agreement that the spouse or civil partner will share any benefit with the settlor, otherwise HMRC could claim this was effectively a reservation of benefit.

4.3 Split trusts

It is possible to put a life policy into a trust which retains some benefit for the settlor, but gives other benefits to other beneficiaries (eg the settlor's family). However, care has to be taken to avoid the gift with reservation rules.

For example, an endowment could be effected under a trust whereby the death benefit is for the family, but the maturity benefit is retained by the settlor. HMRC confirmed to the Association of British Insurers (ABI) in 1986 that this is not a gift with reservation as long as the only benefit the settlor retains is the maturity value – ie he would not be entitled to any surrender value.

It is also possible on a life policy with a critical illness cover (CIC) benefit to have a trust under which the death benefit is for the family, but the CIC benefit is retained by the settlor. HMRC has confirmed that this is not a gift with reservation, and not subject to the POAT rules.

5 Protection for Lifetime Gifts

In a number of cases the taxation consequences of a lifetime gift depend on how long the donor survives after making the gift. If the donor dies before a specified time, the tax liability can often be higher than it would otherwise be. In these cases it may be wise to arrange insurance on the life of the donor to cover this contingency. This problem can arise in two different ways and these will be dealt with in turn.

5.1 Chargeable transfers

As has been explained earlier, if a chargeable transfer during life is taxable (ie because the seven-year cumulation exceeds the threshold), the life rate of 20% applies. However, if the donor dies within seven years of the transfer, then the death rate of 40% retrospectively applies. However, the death rates which apply are those in force at the date of death, not the date of the transfer. In addition, the taper relief will help to reduce the burden of the extra tax liability.

Thus, when the donor dies the taxman works out the tax due on the transfer at the death rate, applies any taper relief (if the donor survived for at least three years) and then deducts the lifetime tax actually paid at the time of the transfer. The resulting tax bill is payable by the recipients of the transfer – normally the trustees. The operation of this principle can be seen from the following table:

Chargeable transfer of £500,000
(assuming no previous transfers and no exemptions available)

Years survived until death	Lifetime tax paid at outset	Death tax (after taper relief)	Balance payable
	£	£	£
0–3	43,000	86,000	43,000
3–4	43,000	68,800	25,800
4–5	43,000	51,600	8,600

5–6	43,000	34,400	0
6–7	43,000	17,200	0
7 +	43,000	0	0

This table assumes continuation of the current rates and bands and shows that extra tax is only payable if the donor dies in the first five years. If the nil rate band rises (as it normally would) the survival period might be reduced, but if the nil rate band was lowered the period might be extended. It will also be noted that if the death tax (after taper relief) is less than the lifetime tax paid, no refund is available.

Trustees will thus hope that the donor lives for long enough to avoid this extra liability and may wish to insure against it. Clearly, the tax bill could be for a large amount and might come at an inconvenient time for the trustees and some form of insurance would be advisable.

The most obvious answer would be a five-year term assurance reducing in the manner shown in the last column in the table, although this is vulnerable to future changes in the rate bands. Thus, a seven-year decreasing term assurance might be a better answer and a number of offices have term assurances with sums assured which are level for three years and then decrease in line with the taper relief.

There are three ways to arrange the cover. First, the donor could effect the policy on his own life under the same trust as the chargeable transfer and pay the premiums himself. This would be a further lifetime gift but possibly exempt under the annual exemption (if there is any left after the main gift).

The second way would be for the trustees to effect the policy on the life of the donor. The potential tax liability gives the trustees the necessary insurable interest. The donor could give the trustees amounts equivalent to the premium for them to pay over to the life office, although these would be further transfers.

The third option would be for the trustees to effect the policy and pay the premiums themselves, in which case no further transfer would be involved, although it requires the trust to have the necessary funds.

However, a term assurance decreasing in line with the taper relief is not the whole answer to the problem. This is because it is only the tax on the lifetime transfer which is tapered. The value of the transfer to be included in the cumulation to calculate the death tax on the estate is not tapered. An example using the transfer shown in the previous table will make this clearer.

Example G

Chargeable transfer of £500,000 (assuming no previous transfers and no exemptions available). Value of estate on death £500,000.

Years survived until death	Extra tax on lifetime transfer	Death tax on estate	Total tax payable
	£	£	£
0–3	43,000	200,000	243,000
3–4	25,800	200,000	225,800
4–5	8,600	200,000	208,600
5–6	0	200,000	200,000
6–7	0	200,000	200,000
7 +	0	nil	86,000

It will be seen that the total extra tax payable on death within the seven years does not decrease in neat 20% steps. In fact, the overall decrease is so slight that the simplest plan would be to have level term assurance for the maximum extra liability for the whole seven years. In this case it would mean a sum assured of £243,000. If the beneficiaries of the estate and those of the lifetime trust are the same, then the trust of the policy can follow these trusts. If they are different, then either two policies could be effected or the policy trust split, as to % for the lifetime trust and the balance for the estate beneficiaries.

If the lifetime transfer (plus the previous seven years' cumulation) is less than the IHT threshold, then no lifetime tax is payable at outset and no extra tax is payable on death within seven years because it is within the nil rate band. However, it will still affect the amount of death tax payable on the estate. For example, if there is a chargeable transfer of £70,000, then no tax is payable on this at outset, or on death within seven years. However, that £70,000 remains in the donor's cumulation for seven years and so if death occurs within that time, the death estate is £70,000 higher up the rate bands than it would otherwise be. Thus, if the death estate is £250,000, the tax is £14,000 if death occurs within seven years and nothing if it is after that period.

There is therefore still a need for life cover in these circumstances, ie in this case a level term assurance for seven years for a sum assured of £14,000. As the tax bands tend to move up each year, the actual liability might be less, although the estate should be increasing in value over the years to offset this.

The potential extra tax liability would have to be met out of the estate by the legal personal representatives. The beneficiaries of the estate have no insurable interest as they have no legal relationship with the testator (see Chapter B section 3.3). For example, the testator may change the will or the beneficiary might predecease the testator. It is doubtful whether the legal personal representatives have an insurable interest either, as again there is no legal relationship because the testator could change his executors or they could predecease him.

For this reason it is probably best for the testator to effect the policy himself, on trust for the beneficiaries of the estate. Ideally, a power of appointment trust should be used – so that the trust beneficiaries can be varied if the will is altered. This would give the beneficiaries the liquid cash to pay the extra tax. The policy will probably be an annual premium contract. Premiums paid by the testator would be lifetime transfers but might be exempt under the annual or normal expenditure exemptions.

5.2 Potentially exempt transfers (PETs)

Similar problems arise on PETs. These transfers are exempt when made but become chargeable retrospectively if death occurs within seven years. Thus, a recipient of a PET will hope that the donor lives for the seven years to avoid this liability. Because no lifetime tax would have been paid at outset, the maximum liability is the full death tax and the taper relief applies after three years. The effect can be seen from the following table:

PET worth £500,000
(assuming no previous transfers and no exemptions available)

Years survived until death	Death tax (after taper relief) £
0–3	86,000
3–4	68,800
4–5	51,600
5–6	34,400
6–7	17,200
7 +	Nil

From the donee's point of view, he may wish to insure this liability, as he will be responsible for it, and so a seven-year decreasing term assurance may be required. This could be effected by the donor on trust for the donee with premiums either being exempt (possibly, under the annual or normal expenditure exemptions) or chargeable lifetime transfers.

Alternatively, the donee could effect the policy on the life of the donor, the potential tax liability creating the insurable interest. The donor might then make gifts to enable the donee to pay the premiums (which might well be exempt under the annual or normal expenditure exemptions) or the donee could pay them from his own resources.

However, as shown in the previous section, this is not the complete answer for the estate because of the 'knock-on' effect of increasing the cumulation for the death estate – without the benefit of taper relief. This is illustrated in the next example, which follows on from the previous one.

Example H

PET worth £500,000. Death estate £500,000. No previous transfers and no examptions available.

Years surivied until death	Death tax on PET	Death tax on estate	Total tax
	£	£	£
0–3	86,000	200,000	286,000
3–4	68,800	200,000	268,800
4–5	51,600	200,000	251,600
5–6	34,400	200,000	234,400
6–7	17,200	200,000	217,200
7 +	Nil	86,000	86,000

Thus, in addition to the donee's policy, the client might want a policy to protect the estate's extra liability – in this case a level term assurance for £200,000 – £86,000 = £114,000. The policy should be written by him on trust for the beneficiaries of the estate – preferably a flexible trust for the reasons explained in the previous section. Premiums might well fall within the annual or normal expenditure exemptions. A possible better answer would be a whole life policy for £200,000 to cover the maximum total liability with the sum insured being reduced appropriately if the donor is still alive after seven years.

As with chargeable transfers, there will be no death tax on the PET if it is nil rated, but there will still be the knock-on effect on the tax on the estate.

Appendix A Power of Appointment Trust

Declaration of Trust

This Annex is deemed to form part of and to be incorporated in the attached application form for a . . . .

I/We desire that the . . . .
Policy (which expression wherever used in this Annex shall include the benefit of the insurance contract or contracts completed pursuant to the acceptance of my/our application and any variation or amendment to the said contract(s) hereby authorised to be made) be issued to me/us as Grantee(s) and expressed to be upon an irrevocable trust for the benefit of all or such one or more exclusively of the others or other of

A The Beneficiaries

. . . .

. . . .

in such shares and in such manner and for such limited or other interest as the Trustees (being at least two in number or a trust corporation) shall in their absolute discretion appoint by deed or deeds revocable or irrevocable and executed at any time or times not later than twenty-four months after the date of death of the life assured (the date of death of the last to die in the case of joint lives assured) and in default of appointment or so far as no such appointment shall extend for the benefit of

B The Beneficiaries entitled if no appointment made

. . . .

. . . .
(in equal shares) absolutely

C The Trustees I/We desire to appoint. . . . .

. . . .

as Trustees to receive the moneys payable under the Policy and they or the survivor of them or other the Trustees for the time being are hereinafter called "the Trustees". The receipt of the Trustees shall be a good discharge to the insurance company for all monies payable under the Policy.

The Trustees may at their discretion and subject to the trusts aforesaid either retain the Policy or deal with the Policy in any manner that they may in their absolute discretion think fit including power (where the Policy so permits but without prejudice to the generality of the foregoing) to surrender the Policy or to convert the Policy in accordance with the options available under the Policy.

Any new Policy or increase or decrease of benefits secured by the Policy or by any new Policy or Policies which is or are effected under any options which are contained in the Policy shall be subject to the same trusts as are herein declared. Any monies liable to be invested hereunder may be invested or laid out in the purchase or at interest upon the security of such stocks funds shares securities investments or property of whatsoever nature and wheresoever situate and whether involving liability or not and whether producing income or not (including the improvement repair insurance (in any value and against any risk) rebuilding and decorating of any property for the time being comprised in the property subject to the trusts hereof or the execution of any other works on or for the benefit of any such property) and whether in the name of a nominee or not as the Trustees shall in their absolute discretion think fit to the intent that the Trustees shall have the same full and unrestricted power of investing and transposing investments as if they were absolutely entitled thereto beneficially. The statutory powers of advancement contained in Section 32 of the Trustee Act 1925 or if applicable Section 33 of the Trustee Act (Northern Ireland) 1958 shall apply to the trusts hereof with the following variation that is to say the omission in proviso (a) to sub-section (l) of the said Section of the words "one-half-of". Section 31 of the Trustee Act 1925 or if applicable Section 32 of the Trustee Act (Northern Ireland) 1958 shall not apply to the trusts of this Policy.

All income which is received by the Trustees and which arises from the Policy or from any property from time to time representing the Policy shall be paid to or applied for the benefit of the beneficiaries entitled to an interest in possession under the trust as and when such income is received by the Trustees.

Any Trustee for the time being (other than myself/ourselves) being a solicitor or other person engaged in any profession or business shall be entitled to charge and to be paid all usual professional or other charges for business done by him or by his firm in relation to the Policy or to the trusts thereof.

A power of removal of any Trustee and a power of appointment of a new Trustee and/or additional Trustee(s) shall be vested in me/in ourselves or the survivor of us.

I/We hereby declare that we intend to pay the premium under the Policy for the sole benefit of the person(s) beneficially interested under the foregoing trusts and

I/We hereby irrevocably disclaim any lien or charge on the said Policy or the monies payable thereunder for the repayment of any such premium.

It is hereby certified that this instrument falls within Category N of the Schedule to the Stamp Duty (Exempt Instruments) Regulation 1987.

Names of Grantees . . . .

Signatures . . . .

. . . .

Date . . . .

Any other Policy or Policies [illegible] by the Trustees and any new Policy or Policies which may be effected in lieu of any Policies which are comprised in the Policy shall be subject to the same trusts as are herein declared. Any moneys which may be invested or laid out in the [illegible] upon the security of such stocks funds shares securities investments or property of whatsoever nature and wheresoever situate and whether involving liability or not and whether producing income or not [illegible] to the intent that the Trustees shall have the same full and unrestricted powers of investing and transposing investments as if they were absolutely entitled thereto beneficially. The statutory powers of [illegible] shall be [illegible] of the Trustee Act [illegible] applicable [illegible] Section [illegible] of the Trustee Act [illegible] shall apply [illegible] with the following addition [illegible] either (i) the [illegible] or (ii) [illegible] Trustee Act [illegible] of the Trustee Act [illegible] 1958 shall not apply to the trusts of this Policy.

All [illegible] received by the Trustees and which represent the Policy [illegible] any [illegible] from time to time representing the same shall be paid to or applied for the benefit of the beneficiaries entitled to an interest in the same under the trusts hereinbefore declared by the Trustees.

Any Trustee for the time being [illegible] engaged in any profession or business shall be entitled to charge and be paid all usual professional or other charges for business done by him or his firm in relation to the Policy or to the trusts thereof.

A power to appoint new Trustees and a power to appoint additional Trustees shall be vested in [illegible].

We hereby declare [illegible] to pay the premiums on the Policy for the sole benefit of the persons [illegible] and [illegible].

We hereby [illegible] declare and [illegible] on the [illegible] payable [illegible] of any such premiums.

[illegible] the Stamp Duty [illegible] 19[illegible].

Names and addresses:

M Life Assurance Based Investment

1 **Saving from Income**

2 **Lump Sum Investments for Basic Rate Taxpayers**

3 **Lump Sum Investments for Higher Rate Taxpayers**

4 **Investments for Children**

5 **Investments by Companies**

6 **Second-Hand Policies**

When considering investment policies, one is looking for both good investment performance and maximum tax efficiency. The degree of security required and ease of access to the cash are also important. This chapter deals with the investment contracts currently on offer. The first section considers those contracts used for saving from income. The second section considers lump sum investments for basic rate taxpayers. This chapter continues by covering lump sum investments for higher rate taxpayers, and concludes with a few specialised areas of investment.

1 Saving from Income

Many people use qualifying life policies as a means of saving from income. The fact that the proceeds are tax-free after ten years is a valuable benefit. A number of different types of contract are currently on offer. These are divided basically into with-profits and unit-linked policies.

1.1 With-profits savings plans

Some life offices market with-profits savings plans.

1.1.1 Fixed-term endowments

There are two types of fixed-term savings plans, described below.

- **Standard with-profits endowment**: probably the most basic savings plan is the standard with-profits endowment. Level regular premiums are paid, usually monthly or annually, although quarterly and half-yearly plans are also available. This purchases a guaranteed sum assured, payable on maturity or earlier death. Many such policies have a ten-year term which is the minimum for qualification status[1]. To this guaranteed sum assured are added bonuses, at the office's declared rate, each year. When the policy matures (or on earlier death), an additional terminal bonus is added. This is often based on a percentage of the total annual bonuses already allocated. The eventual return will thus be the total of the guaranteed sum assured, annual bonuses and terminal bonus.

  Estimates of future maturity values can only be based on the FSA assumed investment return rates of 4%, 6% and 8%. When providing estimated benefits the FSA approved wording must be used to explain them.

  One way to judge life offices is to use actual performances achieved in the past. For this reason tables are published from time to time in the trade press showing comparative performances. There is, however, no guarantee that an office which has performed well in the past will do so in future. If a life office uses past performance in promotional literature, it must state that past performance is not necessarily a guide to future performance.

  Because bonuses are not directly linked to investment performance in the same way as unit-linked policies, it is possible for a life office to utilise its reserves and so produce a 'cushioning' effect which irons out the sharp rises and falls which characterise unit-linked investments.

  Virtually all new with-profits savings plans are now unitised with-profits, rather than conventional with-profits.

- **Low-cost endowment savings plans**: some life offices offer low-cost endowment savings plans. These work in the same way as the low-cost endowments used for house purchase (see Chapter F) except that the term will usually be 10 or 15 years. Thus, the basic sum assured – on which bonuses are calculated – is lower than the death sum assured, and the amount payable on maturity is the basic sum assured

[1] Taxes Act 1988 Sch 15 para 2

plus bonuses. A number of life offices offer low-start, low-cost endowment savings plans, similar to the low-start endowment mortgage plans (see Chapter F). The attraction to savers is that premiums start at a low level and build up over five or ten years to the full premium which, for qualification reasons, cannot be more than double the initial premium. Many savers like the idea of being able to gradually increase their savings each year as their income increases.

1.1.2 Encashment

The best return on a fixed-term savings plan is almost always achieved by letting the contract run until maturity. Any encashment before maturity can lead to a much lower return as most offices' endowment surrender values incorporate a 'penalty' element to compensate for the fact that they have costed the premium on the basis that the contract will run its full term and that, if it is cashed in early, they will not be able to recoup the expense loadings from the unpaid premiums. In addition, a full terminal bonus is only payable on maturity or death and therefore is lost on earlier encashment. This is important because terminal bonuses still form an appreciable part of the total return on longer-term policies – about a third for 25-year plans maturing in 2005. However for 10-year plans terminal bonuses are now a very small element – about 3% on average. Fixed-term endowments are normally only suitable where the saver is sure that he will not want the money until the end of the term.

1.1.3 Flexidowments

The lack of flexibility of fixed-term savings plans, when it comes to encashment, led to the development of open-ended endowment savings plans, often called flexidowments. These contracts (described earlier in Chapter A) were usually written as endowments to age 65 but could be cashed in at any time after ten years with no penalty and no loss of terminal bonus. In this way, the saver was not committed to take the money at any particular time and so, once the initial ten-year period had expired, could encash the policy whenever it suited them.

Further flexibility was given by writing the plan as a cluster of identical individual policies. This is known as segmentation. For example, a £20 per month plan might have been written as 20 £1 policies or four £5 policies. If this were done, the saver was not committed to taking all the money in one go. After ten years, individual policies could be encashed as required. The remaining policies could be continued independently, either with premiums being maintained or as paid-up policies. If policies were made paid-up, no further premiums were payable – the guaranteed sum assured would be reduced accordingly, but bonuses continued to be allocated, albeit at a lower rate than on fully in-force policies. However, for policies certified since February 1988 Her Majesty's Revenue and Customs (HMRC) has refused to allow the policy to give the policyholder the right to go paid-up. In practice flexidowments have largely been replaced by unitised with-profit policies.

1.2 Unit-linked savings plans

The alternative to a with-profits savings plan is a unit-linked contract. Under these contracts, premiums are applied to buy units in a unit-linked fund run by the life office or possibly in a unit trust run by the life office or an associated institution. For some years there has been a steady trend away from conventional with-profits savings plans towards unitised with-profits versions. As a result there are now very few offices marketing the conventional contract.

1.2.1 Charging structure

The charging structures of different policies vary, some having 'initial units' with a heavier in-built charge element and some having an initial non-allocation period. Under some policies, the charges for expenses and life cover are deducted from the premium before it is applied to units, and under others the whole premium is applied, enough units being cancelled by the life office each month to pay for that month's expenses and life cover.

Some offices have reduced charges by giving higher unit allocations from outset and compensating for this by introducing a surrender penalty for early encashments. A typical penalty might be 5% of unpaid premiums due up to the tenth anniversary. The idea is to discourage early surrenders and reward those investors who keep their policies for the full term.

1.2.2 Purchase of units

When units are allocated they will be purchased at the current offer price. The total amount of units allocated to the policy will increase each time a premium is paid and the eventual value of the policy is determined by the total value of the units, which in turn depends on the performance of the underlying fund or funds.

1.2.3 Types of funds

Most offices offer a choice of funds such as Equity, Fixed Interest, Property, International, Cash and Managed. These funds are explained in more detail in Chapter A. Some offices have more specialised funds available, such as United States, Japan, Recovery, Index-Linked Gilt or Building Society Funds. There is an increasing trend for offices to offer funds managed by third parties, eg external open-ended investment company (OEIC) managers. All offices will allow switching between funds both as regards existing units and future premiums. Sometimes switches are free, but often a small charge (say, 0.5% of the value of the units or a fixed fee of £25) is made if more than one switch is done in a year. Policies can often be invested in more than one fund if required.

Some offices have savings plans linked to unitised with-profits funds. The investment performance will be more akin to a conventional with-profits plan than a true unit-linked plan in that the with-profits concept smoothes the investment performance avoiding the more extreme fluctuations of, say, the equity fund. However, offices marketing this type of plan have a market value reduction factor system which could apply to reduce surrender values (or switches) at times of low stock market prices. The factor would not be applied on death or maturity.

1.2.4 Writing of plans

Most unit-linked savings plans are written as endowments. These usually have a ten-year term with a right to extend the policy if required. After ten years the value of units can be taken as a lump sum, or premiums continued for a further ten years, or the units left as they are to be withdrawn as and when required. These contracts are often known as maximum investment plans or MIPs. Other policies are written as whole life assurances, and these can be cashed in at any time for the value of the units then allocated. Increasing premiums are also available.

Whether the contract is written as an endowment or as a whole life, it is likely to include only enough life cover to ensure it is qualifying. For this reason, unit-linked savings plans commonly have a guaranteed sum assured of 75% of premiums payable – over the whole term for an endowment, or up to age 75 for a whole life.

Like flexidowments, unit-linked savings plans are frequently issued as clusters of small policies for maximum flexibility.

One office offers a variable premium unit-linked endowment savings plan, whereby the premium on any policy anniversary can be varied up or down. If the premium is reduced, it cannot drop to less than half the previous highest premium. The increase can be any amount allowed by the office at the time. If this option is exercised, the policy is extended by a further ten years – and it must be remembered that, if the premium is increased, the ten-year period for chargeable events starts to run again from the date of increase[2].

1.2.5 Unit-linked returns

The returns available on unit-linked policies depend mainly on the investment performance of the funds to which they are linked, but this in turn often depends on the exact days on which the policy is effected and cashed in.

Performance

There is a big difference between the performances of the best and worst offices and the best and worst funds within offices. Naturally, the more specialised a fund, the greater the chance of spectacular rises and also of spectacular falls. The more broadly-based a fund, the more likely it is to conform to an average return and the less likely it is to suffer a disastrous fall. There is some evidence to suggest that new funds tend to perform very well in their early years as their small size tends to make dealing easier. On the other hand, very large, long-established funds may tend to have a lower incidence of meteoric rises but can also avoid sharp dips owing to an adverse performance by one individual investment. There have been problems in the past with small funds investing too high a proportion in one single investment.

Cashing-in

As has already been said, the yield obtained from the policy depends on the prices of units on the day the money is taken, and if unit prices are low at times during the term of the policy this can actually work to the saver's benefit – because when prices are low the premiums will buy more units than they would if prices were higher. The saver will receive a better return if prices are low for a long period and then rise just before the policy is encashed, than if the prices rise to the same eventual height but at a consistent gentle growth rate. This is because units will have been bought on average at a lower cost because of the years of low prices. This factor is known as 'pound cost averaging', and works to the investor's advantage in fluctuating market

[2] *ITTOIA s485(6)*

conditions. An example of how this could operate is shown below, using a ten-year policy for £300 pa.

Example A

Case A –
Prices rise at a constant rate for ten years from £1.00 to £1.90.

Year	Investment	Unit price £	Number of units bought £
1	300	1.00	300.00
2	300	1.10	272.73
3	300	1.20	250.00
4	300	1.30	230.77
5	300	1.40	214.29
6	300	1.50	200.00
7	300	1.60	187.50
8	300	1.70	176.47
9	300	1.80	166.67
10	300	1.90	157.89
Total units			2,156.32

Total unit value 2,156.32 x £1.90 = £4,097.00

Case B –
Prices fluctuate, going down and up for ten years between £1.00 and £1.40.

Year	Investment	Unit price £	Number of units bought £
1	300	1.00	300.00
2	300	0.50	600.00
3	300	0.70	428.57
4	300	0.60	500.00
5	300	0.90	333.33
6	300	1.10	272.73
7	300	0.90	333.33
8	300	1.20	250.00
9	300	1.10	272.73
10	300	1.40	214.29
Total units			3,504.98

Total unit value 3,504.98 x £1.40 = £4,906.97

All charges etc have been ignored for simplicity, but the example clearly shows that fluctuating prices, and even the final price, need not damage the overall return.

1.3 Taxation considerations

1.3.1 Early encashment

As has been explained earlier, the best return on a savings plan will usually be obtained by holding it for the full term. If the plan is encashed at an earlier stage, the investment return may be lower than anticipated and there may also be a taxation liability. However, before going into detail about this taxation, it should be stressed that savings policies, both with-profits and unit-linked, frequently have no surrender value at all in the first year. Thereafter, surrender values up to year ten often incorporate some element of penalty, although this is possibly less severe on a unit-linked contract.

Income tax

A surrender of a qualifying policy within the first ten years, or three-quarters of the term if sooner, can be subject to income tax, because it is a chargeable event (see Chapter D). Tax will only be payable if the surrender value exceeds the total gross premiums and then only at the saver's top rate minus lower rate. Thus, if the saver is only a basic rate taxpayer (after addition of the top-sliced chargeable gain – see Chapter D) there will be no tax liability.

1.3.2 Tax-free lump sum

The proceeds of a qualifying policy on maturity are completely tax-free. There is no income tax or capital gains tax (CGT). If the policy is surrendered after ten years, it will also be tax-free. Thus, a flexidowment or a unit-linked whole life policy can be cashed in with no tax liability at any time after ten years. The qualifying rules also provide that proceeds are tax-free on surrender after three-quarters of the policy term if sooner. Thus, a ten-year endowment can be surrendered after seven and a half years free of tax.

It should be remembered, however, that the underlying life fund has already borne corporation tax (at up to 20% on income and 20% on realised gains respectively).

1.3.3 Tax-free 'income'

Some policyholders want to take an 'income' from their plans instead of a lump sum. This can be achieved by applying the maturity value as the single premium for a whole of life policy or endowment for at least ten years. The new policy will be a qualifying policy and withdrawals of up to 5% can be taken without incurring a tax charge under the 5% rule. As long as full encashment is made at least ten years after the reinvestment, there will be no tax charge on that either. Alternatively the term of the policy may be extended for at least ten years and sufficient monies withdrawn to provide the 'income' required and fund the premiums due. Each time a premium is paid in this way, the policy term is extended by ten years to maintain qualifying status. This process is sometimes referred to as 'recycling'.

Another way to produce 'income' is to write the plan as a cluster of small policies and encash one or more each year as required after the tenth anniversary.

It used to be possible to provide 'income' by a so-called peppercorn premium option, but HMRC decided that this could not be included in qualifying policies after 24 February 1988, although there are many existing policies where this option is being used.

1.4 Friendly society policies

Friendly societies offer very tax-efficient savings plans, although there are limits on the size of contracts they can offer. There are around 250 societies, but only a few large ones actively market tax-exempt savings plans.

The advantage of these plans is that the friendly society does not have to pay any income, corporation or capital gains tax on the investment of its funds[3]. Friendly societies can no longer reclaim the 10% tax credit on dividends. The return to the saver is therefore potentially greater than on a policy issued by an ordinary life office where the underlying funds are taxed. The policy has to be a qualifying policy.

The limit for tax-exempt business is £270 pa. If premiums are payable weekly or monthly, 10% of the total annual premium can be ignored, thus permitting premiums of £5 per week or £25 per month[4]. Policies can be effected by any adult up to age 70 on his or her own life, and therefore a husband and wife can each invest £270 pa into these policies. The limit applies to the total of all friendly society policies owned by an individual. Thus, if someone has one £270 pa policy he cannot have any more tax-exempt policies with that society or any other. A friendly society can also write ordinary taxable business without limit.

The Finance Act 1991 permitted children under 18 to effect tax-exempt friendly society policies – the so-called baby bonds. Thus, a parent can have his own friendly society policy for £270 and one for each of his children. However, the advent of Child Trust Funds, with a maximum overall top up of £1,200 a year, has reduced the appeal of baby bonds.

Friendly societies are covered by the Financial Services Compensation Scheme and are supervised by the Financial Services Authority.

Friendly societies currently market a variety of ten-year savings plans, including unit-linked and with-profits plans. Many advisers recommend savers to invest the maximum annual premium into a friendly society ten-year savings plan for the following reasons:

- The funds grow tax-free.
- There is a fairly high degree of security.
- The return is tax-free provided it is taken after seven and a half years.

The plans will have the minimum amount of life cover to remain qualifying – ie 75% of total premiums. On unit-linked plans the life cover will be paid for by the unit

[3] Taxes Act 1988 s460; [4] Taxes Act 1988 s460(2)

cancellation method. Early surrender values will depend on unit prices. If a chargeable gain is made on a tax-exempt friendly society policy, there is no lower rate credit and the full rate of tax is payable.

In view of the fact that the underlying funds are free of tax, the FSA allows friendly societies to project benefits at 5%, 7% and 9% rather than the normal 4%, 6% and 8%.

A number of societies also offer lump sum investments. The lump sum buys a capital protected annuity, which provides an annuity which feeds each annual premium under the friendly society policy. If the saver dies during the policy term, the annuity pays out the difference between the single premium and the total annuity payments. This is in addition to the sum assured under the friendly society policy.

Other societies use guaranteed bonds or unit-linked bonds as a funding vehicle. If the bond has any value remaining in it after the ten-year funding period, it can be encashed or left to grow.

The Friendly Societies Act 1992 enabled friendly societies to incorporate themselves and do other types of business via subsidiaries. This has enabled them to increase their range of services to include unit trusts, ISAs, Child Trust Funds and mortgages (up to £200 per member).

1.5 Non-qualifying savings plans

Some offices have offered short-term savings plans, often for a term of five years, although these have not proved to be very popular in competition with personal equity plans (PEPs) and now individual savings accounts (ISAs). Because they do not have a ten-year term, they are non-qualifying contracts. For this reason they were aimed at basic rate taxpayers to whom a theoretical higher rate tax liability on maturity was not relevant. However, the investor needed to be sure that he would still be a basic rate taxpayer when the policy matured. These policies were generally unit-linked endowments with an income option and a reinvestment option. Thus, on maturity, the investor could take the lump sum or draw an 'income' which would still be tax-free if he were not a higher rate taxpayer. Alternatively, the proceeds of the plan could be transferred into a unit-linked single premium bond. This avoided any immediate chargeable gain and deferred it until the bond was encashed, in which case there would still be no tax charge if the investor remained a basic rate taxpayer.

Because these policies were not restricted by the qualifying rules they were flexible as regards premium payments. Some allowed premiums to be increased or decreased by whatever amount the investor wished on any anniversary and single premiums could often be added in at any time.

In addition, because it was not necessary to comply with the 75% rule, life cover was negligible (usually 101% of the unit value) and so this did not absorb much of the premium and enabled applications to be made easily, as no underwriting was required.

It must always be remembered that, when deciding whether the policyholder was in the higher rate tax band or not, the gain from the policy (after top-slicing) had to be added to their other income for that tax year. Full details of these calculations are given in Chapter D.

1.6 Stakeholder life policies

These have been available since 6 April 2005 and could, at least in theory, be either single premium or regular premium. There are two types of stakeholder life policy – unit-linked and smoothed.

1.6.1 Unit-linked stakeholder life policies

Unit-linked stakeholder life policies must have no more than 60% invested in shares listed on a recognised stock exchange or units in a unit trust or OEIC invested in shares or land or buildings. Investments must be managed to balance growth potential against the risk of loss in value. Thus they would normally have to have a substantial element in cash or fixed interest securities. The managers must have regard for diversification and suitability of investments. The minimum investment must be £20 or less by cheque, direct debit or direct credit. There is a charge cap of 1.5% a year for the first 10 years and 1% thereafter, plus any stamp duty or tax incurred in running the fund. The units must be single priced and quoted daily.

1.6.2 Smoothed stakeholder life policies

Smoothed stakeholder life policies basically have the same rules as unit-linked ones, but the fund must be managed so as to reduce the volatility of returns and the charging structure can reflect this. The fund must also be managed with the aim of giving each investor on maturity or surrender a value falling within a target range notified at outset to the investor. There can be a death sum assured guarantee of no more than 101% of the value of the units.

Both types of plan form part of the Treasury's stakeholder suite of products. However, the FSA has ruled that the smoothed stakeholder plan cannot be sold using the 'basic advice' regime. To date few product providers have shown much interest in developing a stakeholder savings plan and promoters have generally shown a similar lack of enthusiasm for 'basic advice'.

2 Lump Sum Investments for Basic Rate Taxpayers

This section covers the various lump sum investment contracts available for basic rate taxpayers, and then goes on to outline a taxation problem that can affect such policyholders.

2.1 Guaranteed income bonds

A guaranteed income bond is a very simple contract. In return for a single premium, the bond provides a guaranteed income each year for a specified period and then on maturity returns the investor's capital. Life offices offer these contracts from time to time depending on their own internal taxation position. At any one time there will usually be a handful of offices in this market although most tranches are for a limited time or for a limited total amount. The income is usually payable yearly in arrears, although some providers now offer monthly income, and most bonds are for terms of up to five years. The attraction of these bonds is that the income is guaranteed. The rate offered at any particular time varies according to market conditions but is presently around 3.5%. Although called income bonds, technically the 'income' is capital.

2.1.1 Tax

For a basic rate taxpayer, there is no liability to tax at all on the income. However, it must be remembered that any income in excess of 5% must be added to the investor's other income for that tax year to decide whether he is still a basic rate taxpayer. Thus, for a basic rate taxpayer, a bond offering 3.5% free of tax is equivalent to a taxable investment offering 4.375% gross interest.

The maturity value is a guaranteed return of the single premium and so the investor will have had a guaranteed tax-free income, plus a return of capital. The combination of security and good net returns make this an attractive investment for a basic rate taxpayer.

However, there is a possibility of a tax liability on maturity if, by then, the investor is a higher rate taxpayer. On maturity, there is a chargeable gain of the last year's income plus the first 5% of each previous years' income (or total income of the bond was paying less than 5%). This gain, top-sliced by the term of the bond, is then added to the investor's other income in the tax year when it matures. If this brings the investor into the higher rate tax band, he will have to pay tax at his top rate minus the lower rate on some or all of the gain.

For this reason, these bonds are especially attractive to investors who are sure that they will continue to be basic rate taxpayers for the term of the contract. This would include many retired people whose expectations of increased future income are normally less than those of younger people who are still working.

2.1.2 Other versions

Another version works by combining a temporary annuity with a deferred annuity. The temporary annuity provides the income and the deferred annuity has a cash option which returns the original capital at maturity. The taxation of this version is entirely different from the standard guaranteed income bond. The temporary annuity is a purchased life annuity and is split into a tax-free capital content and a fully taxable interest content. When the deferred annuity matures to provide the return of capital this is a chargeable event and there could be an income tax liability, again at higher rate less lower rate.

A guaranteed income bond could also be constructed as a series of policies, one of which is surrendered each year to pay the income and the final one providing the return of capital.

2.2 Guaranteed growth bonds

These are similar to guaranteed income bonds except that no income is paid. The investor pays a single premium and is guaranteed a capital sum in three, four or five years' time. The current market rate is about 3.5% pa and so a five-year bond for £10,000 would pay out £11,876 on maturity. The investor is thus getting a guaranteed capital appreciation which is free of CGT[5] and basic rate income tax.

As mentioned above, the security and good net return make these bonds attractive to a basic rate taxpayer. However, to be sure of being free of tax, the investor must still be a basic rate taxpayer in the year of maturity, after taking into account the whole top-sliced gain as explained earlier. Neither type of guaranteed bond should be used if the investor might wish to cash in early, because often surrender values are not available and, if they are given, they will usually result in a yield much lower than the guaranteed rate.

2.3 Unit-linked bonds

Under a unit-linked bond, the single premium buys units in the fund of the investor's choice. This might be run by the life office itself or be a unit trust run by the life office of another institution. The value of the policy is measured by the total value of the units allocated to it. Immediately the bond is effected, its surrender value will be lower than the single premium because of the difference between the buying and selling price of the units, usually 5%, or an early surrender charge under a contract with no initial charge. From then on, the bond's value will depend on the performance of the fund (or funds) to which it is linked. There has been a trend towards replacing initial charges and bid-offer spreads with early exit charges, eg 5% in the first year, reducing to 1% in the fifth year. The comments made in section 1 regarding the funds available, investment performance, and switching are also valid here.

2.3.1 Investment funds

Most offices have a variety of funds on offer with different risk and growth prospects. The funds most usually available are as follows:

- **Cash fund:** Invested in the short-term money markets such as bank deposits and Treasury Bills. It should produce steady but secure growth and is often used to provide capital protection at a time when the outlook in other investment markets may be uncertain.

- **Building society fund:** Invested in building society accounts aiming to offer a return at least equal to the building societies' ordinary share rates. The interest rate will vary from time to time but the unit price is guaranteed not to fall.

- **Gilt and/or fixed interest fund:** Invested in British government fixed interest stocks and/or other readily marketable fixed interest securities. Some offices may also invest in quoted marketable stocks of overseas governments and companies. Relatively secure, because of the underlying guarantee on government stocks.

- **Index-linked gilt fund:** Invested in index-linked securities issued by the British government. The income element and capital return at maturity are both linked to

[5] *Taxation of Chargeable Gains Act 1992 s210*

the rate of inflation and so returns are likely to be more favourable in times of high inflation.

- **Equity fund:** Invested in shares quoted on the UK stock market and maybe also convertible loan stock and overseas securities. Prices can fluctuate considerably, reflecting the fortunes of the underlying shares and the economy as a whole.

- **International fund:** Invested in securities on foreign stock markets. Some offices might also include shares in UK companies if they earn a large proportion of their profits from overseas earnings. Prices can fluctuate substantially because there is a currency risk as well as an investment risk.

- **Property fund:** Invested in freehold and leasehold interests in commercial and industrial property, such as warehouse buildings, shopping units and office blocks. Should provide reasonable long-term performance but prices can still drop substantially. There is often a proviso that encashments or switches can be delayed for a specific period in times of difficult market conditions because of the relative illiquidity of the underlying investments. Some property funds, particularly smaller ones, also invest in the shares of property investment or development companies.

- **North American fund:** Invested in securities on US and Canadian stock markets. Prices can fluctuate substantially because of currency and investment risks.

- **Far Eastern fund:** Invested in securities on Far Eastern stock markets. Prices can fluctuate very substantially due to currency, investment and political risks.

- **Managed fund:** Invested in a balanced spread of equities, both in the UK and overseas, fixed interest stocks, property and cash either directly or via the other funds. The life office's investment managers will vary the distribution of the investments according to the relative current attractiveness of the various markets. Usually the objective is steady, long-term growth while avoiding undue risk. The spread of investment should reduce risk but prices can still fluctuate. Particularly in the larger managed funds, the managers' abilities to switch actively between investment sectors will be limited, and consequently their sector distribution policy will be directed mainly to new money coming into the fund.

- **External funds** Many offices allow links to other fund managers' funds. There is a trend for some life companies to offer investment bonds which are effectively wrappers for externally run funds.

2.3.2 Switching

Switching tends to be more frequent on bonds than on regular premium policies. An active switching service is offered by some intermediaries. A very skilled adviser can undoubtedly increase returns by switching, but the cost of doing so regularly (as much as 0.5% of the units switched and possibly the cost of the switching advice service) must be borne in mind. However, many offices now offer free switching. There is also some evidence that many switching advisers have achieved returns less than those that would have been obtained by staying in the managed fund of the office concerned.

2.3.3 Encashing

These bonds are written as whole life policies and so can be cashed in at any time or left until death. The investor can take an 'income' from the bond and this can be at regular or irregular intervals and of any amount, as and when required. However, the 'income' is obtained by cashing in part of the unit holding. Thus, it must be remembered that if the rate of 'income' exceeds the growth rate of the units, the bond will decline in value and may extinguish itself altogether if this is continued for long enough.

2.3.4 Tax

For a basic rate taxpayer, all encashments from these bonds are tax-free. However, any part encashment over 5% pa of the single premium (top-sliced by the number of years since the last chargeable event or the policy date, whichever is less) must be added to the investor's other income for that tax year, to ascertain whether he is still a basic rate taxpayer. In addition, on full encashment, the final gain plus the first 5% of any previous encashments must be similarly treated, although in this case the number of years for top-slicing is the number of complete years since the bond was effected.

It should be remembered, however, that the underlying life fund has already borne tax on underlying re-invested income and realised gains at up to 20%.

2.3.5 Advantages and disadvantages

The advantage of unit-linked bonds is their flexibility – cash can be taken out as and when required. This is a big improvement over the guaranteed bond where the dates of payment are fixed in advance and cannot be altered. However, guaranteed bonds have the advantage of security in that the return is guaranteed both as to capital and income. Unit-linked bonds have the prospect of providing a much better return but also the possibility of losing money, depending on the investment performance of the funds concerned.

2.4 Distribution bonds

Ordinary unit-linked bond funds do not separate income and capital, and the investment returns from reinvested income are simply reflected in the unit price. Any withdrawals taken as a form of income are achieved by cashing in units, which thus have no particular relationship to the actual income generated by the fund.

Distribution bonds effectively distinguish between income and capital so that the amount withdrawn reflects the income generated by the fund. This leaves the capital intact, although this could still rise or fall. The way these bonds work is that the money is invested in a special distribution fund which pays out the 'natural' accrued income of the fund (ie dividends, interest, rental income) twice or four times a year. Some offices can pay monthly. Investors can take these payments as income but there are no unit encashments and thus the number of units in the bond remains constant. However, the unit price will fall in line with the payout on each distribution date. The investment managers of the fund have to bear in mind the requirement for income in the way they manage the fund's assets which tend to be well spread with a high proportion of gilts and other fixed interest securities to lessen the risk.

These bonds should be looked on as a medium to long-term investment as a number of offices have early surrender penalties. The taxation of these bonds is the same as for ordinary unit-linked bonds, ie the 5% rules for the 'income' distributions.

A distribution bond would be a good investment for someone requiring income but who is a cautious investor, as the risk profile in general is fairly low – yet there is still a reasonable chance of capital growth. Although withdrawals are derived from the income of the underlying life fund, they are still legally capital, and subject to the normal 5% chargeable gains rules.

2.5 Guaranteed equity bonds

A number of companies have introduced various types of unit-linked bonds with some form of guarantee. The guarantee is often that on the fifth anniversary the bond is guaranteed to return at least 100% of the original capital investment regardless of the performance of the underlying funds. The guarantee is normally achieved by some form of traded option arrangement made by the life office. The guarantee will operate only on the fixed date and if the bond is surrendered before or after that date the normal unit value principle will apply. Many of these bonds are available in limited amounts for short periods only.

Some bonds also guarantee a percentage of the growth in the FTSE 100 Index or some other index and a few have an option (for an extra charge) to lock in growth if the index goes over a set limit.

These investments are worthwhile for those who like the idea of an equity-linked product but who do not want to risk losing money. However, it should be remembered that although getting your capital back after five years is not on the face of it a loss, it is in real terms because of inflation. Also an investor should appreciate that he needs to hold the bond for the full term to benefit from the guarantee and thus these bonds are not suitable as short-term investments or where the money will be needed at an indeterminate time.

Another point to be made is that the FTSE 100 Index measures the price of shares in the UK's top 100 companies and makes no allowance for dividend income which can be a useful part of normal unit-linked fund growth. It should also be remembered that all guarantees cost something. Thus, in general terms the better the guarantee the less will be the ultimate return when compared to a non-guaranteed equity bond if stock market performance over the period is very good.

2.6 With-profits bonds

A number of offices offer with-profits bonds. This is usually done by having a unitised with-profits fund as an addition to the office's normal unit-linked funds. The fund may have a unit price which is increased only once a year when bonuses are declared. Alternatively, the unit price could be fixed and when bonuses are declared this is reflected by an additional allocation of units. Sometimes, there is a terminal bonus on the tenth anniversary, when the money can be taken out or reinvested. There might also be some guaranteed minimum return on the tenth anniversary, via a guaranteed minimum bonus rate.

These bonds should avoid the dramatic rises and falls in unit values seen on full unit-linked contracts due to the cushioning effect of bonus declarations. Also, once bonuses are allocated they cannot be taken away, although there may well be penalties on early surrender resulting in the full value of bonuses not being available.

The policies will be written as whole life policies but perhaps with some form of guaranteed minimum performance on, say, the tenth anniversary. However, changes in valuation rules have made such 'spot guarantees' a rarity on new contracts. There will usually be the right to switch into a unit-linked fund, although penalties similar to those on surrender may be incurred if this is done in the early years. There will be the standard 5% bid–offer spread, or an early exit penalty in the first five years.

Most offices operate an MVR (Market Value Reduction Factor) to protect the interests of investors remaining in the with-profits funds. The MVR can be applied at the life office's discretion to reduce the amount payable on surrenders or switches and may be applied in times of adverse investment conditions – eg a stock market crash. Under older policies usually the MVR will not apply on death or at any time when benefits are in part guaranteed – such as the tenth anniversary. The idea is to prevent the value leaving the fund exceeding the value of the underlying assets.

When these bonds are being sold, the FSA requires the bonus system and MVR to be explained properly and forbids the bonds to be presented as guaranteed. They should therefore be sold as long-term investments. The Association of British Insurers (ABI) has published a note of best industry practice for the marketing of with-profit bonds.

The with-profits bond market has contracted dramatically in recent years, as the problems with Equitable Life, falling bonus rates and MVRs have all deterred investors. Sales of with-profit bonds in 2004 were just over £1.5bn, about 10% of the level achieved in 2001.

2.7 The age allowance trap

Although all proceeds of bonds are tax-free to basic rate taxpayers, they can involve a tax problem for some investors. This is the so-called 'age allowance trap'.

Age allowance is an extra income tax allowance for taxpayers over 65. The normal personal allowance (for 2006/07) is £5,035 and the normal married couple's allowance is £2,350. The age allowances are as follows:

Age 65–74	£7,280 single; £6,065 married couple's allowance
Age 75+	£7,420 single; £6,135 married couple's allowance.

The married couple's allowance only gains relief at 10%, and it is only given where one of the spouses or civil partners was born on or before 5 April 1935.

To qualify for the married couple's allowance, only one of the taxpayers need be over the relevant age, but for the single allowance it is that individual's age only that counts.

Because extra income can be received before tax is payable this means maximum savings of:

£493.90	age 65–74	(single)	£865.40	age 65–74	(with married couple's allowance)
£524.70	age 75+	(single)	£903.20	age 75+	(with married couple's allowance)

for basic rate taxpayers over and above tax levels for couples not entitled to any age allowance.

However, the age allowance is reduced by £1 for each £2 of income over £20,100. Thus, age allowance is only received in full by people with income up to £20,100. It disappears altogether (by reducing to the normal personal allowance) for those with incomes over the following limits:

£24,590	age 65–74	(single)	£32,020	age 65–74	(with married couple's allowance)
£24,870	age 75+	(single)	£32,440	age 75+	(with married couple's allowance).

The marginal rate of tax on income between these limits can be up to 33%. This can be demonstrated as follows taking the example of a single man over 75.

Example B

A Income		£24,870	
Less personal allowance		£5,035	
Taxable		£19,835	
£2,150 @ 10%			£215.00
£17,685 @ 22%			£3,890.70
			£4,105.70
B Income		£20,100	
Less personal allowance		£7,420	
Taxable		£12,680	
£2,150 @ 10%			£215.00
£10,530 @ 22%			£2,316.60
			£2,531.60
Extra income of A	£4,770		
Extra tax of A	£1,574.10		
Therefore marginal tax rate	33%		

Thus, for investors with existing incomes below the limits, it must be appreciated that any investment producing an income which takes total income over £20,100 will push the investors into this trap. It is also important to note that top-slicing is not available to reduce the addition to income for this purpose. Top-slicing is only used to calculate any higher rate tax liability. Thus, if a basic rate taxpayer has a unit-linked or guaranteed bond and is receiving withdrawals in excess of 5% pa, then even though no tax is payable on the excess itself, if the excess takes the investor over the £20,100 limit it will result in extra tax on the income by reducing the age allowance. However, it should be noted that while the age allowance could be eroded by interest or dividends it will not be eroded by bond withdrawals within the 5% allowances.

Thus if income can be replaced by bond withdrawals within the 5% allowance this can increase the age allowance and reduce the tax bill.

A similar effect can be obtained by using a personal pension because under HMRC Extra Statutory Concession A102 the gross pension contribution is deducted from total income to work out the age allowance. As long as the client is under age 75 he or she can contribute £2,808 (net of 22% tax relief) to a personal pension regardless of earnings and get the total income for age allowance reduced by £3,600. This can increase the effective rate of relief to 42% as shown below.

Adam, age 70, has pension income of £24,590, so his personal allowance is reduced to £5,035. Therefore his tax bill is:

	£
£2,150 x 10%	215.00
£17,405 x 22%	3,829.10
Total	**£4,044.10**

If Adam pays a pension contribution of £3,600 gross, this will only cost him £2,808, but will reduce his income for age allowance to £20,990. His age allowance will increase by £1,800 to £6,835, so his tax bill is now:

	£
£2,150 x 10%	215.00
£15,605 x 22%	3,433.10
Total	**£3,648.10**

Adam has thus saved tax of £396 at a cost of £2,808 and got £3,600 worth of pension rights due to the £792 tax relief. Total tax relief is £1,188, which is 42% of £2,808.

3 Lump Sum Investments for Higher Rate Taxpayers

This section covers the lump sum investment contracts that can be used by higher rate taxpayers, together with their taxation consequences.

3.1 Guaranteed growth bonds

These contracts, explained in section 2.2, are also frequently used by higher rate taxpayers. The advantage of a guaranteed growth bond is that it pays no income and the investment is rolled up in the life office's funds where it suffers tax at up to 20%

on income and 20% on capital gains (rather than possibly 40% in the investor's own hands). However, the total profit on maturity is subject to the investor's top rate of tax minus lower rate, taking the rates current in that tax year.

3.1.1 Returns

The guaranteed growth bond can still give a good return, as the following table shows, using the example of a 3.5% bond and an assumed additional tax charge of 20% at maturity.

Tax rate	Net yield	Equivalent gross yield
%	% pa	% pa
40	2.8	4.67

The yield in the third column would be what the investor would have to achieve on a fully taxable investment to achieve the same net return.

If the investor stood a chance of moving down the tax brackets in the future and becoming a basic rate taxpayer by the maturity date, the bond would be even more attractive.

3.2 Guaranteed income bonds

If a higher rate taxpayer requires 'income' from the investment, a guaranteed income bond can be very attractive because there is no immediate tax liability on the first 5% and any balance is only subject to top rate tax minus lower rate. Thus, the bond can provide a net 'income' comparable to that produced by a much higher-yielding fully taxable investment, as the following table shows:

The income yield of guaranteed bonds providing 4% 'income'

Tax rate	Net yield	Equivalent gross yield
%	% pa	% pa
40	3.5	5.83

However, it must be remembered that the 5% withdrawals are not tax-free, as they are added into the final profit calculation on maturity when there will be a tax liability, even though only the single premium is returned at that time. Some income bonds contain an option for the investor to extend the bond on maturity on whatever terms the office may offer at that time.

On a joint life income bond, any excess over the 5% is shared between the joint owners for tax purposes even if it is actually paid to just one of them (Income Tax (Trading and Other Income) Act 2005 (ITTOIA) s469).

Considerable savings are also made because tax payments are substantially deferred, particularly if the bond income is paid yearly in arrears so that the first instalment is paid on day one of the second policy year. This is because any tax will probably only be payable on 31 January after the tax year of the gain, and the chargeable gain on the income only arises at the end of that policy year. The effects of this can be seen from the following table, using a 3.5% bond to show the working of the tax. In this case, as income is not over 5%, no gains arise before maturity.

Example C

Savings made, through deferred tax payments, on a 3.5% Guaranteed Income Bond for £10,000 effected 1 January 2006 – payable yearly in arrears – for four years:

Income payment	Payable	Amount	Total allowances	Gain	Top-sliced sliced gain	Tax due date
1	1 Jan 2007	£350	£1,000[1]	0	0	
2	1 Jan 2008	£350	£1,150[2]	0	0	
3	1 Jan 2009	£350	} 4			
4	1 Jan 2010	£10,350[3]		£1,400[5]	£350[6]	31 Jan 2011

[1] In 2nd policy year – thus 5% x 2 = 10%
[2] 5% for 3rd policy year + 6.5% unused from previous years
[3] Including return of capital
[4] Both payments taxed in final calculation
[5] 4 x £350 = £1,400
[6] Top-slicing = 4 years

Thus, in this example all of the tax will be payable over five years after the policy was effected.

Some offices have guaranteed bonds which minimise the higher rate tax liability by segmenting the bond into a large number of mini-bonds with a nominal maturity value taken each year as income. The way one office works it is to issue a £10,000 one-year plan at, say, 10% (for the sake of the example) as 11,000 policies with a premium of 90.9p, a maturity value of £1 and a reinvestment option at the then current terms. At the end of the first year, the client uses the reinvestment option on 10,000 policies, thus deferring the tax until the eventual maturity. The other 1,000 policies are encashed for £1,000 giving the guaranteed 'income' of 10%. The chargeable gain on each policy is 9.1p (£1 – 90.9p), making £91 in all, giving a maximum tax charge of £18.20 (£91 x 20%) which is an effective rate of 1.82% on the £1,000 payment. However, more tax will be paid on the eventual final payout on the reinvested policies.

3.3 Unit-linked bonds

Many higher rate taxpayers invest in unit-linked bonds either for capital gains or income. As explained earlier, income within the life office's funds is rolling up after tax at a rate lower than the investor's personal rates and any 'income' taken gets the benefit of freedom from any immediate tax liability on the first 5%. For this reason, many higher rate taxpayers take an automatic withdrawal of 5% of the single premium, thus avoiding any immediate payment of tax. This can be continued for 20 years until all these allowances have been used up.

The effect of this is to give the investor quite a high net return when compared to fully taxable investments.

To obtain a net return of 5% on a fully taxed investment, a 40% taxpayer would need a gross yield of 8.33%. If the underlying funds are growing at a rate of more than 5%, then the capital sum payable on final encashment will also be growing.

Even if higher withdrawals are being taken, this can still be very tax efficient for a higher rate taxpayer, both in terms of equivalent gross yields and deferment of tax, as the previous section showed.

Although the withdrawals may be treated as income by the policyholder, and be subject to income tax if they exceed the 5% limit, they are in fact capital payments as a matter of general law.

It should not be forgotten that the 5% allowances taken have to be brought into account in the calculation of the gain on final encashment, and tax paid on them at this stage. However, that might be many years in the future when the investor might be in the basic rate band. Because these bonds are whole life contracts, the investor can choose when he wishes to make final encashment and it might be possible to do this in a year when the investor's tax rates are lower (eg after retirement) and, of course, tax deferred is effectively tax saved.

On a joint life bond, any chargeable gain is shared between the joint owners for tax purposes even if it is actually paid to just one of them (ITTOIA s469).

Many investors will hold on to these bonds until death. Under these circumstances, the tax liability may be reduced, in that total income in the year of death will be less than usual. This is especially true if the investor dies early in the tax year. The extreme case would be an investor who died on April 6, whose other income in that tax year would probably be negligible, thus avoiding any tax at all on the bond proceeds.

A further advantage of unit-linked bonds is that the investment is sheltered from the higher rate of tax while it is within the life office's funds. This is because the rate of tax payable by the life office is 20% on interest income. This contrasts with possibly 40% for the top rate taxpayer. The higher rate liability is deferred to encashment, rather than being paid each year as it would be on an individual investment. Also, the way the gain is taxed can reduce the tax itself, as the following example shows.

Example D

	£	
Interest income	100	Held directly by 40% taxpayer
Tax at 40%	40	
Net income	60	
Interest income	100	Within life office's fund
Life office's tax at 20%	20	
Net income in life fund	80	
Higher rate tax at 20%	16	
Net income	64	A gain of 6.7%

The difference is similar for UK dividend income.

	£	
Net dividend £100 held directly by 40% taxpayer.		
Plus tax credit	11.11	
Gross dividend	111.11	
Tax at 32.5%	36.11	
Net income	75.00	
Net dividend £100 within the life office's fund.		
Tax credit covers life office tax.		
Net income in life fund	100	
Higher rate tax at 20%	20	
Net income	80	A gain of 6.7%

The life office pays CGT on realised capital gains within the life fund at 20%, but is entitled to full indexation allowance up to the date of disposal. Indexation for life funds did not cease in April 1998, as it did for individuals. However the life office gets neither annual exemption nor taper relief, and thus pays tax on all its post-inflationary gains, whereas most individuals do not pay CGT because any gains are within the annual exemption. Thus from a CGT point of view the position of the life fund is different from the individual higher rate tax paying investor, although the eventual total tax rate will be the same – 40%. The life fund has the advantage of indexation, but the disadvantage of no annual exemption and no taper relief.

3.3.1 Segmentation

It can often be beneficial for a higher rate taxpayer to 'segment' his unit-linked bonds. This means taking out a cluster of identical small bonds rather than one large bond. If this is done, then an income can be taken by encashing whole policies rather than making part surrenders of a single bond. This can result in a smaller chargeable gain and thus a lower tax charge.

The following example contrasts the treatment of a single £10,000 bond and a cluster of 20 £500 segments, and assumes a unit growth rate of 7.5% and a 5% bid–offer gap.

Example E

1. After three years the investor wishes to withdraw £2,360. The investment has now grown to £11,800 (£590 x 20).

One policy	**£**
Encashment	2,360
Cumulative allowance (5% x £10,000 x 3)	1,500
Chargeable gain	860
Top-slicing	3
Top-sliced gain	286

Twenty segments	**£**
Amount encashed (4 segments)	2,360
Original investment (4 x £500)	2,000
Chargeable gain	360
Top-slicing	3
Top-sliced gain	120

The maximum tax liability is thus reduced from £172 (£860 x 20%) to £72 (£360 x 20%).

2. After another three years the investor wishes to draw a further £2,932. The investment has now grown to £11,728 (£733 x 16).

One policy	**£**
Encashment	2,932
Cumulative allowance (5% x £10,000 x 3)	1,500
Chargeable gain	1,432
Top-slicing	3
Top-sliced gain	477

Twenty segments (16 left)	**£**
Encashment (4 segments)	2,932
Original investment (4 x £500)	2,000
Chargeable gain	932
Top-slicing	6
Top-sliced gain	155

The maximum tax liability has been reduced from £286.40 (£1,432 x 20%) to £186.40 (£932 x 20%) and, in addition, the possibility of the higher rate being attained has been reduced by the greater top-slicing relief.

3. Final encashment after another three years. The investment has now grown to £10,920 (£910 x 12).

One policy	**£**
Final encashment	10,920
Plus allowances used (5% x £10,000 x 6)	3,000
	13,920
Less original investment	10,000
Chargeable gain	3,920
Top-slicing	9
Top-sliced gain	435

Twenty segments (12 left)	**£**
Encashment	10,920
Original investment (12 x £500)	6,000
Chargeable gain	4,920
Top-slicing	9
Top-sliced gain	546

On final encashment the chargeable gain is higher but the total gains are the same for each method, ie £6,212. However, segmentation is preferable for the following reasons:

- Most investors prefer gains to occur later rather than sooner – eg final encashment after retirement when the tax rate may be lower. Segmentation will always effectively defer gains.

- The cash flow effect of deferring gains and thus tax for as long as possible – tax deferred is tax saved.

- Although total gains are the same in each case, the greater top-slicing relief given by segmentation can lead to less tax being paid. This will be especially true if frequent withdrawals will be taken.

- If the bond is held until death, the deferring of much of the gain until then will be beneficial, in that the investor's tax rate in the year of death is often lower than normal – especially on death early in the tax year. Also any income tax liability reduces the estate for inheritance tax purposes.

Another area where segmentation can be of benefit is if the investor wishes to continue to take withdrawals after his 5% allowances for 20 years have been exhausted. In the 21st year, the top-slicing relief is 21 for both methods. However, in the 22nd year the top-slicing relief for a single bond is one because it relates back to the previous chargeable event which was the part surrender in the 21st year. On a segmented investment, the top-slicing relief would be 22 because as each complete segment(s) is being surrendered it is the number of full years back to the date of the investment. This can have the effect of reducing the amount of tax payable by reducing the rate of tax, even though the actual gain is the same.

3.3.2 Topping-up

Most life offices' unit-linked bonds have a 'topping-up' facility whereby the investor can invest an additional premium at any time should he wish to make a further investment instead of taking out a new policy. This makes no difference to the investment return but can be beneficial on taxation grounds.

This is because the top-slicing relief is related to the full policy term, even if some of the eventual profit is produced by a premium paid only part-way through the term.

Example F

Suppose an investor effects a £10,000 bond and after five years takes out a further £10,000 bond and then cashes them in after ten years, having achieved a unit growth rate of 7.5% pa, assuming a 5% bid–offer gap.

Bond A	**£**
Encashment	19,580
Less investment	10,000
Chargeable gain	9,580
Top-slicing	10
Top-sliced gain	958

Bond B	**£**
Encashment	13,638
Less investment	10,000
Chargeable gain	3,638
Top-slicing	5
Top-sliced gain	727

Total chargeable gain (£9,580 + £3,638) = £13,218
Total top-sliced gain (£958 + £727) = £1,685

If instead the top-up facility had been used the situation would have been as follows:

	£
Encashment (£19,580 + £13,638)	33,218
Less investment (£10,000 + £10,000)	20,000
Chargeable gain	13,218
Top-slicing	10
Top-sliced gain	1,321

The top-sliced gain has been reduced by £364 and this could lead to a reduction in the investor's top rate and thus the amount of tax payable. Topping-up cannot increase the investor's liability and so it follows that, if an investor wishes to put more money into that life office's funds, it will always be preferable to top-up an existing bond rather than effect a new one. In addition, the documentation should be simpler and the processing swifter.

3.4 Bonds as trust investments

In some cases bonds, either guaranteed or unit-linked, are used as investments by trustees. Investment in bonds used to be restricted for some trusts by the Trustee Investments Act 1961, but this limitation was removed by the Trustee Act 2000 from 1 February 2001 in England and Wales. Similar provisions now also apply in Northern Ireland and Scotland. Now that the Trustee Act 2000 has replaced the Trustee Investments Act 1961 all trusts have power to invest in bonds, unless the trust wording specifically prohibits this. Bonds are non-income producing assets which may be very useful for some trusts. If withdrawals within the 5% limit are taken, this is not income and no tax return is required, although it could be spent as income. Any eventual chargeable gain might be free from higher rate tax if the bond was effected, and the settlor died, before 17 March 1998 under the dead settlor trick[6]. If this was not the case, then the tax liability is charged under the 1998 rules – see Chapter D section 2.7. There is no CGT as the policy has not changed hands for actual consideration[7].

If the trustees require income, then it has been suggested that the withdrawals from the bond could possibly be subject to full taxation in the hands of the beneficiaries as pure trust income, with no 5% or lower rate allowance[8]. However, the 1987 decision in *Stevenson v Wishart* has substantially reduced this possibility where the trustees have discretion to advance capital as well as pay income, and it is thought that the chances of HMRC trying this argument are very low. The difference between the *Brodie* case and *Stevenson v Wishart* is that in *Brodie* the trustees had a duty to provide a fixed annual payment to the beneficiary and if the natural income of the trust was less than this, the trustees had to top it up with capital. It was this feature that made the capital top-ups subject to income tax. However in the *Stevenson* case the trustees merely had a discretion to advance capital, not a duty, thus meaning that even if regular capital payments were made they were not income for income tax purposes.

Trustees should not pay bond withdrawals to a beneficiary who is only entitled to income (eg a life tenant) because the withdrawals are technically capital rather than income. It would be permissible, however, if the trustees had the power to advance capital to that beneficiary or all the other beneficiaries, being 18 or over and sane, agreed.

Bonds can be convenient investments for trustees because they do not generate income, and provide access to a diversified portfolio of underlying investments. Most trusts do not have large sums to invest; it is thought that the majority of trusts have less than £50,000. Most trusts cannot achieve economically a very diversified portfolio of investments from direct investments in stocks and shares. However access to a widely diversified portfolio is available via a bond. Diversification is now one of the standard investment criteria imposed by the Trustee Act 2000.

Bonds are also simple to operate in practice. If a trust had a portfolio of, say, 20 shares to get an acceptable degree of diversification, that would mean 40 dividend payments each year and a tiresome (or expensive) job for the trustees to complete the tax return every year. If a bond is used and either no withdrawals taken, or they are kept within

[6] ITTOIA Sch 2 para 112; [7] Taxation of Chargeable Gains Act 1992 s210;
[8] Brodie's Will Trustees v Inland Revenue Commissioners (1933) 17 T.C. 432

the 5% limit, no tax return needs to be completed at all. The only time a tax return would be needed would be the year in which the bond is finally encashed, when the life office's chargeable gain certificate would show the relevant figures for the return.

The changes to the taxation of share and unit trust dividends from April 1999 increased the attractiveness of bonds for trust investments. One change means that non-taxpayers can no longer reclaim the tax credit. Trusts for children, or anyone else who is a non-taxpayer, suffered a 20% drop in spendable income from equities. The same result was produced by another change which meant that for accumulation and discretionary trusts the tax credit could not be claimed by any beneficiary. This was because in these circumstances the income derived from dividends is re-characterised as trust income rather than dividend income, preventing the tax credit being claimed against the ultimate tax liability.

This 20% drop in income can be avoided by using a bond where the tax credit is used by the life office to satisfy its tax liability on dividends. Withdrawals can be taken within the 5% tax limits or not taken at all, deferring all tax until final encashment. Even then the tax can be minimised if the settlor has died or is non-UK resident by using the rules explained in Chapter G section 5.2. The tax could even be eliminated altogether in some cases if the trustees assign the policy *in specie* to a trust beneficiary before encashment. The beneficiary can then encash the policy independently of the trust, and avoid any taxation liability if he is not a higher rate taxpayer (after addition of the top-sliced chargeable gain).

For these reasons a few life offices offer special bonds for trustees with capital guarantees. This gives the trustees a well diversified investment, which is tax efficient, and protects the trustees against any complaint from a beneficiary that the investment has gone down in value.

3.5 Independent taxation

There is a way in which independent taxation can be used to reduce the tax liability on gains on bonds. If an investor is a higher rate taxpayer but his or her spouse or civil partner is not, then the bond could be assigned to the lower rate taxpayer prior to a surrender being made. The assignment is not a chargeable event and is free of CGT and IHT, but puts the money in the hands of someone who will not be taxed on it. Thus, if the spouse or civil partner can be sufficiently trusted, a tax saving of 20% of the gain can be made.

This can even be done if the higher rate taxpayer has been taking 5% withdrawals during his period of ownership, as those withdrawals will be added to the basic rate taxpayer's gain.

3.6 Offshore bonds

These bonds are generally issued by subsidiaries of well-known UK life offices in countries such as Luxembourg, the Channel Islands or the Isle of Man.

The perceived advantage of these bonds is that the country concerned imposes little or no tax on the income and gains of the underlying life fund – thus allowing what is often called a gross roll-up which is valuable to a higher rate taxpayer. This is in contrast to an onshore bond where the fund suffers tax at 20% on most income and 20% on gains.

However, when an offshore bond is encashed a UK policyholder is chargeable to income tax on the gain at the lower and higher rates although top-slicing relief is available for the higher rate tax calculation.

It might seem therefore that an offshore bond will always be preferable, however this is not necessarily so for a number of reasons:

- Indexation relief will apply to gains in an onshore fund leaving the net gain to be taxed at 20% on encashment by the investor. However, on an offshore bond tax is payable at 40% on encashment with no indexation allowance, or taper relief.
- Some investment income of an offshore fund may be received after deduction of non-reclaimable withholding tax, reducing the effect of the gross roll-up. In addition, there would be no credit for this in the chargeable gain leading to possible double taxation.
- In an onshore fund, management expenses are in general deductible from the fund's income (other than UK dividend income) for tax purposes, whereas an offshore fund will have no tax to deduct management expenses from – thus reducing the effect of gross roll-up. However, relief is effectively obtained as charges reduce the gain subject to tax for the investor.
- On an onshore bond, the 20% tax is charged on the net return of the fund whereas on an offshore fund the 40% is on the gross return. The difference this makes is shown by the following example which contrasts an onshore gain from income of £100,000 with an offshore one of the same amount.

Onshore	**£**
Gain in fund	100,000
Less tax at 20% in fund	20,000
Net gain	80,000
Investor's tax at 20%	16,000
Net gain	64,000

Offshore	**£**
Gain in fund	100,000
Investor's tax at 40%	40,000
Net gain	60,000

It will be seen that the net gain is appreciably higher on the onshore bond.

However, one advantage of an offshore bond is that the income rolls up gross and over the long term the compounding effect of this can make a big difference to the eventual overall return, despite the higher tax on final encashment. But as against this, charges on offshore bonds are generally higher than onshore ones.

Offshore life offices are not subject to UK law and until recently most did not issue chargeable event certificates to HMRC. If the policyholder omits to tell HMRC about the offshore chargeable gain, HMRC would probably never find out, although it must be stressed that this is a criminal offence. To combat this problem the government introduced provisions in the Finance Act 1998 to require any offshore life office with UK resident policyholders whose policies have had premiums paid in excess of £1 million in total to appoint a UK tax representative. That UK tax representative is then responsible for issuing chargeable gain certificates. There are powers for HMRC to appoint a tax representative if the overseas life office does not do this itself. An overseas life office does not have to appoint a tax representative if its head office is in an EEA state and disclosure of information to HMRC would be a criminal offence under that country's law as it stood on 17 March 1998. As an alternative to appointing a tax representative, an offshore office may make its own returns to HMRC, supplying similar information to that which would be found on a chargeable event certificate. Most offices have opted for the alternative arrangement.

3.7 Capital conversion plans

There are a number of different types of capital conversion plans which have been marketed. The details vary, but the basis of all these plans is to start with a lump sum investment and transfer it gradually into a qualifying policy where the proceeds will be tax-free after seven and a half years. These plans are now rare, as ISAs and unit trusts/OEICs are offering a more attractive combination.

3.7.1 Unit-linked plans

The most common type of plan involved a series of unit-linked bonds funding a unit-linked regular premium savings policy. For example, if the plan were to last ten years, there would be nine unit-linked bonds and one policy. Most of the lump sum investment would go into the bonds. The balance would pay the first premium on the savings policy. At the end of each year, one bond would be fully surrendered to pay a further premium into the savings policy. The bonds were arranged so that if they grew at the assumed rate, they would provide the required amount. Often the first bond was substantially larger than the others to provide a safety margin. Any surplus after the premium has been met would be reinvested as an additional premium into the next bond. Each surrender was a chargeable event giving rise to a higher rate tax liability on the profit, but eventually all the money would end up in the qualifying policy where it is tax-free after seven and a half years. When the last bond paid out, depending on the investment performance, there could be a surplus for the investor or he may have had to make up any shortfall. The proceeds of the qualifying policy could then be taken as a cash sum at any time after seven and a half years, or as a tax-free income at any time after ten years (using a peppercorn premium if the policy was issued on or before 24 February 1988).

3.7.2 Maximum growth plans

There was a conventional version of this type of plan involving a nine-year temporary annuity feeding a ten-year with-profit endowment. Part of the annuity was tax-free capital, the balance being paid after deduction of tax at 20% – with any higher rate liability being collected by HMRC direct from the policyholder. These were often called maximum growth plans, and had the advantage that, because the annuity is fixed in advance, it guaranteed to pay the endowment premium – although any increase in tax rates generally, or for the investor as an individual, could reduce the net annuity and thus cause a shortfall. The unit-linked version was always the more popular, but the disadvantage of having to go through the bid–offer gap twice (once on the bonds and once on the qualifying policy) rendered these plans generally less competitive against a straight bond investment.

3.7.3 Share exchange schemes

In most cases an investor will buy a unit-linked bond with cash. However, some life offices active in this market offer share exchange schemes whereby the investor with an existing portfolio of securities can use these to make the investment rather than selling them himself and using the proceeds to make the investment. The attraction of these schemes is that the life office may offer a better price than the investor could get himself and/or pay some or all of the dealing costs. Details of individual schemes vary but they all work by the investor giving the life office power to sell the securities on his behalf. If the life office wishes to hold the shares itself, it will buy them – usually at a 'mid-market' price (thus giving the investor a higher price than he would otherwise receive) – and pay some or all of the dealing costs. If the office does not want the shares, it will sell them on the market for the best price it can get and still pay some or all of the dealing costs.

Offices tend not to accept shares that are not quoted on the UK markets, but will usually take gilts or unit trust/OEIC holdings. These schemes can save investors up to 2% of the total value of the securities, and many offices will return a balance in cash to the investor to enable any CGT liability to be met.

An appreciable proportion of bond investments come from share exchanges. It should be remembered, though, that the investor loses all ownership of the securities and has made a disposal of them for CGT purposes. However, a side effect is often that a portfolio of a number of shares is replaced by a single policy – vastly simplifying problems of managing the investment portfolio, collecting income and preparing tax returns.

3.8 Personal portfolio bonds

Personal portfolio bonds are bonds where an investor effectively wraps a bond around his own portfolio of investments instead of investing in the life office's publicly available funds,. The bond is linked to the investor's private fund, and no other investor has access to it. The fund may continue to be managed by the investor's own stockbroker. These bonds were set up to shelter the investments from the high rates of tax they might otherwise suffer in the investor's own hands. For this reason, many personal portfolio bonds were offshore policies.

HMRC acted against these bonds in the 1998 Budget and the penal rules which were introduced then are covered in Chapter D section 2.11. For this reason, the number of these bonds in existence has reduced substantially and no further new sales are now made in the UK, although this product is still offered offshore.

3.9 Broker bonds

Another variant on this theme is the broker bond. This is really an ordinary single premium unit-linked bond arranged via an intermediary where the money goes into a managed fund. However, it is not the life office's own managed fund but a special managed fund managed by the intermediary.

This fund has its own special price, separate from that of the life office's ordinary managed fund, and invests in a mixture of the life office's other funds and/or collective investments as selected by that intermediary. Thus the investor is actually replacing the life office's fund selections with those of the intermediary, although of course the ultimate investment management within the individual specialised funds is done by the life office or collective fund manager.

The investor usually has to pay an extra fee for the intermediary's advice, commonly between 0.5% and 1.5% pa. This will often be administered by the life office making an extra charge in its unit price structure and paying the broker the total sum for all his bonds with that office on a regular basis.

The FSA has considered the marketing of broker bonds and how it should be regulated. The FSA wishes to ensure that:

- There is clear accountability of the life office for the management of its funds by the broker fund adviser.
- An independent adviser's recommendation of his broker fund is consistent with his duty to act impartially and in the clients' best interests.
- There is adequate information to the investor about the broker fund adviser's services, performance and remuneration.
- Broker fund advisers possess the necessary expertise and resources.

An IFA, who is a broker fund adviser, performs two different conflicting functions of an independent advisor in recommending a suitable investment and giving best advice, and acting as manager of the broker bond recommended. This conflict of interest should be disclosed to the client and the broker fund adviser must obtain an acknowledgement from the client that he understands the dual role. The adviser has to be able to demonstrate that best advice has been given at the outset which might be difficult if the broker bond charges are higher than the normal bond charges. The charges disclosed in the key features must include those paid to the broker fund adviser by the life office. At the same time as the suitability letter the broker fund adviser must inform the client of the investment objectives and strategies of the fund together with a relevant published index or other fund with which the broker fund may be compared, which will normally be the life office's managed fund.

The broker fund adviser must provide six-monthly statements showing the performance of the fund and a comparison with the life office's managed fund and a suitable published index or sector average. The report must be followed up with a recommendation in writing to the client either to continue with the broker fund investment or to switch to an alternative investment, together with reasons. Any significant changes in the investment strategy of the fund should be notified to the client in advance.

IFAs wanting to be broker fund advisers have to clear this with the FSA and demonstrate sufficient competence. The life office must ensure that the way broker bonds are operated does not cause any detriment to other investors in the office's funds. Therefore there should be no special pricing deals for these bonds. The life office must satisfy itself as to the competence of any IFA running a broker fund and monitor its performance.

4 Investments for Children

There has been much interest over the last few years in the subject of investments for children. Many parents wish to put money away regularly for their children. This can obviously be done informally by any of the savings plans mentioned in section 1 or, if the child is eligible, via the recently launched Child Trust Fund. However, some life offices offer more formal arrangements where a parent can effect a policy on their own life on trust for the child absolutely. The policy will usually be some form of savings plan. The premiums will be gifts for IHT but normally exempt, either under the annual or normal expenditure exemptions. When the policy matures, the maturity value is payable to the trustees (normally the parents) for the absolute benefit of the child free of all tax.

Such policies are often designed to mature when the child is aged 18 or 21 and frequently give the child an insurability option so that it can effect a further policy on its own life, possibly using the maturity value of the maturing policy.

A number of offices will allow a parent to effect a policy on the life of a child if it is to be under absolute trust for the child. Often life cover will be deferred until a certain age, maybe 16. In these cases the qualifying rules restrict the amount payable on death to a refund of premium. Again, there may be options to effect further policies on the life of the child at maturity. The reason for arranging contracts in this way is the child's lack of contractual capacity. A child only has full contractual capacity at age 18, although many offices will allow children of 16 or 17 to effect policies. A couple of offices are allowed by special Act of Parliament to write policies for children at any age, although parental consent is necessary.

A friendly society is particularly well suited for childrens' policies because the investment is often fairly small, so that it falls within the friendly society limit and the underlying funds are tax-free. Also, the Finance Act 1991 allows children to have their own friendly society policies (often called baby bonds). These are usually effected and paid for by a parent or guardian on behalf of the child.

It should be remembered that if a policy effected by a parent on trust for a child produces a chargeable gain, then that gain is taxed on the parent as the creator of the trust (s465 ITTOIA 2005).

The advent of stakeholder pensions has encouraged parents and grandparents to use these for gifts, rather than less tax-efficient life policies.

An investment of £2,808 per annum per child (which grosses up to £3,600) can be made into personal or stakeholder pensions for a child, even though the child has no earnings. This is a gift for IHT purposes, but may be exempt under the annual or normal expenditure exemptions. For a minor child the guardian must sign the application and be responsible for the contract until the child reaches age 18.

(See also Child Trust Fund – in Chapter N section 13.)

5 Investments by Companies

Sometimes companies wish to effect life policies as investments, particularly single premium bonds. However, the Finance Act 1989 substantially reduced the attraction of life policies for companies. The detailed provisions are set out in Chapter D, but the main problem is that the chargeable gain is treated as income of the company and thus subject to corporation tax. Because there is no credit for the tax paid by the life fund, the gain is effectively taxed twice.

However, there would be little or no double taxation on an offshore bond because these are generally set up in countries where there is little or no taxation of the underlying fund. A company could also receive 5% tax deferred withdrawals for up to 20 years.

6 Second-Hand Policies

There has been much interest in the selling and buying of existing life polices – often called the second-hand policy market. The attraction for the original policyholder who needs the cash is that the selling price of the policy on the market may be better than the surrender value offered by the life office – sometimes by a substantial margin. The attraction for the buyer is that although future premiums will have to be paid, the yield on maturity may be very good and there is always a chance of an early profit if the life assured dies. Most second-hand policies are endowments, giving rise to the alternative term 'traded endowment policy', or TEP.

There are now a number of firms active in this market including market makers who buy policies themselves and hope to sell later at a profit, agents who try to put buyers and sellers together for a fee and a firm of auctioneers who have been going since 1843. The seller has to execute a deed of assignment in favour of the buyer and hand the policy over to him. The buyer should serve notice on the life office under the Policies of Assurance Act 1867 to protect his interest and prevent the life office paying the original owner by mistake. The buyer will be responsible for premiums falling due after the sale and will have to make arrangements to pay them. It would also be a good idea for the buyer to keep in touch with the life assured so as to be aware of any death claim. Some market makers are willing to buy back policies sold by them. This increases the liquidity of the investment and is in effect a tertiary market.

Participating in this market, whether as market maker, agent or auctioneer is investment business requiring authorisation under the Financial Services and Markets Act. The policies traded are mostly with-profits endowments (including unitised with-profit) and some guaranteed bonds. Each firm has its business criteria usually based on acceptable life offices, minimum surrender values and years to run. Older with-profits policies with a few years to run to maturity from sound, well-established offices are the most popular. Each firm also has its own scale of charges for buyers and sellers. The market maker or agent should check that there are no assignments registered with the life office and that premiums are paid to date.

If a firm deals in second-hand policies, it can only quote estimated maturity values at the FSA rates of 4%, 6% and 8%, unless within five years of maturity, in which case the office's current bonus rates can be used.

The FSA now requires life offices to inform policyholders considering surrender of the option of selling their policy.

The state of health of the life assured of a policy to be sold is normally assumed to be average for his age and so underwriting is not a consideration in determining the sale price of the policy.

For the taxation of second-hand policies, see Chapter D section 2.10 (for income tax) and section 5.1 (for CGT).

6.1 Viatical settlements

A viatical settlement is a sale of an existing life policy by a terminally ill person to a viatical company who will pay a cash price for it, usually expressed as a percentage of the expected death claim value. This might be attractive to someone who is terminally ill and needs the money to ease the last few months of life, as the viatical settlement price will probably be substantially higher than the standard surrender value. It will also be higher than the second-hand market value. However, it does involve losing the death cover provided by the policy because it is the viatical company that will claim the sum assured from the life office.

There are currently only a few companies in this market and each has its own criteria as to which policies it will buy. The viatical company will require medical evidence of the terminal illness, as well as details of the policy. The policy is assigned to the viatical company in a similar way to a second-hand policy, and the viatical company will give notice to the life office of this. The tax situation for the seller is the same as for second-hand policies (see above), although the impact of the receipt of the sales price in cash on the policyholder's right to receive state benefits should be borne in mind.

There have been some doubts expressed over the ethics of this market, but it clearly could be a good deal for some policyholders in the right circumstances. Policies under trust and life of another cannot be viatically sold by the life assured as they do not belong to the life assured. A viatical company is covered by the Financial Services and Markets Act 2000, and so these firms are regulated. Policyholders whose policies have critical illness or terminal illness cover may well not need to sell to a viatical company, as they can probably claim the full sum assured under the critical illness cover or terminal illness cover.

The buyer takes the risk of not getting paid the sum assured, if the original policyholder failed to disclose a material fact at outset. The buyer should keep in contact with the life assured so as to know when to claim. Some policies are bought by individuals and some by pooled funds.

N Other Investments

1 Bank Accounts

2 Building Society Accounts

3 Currency Funds

4 National Savings and Investments

5 Gilts

6 Corporate Bonds

7 Shares

8 Investment Trusts

9 Unit Trusts

10 Open-Ended Investment Companies (OEICs)

11 Individual Savings Accounts (ISAs)

12 Personal Equity Plans (PEPs)

13 The Child Trust Fund

14 Enterprise Investment Scheme (EIS)

15 Venture Capital Trusts (VCTs)

16 Derivatives

17 Hedge Funds

18 Wrap Accounts

19 Commodities

20 EU Investments

21 Other Investments

The previous chapter dealt with life assurance based investments. However, following the best advice requirements of the Financial Services and Markets Act 2000, all advisers should be aware of other non-life assurance investments and this chapter deals briefly with those.

1 Bank Accounts

Most adults in the UK keep a bank account as a home for money that will be needed immediately, eg to pay household bills. Most traditional current accounts do not pay anything more than a token rate of interest and are thus not really investments at all, but merely a secure and convenient place to store cash. Cash can be withdrawn at any time without notice and the cash is very secure as it cannot go down in value, although most banks have some form of charge for their services. If there is no income or capital gain there is no tax. Banks have to be authorised under the Financial Services and Markets Act 2000, and are supervised by the Financial Services Authority (FSA).

The security of a bank account is provided by the soundness and reputation of the bank concerned. In addition, there is the protection of the Financial Services Compensation Scheme (FSCS). This will compensate a depositor in an authorised bank which becomes insolvent. The deposit has to be a sterling deposit at a UK branch and currently protection is limited to 100% of the first £2,000 plus 90% of the next £33,000 (capital and interest). The maximum compensation is thus £31,700. The Financial Ombudsman Service (FOS) can handle complaints about banking services.

1.1 Bank deposit accounts

These are accounts, operated by banks, which pay interest. Different types of account have different conditions but generally the higher the rate of interest the longer the notice of withdrawal or the smaller or less well-known the bank. Often, small amounts can be withdrawn without notice. The capital invested will not go down but the interest will usually be variable at the discretion of the bank.

There is no capital gains tax (CGT) but the interest is subject to income tax. The banks will deduct 20% from the payment and credit the balance to the account holder. Higher rate taxpayers will have to pay extra tax on the gross interest on their annual assessment and non-taxpayers can reclaim from Her Majesty's Revenue and Customs (HMRC) the tax deducted. Alternatively, non-taxpayers can be paid without deduction of tax on completion of the appropriate certificate (R85). Basic rate taxpayers have no further liability, and starting rate taxpayers can reclaim 10%.

The Financial Services Compensation Scheme described above applies to deposit accounts as well as current accounts.

A deposit account with a major UK bank is a safe home for money as the capital cannot go down, some interest is paid and there is the security provided by the Financial Services Compensation Scheme. However, the interest rate is not guaranteed and can be reduced in the future without notice. In addition, although the nominal value of the capital does not go down, its real value will be reduced by inflation. A deposit account is therefore not the best medium for a long-term 'serious' investment – it is better looked at as a home for short-term cash.

In the past few years a number of supermarket chains, other national retailers and insurance companies have started to offer 'no frills' postal deposit accounts paying higher rates of interest than most clearing banks.

There is a Banking Code of good practice, which is followed by most banks and building societies. Under the code banks must:

- Send annual details of interest rates.
- Tell depositors when interest rates change.
- Inform depositors of any changes to the terms of the account.
- When an account is superseded maintain interest rates at the same level as similar accounts which are current.
- Advertise rates as the Annual Equivalent Rate (AER) to enable fair comparisons to be made.

1.2 Stakeholder deposit accounts

These accounts have been available since 6 April 2005. The minimum deposit must be £10 or less by cash, cheque, direct debit or direct credit. Interest must accrue daily at not less than the Bank of England base rate less 1%. When the base rate increases the interest rate must increase within one month. Withdrawal instructions must be executed within seven days and there must be no limit on the number or frequency of withdrawals.

2 Building Society Accounts

Building societies offer interest-bearing accounts with a huge variety of terms. In most cases the interest is variable at the discretion of the building society. Often, higher rates are offered for higher deposits. Instant access is a feature of basic accounts, but many higher rate accounts require a period of notice before money can be withdrawn. Generally, the higher the rate the longer the period of notice. Some accounts may offer a guaranteed rate for a defined period but on no account can the capital go down.

However, there is a vital difference in the legal structure of a building society account as opposed to a bank account. Because a building society is a mutual organisation, it is actually owned by its account holders. Thus, an account holder is technically a part owner, which is not the case with a bank where the depositor's rights are restricted to what is in his account.

The taxation situation is exactly the same as for bank deposit accounts as explained above. Building societies can also offer stakeholder deposit accounts.

Building societies have to meet the requirements of the Financial Services and Markets Act 2000 and are supervised by the FSA. The Act set up the Financial

Services Compensation Scheme which provides protection against a society becoming insolvent. The protection is 100% of the first £2,000 plus 90% of the next £33,000. The maximum payout would thus be £31,700. The Financial Ombudsman Service handles complaints about building societies.

A building society account is a good, safe investment as the capital cannot go down, a competitive rate of interest is paid and it is backed by the Financial Services Compensation Scheme. However, interest rates are not guaranteed and can be reduced in the future with little notice. Although the capital cannot fall in nominal terms, its real value is constantly being eroded by inflation. A building society account is therefore not the best home for a long-term investment particularly of a large sum. It is an ideal place for an emergency cash reserve because of its liquidity and easy access. It is also a good home for money 'in between' other investments, especially at times of falling equity markets. Building society accounts are also used for investors who cannot afford to see the value of their investment fall, even temporarily – what one might describe as 'widows and orphans' money. Anyone investing over £33,000 should consider dividing it among several societies to maximise the protection of the Financial Services Compensation Scheme.

Some building societies offer permanent interest bearing shares (PIBS). These pay a fixed rate of interest, but are not as safe as a traditional building society account because the Financial Services Compensation Scheme does not apply to them. They will rank behind ordinary accounts in priority for payment should the society become insolvent. They are like gilts (see section 4) in that interest is paid twice yearly (paid gross) and they are free of CGT. The capital value of PIBS should fluctuate like an undated gilt, and so there is no certainty that an investor will get all his capital back.

There is no fixed redemption date so the building society does not have to buy them back. They can, however, be bought and sold on the Stock Exchange. PIBS are regulated investments under the Financial Services and Markets Act 2000.

2.1 Building society demutualisations

When a building society demutualises, it converts from a mutual organisation owned by its members to a company owned by its shareholders. The building society may give its members a cash bonus or free shares as an incentive for voting for the demutualisation. The question thus arises as to how these are treated for tax purposes, and there has been some dispute about this between taxpayers and HMRC.

It has now been held (and HMRC has accepted the decision) that where a person invests with a building society in an account giving membership rights, he is buying one asset comprising the right to whatever money is in the account and the membership rights. If a cash bonus is paid to members on demutualisation, this is effectively a payment made for the giving up of membership rights. This is a disposal for CGT purposes, with the indexation allowance being due on the capital invested from the date of investment to April 1998 or the date of demutualisation, if earlier and taper relief. This should mean in any future demutualisation that most investors will have no tax to pay as the combination of the indexation allowance and annual CGT exemption will be more than the cash bonus.

Where a building society account did not give membership rights, it was effectively a loan to the building society and no asset was disposed of. There is thus no income tax or CGT on the cash bonus.

Where a building society issues free shares rather than making a cash payment, the situation is different. The issue of free shares is not subject to income tax or CGT. If the investor then sells the shares, there could be a CGT liability under normal CGT rules. The base value of the shares would be nil, because there was no acquisition cost.

3 Currency Funds

Currency funds aim to make a profit by buying and selling the various currencies of the world. They are run by fund managers on behalf of investors and try to limit exchange rate risks by investing in a spread of currencies. Money will actually be invested in short-term money market instruments in a variety of currencies and will be switched between currencies at the manager's discretion. Overall returns will be determined by interest rates and exchange rate fluctuations. Some funds have a bid–offer spread like a unit trust, others have a single price structure but all will have some form of charge. Many funds operate offshore.

There are two types of offshore fund: accumulation and distributor.

3.1 Accumulation funds

Accumulation funds roll up gross income within the fund rather than pay it out regularly. Investors pay income tax on the whole gain, both rolled-up income and any currency or capital gains, but only when it is paid out – effectively deferring the tax.

3.2 Distributor funds

Distributor funds have to distribute at least 85% of their income as a dividend which is taxable in full, although paid out gross. However, if total income is less than 1% of the fund value, no distribution is necessary. Any capital gain made on cashing in the investment is subject to CGT in the normal way.

4 National Savings and Investments

National savings products are government products which can be bought easily through post offices, via the post or the internet. They are all guaranteed by the government and are effectively a fund raising device for the government. National Savings is now officially called National Savings and Investments (NS&I). The Financial Ombudsman Service has been able to deal with complaints about National Savings since 1 September 2005. There are various different types of product as follows:

4.1 National Savings bank accounts

NS&I bank accounts are operated mainly across post office counters. There are two types of account – investment accounts and easy access savings accounts, and both have variable tiered rates of interest. National Savings subscribes to the Banking Code.

4.1.1 Investment accounts

Investment accounts pay a relatively uncompetitive rate of interest, with one month's notice required to withdraw money without penalty. Alternatively, money can be withdrawn immediately but with a 30 day interest penalty.

- The account is available to anyone over the age of seven.
- Interest is paid without deduction of tax but is taxable as savings income in full.
- An investment account might be a suitable investment for a non-taxpayer, such as a child, with a total income below the personal allowance.

4.1.2 Easy access savings accounts

The easy access savings account has replaced the ordinary account. All ordinary accounts were closed for transactions after 31 July 2004, except to withdraw or transfer the whole balance.

- Interest is paid gross but it is taxable as savings income in full. The advantage of the ordinary account, namely that the first £70 of interest a year was tax-free, was not carried through to this account.
- There are tiered interest rates, which are more competitive than the investment account, but are easily beaten elsewhere.
- Anyone age 11 or over can open an account.
- Withdrawals require no notice and the account can be operated by telephone and cash card as well as at post offices. Up to £300 cash can be withdrawn daily, but larger withdrawals must be paid into a bank or building society account.
- The account must hold a minimum balance of £100, so it is not suitable for children saving small amounts of pocket money.

Because these accounts are guaranteed by the government, they are safer than bank or building society accounts, although the interest rates are less competitive.

4.2 National Savings certificates

National Savings certificates are savings contracts which are on virtually continuous offer from the government. There have been over 100 issues of these certificates, each with a different fixed rate of return. The certificate is bought with a lump sum and no interest is paid, but after a set period it can be redeemed at a guaranteed higher value.

If it is not redeemed, the proceeds of a matured certificate are automatically reinvested in the latest issue. The capital appreciation of the certificates is free of all taxes. The certificates cannot go down in value, although if cashed in early the guaranteed rates will not usually apply. These certificates can be bought and redeemed at post offices.

These investments are suitable for people who do not require an income and can afford to tie up their capital for a fixed period of either two or five years. If no capital access is required, the security and tax-free status of these certificates make them a good investment, mainly for higher rate taxpayers. They are also easy and cheap to purchase and encash as they can be dealt with over the post office counter.

If the rate of interest paid is higher than the average rate of inflation over the life of the certificate, the investment will have given a positive real rate of return. However, there is no guarantee that this will be so and a real loss is therefore possible, although because of the government guarantee there will always be the fixed nominal rate of return.

4.3 National Savings index-linked certificates

Index-linked certificates are National Savings certificates with a return that is not fixed but linked to the rate of inflation. If a certificate is encashed in the first year, only the purchase price is repaid. However, if it is held for over a year the redemption value is index-linked so that the return will match inflation, as measured by the Retail Price Index (RPI). In the unlikely event of the RPI falling, the value will not drop below the original purchase price.

Some certificates offer an extra rate of interest over and above indexation. The extra rate depends on the exact issue. These certificates are free of income tax and CGT and can be bought and encashed at post offices.

These investments have the same advantages as the ordinary certificates but the added benefit of avoiding a real capital loss because of index-linking.

4.4 National Savings income bonds

National Savings income bonds are bonds which are guaranteed by the government and which pay interest monthly at a variable rate. Rates are changed from time to time and are usually announced in the newspapers. The interest is taxable but is paid without deduction of tax, which is convenient for non-taxpayers such as children. Bonds can be cashed in at any time. They can be bought from post offices.

The bonds are suitable for investors who need a simple, safe, income-producing investment. However, they should not be used by those who need instant capital access and their attraction largely depends on how competitive the interest rate is as against those offered by banks and building societies.

4.5 National Savings capital bonds

Under National Savings capital bonds the interest is not paid out but is reinvested to increase the bond's capital value. The bond has a guaranteed fixed rate for a fixed term of five years. At the end of the term the capital plus guaranteed interest is paid out.

The interest is taxable each year, but tax is not deducted and the gross amount is reinvested. Early encashment reduces the rate of interest credited. The bonds can be purchased at post offices.

This bond is only suitable for an investor who can afford to tie up capital for a fixed period and is happy to pay tax on money that cannot be realised until a fixed future date or is a non-taxpayer. The investment cannot produce a nominal loss but will produce a real loss if inflation over the period turns out to be higher than the guaranteed rate of interest.

4.6 Fixed rate savings bond

These bonds pay a fixed rate of return, either monthly or annually, for a choice of one, three and five-year terms. Interest is taxable and paid net of 20% tax. The minimum investment is £500 and the maximum is £1,000,000. Rates depend on the term selected and are tiered according to the amount invested.

4.7 Pensioners guaranteed income bond

The pensioners guaranteed income bond is available to anyone aged 60 or over wanting to invest from £500 to £1,000,000. It pays a monthly income at a fixed rate for one, two or five years. The income is taxable but is paid without deduction of tax. The capital is repayable after one, two or five years but can be paid earlier subject to 60 days' notice and 60 days' loss of interest or no notice and 90 days' loss of interest.

4.8 Children's bonus bond

The children's bonus bond is a fixed rate bond for children under 16. It can be bought by anyone over 16, such as a parent, friend or relative. It pays a rate of interest guaranteed for five years, plus a bonus every five years which is non-taxable, and can be continued until the child is 21 or cashed in earlier.

4.9 Premium bonds

Premium bonds are effectively a cross between a lottery and a no gain, no loss investment. Once a premium bond is bought it is entered into a monthly draw and a few lucky holders win money prizes. However, unlike the lottery, the holder can always get his money back although no interest or growth is paid. Some people use these as a form of investment. The underlying interest rate, which determines the level of prizes, is variable. Prizes are free of all taxes.

4.10 Individual savings account

National Savings offer a mini-ISA with a cash component only. The interest rate is variable and interest is credited annually on 5 April. It can take transfers.

4.11 Guaranteed equity bonds

There have been a number of different issues of these bonds, each a five-year term linked to the FTSE 100 index. When the bonds mature they pay a return of capital, plus a specified percentage of the growth in the index, which may be subject to a stated maximum. If the index drops the capital is guaranteed. Any gain is subject to income tax (not CGT) in the year of maturity, but is paid gross. They are only suitable for investors who will not need access to their money as they cannot be cashed in before maturity.

5 Gilts

Gilts, or more properly gilt-edged securities, are British government stocks and are effectively loans to the government. They are often called fixed interest stocks because the interest rate (or coupon) is fixed and guaranteed by the government. The fixed rate of interest is expressed as an annual rate per £100 of stock. Thus, someone who holds £100 of Treasury 9% 2012 will get £9 pa until 2012.

Gilts can be bought direct from the government if they are being currently issued, or via the Stock Exchange because they are listed securities. Gilts need not be issued at par value: a £100 stock could be issued at a discount such as £95. Interest is based on £100 and that is the price the government will pay to redeem the stock. Once a stock has been issued its price will be quoted on the Stock Exchange and thus can vary daily. The holder of gilts can sell them at any time on the Stock Exchange at the current price.

The government has to pay interest on the stock at the fixed rate, usually half-yearly. It also has to redeem (buy back) the stock at its par value at some time in the future. The exact time depends on the conditions of the stock. It could be on a fixed date: eg Treasury 9% 2012 must be redeemed in 2012. It could be a specified period: Treasury 7.75% 2012–15 must be redeemed at some time in those years. On some low interest stocks, the redemption date is at the government's discretion: eg War Loan 3.5%. Where the government has a choice, it is most unlikely to redeem stocks where the rate of interest is less than market rates.

A large range of stocks is available and these are classified according to the length of time to redemption:

- Short-dated stocks have less than five years before redemption.
- Medium-dated stocks have between five and 15 years to run.
- Long-dated stocks have over 15 years to go.

- Undated stocks have no fixed final date for redemption.

A wide range of terms and interest rates is available so an investor requiring a specified rate for a specified period should be able to find a stock to fit the bill.

5.1 The benefits from gilts

Gilts give the investor two benefits: first, the income and, second, the capital gain if a stock bought at below par is redeemed at par or sold on the Stock Exchange at more than the purchase price. The income yield to the investor is related to his purchase price rather than to the redemption or the par value. For someone buying £100 of 10% stock at £120, the interest yield is 10/120 = 8.33%.

The capital profit (or loss) for a redeemable stock will never be less than the difference between the purchase price and par if the stock is held until redemption. However, if the stock is sold on the Stock Exchange, any profit (or loss) will depend on the price when sold.

The price depends basically on the attractiveness of gilts as against other investments. Thus, if general interest rates rise, a fixed rate is less attractive and gilt prices should fall. Virtually all gilt prices are above par as a result of the fall in interest rates since the late 1980s.

Gilts can be bought and sold through stockbrokers, who charge commission. Most gilts can be bought or sold via a postal service run by Computershare on behalf of the Debt Management Office, the Treasury department that manages government debt. The dealing costs via Computershare are lower than the usual stockbroker's commission. A gilt certificate is evidence of title, although most stocks are registered in any case.

Gilts are an attractive investment to anyone wanting a fixed rate of income with a capital guarantee. They are very safe because they are backed by the government, easily realisable because they can be sold on the Stock Exchange and, for individual investors, have a taxation advantage over other investments which might produce a capital gain which is not free of CGT.

With the variety of gilts on the market there should be one with a redemption date to suit any investor. Because of these features, life assurance companies are major investors in gilts as they have fixed future liabilities for which they must have the money available, eg guaranteed maturity values on life policies.

The nominal loss on gilts held to redemption will become a greater real capital loss as inflation over the period the gilt is held will erode the purchasing power of the maturity value. Because gilts are free of CGT for individuals any capital loss cannot be offset against other capital gains.

5.2 Index-linked gilts

Some gilts are index-linked in that both the interest and the capital gain are linked to the RPI. There are a number of these issues, with varying redemption dates. The interest on these stocks tends to be low, as the real attraction is the guarantee of inflation-proofing on the capital. However, the stock will be inflation-proof only if it is held to redemption. If it is sold on the Stock Exchange before redemption, the price will not necessarily give an overall index-linked return.

Index-linked gilts are attractive to investors who want to be sure that their return will keep pace with inflation, although the investor will need to be sure he will not need the money until the redemption date otherwise the inflation-proofing could be lost. They are thus suitable for those with fixed future liabilities, particularly long-term ones. For this reason, life offices and pension funds are major purchasers of index-linked gilts.

5.3 Gilt taxation

Gilt interest is normally payable without deduction of tax, but holders can opt to be paid net of tax. This does not alter the fact that interest is taxable. If tax is deducted, it will be at 20%, which will be the full liability for a basic rate taxpayer. A non-taxpayer can reclaim all the tax, a starting rate taxpayer can reclaim 10% and a higher rate taxpayer will have to pay the balance on the gross interest.

When a gilt is sold or held to redemption by an individual investor, any capital gain is free of CGT. However, a seller is treated generally as having received interest accruing up to the date of sale and is liable to income tax on this. Rules charging capital gains to corporation tax apply to companies (including life companies).

6 Corporate Bonds

The previous section dealt with stocks issued by central government. Companies also issue loan stocks, popularly called corporate bonds. These investments are listed on the Stock Exchange and thus can be bought and sold through stockbrokers. There are basically three types of corporate bonds:

- Debenture stocks.
- Loan stocks.
- Convertible stocks.

6.1 Debenture stocks

Debenture stocks are effectively secured loans to a company. The security is either a fixed charge on the company's property or a floating charge on some of its assets (such as trading stock). If the company defaults on the loan, the debenture holder can take over and sell the property charged to get his money back. In the case of a floating charge, default is said to 'crystallise the security', which means that the floating charge is converted into a fixed charge on the company's assets at the date of default.

Trustees are appointed on the issue of debentures to supervise the way the company performs its obligations concerning the payment of interest and repayment of capital. In the event of any default, the trustees act for the debenture holders.

Like gilts, debentures pay a fixed rate of interest for a fixed term, at the end of which the capital is repaid, although often the company can repay earlier if it wishes. Debentures are not as secure as gilts, because they are not guaranteed by the government. A company can become insolvent and be unable to pay the interest due. Hopefully, the charge on property would mean that this could be sold to repay the capital, but a forced sale might not raise enough money to do this, particularly in the case of a floating charge.

Because the security is less than for gilts, interest rates tend to be higher.

Interest is paid net of 20% tax, with the normal consequences for non-taxpayers and basic, starting and higher rate taxpayers. As debentures are traded on the Stock Exchange, it is possible to buy and sell at a profit (or loss). If the debenture meets the conditions for qualifying corporate bonds, any gain is exempt from CGT for individuals.

6.2 Loan stocks

Loan stocks are unsecured loans to a company. Interest is fixed, as is the term. If the company defaults, the investor has no security and thus is in the same position as all the other unsecured creditors of the company. If the company's assets are not sufficient to pay off all creditors, the loan stockholder may receive only part of his money back. It is also possible for him to get nothing back if the company's assets are all used up in paying off secured creditors (such as debenture holders). Loan stocks are thus much less secure than debentures and may therefore carry higher rates of interest. Trustees are appointed to act for the stockholders. The taxation rules are the same as for debentures.

6.3 Convertible stocks

Convertible stocks are debentures or loan stocks which have the additional right to convert on a fixed date to a certain number of ordinary shares in the company. On this date the holder can thus change his investment from a fixed interest loan to part ownership of the company, with a right to share in its profits by way of dividend. Whether it is worthwhile exercising the conversion option depends on the fortunes of the company at the time and the price at which the convertible stock can be converted into ordinary shares. The decision will also depend on whether the expected dividend income and capital growth in share price is better than the fixed interest and more secure capital growth in stock price.

Reverse convertibles are stocks, where the borrowing company has the choice of repaying in shares or cash. If the share price falls, the borrower will repay in shares and the investor will suffer a loss. The risk will usually mean the company has to pay a higher rate of interest.

6.4 Suitability of corporate bonds

All corporate bond investments involve a degree of risk because there is not the guaranteed backing available with gilts and local authority bonds. If the company goes into liquidation, it is possible for investors to lose all their money, although a debenture holder should get something back via the fixed or floating charge. However, even then there is no guarantee of a full return of capital. For this reason, these investments are not suitable for those who cannot afford to lose money. They are, however, used by institutions for whom they will only form one part of a much wider portfolio. They are also used by 'venture capital' investors. The larger and more financially sound the company is, the more secure will be its corporate bond, although recent events have shown that size and apparent financial soundness is not proof against disaster. Corporate bonds can be held in PEPs and ISAs and have become increasingly popular as yields have fallen on other, more secure interest-paying investments.

7 Shares

Shares are different from stock in that a shareholder is a part owner of the company. A company is a separate legal person which is owned by all of its shareholders. The shareholders control the company through the fact that basically each share carries one vote at company meetings. The shareholders can thus decide major issues and vote in new directors to run the company if they wish. Shareholders are not liable for the debts of their company.

Each company maintains a register of shareholders and each shareholder receives a share certificate as evidence of title or (more commonly now) will have his evidence of ownership held electronically on Crest. Companies can be public or private. Generally speaking, private company shares are not listed on the Stock Exchange and are not available to ordinary investors. Public limited company (plc) shares can be quoted on the Stock Exchange if they meet the requirements of the UK Listing Authority (run by the FSA) and the trading requirements set by the Stock Exchange. The workings of the Stock Exchange are regulated by the FSA to protect the investing public. The shares in all major public companies are traded on the Stock Exchange, which means that there is a daily list of their prices which appears in the newspapers. Listed company shares are thus easy to buy and sell through stockbrokers. The shares can in theory be bought and sold on any working day, although on a new issue of shares in a popular company there may be more would-be buyers than shares available. Equally, if a company is in bad trouble, there may be no buyers at all.

The value of a share fluctuates according to the market's view of the worth of the company. If a company is doing well, its share price will tend to rise; and if it is doing badly, it will tend to fall. However, share prices are also influenced by other factors, such as how the country's economy is doing overall and the general level of interest rates. A share can thus be a volatile investment. A share price could rise very quickly, giving huge capital gains to investors who get in early; eg a new oil exploration company which makes a major discovery. The share price can also fall rapidly; eg the same company a few years later when the discovery proves to be smaller than originally thought and other wells are dry. In the extreme, a share can become worthless if the company becomes insolvent and all its assets are used to pay off creditors. A shareholder must therefore realise that he could lose all his money. In theory, the chances of this happening should be reduced by investing in shares of large, well-established, reputable companies, but history has shown that this does not always work in practice.

The costs of buying and selling shares include the stockbroker's commission and, assuming the Stock Exchange Electronic Trading Service (SETS) is not used for the transaction, the difference between buying prices and selling prices quoted by market makers.

7.1 The Alternative Investment Market (AIM)

The Alternative Investment Market (AIM) is a market for smaller and growing companies with less onerous access requirements and lower costs than a full listing. For these reasons, there are no rules concerning how long the companies have been in existence or their market capitalisation or the availability of shares. The AIM is open to all UK plcs. AIM shares are treated as unlisted shares for tax purposes.

7.2 Other markets

There is no rule which says that a company's shares must be traded on the Stock Exchange or the AIM. Shares not dealt in these markets can still be bought and sold by investors. However, protection is limited and once bought the shares may prove to be unsaleable and thus effectively worthless. Shares in foreign companies may be dealt in other stock exchanges throughout the world. Shares traded on major, recognised stock exchanges such as New York, Tokyo and Paris may be as easily marketable as UK-listed securities, although this may not be so of other, less-developed exchanges. Currency risks also need to be borne in mind for foreign shares.

7.3 Ordinary shares

The holder of an ordinary share in a company is a part owner of the company and is entitled to share in its profits in the form of a dividend. Dividends are paid out of the company's profits as decided by the directors. There is no certainty that a company will make profits and thus no certainty there will be a dividend. However, a company's track record can be inspected to judge whether profits are likely to be made and dividends paid. Dividends are usually paid half-yearly and provide income from the investment.

An investor will also hope to make a capital gain from the shares by an increase in the share price, although this is in no way guaranteed. The price of a listed share will fluctuate from day to day according to the company's progress and general economic conditions. Announcements of high profits, and thus high dividends, will tend to increase the price. Low profits have the opposite effect. A shareholder can always realise his investment by selling the shares. This may be easy for a successful, listed company but impossible for an unsuccessful, unlisted company. Shares are thus a risk investment: an investor could lose all his money, particularly if he invests in only one company's shares. A portfolio of shares in different companies is thus more advisable than having all one's eggs in one basket.

Dividends on shares are paid with an accompanying 10% tax credit, recognising the fact that the company will be paying corporation tax on its profits. This tax credit satisfies the full liability of starting and basic rate taxpayers. Higher rate taxpayers have a 32.5% liability, resulting in a further 22.5% to pay. This is calculated on the gross dividend – i.e. the dividend plus the tax credit. Non-taxpayers cannot reclaim the tax credit, although ISA and PEP managers could until 5 April 2004.

If shares are sold at a profit, this is subject to CGT. If shares are sold at a loss, then the loss may be used to offset gains made on other assets or carried forward to future years. Purchases of shares are subject to stamp duty reserve tax at 0.5% of the purchase price, payable by the buyer.

7.4 Preference shares

Preference shares give the holder a right to a fixed dividend provided enough profit has been made to cover it. This right takes preference over the right of ordinary shareholders to dividends. Preference shares differ from stocks in that although the income is fixed, it is not interest and may not be paid if profits are not made. They differ from ordinary shares in that the dividend will never be more than the fixed rate even if profits are more than enough to cover it. They are thus slightly more secure than ordinary shares but potentially less profitable. However, preference shareholders are part owners of the company and have similar rights to ordinary shareholders.

7.5 Suitability of shares

Shares are risk investments. There is no guarantee that a share will ever pay a dividend, nor that its market price will not fall to zero. Some comfort can be gained from Stock Exchange listing requirements and previous dividend and share price records, but none of these is proof against disaster. Some shares are particularly risky, eg foreign shares with political and currency risks and mining shares where the minerals can run out. Anyone putting all his money into one share must be prepared to lose it and thus it is preferable to invest in a wide spread of shares. It is certainly better for a smaller investor to invest in shares via an OEIC, unit trust, an investment trust or a unit-linked bond to get a wide spread of investment and reduce the risks of any one share rendering the whole investment worthless. Investing through an ISA may have tax advantages.

However, for those willing to take the risk, shares can be an extremely rewarding investment. Those buying shares in the early days of a company have sometimes seen the value of their investment increase over a hundred-fold in a decade or so. Economic history also suggests that, on average, a long-term investment in shares should perform better than an investment in an interest-bearing account, although there is no guarantee of this.

8 Investment Trusts

The companies whose shares were discussed in section 7 would be trading companies doing business in one or more areas; for instance, brewers, manufacturers, mining companies, retailers, oil companies and insurance companies. However, it is possible to invest in a company whose object is not some sort of business or trade but to invest its shareholders' money in other stocks and shares. This is an investment trust. The name is really a misnomer, as it is a limited liability company and not a trust. In effect it is a way in which individual investors can pool their resources to get professional investment management in a large number of companies, which would be impossible for the normal private investor.

In this way, it is similar to a unit trust (see section 9), although their legal structures are entirely different. Investment trusts sometimes take the lead in launching new companies and providing development finance for existing companies, rather than just being passive investors.

An investment trust is a limited company in which the investor buys shares, making him a part owner of the company. The shareholder receives his income in the form of dividends, which effectively come from the dividends on the shares held by the investment trust. Unlike a unit trust, which is open-ended in the sense that the managers can always create new units for new investors or cancel units for departing investors, an investment trust has a fixed number of shares. A unit trust can repurchase its own units, whereas an investment trust generally cannot repurchase its own shares. The shares are, however, marketable as they are listed on the Stock Exchange and thus can be bought or sold like any other shares.

An investment trust will invest mainly in shares quoted on the world's major stock exchanges, although many specialise in specific types of companies (eg energy or technology) or geographical areas. Trusts may invest in unlisted shares and some trusts specialise in this area. No more than 15% can be invested in any one company, except another investment trust.

Also, unlike most unit trusts, an investment trust can raise money by borrowing, for instance, in the form of a bank loan, unsecured loan stock or debentures. It can thus 'gear up' its investment by borrowing. This will be beneficial if its investments produce more than is required to service the loans, but not otherwise. An investment trust thus has the potential to make a greater profit or loss than a unit trust.

The value of the investment is simply the price quoted on the Stock Exchange for the shares. This will not necessarily reflect the exact value of the trust's investments in the same way as with a unit trust, and in general investment trust shares trade at a discount to the value of the underlying investments.

An investment trust is run by its directors, although the day-to-day investment management is usually undertaken by a firm of professional investment managers under a contract with the investment trust.

An investment trust enables a small investor to benefit from professional investment management and a wide spread of investment. Investment trusts can specialise in certain areas or sectors but can also change their investment strategy if they wish. Investment policy will be set out in the initial prospectus and the annual reports and accounts. Investment trust shares can be bought and sold through stockbrokers and other investment advisers.

Some investment trusts are known as split-capital trusts. These have income shares and capital shares and are set up for a fixed period. During that period, income shareholders receive all or most of the income generated by the trust's investments. At the end of the period, capital shareholders receive all or most of the money raised by selling the investments.

There are also zero coupon preference shares which give investors a fixed sum on repayment, usually expressed by way of an annual rate which accrues annually but is not paid until the payment date – hence zero coupon.

An investment trust costs money to run, as there will be operating expenses and fees payable to the investment managers. These vary considerably between trusts, with a typical range of 0.25% to 2% pa of the value of the investment portfolio. These costs are usually deducted from the income of the trust before it is distributed to shareholders. The shareholders have all the rights of ordinary shareholders to vote at company meetings etc.

Although investment trusts are effectively an investment in a collection of other shares, they reduce risks by their spread of investments. The wider the spread the safer will be the investment. However, they still involve a degree of risk as the market price of an investment trust share will be influenced by the general economy and level of share prices, as well as the prices of its constituent shares. The capital is thus not guaranteed and neither is the income. Highly geared investment trusts are clearly more risky than non-geared or lowly geared trusts. It can be, however, a reasonable, safe and cost-effective way of investing in shares.

There are a number of investment trust savings schemes on the market under which investments can be made by regular monthly payments or as a lump sum. The regular investment schemes can be viewed as a savings medium in the same way as a unit-linked life policy. The pound cost averaging effect can thus apply – see page 305.

8.1 Taxation of investment trusts

The income of an investment trust will probably come largely in the form of dividends paid by UK companies in whose shares the trusts invest. This is called franked income, as it has already borne UK corporation tax. It can thus be passed on to the shareholders of the investment trust in the form of a dividend with no further tax liability within the investment trust.

The trust may have other income (such as bank interest and dividends from foreign companies) which has not borne UK tax. This is called unfranked income, and is subject to corporation tax in the hands of the trust, although management expenses and loan interest can be set against this.

When the trust pays out income to its shareholders in the form of a dividend, this is subject to income tax in the same way as for ordinary shares: see section 7.

Capital gains made by investment trusts are exempt from CGT. Capital gains made by investment trust shareholders when they sell their shares are taxed in the same way as for ordinary shares.

8.2 Real estate investment trusts (REITs)

Real estate investment trusts, or REITs, should become available from 1 January 2007. They will be UK resident companies listed on a recognised stock exchange, like other investment trusts. No one person can own 10% or more of the shares.

For tax purposes a REIT will consist of two components – a tax-exempt business of property letting and a taxable business including ancillary property services and associated development. The REIT must derive at least 75% of its total profits from the tax-exempt business, which must also represent at least 75% of gross assets. It must hold at least three properties, with no one property worth more than 40% of the total. However, a large property consisting of *n* separate commercial or residential units is treated as *n* properties, rather than one. A REIT could invest in just one site consisting of a number of individual separately let blocks or flats.

A REIT must distribute at least 90% of the profits of the tax-exempt business as dividends within six months of the end of its accounting period. This dividend will be subject to deduction of tax at 22% and will be classed as profits of a UK property business for the individual investor. The tax deduction can be reclaimed by non-taxpayers, but higher rate taxpayers would have to pay an extra 18% on the gross dividend. Any distribution from the non-exempt business will be taxed as a normal UK dividend.

There is a conversion charge for existing property companies converting to REITs of 2% of the gross market value of investment properties.

9 Unit Trusts

A unit trust is similar to an investment trust in that it is a vehicle for small private investors to obtain professional investment management and a wide spread of investments. However, it is totally different from an investment trust in its constitution. A unit trust is a trust: a trust deed is executed whereby one company, the unit trust manager, agrees to manage the trust in return for certain fees, and another company, the trustee, agrees to hold the investments of the trust for the benefit of the unit holders. Unit holders do not own the unit trust in the way that shareholders own their company.

The trust deed sets out:

- The manager's investment powers.
- The price structure.
- The registration of unit holders.
- The remuneration of the managers.
- The accounting and auditing rules.

Unit trusts have to be authorised by the FSA and their operations are regulated by the FSA. The investments of the unit trust are selected and managed by the managers but are legally owned and held by the trustee for the benefit of the unit holders. The trustee, which is usually a bank or insurance company subsidiary, must ensure that the managers adhere to the provisions of the trust deed and act generally to protect the unit holders.

The investor buys units in the unit trust from the managers at the buying (or offer) price calculated as per the trust deed. Units can be sold back to the managers at any time at the selling (or bid) price. Units are thus very easy to buy and sell. It is not necessary to use a stockbroker (or other adviser) and sales can be made very quickly without the need to find a purchaser as would be the case with shares. The managers can create as many new units as investors require and can cancel units if new purchases are exceeded by encashments. A unit trust is thus open-ended.

The price of a unit is not set by any market opinion, as the calculation basis is set by the FSA. The buying price is based on the amount required to purchase the underlying investments (plus costs, including any initial charge levied by the manager) and the selling price is based on the amount for which they could be sold (less costs of sale). The prices are recalculated every day and quoted in the newspapers. The price accurately reflects the value of the underlying investments: if the unit trust has 1,000,000 units and the investments could be sold for £10,000,000 then the bid price will be £10 per unit.

There is a spread, generally around 3% to 6%, between the selling and buying prices, which is effectively the cost of purchase for an investor. There is also an annual management fee, typically 0.5% to 1.5%, deducted by the managers from the income of the trust. Some unit trusts have no initial charge but this may be offset by an exit charge for early encashments.

When an investor invests in a unit trust, he is allocated however many units his investment will buy at that day's buying price. The investor may receive a certificate in proof of title, although most groups now only issue contract notes. The money will be used by the managers to purchase further investments. Every day, the total assets of the trust are valued and divided by the number of units to calculate the next day's prices. When an investor wishes to cash in his units, the managers will buy them back at the selling price on that day. The FSA proposes to replace the current dual pricing system with a single price system, based on a single mid-market price, designed to be simpler and clearer for investors. Single pricing is now permissible, but compulsion is still some way off.

A unit trust cannot normally borrow money to 'gear up', although regulations introduced in 2004 by the FSA permit registered non-UCITS (Undertakings for Collective Investments in Transferable Securities) funds to borrow up to 10% on a permanent basis. Unit trusts can invest in shares, stock, gilts, property and other collective funds. Foreign securities are also permissible. Half-yearly reports are sent to unit holders.

9.1 Types of unit trust

There are many types of unit trust, according to the investment objectives of the trust. A trust may aim for a high income or a high capital growth, or a combination of growth and income. There are fixed interest trusts investing solely in corporate bonds. Other trusts invest solely in shares. Some trusts are general trusts and may thus invest in any shares. Others are specialised trusts investing in specific sectors of the market such as high-tech shares, small companies or commodities. There are also trusts investing in specific geographical areas such as North America, Japan and Australia. Trusts can be even more specialised: Japanese smaller companies; healthcare; gold shares. Fund of funds trusts invest in a spread of other trusts and OEICs. This might involve an extra layer of charges, although this could be mitigated by the buying power of large investment managers.

The risks involved vary according to the type of trust chosen. A gilt trust is relatively secure because of the security of the government backing for gilts. A specialist trust such as gold mining will be very much less secure because of the inherent volatility of the underlying shares. However, the idea is that due to the wide spread of securities held the investor will be protected against the consequences of one individual share becoming worthless because of the company going bankrupt.

A number of unit trust managers have regular savings schemes enabling investors to make monthly investments into unit trusts. This can bring the advantages of pound cost averaging (see Chapter M section 1.2.5).

In theory, the larger the unit trust the wider the spread of investments and the greater the degree of security against a sharp fall in value due to the collapse of one company's share price. Equally, however, the wider the spread the less likelihood there is of dramatic gains being produced by the success of one individual share. There are a number of trusts which try to give an extra degree of security by tracking one of the Stock Exchange indices, eg the FTSE Actuaries All-Share Index. These trusts try to match their investments to that of the index and (ignoring management charges) should thus never underperform (or outperform) the market. However, even tracker trusts will drop in value if the market as a whole drops in value – as happened during 2000–2002.

Security of the trust itself is provided by the approval requirements and monitoring of the FSA and the role of the trustee in holding assets and protecting the unit holders.

9.2 Taxation of unit trusts

The unit trust will generate income from its investments in the form of dividends on shares and interest on gilts, fixed interest securities and cash. Dividends on UK shares are franked income and have already borne UK corporation tax. This income can thus be passed on to unit holders in the form of a dividend with no further tax liability on the unit trust. Other income (such as gilt interest and dividends on foreign shares) will not have borne UK tax and is unfranked income. The unit trust will pay corporation tax at 20% on foreign dividends and gilt interest. Management expenses can be set against the corporation tax bill on this income.

A unit trust will pay out its income (less charges), usually half-yearly in the form of a dividend. Dividends from trusts are payable like share dividends – with a 10% tax credit which covers liability up to the basic rate. A higher rate taxpayer has a further liability of 22.5% of the gross dividend but a non-taxpayer cannot reclaim the tax credit. Some unit trusts do not physically pay out a dividend but use it to purchase further investments for the unit holders. This is effectively an automatic reinvestment facility, but it does not alter the taxation consequences for a taxpayer as the unit holder is deemed to have received a dividend. Unit trusts are exempt from CGT, but unit holders are liable to this tax if they sell units at a profit, or can set losses against other gains.

Fixed interest trusts deduct income tax at 20% from their interest payments. This is reclaimable, unlike the dividend tax credit. However, the higher rate taxpayer faces a total charge of 40%.

Surrenders of units to the managers of a unit trust are chargeable to stamp duty reserve tax at 0.5% of the encashment value. The charge is reduced where the trust is shrinking, and sales of the trust's underlying assets are liable to stamp duty reserve tax in their own right.

9.3 Stakeholder unit trusts

Stakeholder unit trusts have been available since 6 April 2005. No more than 60% of the investments of the trust can be in shares listed on a recognised stock exchange, or units in a unit trust invested in shares or land and buildings. The investments must be managed to balance growth potential against the risk of loss in value. This would normally involve a substantial element of cash and/or gilts. The manager must have regard for diversification and suitability of investments. The minimum investment must be £20 or less by cheque, direct debit or direct credit. There is a charge cap of 1.5% a year for the first 10 years, and 1% thereafter, plus any stamp duty or tax incurred in running the fund. The units must be single priced and quoted daily.

10 Open-Ended Investment Companies (OEICs)

Open-ended investment companies (OEICs) are investment funds in a corporate form, but with a variable share capital – they are open-ended like a unit trust. Each OEIC must have an authorised corporate director (ACD) responsible for day-to-day management and compliance with the regulations. There must also be a depository responsible for the safekeeping of assets (like a trustee in a unit trust). To be marketed in the UK, the OEIC must be authorised by the FSA. The FSA also regulates the ACD and the depository. The FSA also regulates the selling and marketing, where the non-life disclosure rules apply. It is possible to have a range of funds within one OEIC. OEICs will normally qualify as UCITS.

Although an OEIC is a company, and the investment is a share in it, in other respects an OEIC is like a unit trust in that the number of shares can go up or down according to whether there is a net inflow or outflow of investment. The price paid for a share is determined by the value of the investments of the fund, like a unit trust, rather than supply and demand on the Stock Exchange (like ordinary shares and investment trusts). Stock Exchange listing is optional. There is a single price structure (ie no bid–offer spread) with initial charges shown separately. There can be a limited ability to borrow in order to gear up the investments – up to 10% of the fund.

A charge, called the 'dilution levy', can be added to the single price on share purchases or deducted from the price on redemptions, at the ACD's discretion. The dilution levy is paid to the OEIC to cover dealing costs and the spread between the buying and selling prices of the underlying investments if there were to be unusually large inflows and outflows of funds. The levy goes to the fund, not the managers.

The OEIC pays income in the form of dividends and it is possible to make capital gains or losses on selling the shares. The taxation of an OEIC is effectively the same as for a unit trust. OEICs are ISAable in the same way as unit trusts. There has been a steady pattern of unit trusts converting themselves into OEICs. This conversion process and the launch of most new funds with an OEIC structure means that about 63% of the UK authorised fund market is now OEICs. An OEIC can be a stakeholder OEIC if it meets the conditions set out in section 9.3 for unit trusts.

11 Individual Savings Accounts (ISAs)

The Individual Savings Account (ISA) was introduced on 6 April 1999 and is guaranteed to run for at least eleven years. It is available to anyone resident and ordinarily resident in the UK who is 18 or over. Since 6 April 2001 mini cash ISAs and the cash component of a maxi ISA have been available to 16 and 17 year olds. However if the money is given to them by a parent, any income arising in the ISA is taxable on the parent while the child is under 18. Crown employees serving abroad are eligible as are their spouses and civil partners. An ISA can only have a single owner. An ISA cannot be assigned or put into trust. There is no minimum investment and no minimum holding period. ISA conditions are not allowed to lock investors in for a fixed period, they must be transferable on request. The permitted components within the ISA envelope are:

- Cash deposits.
- Stocks and shares.

11.1 Cash deposits

Cash deposits are deposits in banks and building society accounts (including their Euro equivalents), authorised cash unit trusts, National Savings ISA product, deposits with credit unions, stakeholder cash deposit accounts, cash-like stakeholder medium-term products and cash-like life policies.

11.2 Stocks and shares

Stocks and shares can be listed on any recognised stock exchanges anywhere in the world. They comprise:

- Shares and corporate bonds issued by companies listed on a recognised stock exchange anywhere in the world.
- Gilt edged securities ('gilts'), similar securities issued by governments of other countries in the European Economic Area and 'strips' of all these securities, provided there is at least five years to run until redemption when they are purchased.
- Units or shares in UK authorised unit trusts or OEICs which invest in shares and securities (called securities schemes and warrant schemes) and fund of funds schemes which invest in them.
- Shares and securities in approved investment trusts (except property investment trusts).
- Units or shares in UCITS funds based elsewhere in the European Union.
- Any shares which have been transferred from an HMRC approved all employee scheme under the special rules.
- Life insurance policies that would have qualified for the separate life insurance ISA component that existed before 5 April 2005.
- Non UCITS retail schemes (NURS) provided they are not quasi-cash funds and they allow investors to access their funds at least twice a month. This could include property funds.
- Stakeholder medium-term products.

Collective funds which guarantee or offer protection that the investor will receive at least 95% of their original capital within five years of investment are only eligible for the ISA cash component. Unlisted and AIM shares are not allowed.

The pre-6 April 2005 insurance component includes friendly society policies and is separate from any existing ordinary life policies. The policy must be a single premium policy, although recurrent single premiums are possible. It must be on the life of the investor and is non-assignable. It does not include annuities, personal portfolio bonds or pension contracts. The policy must not be linked to a non-ISA policy and policy loans are not allowed. The policy can only exist as part of an ISA. Few providers offered the insurance component and their inclusion within the stocks and shares component was recognition of this.

The maximum overall annual investment into an ISA is £7,000, but limited to £3,000 for the cash element. Investments must be made with the investor's own cash (except for shares transferred within 90 days from approved profit sharing, approved share incentive plans and SAYE share options).

The ISA is exempt from income tax and capital gains tax and could reclaim the 10% tax credit on UK dividends until 5 April 2004. This also applied to shares which backed policies in any life assurance element. Withdrawals can be made in full or in part at any time with no loss of tax relief or tax liability.

The ISA has to be run by an HMRC approved manager. This could be a product provider offering one or more of the approved investment components or an independent person offering other people's products. Savers have a choice of managers – each year there are two options.

11.2.1 Single manager – maxi ISA

The first option is to choose a single manager. This manager must offer a maxi account which can accept the overall subscription. It must include the stocks and shares component, but not necessarily cash. The saver can subscribe up to £7,000 to the stocks and shares component. If the manager offers the cash component as well, savers can invest up to £3,000 to the cash component, with the balance invested in stocks and shares. An investor can only subscribe to one maxi account each tax year.

11.2.2 Separate managers – mini ISA

The second option is for savers to choose separate managers for each component (mini accounts) and invest up to £4,000 in stocks and shares and £3,000 in cash. An investor can only subscribe to one mini account for each component each year and cannot subscribe to both a mini ISA and a maxi ISA in the same tax year.

11.2.3 TESSA only ISA

It was also possible to transfer into a TESSA only ISA the capital proceeds (but not accumulated interest) of a matured TESSA, without affecting the normal ISA subscription. Reinvestment had to take place within six months of the TESSA's maturity date, so the final date for this was 5 October 2004. TESSA only ISAs have now effectively become cash ISAs.

11.2.4 Transferring an ISA

An investment can be transferred from one ISA manager to another, but must stay within the same component. A current tax year ISA can only be transferred in full, but a previous year's ISA can be transferred in full or in part.

11.2.5 Regulation

The ISA is regulated in the same way as the individual components which make it up. There used to be CAT (charges, access terms) standards for ISAs but these were withdrawn by the government on 6 April 2005 with the introduction of the stakeholder suite of products.

An ISA holder who ceases to be resident and ordinarily resident in the UK can keep the ISA with its tax benefits, but cannot pay in any further money.

The government has promised to keep the current ISA limits until 5 April 2010.

12 Personal Equity Plans (PEPs)

Personal equity plans (PEPs) are tax-free investment plans owned by an individual, but run by a PEP manager registered with HMRC, and authorised under the Financial Services and Markets Act 2000. They can invest in the same assets as ISAs (see section 11).

Dividends on the underlying shares or units are free of income tax and the PEP manager could reclaim the 10% tax credit until 5 April 2004. Any capital gains made within the PEP or by encashment of the PEP are free of CGT. Interest on bonds and fixed interest fund holdings is tax-free, ie the 20% tax deducted can be reclaimed. There was no 2004 cut-off date for this reclaim.

No new money could be invested in a PEP after 5 April 1999, when they were effectively replaced by ISAs – see section 11. However, PEPs in existence on that date could be continued with tax advantages very similar to ISAs. The amount held in a PEP does not affect what can be paid into an ISA. A PEP can still be transferred from one PEP manager to another PEP manager, but not into an ISA.

13 The Child Trust Fund

The Child Trust Fund (CTF) applies to all children resident in the UK born from 1 September 2002 onwards, although CTF accounts have only been available since 6 April 2005. Each child can have only one CTF.

CTF providers must be approved by HMRC and be authorised by the FSA. Firms must inform the FSA before they launch a CTF account. All providers have to offer a stakeholder CTF which must include shares and can also include cash, unit trusts, OEICs, fixed interest securities and single premium policies on the life of the child. The CTF is effectively an investment wrapper like an ISA. There is an annual charge cap at 1.5% plus any stamp duty reserve tax for a stakeholder CTF.

The government contributes £250 to each CTF at birth. Children of families receiving child tax credit (CTC) and with an income below the CTC threshold (currently £14,155) will receive an extra £250. The government will then make a further payment into the CTF on the child's 7th birthday of £250, or £500 for families with an income below the CTC threshold. The government is also consulting about a payment at age 11, likely to be £250/£500.

Anyone else (including the child) can contribute up to £1,200 a year in total per child, although there can be no carrying forward of unused allowances. These contributions are transfers of value for inheritance tax (IHT) purposes (unless from the child itself).

Normally the CTF will be opened by a parent or guardian (designated as the registered contact) but if they do not do this within a year of birth HMRC will open an account for the child anyway.

The registered contact can change the CTF provider at any time and manages the CTF, although it will still be owned by the child. The child will take over management of the CTF as the registered contact at age 16.

The CTF is administered by the issue of vouchers via the child benefit system. All income and gains of a CTF are exempt from personal tax, like an ISA. Chargeable gains certificates are not required for life assurance CTFs. The parental settlement rules do not apply. A CTF cannot be assigned or charged, and does not pass to any trustee-in-bankruptcy.

The CTF will not be accessible until age 18. On the 18th birthday, the CTF will cease and the funds can be spent as the child wishes, or remain invested as a non-CTF investment subject to normal tax rules, although there will be no CGT on any gain made during the CTF period.

13.1 Regulation

The CTF is regulated by the FSA and covered by the FOS and the FSCS. There are specific FSA rules for CTFs and the registered contact counts as the customer for those rules. CTF vouchers count as client money for the client money rules.

Product disclosure documents must make it clear that once money has been paid into a CTF it cannot be taken out, except by the child when it reaches age 18. CTF providers should also make it clear to third party subscribers that the subscription is a gift. Product disclosure documents must also explain the difference between stakeholder equity based CTFs and non-stakeholder cash CTFs. Projections are not required but if done should be done at the higher rates, as for pensions and ISAs. Life policy CTFs have a 30 day cancellation period, but the life office does not have to issue a cancellation notice, although information about the cancellation rights must be given in the point of sale material.

CTF providers can rely on the CTF vouchers for money laundering identification purposes for both the child and the registered contact.

14 Enterprise Investment Scheme (EIS)

Enterprise investment schemes (EISs) give tax incentives for equity investment in unlisted trading companies. Individuals can obtain income tax relief at 20% on investments up to £400,000 a year. Gains on disposal will not be subject to CGT but losses are allowable against CGT or income tax. There is a three-year minimum holding period and investors cannot be connected with the company prior to investing although they can become directors afterwards. Companies providing rented housing are not allowed in the EIS. An EIS company must carry on a qualifying activity in the UK for at least three years. It must have gross assets of less than £7 million before an investment, and no more than £8 million after it. Where an EIS investor disposes of assets, they are allowed to defer any chargeable gain on those assets up to the amount of their EIS investment, thus effectively getting CGT relief at up to 40% in addition to income tax relief at 20%. There is no limit on CGT deferral relief. EIS shares get 100% business property relief for IHT after two years' ownership.

The government has restricted EISs from offering arrangements where a substantial part of the return to investors is guaranteed or backed by property.

15 Venture Capital Trusts (VCTs)

Venture Capital Trusts (or VCTs) were introduced to encourage investment in unquoted trading companies. A VCT is similar to an investment trust in that it is a company quoted on the Stock Exchange which invests in other companies. At least 70% of a VCT's investments must be in unlisted trading companies, with not more than 15% in any one group of companies. The investments can include loans for at least five years, but at least 30% must be in new ordinary shares. VCTs have up to three years to meet these requirements. VCTs have to be approved by HMRC and investors have to be 18 or over.

When an investor buys new shares in a VCT, he gets income tax relief at 30% on up to £400,000 in any tax year, provided the shares are held for at least five years. The dividends from a VCT are not taxable and any gains on disposal of VCT shares are exempt from CGT.

EISs and VCTs must not be invested in companies carrying out farming, forestry, property development, hotel management or care home operations.

16 Derivatives

Instead of buying or selling a security outright, an investor can buy a right to purchase or sell a security at a future time. This is called an option. A share option gives the right to deal in a fixed number of a company's shares at a fixed price during the option period – usually three months. A call option gives the right to buy and a put option the right to sell. The option is bought for a price, or premium, usually expressed in pence per share. Options are often called derivatives to distinguish them from actual shares.

There are also traded options on leading shares and gilts. These options can be bought and sold on the Stock Exchange. An option to buy shares in the future is often called a future.

An investor purchasing a call option will be hoping that the share price will rise, so that when the option is exercised the premium plus the fixed price will be less than the value of the shares. The seller of the option will be wanting the reverse to happen so that the option will not be exercised and he will profit by the amount of the premium.

An investor purchasing a put option will hope the share price will fall, so that he can sell for an amount greater than the value of the shares plus the premium. He can then buy the shares on the market and sell them at an immediate profit. The seller of the option will be hoping the reverse happens.

Investing in options is inherently risky and an investor must be prepared to lose all his money. Gains on options are generally subject to CGT unless HMRC deems the investor to be trading, in which case income tax would apply.

17 Hedge Funds

There is no real agreement on what exactly a hedge fund is. One definition used by the FSA was 'any pooled investment vehicle that is privately organised, administered by professional investment managers and not widely available to the public'. Hedge funds are certainly not about hedging investments. They are more about speculating in the pursuit of above average gains.

Hedge funds use techniques such as short selling and leverage not used by traditional investment managers. Short selling is borrowing shares in a company thought to be overvalued, selling them and then buying them back at a lower price by the date they have to be returned to the original owner. In this way hedge funds claim to be able to make money in a falling market. However, if the market rises it will lose on the deal. Leveraging is borrowing to invest which magnifies gains if the market goes up, but magnifies losses if it goes down.

These techniques can destabilise markets and have attracted the attention of regulators. One hedge fund in the USA collapsed some years ago, having a drastic effect on the whole market and requiring federal intervention. There are now thousands of hedge funds, mostly based in the USA, but some in the UK. They can be open ended (like unit trusts) or close ended (more like an investment trust). Many have initial lock-in periods and set redemption dates. They are rarely transparent and often poorly regulated. Undoubtedly large gains can be made, but equally so can large losses. Total failures are not uncommon.

Charges tend to be high compared to more conventional investments and they often include a performance-related element, so that the better the fund performs, the more the managers get paid. Minimum investments tend to be high. They might be suitable for professional and sophisticated investors but not for the average client. The risks could be spread by investing in a fund of hedge funds but this might involve an extra layer of charges.

18 Wrap Accounts

There is no real definition of a wrap account but they are not products in themselves. They are just computer systems (or administrative platforms) that consolidate the valuation of some or all the savings and investments products belonging to a particular client. They enable advisers to view the value of the client's investments and advise on asset allocation across the board at any time.

In theory, a wrap account could hold details of any asset a client might hold. In practice, most wrap accounts are restricted to listed shares, authorised unit trusts, bonds, OEICs, ISAs, PEPs and self-invested personal pensions (SIPPs). They may be particularly useful for advisers who operate discretionary investment management arrangements, although this is not the same thing as a wrap account.

Wrap account providers charge fees, usually based on the market value of assets held within them. These fees may be on top of any charges made by the providers of the underlying products, although the product provider may cut its charges for dealing with wrap accounts. However, they may make the job of the investment adviser easier, and therefore reduce other fees. They may also make tax reporting easier by providing all the required details in one place and simplify IHT negotiations by providing details of valuation on death.

Increasing competition in this area lately has resulted in wrap managers trying to include as many products within their accounts as possible. Competitive pressures are also making the computer systems more flexible and easier to access and use. However there is nothing magic about a wrap account and it should be viewed as an administrative tool rather than a substitute for good investment advice.

A wrap account is not the same as a fund supermarket, or fund of funds or manager of managers. It is also not a back office system for advisers as it handles only investments, not protection products or mortgages.

19 Commodities

The commodity markets exist primarily for commercial buyers and sellers of the commodity concerned.

Examples

Examples are:

- For oil – producers, refiners, petrol sellers.
- For coffee – growers, roasters, drinks companies.
- For wheat – farmers, bakers, food manufacturers.

Commodities can be bought as:

- Physicals, where the goods exist and are delivered immediately: for instance, 1,000 bags of coffee for delivery at the warehouse tomorrow.
- Futures, where the goods may not yet exist and will be delivered in the future: for instance, 1,000 bags of coffee to be delivered in a year's time.

An investor may try to make money by buying a commodity future, which is the right to have a certain quantity of a specified commodity for a set price at a fixed date in the future. He will be hoping that the market prices will rise so that when the goods are delivered he will be able to sell immediately at a profit. He will not be interested in the goods themselves and will almost certainly never see them.

Commodity prices can be very volatile as they depend on supply and demand, and on other variable factors such as the weather. For example, an unseasonable frost in Brazil may reduce the coffee crop and thus greatly increase prices for the coffee to be harvested in a few months' time. Large profits can be made from commodity futures. Equally, large losses can be made.

As well as dealing directly in commodities, an investor can deal in commodity options, which work in a similar way to share options (see section 16).

Investors can invest via commodity brokers in a number of markets such as coffee, tea, oil, gold and metals. London has a Commodity Exchange and a Metal Exchange and there is the International Commodities Clearing House to administer these contracts. There is also the London International Financial Futures Exchange (LIFFE) dealing in financial futures.

Investing in commodity futures and options is extremely risky and can involve not only the loss of the whole investment but also the loss of all one's other assets. It is therefore not recommended except possibly for those with rich and understanding relatives. For investors, profits on non-trading transactions on recognised dealing exchanges in commodity or financial futures are charged to CGT. Any losses can be offset against other gains.

20 EU Investments

A number of European investments are now available for UK investors.

20.1 UCITS

These are Undertakings for Collective Investments in Transferable Securities and are the European equivalent of a unit trust. A UCITS from an EU state can be sold in the UK if registered with the FSA.

20.2 SICAV

These are Sociétés d'Investissement à Capital Variable and are mutual funds with no fixed capital which can issue and redeem shares without shareholder approval (similar to a UK OEIC). They are effectively a cross between unit trusts and investment trusts.

21 Other Investments

There are other things that people sometimes use for investments. Examples would be land, forests, stamps, coins, antiques, vintage cars and works of art. These alternative investments are not covered by the Financial Services and Markets Act 2000, are in no way in competition with insurance products and are thus beyond the scope of this book.

O Pensions Funding

The introduction of pensions simplification is the most radical overhaul of pensions for a very long time. Previous attempts at reforming the tax aspects of pensions have resulted in increasing the complexity. The stated objective of pensions simplification was to replace all the previous regimes with one set of rules which applies to all types of pension, existing and new. This came into force on 6 April 2006 – the so-called A Day.

The new regime is designed to be more flexible than the previous ones. However, the original simple proposals have become much more complex as the details have been worked out and no doubt this process will continue into the future as pensions is still a hot political topic.

This chapter deals basically with the rules relating to the funding of pension schemes, whereas the next chapter deals with the rules relating to benefits. This distinction might be summarised as: Chapter O money in, Chapter P money out.

The legislation is contained in the Pensions Act 2004, plus the Finance Acts 2004, 2005 and 2006.

1 State Pensions

The state provides pensions for virtually all UK residents in some fashion. Fuller details of benefits are given in Chapter P. This is effectively funded by the National Insurance system described in Chapter C section 6. However, it should be appreciated that as one of the originators of the system said – 'the secret of the state pension fund is that there is no fund'. Current pensions in payment are paid for by the current working population and there is no link between the level of pensions paid out and the contributions paid in.

2 Historic Pensions Arrangements

While pensions simplification has brought in one regime of tax rules for all types of pension there is still a historic distinction between occupational pension schemes and personal pensions.

An occupational pension scheme is a scheme established by an employer for the benefit of its employees, whereas a personal pension is an individual contract with a pension provider effected by an individual who might be employed, self-employed or even unemployed. While the new regime has altered what contributions and benefits the tax laws now allow, this does not of itself alter the legal rights of members of pension schemes or personal pension holders. Their rights are still determined by the rules of the scheme or contract. However, it is expected that most schemes and pension providers will allow members/holders to exercise any of the new rights subject to there being enough money in the scheme/contract.

Therefore some explanation must be given of the structures of the two types of pension. Either type of pension could provide life cover as well as retirement benefits.

3 Occupational Pension Schemes

3.1 Scheme funding

3.1.1 Pay-as-you-go

This is the basis on which the state pension scheme and some public sector schemes work. Pensions are paid out of current income, rather than from accumulated funds. To operate on this basis there must be some guarantee that money will be available many years in the future to pay the pensions of current employees. For this reason such schemes are almost exclusively in the public sector – where the liabilities can be underwritten by the government – ie they take the money from the general body of taxpayers.

3.1.2 Advance funding

This is the basis under which most other schemes work. Contributions are paid by the employer, and, usually, the employee, into an investment fund. The benefits are then paid out of this fund as and when they fall due. The fund is usually a trust fund, separate from the employer's business, so the payment of pensions does not depend on the future profitability or solvency of the employer.

If an employer deducts employee contributions from wages, it must pay those contributions over to the pension scheme by the 19th day of the month after that in which the deduction was made. Failure to do this is a civil wrong under the Pensions Act 1995 for which The Pensions Regulator can impose a fine. Life offices which become aware of late payments should inform The Pensions Regulator, although it does not wish to be told of isolated late payments or short periods of lateness for small contributions.

3.1.3 Benefit bases

There are, broadly speaking, two ways of calculating pensions:

- Define the benefits that will be payable and pay sufficient contributions into the fund to provide those benefits.
- Define the level of contributions to the fund. The resulting benefits will then depend on the accumulated amount available when the benefit falls due.

3.1.4 Defined benefit schemes

Many members of occupational pension schemes are in schemes that provide a pension that is a fraction of pay at, or shortly before, retirement. The benefit to the employee is that planning for retirement is made easier because the pension is directly related to the standard of living before retirement. They are often called final salary schemes.

The employer, however, is unable to forecast accurately the cost of the scheme as the ultimate pension is dependent on final earnings. Thus, a period of high wage inflation shortly before an employee's retirement could dramatically increase the contributions needed for that employee's pension.

The way in which a defined benefit scheme is costed will largely depend on the number of scheme members. In a small scheme, each member's benefits are likely to be costed individually. Each employee would effectively have his own pension fund. In practice such small schemes are now very rare.

In larger schemes, say over 20 members, the cost is likely to be calculated as a percentage of the total pensionable payroll. The scheme actuaries will make assumptions about the age and sex distribution of the scheme, future wage inflation and investment returns, staff turnover, deaths, early retirements, etc, and produce an overall cost for the scheme. As circumstances change, and assumptions are borne out (or not), this overall cost will be revised, often annually. In this sort of scheme, money is not usually allocated to individual members until a benefit falls due.

3.1.5 Defined contribution schemes

A defined contribution (or money purchase) scheme is much simpler. Contributions are invested for each individual member and his accumulated fund is used to purchase his benefits when due. The pension depends largely on the investment performance of the fund, and annuity rates at the date of retirement.

The employer has the advantage of always knowing how much the pension scheme will cost. The employee, however, does not know how his pension will relate to his standard of living before retirement as his pension will depend on the funds available. A period of high inflation or low interest rates shortly before retirement could drastically reduce the real value of the pension.

There is a trend to moving from defined benefit to defined contribution. According to the National Association of Pension Funds, 10% of private sector defined benefit schemes closed to new entrants in 2001, 19% closed in 2002, 26% closed in 2003 and 10% in 2004.

3.1.6 Hybrid schemes

There are also some hybrid schemes which are partly final salary and partly money purchase. These are designed to give the employee some idea of the eventual pension and enable the employer to keep some control over future costs.

3.2 Scheme structure

Most occupational pension schemes are established under irrevocable trusts. This ensures that, apart from in exceptional circumstances, the assets of the fund are held by a trustee or trustees and are not available to the employer or its creditors.

It is not necessary to set up a formal trust deed in order to establish a trust – a resolution of the board of directors may be sufficient. However, in all but the simplest of schemes there will need to be some kind of formal documentation.

For most schemes there is a trust deed which establishes the scheme, describes how trustees are appointed or discharged, defines the acceptable range of investments for the assets of the scheme, and sets out the circumstances in which the scheme can be altered or discontinued.

In addition to, or as part of, the trust deed, there are the rules of the scheme. This document defines the contribution and benefit structure of the scheme. It lays down the categories of employees who are eligible to join the scheme, the circumstances in which a benefit becomes payable, the level of benefits and who is entitled to those benefits.

Both of these documents are written in a form that puts the scheme on a sound legal footing and can be used to resolve disputes. So, most schemes will supplement the rules with a simplified booklet which describes the principal features of the scheme, in language which the members will find easy to follow.

The trustees' job is to protect the interests of the members of the scheme, and to ensure that the assets of the scheme are only used for their benefit, in accordance with the scheme rules.

There normally has to be a schedule of contributions (for a defined benefit scheme) or a payment schedule (for a defined contribution scheme). The trustees must inform The Pensions Regulator if the employer does not make payment within 30 days (other than for minor breaches) and also tell members if payments are still outstanding after 60 days.

3.3 Member-nominated trustees

Under provision in the Pensions Act 2004 at least a third of an occupational pension scheme's trustees must be member nominated. However, when a scheme has an employer opt-out under the Pensions Act 1995 rules, the opt-out will be allowed to continue until its approval expires, subject to a final cut-off date, probably 31 October 2007. The Pensions Act 2004 also gave the Department for Work and Pensions (DWP) powers to increase the proportion of member-nominated trustees to 50%, but no decision has yet been made on when or how the change will be implemented.

The removal of a member-nominated trustee requires the agreement of all the other trustees. This requirement does not apply if every member of the scheme is a trustee and no other person is a trustee. Where every trustee of a scheme is a company at least a third of the directors of the company must be member nominated trustees.

3.4 Independent trustees

If an employer becomes bankrupt or goes into liquidation, the insolvency practitioner or Official Receiver must ensure that at least one trustee is an independent person and, if not, appoint one. The independent trustee must not be connected with the employer, or the insolvency practitioner or Official Receiver in any way. The idea is that the independent trustee will protect the interests of members during the insolvency proceedings. During the insolvency any discretionary powers of the trustees or the employer can only be exercised by the independent trustee.

3.5 Trustees

No trustee of a scheme can be its auditor or actuary. Trustees are disqualified if they are convicted of an offence involving dishonesty or deception, are judged bankrupt, are involved in any voluntary arrangement with creditors or have been disqualified as a company director. Where a trustee is a company the company will be disqualified if any director would have been disqualified under the above provisions. The Pensions Regulator can also disqualify a trustee if he is incapable by reason of mental disorder or a trustee company if it has gone into liquidation. Acting as a trustee while disqualified is an offence.

A trustee's liability for breach of duty of care when investing the scheme's money cannot be excluded or limited. However the trustees are not responsible for the acts or defaults of a fund manager to whom they have delegated investment powers if they took reasonable steps to satisfy themselves that the fund manager had appropriate knowledge and experience and was carrying out the work competently. The trustees must ensure that there is a written statement of investment principles arrived at after consultations with the employer. This must include details of ethical investment and voting policies. The trustees and the fund manager must have regard for the need for diversification and suitability of investments for the scheme and the trustees must take proper advice on this. Any powers to pay surplus money to the employer can only be exercised by the trustees if they are satisfied that it is in the interests of members, the members are given notice, pensions have been improved to LPI standard, and The Pensions Regulator is satisfied with this.

Trustee decisions can be by majority, although a unanimous vote is needed to remove a member-nominated trustee.

Under the Pensions Act 2004 the trustees of a pension scheme must arrange for a statement of investment principles to be prepared and maintained. It must be reviewed regularly (at least every three years) and revised if necessary.

The Act also states that every trustee must be conversant with the trust deed and rules, the statement of investment principles, any statement of funding principles and the law relating to pensions and trusts.

3.6 Whistle blowing

Each occupational pension scheme must have an auditor, an actuary (if final salary) and a fund manager (unless fully insured). If an auditor, actuary or anyone involved in scheme administration, other adviser or trustee has reason to believe that any duty on any person connected with the scheme is not being complied with in a materially significant way, he must 'blow the whistle' to the Pensions Regulator. Any other professional adviser can also do this. Such disclosures are not a breach of any duty of confidentiality. The professional advisers must be appointed by the trustees and work for them (not the employer).

3.7 Records

Trustees must keep the scheme's money in a separate bank account. Regulations under the Pensions Act 1995 specify what other records must be kept.

3.8 Disputes

Trustees must have appropriate internal arrangements for resolution of disputes, and members must be informed of the Pensions Advisory Service (PAS) and the Pensions Ombudsman. Disputes can be referred to the Pensions Ombudsman – see Chapter R.

3.9 Compensation

The Pensions Act 2004 established the Pension Protection Fund (PPF) with effect from 6 April 2005. The fund applies to private sector defined benefit occupational pensions schemes only, and is funded by a levy on those schemes. It will compensate scheme members if the employer becomes insolvent and the scheme is under-funded. When the PPF assumes responsibility for a scheme the assets and liabilities of the scheme are transferred to the PPF. The PPF itself is not a pension scheme but benefits from the same tax treatment as authorised pension schemes.

Protection for pensions in payment is at 90% for members under normal pension age at the time the PPF steps in, and 100% in other cases. For members who have not yet reached normal pension age protection is at 90% of the pension accrued so far. Protection also extends to deferred members, transfer payments, and survivors and dependants' benefits. There is a compensation cap of £26,050 per annum, based on a normal pension age of 65, which applies only to those under normal pension age.

The fund can also pay compensation where the value of any occupational pension scheme's assets has been reduced by fraud and the employer is insolvent (or is unlikely to continue as a going concern). Such a payment would be made to the trustees of the scheme and is limited to the loss less any amounts recovered. This part of the PPF is called the Fraud Compensation Fund and effectively took over from the previous Pensions Compensation Board.

There is a PPF ombudsman for disputes about how the PPF carries out its function.

To reduce the number of cases where an employer might try to push a scheme into the PPF to reduce their own liabilities, the Pensions Regulator can issue a Contribution Notice to anyone involved in an act or failure to act after 26 April 2004, which had as one of its main purposes the avoidance of pension liabilities. The Notice would aim to recover, where reasonable, an amount up to the full statutory debt. The Pensions Regulator can also issue a Restoration Order requiring any money or property that has been transferred out of the scheme at under value in the two years before insolvency to be returned to the scheme.

The PPF is funded by a levy on all schemes covered, 80% of which is risk based.

3.10 Winding up

The provisions in the Pensions Act 2004 override the terms of an occupational scheme's winding up clauses to give priority to 'preferential liabilities'. These were changed from 6 April 2005 under the Pensions Act 2005. The priority order is now, after meeting scheme expenses and debts to third parties:

(a) Benefits covered by insurance contracts taken out before 6 April 1997 which cannot be surrendered.

(b) All other benefits not exceeding the corresponding Pension Protection Fund liabilities (ie the cost of securing benefits if the Pension Protection Fund assumed responsibility for them).

(c) Benefits from additional voluntary contributions (AVCs).

(d) All other benefits under the scheme.

Any money purchase benefits in the scheme, and the assets linked to them, are treated entirely separately. Thus AVCs paid on a money purchase basis have effective priority as they are treated separately. However, AVCs which buy 'added years' fall within (c) above.

4 Personal Pensions

Personal pensions are individual contracts with a pension provider. The pension provider is usually a life office but could be a friendly society, bank, building society or authorised unit trust manager. They are effectively investment contracts where the pot of money at retirement is applied to provide some form of pension. This contract could be a with-profit or unit-linked policy, a deposit account or a unit trust.

4.1 Group personal pensions

A number of life offices have group personal pensions – or GPPs. Legally speaking there is no such thing, because a personal pension is a contract between an individual and a pension provider. They are actually a collection of individual contracts where an employer agrees to deduct contributions from wages and/or pay contributions itself and pass them on to the pension provider. The employer may also provide facilities for a life office or intermediary to promote the arrangement. Because of the cost savings of selling large numbers of contracts in one go, charges can be lower than on standard 'one-off' personal pensions (or benefits improved).

Because each pension is an individual contract, a 100 member scheme will consist of 100 contracts. This means that there are 100 clients and if advice is being given, a separate fact find would be required for each employee. An employer cannot instruct its employees to use a particular provider's GPP, but from 1 July 2005 there has been an Financial Services and Markets Act 2000 (FSMA) exemption which enables employers to promote the uptake of their personal (or stakeholder) pensions scheme to their employees without needing to be authorised by the Financial Services Authority (FSA), and without needing to be approved by someone authorised by the FSA. This applies provided:

- The employer confirms it will make a contribution to the plan.
- The employer has not and will not receive any financial benefit from the plan.
- The employee is told before becoming a member how much the employer will contribute.
- The employee is told of his or her right to seek advice from an authorised person.

4.2 Stakeholder pensions

Stakeholder pensions were introduced on 6 April 2001 by the Welfare Reform & Pensions Act 1999. They are a type of personal pension, in that they are individual pension contracts with the same rules for eligibility, transfers, benefits, contributions and taxation. However, a stakeholder pension provider must be authorised under the FSMA, register with Her Majesty's Revenue and Customs (HMRC) and register the scheme with Pensions Regulator. Stakeholder pensions can be used for contracting out of the state second pension (S2P). The tax treatment of stakeholder pensions is identical to that of other pensions.

Life cover can be provided within a stakeholder plan on the same basis as for other pensions. Protection for contributions in the event of illness must be provided outside the plan as for other pensions. The pension can be taken from age 50 (55 from 6 April 2010) to 75.

Stakeholder pensions are subject to a number of DWP regulations that do not apply to other pensions. The most important are as follows.

- The maximum plan charge is 1.5% of the fund value per year for the first ten years and 1% thereafter for contracts effected on or after 6 April 2005. A 1% maximum charge continues to apply to pre-6 April 2005 plans and future contributions to such plans. All charges must be levied as a percentage of fund. An adviser can charge a fee for advice, but this must be payable under a separate contract between the adviser and the client.

- The minimum stakeholder contribution cannot be higher than £20, single or regular. The figure is net for individual contributions and gross for employer contributions.

- A new stakeholder plan must incorporate a 'lifestyling' default investment option. Plans started before 6 April 2005 had only to offer a default fund.

- A stakeholder pension must be able to accept a transfer payment from another pension scheme (including pension sharing credits).

- Since 8 October 2001, all employers with more than four employees have been required to nominate a stakeholder pension arrangement to which their employees can contribute. The following groups of employees are exempt from this requirement:

    - Employees who would normally qualify to become members of an occupational pension scheme not more than 12 months after starting work, or on attaining age 18.

    - Employees who qualify for membership of a group personal pension with no exit charges to which the employer contributes at least 3% of basic pay.

    - Employees who earn less than the lower earnings limit, currently £84 per week in any week in the last three months.

    - Employees who are within five years of the normal pension age under an occupational pension scheme but could otherwise join.

- Employees who have worked for the employer for less than three months.
- Employees who have been offered membership of an occupational pension scheme and have declined to join or who have left the scheme and are now unable to rejoin.

Many stakeholder schemes have been set up for employers, trade associations and affinity groups. Employers are not required to contribute to their nominated stakeholder scheme (and only 5% of employers do so according to the Pensions Commission Report), but must be able to deduct employee contributions from wages and pay them to the scheme. Many nominated schemes – 82% in 2003 according to the Association of British Insurers (ABI) – have no members and no money in them.

The Pensions Regulator can fine employers who do not comply and in early 2004 its predecessor the Occupational Pensions Regulatory Authority (OPRA) levied its first fine of £10,000. Most schemes are run by insurance companies, but some are operated by other groups, eg the TUC.

If, after 8 October 2001, an employer employs more than four employees for the first time, it has three months in which to designate a stakeholder scheme.

5 The New Tax Regime

The main features of the new tax regime for pensions are as follows. Fuller details are given later in this chapter, and the next.

5.1 Lifetime allowance

Everyone has a maximum tax-exempt fund called a lifetime allowance. This is currently £1,500,000 for 2006/07. Any excess over this allowance is taxed at 55% if drawn as a lump sum, or 25% if used to provide taxable income benefits.

5.2 Annual allowance

There is an annual contribution allowance of £215,000 for 2006/07, with a further ceiling of the greater of 100% of earnings or £3,600. Any contribution in excess of this limit is subject to tax at 40% for the individual. The limit does not apply to a pension arrangement in the tax year when the individual has become entitled to all the benefits from that arrangement.

5.3 Tax-free cash sum

The maximum tax-free cash sum from any pension arrangement is 25% of the value of the pension rights.

5.4 Retirement age

The minimum age for drawing benefits is 50, rising to 55 on 6 April 2010. There is no maximum or normal retirement age.

5.5 Death benefits

The maximum lump sum death benefit is the same as the lifetime allowance – currently £1,500,000. Any excess is subject to income tax at 55% on the recipient(s).

5.6 Income in retirement

Income in retirement can be provided in four ways:

- Lifetime annuities.
- Scheme pensions.
- Unsecured pensions.
- Alternatively secured pensions.

6 Registration

The system of HMRC approval of pensions was abolished on 6 April 2006. It has been replaced by registration. A pension arrangement must now be registered with HMRC if it is to benefit from the tax privileges of the new regime. There is just one on-line registration form for all types of pension. HMRC must register the scheme unless it believes the information on the form is incorrect.

To be registered a scheme must be either an occupational pension scheme established by one or more employers, or be set up by one of the following:

- The government.
- An insurance company.
- A unit trust scheme manager.
- An operator, trustee or depositary of a recognised EEA collective investment scheme.
- An authorised open-ended investment company.
- A building society.
- A bank.

- An EEA investment portfolio manager.

6.1 Existing arrangements

All approved pension arrangements in force on 5 April 2006 became registered arrangements on 6 April 2006, unless they decided to opt out. However, opting out is very uncommon as it triggers a 40% tax charge on the assets held on 5 April 2006, payable by the scheme administrator.

6.2 Deregistration

HMRC can deregister an arrangement in the following cases:

- If the total chargeable unauthorised payments in any year are 25% or more of the value of the fund.
- If the scheme administrator fails to pay a substantial amount of any tax or interest due.
- If the scheme administrator significantly fails to provide information requested by HMRC.
- If any information provided to HMRC is materially incorrect.
- If any declaration in a registration application (or otherwise) to HMRC is false.
- If the scheme does not have an administrator.

HMRC has to serve notice of deregistration on the scheme administrator stating the effective date.

7 Eligibility

In order to get tax relief on personal contributions to a registered scheme you have to be 'a relevant UK individual'. You are a 'a relevant UK individual' for a tax year if you are under 75 and:

- Have relevant UK earnings chargeable to income tax for that tax year. Relevant UK earnings are employment income, income from a trade, profession or vocation, and patent income; or
- You are resident in the UK at some time in that tax year; or
- You were resident in the UK both
    - at some time in the five tax years immediately before that year, and
    - when you became a member of the scheme.

In this case relief is restricted to a maximum contribution of £3,600 per tax year and only by deduction at source; or

- You, or your spouse (or civil partner) have earnings for the tax year from an overseas Crown employment subject to UK tax.

If you do not satisfy these rules you can make unlimited personal contributions to a registered scheme, but you do not get any UK tax relief.

8 The Lifetime Allowance

The lifetime allowance is the upper limit of the fund value for tax exemption. It includes the value of all benefits, including dependants' benefits. The lifetime allowance is as follows:

Tax year	Lifetime allowance £
2006/07	1,500,000
2007/08	1,600,000
2008/09	1,650,000
2009/10	1,750,000
2010/11	1,800,000

Allowances for 2011/12 and thereafter will be set by the Treasury. For a defined benefit scheme the notional fund value is based on a 20:1 valuation factor, ie a pension of £75,000 pa equates to the limit of £1,500,000.

9 The Annual Allowance

The annual allowance is the limit on personal tax-relieved contributions from all sources that can be made to all the pensions arrangements of an individual in a tax year. In general this limit is much more generous than under the pre-A Day regimes.

The annual allowances are as follows:

Tax year	Annual allowance £
2006/07	215,000
2007/08	225,000
2008/09	235,000
2009/10	245,000
2010/11	255,000

Allowances for 2011/12 and thereafter will be set by the Treasury.

There is also a further limit of the greater of 100% of earnings or £3,600. The operation of the rules is shown in the following examples.

Earnings £	Allowance £
0	3,600
3,600	3,600
50,000	50,000
100,000	100,000
300,000	215,000

9.1 The total pension input amount

Like a lot of pensions simplification, the annual allowance is much more complicated than it first seems. It consists of the 'total pension input amount'. This comprises the total of:

- For defined contribution arrangements, all contributions made by or on behalf of an individual, excluding contracting out minimum payments. A reallocation of funds between members within a scheme counts as a contribution, but any investment growth (or loss) is ignored.

- For active members of defined benefit schemes, all increases in the capital value of the member's pension and tax-free cash benefits (except death benefits).

- For deferred members of defined benefit schemes, the capital value of increases to their pension and tax-free cash sum benefits that exceed the greater of 5% and the increase in the Retail Prices Index (RPI). Death benefits are excluded.

9.2 Exclusions

The following are excluded from the total pension input amount:

- Contributions and defined benefit growth in any year when the member wholly crystallises benefits in that scheme.

- Contributions and defined benefit growth in the year in which the member dies.

- Personal contributions which are in excess of 100% of earnings and so do not receive income tax relief.

- Contracted out rebates paid by HMRC.

9.3 Defined benefit schemes

For defined benefit schemes the notional contribution for annual allowance purposes is the increase in value of the employee's pension and any separate lump sum benefits. The accruing pension benefits are valued on a 10:1 basis, ie if pension benefits (before commutation) increase by £10,000 pa the notional contribution is £100,000.

9.4 The Annual Allowance Charge

If total contributions exceed the annual allowance, the individual is subject to an annual allowance charge on the excess at 40% (whatever the individual's marginal income tax rate). The object of this is to claw back the income tax and National Insurance contribution (NIC) relief. However, employer contributions in excess of the limit still attract tax relief as an allowable business expense, and tax relief is still available to the individual on contributions above the limit, provided they do not exceed 100% of earnings for that year.

9.5 Collection of the charge

The annual allowance charge is taxed on the individual under the normal self-assessment procedure for income tax. However, the excess on which it is charged does not count as income for tax purposes, so no allowances, reliefs or losses can be set against it. There is an element of double taxation here because when the pension provided by the excess contributions emerges from the scheme it will be taxed again in the normal way.

10 Tax Treatment of Contributions

The tax treatment of contributions is largely the same as pre-A Day. In general all pension arrangements will operate tax relief by deduction at source as was done before A Day for personal pensions, often called Pension Tax Relief at Source (PTRAS).

The deduction has to be made at the basic rate in force at the date of payment. The pension provider will then reclaim the relief deducted from HMRC each month. So if a gross contribution is £1,000 the individual pays £780 to the pension provider, which will reclaim £220 from HMRC. Higher rate taxpayers can get higher rate tax relief by adjustment of their PAYE code or on their tax assessment. The pension provider can issue a certificate of payment for this purpose, although HMRC does not normally require to see this. A non-taxpayer or a starting rate taxpayer does not have any tax relief clawed back.

Higher rate relief is actually given by extending the basic rate band by the amount of the gross pension contribution. Total income for age allowance is reduced by the gross amount of any contribution subject to relief at source. It can thus be used to avoid the age allowance trap (see Chapter M) by reducing income below the age allowance limit. In this way (provided the individual is under 75) relief can be obtained at the basic rate on the pension contribution, plus further effective relief by preserving the age allowance. The extension of the basic rate band also applies to deciding whether it has been exceeded for capital gains tax (CGT) purposes.

A Day marked the end of carry back and carry forward for personal pensions and retirement annuities. However, there is transitional relief to allow an election until 31 January 2007 to carry back retirement annuity contributions made in 2005/06 to 2004/05, or 2003/04 if there were no net relevant earnings in 2004/05.

10.1 Occupational pension schemes

An occupational scheme can operate a 'net pay' system whereby personal contributions are deducted from gross pay for income tax (but not NIC) purposes. This system must apply to all contributing members. The system can even be operated for a GPP if it is established under a separate employer trust for the benefit of employees.

10.2 Retirement annuities

Contributions to old pre-1988 retirement annuities can continue to be paid gross, with tax relief being given via the PAYE code or tax assessment.

10.3 Public service pensions

Members of public service pension schemes who are not employees (eg many doctors and dentists) can pay gross and claim tax relief through their self-assessment returns.

10.4 Limits

Any eligible scheme member can contribute up to £3,600 gross (£2,808 net) regardless of earnings if relief is deducted at source. Where this does not apply and earnings are less than £3,600, the contributions are limited to 100% of relevant UK earnings.

10.5 Share contributions

Employees can make contributions by transferring shares emerging from approved save as you earn (SAYE) option and share incentive plans. The transfer must be made within 90 days of the request to exercise the option, or release of shares to the employee. The transfer of shares is a disposal for CGT purposes.

10.6 Refunds for early leavers

Members leaving service with less than two years service are entitled to a refund of their personal contributions. The first £2,800 of any refund is taxed at 20% and any excess at 40%. The tax liability falls on the scheme administrator who will deduct it from the refund.

10.7 Commission

Where commission is payable to a personal pension policyholder, the rules for tax relief are as follows:

- Where a policyholder pays the full premium and receives commission separately, tax relief is given on the full premium without taking the commission into account.
- Where an amount of commission due is reinvested into the personal pension, tax relief is given on that amount.

- Where a policyholder deducts commission in respect of his own pension contribution from the gross amount payable, relief is only due on the net amount paid.
- Where a policyholder pays discounted premiums, tax relief is only due on the discounted amount paid.
- Where extra value is added to the pension by the provider (eg bonus units), relief is due on the amount paid by the policyholder without taking the extra value into account.

10.8 Employer contributions

Tax relief for employer contributions to any registered scheme is available with no limit, provided they meet the normal rules for allowable business expenses. Thus they must be wholly and exclusively for the purposes of the trade. So the situation is not as clear-cut as pre-A Day where contributions to approved schemes were automatically allowable.

Relief is given for the accounting period in which the contribution is paid, except where a loss is created (when it can be carried back) or where the spreading rules apply. The spreading rules are as follows.

10.8.1 Spreading

A contribution must be spread if it exceeds 210% of the contributions paid in the previous accounting period, and the amount paid in excess of 110% of the previous contribution is £500,000 or more. The contribution does not have to be spread to the extent that the increased cost is attributable to the funding of cost of living rises for pensioner members or future service liabilities for new scheme entrants.

Where spreading applies, the excess is spread as follows:

Excess **£**	**Spread**
500,000–999,999	2 accounting periods
1,000,000–1,999,999	3 accounting periods
2,000,000+	4 accounting periods

The rules apply to accounting periods ending on or after 6 April 2006 even if the actual contribution was made before then.

Example

S McLean Ltd normally makes an annual contribution of £500,000 but this year decides to contribute £2 million because it has had a very good year. The calculation is as follows:

Previous contribution £500,000 x 210% = £1,050,000

Thus spreading will apply if the excess is £500,000 or more.

The excess over 110% of the previous contribution is £2,000,000 – (£500,000 x 110%) = £1,450,000.

So the excess of £1,450,000 will be spread over three periods at £483,333 per period. In the first period relief will be given on £500,000 + £483,333 = £983,333.

10.9 Salary sacrifice

Salary sacrifice involves an employee voluntarily giving up part of his salary in return for a contribution (of an equivalent amount) to his pension plan. Although this would appear to be a personal contribution, it is nonetheless a company contribution and accordingly will be eligible for relief against corporation tax subject to normal HMRC limits.

Salary sacrifice can be beneficial for both employer and employee alike. For employees:

- It reduces the income tax bill by reducing overall taxable income (this obviously has greater significance for higher rate taxpayers).
- It provides an efficient means of avoiding tax on commission and bonuses.
- For directors who wish to top up their benefits by way of a separate arrangement but find their employer unwilling to meet any extra costs.
- It saves on NICs.

For employers:

- It involves no extra expenditure.
- It saves on NICs.
- Contributions are eligible for relief against corporation tax.

Any agreement to sacrifice an element of salary must be effected by means of a simple exchange of letters between the employer and employee. It is essential that the exchange of letters takes place before the reduction in salary and omits any reference to pension contributions. It should be borne in mind that the lower level of salary is what would be taken into account to calculate S2P benefits.

11 Tax Treatment of Pension Funds

The tax treatment of registered pension funds is effectively the same as for approved pensions before A Day.

- Investment income is tax-free.
- No CGT on investment gains.
- Tax credits on UK dividends cannot be reclaimed.
- Trading income is taxable.

If a pension fund invests in prohibited assets (section 14.1) this is treated as an unauthorised member payment triggering a tax charge (see section 12).

12 Tax Charges on Pension Schemes

There are four sets of tax charges on pension schemes which are designed to prevent abuse of the tax privileges of registered schemes. These are as follows:

- Unauthorised payments charge.
- Unauthorised payments surcharge.
- Scheme sanction charge.
- De-registration charge.

12.1 Unauthorised payments charge

This applies to any payment that is not authorised. Authorised payments are as follows:

- Pensions or pension death benefits permitted by the Finance Act 2004.
- Lump sums and lump sum death benefits permitted by the Finance Act 2004.
- Transfers permitted by the Finance Act 2004.
- Certain scheme administration payments.
- Payments pursuant to a pension sharing order.
- Any payments prescribed in HMRC regulations.
- Authorised surplus payments.

- Compensation payments made in respect of a member's liability to the employer because of a criminal, fraudulent or negligent act.

- Authorised loans to an employer.

If an unauthorised payment is made there is an income tax charge at 40% of the payment. The charge is on the recipient, but the unauthorised payment is not income for tax purposes and so cannot be offset by reliefs, allowances or losses.

12.2 Unauthorised payments surcharge

This is an additional charge on the recipient of an unauthorised payment when the value of total unauthorised payments in a year is 25% or more of the fund value. The surcharge is an extra 15% income tax, bringing the total charge to 55%.

12.3 Scheme sanction charge

This is an income tax charge on the scheme administrator if the scheme has made an unauthorised payment or indulged in unauthorised borrowing. The charge is at 40%, but it can be offset by the amount of any unauthorised payment charge paid by the member or employer. This offset is limited to the lesser of:

- 25% of the total unauthorised payments made by the scheme on which tax was paid under the unauthorised payments charge in that tax year; and

- The actual unauthorised payments charge paid by the recipient, but not any surcharge.

Example

The ABC scheme makes total unauthorised payments of £20,000 so the scheme sanction charge is £8,000. If the recipients of the £20,000 unauthorised payments have paid their £8,000 tax bill then the offset is £5,000 (ie 25% of £20,000), resulting in £3,000 to pay. The total tax charge on recipients and scheme is therefore £11,000 – an effective rate of 55%.

12.4 Deregistration charge

When a scheme is reregistered by HMRC (see section 6.2) there is a charge at 40% of the total value of the scheme's funds at deregistration. This is to combat 'trust busting' and investing in prohibited assets.

13 Reporting to HMRC

13.1 Reporting by the member

The member must report any tax charge falling on them on the normal tax return. This would include:

- Unauthorised payments.
- Annual allowance charge.
- Lifetime allowance charge.
- Benefits in kind from scheme assets.

Reports also have to be made for:

- Crystallising benefits.
- Trivial commutation.
- Transitional protection.

13.2 Reporting by the scheme

The scheme administrator is responsible for the tax affairs of a registered scheme. There is a list of reportable events which trigger an event report to HMRC by 31 January following the end of the tax year in which the event occurred. Reportable events include:

- Unauthorised payments.
- A payment on a member's death that exceeds 50% of the lifetime allowance.
- A benefit paid before normal minimum pension age to a member who is (or was) a director of, or participator in, the employer.
- A serious ill-health payment to a member who is (or was) a director of, or participator in, the employer.
- Benefits crystallising in excess of the standard lifetime allowance.
- Winding up.
- The provision of an alternatively secured pension for the first time in the year.
- Change of scheme administrator.

13.3 Other reports

There are also detailed regulations requiring the scheme administrator to supply prescribed information to scheme members including:

- Unauthorised payments.
- Tax deductions.
- Pensions in payment.
- Benefits on impending retirement.
- When the lifetime allowance is exceeded.

14 Pension Scheme Investments

In general there are many fewer restrictions on investments than before A Day. However, a number of provisions do apply.

14.1 Prohibited assets

Prohibited assets include the following:

- Residential property.
- Personal chattels.
- Works of art.
- Antiques.
- Fine wine.

While these assets are not actually banned, they are highly tax inefficient because:

- They are treated as unauthorised member payments, resulting in a tax charge at 40%, or 55% (see sections 12.1 and 12.2).
- There is no income tax or CGT relief for prohibited assets within the scheme.

14.2 Investments in the employer

An occupational scheme cannot invest 5% or more of its assets in any one sponsoring employer. If there is more than one sponsoring employer the scheme cannot invest 20% or more in the employers.

14.3 Loans

Loans to members are allowed. Loans to sponsoring employers by occupational schemes must:

- Not exceed 50% of the value of the scheme's assets at the date of the loan.
- Be secured with a first charge on assets with an initial value at least equal to the loan.
- Bear interest of at least 1% over the average base rate of the main clearing banks.
- Last for less than five years.
- Be repaid by equal annual instalments.

If any of these conditions is broken this is an unauthorised payment. Pre-A Day loans that fail these tests may continue. These rules do not apply to loans in the form of bonds issued on the open market or listed on a recognised stock exchange.

14.3.1 Borrowing by a scheme

The maximum loan to a pension scheme for any purpose is 50% of net scheme assets before the loan. Pre-A Day borrowing which fails this test can continue.

14.4 Scheme assets used by members

If any scheme asset is used by a member, this is likely to be a prohibited asset taxable as set out in section 14.1. If it is not a prohibited asset, use of the asset by a member (or their family) is treated as an unauthorised payment (see section 12.1) anyway, with the value being calculated using the normal benefit in kind tax rules.

However, it does not undertake formal arbitration and will refer complaints to the Pensions Ombudsman (see Chapter R) for this.

The Pension Advisory Service (PAS) is now funded by a grant from the Pensions Regulator, which itself draws funds from a levy on pension schemes (see section 20.1).

15 Transitional Protection

There is a whole raft of transitional rules which apply to protect rights acquired before A Day. These are extremely complex and have led many to regard pensions simplification as an oxymoron. The following is an explanation of the most important points. There are two main types of transitional protection:

- Primary protection.
- Enhanced protection.

Scheme members must register for these by 5 April 2009. They are options and are thus not compulsory.

15.1 Primary protection

This is a way of protecting pension rights in excess of the standard lifetime allowance of £1.5m on 5 April 2006. For defined contribution schemes the value is simply the fund value. For defined benefit schemes the 20:1 factor is used to value benefits, so a pension of £75,000 pa would equate to the allowance. Where an individual has crystallised benefits by 5 April 2006 these benefits are valued at 25 times the pension payable on that date, so a pension of more than £60,000 would be eligible for protection.

15.1.1 The primary protection factor

Once benefits have been valued as explained in section 15.1, the primary protection factor can be calculated. This is:

$$\frac{\text{Total value of benefits at 5/4/06} - £1{,}500{,}000}{£1{,}500{,}000}$$

Thereafter, whenever a lifetime allowance test is required because of a benefit crystallisation event this factor is used to calculate the increased lifetime allowance.

15.1.2 Example

Joanna has defined benefit accrued pension rights of £70,000 pa, and a personal pension with a fund value of £500,000, as at 5 April 2006. The total value is:

£70,000 x 20	=	£1,400,000
+ £500,000	=	£1,900,000

Her primary protection factor is therefore:

$$\frac{1{,}900{,}000 - 1{,}500{,}000}{1{,}500{,}000}$$

$$= \frac{400{,}000}{£1{,}500{,}000}$$

$$= 0.2667$$

Thus if she draws her pensions in 2010/11 when the standard lifetime allowance (see Chapter P) is £1.8m, her increased lifetime allowance will be £1,800,000 x 1.2667 = £2,280,060.

15.2 Enhanced protection

This provides full protection for the whole of an individual's pension rights accrued on 5 April 2006 regardless of any fund growth after then. It is available even if pension rights do not exceed £1,500,000. Enhanced protection can be elected as well as primary protection. Enhanced protection takes preference so primary protection will only be effective if enhanced protection is lost or revoked.

Enhanced protection means that any future lifetime allowance charge is avoided, regardless of the level of fund growth.

15.2.1 Conditions for enhanced protection

Four conditions have to be met from 6 April 2006 to elect enhanced protection.

1. There must be no subsequent transfers out of benefits unless it is of all benefits to a money purchase arrangement where the benefits of the old and new schemes have equivalent actuarial values.

2. No new registered scheme can be established for the individual, other than for a transfer permitted under condition 1 above.

3. No further pension benefits can accrue under a registered scheme.

4. No impermissible transfers can be made into existing money purchase arrangements. Impermissible transfers are transfers from other individuals' pension arrangements, transfers from non-pension sources and the transfer lump sum benefit under an alternatively secured pension.

The effect of condition 3 is that no further contributions can be made on or after 6 April 2006 by or on behalf of the individual.

15.2.2 Revocation

Enhanced protection is revoked by the member if at any time before their 75th birthday they:

- Resume active membership of a registered scheme where relevant benefit accrual occurs.

- Become a new member of a registered scheme.

- Make an impermissible transfer (see condition 4).

- Arrange a transfer that is not permitted (see condition 1).

If enhanced protection is revoked, primary protection will apply instead, provided the conditions in section 15.1 were met on 5 April 2006, and election is made for primary protection by 5 April 2009. It would only be advisable to revoke enhanced protection where the value of benefits would be greater under primary protection. Revocation is irrevocable. The individual must inform Her Majesty's Revenue and Customs (HMRC) of revocation within 90 days or risk a fine.

15.3 The choice

Enhanced protection will protect money purchase schemes whatever the fund growth, so would be preferable if it was believed that fund growth would be greater than the increase in the lifetime allowance under primary protection. However, the consequence is that no further contributions can be made, so it might not be suitable for those with a large portion of their working life to go. Nevertheless if further contributions were desired, enhanced protection could always be revoked in favour of primary protection.

15.4 Tax-free cash

Where tax-free cash rights were £375,000 (ie 25% of the lifetime allowance) or less as at 5 April 2006, and neither enhanced nor primary protection apply, there is still some transitional protection. A member of an occupational pension scheme is automatically entitled to transitional protection if the value of the tax-free cash on 5 April 2006 would have exceeded 25% of the total benefit value if all benefits had come into payment simultaneously.

Where tax-free cash rights exceed £375,000 as at 5 April 2006 they could be protected through enhanced or primary protection.

16 Early Leavers

Individuals who leave an employer's service before the normal retirement age set by an occupational pension scheme have the following choices:

- Keep the pension rights in the scheme – known as preserved or deferred pensions.
- Transfer the rights to another occupational pension scheme or group personal pension scheme (GPP).
- Transfer to an individual pension, possibly a stakeholder one.
- Claim a refund of personal contributions but only if there is less than two years' pensionable service with that employer. Service for this purpose includes pensionable service transferred in from previous employment. There can be no refund of any transfers in from individual pensions. The refund is taxable as set out in section 10.6.
- Take early retirement benefits, but only where the member is over 50 (increasing to 55 from 6 April 2010).

For members with at least two years' pensionable service a preserved pension must be held until the member reaches the scheme's normal retirement age.

16.1 Transfer values

Provided an employee has been a member of an occupational pension scheme for at least three months, he or she is entitled to a transfer value. This reflects the rights produced by contributions from the employer and the employee. For a money purchase scheme the transfer value will be the cash pot. For a defined benefit scheme the transfer value must be calculated by the scheme's actuary within three months of a request, and then be guaranteed for three months.

The transfer value cannot be paid to the member but must be paid into the new pension arrangement where it will be applied to purchase pension benefits according to the rules of the new arrangement.

What is offered in exchange for a transfer payment into a new scheme can vary from scheme to scheme and according to the negotiating position of the employee:

- A fixed pension, which if the new scheme is similar to the old scheme will be similar to the preserved pension that was offered by the old scheme.

- Added years of service in the new scheme if it is a final salary scheme. Except for transfers between public sector schemes, these added years are unlikely to be as many as were served in the old scheme.

  Transfers are often a source of contention because employees do not appreciate what the transfer value is. They often wrongly believe that if they transfer their pension it will be as if their service was continuous. There are two principal reasons why this is not so:

- The transfer value is the discounted value of the cost of providing the preserved pension at normal retirement age. So, if the new scheme is to provide more than that amount, more money must be put in.

- It is unlikely that the two schemes are identical. Even if only one feature, such as the rate at which pension is increased after retirement, is different then the transfer value will not purchase identical benefits in the two schemes.

The benefits offered in exchange for a transfer value will largely depend on an actuary's assumptions about future interest rates. Even if interest rates are lower than assumed, the benefit is unlikely to be reduced. Conversely, the benefit will not reflect higher interest rates than those assumed. Transfer values do not always take discretionary increases to pensions under the transferring scheme fully into account.

Transfer values are sensitive to current long-term interest rates.

17 Pension Transfers

The basic proposition is that a member of any registered pension scheme is entitled to transfer the value of the rights under that scheme to any other registered pension scheme, whether leaving service or not. The comments about transfer values in section 16.1 apply here too.

The right to a transfer includes what used to be called the open market option on a personal pension, ie the right to transfer the benefit on retirement to the insurance company (or friendly society) of the individual's choice to provide an annuity. The

FSA rules require that personal pension holders are told at an appropriate time before taking benefit that they may buy their annuity from an insurance company other than the pension provider.

17.1 Transfer to a personal pension

Advisers sometimes consider whether to advise a client to transfer out of an occupational pension scheme into a personal or stakeholder pension. This subject has attracted much attention from the regulators. The FSA in particular has stated its view that the starting point should be that it is not best advice for an active member of an occupational scheme to transfer into a personal pension. The onus is therefore on an adviser to demonstrate in respect of any recommended transfer that it is *bona fide* in the client's interest to do so. Any adviser giving advice on pension transfers (or opt-outs) from final salary schemes should at least have passed the AFPC G60 exam or its equivalent.

Under a transfer review, the adviser will need full details of all the client's rights and benefits under the existing scheme so that they can be compared with the potential benefits of a personal pension. This will require examination of the current scheme booklet and possibly further information from the trustees of the scheme.

Factors to be taken into account include the following:

- **The guaranteed nature of the client's pension**
  Subject to the impact of escalation, benefits under final salary schemes are effectively guaranteed. The relevance of this must be considered on an individual basis for each client. Broadly speaking, the older the client, the greater the significance of guarantees. Effectively all guarantees are lost under personal pensions. How relevant is this to the client? Is the greater investment potential of an unguaranteed contract of more importance?

- **Spouse's and children's pensions**
  Preserved benefits usually include a spouse's pension payable on the death of the member before or after retirement. In addition, there may also be pension benefits for children and, possibly, other dependants, eg common law spouses.

- **Early retirement provisions, including those for ill-health.**

- **Indexation or other increases of pensions in payment** and whether they are guaranteed or discretionary.

  The majority of final salary schemes provide increases to pensions in payment (and have to do so in respect of post-April 1997 accrual benefits). These may take the form of guaranteed and/or discretionary increases, details of which should be obtained. A guarantee of full inflation proofing is common in statutory schemes, but rare in the private sector. Since 6 April 1997, any available surplus must first be used to provide for increases to pensions in payment up to the LPI level before any refund to the employer is made. Unless LPI or better already applies to pensions in payment, a scheme's surplus position must therefore be investigated.

Under the Pensions Act 2004, from April 2006 surplus may only be refunded if a scheme is fully funded (including LPI increases) on a buy out basis.

- **Employee's and employer's contributions**
  A very low or nil employer contribution may indicate that a contribution holiday is being taken, although these are now very rare.

- **Ancillary benefits – eg lump sum death benefit.**
  A number of schemes provide lump sum and/or disability pensions as part of their pension package, although these are not normally part of preserved benefits.

- **The financial security of the scheme**
  Post-Maxwell, this is not an area which can be ignored, although the Pensions Act 1995 attempted to provide additional security. The financial standing of the early leaver's scheme should be reviewed in the light of the scheme's reports and accounts, the composition of the Board of Trustees and, to a lesser extent, the financial health of the sponsoring company. The difficult stock market conditions between 2000 and 2003 have meant most final salary schemes are facing substantial deficits. This has increased the importance of checking a scheme's financial security.

- **Any 'transfer club' facilities** under schemes for employees changing jobs in the public sector.

The public sector schemes operate a 'transfer club' which allows members to transfer between public sector jobs with full credit for past pensionable service. This will normally be more favourable than an outside transfer. Moreover, a former public sector employee now in a private sector job, but possibly returning to the public sector later (eg a teacher or nurse) would lose future 'transfer club' benefits if they move their benefits elsewhere.

- **Initial charges** (including any nil allocation period) under the personal pension.

  Although initial charges are taken into account in illustrations, they must still be borne in mind, particularly when there is only a short timespan to retirement.

- Whether **the employer would contribute** to a personal or stakeholder pension.

- Whether eligibility for other benefits (such as income protection) is dependent on membership of the scheme.
- **Future career plans and earnings prospects.**

- **Age** and **attitude** towards the merits of final salary against money purchase.

- **Psychology**
  This is probably the most difficult area. Many ex-employees may want to transfer their pensions simply to remove themselves from any link with the former employers. This desire can be especially strong if redundancy has been the cause of

leaving service. In such cases, it is vital that the client is made aware that to transfer regardless of the outcome could involve considerable loss of benefits. Similar considerations arise where 'consolidation' or 'personal control' are the client's main reasons for wanting a transfer.

For these reasons many life offices do not allow their representatives to arrange transfers for active members of occupational schemes into personal or stakeholder pensions. If an employer will not contribute to a personal or stakeholder pension, it is most unlikely to be good advice to recommend such a transfer.

Similar considerations apply to transfers from schemes which the individual has left but has preserved benefits. These are often known as 'frozen' benefits, although the FSA does not like this expression, as it is increasingly rare to find any scheme where benefits are not increased in one form or another in deferment.

If a firm uses representatives of ordinary competence to arrange transfers and opt outs, it must have a system for checking such advice by expert staff or buy in that expertise from an authorised person. A transfer value analysis must be done for all transfers to show the rate of return needed under a personal or stakeholder pension to match the scheme's benefits. Most firms set maximum rates of return above which they will not allow their representatives to advise transfers. Life offices have to have a transfer value analysis system complying with the FSA rules. Independent financial advisers can either use their own system complying with the rules or obtain an analysis from a life office.

A copy of the transfer value analysis must be given to the investor with the key features, and it must be explained to the client. Fact-finds for these cases must be kept indefinitely. For execution-only cases, the firm must have a written request from the investor for this in his own words and have reasonable grounds for believing the investor has sufficient experience and understanding to do this. A similar system operates for cases where the investor wants to go ahead despite a recommendation not to. Where a transfer or opt out is recommended, a suitability letter must be sent to the investor explaining why the advice is suitable, taking explicit account of the alternative of remaining in the scheme and setting out the pros and cons.

Firms must also notify the FSA quarterly of the numbers of transfers and opt outs made and also give further details if the number of execution-only cases, or the number of clients going ahead despite advice not to.

18 Contracting Out

It is possible to contract out of the S2P through an occupational pension scheme or a personal (or stakeholder) pension. However the rules are extremely complex and are becoming increasingly irrelevant. This is for two reasons:

- Most contracted out defined benefit schemes are closed to new members and in the not too distant future many will probably also close to future accrual.

- For money purchase schemes and personal pensions the current level of National Insurance reductions and rebates has led most experts to believe that contracting out is no longer justifiable in financial terms.

For these reasons this book does not cover the detailed regulations for contracting out.

19 Defined Benefit Scheme Funding

19.1 Solvency

The Pension Act 1995 introduced a Minimum Funding Requirement (MFR) for defined benefit schemes to try to ensure their continued solvency.

As part of the MFR, trustees must have a schedule of contributions to which the employer must adhere. If an employer fails to pay these contributions, this must be reported to the Pensions Regulator and the members.

The Pensions Act 2004 replaced the MFR with a new statutory funding objective, which is to 'have sufficient and appropriate assets to cover its technical provisions', ie liabilities. Trustees or scheme managers must have an up to date statement of funding principles and if the statutory funding objective is not satisfied, the trustees must prepare a recovery plan. A similar contribution schedule to the MFR schedule is also required, which must be certified by an actuary as being consistent with the funding objective. Failure to meet the statutory funding objective or payments due under the contribution schedule must be reported to the Pensions Regulator.

These regulations came into force on 30 December 2005 but are being phased in over three years from 23 September 2005. The new funding standard must reflect the circumstances of the employer (ie its financial strength), and the scheme actuary now has a statutory duty of care in this respect to scheme members.

19.2 Winding up

When a scheme is wound up and the employer is still solvent, the employer is required by law to 'stand behind' the benefits promised. This covers:

- The administrative cost of winding up the scheme.
- The cost of annuities for pensioner members.
- The cost of deferred annuities for non-pensioner members.

Therefore the effect is that the employer is saddled with a debt equivalent to the difference between the full buy out cost of the benefits and the value of the scheme's assets.

The FRS 17 accounting standard requires any pension deficit to be shown in the employing company's accounts.

19.3 Surplus

There are rules about occupational pension schemes where the valuation reveals a surplus. Current conditions and the pensions simplification rules have rendered these largely redundant. In the unlikely event of a surplus, benefits could be increased within the overall HMRC limits. Alternatively the surplus can be refunded to the employer less tax at 35% deducted by the trustees of the scheme. A surplus cannot be paid to the employer unless the scheme is fully funded on a buy out basis. A surplus could also be reduced by the employer taking a contribution holiday.

The Pensions Ombudsman has decided that trustees of a scheme must consider the interests of members when deciding what to do with a surplus. If there is a surplus, the court ruled in the National Grid case that the employer can use it to reduce contributions. The court also said that while the members had no right to any surplus they had a reasonable expectation that any dealings with the surplus would pay fair regard to their interests.

20 The Pensions Regulator

The Pensions Regulator took over from the previous regulator, the Occupational Pensions Regulatory Authority (OPRA), with effect from 6 April 2005. Objectives of the Pensions Regulator are as follows:

- To protect benefits under occupational pensions schemes and personal pensions for employees.
- To reduce the risk of compensation being payable by the Pension Protection Fund.
- To promote and improve the understanding of the good administration of work based pension schemes.

The Pensions Regulator must maintain a register of occupational pensions schemes and personal pensions for employees plus a register of prohibited trustees. There is a duty to report breaches of law to the Pensions Regulator on trustees, managers, administrators, employers and professional advisers in writing as soon as reasonably practical. The Pensions Regulator can require anyone to furnish information and documents and inspect premises. Refusal to assist is an offence, as is providing false or misleading information.

The Pensions Regulator can prohibit a person from being a trustee of a pension scheme if that person is in serious or persistent breach of duties. The Pensions Regulator can then appoint a replacement. The Pensions Regulator can suspend a trustee if, for example, he is involved in proceedings for an offence involving dishonesty or deception or is the subject of insolvency proceedings. It is an offence to act as a trustee following prohibition or suspension. The Pensions Regulator can appoint a trustee for a scheme, if this is necessary, to ensure the proper running of the scheme. It can fine any person up to £5,000 (for an individual), or £50,000 (for a company) for a breach of the law. It can wind up a scheme if necessary to protect members.

The Pensions Regulator can get an injunction from a court to prevent any misuse of the assets of an occupational pensions scheme, and can also go to court for an order for restitution of assets for certain breaches of the law. It can require production of any documents from anyone connected with a scheme and appoint an inspector to investigate a scheme and question anyone involved with it.

The Pensions Regulator is financed by levies on pension schemes. It aims to be a much more proactive regulator than its predecessor OPRA. It may report a life office or Independent Financial Adviser (IFA) to the FSA if they give misinformation to trustees of a pension scheme or demonstrate a lack of relevant knowledge.

The Pensions Regulator also runs the Occupational Pensions Registry. This is a register of all occupational and personal pension schemes with two or more active members and all stakeholder schemes. The trustees of each scheme have to register each scheme and pay an annual levy to fund the running costs of the Registry. The Registry records all details of the scheme which are regularly updated. The object is to enable people who leave service with pension rights to trace their scheme, which can be difficult if they left years ago and the scheme has been terminated or merged or the employer has gone out of business.

Appeals against decisions of the Pensions Regulator can be made to the Pensions Regulator Tribunal.

20.1 The Pensions Advisory Service

The Pensions Advisory Service (PAS) is an independent and voluntary organisation established for the purpose of giving help and advice to members of the public on all matters concerning pension schemes (other than state schemes) including personal pensions. The service is available to all those who think they have pension rights, including scheme members, pensioners, those with deferred pensions and dependants.

The PAS operates through a nationwide network of 250 voluntary advisers who can be contacted via Citizens' Advice Bureaux. The local advisers are backed up by a central panel of pensions experts who deal with particularly complex problems. However, it does not undertake formal arbitration and will refer complainants to the Pensions Ombudsman (see Chapter R) for this.

The PAS is now funded by a grant from the Pensions Regulator, which itself draws funds from a levy on pension schemes.

P Pensions Benefits

This chapter deals with those aspects of pensions law and tax relating to benefits. It also deals with associated issues such as sex equality, divorce and bankruptcy.

1 State Pensions

1.1 The basic pension

The basic pension is the flat rate pension of £84.25 per week as at April 2006. A married woman who is not entitled to a pension in her own right can claim a pension on her husband's contributions of £50.50 per week, making a total pension for a married couple of £134.75. These are all maximum entitlements, which depend on the relevant National Insurance Contributions (NIC) record.

There is also an age addition of 25p per week for those aged 80 or over. Where a married woman has paid sufficient NICs herself she may receive the better of the basic state pension accrued in her own right or the married person's addition.

A full pension is payable to those who have paid NICs (or had credits) for at least 90% of their working lives. Lesser contribution records result in a lower pension. NI credits are given to those unable to pay contributions due to sickness, unemployment, home responsibilities, attendance on an approved training course and those receiving certain Social Security benefits.

The pension is currently payable from the 65th birthday for males and the 60th birthday for females. However, under the Pensions Act 1995, the retirement age will be equalised at 65 from 2020. A gradual increase in the state pension age will be phased in over ten years starting in April 2010 and will ensure that females who were born on or before 5 April 1950 will still be able to collect the pension at age 60. Those born after 5 April 1950 will have an extra month added to their state pension age for each month their birthday falls after that date.

Thus a female born in April 1950 will have a pension age of 60 and one month and will retire in 2010. A female born in April 1953 will have a pension age of 63 and one month and will retire in 2016 and a female born in April 1955 or later will have a pension age of 65.

Individuals wishing to defer collecting their pension until after age 65 can now do so for as long as they wish. The Pensions Act 2004 raised the rate of increase from 7.5% to 10.4% with effect from 6 April 2005. The Act also allows those who defer their pension for at least 12 months to exchange the increase in basic state pension for a lump sum, taxable at their marginal rate of tax. The lump sum is calculated by accumulating the pension foregone at base plus 2%.

1.2 State earnings related pension scheme (SERPS)

In 1978 a second tier of state pension was introduced for employees (not the self-employed) to provide earnings related pensions. It is not an easy scheme to understand as the pension entitlement the scheme provided is calculated in several stages. While no new benefits are accruing under SERPS, many people built up benefits before SERPS was replaced in 2002.

- Not all earnings counted for SERPS. Earnings below a lower earnings limit, roughly equivalent to the level of the basic pension, did not count. Neither did earnings above an upper earnings limit, roughly eight times the lower earnings limit. Only earnings since 6 April 1978 counted. As SERPS ended on 5 April 2002 and was replaced by the State Second Pension (S2P), 2001/02 was the last year in which SERPS benefits accrued.

- Each year's earnings were revalued in line with increases in national average earnings. A year is 6 April to 5 April. No revaluation took place for the tax year in which age 64 (males) or age 59 (females) was attained.

- The annual rate of SERPS was then determined according to the tax year in which the individual retired as follows:

  - Retired/Retiring in 2005/06–2008/09

    Where an individual reaches state pension age in tax year 2009/10 or later, his/her maximum SERPS pension accrual rate 2001/02 was based on 20% of his/her revalued earnings. Where he/she reaches/reached state pension age before 2009/10, the SERPS pension is reduced on a sliding scale as follows:

Tax year	**SERPS entitlement**
	%
2005/06	22.0
2006/07	21.5
2007/08	21.0
2008/09	20.5

The transitional arrangements that apply in respect of periods in SERPS completed for tax years 1978/79 to 1987/88 are shown below.

An individual would be entitled to a pension based on:

$\frac{25\%}{N}$ of the revalued earnings for tax years 1978/79 to 1987/88 inclusive

plus

$$\frac{\text{(appropriate \% based on: tax year reaching state pension age – eg 22 if year 2005/06)}}{N}$$

of the revalued earnings for tax year 1988/89 to 2001/02 inclusive where *N* is the number of years in SERPS (and its S2P successor) to state pension age after 5 April 1978.

- Retiring in 2009/10 or later

$\frac{25\%}{N}$ of the revalued earnings for tax years 1978/79 to 1987/88 inclusive

plus

$\frac{25\%}{N}$ of the revalued earnings for tax years 1988/89 to 2001/02 inclusive.

1.2.1 SERPS inheritance

One spouse's SERPS entitlement can be inherited (at least in part) by a surviving spouse. The situation is as follows:

- Anyone over state pension age on 5 October 2002 can pass on up to 100% of their SERPS entitlement.
- Anyone with at least eight years to go until state pension age on 5 October 2002 can pass on up to 50% of their SERPS entitlement.
- For those within eight years of state pension age on 5 October 2002 there is a phased entitlement. For example, someone who reaches state pension age between 6 October 2004 and 5 October 2006 will be able to pass on up to 80% of their SERPS entitlement.

The above percentages are the maximum that the surviving spouse can inherit because when adding a person's own entitlement and inherited SERPS the total cannot be over the prescribed maximum payable to a surviving spouse.

1.3 Graduated pension

In addition to the basic pension, some people receive a graduated pension. This is a pension earned under the National Insurance scheme which ran from 1961 to 1975 but the amounts are very small often – only a few pounds a week. The maximum value in 2006/07 is £8.54 per week for a man and £7.15 per week for a woman.

1.4 The State Pension Credit

This was introduced on 6 October 2003 to replace the Minimum Income Guarantee (MIG). It is paid to pensioners and the amount depends on age, income and savings. The stated intention is to reward savers rather than penalising them as tended to happen before.

The credit can be claimed by any single pensioner with a weekly income of up to about £151 or a married couple with a weekly income of up to about £222. It consists of two parts – a guarantee credit and a savings credit. The guarantee credit is available to men and women but is based on the state pension age for women – 60 for those born before 6 April 1950, and 65 for those born after 6 April 1955, with a sliding scale between these two.

If a single claimant's weekly income is below £114.05, a guaranteed credit top-up will be paid to bring total income up to that level. For a married couple the figure is £174.05. These figures are expected to increase annually in line with earnings.

If a pensioner has savings income or a private pension, they may be eligible for a savings credit in addition to the guarantee credit. This is available from age 65. For couples only one spouse has to be 65 or over. The savings credit provides an extra 60p for every £1 per week of income above the level of the basic state pension. This can increase income by up to £17.88 for a single person and £23.58 for a married couple. This is then reduced by 40p for every £1 of income above the guaranteed income level.

Total income for this purpose is income from all sources plus assumed income from savings of £1 per week for every £500 (or part of £500) of savings above £6,000 (or £10,000 for those in residential care or a nursing home).

Example A

A single person aged 70 has a basic state pension of £84.25, a private pension of £20 pw and savings of less than £6,000.

Guarantee credit	£114.05 – (£84.25 + £20) = £9.80
Savings credit	£20 x 0.6 = £12

No reduction as income is less than £114.05

Total income is now:

State pension	£84.25
Private pension	£20.00
Guarantee credit	£9.80
Savings credit	£12.00
Total	£126.05

Example B

A married couple both over 65 have a basic state pension of £134.75 plus £35 from a private pension and savings of £10,160.

Assumed savings income	£10,160 – £6,000 ÷ 500 = £8.30
Rounded up to	£9
Total income	£134.75 + £35 + £9 = £178.75
No guarantee credit as income is greater than	£174.05
Savings credit	£178.75 – £134.75 x 0.6 = £26.40
but restricted to a maximum of	£23.58
Less £178.75 – £174.05 x 0.4	£1.88

Total income is now:

Basic state pension	£134.75
+ private pension	£35.00
+ savings credit	£23.58
– savings credit reduction	£1.88
Total	£191.45

1.5 State Second Pension

From April 2002, the S2P replaced SERPS. Any benefit already built up under SERPS will remain but since 6 April 2002 benefits have been built up under S2P. The scheme was originally planned to be introduced in two stages, but it is now unclear when – or even if – the second stage will arrive. The structure contained in the Child Support, Pensions and Social Security Act 2000 for S2P is as follows:

- In both stages, S2P will give those earning above the Lower Earnings Limit (LEL) but not more than the Lower Earning Threshold (LET) a pension of 40% of their earnings between the LET and LEL. The LET is currently £12,500 and is index-linked to earnings, so the gap between it and the LEL (normally linked to prices) will gradually widen. In effect S2P is an additional flat rate pension for the lower paid.

- In the first stage of S2P, for employees earning more than the LET, the rate of S2P accrual is:

  - 40% of their earnings between the LET and the LEL

  plus

  - 10% of their earnings between (3 x LET – 2 x LEL), known as the Secondary Threshold (ST), a year and the LET

  plus (for those earning over the ST)

  - 20% of their earnings between the upper earnings limit (UEL), set for 2006/07 at £33,540 per year, and ST.

  This gives the following accrual rates for 2006/07:

Band	**Yearly earnings in 2005/06**	**% of earnings**
Below LEL	£0–£4,368	0
LEL to LET	£4,368–£12,500	40
LET to ST	£12,500–£28,800	10
ST to UEL	£28,800–£33,540	20

Anyone earning between £4,368 and £12,500 is treated as earning £12,500. Calculations are based on average lifetime earnings by totalling the benefits that accrue from income falling within each band.

Increases in accrual rates are made for those reaching state pension age before 6 April 2009 to ensure nobody is worse off under the first stage of S2P than they would have been under SERPS.

In the second stage – if it arrives – S2P is set to become a flat rate scheme providing benefits only in relation to earnings up to the LET. Only those with a significant part of their working life ahead of them (under age 45 was suggested) would switch across to the flat rate scheme. Older employees would stay in the earnings related version of S2P.

It is possible for individuals and pension schemes to contract out of S2P, just as it was possible to contract out of SERPS. The government's aim is to encourage all those earning above the LET to contract out, while those earning less than the LET a year are likely to stay in S2P. The mechanism for contracting out is extremely complex for occupational pension schemes, as it involves a pension top-up from the state for those earning between the LET and ST in a year. The National Insurance contribution rebate approach applies to personal pensions and stakeholder pensions as it did for SERPS, but with different levels of rebate for each earnings band. Those previously contracted out of SERPS were automatically contracted out of S2P.

The long-term thrust of S2P – turning the earnings related SERPS scheme into an additional flat rate pension – was a radical change. The self-employed are not eligible for S2P at present. Although the Pensions Green Paper suggested that they should have the option to join S2P, this idea did not make its way into the Pensions Act 2004 and seems to have been dropped. S2P does apply to those who are unable to work because they are caring for somebody, or because of long-term illness or disability. These individuals will be treated as if they had earned the LET for each complete tax year they qualify.

2 The Lifetime Allowance

The lifetime allowance is the upper limit of the fund value for tax exemption. It includes the value of all benefits, including dependants' benefits. The lifetime allowance is as follows:

Tax year	Lifetime allowance £
2006/07	1,500,000
2007/08	1,600,000
2008/09	1,650,000
2009/10	1,750,000
2010/11	1,800,000

Allowances for 2011/12 and thereafter will be set by the Treasury. For a defined benefit scheme the notional fund value is based on a 20:1 valuation factor, ie a pension of £75,000 pa equates to the limit of £1.5 million.

The lifetime allowance test applies whenever a benefit crystallisation event occurs – see section 5.

2.1 Enhanced lifetime allowance

The standard lifetime allowance can be enhanced in the following cases:

- Where pension credits (on divorce) existed before A Day – see section 13.
- Where pension credits arise from rights that came into payment after A Day – again see section 13.
- Where transitional protection applies – see Chapter O section 15.

2.2 The lifetime allowance charge

When a benefit crystallisation event occurs (see section 5), the total value of an individual's pension rights in payment and being crystallised has to be calculated. This is then compared to the lifetime allowance. If the lifetime allowance is exceeded, the lifetime allowance charge applies to the excess. The object is to claw back the income tax and NIC relief given.

The excess is taxable at 55% if it is paid as a lump sum, or 25% if used to provide pension income. The total charge is effectively the same for a 40% taxpayer, as shown below.

Example

Elizabeth has an excess over the lifetime allowance of £250,000. She can take it as cash or pension.

If she takes cash the tax will be:

£250,000 x 55%	£137,500

If she takes pension the tax will be:

£250,000 X 25%	£62,500
The remaining £187,500 is used to buy pension taxable at 40%	
£187,500 x 40%	£75,000
Total tax	£137,500

The excess does not count as income for other tax purposes and so cannot be offset by any allowances, reliefs or losses.

2.3 Administration of the charge

The member and the scheme administrator are jointly and severally liable to pay the tax. The scheme administrator is primarily liable and can pay it out of scheme funds, or more probably by reducing the member's benefits. If payment comes out of scheme funds this is treated as a further excess, attracting additional tax.

If the member's benefits are reduced to pay the tax the member can choose to have this done by deduction from any lump sum payable or by reducing future pension payments. The member has to declare the excess on his/her tax return.

2.4 Example of the charge

Judith retires in 2010/11 with a pension of £60,000 from a defined benefit scheme and a personal pension fund of £1 million. She has no transitional protection so the standard lifetime allowance of £1,800,000 applies. The value of her pension benefits is:

Defined benefit pension £60,000 x 20	£1,200,000
Personal pension fund	£1,000,000
Total	£2,200,000

The excess is £2,200,000 – £1,800,000 = £400,000. She can draw the whole excess as cash with £220,000 being deducted as tax (at 55%), leaving her with £180,000. Alternatively she can use £300,000 to buy an annuity, with the balance of £100,000 having paid the tax at 25%. She could also combine the two methods, taking some of the excess as cash and some as annuity.

2.5 Is it worth overfunding?

With an effective tax rate of 55% this charge makes deliberate funding of pension over the lifetime allowance tax-inefficient. Where an employee has a choice of a bonus or a pension contribution taking them over the lifetime allowance, then in pure tax terms the bonus is preferable. This is shown by the following example using a bonus of £10,000.

A	**Take it as a pension contribution**	**£**
	Cost to employer	10,000
	Tax at 55%	5,500
	Net benefit to employee	4,500
	Effective tax rate	55%
B	**Take it as a bonus**	**£**
	Bonus	8,865
	Employer's NIC at 12.8%	1,135
	Total cost to employer	10,000
	Employee's tax £8,865 at 40%	3,546
	Employee's NIC £8,865 at 1%	89
		3,635

Net benefit to employee £8,865 – £3,635	5,230
Effective tax rate	47.7%

Deliberate overfunding could trigger the annual allowance charge at 40% as well as the lifetime allowance charge at 55%, making a total tax charge of 95% – a very unattractive proposition.

3 Pension Age

The concept of a normal retirement age has disappeared under the new regime, at least for tax purposes. The previous restriction on drawing occupational pension scheme benefits while still working for the employer has also been abolished. However, many employers may still have a normal retirement age in their scheme.

3.1 Normal minimum pension age

The new regime has introduced the concept of a normal minimum pension age. This is 50 from 6 April 2006 to 5 April 2010, and 55 thereafter. This produces a strange quirk for anyone born between 7 April 1955 and 5 April 1960 (inclusive). They can retire at 50 if they do this before 6 April 2010, but if they do not they will have to wait until age 55. For example, someone aged 53 on 6 April 2010 cannot take their pension then, even though they could have done so in the previous three years. They would now have to wait another two years.

The special early retirement ages for certain occupations (eg sportspeople) have disappeared – but see section 3.3.2.

3.2 Maximum pension age

In theory there is now no maximum pension age, but in practice it is still 75. This is because:

- Tax-free cash can only be paid before the 75th birthday. If paid on or after that date it would be a taxable unauthorised payment.
- Any money purchase scheme benefit is deemed to convert to unsecured pension at age 75.
- Any defined benefit scheme benefits are deemed to crystallise at age 75.

3.3 Exceptions

There are three exceptions to the normal minimum pension age rules:

- Existing contractual rights (see section 3.3.1).
- Special retirement ages (section 3.3.2).

- Ill-health (see section 4).

3.3.1 Existing contractual rights

A member of an occupational, statutory or parliamentary scheme who had a contractual right on 5 April 2006 to take pension benefits from 50 to 54 can still do so. This right must have been in the scheme rules on 10 December 2003. This exception only applies if all benefits are vested and the member is no longer employed by the sponsoring employer. This exception is normally lost if benefits are transferred.

3.3.2 Special retirement ages

Holders of personal pensions or retirement annuities with special retirement ages below 50 (eg sportspeople) at 5 April 2006 can keep their right to draw benefits early in respect of pre-A Day arrangements. They must vest all benefits from that arrangement in full. See Appendix for a list of special retirement ages.

3.3.3 Reduction in lifetime allowance

Where benefits are drawn before the normal minimum pension age, the lifetime allowance is reduced by 2.5% for each full year below the minimum age. So if a footballer draws benefits this year on his 40th birthday, the lifetime allowance would be reduced by 10 x 2.5% = 25%. It would thus be £1,500,000 x 75% = £1,125,000.

4 Ill-health Benefits

It is possible to take pension benefits before normal minimum pension age on grounds of ill-health. This is allowed by the Finance Act 2004 if 'the scheme administrator has received evidence from a registered medical practitioner that the member is (and will continue to be) incapable of carrying on the member's occupation because of physical or mental impairment, and the member has in fact ceased to carry on the member's occupation'.

This envisages permanent incapacity although it is possible for a scheme to suspend payment of an ill-health pension if the member recovers. Any scheme can have a stricter definition in its rules, eg providing an ill-health pension only if the member is incapable of carrying on any occupation, rather than their own occupation.

Taking this benefit is a benefit crystallisation (see section 5) and the lifetime allowance test applies, although without a reduction for early retirement. If this benefit was taken under a money purchase scheme, the cash pot could be used to buy an impaired life annuity if it was desired to maximise income. If this was not the main objective then it might be better to use an unsecured pension to maximise death benefits.

4.1 Commutation before age 75

If a member is under 75 and there is proof from a registered medical practitioner that the expectation of life is under a year, then all uncrystallised benefits can be commuted for a 'serious ill-health lump sum'. This is a benefit crystallisation triggering the lifetime allowance test.

5 Benefit Crystallisation Events

Under the new regime there are no limits on the amount of pension payable, or the rate of increase after retirement. Instead there is the lifetime allowance test (see section 2) which is triggered by a 'benefit crystallisation event'. There are nine of these as follows:

	Event	Valuation basis
1	The designation of money purchase arrangement assets to provide payment of an unsecured pension.	The value of the fund used to provide unsecured pension.
2	The member becoming entitled to a scheme pension.	Every £1 of pension pa = £20. The 20:1 factor.
3	A payment of a scheme pension above the maximum level set when the pension started.	The increase using the 20:1 factor.
4	The member becoming entitled to a lifetime annuity purchased under a money purchase arrangement.	The fund value used to purchase the annuity.
5	The member reaching age 75 with uncrystallised scheme pension and lump sum benefits from a defined benefits scheme.	The value of the pension using the 20:1 factor plus the lump sum at 75.
5A	The member reaching age 75 with designated money purchase scheme assets available for payment of unsecured pension.	The value of the unsecured pension fund less the amount used to provide payment of an unsecured pension.
6	The member becoming entitled to a lump sum.	The lump sum.
7	A lump sum death benefit being paid in respect of the member from a defined benefits scheme or the uncrystallised funds of a money purchase scheme.	The lump sum death benefit.
8	A transfer to a qualifying recognised overseas pension scheme.	The transfer value.
9	Moving from an unsecured pension to alternatively secured pension at age 75.	The fund value.

5.1 Benefits started after A Day

There is no need to draw all retirement benefits at the same time. So any lifetime allowance test has to take account of benefits already drawn. This is done by each crystallisation using a percentage of the allowance and carrying that forward to the next crystallisation. This is shown in the following example.

Example

Nicole draws pension scheme benefits of £48,000 in 2006/07.
Value £48,000 x 20 = £960,000.
This is 64% of the lifetime allowance of £1,500,000 so only 36% is left.
If she takes further benefits in 2010/11 when the allowance is £1,800,000 she has only 36% of this left = £648,000.

5.2 Benefits started pre-A Day

For benefits started before A Day a 25:1 valuation factor is used. So for example a pension of £25,000 is valued at £625,000.

If the benefits were income withdrawals, the 25:1 factor applies to the maximum withdrawal at the last review, or commencement if there has not yet been a review. The actual amount of withdrawal taken is ignored.

6 Retirement Income

The new regime allows four methods of retirement provision:

1 Scheme pension.
2 Lifetime annuity. } Secured pensions
3 Unsecured pension. }
4 Alternatively secured pension.

There are no maximum pension limits as the lifetime allowance test applies instead. There is no obligation to draw income benefits by age 75, but if tax-free cash is required it must be drawn before age 75.

6.1 Scheme pensions

These are pensions paid to a member by a registered pension scheme, or on its behalf by an insurance company chosen by the scheme administrator. Defined benefit schemes can only provide scheme pensions.

Defined contribution schemes can offer scheme pensions, but do not have to. They can only offer them if the member was also offered a lifetime annuity and declined it. In practice very few defined benefit contribution schemes are likely to offer them.

The scheme pension:

- Must be payable annually.
- Cannot reduce in amount, unless the same proportionate reduction applies to all members.
- Cannot be guaranteed for more than ten years (see section 6.1.3).
- Can be temporarily increased until state pension age as a bridging pension, provided the increase is no more than the basic state pension (plus any graduated pension).
- Can be transferred in payment to another insurance company, if paid by an insurance company.
- Can incorporate pension protection (see section 6.1.3).

Any artificially high initial pension designed to boost tax-free cash under the 20:1 factor is prevented by a rule saying that a reduction in pension to less than 80% of the original level in the first 12 months triggers an automatic unauthorised payment charge at 40%.

6.1.2 Taxation of scheme pensions
Scheme pensions are subject to income tax deducted under PAYE as employment income. However, they are not subject to NICs.

6.1.3 Scheme pension death benefits
There are two mutually exclusive death benefits:

- Guaranteed periods.
- Pension protection.

Pensions may be guaranteed for up to ten years. There can be no commutation and the guaranteed payments are taxable as income under PAYE on the recipient.

Under pension protection there can be a lump sum payment on death before age 75, being the original pension cost, less gross income payments made, less a tax charge at 35%.

However a defined benefit scheme can pay a defined benefit lump sum instead and avoid the 35% tax. This can be a monetary amount or a multiple of salary. This payment would be a benefit crystallisation event, triggering the lifetime allowance test. Thus to avoid a tax charge, the lump sum should be less than the remaining lifetime allowance. Tax on any excess could be avoided by using it to provide dependants' pensions.

6.1.4 Dependants' benefits

Dependants' benefits from a defined benefit scheme must be paid as a scheme pension. Dependants' benefits from any other scheme can be paid as:

- An annuity.
- An unsecured pension if the dependant is under 75.
- An alternatively secured pension if the dependant is 75 or over.
- A scheme pension.

Dependants' benefits do not have to be payable for life. A dependant is:

- A person who was married to (or a civil partner of) the member at death, or when retirement income started.
- A child of the member aged under 23 at death. Payment cannot go beyond age 23.
- A child of the member aged 23 or over who was dependent on the member because of their physical or mental impairment at death.
- A person who at the member's death was:
    - Financially dependent on the member;
    - In a financial relationship of mutual dependence with the member;
    - Dependent on the member due to their physical or mental impairment.

Dependants' benefits:

- Must not have a guaranteed period.
- Cannot have pension protection.
- Cannot be transferred in payment.
- Cannot provide any further payment on the dependant's death.
- Cannot be surrendered or assigned.

6.2 Lifetime annuities

All defined contribution schemes must offer a lifetime annuity. The lifetime annuity:

- Must be paid by an insurance company of the member's choice (an open market option).

- Must be paid at least yearly.
- Cannot be guaranteed for more than ten years (see section 6.1.3).
- Cannot reduce, unless they are:
    - Linked to the Retail Prices Index (RPI);
    - Unit-linked;
    - With-profits;

  or a combination of these.
- Can be transferred while in payment to another insurance company or registered pension scheme.
- Can include pension protection (see section 6.1.3).

6.2.1 Taxation of lifetime annuities

Lifetime annuities are subject to income tax by deduction under PAYE, with the exception of retirement annuity contracts. These are currently paid with deduction of basic rate income tax at source, but will be brought under PAYE from 6 April 2007.

6.2.2 Types of lifetime annuity

A lifetime annuity could be:

- Level.
- Increasing at a fixed rate.
- Index-linked to RPI.
- Unit-linked (see chapter A section 7.8).
- With-profits (see chapter A section 7.9).
- Impaired life (see chapter A section 7.11).

6.2.3 Death benefits

These rules are the same as for scheme pensions – see section 6.1.3.

6.2.4 Dependants' benefits

These rules are the same as for scheme pensions – see section 6.1.4.

6.3 Unsecured pensions

There are two types of unsecured pension. They are only available from money purchase schemes.

- Income withdrawal.
- Short-term annuities.

Neither can be extended beyond 75 but the introduction of alternatively secured pensions (see section 6.4) means that there no longer has to be an annuity purchase at 75.

6.3.1 Income withdrawal

Income withdrawal is sometimes known as pension fund withdrawal, and is designed to prevent people being locked into low annuity rates at retirement. It enables the member to buy an annuity later when rates may be better and to retain control over investment for longer. Starting income withdrawal is a benefit crystallisation triggering the lifetime allowance test.

The pension fund, less any tax-free cash taken, is invested and withdrawals are taken from that investment fund. There is a maximum withdrawal, but no minimum, so tax-free cash can be taken with no withdrawals until age 75. There is a complex formula for calculating maximum withdrawals based on 120% of the Government Actuary's Department (GAD) annuity rates, which in turn are based on the yield on 15-year gilts.

The level of withdrawals must be reviewed every five years, using the fund value up to 60 days before the review date. If part of the arrangement is used to buy an annuity or scheme pension there must be a review on the next anniversary. Pre-A Day income withdrawals come within this regime and must be reviewed within two years of A Day. In practice it might be advisable to review the level of withdrawals every year in the light of income requirements, personal circumstances and investment conditions.

Income withdrawals are subject to income tax by deduction under PAYE, but not NICs.

6.3.2 Short-term annuities

The way these work is that after taking tax-free cash the remaining fund stays invested but part of it is used to buy a temporary annuity. This must be payable at least yearly by an insurance company of the member's choice. The maximum initial annuity is the same as for income withdrawals and reviews have to be done in the same way. The annuity cannot be payable for more than five years and must cease at age 75.

The annuity cannot incorporate pension protection. It can be transferred to another insurance company and can vary like a lifetime annuity (see section 6.2.2). The annuity is subject to income tax by deduction under PAYE, but not NICs. Starting the annuity is a benefit crystallisation event triggering the lifetime allowance test.

6.3.3 Death benefits

On death while drawing an unsecured pension the residual fund can provide:

- A lump sum subject to tax at 35%.
- Dependants' scheme pensions with no guarantee or pensions protection.
- Dependants' annuities with no death benefits.
- Dependants' unsecured income provided the dependant is under 75. On the dependant's death before 75 the remaining fund is payable as a lump sum subject to 35% tax.
- An alternatively secured dependant's pension if the dependant is 75 or over.

If an unsecured or alternatively secured pension is selected, the maximum income depends on the age and sex of the dependant.

6.3.4 Risks of unsecured pensions

Unsecured pensions expose the member to investment risk, unlike scheme pensions and most lifetime annuities. What happens at a review will largely depend on the investment performance over the previous five years, relative to 15-year gilts (the basis for GAD annuity rates). This would be exacerbated by a review date coinciding with a market low. The problem is particularly acute for those taking the maximum level of withdrawals. Poor investment performance might lead to a drastic reduction in withdrawals.

There is also no guarantee that annuity rates will improve in the future as life expectancy has tended to lengthen historically, thus making annuities more expensive regardless of interest rates.

Under secured pensions there is an inherent cross-subsidy, with those who die early subsidising those who live longer than average. This cross-subsidy does not exist for unsecured pensions, but there is a fund left on death for the member's beneficiaries. Unsecured pension funds must achieve additional investment returns to combat this 'mortality drag'.

6.3.5 Advantages of unsecured pensions

Unsecured pensions are attractive in the following cases:

- The client wants maximum tax-free cash but does not need much, or any, income.
- The client is relatively young when it begins, providing a longer potential investment period.
- The client is not overdependent on pension income due to other income sources and assets.

- The client believes long-term interest rates are at temporarily low levels and will increase in the future.

- The client wants flexibility of income that cannot be provided by secured pensions.

- The client wants to maximise death benefits. However, IHT must be considered (see section 10).

- The client is a sophisticated investor who can understand the risks and has other investments.

6.3.6 Disadvantages of unsecured pensions

There are number of disadvantages which make unsecured pensions unsuitable for many clients.

- Charges tend to be relatively high. These could be by the pension provider for administration, or from an intermediary for advice.

- Investment in safe media (eg cash or fixed interest) is almost certain to produce a lower lifetime income than annuities and scheme pensions with their mortality subsidy and lower costs.

- There is an investment risk, which gets higher as the time until a secured pension is planned reduces.

- Annuity rates could continue to reduce.

6.4 Alternatively secured pensions

According to the Government, alternatively secured pensions (ASPs) were introduced by the new regime 'to provide an alternative to annuitisation for those with religious objections to risk pooling'. They were not meant as a method for intergenerational transfers of pension funds by scheme members generally – hence the IHT provisions explained in section 10.

Starting an ASP is a benefit crystallisation event triggering the lifetime allowance test. Someone who chooses unsecured pension to 75 and then ASP will face two tests:

- Firstly when the unsecured pension starts.

- Then when the ASP starts at 75.

Example

In 2006/07 Judith has a fund of £1,200,000. She takes tax-free cash of £300,000 and income withdrawals of £1,000 pa from the balance of £900,000. In 2010/11 she reaches age 75 and switches to an ASP when the fund is worth £1,300,000.
Her first benefit crystallisation event in 2006/07 uses 80% of her lifetime allowance (ie £1,200,000/£1,500,000). So only 20% is left.

In 2010/11 for the second test the allowance is £1,800,000 x 20%	£360,000
The fund is £1,300,000 less the £900,000 put into income withdrawal	£400,000
Less the remaining allowance	£360,000
Excess chargeable	£40,000

It might have been possible for Judith to avoid this charge by increasing the income withdrawal in the year before her 75th birthday.

A subsequent use of the ASP funds to buy a lifetime annuity would not require a third test.

6.4.1 Requirements for ASP

The main requirements for ASP are:

- It cannot be taken before the 75th birthday.
- It cannot be provided by a defined benefit scheme.
- The initial ASP income cannot exceed 70% of the GAD rate.
- There is no minimum income so funds can just be left to roll up.
- Reviews must be done at yearly intervals with the GAD rate based on age 75 not the actual age.
- An ASP in payment can be transferred.
- The ASP can be guaranteed for up to ten years, provided it is not a dependant's ASP. On death, payments continue until the end of the guaranteed period with the maximum recalculated annually based on the deceased member's sex and age 75. The guaranteed payments can be paid to anyone but cannot be commuted.
- At the end of any guaranteed period the residual fund can be used to provide death benefits as explained in section 6.4.2.

The ASP income is subject to income tax by deduction under PAYE, but not NICs.

6.4.2 Death benefits

If there are any dependants of the member alive at his or her death, the remaining ASP fund must be used to provide dependants' pensions as set out in section 6.1.4.

If there are no dependants to whom pension benefits can be paid there are two choices:

- A transfer lump sum death benefit; and/or
- A charity lump sum death benefit.

Neither of these is subject to the 35% tax charge.

The transfer lump sum death benefit is a transfer of the remaining fund to a member (or members) of another arrangement within the deceased member's registered pension scheme. The recipient can be nominated by the member, and this is binding on the scheme administrator. If there is no nomination, the administrator can decide which surviving scheme member should benefit.

Alternatively the member can nominate a charity (or charities) to receive all or part of the remaining fund.

For the IHT situation see section 10.

6.4.3 Advantages of ASP

These are:

- It provides a death benefit whenever death occurs, unlike secured pensions where the best option is a ten-year guarantee.

- It is more flexible than secured pensions.

- It is always possible to switch from an ASP to a secured pension – but not vice versa.

- It could be used to pass pension assets between generations, eg property used by a family business.

6.4.4 Disadvantages of ASP

There are some serious disadvantages:

- No security of income, although the maximum is set low to reduce the risk of fund erosion.

- Annual reviews are required, which increases the costs of administration and advice.

- The mortality drag effect is high due to the advanced age. The older the member the higher the investment performance needed to overcome this and the additional costs.

- It is complex and difficult to understand.

- The IHT situation – see section 10.

6.4.5 Suitability

ASPs might be suitable for clients who:

- Have limited, or no, need for income, maybe due to other income sources.
- Have large funds available.
- Desire to pass fund assets on to other members of their scheme.
- Desire to give their fund to charity on death.
- Are uncertain about their health and do not want to commit to a secured pension.
- Understand and accept the risks involved.
- Are willing to accept the complexities involved, particularly annual reviews.

7 Tax-Free Cash

Under the new regime the general limit for tax-free cash when benefits are taken is 25% of the total value of benefits for any pension arrangement. Tax-free cash must be taken before the 75th birthday.

The total value of benefits is the cash fund for a money purchase scheme and 20 times the pension for a defined benefit scheme. However, bridging pensions (see section 6.1) are ignored for this calculation. It is now possible to draw tax-free cash from protected rights (funds built up from contracting out of SERPS/S2P) and all forms of additional voluntary contributions.

There is no monetary limit on tax-free cash, other than the £375,000 produced by 25% of the £1,500,000 lifetime allowance. However, larger sums can be taken if transitional protection applies – see Chapter O section 15.

Example

Colin Smith retires at age 65 in 2006/07. He has a defined benefit scheme paying a pension of £50,000 pa plus a personal pension fund of £100,000. His maximum tax-free cash is:

DB scheme £50,000 x 20 x 25%	£250,000
Personal pension £100,000 x 25%	£25,000
Total	£275,000

If an occupational scheme member drew tax-free cash before A Day under the old rules, but deferred their pension until after A Day, they cannot take any more of the remaining fund as cash.

Where benefits are taken in stages after A Day the amount of any previously taken benefits is revalued in line with the standard lifetime allowance to preserve the effect of the 25% of the lifetime allowance limit. This is shown in the following example.

Example

Daniel Smith takes his money purchase occupational pension benefits in 2006/07. The fund is £800,000 so his tax-free cash is £200,000. He then takes his personal pension benefits in 2010/11 when the fund is £1,200,000.

	£
Standard lifetime allowance for 2010/11	1,800,000
Revalued 2006/07 benefits	
£800,000 x (£1.8m/£1.5m)	960,000
Balance of lifetime allowance left	840,000
Maximum tax-free cash £840,000 x 25%	£210,000

As Daniel's personal pension fund exceeds his lifetime allowance by £360,000 this is subject to the lifetime allowance charge.

7.1 Defined benefit schemes

On a defined benefit scheme if cash is taken the pension must obviously be reduced proportionately. While the 20:1 factor applies for the tax-free cash test in the legislation, many schemes only allow cash to be taken on a much less generous basis – eg commonly 12:1. So to get the maximum cash, much more than 25% of the possible maximum pension has to be given up – simply because each £12 of cash costs £1 of pension.

For this reason many schemes are under pressure to improve their commutation factors, although scheme deficits may make this hard to do. Thus it may not always be advantageous to take the maximum cash available.

7.2 Recycling

Recycling (sometimes called turbocharging) is the practice of taking money out of a pension using tax-free cash and putting it straight back in as a new contribution to attract further tax relief and more tax-free cash. This exercise could be repeated a number of times in quick succession to boost tax relief and tax-free cash further.

HMRC acted against this in the Finance Act 2006 for tax-free cash sums paid on or after 6 April 2006. The new rules provide for the tax-free cash to be treated as an unauthorised payment if it is used as part of a recycling device. They are not intended to apply to people who simply increase contributions with the intention of increasing the ultimate benefit. The rules apply only where contributions are significantly increased because of the lump sum. The rules do not apply where, when taking the lump sum, the individual had no intention of using it to pay contributions to a registered pension scheme.

7.2.1 The rules

The legislation applies where:

- An individual receives tax-free cash; and
- Because of it the amount of contributions paid into a registered pension scheme is significantly greater than it would otherwise have been; and
- The additional contributions are paid by the individual or anyone else; and
- The recycling was preplanned.

The HMRC view is that a significant increase in contributions occurs where, because of the tax-free cash, the amount of additional contributions is more than 30% of the contributions that might have been expected.

In addition, for the new rules to apply:

- The amount of the tax-free cash plus any other such tax-free cash taken in the previous 12 months exceeds 1% of the standard lifetime allowance (ie £15,000 for 2006/07); and
- The cumulative amount of additional contributions exceeds 30% of the tax-free cash.

The fact that the individual has other funds from which the extra contributions are, or could have been, paid does not mean that the rules are avoided.

7.2.2 The tax charge

When the rules apply, the tax-free cash is deemed to be an unauthorised payment, although any part of it that is subject to the lifetime allowance charge is excluded (to prevent double charging).

This payment would therefore be subject to a tax charge on the recipient of 40% or 55% – see Chapter O sections 12.1 and 12.2. The scheme administrator would also be subject to a scheme sanction charge of between 15% and 40% – see Chapter O section 12.3.

A scheme administrator can apply to HMRC to discharge this liability if it is just and reasonable to do so. This could apply where the member declares to the administrator that they are not recycling, but it turns out that this was false. Regulations require a member who intends to take tax-free cash as part of a recycling device to inform the scheme administrator within 30 days.

These rules have been widely condemned as impractical, unfair to scheme administrators and unnecessary.

8 Trivial Commutation

If pension benefits are trivial they can be commuted to a lump sum, assuming the pension provider is willing to do so.

8.1 Commutation by the member

A member can commute one, or more, pension arrangements if:

- It is after their 60th birthday.
- All benefits from that scheme or annuity are commuted.
- All commutations occur within 12 months of the first trivial commutation, the commutation period.
- It is before their 75th birthday.
- The value of all the member's pension rights does not exceed 1% of the standard lifetime allowance (currently £15,000) on the nominated date. This is any date within three months of the start of the commutation period. If no date is nominated, it will be the start of the commutation period.

A trivial commutation payment is subject to income tax under PAYE, other than for unvested plans where 25% (corresponding to the tax-free cash) is tax-free.

8.2 Commutation by a dependant

A dependant can commute pension death benefit if:

- The member died before age 75.
- The payment is made before the day when the member would have attained age 75.
- The commutation extinguishes the dependant's entitlements under the scheme to any pension or lump sum death benefit in respect of the member.

The whole payment is taxed on the dependant under PAYE. If the amount exceeds 1% of the standard lifetime allowance the excess is an unauthorised payment.

9 Benefits on Death Before Crystallisation

The new regime provides a much simpler structure for what might be called death in service benefits. This is resulting in much greater use of pensions term assurance where ordinary term assurance might have been used previously.

9.1 Lump sum death benefits

A registered pension scheme can pay a lump sum on death before age 75, either as a monetary sum or a multiple of salary. It can even be paid after the member has drawn pension benefits as long as this is before their 75th birthday.

Payment of a lump sum death benefit is a benefit crystallisation event triggering the lifetime allowance test. The maximum tax-free lump sum is therefore whatever remains of the lifetime allowance. So for someone who has drawn no pension benefit previously, the maximum is £1,500,000. If the lump sum exceeds the lifetime allowance, the 55% tax charge will be payable by the recipient on the excess. This charge could be avoided by using the excess to provide dependants' benefits – see section 9.2.

9.2 Dependants' benefits

Dependants' benefits can be paid as set out in section 6.1.4. That section also gives the definition of a dependant.

There is no limit on a dependants' pension if the member dies before their 75th birthday. If death occurs after then and the member was in receipt of a scheme pension, the maximum total dependants' pension is 100% of the member's actual and prospective pension in the year to death plus 5% of any tax-free cash the member had drawn. If the member died within 12 months of the start of their pension the actual pension is deemed to be the expected pension for the full year.

If the limit is exceeded the excess dependants' pensions are unauthorised payments and so taxable as set out in Chapter O section 12.1

9.3 Pensions term assurance

The new regime has generated much more interest in what might be called pension term assurance (PTA), as this can now be done for much greater sums assured than previously. Thus stand-alone PTA is increasing in popularity.

The gross premiums are somewhat higher than for ordinary term assurance, as there is no tax relief for expenses within the pension fund. However, full tax relief on the premiums means that the effective net premium will often be lower than for ordinary term assurance, particularly for higher rate taxpayers. Premiums are payable net of 22% basic rate tax relief, with higher rate taxpayers claiming the extra 18% through PAYE or their tax return.

Thus for sums assured under £1,500,000, PTA may well be the starting point, unless cover is required beyond age 75. For this reason the FSA has said that PTA can be sold under either the Insurance Conduct of Business rules (ICOB), or the full COB rules – see Chapter Q. However, advisers should consider what effect a PTA might have on the client's other pension arrangements.

PTAs can be issued under trust to avoid IHT, just like ordinary term assurances. The benefits of a PTA could be assigned, eg to a lender. PTAs must be single life and own life – so joint life and life of another are not allowed. Premiums can be paid by the member, or anyone else.

10 Inheritance Tax

10.1 IHT on contributions

Any contribution an employer makes to a registered pension scheme for the benefit of employees, or their dependants, is exempt from Inheritance Tax (IHT).

However, if one individual (who is not the employer) pays a contribution into another individual's pension arrangement this is a transfer of value for IHT. The value of the transfer will be the contribution net of basic rate tax relief under the loss to the estate principle. If an individual pays a premium on a PTA (or its pre-A Day equivalent) which is on trust for someone else, this is also a transfer of value of the net premium. In these cases the transfer might be exempt if it was for a UK domiciled spouse (or civil partner), or under the £3,000 or normal expenditure exemptions.

10.2 Death benefits

Most occupational pension schemes provide the death in service benefit under a discretionary trust whereby the employee completes an 'expression of wish' form saying to whom he or she would like the benefit payable. The trustees then have a discretion as to whom to pay but would normally follow the employee's wishes. Because it is a discretionary trust, the benefit is not part of the employee's estate for IHT purposes. It is also not part of the named beneficiary's estate if he or she predeceases the employee. Registered pension schemes are exempt from the normal IHT charges on discretionary trusts. However, the benefit must be distributed by the pension trust within two years of the member's death to avoid IHT.

If an individual dies while owning a right to an annuity under a registered pension this is ignored for IHT. However, if the balance of a guaranteed pension was payable to the estate this could be subject to IHT. Any other payments to the estate could also be subject to IHT.

When a pension term assurance (or its pre-A Day equivalent) is under trust the sum assured is not part of the individual's estate and is thus not subject to IHT. Any such policy payable to the estate could be subject to IHT.

10.3 Lifetime charges

An IHT charge can arise during a member's lifetime under the omission to exercise a right rules in s3(3) Inheritance Tax Act 1984 (IHTA), if he or she does not exercise their right to take pension benefits. The charge applies at the latest time when the right could be exercised – ie immediately before death. Thus if a member found out that their life expectancy was seriously impaired and deliberately decided not to take their pension and this resulted in an enhanced death benefit being paid to their beneficiaries the IHT charge could apply.

There is no charge if the beneficiary is a spouse, civil partner or person who is financially dependent on the member. IHT also does not apply where a member chooses not to take a pension when he or she is in good health and does not later vary that decision even when a reduction in life expectancy could strictly result in a charge.

10.4 Alternatively secured pensions

The government did not intend that ASPs should be able to be used to pass on tax privileged retirement savings to their dependants. Therefore left over ASP funds on death are subject to IHT.

Any funds paid as a transfer lump sum death benefit (see section 6.4.2), or refunded to an employer, or used to provide benefits for a dependant (in the pension sense) who is not a spouse, civil partner or person who is financially dependent will be subject to IHT as if the sums were part of their taxable estate on death.

Any funds payable to charity will be exempt, as will funds expended for the member's spouse, civil partner or financial dependant. Any left over funds, once use by the spouse, civil partner or financial dependant has ceased, will be chargeable to IHT on the earlier of the cessation of those benefits and the death of the beneficiary. Again these will be treated as part of the original member's estate.

Where a dependant chooses an ASP from benefits inherited from a member who died before 75, any left over funds on the dependant's death will be chargeable to IHT as if they were part of the dependant's taxable estate on death.

10.4.1 Administration of the tax

In the circumstances above, IHT will be payable on the value of the fund at the time the charge arises according to the rates in force at that time. The scheme administrator will be responsible for paying any IHT due on ASP funds, which is bound to lead to problems in practice. There are two cases where the tax charges on ASP funds overlap.

- Where the funds are paid to an employer.
- Where, on the death of a dependant under 75, any remaining funds are paid out as a lump sum, other than to charity.

In these cases the IHT charge takes priority over the pension scheme tax charge, which is applied to the net fund after deduction of IHT.

11 Sex Equality

11.1 Equal access

One aspect that must not be taken into account in the eligibility conditions for a scheme is the sex of the employee. Schemes are not permitted to have eligibility conditions that discriminate between men and women. As a result:

- The lower entry age must be the same for men and women.
- The upper entry age may be different for men and women, but only to the extent that retirement ages differ. For example, if retirement ages in a scheme are 65 for men and 60 for women then the upper entry age can be 59 for men and 54 for women so that both are six years before retirement age. Following the *Barber* case almost all schemes have now equalised retirement ages for men and women.
- Qualifying service must be the same for men and women.

Employers have to be careful not to exclude any of their employees from a scheme indirectly by imposing rules which disproportionately affect a much greater number of members of one sex, unless the exclusion can be objectively justified on grounds other than sex. The main thrust of this used to be in respect of part-time workers, who were more frequently women than men.

However, legislation now ensures that as a general rule part-timers will be included in pension schemes if their full-time counterparts are scheme members.

The equal access rules only affect eligibility for membership. There are no legal requirements for a scheme to provide equal benefits for men and women. Pensions and Social Security were specifically excluded from the sex discrimination legislation, largely because the State itself discriminates both on retirement ages and survivor benefits.

11.2 Equality of benefit

The Sex Discrimination Act 1986 prevents an employer from imposing different compulsory retirement ages for men and women, but does not force equalisation of the age at which the pension normally starts.

The case of *Barber v Guardian Royal Exchange Assurance Group* decided that no pension scheme member retiring, dying or leaving service on or after 17 May 1990 can be treated unequally on the grounds of sex in respect of service after that date.

Since then, pension schemes have been required to take whatever action is necessary to bring their schemes into line, eg by adopting a common retirement date and

extending widows' benefits to widowers. In addition, the Pensions Act 1995 provides that all schemes should be treated as having an equal treatment rule requiring males and females to be treated equally. However, differential treatment is allowed to the extent that the state retirement pension differentiates, and as a result of actuarial factors.
The *Neath* case decided that funded defined benefit schemes can use gender specific actuarial factors in calculating transfer values, early retirement benefits and lump sums. It also decided that they did not have to use unisex annuity rates.

Equalisation does not apply to additional voluntary contributions (AVCs), personal or stakeholder pensions, group personal pensions or retirement annuities.

Following a decision by the European Court of Justice, part-timers refused membership of a pension scheme have been able in certain circumstances to claim equal treatment if it can be shown that their exclusion was the result of indirect discrimination.

12 ABI Pensions Maturities – Statement of Good Practice

The Association of British Insurers (ABI) Statement applies to personal pensions, stakeholder pensions, retirement annuities, free-standing AVCs (FSAVCs) and section 32 buy-out plans. It is supported by the FSA.

The pensions provider must issue a pre-retirement letter four months before the retirement date setting out all the options and any implications of market value reductions if retirement is deferred. There must be details of the open market option (also an FSA requirement), including the fact that another provider might pay a higher annuity. There need only be broad descriptions of the options, not detailed figures.

There should then be a detailed retirement letter at least six weeks before retirement date including a retirement annuity quote and a reminder about the open market option.

If all the required information is received before retirement date, the tax-free cash should be paid within 14 days of the retirement date, plus details of the annuity and its taxation. If the annuity is to be provided by another provider the pension fund must be sent to the annuity provider within 14 days of the retirement date. The annuity provider must then pay the tax-free cash and confirm details of the annuity and its taxation within 14 days of receiving the pension fund.

13 Divorce

There are three main ways of dealing with pension on divorce:

- Offset.
- Earmarking.
- Pensions sharing.

13.1 Offset

Offset takes into account the value of pension rights (only those accrued since marriage in Scotland) as part of the overall assets of the divorcing parties. The divorce settlement then divides up the matrimonial assets, leaving pensions untouched. So, for example, a common situation would be for the breadwinner to retain their pension rights, but to transfer other assets – typically an interest in the family home – to their spouse. The result is often that one party ends up with assets but no pension, while the other has pension, but few if any assets.

Offset remains the most popular way to deal with pensions on divorce because:

- Pension sharing has only applied to divorce proceedings started on or after 1 December 2000.
- It is relatively easy to implement, provided there are sufficient non-pension assets available.
- It does not reduce pension entitlements.
- It is widely understood, which is more than can be said for earmarking or pension sharing.

Offset will not be a practical proposition where there are insufficient other assets with which to offset or where both parties want to retain an interest in pension rights.

13.2 Earmarking

Earmarking was introduced by the Pensions Act 1995, but has not proved popular. The basis of earmarking is that the court issues an order to pension scheme trustees (or providers of personal pensions, stakeholder pensions and retirement annuities) requiring that a proportion of the member's benefits are paid directly to the former spouse when the member retires: in effect a deferred maintenance order. Nevertheless, the pension is fully taxed as the member's income. The court may also order that a proportion of the lump sum death in service benefits is paid to the former spouse, overriding the normal trustees' discretion.

Earmarking has not been extensively used because:

- There is a much greater familiarity with offset amongst courts and solicitors.
- The former spouse is dependent upon the pension scheme member's retirement for benefits to begin. This might mean waiting until their 75th birthday.
- Pension benefits to the former spouse cease on the member's death. It is therefore possible that the former spouse will receive little or no benefit from an earmarking order. Similarly, if the former spouse dies or remarries, the earmarked benefits will revert to the member.
- There is no clean break.

In Scotland lump sums can be earmarked but pensions cannot, although a spouse who remarries retains the rights to earmarked benefits.

13.3 Pension sharing

Pension sharing was introduced by the Welfare Reform and Pensions Act 1999. It applies to divorce petitions filed on or after 1 December 2000. The court can divide pension benefits between the divorcing parties, giving each party their own share of the pension rights. It thus achieves the clean break which earmarking does not. The split can be any percentage decided by the court and is based on the Cash Equivalent Transfer Value (CETV). The pension sharing rules apply to all types of pension, including personal pensions, retirement annuities, stakeholder pensions and unapproved schemes. They apply to SERPS and S2P, but not the basic state pension. They apply to pensions in payment, as well as rights to a future pension. Life offices must be able to quote CETVs within strict time limits for retirement annuities and stakeholder and personal pensions, as must trustees for occupational pension schemes. Pension schemes are allowed to charge for the costs of pension sharing.

For unfunded schemes (eg many public sector schemes), the regulations require an internal transfer to be made, giving ex-spouses their own independent membership of the scheme. A transfer to another scheme does not have to be offered.

Funded schemes have the choice of giving a transfer value or separate membership to the ex-spouse. Many schemes offer a transfer value only for ease of administration. For a personal pension, the ex-spouse will be given a sum of money to establish their own personal pension either with the existing pension provider or through a transfer to another provider.

For a retirement annuity there has to be a transfer to a personal or stakeholder pension, or an occupational scheme of which the ex-spouse is a member, because no new retirement annuity can be effected now.

A pension share given to an ex-spouse is called a pension credit. From the original member's point of view the share is a pension debit. For lifetime allowance purposes, a pension credit counts as part of the recipient's allowance, while a pension debit is deducted from the fund to value the original member's benefits.

Credits (subject to an appropriate election) and debits granted before A Day will be ignored under the new regime, ie they will neither count as part of the recipient's nor the donor's pension rights. A pension credit paid in respect of a member's pension already in payment that started after 5 April 2006 is subject to special treatment. The member giving the credit can elect for an enhanced lifetime allowance to reflect the loss of a benefit that will have already been subject to a lifetime allowance test.

The pension resulting from a pension credit is taxable as income of the payee, not the original member.
Scottish courts can only take account of benefits which accrued during the period of the marriage, whereas in England all accrued benefits are taken account of.

Few pension sharing orders have actually been made.

14 Bankruptcy

There has been considerable interest in the rights of a trustee-in-bankruptcy over a bankrupt's pension contracts. The law changed some years ago – the situation now depends on whether the bankruptcy order was made on or after 29 May 2000.

Under the Welfare Reform and Pensions Act 1999 in a bankruptcy where the bankruptcy order was made on or after 29 May 2000 any rights under any registered pension scheme are excluded from the bankrupt's estate and therefore cannot be taken by the trustee-in-bankruptcy. This applies to occupational schemes, personal pensions, stakeholder pensions and retirement annuities but not to unregistered schemes.

Also under the Welfare Reform and Pensions Act 1999 a trustee-in-bankruptcy can apply to the court and if the court thinks that payment of excessive pension contributions has unfairly prejudiced the individual's creditors it can order the position to be restored to what it would have been if the excessive contributions had not been made. The court can thus order a pension provider to make payment to the trustee-in-bankruptcy, and adjust the liability to the bankrupt appropriately.

However, the law is completely different for bankruptcies where the bankruptcy order was made before 29 May 2000. In these cases the law provides that the trustee-in-bankruptcy takes over the bankrupt's assets and pension rights are clearly assets for this purpose. However, the trustee only takes over the bankrupt's rights and cannot claim any greater rights than the bankrupt could. Protected rights do not pass to the trustee-in-bankruptcy.

Thus on a personal pension (or retirement annuity) the trustee cannot surrender the contract for cash. The trustee can only wait until the retirement date and claim the maximum lump sum and then residual pension as and when it is payable. However if the contract allows the client the right to take early retirement (eg at any time after age 50 on a personal pension) the trustee can exercise this right and claim the benefits as early as the contract and legislation allow. This was confirmed in the case of *Re Landau* (TLR 1 Jan 97) which also confirmed that the trustee's title to the benefits continued after the bankrupt's discharge (which, under the Enterprise Act 2002, is now likely to be after 12 months). Thus someone made bankrupt before 29 May 2000 at age 30 and who got his discharge at 33, can still have the pension benefits taken by the trustee-in-bankruptcy at age 50. If a bankrupt is already being paid a pension the trustee can claim the regular payments for the creditors – with the exception of any protected rights (159 Pension Schemes Act 1993).

Most occupational pension schemes have traditionally contained a clause providing for forfeiture of benefits if the member becomes bankrupt, leaving the trustees with a discretion to pay the bankrupt's family. This was almost certainly effective against claims from a trustee-in-bankruptcy, so long as it expressed the member's entitlement to pension as ceasing on bankruptcy – (*Kemble v Hicks*). As explained above, where the bankruptcy order was made on or after 29 May 2000 any rights under a registered occupational pension scheme cannot be taken by a trustee-in-bankruptcy.

Whether a bankruptcy was before or after 29 May 2000 the trustee-in-bankruptcy can get an income payments order from a court against a pension in payment under the Insolvency Act 1986 (as amended by the Enterprise Act 2002). This will generally run for three years from the date of the order, even though the bankrupt will usually be discharged after 12 months. However under the Social Security Pensions Act 1975 s48 (3) for a contracted out pension scheme, the debtor's guaranteed minimum pension (GMP) does not pass to the trustee-in-bankruptcy so he could only claim the balance.

Unregistered pension arrangements (eg funded unapproved retirement benefits schemes (FURBS)) are not protected by the 1999 Act and thus still pass to the trustee-in-bankruptcy, however the bankrupt can apply to the court to keep the pension rights if it is his or her main means of pension provision, bearing in mind the needs of the bankrupt and his family and other pensions.

Appendix Early Retirement Ages

The list below shows for certain professions and occupations the pension ages for personal pensions agreed by HMRC. Individuals in other professions and occupations may not take benefits from their pension arrangements before age 50.

Profession or occupation	Retirement age
Athletes	35
Badminton players	35
Boxers	35
Cricketers	40
Cyclists	35
Dancers	35
Divers (saturation, deep sea and free swimming)	40
Footballers	35
Golfers	40
Ice hockey players	35
Jockeys – flat racing	45
Jockeys – National Hunt	35
Members of the Reserve Forces	45
Models	35
Motor cycle riders (motocross or road racing)	40
Motor racing drivers	40
Rugby League players	35
Rugby Union players	35
Skiers (downhill)	30
Snooker/billiards players	40
Speedway riders	40
Squash players	35
Table tennis players	35
Tennis players (including real tennis)	35
Trapeze artistes	40
Wrestlers	35

Notes

1. The pension age shown applies only to pension arrangements funded by contributions paid in respect of the relevant earnings from the occupation or profession carrying that age. If an individual wishes to make pension provisions in respect of another source of relevant earnings to which the pension age shown above does not apply then a separate arrangement must be set up, with a pension age within the normal range.

2. The ages shown above for professional sportsmen apply only to arrangements made in respect of relevant earnings from activities as professional sportsmen eg tournament earnings, appearance and prize money. They do not apply to relevant earnings from sponsorship or coaching for which, if desired, a separate arrangement with a pension age within the normal range should be made.

Appendix: Early Retirement Ages

[illegible]

[illegible]	[illegible]
Athletes	[illegible]
Badminton players	[illegible]
Boxers	[illegible]
Cricketers	[illegible]
Cyclists	[illegible]
Dancers	[illegible]
Divers (saturation, construction etc, [illegible])	[illegible]
Footballers	[illegible]
Golfers	[illegible]
[illegible]	[illegible]
Jockeys—Flat racing	[illegible]
Jockeys—National Hunt	[illegible]
Members of the Reserve Forces	[illegible]
Models	[illegible]
Motor cycle riders (motocross or road racing)	[illegible]
Motor racing drivers	[illegible]
Rugby League players	[illegible]
Rugby Union players	[illegible]
Speedway riders	[illegible]
Squash players	[illegible]
Table tennis players	[illegible]
Tennis players (including real tennis)	[illegible]
Trapeze artistes	[illegible]
Wrestlers	[illegible]

Notes

[illegible]

[illegible]

Q The Financial Services and Markets Act 2000

The Financial Services and Markets Act 2000 brought together the regulation of all parts of the financial services industry under one regulatory system. This chapter covers the aspects of this relevant to life assurance and pensions, including the Financial Ombudsman Service and the Financial Services Compensation Scheme.

1 The Act

The object of the Financial Services and Markets Act 2000 (FSMA) was to bring together the regulation of all parts of the financial services industry under one regulatory system.

Previously different parts of the financial services industry were regulated under different Acts, for example:

- Banking by the Bank of England under the Banking Act 1987.
- Building societies by the Building Societies Commission under the Building Societies Act 1986.
- Friendly societies by the Friendly Societies Commission under the Friendly Societies Act 1992.
- The prudential regulation of insurance companies by the Treasury under the Insurance Companies Act 1982.
- Investments (including long-term insurance) by the self-regulatory organisations (SROs) under the Financial Services Act 1986.

The FSMA established the Financial Services Authority (FSA) as the sole regulatory body with effect from the so called N2 Day – 30 November 2001. The FSA was developed from the Securities and Investments Board (SIB) which was the lead regulator under the Financial Services Act 1986.

All firms authorised by SIB or the SROs under the Financial Services Act became automatically authorised by the FSA under the FSMA on 30 November 2001.

1.1 Scope of the Act

The scope of the FSMA is much wider than the Financial Services Act in that it covers:

- Deposit taking (eg bank and building society accounts).
- Stocks and shares.
- Gilts and local authority bonds.
- Debentures.
- Futures.
- Unit trusts.
- Open-ended investment companies (OEICs).

- All contracts of insurance (including general insurance and the Lloyd's market).
- Loans secured on land (ie mortgages), but only with effect from 31 October 2004.
- Funeral plan contracts.

The Treasury has also decided that the FSA should regulate home reversion schemes, but this will not be for some time as primary legislation is needed to do this.

Regulated activities include dealing in, arranging, managing or giving advice on any of the above. It also includes using a computer based system for giving investment instructions. However, giving advice on deposits is not currently regulated.

The objectives of the Act are to bring together the regulation of all the different types of financial services under one regulator – the FSA, with one Ombudsman – the Financial Ombudsman Service (FOS), and one compensation scheme – the Financial Services Compensation Scheme (FSCS).

The Act was passed on 14 June 2000 and is extremely long and complex, consisting of 433 sections and 22 schedules. However the Act is mostly enabling legislation in the sense that all the detailed requirements for firms regulated under the Act are in Regulations and Rules made under the Act by the Treasury or the FSA.

The FSA's rulebooks are incredibly lengthy and complex comprising 27 separate volumes, costing £1,300 if bought in one go and more if bought separately! They are however available on CD-ROM. There have also been over 200 FSA consultation papers.

National Savings and Investments products are not regulated by the FSA.

1.2 The objectives of the FSA

Under Section 2 of the FSMA the FSA has four regulatory objectives:

- Market confidence.
- Public awareness.
- The protection of consumers.
- The reduction of financial crime.

The FSA must, so far as is reasonably possible, act in a way which is compatible with these objectives and which it considers most appropriate to meet them. The FSA must have regard to:

- The need to use its resources in the most efficient and economic way.

- The responsibilities of those who manage the affairs of authorised persons.
- The principle that burdens and restrictions should be proportionate to the benefits expected from them.
- The desirability of facilitating innovation.
- The international character of financial services and the desirability of maintaining the competitive position of the UK.
- The need to minimise the adverse affects on competition.
- The desirability of facilitating competition.

1.3 The FSA's powers

The FSA has the following powers over individuals and firms carrying on regulated activities:

- To grant, vary and cancel authorisations and permitted activities.
- To approve individuals to perform certain controlled functions, to issue codes for their conduct and take action for misconduct.
- To be represented in court in cases of banking or insurance transfers.
- To impose penalties for market abuse.
- To make rules including those for:
    - Conduct of business;
    - Client money;
    - Financial promotions;
    - Money laundering.
- To require an authorised person to provide information or documents.
- To carry out investigations.
- To regulate changes of control over UK authorised persons.
- To take disciplinary action against authorised persons.
- To establish a compensation scheme – the Financial Services Compensation Scheme (see later).

- To establish the Financial Ombudsman Scheme (see later).
- To authorise unit trusts.
- To recognise overseas collective investment schemes.
- To recognise investment exchanges and clearing houses.
- To keep the Lloyd's insurance market under review.
- To maintain a public record of authorised persons and prohibited persons.
- To co-operate with other regulators.
- To institute criminal proceedings for offences under the FSMA.

The FSA is answerable to the Treasury for the way it does its job. It also makes an annual report to Parliament.

The FSA and its employees are not liable for acts done in discharge of its functions unless done in bad faith or in breach of the Human Rights Act 1998.

1.4 The FSA's methods of operation and enforcement regime

The FSA operates as a reactive and a pro-active regulator. It is reactive in that it receives a regular flow of information from regulated firms as a result of which it can institute investigations and/or take disciplinary action. This information would include:

- Accounts and auditors' statements.
- Banking returns under the banking rules.
- Insurance returns under the Prudential Rulebook.

If any of this information gave cause for concern then the FSA could take the appropriate action.

The FSA can also react to any concerns expressed by:

- The Consumer Panel.
- The Practitioner Panel.
- The Office of Fair Trading.
- The Complaints Commissioner.

- The Financial Ombudsman.
- The media.
- The government.
- Individual complaints.

The FSA is also a proactive regulator in the sense that it has a regular programme of inspection visits for regulated firms as part of its enforcement regime.

The FSA has teams of enforcement officers whose job it is to investigate complaints and ensure compliance with the rules by regular visits to regulated firms. FSA officers can visit any premises, with or without notice and question staff. They can demand access to documents and records and require copies. The staff of regulated firms have to co-operate with FSA officers. The FSA can get a warrant to enter and search premises and take documents by force if necessary.

1.5 Disciplinary action

If as a result of complaints, inspection visits or investigations the FSA decides the law or its rules have been broken it can take disciplinary action. This could include:

- Public announcements.
- Fines.
- Conditions on future business.
- Obtaining a court injunction.
- Ordering compensation for customers.
- Withdrawing authorisation.
- Prohibiting any individual from carrying out regulated activities.

Because of individual registration of controlled functions disciplinary action can be taken against individuals as well as firms.

Any disciplined person can appeal to the Financial Services and Markets Tribunal.

The FSA has stated that firms must not use insurance to pay FSA fines.

1.6 Authorisation

Under s19 of the FSMA it is an offence to carry on a regulated activity unless the person is authorised or exempt. This is termed the general prohibition. Authorised persons can only carry on the activities permitted by the FSA. Thus a firm that was authorised as an independent financial adviser only could not suddenly provide deposit taking services, without getting FSA permission for that extra activity.

1.7 Previously authorised firms

Firms previously authorised under the Banking Act 1987, the Insurance Companies Act 1982 and by the FSA or an SRO under the Financial Services Act 1986 were automatically authorised by the FSA for the previously authorised activities. Thus firms authorised by the Personal Investment Authority (PIA) under the previous regime were 'grandfathered' into authorisation under the new regime.

Professional firms previously authorised by a Recognised Professional Body (RPB) under the Financial Services Act 1986 were not grandfathered in and thus may need authorisation. They do not need authorisation for regulated activities which are incidental to their professional services, but do for arranging, managing or dealing in particular investments. Thus a solicitor would not need authorisation for assisting a policyholder to make a claim under a life policy, and an accountant would not need authorisation for advice on the taxation of a life policy as these are incidental to their professional services. However authorisation would be needed if a firm of solicitors or accountants wanted to sell life policies.

Grandfathering does not apply to newly regulated activities, such as mortgage lending where authorisation has to be obtained.

1.8 New firms and activities

Any new firm wishing to undertake regulated activities and any existing regulated firm wishing to undertake a regulated activity that it is not currently permitted to do, must apply to the FSA for authorisation. The firm cannot start that business until it has received authorisation. The FSA can grant authorisation or refuse it at its discretion. Any firm refused authorisation can appeal to the Financial Services and Markets Tribunal.

1.9 Appointed representatives

A firm is exempt if it has a contract with an authorised person whereby that authorised person has accepted responsibility in writing for its activities. The contract must comply with various regulations and can restrict the permitted business. Such firms are called 'appointed representatives' (ARs) and the authorised person is known as the 'principal'. The principal is liable for the acts and omissions of the appointed representative for business covered by the contract as if they were its own.

An AR could be a full AR able to give advice on life and pensions or just an introducer restricted to making introductions and distributing advertisements. An AR could also restrict its activities to a particular category of product, eg pension products, provided this is clear to customers.

1.10 Individual registration

Individuals undertaking a 'controlled function' within an authorised firm must be individually approved by the FSA. Controlled functions are those that involve either:

- A significant influence on the conduct of an authorised person's affairs; or
- Dealing with customers in connection with regulated activities; or
- Dealing with the property of customers in connection with regulated activities.

Thus individual registration is necessary for:

- Directors and chief executives.
- Appointed actuaries of insurance companies.
- Money laundering reporting officers.
- Heads of compliance.
- Internal auditors.
- Senior managers.
- Customer advisers and traders.
- Discretionary investment managers.

The individual registration gives the FSA disciplinary powers over the individual as well as the firm.

The FSA can withdraw approval if it decides an individual is no longer fit and proper for that function. It can also make a prohibition order against an individual, which would effectively ban that person from working in any regulated activity.

The FSA has said it will only discipline an individual for personal culpability where behaviour was deliberate or fell below a reasonable standard. It also said it will not discipline for vicarious liability.

Individuals who previously held equivalent individual registrations under the Financial Services Act regime did not need fresh approval by the FSA but all new appointees to controlled functions do need approval.

An approved individual must remain fit and proper for the function under the following criteria:

- Honesty.

- Integrity.
- Reputation.
- Competence.
- Capability.
- Financial soundness.

For senior managers, a firm must maintain a clear and appropriate apportionment of significant responsibilities and these must be recorded. There must be appropriate systems and controls. There must be an effective compliance system under a director or senior manager.

1.11 Polarisation

Polarisation was a requirement of the previous Financial Services Act regime which continued under the FSMA. It applied to life assurance, pensions, annuities, unit trusts and unit trust ISAs.

In order to sell or advise on any of these contracts a person had to be either a representative of the life office/unit trust manager or an independent financial adviser (IFA). No one individual or company could be both.

A representative of a life office/unit trust manager could have been an employee or self-employed representative of the product provider or one of its appointed representatives. An IFA could have been an employee or self-employed representative of an authorised IFA firm or of an appointed representative of an authorised IFA firm (known as a network). There are a number of IFA networks that provide authorisation for member firms and individuals.

A representative of a product provider could only sell his provider's contracts and no-one else's. An IFA had to be able to sell the contracts of any provider in the market place.

The duty of a provider's representative was to select the best contract from their own provider's range for the client. The duty of an IFA was to select the best contract for the client from all the providers in the market.

Polarisation led a lot of firms, particularly lenders and estate agents, to become ARs of (or to 'tie to') a particular life office. Sometimes an AR (such as a bank or building society) may actually own its principal life office. It also led to IFA networks being formed to provide authorisation and support for many small firms of IFAs, who might otherwise have found all the requirements of authorisation and compliance too onerous and time consuming. It is now virtually impossible for a one or two man firm to be authorised in its own right and still find time to do business and make a profit.

There is a vital difference in legal status between a representative of a product provider and an IFA. A provider's representative is the agent of his or her provider and the provider is fully responsible for their acts and omissions. An IFA is the agent of the client and either the individual IFA firm, or its authorising network, is responsible for its acts and omissions.

An investor would always have known whether his adviser was tied to a provider or was independent.

1.12 Depolarisation

The FSA replaced the polarisation regime on 1 December 2004 with a six month transitional period ending 1 June 2005. Between these dates firms could operate under the new or old rules but had to tell the FSA when they converted. All firms had to be operating under the new rules from 1 June 2005.

Under the new rules an intermediary could be one of three basic types:

- A single tied agent (possibly an appointed representative) of one product provider.
- A multi tied agent of a limited range of product providers.
- An IFA with access to the whole market (or a whole segment of it).

A single tied agent can only advise on the products of the provider to which it is tied. A multi tied agent can only advise on the products of the range of providers to which it is tied.

An IFA must have access to the whole market, or a whole segment of it, and must regularly analyse the market to ensure its advice remains suitable. However, an IFA can use a panel of product providers, provided this is reviewed regularly. An IFA must offer customers the option of paying fees, rather than taking commission. An IFA could be independent for this purpose, even if it is not for mortgage business, as long as this is clear to the customer.

Within the three basic types of intermediary there is an almost infinite variety of business models.

Some tied agents are appointed representatives of a product provider, some are individually authorised firms within the same group as a product provider and some are individually authorised businesses which are not in the same group of companies as the product provider.

Some multi-tied agents are tied to one producer for each product type they deal in, eg life office A for term assurance and whole life policies, office B for single premium bonds, unit trust managers C for unit trusts and life office D for pensions. Other multi tied agents could be tied to more than one producer for a particular product type.

There are also intermediaries who have access to the whole market, or a whole segment of the market, but cannot call themselves IFAs because they do not offer clients a fee option.

1.13 Status disclosure

These rules were introduced on the back of the depolarisation rules and came into force for all firms on 14 January 2005. On first contact with a private customer where advice and arrangements in packaged products are contemplated a firm must provide an Initial Disclosure Document (IDD) and a fees and commission statement (the Menu). These documents give basic information about the firm's status, services provided and how they will be paid for. The format is set by the FSA and must incorporate their key facts logo.

These two documents do not have to be given:

- If one has already been given to the customer and is still valid.
- Where the initial contact is by telephone.
- For execution-only transactions in non-life packaged products.
- By an insurer for a customer which it is not advising on investments.
- By a discretionary investment manager unless life policies are involved.
- By a non-discretionary investment manager acting under a fee based whole market agreement that permits it to recommend securities as well as packaged products.

The IDD states:

- That the firm is regulated by the FSA.
- The firm's status as a single tied agent, multi tied agent or IFA.
- What services are provided.
- That details of how the firm is paid will be given in the Menu.
- Details of loans and ownership.
- How to complain.
- Coverage by the FSCS.

The Menu must explain whether the firm charges a fee, or operates on a commission basis or offers a choice of these. If commission is possibly payable there must be details of the firm's maximum commission rates and the FSA provided market average commission.

Where a fee is to be charged the customer's agreement must be obtained to the fee basis before the firm starts to act. Any commission must be transferred to the customer by reducing the fee, increasing the investment or direct payment to the customer. However the firm can still agree with the customer (in writing) that it will retain any trail or renewal commission if it is small relative to the overall fees, and it would be disproportionate for the firm to have to account for it to the customer. The firm must keep its Menu up to date and keep records for six years.

Firms which operate with a range of packaged products must produce a record of the range for distribution to private customers on request.

Where the initial contact with the customer is by telephone, the IDD and Menu do not need to be given, but the equivalent information must be provided on the telephone and later confirmed in writing.

1.14 Responsibilities of regulated firms

All regulated firms are responsible to make sure that they are authorised and have permission for all the regulated activities they undertake. Permission must be obtained for any new regulated activities.

Regulated firms are responsible for the conduct of all their employees, agents and ARs. The firm must ensure that all those for whom it is responsible comply with all the requirements of the FSMA and rules made under it. A regulated firm must not use the services of an individual prohibited by the FSA.

A product provider is not responsible for the acts or omissions of an intermediary.

An authorised firm is responsible for advice given by its representatives. If such advice is in breach of the Act or the FSA rules, the authorised firm is liable to compensate the client for any loss sustained as a result of the advice. However the mere fact that an investment has lost value does not give rise to any duty to compensate as this may be due to factors unconnected with the quality of the advice eg a stock market crash.

An authorised firm must ensure that all its individuals carrying out controlled functions are approved by the FSA. However in order to cover for illness and holidays an individual can perform significant influence functions on a temporary basis for up to 12 weeks in a year without approval.

All authorised firms thus have a Compliance Officer, assisted by a Compliance Department to ensure that all the myriad rules are complied with.

1.15 Offences

There are a number of offences under the FSMA for which the FSA can institute prosecutions. These include:

- Carrying on a regulated activity without authorisation or exemption.

- Describing oneself as authorised or exempt if this is not true.
- Promoting an investment unless you are authorised, or the promotion is approved by an authorised person.
- Breaching a prohibition order.
- Failure to co-operate with a FSA investigation or falsifying, concealing or destroying documents in connection with a FSA investigation.
- Failure to inform FSA of a change of control of an authorised firm.
- Giving materially false or misleading information to the FSA.

It is also an offence under s397 to:

- Make a statement, promise or forecast known to be misleading, false or deceptive in a material particular;
- Dishonestly conceal any material facts; or
- Recklessly make (dishonestly or otherwise) a statement, promise or forecast which is misleading, false or deceptive in a material particular,

if this is for the purpose of inducing another person to enter into, or offer to enter into, or refrain from entering into a regulated investment or to exercise, or refrain from exercising rights under a regulated investment.

Any offence by a company is also an offence by an officer of the company if it was done with his/her consent or connivance or is attributable to his/her neglect.

1.16 The FSA Principles of Business

The FSA Principles are a general statement of the fundamental obligations of all authorised firms. The Principles only apply to deposit taking in the prudential field, not in the conduct of business.

The principles are:

1. **Integrity** A firm must conduct its business with integrity.
2. **Skill, care** and **diligence** A firm must conduct its business with due skill, care and diligence.
3. **Management** and **control** A firm must take reasonable care to organise and control its affairs responsibly and effectively, with adequate risk management systems.
4. **Financial prudence** A firm must maintain adequate financial resources.

5. **Market conduct** A firm must observe proper standards of market conduct.

6. **Customers' interests** A firm must pay due regard to the interests of its customers and treat them fairly.

7. **Communications with clients** A firm must pay due regard to the information needs of its clients, and communicate information to them in a way which is clear, fair and not misleading.

8. **Conflicts of interest** A firm must manage conflicts of interest fairly, both between itself and its customers and between a customer and another client.

9. **Customer's relationship of trust** A firm must take reasonable care to ensure the suitability of its advice and discretionary decisions for any customer who is entitled to rely on its judgment.

10. **Clients' assets** A firm must arrange adequate protection for clients' assets when it is responsible for them.

11. **Relations with regulators** A firm must deal with its regulators in an open and co-operative way, and must disclose to FSA appropriately anything relating to the firm of which the FSA would reasonably expect notice.

1.16.1 Treating customers fairly

The FSA has talked a lot recently about the need for all authorised firms to treat their customers fairly. It regards this as fundamental to all aspects of the way in which business is done. Therefore firms not only have to ensure that all the myriad of detailed rules is complied with, but that the overall effect of their procedures results in clients being treated fairly. The FSA believes that this will reduce complaints and regulatory intervention.

While no one could argue with this as a general principle, it must be said that treating customers fairly is a pretty nebulous concept. What one person may regard as fair, another may not. Shareholders of an insurance company might not regard it as fair for the company to pay claims that are not really due just because the policyholder might otherwise complain. Life offices in particular have a duty to be fair to all classes of policyholder and should not favour one class to the detriment of another, eg with-profit policyholders. There is also a suspicion that the FSA might use the principle as a way of criticising firms whose actions they do not like, but where no law or rule or guidance has been broken. It is also possible that large doses of hindsight could be used to criticise advice that turned out badly through no fault of the adviser (eg stock market crashes).

1.17 The FSA Principles for Approved Persons

The FSA also has Principles for Approved Persons, ie those subject to individual registration (see earlier). The Statements of Principles are:

1. An approved person must act with integrity in carrying out his controlled function.

2. An approved person must act with due skill, care and diligence in carrying out his controlled function.

3. An approved person must observe proper standards of market conduct in carrying out his controlled function.

4. An approved person must deal with the FSA and with other regulators in an open and co-operative way and must disclose appropriately any information of which the FSA would reasonably expect notice.

5. An approved person performing a significant influence function must take reasonable steps to ensure that the business of the firm for which he is responsible in his controlled function is organised so that it can be controlled effectively.

6. An approved person performing a significant influence function must exercise due skill, care and diligence in managing the business for which he is responsible in his controlled function.

7. An approved person performing a significant influence function must take reasonable steps to ensure that the business of the firm for which he is responsible in his controlled function complies with the regulatory requirements on that business.

2 Prudential Regulation

The prudential regulation of insurance companies used to be carried out by the Treasury under the Insurance Companies Act 1982. However that changed with the full implementation of the Financial Services and Markets Act 2000 on 30 November 2001. The FSA is now the prudential regulator of insurance companies under its Prudential Sourcebook for Insurers. The Insurance Companies Act and its attendant regulations have been repealed.

Any insurer wishing to commence business in the UK will have to obtain authorisation from the FSA. Authorisation is also necessary for an existing insurer wishing to transact a new class of business. The FSA can refuse authorisation if it believes a director, controller or manager is not a fit and proper person for that purpose or the insurer does not have sufficient financial resources. It is a criminal offence to carry on insurance business without being authorised by the FSA.

However, an insurance company with its head office in an EEA state other than the UK is automatically authorised if it is so authorised in its home state. The home state will supervise all that company's business in the EEA. No member state can prohibit a person from having an insurance contract with a company authorised anywhere in the EEA. Member states cannot require prior approval of policy conditions or premium rates. Assets relating to EEA business can be located in any EEA state.

The Prudential Sourcebook contains many provisions on the following:

- Accounts.
- Balance sheets.
- Actuarial investigations.
- Audits.
- Separation of assets attributable to long-term business ie life, annuity and pensions.
- Application of assets.
- Allocations of surplus.
- Transactions with connected persons.
- Solvency margins.
- What types of property can be used for unit-linked policies.

Insurers have to supply large volumes of information regularly to the FSA to show they are complying with all these rules.

2.1 Supervisory powers

The FSA has wide-ranging powers of control and intervention. These powers are exercisable on any of the following grounds:

- If it considers it desirable to protect policyholders against the risk that the insurer might be unable to meet its liabilities or to fulfil the reasonable expectations of policyholders.
- If it appears that the insurer has broken a rule (eg an accounting regulation).
- If it appears that misleading or inaccurate information has been supplied.
- If it is not satisfied with the reinsurance arrangements of the insurer.
- If it believes that a director, controller or manager is not a fit and proper person.

The powers that can be used include the following:

- To restrict new business of a specified description.
- To make requirements as to prohibited investments or realisation of existing investments.

- To place assets in the control of an approved trustee.
- To limit premium income for specified types of business.
- To require an actuarial investigation and report.
- To obtain information and production of documents.
- To suspend or terminate authorisation.

These powers, together with the accounting and valuation rules, enable the FSA to exercise its overall supervisory functions. The powers cannot in themselves stop an insurer from running into difficulties but they give the FSA the ability to monitor the situation and step in before failure occurs.

To strengthen this control, notice must be given to the FSA of the appointment of a managing director or chief executive, or of a change in the person controlling an insurer.

3 The Conduct of Business Rules

The detailed rules for individuals working in regulated businesses are not in the FSMA at all. They are in the various rules made by the FSA. Most of those affecting the day to day work of advisers are in the Conduct of Business Rules (COB).

3.1 The purpose of the Conduct of Business Rules

The purpose of the Conduct of Business rules is to set out the detailed rules for how staff and representatives of regulated businesses deal with customers.

The COB rules basically apply to all regulated businesses, although many individual rules only affect specific regulated activities. Some rules cover how regulated firms carry on unregulated activities. The COB rules mainly address investments that were previously regulated under the Financial Services Act 1986 eg most long-term insurance and unit trusts. For this reason they have limited application to deposit taking, pure protection life insurance and general insurance. There are separate rules for the last two – see section 10.

Many of the COB rules distinguish between various types of customer as follows:

3.1.1 Private customer

A private customer is a client who is not a market counterparty or an intermediate customer.

3.1.2 Intermediate customer

An intermediate customer is a client who is not a market counterparty, but is:

- A local or public authority.

- A company listed on a recognised stock exchange.
- A company which has share capital or net assets of at least £5 million.
- A partnership which has net assets of at least £5 million.
- A trustee of a trust (other than a pension trust) which has assets of at least £10 million.
- A trustee of a pension trust with a least 50 members and assets of at least £10 million.

3.1.3 Market counterparty

A market counterparty is a client who is:

- A government of a country.
- A central bank of a country.
- Various other state or supranational bodies.
- Another authorised firm.

Private customers get the greatest protection by the rules, followed by intermediate customers, then market counterparties.

Most of the COB rules only apply to dealings with private and intermediate customers. Contravention of a rule is not an offence and does not make legally void any resulting transactions. However it can result in an authorised person being liable to any private person who suffers a loss due to the rule breach. For this purpose a private person is an individual or a corporate body (unless it suffers the loss in the course of any kind of business), but not a government, local authority or international organisation.

3.2 Records

The standard periods of record keeping under the COB rules are:

- Indefinitely for pension transfers, pension opt-outs and free standing additional voluntary contributions (FSAVCs).
- Six years for life policies and pension contracts.
- Three years in other cases.

3.3 The COB rules

For this purpose investment business includes life and pension policies, shares, gilts and unit trusts, but not reassurance or pure protection policies. The most important rules are as follows.

3.3.1 Clear communication

When a firm communicates information to a customer it must take reasonable steps to communicate in a way which is clear, fair and not misleading, having regard to the customers' knowledge of the business. The FSA's key facts logo can only be used where required by the rules.

3.3.2 Inducements

A firm must take reasonable steps to ensure it does not offer, give, solicit or accept an inducement or place business in any way likely to conflict to a material extent with any duty owed to customers. For packaged products (life and pension policies, OEICs and unit trusts) volume overrides of commission are forbidden. Commission can only be paid to the firm responsible for the sale unless:

- The firm responsible for the sale has passed on its right to the commission to the recipient, or
- Another firm has given advice on investments to the same customer after the sale, or
- It relates to the sale of a packaged product by a direct offer advertisement to a customer of the firm.

A product provider can only invest in an intermediary if it is on commercial arm's length terms, unless the intermediary is in the same corporate group as the provider.

3.3.3 Indirect benefits

The FSA has many other rules on commission, designed to prevent multi tied agents and independent intermediaries being swayed in their recommendations by incentives other than straight monetary commission. The rules thus seek to ban many indirect benefits and 'under-the-table' payments and services.

Providers can supply goods and services, either free or for a charge, only in accordance with the following rules.

Product literature can be supplied provided:

- It does not contain the name of the intermediary, or
- The name of the intermediary is printed less prominently than the provider's on generally available literature.

Life office employees cannot do the selling for intermediaries. A provider can assist an intermediary to promote its products so that the quality of its service to customers is enhanced.

A provider can pay reasonable travelling and accommodation costs of an intermediary visiting an office of theirs in the UK. It can also supply reply paid envelopes for communicating with it, plus a free phone link if these are available to intermediaries generally.

A provider can give an intermediary quotations, projections, training and advice on its own products but cannot give more general services such as a financial or tax planning service. An intermediary can also be given access to data processing facilities specifically related to the provider's products, and software to produce its quotations and give details of its products. Provision of IT hardware is only allowed where it forms part of a software project and cannot be given as a free standing gift.

An intermediary can be given gifts, hospitality and promotional competition prizes of a reasonable value. A provider's staff can take part in seminars given by intermediaries and can contribute to the costs of the seminar if it is for a genuine business purpose and the contribution is reasonable and proportionate. Providers can hold seminars or conferences for intermediaries for *bona fide* business purposes (such as a new product launch) but must not pay travel or overnight expenses.

A provider can supply written technical information which does not relate to its own products, provided it is available to intermediaries generally and clearly states that it is produced by the provider. Training facilities can be supplied with or without charge, if the provider makes them generally available for intermediaries. In addition, the provider can pay or contribute to any reasonable travelling or accommodation expenses of the intermediary for this training. A provider can pay a reasonable fee to an intermediary for taking part in market research.

Records must be kept of benefits given to intermediaries for six years.

3.3.4 Exclusion of liability

A firm must not seek to exclude or restrict any duty or liability it may have to a customer under the regulatory system. This is to prevent firms trying to 'contract out' of the rules.

3.4 Financial promotions

The rules apply to all financial promotions by any means except for deposits, general insurance, pure protection life insurance and reinsurance. The rules are aimed at advertisements and general promotions and do not apply to:

- Communications to one recipient only.
- Specific products for a specific recipient.

- Personal quotations or illustrations.
- A promotion containing only:
  - the name of the firm,
  - the name of the investment,
  - a contact point,
  - a logo,
  - a brief factual description of the firm's activities, fees and products,
  - the price or yields of investments and charges.

Real time financial promotions are those done in the course of a personal visit, telephone conversation or other interactive dialogue. Non-real time financial promotions are all others, such as advertisements.

3.4.1 Approval

Before doing a non-real time financial promotion a firm must get an individual with the appropriate expertise to check it meets the rules. Thus all advertisements will be checked probably by someone in the compliance department. Any promotions which cease to be compliant must be withdrawn.

3.4.2 Records

A firm must keep a record of all its non-real time financial promotions for the standard periods. The record must include a copy of the item and the name of the individual who checked it.

3.4.3 Content

A non-real time financial promotion must contain the name of the firm and its address or contact point, and whether it is single tied, multi tied or independent.

A firm must take reasonable steps to ensure that a non-real time financial promotion is clear, fair and not misleading. Those containing comparisons must compare investments for the same need or purpose. Comparisons must be objective, material, relevant and verifiable. There must be no denigration of a competitor.

The promotional purpose must not be disguised or misrepresented. Any statements of opinion must be honestly held and given with the consent of the person concerned. There must be no false indications of a firm's independence, resources and scale of activities or of the scarcity of an investment or service.

There must be no reference to approval by the FSA or any government body unless it has been obtained in writing.

Except for life policies or deposits an investment must not be described as guaranteed unless there is a contract with a third party to meet a claim in full.
A specific non-real time financial promotion must include a fair and adequate description of the nature of the investment or service, the commitment required and the risks involved.

A specific non-real time financial promotion that mentions past performance must state in the main text unambiguously and without reservation that past performance should not be seen as an indication of future performance. The past performance data must be relevant and for a sufficient period to provide a fair and balanced indication of the performance. Any past performance information should make clear the period of time to which it relates. The information should normally be based on the actual performance of the fund for the entire period.

Where actual past performance does not exist, hypothetical past performance can only be used if the result is clear, fair and not misleading. For past performance of a packaged product there must be information about the performance for the previous five years. Past performance must not be shown so as to constitute a projection of possible future values.

A provider firm must not do a specific non-real time financial promotion for a packaged product unless it states that it can only advise on the products of its marketing group (and any adopted packaged products).

3.5 Real time financial promotions

A firm must take reasonable steps to ensure that an individual who makes a real time financial promotion on its behalf:

- Does so in a way which is clear, fair and not misleading.
- Does not make any untrue claims.
- Makes clear the purpose of the promotion at the start and identifies themself and their firm.
- If the communication was not previously agreed with the recipient, check that the recipient wishes them to proceed and stops if not.
- Gives the recipient a contact point.
- Does not communicate at an unsocial hour, or on an unlisted telephone number without permission.

3.6 Direct offer financial promotions

Direct offer financial promotions must not relate to broker funds. They must not relate to unregulated collective investment schemes, derivatives or warrants unless the firm has evidence that it is suitable for the recipient. They must contain sufficient information to enable a person to make an informed assessment of the investment or service. The following information must be given:

- That the firm is regulated or authorised by the FSA.
- That if there is any doubt about the suitability of the investment the firm should be contacted for advice (or an IFA if the firm does not offer advice).
- The full name and address of the person offering the investment and, if different, the full name and address of the firm communicating or approving the promotion.
- If the promoter can't hold the client money the name of the person to whom payment should be made.
- Details of any charges and expenses.
- Details of any commission or remuneration payable by the firm to another person.

A promotion of a packaged product must contain the information required by the key features rules (see later). If investments can fluctuate in value this must be clearly stated. If the investment is a life policy the promotion must state which benefits are fixed and which are not.

The promotion must contain a summary of the taxation of the investment and the tax consequences for investors generally. There must be a warning that tax levels and reliefs can change. Any assumed rates of tax must be given. Statements about tax relief must distinguish between reliefs which apply directly to investors and anyone else, and that the reliefs are those which currently apply and their value depends on the circumstances of the investor. Where words such as tax-free are used it must be made clear that this describes the benefits when paid to the investor, and there must be an equally prominent statement that it is paid out of a fund which has already paid income tax, corporation tax or capital gains tax if this is the case. If cancellation rights apply these must be explained.

3.7 Unsolicited real time financial promotions

Unsolicited real time promotions are often termed 'cold calling'. This must not be done unless the recipient has an established customer relationship with the firm such that he envisages this, or the promotion relates to a generally marketable packaged product which is not a higher volatility fund (or a life policy linked to one).

3.8 Accepting customers

Before doing business with a client a firm must take reasonable steps to establish whether the client is a private customer, intermediate customer or a market counterparty. A firm can treat an expert customer as an intermediate customer if the client is warned of the protection lost, has had time to consider it and gives his written permission. Similarly some large intermediate customers can be treated as market counterparties. Records of classification must be kept for the standard periods.

3.9 Terms of business

A firm must provide a private customer with its terms of business before conducting the business, or within five business days for an oral offer to enter into an ISA or a stakeholder pension scheme. For an intermediate customer the terms of business must be provided within a reasonable period of the start of conducting business.

Terms of business or client agreements are not required for:

- Execution only transactions.
- Direct offer financial promotions.
- Life offices selling life and pension policies.
- Collective investment scheme operators selling units in their scheme.

Terms of business documents and client agreements must set out in adequate detail the basis for conducting the business such as:

- Commencement.
- Regulation by the FSA.
- Investment objectives.
- Restrictions.
- Services provided.
- Payment.
- Status.
- The giving of instructions.
- Accounting.
- Withdrawal rights.
- Conflicts of interest.
- Risk warnings.
- Complaints.
- Compensation.
- Termination.

Records of terms of business provided for customers must be kept for the standard periods.

3.10 Best advice

The adviser must find out and record sufficient personal and financial information about the client as to enable best advice to be given. The collection of relevant information is a process often called fact finding. Relevant information would include:

- Marital status.
- Dependants.
- Income.
- Existing insurance, investments and pensions.
- Needs.
- Priorities.
- Attitude to risk.
- Taxation situation.

Life offices and intermediaries have fact find forms for their salesmen to complete to show that the relevant facts were obtained at the time of the sale. These forms can then be retained as evidence to defend any allegation of bad selling. The investor is not required to sign the form although this is obviously helpful. Having elicited all the relevant facts the company representative or single tied agent must recommend the most suitable contract for the client's needs and circumstances from his office's range. A multi tied agent must recommend the most suitable contract from those providers to which it is tied. An IFA must recommend the most suitable contract from all those available on the market. The contract must be suitable for the client and if no contract is suitable no sale should be made. The client must be able to afford the recommended product, which is particularly relevant to future increases of premiums on low-start contracts.

The fact find should contain details of all existing contracts and if any of them are to be cancelled or replaced a full justification must be given. The fact find must be kept for the standard periods. Where a firm arranges a pension opt-out or pension transfer from an occupational pension scheme for a private customer it must keep a clear record, even if no advice was given, indefinitely. Poor completion of fact finds has been a major cause of problems since the rules were originally introduced in 1988 and the value to advisors and clients of a well completed fact find cannot be over emphasised. A fact find can either be on paper or stored electronically, but if it is the latter, it should be capable of being reproduced on paper.

There is a set of ten decision trees in the FSA rules for decision making for pensions business. A copy of the decision trees must accompany any written information on stakeholder pensions given to a private investor, unless the advisor had already recommended a stakeholder pension. The decision trees must be incorporated in or with key features documents.

3.11 Suitability letter

A firm is required to provide a private customer with a suitability letter, if following a personal recommendation the customer:

- Buys, sells, surrenders, converts, cancels or suspends premiums or contributions on a life policy or pension contract; or
- Elects to make income withdrawals on a pension contract; or
- Buys or sells a unit trust or OEIC holding; or
- Enters into a pension transfer or opt-out from an occupational pension scheme.

The letter must explain why the transaction is suitable for the customer, having regard to his circumstances and contain a summary of the main consequences and any possible disadvantages of the transaction. For a personal pension or an FSAVC it should explain why it is considered at least as suitable as a stakeholder pension. For an FSAVC it must also explain why it is at least as suitable as an AVC.

The letter must be sent no later than the cancellation notice, or as soon as possible after the transaction if no cancellation notice is required.

The letter is not required for friendly society life policies with premiums not exceeding £50 pa or £1 per week. It is also not required for increases to regular premium contracts and single premium top-ups of single premium contracts.

There are specific detailed rules for broker funds, pension transfers and opt-outs, and group personal pensions.

3.12 Charges and commission

A firm must ensure its charges to a private customer are not excessive, compared to the prevailing level in the market. Before doing business the firm must disclose in writing to a private customer the basis of its charges and the nature or amount of any other income receivable by it (or its associate) due to that business.

Before selling a packaged product to a private customer a firm must disclose any remuneration payable by it to its employees or agents, and any remuneration or commission received by it. This is often called commission disclosure.

For remuneration of employees and agents a firm must put a proper value on any benefits or services provided as well as cash. These benefits include cars, loans, pensions and any support services that could not be provided for an IFA. The remuneration disclosed for a provider's representative could thus be much greater than the actual cash commission paid.

4 Product Disclosure

These rules regulate the information given to the client to enable him to be aware of all the details of the contract.

4.1 Key features

Every product provider must produce a key features document for each of its packaged products. This could be hard copy or in electronic format. It must be produced to the same standard as its marketing material. The key features must be given to every private customer before the application form is completed, although a product provider is not responsible for this for sales made by intermediaries. This rule applies for new sales and variations of existing post 1 January 1995 life policies where the premium is increasing by more than 25%. For a collective investment scheme sold without a written application the key features must be sent within five business days of the date of the sale.

There are special rules for occupational pension schemes, self invested personal pensions, pension income withdrawals, cash ISAs, traded life policies and stakeholder pensions.

4.2 Contents of key features

The key features document must include all the details required by the rules which include:

- The nature of the investment.
- The risk factors.
- A projection of future benefits.
- The principal terms of the investment.
- Projected surrender values for life policies or cash-in values for collective investment schemes.
- An explanation of charges and their effect in reducing the yield.
- Commission payable to an intermediary.
- Remuneration payable to a provider's representative.
- The information required by the Third Life Directive.

The Third Life Directive required information includes:

- Name of life office.
- The address of the head office or branch concerned.
- Definition of each benefit and option.
- Policy term.
- Means of termination.
- Means of payment of premiums and duration.
- Means of calculation and distribution of bonuses.
- Indication of surrender and paid-up values and whether they are guaranteed.
- Premiums.
- Unit-linking details.
- Cancellation rights.
- Tax arrangements.
- Complaints arrangements.
- Law applicable.

4.3 Post sale confirmation

Where a private customer buys a life or pension contract (or increases an existing post 1 January 1995 one by more than 25%) the life office must send him a post sale confirmation. This must be sent no later than the cancellation notice, or as soon as reasonably practicable after the contract is effected if there is no cancellation notice. It is not required for policies purchased by the trustees of an occupational or stakeholder pension scheme. The post sale confirmation repeats a lot of the information already given in the key features.

4.4 Projections

Whenever a firm produces a projection of future benefits the projections rules apply. This could be in an advertisement, letter, key features document or post sale confirmation.

The rules impose a common calculation basis using FSA's assumed rates of interest and the provider's own charges. The FSA assumed rates are currently 4%, 6% and 8% for life policies and collective investment schemes, and 5%, 7% and 9% for tax-exempt pension, ISA, PEP and friendly society business.

There are various prescribed wordings to accompany projections to explain that the figures are only examples and are not guaranteed.

Generic projections can be given at a single rate in certain circumstances, eg in comparative tables and to estimate the likely cost of a proposed transaction. The single rate projection cannot relate to an existing contract and cannot exceed the higher FSA rate for the class of business concerned. It must be stated that the figures are only illustrations and that an assessment of the client's needs will be confirmed before a recommendation can be made.

4.5 The cancellation notice

Cancellation notices are required by the FSA Conduct of Business Rules. A cancellation notice must be issued for all long-term insurance policies except for:

- Life policies for six months or less.
- Traded life policies.
- Policies issued to corporate bodies (other than pension scheme trustees).
- Pure protection contracts effected by the trustees of an occupational pension scheme, an employer or a partnership to secure benefits for employees or the partners in the partnership.
- Pension fund management policies.
- Defined benefit occupational pension schemes or AVCs associated with them.
- Pension policies where all or part of the premium is all or part of a transfer payment from another pension scheme.
- Buy-out policies effected by the trustees of an occupational pension scheme.
- Pension annuities starting within one year and a day.
- Without-profit deferred annuities purchased by the trustees of an occupational pension scheme, or by an employer.
- Personal pensions or pension annuities which are all or part of redress on a pension mis-selling review case.
- A single premium contribution to an occupational pension scheme with a pooled fund.

- A purchase made to insure and secure members' pension benefits under a money purchase occupational scheme or stakeholder pension scheme (unless it is the master, first or only policy).
- Policies where the customer, at the time he signs the application, is habitually resident in an EEA state other than the UK, or outside the EEA and is not present in the UK.

Where a policy is varied there must be a cancellation notice if the premium increases by more than 25% (except for pre-selected options).

The notice must be sent by post or electronically to the policyholder (not via an intermediary) in the 14 days after the conclusion of the contract. The period is eight days for single premium policies. For industrial policies the notice can be given to the policyholder as opposed to being sent by post. Where the policyholder is a trustee reasonably believed by the life office to be expected to act on the instructions of a beneficiary, the notice must be sent to the beneficiary as well and the beneficiary should be told that he should give timely instructions to the trustees if he wishes to cancel. The notice is not invalid if sent out after the time limit, but the office cannot deduct any shortfall on cancellation (see later). If a life office fails to send out a notice, the policy can be cancelled by the policyholder at any time within the first two years.

The notice must be clear, prominent, timely and comprehensive. It must set out full details of the following:

- The right to cancel and when it begins and ends.
- The steps the investor must take to cancel the contract.
- The consequences of cancellation.
- Any shortfall costs the investor may have to bear.
- That the investor is entitled to key features.

The notice may include a cancellation form for the investor to use if he wants to cancel.

For pensions open market option cases there is a cancellation substitute notice procedure giving a 30-day period of reflection before the pension annuity is processed. It includes key features and an explanation of the open market option and states that if the proposer wishes to go ahead, he should send in the proposal and, if not, he should contact the adviser or the original pension provider. There is a similar procedure for pension transfers whereby the transfer value is not taken out of the original scheme for at least 30 days.

The purpose of the notice is to draw the policyholder's attention to the fact that he has a right to change his mind and withdraw from the contract. It asks him to consider the policy details and gives a name and address where further information about the policy can be obtained. This will normally be the branch or head office of the insurer.

The notice does not give individual policy details as these are given in the key features and post sale confirmation (see sections 4.2 and 4.3). The key features should include a summary of the cancellation rights.

4.5.1 Cooling-off period

The policyholder has a 'cooling-off' period of 30 days from when he receives the cancellation notice. If a cancellation notice is not issued within this period, the policyholder can cool off at any time in the first two years.

During the cooling-off period the policyholder can exercise the right to cancel the policy by signing the cancellation form, which is a 'tear-off' slip at the end of the cancellation notice, and sending it to the life office. Alternatively, the policyholder can write a letter to the same effect. Notice of cancellation dates from when it is served on the life office or its appointed representative or, if put in the post, from the moment of posting. Thus, although the notice of cancellation might reach the office after the expiry of the cooling-off period, as long as it was posted during the period it would still be valid.

If the policyholder exercises his cancellation rights he is entitled to a full refund of any sum paid to the life office or its agent in connection with the policy. On single premium unit-linked contracts, the life office is entitled to deduct any shortfall produced by a drop in the price of units since allocation. This is to prevent investors playing the market by keeping the investment if the price goes up during the cooling-off period but getting a full refund if it goes down. The shortfall provisions do not apply if the cancellation notice is sent after the eight-day period or if the shortfall provisions are not prominently mentioned in the cancellation notice.

For a pension annuity, a cancellation is not valid if done after the death of the annuitant. Cancellation by one joint policyholder is valid as a cancellation by all.

4.6 Pure protection life policies

The FSA rules on selling and marketing do not apply to pure protection policies, but providers of pure protection life policies must send the customer before entering into the contract the information required by the Third Life Directive – see earlier. A record of this must be kept for six years.

Pure protection policies are long-term insurance contracts, other than reinsurance, where:

- The benefits are payable only on death or incapacity due to injury, sickness or infirmity.

- The contract provides that benefits are payable on death only within ten years, or where death occurs before an age not exceeding 70.
- The contract has no surrender value, or the surrender value does not exceed the single premium.
- There are no conversion or extension options which might cause it to fail any of the previous tests.

Thus it mainly applies to term assurance, income protection insurance and critical illness cover. These contracts are covered by the general insurance COB rules – see section 10.

4.7 Long-term care insurance (LTCI)

Originally only LTCI which had an investment element was fully within the FSA COB rules. All LTCI products became subject to full FSA regulation as regards sales and marketing from 31 October 2004. All advisers have to pass an appropriate LTCI exam within two years. Key features documents are required and for LTCI products based on single premium bonds, an annual performance statement must be sent to the policyholder. Claims must be handled promptly (normally within five business days) and fairly and the insurer must give the policyholder reasonable guidance to help them make a claim. An insurer must not unreasonably reject a claim, nor refuse a claim due to non-disclosure of a material fact which the policyholder could not reasonably be expected to have disclosed. Claims should normally be paid within five business days of being agreed.

4.8 With-profit business

Every life office doing with-profit business must have a Principles and Practices of Financial Management (PPFM) document setting out how they manage their with-profit business. A customer friendly PPFM must be sent to all existing with-profit policyholders with their annual statements. PPFMs must also be sent to existing policyholders where there is any change and must be given to new policyholders at the point of sale. There is also a whole raft of FSA rules which are extremely complex and govern how the office runs its with-profit business.

4.9 E-commerce

If a life office does business online, or even advertises online, it is subject to the FSA E-Commerce Directive Rules. The main provisions are as follows:

- Certain minimum information must be easily, directly and permanently accessible – name, geographic address, e-mail address and FSA registered number.
- There must be clear information as to the services provided.
- Customers must be clearly told how to place an order.

- Customers must have a means of identifying and correcting input errors prior to making an order.
- Orders must be acknowledged without delay, although they do not have to be accepted.

All the normal COB rules also apply.

In a case involving non-disclosure in an online proposal the Financial Ombudsman has ruled that the proposer should be given a complete printed copy of the proposal before being asked to sign – thus destroying much of the point of doing online business.

4.10 Financial Services (Distance Marketing) Regulations 2004

The Financial Services (Distance Marketing) Regulations 2004 resulted from the EU Distance Marketing Directive and came into force on 31 October 2004. They set common minimum standards for information which must be given to consumers of financial services prior to a distance contract becoming binding on a consumer. They apply when a supplier makes exclusive use of one or more means of distance communication – telephone, fax, internet or mail. So the regulations will not apply where face to face advice is given, whether this is by the product provider or an intermediary. Financial services for these purposes includes banking, credit, insurance, personal pensions and investments but not occupational pensions.

The product provider must, in good time prior to the consumer being bound, provide specified information in a clear and a comprehensible manner, appropriate to the means of distance communication. Items which must be disclosed include the following:

- Identity, business and address of the supplier.
- Authorising body.
- Total price to be paid for the services plus any specific costs for distance communication.
- Cancellation rights.
- Law applicable.
- Complaints and compensation arrangements.

This information must be provided on paper or in another durable medium.

There is a cancellation period of 30 days for life and pension contracts and 14 days for other contracts. However, some contracts have no cancellation period, for example those where the price depends on fluctuations in the financial market which are outside the supplier's control, eg unit trusts. If the contract is cancelled the supplier must refund any sums received from the consumer, less a proportionate charge for any services already supplied.

5 The Training and Competence Rules

The training and competence rules are designed to ensure that firms' employees are (and remain) competent for the work they do, and are properly supervised. Competence must be regularly reviewed and the level of competence must be appropriate to the business.

When recruiting individuals to deal with private customers the firm must take into account the knowledge and skills of the individual and his role and obtain sufficient information about his previous activities and training. This would include any appropriate examinations.

If an employee deals with private customers the firm must determine the training needs and organise training to meet those needs. Training must take account of changes in the market, products, legislation and regulation.

An employee must not engage in or oversee an activity unless he has been assessed as competent in that activity or is under supervision. An employee must not deal with private customers (even under supervision) until he has passed the regulatory module of an appropriate examination and has an adequate level of knowledge and skills. For various different specialised activities such as broker funds and pension transfers there are specific appropriate examinations which must be passed first. An employee must not be assessed as competent unless he has passed each module of the appropriate examination within the specified time scale. An employee who doesn't pass within the time limit must cease to engage in that activity.

A firm must ensure that an employee assessed as competent maintains that competence. Supervisors of employees advising private customers on packaged products must also pass an appropriate approved examination and have the knowledge and skills to act as a supervisor.

Records must be kept of training for at least three years from the cessation of the employee's appointment, or indefinitely for pension transfer specialists. For these purposes employees include self-employed representatives, appointed representatives and their employees.

There is a list of appropriate examinations for various different activities, administered by the Financial Services Skills Council.

6 Rules Specific to Intermediaries

6.1 Client money rules

These rules apply to firms which receive or hold money from or on behalf of a client. They do not apply to banks, building societies or life offices.

A firm must hold client money separate from its own money in a client bank account. The money must normally be paid into the client bank account within one business day of receipt. The client bank account must be so designated and be with an approved bank. This ensures that the money in the account is effectively held on trust for the clients and is thus not available to the creditors of the firm if it becomes insolvent.

Interest on client money belongs to the client unless agreed otherwise. Client money reconciliations must be done at least every 25 business days and discrepancies corrected as soon as possible.

Many intermediaries do not have authority to handle client money and so must ensure that all cheques or other payments for investments arranged are payable direct to the product provider. They do not need client money accounts.

6.2 Financial requirements

Because FSA is concerned with the solvency of the intermediaries it regulates there are a host of financial requirements which vary according to the type and volume of business done. Full accounting records must be kept to disclose at any time the financial position of the firm, in particular all money received and expended and all assets and liabilities. Annual financial statements have to be submitted to FSA, details of which vary according to the type and scale of business. The FSA can require more regular financial statements if they so decide. Auditors' reports are also required and these requirements also vary according to the type and scale of business.

6.3 Professional indemnity insurance

Professional indemnity insurance is a requirement for all intermediaries, except those with a stock market capitalisation of over £50 million or those which are subsidiaries of banks, building societies, insurance companies or friendly societies who use their parent's name, or whose liabilities have been guaranteed by the parent company. The policy must comply with the minimum requirements, although it does not specify policy wordings. Cover is required for the negligence of the member, its staff and appointed representatives, to certain specified limits. Cover must apply retrospectively to claims arising from work carried out in the past. It must also include the Ombudsman's awards and the dishonesty of employees, appointed representatives and principals of appointed representatives firms. Cover can exceed the FSA requirements if the firm so desires. The insurer must be authorised to transact professional indemnity insurance in the UK.

From 15 January 2005 the European Insurance Mediation Directive has required all intermediaries to have at least €2.5 million cover. This prevents the FSA granting waivers.

6.4 Networks

A number of IFAs are members of networks. The network itself is authorised by the FSA with its members being appointed representatives. The network is thus the authorised person and is responsible for the conduct of its appointed representatives. It will thus have to have a compliance department and procedures to monitor its representatives. Commission from a life office must be paid to the network (as this is the authorised firm) which will then pay it on to its members, usually after some deduction.

Equally, it is the network that is responsible to the life office for any indemnity commission clawback even if the firm that sold the policy has at that stage left the network. The network would also be responsible for any complaints about its members and about ex-members in relation to business done during membership.

The network will have to show the FSA that it can monitor its members and have a written contract whereby the network agrees to take responsibility for the member's actions and the member agrees to comply with the rules.

Around half of all firms of independent intermediaries are members of networks and some 30% of individual independent financial advisers are authorised in this way. It is now recognised as the easiest route to authorisation for a new firm.

Some networks provide other services for their members as well as compliance – eg commission tracking, marketing support, technical back-up and best advice panels.

7 Complaints

If someone wishes to make a complaint it should be made in the first place to the firm that provided the relevant product or service. Complaints about the sale of contracts arranged by an intermediary should be made to the intermediary, rather than the product provider. Complaints about a sale made by an employee or representative of a provider should be made to the provider.

7.1 Complaints procedures

The FSA rules require every authorised firm to have and publicise an appropriate written complaints handling procedure to handle complaints from eligible complainants about its provision (or non-provision) of a financial services activity. The procedures should include provisions for referring the complaint to another firm if they are the subject of the complaint, within five business days of ascertaining this, and so informing the complainant.

An eligible complainant is:

- A private individual.
- A business with an annual turnover of less than £1 million.
- A charity with an annual income of less than £1 million.
- A trust with a net asset value of less than £1 million.

An intermediate customer or market counterparty is not an eligible complainant. A complaint for this purpose is any expression of dissatisfaction, whether oral or written and whether justified or not. The complainant might be a customer, eg a policyholder, but could be someone who has never been a customer of the firm, eg a proposer whose application for life assurance has been declined on medical evidence. While no life office has to insure someone just because they have applied, it does have to deal with the complaint. The complaint might even be about something entirely inconsequential, eg a spelling mistake in a letter. A complaint has to be dealt with under the rules even if it is entirely fabricated and totally unjustified.

There may often be a fine line between a request for clarification or information and an expression of dissatisfaction. If the firm is in doubt it is best to treat it as a complaint to avoid subsequent criticism by the FSA or FOS.

A firm must refer in writing to the availability of its complaints procedure at, or immediately after, the point of sale. It must publish details of its procedures, supply a copy on request and supply a copy to the complainant when it receives a complaint (unless it is resolved by close of business on the next business day). The firm must also display in each of its branches to which eligible complainants have access a notice indicating that it is covered by the Financial Ombudsman Service.

The firm's complaints procedure must ensure that a competent and independent employee investigates the complaint. That person must have the authority to settle the complaint.

Complaints must be handled fairly, consistently and promptly. All relevant employees must be aware of the complaints procedure.

A complaint must be acknowledged within five business days of receipt. A final or holding response must be sent within four weeks. After eight weeks there must be a final response or further holding response.

Once the complaint has been considered a decision must be made whether to reject or uphold it. This final response must be notified to the complainant and refer to his right to refer the matter to the Financial Ombudsman Service. If a final response is not sent by eight weeks the complainant must be informed of his right to refer the matter to the FOS.

If the complaint is upheld the firm must make an offer of appropriate compensation or remedial action. If the complainant accepts, this should be the end of the matter. If he thinks the offer is insufficient, he can still refer it to the FOS, as he can if the complaint is rejected.

Complaints records must be kept for at least three years.

A firm must supply complaints statistics to the FSA twice a year.

7.2 The Financial Ombudsman Service

The Financial Ombudsman Service replaced a number of previous ombudsmen:

- The Insurance Ombudsman.
- The Banking Ombudsman.
- The Building Society Ombudsman.
- The Investment Ombudsman.
- The PIA Ombudsman.

The FOS was set up under s225 of the FSMA as the ombudsman for all complaints against authorised persons about regulated activities. All authorised firms have to inform complainants of their right to refer their complaint to the FOS. The object of the FOS is to resolve disputes quickly with the minimum of formality.

There is a panel of ombudsmen within the FOS and a Chief Ombudsman. They are not liable for their actions unless there is bad faith or a breach of the Human Rights Act 1998.

Only an eligible complainant (see earlier) can refer a complaint to the FOS. The complainant must refer the matter to the FOS within the earliest of:

- Six months after the firm's final response.
- Six years after the event complained about, or if later, three years after the complainant knew or should have known he had cause for complaint.

However the FOS can consider complaints outside these limits in exceptional circumstances and for cases stemming from the pension transfer, opt-outs and FSAVC reviews.

The FOS can require the parties to the complaint to produce any necessary information or documents and failure to do so can be treated as contempt of court. All authorised firms must co-operate with the FOS. The FOS must investigate and can give the parties an opportunity to make representations and can hold a hearing. The FOS must decide the complaint on what is fair and reasonable in all the circumstances, taking into account the law, the FSA rules and guidance and good industry practice. The decision must be notified in writing to the complainant and the respondent. Reasons must be given for the decision. The complainant must then accept or reject the decision within the time limit specified by the FOS.

If the complainant accepts the decision it is binding on the respondent. If the complainant rejects the decision he is free to pursue the matter in court. If the complainant does not respond to the FOS decision letter it is treated as a rejection, and the respondent is not bound by the decision.

The FOS can award compensation for any loss including an amount for suffering, damage to reputation, distress or invonvenience and/or order the respondent to take remedial action. The respondent must comply with any award. The maximum monetary award is £100,000 plus the complainant's costs. The FOS can recommend a higher award but this would not be binding on the respondent. The FOS cannot award the respondent costs against the complainant, but can charge the complainant its own costs if the complainant's conduct has been improper or unreasonable.

The FOS jurisdiction is compulsory for authorised firms, but there is also a voluntary jurisdiction for firms not needing authorisation.

The compulsory jurisdiction takes in all regulated activities plus mortgage lending, unsecured lending, paying money by a plastic card and ancillary banking services. The activities must be carried on in, or from an establishment in, the UK.

The FOS is funded by a general levy on all participating firms, determined by reference to membership of ten industry sectors and the firm's turnover, plus a flat rate case fee for complaints made against individual firms. The FSA has said that it is unfair for a firm to try to recoup the case fee from an unsuccessful complainant.

The FOS has been able to deal with complaints about National Savings since 1 September 2005.

8 The Financial Services Compensation Scheme

The Financial Services Compensation Scheme (FSCS) was established under s212 of the FSMA to compensate claimants where authorised persons (or their ARs) are unable to satisfy claims against them in connection with regulated activities. The FSCS effectively replaced the previous Policyholders Protection Act regime, the deposit protection scheme for banks and building societies, and the Investors Compensation Scheme, under the Financial Services Act 1986.

In order to get compensation a claimant must be eligible. Eligible complainants are any person except:

1. Firms (other than a sole trader firm or a small business whose claim arises out of a regulated activity for which they do have a permission).
2. Overseas firms.

3. Collective investment schemes, and anyone who is the operator or trustee of such a scheme.

4. Pension and retirement funds, and anyone who is a trustee of such a fund (except a trustee of a small self administered scheme or an occupational pension scheme of an employer which is not a large company or large partnership).
5. Supranational institutions, governments, and central administrative authorities.

6. Provincial, regional, local and municipal authorities.

7. Directors and managers of the relevant person in default. However, this exclusion does not apply if:

   (a) the relevant person in default is a mutual association which is not a large mutual association; and

   (b) the directors and managers do not receive a salary or other remuneration for services performed by them for the relevant person in default.

8. Close relatives of persons excluded by (7) above.

9. Bodies corporate in the same group as the relevant person in default.

10. Persons holding 5% or more of the capital of the relevant person in default, or of any body corporate in the same group.

11. The auditors of the relevant person in default, or of any body corporate in the same group as the relevant person in default, or the appointed actuary of a friendly society or insurance undertaking in default.

12. Persons who in the opinion of the FSCS are responsible for, or have contributed to, the relevant person's default.

13. Large companies.

14. Large partnerships or large mutual associations.

15. Persons whose claim arises from transactions in connection with which they have been convicted of an offence of money laundering.

16. Persons whose claim arises under the Third Parties (Rights against Insurers) Act 1930.

However the following are eligible:

- Persons in 14 for deposits.

- Persons in 1–4 for deposits if they are not a large company, large mutual or a credit institution.

- Persons in 1–6, 13, 14, and 16 for long-term insurance.
- Persons in 1–4 for general insurance if they are small businesses.
- Any person for compulsory insurance.

The claim must be for:

- A protected deposit.
- A protected insurance contract.
- Protected investment business.

Protected deposits are basically deposits at UK branches.

Protected insurance contracts are ones issued through an office in the UK, another EEA state, the Channel Islands or the Isle of Man, if the risk is situated in one of these countries. For life and pension policies the risk is situated where the policyholder is habitually resident at the date the policy was effected.

Protected investment business is:

- Any investment business carried on by the firm with the claimant or as agent for him,
- The activities of a manager or trustee of an authorised unit trust if the claim is made by a unitholder,
- The activities of an authorised corporate director (ACD) or depository of an OEIC if the claim is made by the holder,

provided the business was carried on from a UK office.

The FSCS must decide whether the firm is in default which means it is unable (or is likely to be unable) to satisfy protected claims against it. The FSCS can require a firm to produce information and documents for this purpose and that power extends to any insolvency practitioner handling the firm's bankruptcy or liquidation.

If the FSCS judges that a firm is in default it must pay compensation to all claimants affected by the default. The limits of compensation for each complainant are as follows:

Deposits
100% of the first £2,000 plus 90% of the next £33,000 – maximum £31,700.

Investments and mortgage business
100% of the first £30,000 plus 90% of the next £20,000, maximum £48,000.

Long-term insurance
100% of the first £2,000 plus 90% of the remainder with no maximum.

General insurance
For compulsory insurance 100% of valid claims or unexpired premiums, with no maximum. For non-compulsory insurance 100% of the first £2,000 of valid claims or unexpired premiums plus 90% of the remainder, with no maximum.

The costs of the FSCS could be minimal if for example a small IFA that didn't handle client money went bankrupt. However the costs could be enormous if a large bank or insurance company became insolvent.

The costs of the FSCS are funded by a levy on authorised firms. There are three sub schemes for deposits, insurance and investment business. Each firm is allocated to a contribution group within a sub scheme in accordance with their activities. When a member of that group goes into default the other members of that group have to pay a levy to fund the compensation. There will be minimal cross-subsidisation between groups, and none between sub schemes.

The FSCS also has a duty to try to make arrangements to secure continuity of insurance for long-term insurance policyholders by transfer of the business to another insurer. It must also try to safeguard the policyholders of insurance companies in financial difficulties.

The FSCS can require a claimant to assign his rights against the defaulting firm to them. Claims must be paid as soon as possible after the amount has been calculated by the FSCS. Payment can be made to a pension scheme in pension cases to avoid tax law being broken by making a payment direct to the claimant. Compensation cannot be paid for protected investment business in respect of a failure of investment performance to match a guarantee or for the mere fluctuation in value of an investment.

The FSCS may decide to reduce compensation if there is evidence of contributory negligence by the claimant or if paying the full amount would provide a greater benefit than the claimant might reasonably have expected or than the benefit available on similar investments with other firms. Any bonus on a with-profit policy is not part of a claim unless declared prior to the liquidation of a life office. If the FSCS considers that the benefits under a long-term insurance are excessive it must refer the contract to an independent actuary. If the actuary agrees the benefits are excessive the FSCS can reduce the claim.

A deceased person can claim via his personal representatives and trustees can also claim on behalf of the trust.

9 Compliance Monitoring

Compliance monitoring must be undertaken by the FSA and all authorised firms to ensure that all the rules are adhered to.

9.1 FSA compliance monitoring

The mere existence of rules does not mean they will always be adhered to, and thus the FSA has to have monitoring procedures to try to ensure compliance with the rules, and catch and discipline those who don't comply with them.

The FSA does this in a number of ways. It receives a huge amount of information regularly from authorised firms including:

- Accounts.
- Auditors' statements.
- Banking returns.
- Building society returns.
- Insurance returns.
- Complaints statistics.

It can use these to decide whether investigation or intervention is necessary. The Consumer Panel and Practitioner Panel may raise matters of general concern, as may the Office of Fair Trading and the Complaints Commissioner. Reports from the Financial Ombudsman may also alert the FSA to general problems or problems at a specific firm.

The FSA can also react to concerns expressed by the government, the media and individual complainants. The FSA also 'keeps its ear to the ground' in order to detect potential problems as soon as possible.

The FSA is also a pro-active regulator in that a major part of its compliance monitoring is its programme of inspection visits by enforcement officers on authorised firms. The programme works on a 'risk to the public' basis combining the scale and the type of business involved. An inspection visit can vary from one enforcement officer for one day for a small IFA to a team of officers for over a month for a large insurance company.

The FSA enforcement officers will check all the compliance systems at a firm to ensure they are adequate. Typical things checked would be:

- Effectiveness and knowledge of the compliance department.
- Competence of advisers.

- Whether the firm has permission for all its activities.
- Procedures for appointing employees and appointed representatives.
- Procedures for individual registrations for controlled functions.
- Record keeping.
- Control of inducements.
- Checking of financial promotions.
- Giving customers terms of business documents, IDDs and Menus.
- The suitability of recommendations to customers.
- Suitability letters.
- Key features production.
- Post sales confirmations.
- Projection calculations.
- Production of cancellation notices.
- PPFMs.
- Client money systems.
- Complaints systems.
- Training and competence systems.
- Money laundering procedures.

At the end of the visit a report will be prepared detailing any remedial work necessary and giving time limits for that. The firm must then take the required action within the specified time limits.

If the FSA believe it is appropriate they can take disciplinary action against firms and individuals. Disciplinary action can be publicised to encourage other firms or individuals not to make the same mistakes.

9.2 Internal compliance monitoring

Each authorised firm should also have its own compliance monitoring procedures. This is necessary to avoid or reduce accidental rule breaches and problems with FSA inspection visits. The firm's Compliance Officer is responsible for all aspects of FSMA compliance and should be a director or senior manager. The Compliance Officer will usually have a compliance department to assist in this work and that department may well be quite large. Compliance departments have grown more rapidly than most other departments in all large financial services businesses over the last decade.

The compliance department should keep a regular check on all the procedures listed above so that there should hopefully be no surprises on a FSA inspection visit. The department may even have control over functions such as advertisement checking, fact find checking, suitability letter checking and training. The department may do mini inspection visits on branches, ARs and individual advisers.

A failure to adequately monitor compliance could lead to:

- Disciplinary action by the FSA.
- Unwelcome publicity.
- A decline in business.

None of these would be good for the careers of the directors, managers or compliance staff of the firm.

10 General Insurance

The selling and marketing of general insurance and pure protection life assurance has been fully regulated by the FSA since 14 January 2005. The FSA has made the Insurance Conduct of Business Rules, commonly known as ICOB.

Insurers and intermediaries need authorisation and an insurer must make sure that any intermediary it deals with is authorised. The rules distinguish between retail customers and commercial customers (who get less protection). The rules also vary according to whether the sale is with or without advice. The rules apply to renewals as well as new business, as general insurance policies are normally one-year contracts, not permanent ones.

An intermediary must supply the client with an Initial Disclosure Document giving details of the services offered and the authorisation status. An intermediary must have a list of insurers with which it deals available for clients. The intermediary must get details of a client's circumstances and needs, including existing policies and give the client a statement of those needs, and reasons for any recommendations.

Recommendations must be suitable and the intermediary must explain the duty of disclosure of material facts and its importance.

There are product disclosure rules relating to policy details, including claims and compensation. Policy documents must contain all contractual terms and conditions.

For pure protection life policies there is a 30 day cancellation period and if the client cancels the contract, a full refund of premiums must be given. For general insurance policies there is a 14 day cancellation period, but the client will not necessarily get a full refund of premiums as the insurer is entitled to deduct a pro rata charge for time on risk and such of the commission as is necessary to cover the costs of the intermediary. There are no cancellation rights for:

- Travel policies.
- Policies lasting less than one month.
- Policies where performance has already been completed.
- Pure protection life policies for six months or less.

The client must be given 21 days notice of renewal terms or of an insurer which is declining to renew the contract.

In any claim the intermediary must inform the client if it is acting for the insurer as well, and the intermediary must carefully manage any conflicts of interest. If the intermediary acts for the client it must act with due skill, care and diligence.

The insurer must handle claims fairly and promptly and if a claim is rejected the reasons why must be explained. Clients must be given guidance on claims procedures. The insurer must not unreasonably reject a claim. Unless there is evidence of fraud the insurer must not refuse a claim on grounds of non-disclosure of a material fact that a retail customer could not reasonably be expected to have disclosed. Claims cannot be rejected for misrepresentation unless the misrepresentation is negligent. Claims cannot be rejected for a breach of warranty unless the claim is connected with the breach.

General insurance companies can act via appointed representatives (like life offices) but general insurance appointed representatives can act for more than one insurance company. The complaints rules and FOS jurisdiction have been extended to general insurance intermediaries. Records of general insurance business must be kept for at least three years.

11 Mortgages

The FSA took over the regulation of mortgage advice on 31 October 2004 and has made the Mortgage Conduct of Business Rules (MCOB). The rules apply to mortgage lenders, administrators, arrangers and advisers. All these firms must be authorised, either directly or as an appointed representative of an authorised firm.

A firm describing itself as independent must provide a whole of the market service and give clients the option to pay by fee.

Regulated mortgage contracts are those where a lender provides credit to an individual (or trustees) secured by a first legal mortgage on land in the UK which is to be used as a dwelling by the borrower (or a beneficiary of the trust) or a spouse, quasi-spouse, parent, brother, sister, child, grandparent or grandchild of the borrower.

There is a range of rules, similar in many ways to the investment rules, covering subjects such as:

- Clear, fair and not misleading communications.
- Inducements.
- No exclusion of liability under the rules.
- Record keeping (generally for three years).
- Advertising.
- An IDD, detailing the services offered and any charges.
- Illustrations and risk warnings.
- Annual percentage rates of interest (APRs).
- Responsible lending – lenders must take account of a customer's ability to repay before giving a loan.
- Charges.
- Arrears and repossessions.

Selling rules differ according to whether they are with or without advice and whether they involve standard risk mortgages or higher risk (lifetime) mortgages. All advised mortgages must be suitable for the client. There must be a personalised key facts illustration (KFI) setting out the costs, terms and conditions of the mortgage and this must be given to the client before the mortgage application is made. Any commission paid by a lender to an intermediary must be disclosed to the client. Early repayment charges must be disclosed and must reflect the actual cost to the firm of repaying early. Similarly any arrears charges must reflect only the cost of the added administration a firm incurs in managing the arrears. Mortgages are covered by the FOS and the FSCS.

The Consumer Credit Act regime still continues for all the other types of credit not covered by the FSA rules.

12 Stakeholder Products

There is a so called 'lighter touch' regime for basic advice on stakeholder products, except for the smoothed life policy. All the normal FSA rules apply with the following modifications:

- The 'know your customer' rules are replaced by a series of questions about debt levels, investment objectives, tolerance of risk and pension rights. The recommended product only has to be suitable, not the most suitable.
- The Menu is not required but the customer must be given a copy of the range of stakeholder products which can contain no more than one of each of the collective investment scheme or life policy, pension or CTF. Basic advice cannot be given on an independent basis. Commission must be disclosed.
- The customer must be told that only basic advice about stakeholder products will be given and that they are intended to provide a simple, low-cost way of investing and saving. The client must also be told that any recommendation will be based on the answers to the questions. There must be no sale if the product is unaffordable, and a strong warning must be given about the desirability of repaying debt in preference to investing.
- Basic advisers cannot give advice on fund choice, encashment of other investments, or non-stakeholder products. The customer cannot be advised on what contribution level on a stakeholder pension is needed to achieve a specific level of income in retirement.
- The suitability letter is replaced by a recommendation summary including the reasons for the recommendation and the amount of the investment. Post sales information is not required.
- There must be no product bias in the remuneration structure of a basic adviser. Basic advisers do not have to pass any external exams (although they do have to be competent) and basic advice is not a controlled function. Records of basic advice must be kept for six years.

This is an Association of British Insurers (ABI) Model Guide for Customers on Basic Advice and an ABI Guidance for Providers of Basic Advice.

R Other Regulatory Provisions

1 The Statement of Long-Term Insurance Practice

2 The Statement of Best Practice for Income Protection Insurance

3 The Consumer Credit Act 1974

4 The Data Protection Act 1998

5 The Pensions Ombudsman

6 Money Laundering Prevention

7 The Third Life Directive

8 The Unfair Contract Terms Directive

Appendix 1 Statement of Long-Term Insurance Practice

Appendix 2 Statement of Best Practice for Income Protection Insurance

> This chapter deals with various other regulatory measures that apply to the life assurance and pensions industry.

1 The Statement of Long-Term Insurance Practice

The insurance industry gained exemption from the Unfair Contract Terms Act 1977 on the basis that it would publish statements of practice agreed with the DTI.

These statements by and large reflected the existing practice of most reputable offices. The statements apply only to policies effected by individuals resident in the UK in a private capacity. They are not legally binding and a breach does not invalidate the contract concerned. There is one statement for general business and one for long-term business (life and pensions). The current Association of British Insurers (ABI) Statement of Long-term Insurance Practice is shown in Appendix 1.

The Financial Ombudsman expects life offices to comply with the Statement and will almost certainly find against them if they do not.

2 The Statement of Best Practice for Income Protection Insurance

In August 1999 the ABI issued a Statement of Best Practice for Income Protection Insurance, which is mandatory for all ABI members. The statement was revised in 2003. The statement is not legally binding but will be taken into account by the Financial Ombudsman. The statement is shown at Appendix 2.

3 The Consumer Credit Act 1974

The Consumer Credit Act 1974 was passed to regulate the business of providing credit. It affects all individuals or companies who provide any form of credit and is supervised by the Office of Fair Trading.

Life offices are affected as they often give loans on the security of their policies and provide funds for house purchase. The Act covers advice and arrangement of loans, as well as the lending itself. Therefore, brokers and other intermediaries are also affected.

The Act provides that any person carrying on consumer credit business must have a licence from the Office of Fair Trading covering any lending or advisory operations carried out. The OFT supervises licensees and can suspend or revoke the licence if it is not satisfied with the conduct of a licensee. This means that the licensee will have to cease all business covered by that licence. Carrying on consumer credit business without a licence is a criminal offence.

The Act sets out regulations regarding advertisements, quotations, the true rate of interest to be stated, the form and content of deeds and cooling-off provisions. Loans of over £25,000 are exempt from many of the Act's provisions.

Employees of a life office are covered by the office's licence. However, self-employed company representatives and appointed representatives need their own licences as they are not covered by the life office's licence.

The Act continues to apply to those loans not regulated by the FSA under their Mortgage Rules – see Chapter Q section 11.

4 The Data Protection Act 1998

The Data Protection Act 1998 implements into UK law the provisions of the 1995 EC Data Protection Directive. It regulates the use of computers and other automatic data processing equipment, but also covers information recorded in a 'relevant filing system'. This is any set of information relating to individuals to the extent that the set is structured, either by reference to individuals or by reference to criteria relating to individuals, in such a way that specific information relating to a particular individual is readily available. It therefore applies to many manual or paper records. It can also apply to things like telephone recordings, CCTV film and photographs.

The case of *Durant v FSA* [2003] EWCA Civ 1746 established that a 'relevant filing system' is broadly equivalent to a computerised system in ready accessibility to relevant information. Therefore it has to be so referenced or indexed that it enables the data controller to identify at the outset of a search, with reasonable certainty and speed, the relevant files and personal data, without having to make a manual search of them. Therefore many manual files will not be subject to the Act.

All businesses handling such data have to abide by the following Data Protection Principles:

The Data Protection Principles

(1) Personal data shall be processed fairly and lawfully, and in particular, shall not be processed unless:

  (i) One of the conditions in Schedule 2 is met; and

  (ii) In the case of sensitive personal data, at least one of the conditions in Schedule 3 is also met.

(2) Personal data shall be obtained only for one or more specified and lawful purposes, and shall not be further processed in any manner incompatible with that purpose or those purposes.

(3) Personal data shall be adequate, relevant and not excessive in relation to the purpose, or purposes for which they are processed.

(4) Personal data shall be accurate and, where necessary, kept up to date.

(5) Personal data processed for any purpose or purposes shall not be kept for longer than is necessary for that purpose or for those purposes.

(6) Personal data shall be processed in accordance with the rights of data subjects under this Act.

(7) Appropriate technical and organisational measures shall be taken against unauthorised or unlawful processing of personal data and against accidental loss or destruction of, or damage to, personal data.

(8) Personal data shall not be transferred to a country or territory outside the European Economic Area unless that country or territory ensures an adequate level of protection for the rights and freedoms of data subjects in relation to the processing of personal data.

Personal data means any data relating to an identifiable living individual. The data must be biographical and the individual must be the focus of the information rather than the focus being some other event in which the individual is involved. The conditions in Schedule 2 are that:

- The data subject has given consent to the processing.
- The processing is necessary for the performance of, or to enter into, a contract with the data subject.
- The processing is necessary for the data controller to comply with a legal obligation.
- The processing is necessary in order to protect the vital interests of the data subject.
- The processing is necessary for the exercise of functions of a public nature exercised in the public interest.
- The processing is necessary for the pursuit of legitimate interests by the data controller unless such processing prejudices the rights, freedoms, or legal interests of the data subject.

Processing in this context includes disclosure to a third party.

Sensitive data is data about such things as a person's ethnic or racial origin, religious or political beliefs, health or sexual life. Strict conditions usually involving explicit consent of the data subject are required under Schedule 3.

Data must be obtained fairly if it is to be processed fairly. The data subject has various rights such as:

- A right to a copy of the personal data held on him (for a maximum fee of £10 (computer records) or £50 (manual)).
- A right to be informed of any logic in automated decision-making processes relating to him.
- A right to prevent processing likely to cause unwarranted damage or distress.

- A right to prevent processing for purposes of direct marketing.
- A right to compensation for damage or distress caused by a breach of the Act.
- A right to require rectification, erasure or destruction of inaccurate data.

All data controllers must notify the Information Commissioner and give details of the data held, and the purposes for which it is held, although this does not apply to those who only process manual records. The Information Commissioner maintains a register of this information.

The Information Commissioner's duty is to oversee the working of the Act. If it believes that any data controller is contravening any of the Principles it can serve an enforcement notice and the data controller will commit an offence if it fails to comply with it. Data processing without required notification to the Information Commissioner is an offence. It is an offence, without the consent of the data controller, to obtain or disclose personal data.

5 The Pensions Ombudsman

The Pensions Ombudsman was set up in 1990 under the Social Security Act 1990, although his powers are now set out in the Pensions Schemes Act 1993 and various regulations. His function is to investigate and determine complaints made by pension scheme members (or their widows, widowers, civil partners or dependants) alleging that injustice has been sustained in consequence of maladministration in connection with any act or omission of the trustees or managers of an occupational pension scheme or personal pension scheme. He can also investigate and determine any disputes of fact or law between members and the trustees or managers of the scheme.

He can investigate complaints regarding matters which arose prior to 1990 but cannot look at complaints where court proceedings have been commenced. The Ombudsman can require any trustee or manager of a pension scheme to furnish whatever information he wants and can also compel the attendance of witnesses. His decisions are binding on the complainant and the trustees or managers of the scheme, whom he can direct to take such action as he may specify. He must act in accordance with legal principles, *Wakelin v Read*. His decisions can be appealed but only on a point of law to the Courts. He is responsible to the Secretary of State for Work and Pensions.

However, he cannot deal with:

- Schemes with less than two members.
- The Armed Forces Pension Scheme as regards officers who have a right of appeal to the Crown.
- A public service pension scheme other than the nhsss.
- Matters which can be investigated by the FSA.

The complaint must be referred in writing within three years of the problem occurring or coming to the knowledge of the complainant. The complainant must have already taken up the matter with the scheme manager and the trustees, and should also preferably have raised the matter with OPAS. Complaints about the state scheme or rebates are not covered. His services are free to complainants and his costs are paid for by a levy on pension schemes. He has recently decided that he can look at complaints about scheme surpluses and how they are spent. The Appeal Court has decided that he cannot make a decision which adversely affects a third party. It has also held that he can't set aside a decision of the trustees reached in the proper exercise of their discretion on the grounds that it was unfair. His jurisdiction extends to unregistered schemes and insurance companies, but not to matters that are not the subject of a complaint to him.

The High Court has ruled that the Pensions Ombudsman does not have the power to fine trustees for maladministration, despite his attempts to do this in the past. He cannot order a payment which would be *ultra vires* for the payer. However, he does have the power to order trustees to make payments for distress, irrespective of financial loss. The Court has also decided that a mere error of law cannot amount to maladministration.

The Pensions Act 1995 extended the Ombudsmen's jurisdiction to include disputes between the employer and trustees, between the trustees themselves and between the trustees or employer of one scheme and the trustees or employer of another scheme. The Pensions Ombudsman was not taken over by the Financial Ombudsman, unlike the various other Ombudsmen, such as the Insurance Ombudsman.

The Pensions Ombudsman has a memorandum of understanding with the Financial Ombudsman Service for personal pensions and small occupational schemes whereby the FOS will deal with complaints concerning the circumstances of the sale, and the Pensions Ombudsman will handle any problems concerning the management or administration of the scheme.

6 Money Laundering Prevention

The Proceeds of Crime Act 2002 was passed to try to ensure that criminals of all sorts cannot keep and enjoy the proceeds of their crimes. The Act created a number of criminal offences as follows:

- To conceal, disguise, convert or transfer criminal property or remove it from the UK.
- To be concerned in an arrangement to facilitate the acquisition, retention, use or control of criminal property.
- To acquire, use or possess criminal property.

It is also an offence to fail to disclose known or suspected cases of money laundering in the course of business in the regulated sector. The regulated sector includes deposit taking, money changing, dealing in, arranging, advising on or managing investments, and effecting or carrying out contracts of long-term insurance. Disclosure must be made to the Serious Organised Crime Agency (SOCA) or the Money Laundering Reporting Officer of the business concerned. It is also an offence to tip off the subject of a money laundering disclosure.

6.1 Money laundering regulations

The Money Laundering Regulations 2003 were made by the Treasury and came into force on 1 March 2004, replacing various previous regulations.

The Regulations apply to all relevant businesses which include:

- Deposit taking.
- Providing or advising on long-term insurance.
- Providing or advising on investments.
- Money changing.
- Estate agency.
- Casinos.
- Insolvency practitioners.
- Tax advisers.
- Accountants.
- Auditors.
- Legal services.
- The promotion and operation of companies and trusts.
- Dealing in goods for cash over €15,000 (or equivalent).

Relevant businesses must have internal control procedures for detecting money laundering and training for staff on how to recognise and deal with transactions which may be related to money laundering.

Relevant businesses must have procedures for identifying customers with whom they have a business relationship or have a transaction of €15,000 or more. This would include a series of transactions involving paying or receiving money, and as a rough guide €15,000 at the time of writing was worth just over £10,000. The identification procedures require that the customer must produce satisfactory evidence of identity. If satisfactory evidence of identity cannot be obtained the business relationship must not proceed further. If the customer is acting for another person the identity of that other person must also be established eg the donor of a power of attorney.

Where evidence of identity is required it must be obtained as soon as reasonably practicable after first contact is made with the customer. The regulations do not specify what is evidence of identity but documents such as a passport or driving licence are normally acceptable. For a corporate client a check could be made with Companies House. As part of evidence of identity, proof of the client's address is usually required. This can be done by production of a current utility bill or tax bill showing the client's name and address.

Evidence of identity is not required if the transaction is:

- With a third party via an introduction by another relevant business (eg an IFA) which has certified that it has obtained evidence of identity.

- For long-term insurance in connection with a pension scheme where there is no surrender value.

- Long-term insurance where the single premium does not exceed €2,500 (say £1,700).

- Long-term insurance where the annual premium does not exceed €1,000 (say £680).

Businesses must keep records of evidence of identity for at least five years from when the business relationship ends. The business must have internal reporting procedures where:

- There is a nominated officer to receive disclosures of money laundering – the money laundering reporting officer.

- Any staff must report known or suspected money laundering transactions to the money laundering reporting officer or SOCA.

- The money laundering reporting officer must consider the circumstances of the case and if necessary report the transaction to SOCA.

Firms can always operate tougher money laundering rules than the Regulations require, but cannot relax the rules no matter what the reason.

The FSA regards breach of the money laundering rules as a serious matter which may call into question the fitness and propriety of those involved.

6.2 The Assets Recovery Agency

The Proceeds of Crime Act established the Assets Recovery Agency (ARA) to confiscate from criminals the proceeds of their crimes. The ARA can get a court order empowering it to sell a defendant's assets as part of this procedure. There are also wide powers for the ARA to obtain financial information. These powers could be used in relation to life policies and other investments. The ARA can require the trustees or managers of a pension scheme to pay them the value of the pension rights, after deduction of their costs. This overrides the normal prohibition against commuting or surrendering a pension or anything else in the scheme rules. The payment will appropriately reduce (or extinguish) the liability of the pension scheme to the member (or anyone else). These provisions cover occupational pension schemes, personal pensions, stakeholder pensions and retirement annuities and thus affect insurance companies. The ARA can also take over Her Majesty's Revenue and Customs' (HMRC) function to tax profits or gains of criminal conduct. This applies to income tax, capital gains tax (CGT), corporation tax, National Insurance contributuions (NICs) and also inheritance tax (IHT) on transfers of value of criminal property.

7 The Third Life Directive

The EU Third Life Directive was incorporated into UK law by the Insurance Companies (Third Insurance Directives) Regulations 1994, and has now been incorporated in the Financial Services Authority (FSA) rules.

Under these regulations an insurance company with its head office in an EEA state does not need authorisation under the Financial Services and Markets Act 2000 to operate in the UK if it is authorised in its country of origin. Before transacting life or pensions business, an insurance company must satisfy itself that its premiums, income and other resources are sufficient to meet all its commitments on reasonable actuarial assumptions. It cannot rely on other resources if doing so would jeopardise solvency.

An EEA insurer can therefore transact business in the UK without being authorised under the Financial Services and Markets Act 2000. The state which authorises the insurance company will supervise all that company's business in the EEA. No member state can prohibit a policyholder from having a contract with a company authorised in an EEA state. Member states cannot require prior approval of policy conditions or premium scales. Assets relating to EEA business can be located in any EEA state.

All EEA life offices must have sound and prudent management and certify that they have sound administrative and accounting procedures, plus adequate internal control arrangements. In urgent cases the FSA can suspend authorisation in the UK and can appoint an investigator to find out whether a company has sound and prudent management, and the company must cooperate.

Any UK life office selling to policyholders resident in other EEA states must inform the FSA and supply separate statistics for these cases. This actually makes it harder to do occasional business in other EEA states, which is the reverse of the stated objective.

8 The Unfair Contract Terms Directive

The EU Unfair Contract Terms Directive has been put into UK law by the Unfair Terms in Consumer Contracts Regulations 1999. These regulations apply to all contracts between a seller, or a supplier, and a consumer, which includes life and pensions contracts entered into since 1 July 1995. The regulations do not apply to contractual terms reflecting mandatory legal or regulatory provisions, eg the terms required by HMRC for pensions contracts, or the FSA for terms of business agreements.

A contractual term which has not been individually negotiated is regarded as unfair if, contrary to the requirement of good faith, it causes a significant imbalance in the parties' rights and obligations to the detriment of the consumer. Virtually all the terms of a life or individual pension policy will not have been individually negotiated, as a standard wording will be used. The Regulations contain examples of terms which may be regarded as unfair.

The unfairness of a contractual term will be assessed according to all the circumstances prevailing at the time the contract was concluded. However the unfairness test does not apply to terms in plain, intelligible language which define the main subject matter of the contract (eg scope of cover clauses and exclusion clauses) or concern the adequacy of the price (eg the premium).

Sellers and suppliers must ensure that written contracts are expressed in plain, intelligible language. If there is doubt about the meaning of a written term the interpretation most favourable to the consumer will prevail.

An unfair contract term is not binding on the consumer, but the rest of the contract does continue to be binding on both parties, if it is capable of existing without the unfair term.

The Office of Fair Trading (OFT) can consider complaints relating to unfair contract terms and can obtain a court injunction against a business which has unfair terms in general use. The OFT can require a business to supply documents and information for this purpose. Trading Standards Departments and the Consumer's Association can also apply for injunctions.

The FSA is also a qualifying body under the Regulations and is taking lead responsibility for contracts in the areas of investment, pensions, life and general insurance, mortgages and banking. The Financial Ombudsman Service will also take the Regulations into account when considering complaints.

The FSA has expressed views about some life and pensions contracts with variable premiums or charges. Their view seems to be that any terms of this kind which confer an unnecessarily broad discretion on the office or could be used to the advantage of the office, rather than the consumer, is likely to be unfair.

- Where the contractual terms specify the circumstances when the discretion can be exercised and provide for the consumer to be notified of it in advance, this will reduce the chances of it being deemed unfair.

- If a term could only ever be used to the office's advantage, and never to the advantage of consumers, it is likely to be unfair.

- If a review term gives a life office the opportunity, but not the obligation, to review premiums it may be unfair as this would allow the firm to review premiums only where the outcome would be to the office's advantage.

- A term which allows an office to recoup its investment losses on the contract incurred up to the date of the review, or one which gives it discretion to increase profitability margins beyond those assumed at outset, is likely to be unfair.

- The same would apply to terms which allow the office to target a particular group of policyholders unfairly for an increase in premium to cover losses incurred elsewhere in the business.

Appendix 1 Statement of Long-Term Insurance Practice

STATEMENT OF LONG-TERM INSURANCE PRACTICE

The following Statement of normal insurance practice applies to policies of long-term insurance effected in the UK in a private capacity by individuals resident in the UK.

1. **Proposal Forms**
   (a) If the proposal form calls for the disclosure of material facts a statement should be included in the declaration, or prominently displayed elsewhere on the form or in the document of which it forms part:
      (i) drawing attention to the consequences of failure to disclose all material facts and explaining that these are facts that an insurer would regard as likely to influence the assessment and acceptance of a proposal;
      (ii) warning that if the signatory is in any doubt about whether certain facts are material, these facts should be disclosed.
   (b) Neither the proposal nor the policy shall contain any provision converting the statements as to past or present fact in the proposal form into warranties except where the warranty relates to a statement of fact concerning the life to be assured under a life of another policy. Insurers may, however, require specific warranties about matters which are material to the risk.
   (c) Those matters which insurers have commonly found to be material should be the subject of clear questions in proposal forms.
   (d) Insurers should avoid asking questions which would require knowledge beyond that which the signatory could reasonably be expected to possess.
   (e) The proposal form or a supporting document should include a statement that a copy of the policy form or of the policy conditions is available on request.
   (f) The proposal form or a supporting document should include a statement that a copy of the completed proposal form is available on request.

2. **Policies and Accompanying Documents**
   (a) Insurers will continue to develop clearer and more explicit proposal forms and policy documents whilst bearing in mind the legal nature of insurance contracts.
   (b) Life assurance policies or accompanying documents should indicate:
      (i) the circumstances in which interest would accrue after the assurance has matured; and
      (ii) whether or not there are rights to surrender values in the contract and, if so, what those rights are.

      (Note: The appropriate sales literature should endeavour to impress on proposers that a whole life or endowment assurance is intended to be a long-term contract and that surrender values, especially in the early years, are frequently less than the total premiums paid.)

3. **Claims**
   (a) An insurer will not unreasonably reject a claim. In particular, an insurer will not reject a claim or invalidate a policy on grounds of non-disclosure or misrepresentation of a fact unless:
      (i) it is a material fact; and
      (ii) it is a fact within the knowledge of the proposer; and

(iii) it is a fact which the proposer could reasonably be expected to disclose.
(It should be noted that fraud or deception will, and reckless or negligent non-disclosure or misrepresentation of a material fact may, constitute grounds for rejection of a claim.)

(b) Except where fraud is involved, an insurer will not reject a claim or invalidate a policy on grounds of a breach of a warranty unless the circumstances of the claim are connected with the breach and unless:
   (i) the warranty relates to a statement of fact concerning the life to be assured under a life of another policy and that statement would have constituted grounds for rejection of a claim by the insurer under 3(a) above if it had been made by the life to be assured under an own life policy; or
   (ii) the warranty was created in relation to specific matters material to the risk and it was drawn to the proposer's attention at or before the making of the contract.

(c) Under any conditions regarding a time limit for notification of a claim, the claimant will not be asked to do more than report a claim and subsequent developments as soon as reasonably possible.

(d) Payment of claims will be made without avoidable delay once the insured event has been proved and the entitlement of the claimant to receive payment has been established.

(e) When the payment of a claim is delayed more than two months, the insurer will pay interest on the cash sum due, or make an equivalent adjustment to the sum, unless the amount of such interest would be trivial. The two month period will run from the date of the happening of the insured event (ie death or maturity) or, in the case of a unit-linked policy, from the date on which the unit-linking ceased, if later. Interest will be calculated at a relevant market rate from the end of the two month period until the actual date of payment.

(f) In the case of a tax exempt policy with a friendly society, the total of the cash sum due and such interest to the date of the claim cannot exceed the statutory limit on such assurance.

4. Disputes
The provisions of the Statement shall be taken into account in arbitration and any other referral procedures which may apply in the event of disputes between policyholders and insurers relating to matters dealt with in the Statement.

5. Commencement
Any changes to insurance documents will be made as and when they need to be reprinted, but the Statement will apply in the meantime.

Note Regarding Industrial Assurance Policyholders
Policies effected by industrial assurance policyholders are included amongst the policies to which the above Statement of Long-Term Insurance Practice applies. Those policyholders also enjoy the additional protection conferred upon them by the Industrial Assurance Acts 1923 to 1969 and Regulations issued thereunder. These Acts give the Industrial Assurance Commissioner wide powers to cover inter alia the following aspects:

(a) Completion of proposal forms.

(b) Issue and maintenance of Premium Receipt Books.

(c) Notification in Premium Receipt Books of certain statutory rights of a policyholder including rights to:
   (i) an arrears notice before forfeiture,
   (ii) free policies and surrender values for certain categories of policies,
   (iii) relief from forfeiture of benefit under a policy on health grounds unless the proposer has made an untrue statement of knowledge and belief as to the assured's health,

(iv) reference to the Commissioner as arbitrator in disputes between the policyholder and the company or society.

The offices transacting industrial assurance business have further agreed that any premium (or deposit) paid on completion of the proposal form will be returned to the proposer if, on issue, the policy document is rejected by him or her.

Appendix 2 Statement of Best Practice for Income Protection Insurance

1. **Introduction**

1.1 The Association of British Insurers is the trade association for insurance companies in the United Kingdom. Of its more than 400 members around 200 transact long-term insurance business and they account for almost 100% of the life insurance and pension business written in the United Kingdom.

1.2 This revised Statement of Best Practice falls under the ABI Life Insurance (Non Investment Business) Selling Code of Practice, and covers the following:
- The description of Income Protection Cover in a Key Features Document.
- Guidance notes for certain policy terms and conditions.
- Generic Terms.
- The review process.

1.3 The Statement updates part of the industry's response to the second report by the Office of Fair Trading (OFT) on Health Insurance, published in May 1998. It was developed by the ABI's Income Protection Working Party, which produced their original proposals following research to discover what consumers would find most useful as an aid to understanding and comparing income protection products. These proposals were validated by further consumer research and have been subject to wide consultation across the industry and with key external partners such as the OFT, the Financial Ombudsman Service (FOS) and others.

2. **General Principles**

Applicability

2.1 The Statement applies to income protection providers who are members of the ABI. From 29 February 2000, compliance with the Statement of Best Practice has been a condition of ABI membership.

2.2 This Statement applies to individual income protection policies. It is not intended for group income protection policies. However best practice for group income protection is being developed by Group Risk Development (GRID) insurance industry contributors – see their website www.grouprisk.org.uk

Is income protection the right product for the applicant?

2.3 Before a potential applicant gets to the stage of applying for an income protection policy and, for example, comparing key features of different companies products they need to decide if income protection is the right type of insurance policy for them. A model leaflet, which companies may wish to adopt to help their customers come to an informed decision, has been issued at the same time as this Statement.

Products covered by the Income Protection Model Key Features Document (KFD)

2.4 If the product is primarily income protection (which may or may not include waiver of premium) then the model KFD should be used. A similar format should apply to the following contracts with appropriate amendments:
- Housepersons policies (ie policies for housewives, househusbands etc.).
- Expenditure related (eg mortgage) protection plans.

2.5 The Statement does not address policies which incorporate more than one health-related benefit (eg critical illness, private medical insurance or long term care insurance in addition to income protection). Nevertheless we recommend that insurers comply with the spirit of the Income Protection KFD when they print their product literature in respect of such policies in addition to the statements of Best Practice that apply to these products. Protection plans classified as short term under the Insurance Companies Act are not included in the above. Combinations of income protection and unemployment insurance are covered by these provisions, but creditor insurance is not.

2.6 The Statement is based on the following concepts.

Clarity

2.7 Wherever possible to aid consumer understanding, the preferred wording of the Key Features Document will be in 'plain english' provided that this does not dilute or conflict with the meaning.

2.8 The intention behind the guidance notes is that policy terms/conditions should be as robust as possible in differentiating between what is, and is not, covered to:

2.8.1 Create a clear expectation of the scope and limitations of the cover.

2.8.2 Allow valid claims to be paid promptly.

2.8.3. Minimise the number of disputed claims to avoid disappointment.

Key Features Document

2.9 The requirements of the Key Features Document included in this Statement are in addition to (and, in the event of conflict, are overruled by) any regulatory, legal, 3rd Life Directive and product specific requirements for Key Features.

2.10 The Key Features format is intended to ensure that income protection is described in a way that allows consumers to compare the income protection cover of different providers. Providers should give Key Features Documents to enquirers and potential customers (via intermediaries as appropriate) at the earliest opportunity to allow them to make meaningful product comparisons before purchase. They may also wish to issue their version of the model leaflet to consumers. The KFD should be issued in addition to the company's marketing and quotation materials.

Implementation

2.11 The provisions apply to new policies effected on or after the implementation date adopted by the provider. An increment or increase to an existing policy effected after that date as a new policy may be excluded if it mirrors the original contract.

2.12 Companies are currently required to apply the 1999 Statement of Best Practice together with the revised 2001 Key Features document. The timetable for implementing the revised 2003 Statement of Best Practice and Key Features Document is 1 January 2004.

3. Use of the Key Features Document

General

3.1 The model Key Features Document reproduced at Appendix A represents an industry standard template, and should be used taking the points below into account:

3.1.1. The front page and the left hand side (headings and subheadings) of the subsequent pages are mandated.

3.1.2 The right hand side – the answers – on the second and subsequent pages are an example text. We recommend that you use this, subject to the qualifications that:

3.1.2.a The wording accurately describes your product.

3.1.2.b Material in square brackets should only be used if it applies to your product.

3.1.2.c Amendments to the text can also be made to meet PPIAB or other guidelines on plain language. We have tried to incorporate the spirit of these guidelines in the Key Features Document, but brands may amend the text if this is necessary to gain PPIAB or other accreditation.

3.2 Sections should only be omitted where they are inappropriate to the product (eg no relation of benefit to earnings on Housepersons products).

3.3 Providers should ensure that the wording they use accurately describes the limitation of benefits. This may involve changes to the mandated wordings.

3.4 Providers are permitted to use any presentational or print style as long as the order of the questions is the same.

Front Page Headings

3.5 The front page headings ('Its Aims', 'Your Commitment' and 'Risk Factors') are already mandated for regulated business. This is extended under this Statement of Best Practice to non-regulated business.

'Questions and Answers'

3.6 A brief guide to the key features of the product are given in the form of answers to questions. The questions provided in the Model Key Features Document should be adopted as standard.

3.7 Additional questions and answers may be included to describe any material features not covered by the standard questions and answers. Alternatively, such features can be included in the sections headed 'What other benefits can I choose?' and 'What other features are there?'

4. Use of the Guidance Notes on Policy Terms and Conditions

4.1 The guidance notes cover ten of the most important policy terms and conditions:

- Definition of Incapacity – Own Occupation (Appendix B1a).
- Definition of Incapacity – Any Occupation (Appendix B1b).
- Limitation of Benefit (Appendix B2).
- Proportionate/Rehabilitation Benefits (Appendix B3).
- Change of Occupation (Appendix B4).
- Claims Notification Period (Appendix B5).
- Deferred Period (Appendix B6).
- Waiver of Premium (Appendix B7).
- Pregnancy Clause (Appendix B8).
- Linked Claims (Appendix B9).

4.2 For each condition, the Guidance Note describes its purpose, the main features that should typically be covered by the policy wording, the insurer's obligations to the consumer in describing their practice, and recommendations as to how the wordings should be applied.

4.3 For each term or condition included in a policy, the insurer should give proper consideration to the relevant guidance note. The practice of the insurer should be consistent with the guidance unless there is a good business case against such consistency, in which case the actual practice should be clearly explained.

4.4 Insurers should adopt these guidance notes when they next review the wording in their policy conditions. Insurers may choose to enhance cover retrospectively for customers with existing policies, but they are not obliged to do so.

5. Generic Terms

5.1 When generic terms are used, they should have the meanings shown and other terms should not be used in their place. This is to ensure that the terms always have the same meanings.

5.2 The generic terms are as follows:

Deferred Period

5.3 The meaning of this term is: 'The period of incapacity before any benefit is paid'. Please note that terms such as 'waiting period' and 'elimination period' should not be used.

Incapacity

5.4 The term 'incapacity' should be used instead of the term 'disability', in particular as regards the definition of the disability clause in the policy contract, which should be called the definition of incapacity clause.

Generic Product Name

5.5 The terms 'Income Protection Cover' and 'Income Protection' apply to this type of cover. Providers are free to use marketing names for their products and cover, provided that the cover is described either as: 'Income Protection Cover' or by using the words 'Income Protection'.

Model Exclusions

5.6 The following model exclusion wordings have been created for use by Income Protection and Critical Illness insurers.

5.7 Income Protection providers are free to omit or amend any of the model exclusions and may include additional exclusions.

5.8 The heading forms part of the model wording.

5.9 All exclusions and limitations (not only model exclusions) should be contained in one section of the policy (and key features, as set out above).

5.10 Providers should state which exclusions apply to which conditions in their policy (and other benefits as appropriate, eg Waiver of Premium Benefit) and should use an introductory policy wording to suit their individual policy style (see the example below).

> Example introductory wording for policy exclusions
> 'We will not pay an Income Protection claim if it is caused directly or indirectly from any of the following:

Aviation
Taking part in any flying activity, other than as a passenger in a commercially licensed aircraft.

Criminal Acts
Taking part in a criminal act.

Drug Abuse
Alcohol or solvent abuse, or the taking of drugs except under the direction of a registered medical practitioner.

Hazardous Sports and Pastimes
Taking part in (or practising for) [boxing, caving, climbing, horse-racing, jet skiing, martial arts, mountaineering, off piste skiing, pot-holing, power boat racing, under water diving, yacht racing or any race, trial or timed motor sport.]

HIV/AIDS
Infection with Human Immunodeficiency Virus (HIV) or conditions due to any Acquired Immune Deficiency Syndrome (AIDS).
Self-inflicted Injury
Intentional self-inflicted injury.

War & Civil Commotion
War, invasion, hostilities, (whether war is declared or not), civil war, rebellion, revolution or taking part in a riot or civil commotion.

6. Review Process

6.1 This Statement of Best Practice, the Key Features Document and the Guidance Notes will be reviewed regularly to ensure they continue to reflect current legislative and regulatory requirements and market practice. The next review will take place, at the latest, by February 2004, subject to FSA proposals on regulating this product. It could, however, take place earlier if this proves necessary.

6.2 Changes to any of these documents which are recommended as a result of a review will only be made following consultation with the industry and interested parties.

ABI
2003

Life Assurance & Pensions Index – 2006

A

D

E

F

J

K

L

M

N

O

P

Q

R

S

T

U

V

W

Z